U.S. MARINES IN VIETNAM
THE BITTER END
1973-1975

by

Major George R. Dunham
U.S. Marine Corps

and

Colonel David A. Quinlan
U.S. Marine Corps

HISTORY AND MUSEUMS DIVISION
HEADQUARTERS, U.S. MARINE CORPS
WASHINGTON, D.C.

1990

Volumes in the Marine Corps Vietnam Series

Operational Histories Series

U.S. Marines in Vietnam, 1954-1964, The Advisory and Combat Assistance Era, 1977

U.S. Marines in Vietnam, 1965, The Landing and the Buildup, 1978

U.S. Marines in Vietnam, 1966, An Expanding War, 1982

U.S. Marines in Vietnam, 1967, Fighting the North Vietnamese, 1984

U.S. Marines in Vietnam, 1969, High Mobility and Standdown, 1988

U.S. Marines in Vietnam, 1970-1971, Vietnamization and Redeployment, 1986

In Preparation

U.S. Marines in Vietnam, 1968

U.S. Marines in Vietnam, 1971-1973

Functional Histories Series

Chaplains with Marines in Vietnam, 1962-1971, 1985

Marines and Military Law in Vietnam: Trial by Fire, 1989

Anthology and Bibliography

The Marines in Vietnam, 1954-1973, An Anthology and Annotated Bibliography, 1974, reprinted 1983; revised second edition, 1985

Library of Congress Card No. 77-604776
PCN 190-003109-00

Foreword

This is the ninth volume in a nine-volume operational and chronological historical series covering the Marine Corps' participation in the Vietnam War. A separate functional series complements the operational histories. This volume details the final chapter in the Corps' involvement in Southeast Asia, including chapters on Cambodia, the refugees, and the recovery of the container ship SS *Mayaguez*.

In January 1973, the United States signed the Paris Peace Accords setting the stage for democracy in Southeast Asia to test its resolve in Cambodia and South Vietnam. The result was not a rewarding experience for America nor its allies. By March 1975, democracy was on the retreat in Southeast Asia and the U.S. was preparing for the worst, the simultaneous evacuation of Americans and key officials from Cambodia and South Vietnam. With Operation Eagle Pull and Operation Frequent Wind, the United States accomplished that task in April 1975 using Navy ships, Marine Corps helicopters, and the Marines of the III Marine Amphibious Force. When the last helicopter touched down on the deck of the USS *Okinawa* at 0825 on the morning of 30 April, the U.S. Marine Corps' involvement in South Vietnam ended, but one more encounter with the Communists in Southeast Asia remained. After the seizure of the SS *Mayaguez* on 12 May 1975, the United States decided to recover that vessel using armed force. Senior commanders in the Western Pacific chose the Marine Corps to act as the security force for the recovery. Marines of 2d Battalion, 9th Marines and 1st Battalion, 4th Marines played a key role in the events of 15 May 1975 when America regained control of the ship and recovered its crew, concluding American combat in Indochina and this volume's history.

Although largely written from the perspective of the III Marine Amphibious Force, this volume also describes the roles of the two joint commands operating in the region: the Defense Attache Office, Saigon, and the United States Support Activities Group, Thailand. Thus, while the volume emphasizes the Marine Corps' role in the events of the period, significant attention also is given to the overall contribution of these commands in executing U.S. policy in Southeast Asia from 1973 to 1975. Additionally, a chapter is devoted to the Marine Corps' role in assisting thousands of refugees who fled South Vietnam in the final weeks of that nation's existence.

The authors, Major George Ross Dunham and Colonel David A. Quinlan, individually worked on this volume while assigned to the History and Museums Division, Headquarters Marine Corps. Colonel Quinlan, who is now retired and resides in Hartford, Connecticut, began the book in 1976. Major Dunham, who recently retired and resides in Dunkirk, Maryland, inherited his co-author's work and completed the majority of the volume during his tour from 1985 to 1990. Both authors are graduates of the U.S. Naval Academy and have advanced degrees. Colonel Quinlan, who was an infantry officer, has a juris doctor degree from George Washington University (1979) and Major Dunham, who was an aviator, has a master of arts degree in history from Pepperdine University (1976).

E. H. SIMMONS
Brigadier General, U.S. Marine Corps (Retired)
Director of Marine Corps History and Museums

Preface

> Let every nation know, whether it wishes us well or ill, that we shall pay any price, bear any burden, meet any hardship, support any friend, oppose any foe, to assure the survival and success of liberty.
>
> John F. Kennedy, Inaugural Address
> 20 January 1961

U.S. Marines in Vietnam: The Bitter End, 1973-1975 is a story about commitment, sacrifice, and the price America and its ally, South Vietnam, paid. It answers no questions, places no blame, and offers no prophetic judgement, but provides an historical account of the end of a state and the beginning of new lives for those fortunate enough to escape that upheaval. This description of the United States Marine Corps' involvement at the bitter end of America's military presence in Southeast Asia also traces the effects of uncontrolled fear on a society fighting for its survival.

The effect of fear on the fighting man on the battlefield was no different in 1975 in South Vietnam than it was more than 2,400 years earlier, when the Athenians fought to defend their beloved city. In preparing his Marines and sailors for battle in the Peloponnesian War of 429 B.C., and anticipating their fear of death, Phormio of Athens told them:

> Fear makes men forget, and skill which cannot fight is useless.

The South Vietnamese Armed Forces in the spring of 1975 were rendered useless as a fighting force. No level of training or skill, no program of Vietnamization, no amount of money could have reversed the rampant spread of fear that engulfed all of South Vietnam in March and April of 1975. Incredible acts of courage temporarily checked the nation's slide into oblivion, at places like Xuan Loc and Bien Hoa, but fear ruled the day. Its only antidote, courageous leadership at the highest levels, rapidly disappeared as the NVA war machine gained momentum. As one senior leader after another opted to use his helicopter to evacuate rather than to direct and control the defensive battle, strategic retreats turned into routs and armies turned into mobs of armed deserters. Amidst all this chaos, the U.S. Marine Corps aided its country in the final chapter of the Vietnam War, the evacuation of American citizens, third-country nationals, and as many South Vietnamese as conditions permitted.

To describe those events accurately, the authors used, for the most part, original sources, including interviews of many of the participants. A debt of gratitude is owed to many people for the compilation and collation of that material. In particular, we thank the other Services and their respective historical agencies for their contributions, with a special note of appreciation due to Dr. Wayne W. Thompson and Mr. Bernard C. Nalty, both of the Office of Air Force History, and Dr. Edward J. Marolda of the Naval Historical Center. A large portion of the available source material was provided by the staff of the Marine Corps Historical Center and for that contribution we are very appreciative. In particular, we thank the Historical Center librarian, Miss Evelyn A. Englander, and archivist, Mrs. Joyce Bonnett, and their staffs; the Reference Section (Mr. Danny J. Crawford and staff); the Oral History Section (Mr. Benis M. Frank and Mrs. Meredith P. Hartley); and the Publications Production Section (Mr. Robert E. Struder, Mrs. Catherine A. Kerns, Mr. W. Stephen Hill, and Corporal Andre L. Owens III). Of course, history cannot be read until it has been written, and rewritten, and for that demanding task of editing, we thank the Chief Historian, Mr. Henry I. "Bud" Shaw, Jr.; the head of the Vietnam Histories Section, Mr. Jack Shulimson; and our colleagues in the section who had to read our work in its most primitive state (Lieutenant Colonel Gary D. Solis, Major Charles D. Melson, and Mr. Charles R. "Rich" Smith). To those whose names are too many to mention here, we extend our sincerest gratitude for loyalty and special acts of assistance in this project, and for those who reviewed our manuscript and contributed comments and pictures, we offer you a book bearing your imprint, and our thanks. The authors, however, are responsible for the content of the text, including opinions expressed and any errors in fact.

We would like to salute every Marine and American who served in Vietnam and dedicate this book to those who paid the ultimate price for the "survival and success of liberty." In particular, we commend the sacrifice of the four Marines who died in South Vietnam on 29 April 1975: Lance Corporal Darwin D. Judge; Corporal Charles McMahon, Jr.; First Lieutenant Michael J. Shea; and Captain William C. Nystul; and ask that the fourteen Marines who lost their lives on Koh Tang in Cambodia, on 15 May 1975, also not be forgotten.

GEORGE ROSS DUNHAM

DAVID A. QUINLAN

Table of Contents

Foreword iii
Preface v
Table of Contents vii
List of Maps x

PART I THE UNITED STATES PRESENCE IN THE WESTERN PACIFIC 1

Chapter 1 The War Goes On 2
   Paris Peace Accords 2
   The NVA Marshals in the South 7
   A Division of Marines 16
Chapter 2 The United States Presence in Southeast Asia 22
   The Forces in Thailand 22
   The Forces Afloat 27
   The III Marine Amphibious Force 29
   Americans Ashore 36
   The Marines in Vietnam 37
Chapter 3 Contingency Planning 40
   The Plan for Cambodia 42
   Vietnam 52
Chapter 4 The Fleet Marines are Readied 55
   The Air Contingency BLTs 55
   The Eagle Pull Command Element 57
   The 31st MAU 60
   The Other Contingency 65

PART II SOUTH VIETNAM 67

Chapter 5 The North Vietnamese Winter-Spring Offensive, 1974-75:
   The Mortal Blow 68
   The Collapse of the Central Highlands 68
   Defeat in Military Region 1 76
   A Wasted Division 79
Chapter 6 The Evacuation of South Vietnam's Northern Provinces 85
   The Amphibious Evacuation RVN Support Group 85
   Initial Operations in Vietnamese Waters 88
   Military Sealift Command Operations 92
   Meeting the Needs 97

PART III OPERATION EAGLE PULL 99

Chapter 7 The Evacuation of Phnom Penh 100
   The Khmer Rouge 100
   The Khmer Communists' Last Dry Season Offensive 102

  The Marines Move into Position..105
  Final Preparations Ashore..111
  Final Preparations at Sea...115
  The Execution of Eagle Pull..119

PART IV ENDING AN ALLIANCE..125

Chapter 8 The Other Contingency...126
  Marine Security Guard Detachment, Da Nang...................127
  Military Region 2: Nha Trang..131
  III MAF and the NVA Onslaught..132
  9th MAB and Task Force 76..136
  The Brigade..138
Chapter 9 Planning the Evacuation..143
  Brigade Planning and Liaison...143
  The Restructured 9th Marine Amphibious Brigade.............146
  The Concept..148
  Additional Forces, Plans, and Liaison................................152
  DAO Planning: The SPG and Project Alamo......................155
Chapter 10 The Final Days...160
  The AESF...160
  Xuan Loc Remembered..168
  Saigon and the Final Preparation Pieces..........................170
  Consulate Marines..173

PART V OPERATION FREQUENT WIND AND A NEW BEGINNING......177

Chapter 11 The Evacuation..178
  9th MAB..181
  The DAO Compound..183
  The Embassy..195
Chapter 12 Refugee Operations..204
  A Link to Freedom: The Exodus and a New Beginning......204
  Way Stations..207
  Preparations: 1st Battalion, 4th Marines and the Task Force....212
  Evacuation and Passage: Frequent Wind and the AESF's Final Chapter....216
  A Vietnamese City in Guam..222
  The Final Link: Camp Pendleton..228

PART VI AFTER 'VIETNAM'..237

Chapter 13 Recovery of the SS *Mayaguez*.............................238
  The *Mayaguez* Crisis...238
  The Initial Decisions..239
  Assault Preparations..242
  The First Assault Wave..245
  The Linkup...253
  The Second Wave..255
  The Retrograde..257
  The Aftermath...262
Chapter 14 Epilogue..266

NOTES 269

APPENDICES
   A. Command and Staff List, Southeast Asia, 1973-1975 281
   B. Command Staff, BLT 2/4, 29-30 April 1975 284
   C. U.S. Marine Officers Serving in Billets in
      South Vietnam and USSAG, Thailand, 1973-1975 285
   D. Company C, Marine Security Guard Battalion, January-April 1975 286
   E. *Mayaguez* Rescue Force (BLTs 2/9 and 1/4), 12-15 May 1975 287
   F. Glossary of Terms and Abbreviations 288
   G. Chronology of Significant Events, 1973-1975 294
   H. List of Reviewers 296
   I. 1st Battalion, 4th Marines Detachments, 3-11 April 1975 298
   J. Frequent Wind Forces 299
   K. Helicopter Flow Table for Frequent Wind 300

INDEX 302

List of Maps

Ho Chi Minh Trail Network... 9
Southeast Asia, 1973-1975... 41
Phnom Penh Evacuation Sites, 1973-1974................................. 49
The Battle of Phuoc Long, December 1974-January 1975................... 69
The Fall of Ban Me Thuot, 10-18 March 1975............................. 72

Administrative Divisions of South Vietnam.............................. 75
Military Region 1, VNMC Division AO, 1 January-15 March 1975........... 77
Military Region 1, VNMC Division AO, 15-31 March 1975.................. 81
The Khmer Communists' Last Dry Season Offensive....................... 103
Phnom Penh Evacuation Sites, 12 April 1975............................ 112

USS *Okinawa* and 31st MAU, 1200-2000, 12 April 1975.................. 117
Da Nang City, 27-30 March 1975.. 130
Administrative Divisions of South Vietnam............................. 134
The Fall of Xuan Loc, 9-22 April 1975................................. 135
Administrative Divisions of South Vietnam............................. 161

The Fall of Saigon, 25-29 April 1975.................................. 167
Potential Evacuation Sites.. 173
USS *Okinawa* and Task Force 76, 29-30 April 1975..................... 180
DAO/Air America Complex... 191
Mayaguez Recovery, 15 May 1975...................................... 243

PART I
THE UNITED STATES PRESENCE IN THE WESTERN PACIFIC

CHAPTER 1
The War Goes On

Paris Peace Accords—The NVA Marshals in the South—A Division of Marines

---

Fifteen minutes after noon on 29 April 1975, units of the 9th Marine Amphibious Brigade (9th MAB) received the order to execute Operation Frequent Wind, the plan for emergency evacuation of noncombatant civilians from Saigon, and to supply the final episode of Marines in Vietnam. Less than two hours later, the first elements of the 9th MAB's ground security force (GSF) landed in South Vietnam for the last time. Specifically organized to provide security for the evacuation landing zones, the first elements of the 9th MAB entered the Defense Attache Office (DAO) compound at 1506 Saigon time. The men were met by: ". . . the cheers of awaiting evacuees, almost all of whom were overcome by emotion at the sight of the organized and well disciplined Marines."[1]

These troops, many of whom were veterans of previous Vietnam battles, provided protection for the refugees in the DAO Compound. With the departure of the last evacuee, the Marine security force began returning to the safety of Seventh Fleet ships. Elements of the GSF also deployed to the American Embassy in Saigon where a few Marines remained until the bitter end. As the last CH-46 helicopter lifted off the Embassy rooftop at 0753 on 30 April with 11 Marines on board, U.S. involvement in South Vietnam ended.*

Paris Peace Accords

The signing of the Paris Peace Accords on 27 January 1973 represented a formal end to hostilities. Negotiated at the Paris Conference on Vietnam, it would serve as an important backdrop to events in a country where war seemed endemic.

The "Agreement on Ending the War and Restoring Peace in Vietnam" required the United States and its allies to cease military activity and leave South Vietnam within 60 days of the signing. To accomplish this, the Paris Accords required the U.S. to dismantle all its military bases and withdraw all military personnel including its advisors to the Republic of Vietnam Armed Forces. By 27 March the conclusion of the 60-day implementation phase, South Vietnam and the United States had completed most of the changes required by the Accords and its protocols. The absence of the same effort and commitment on the part of the North Vietnamese and the Viet Cong would soon define the meaning of "peace" in Vietnam. In essence, the precarious balance of power in Southeast Asia and the future of South Vietnam rested on a piece of paper.

For the critical transition from war to peace, the Accords empowered three commissions to oversee the implementation phase and resolve any differences. The Four-Power Joint Military Commission (JMC) represented each belligerent: the United States, South Vietnam, North Vietnam, and the Viet Cong. At the conclusion of the 60-day cease-fire, this commission would in theory shed its protective outer garment (U.S. and North Vietnam) and become the Two-Power Joint Military Commission, an insular body representing the interests of the Republic of Vietnam (South Vietnam) and the Provisional Revolutionary Government of South Vietnam (PRG, the Viet Cong). The third commission, and the most important one, involved international participation in the transition to peace. Entrusted to regulate and oversee the implementation of the Accords' articles, the International Commission of Control and Supervision (ICCS) consisted of four members: Canada, Hungary, Poland, and Indonesia.[2] The ICCS bore the implied responsibility of enforcement, but lacked the power to do more than report the violations to the Joint Military Commission. The ICCS was to cease functioning when the Accords' provisions had been fulfilled, signalled by a supervised national election and the installation of the new government's elected officials. The ICCS' goal and the final determinant of its existence would be the attainment of this "peace," but in the interim the commission's immediate and overwhelming problem would be settlement of territorial disputes and ceasefire violations. Final resolution of these and any other matters pertaining to the Accords ultimately required a unanimous vote of the JMC. This rarely happened.

The Four-Power Commission attempted to deal with

---

*For the Marine Corps, involvement began in 1954 with the assignment of the first Marine advisor (Lieutenant Colonel Victor J. Croizat), continued with the insertion of a helicopter task force at Soc Trang in 1962, and increased significantly in March of 1965 with the landing of the 9th Marine Expeditionary Brigade at Da Nang.

THE WAR GOES ON

Photo courtesy of Capt Russell R. Thurman, USMC (Ret)
Two CH-53Ds from HMH-462 carrying elements of 2d Battalion, 4th Marines head for Saigon. The first helicopter landed in the DAO compound at 1506 on 29 April 1975.

The Paris Peace Accords, with this introduction, were signed by the U.S., South Vietnam, North Vietnam, and the Provisional Revolutionary Government on 27 January 1973. It restricted the U.S. to a maximum of 50 military personnel in South Vietnam.

AGREEMENT ON ENDING THE WAR

AND

RESTORING PEACE IN VIET-NAM

The Parties participating in the Paris Conference on Viet-Nam,

With a view to ending the war and restoring peace in Viet-Nam on the basis of respect for the Vietnamese people's fundamental national rights and the South Vietnamese people's right to self-determination, and to contributing to the consolidation of peace in Asia and the world,

Have agreed on the following provisions and undertake to respect and to implement them:

charges and countercharges of landgrabbing, deception, and deceit by both the North and South Vietnamese. Having little or no success, it merely served as a conduit for frustration and diplomatic infighting. The U.S., North Vietnam, South Vietnam, and Viet Cong representatives of the Four-Power group resolved little, leaving as a legacy to the Two-Power Joint Military Commission (South Vietnam and Viet Cong) and the International Commission of Control and Supervision unresolved problems, misguided efforts, and mutual distrust.[3]

The ICCS, virtually powerless, found enforcement of the Paris Peace Accords impossible. The North Vietnamese indifference and flagrant disregard of the peace terms so frustrated Canada that it gave proper notice and quit the commission on 31 July 1973. Announcement of the decision to withdraw came on the heels of the 15 July Viet Cong release of two Canadian observers whom the Communists had illegally seized and held captive since the 28th of June. After a personal request from President Richard M. Nixon to Shah Mohammed Reza Pahlavi, Iran agreed to replace Canada on the ICCS and on 29 August its first observers arrived in South Vietnam. The new member soon learned what Canada and the other members of the ICCS already knew: some of the signatories to the Paris Peace Agreement had chosen to ignore their own words. Just prior to its departure from Southeast Asia, Canada charged that North Vietnam regularly had been violating Article 7 ". . . by moving thousands of troops into South Vietnam and that the infiltration was continuing on a 'massive' scale."[4] The terms of that part of the protocol allowed only a one-for-one replacement of worn-out or damaged armaments, munitions, and war materials, and precluded anyone from introducing troops, military advisors, or military personnel including technical assistants into South Vietnam.[5]

The Communists argued that the United States did not adhere to the spirit of the Accords. General Tran Van Tra, the Viet Cong representative to the Four-Power Commission, maintained that the United States and South Vietnam attempted to use the agreement, "in accordance with their existing plans, . . . to pacify, encroach, and build a strong army in order to change the balance of forces in their favor and gain

Between 27 January and 27 March 1973 the last American military forces left South Vietnam. U.S. Army soldiers and U.S. Air Force airmen board a plane bound for the United States while representatives of the four-power Joint Military Commission observe.

Marine Corps Historical Collection

complete control of South Vietnam."*⁶ He further alleged that the United States violated three articles of the Peace Accords: Article 8 of the Protocol by leaving behind in Vietnam all "their weapons, ammunition, and military equipment"; Article 3 by withdrawing troops prior to a withdrawal plan approved by the Four-Power JMC and supervised by the ICCS; and Article 6 by failing to submit a plan for U.S. base dismantlement and in fact dismantling no bases when it had agreed to dismantle all of them.⁷ Tran Van Tra accused the Americans of a deception "brazen beyond words" because they had told him, " '. . . we have no bases in South Vietnam. All of them were turned over to the Republic of Vietnam prior to the signing of the agreement. [We] are now stationed in camps temporarily borrowed from the Republic of Vietnam.' "⁸

Even more critical than the issue of total removal of U.S. forces and their allies from South Vietnam was the question of what to do with North Vietnamese troops still occupying RVN territory. It represented disagreement between the United States and its ally. In attempting to conclude a peace acceptable to all parties, President Richard M. Nixon authorized Henry Kissinger, head of the U.S. delegation in Paris, to agree to North Vietnam's demands. This decision did not meet with President Nguyen Van Thieu's approval. During the ongoing negotiations in Paris, the leader of South Vietnam repeatedly had voiced his opposition to any agreement which would allow North Vietnam to leave its troops in the Republic of Vietnam. To President Thieu this military arrangement represented an important strategic advantage for the Communists and a decided disadvantage for the government of South Vietnam (GVN), and it only served to intensify his displeasure with the Accords. Neither the events in Paris nor Kissinger's overtures had changed his position. Thieu contended that American estimates placing North Vietnamese military strength in the South at 140,000 were "imaginary and misleading" and suggested that the actual figure was not less than 300,000. Yet in the end when confronted with the possibility of a unilateral signing by the United States and Nixon's repeated pledges that the U.S. would " '. . . take massive action against North Viet-Nam in the event they break the agreement,' " President Thieu reluctantly agreed to comply with the terms of the Paris Peace Accords. It would not be his last tough decision nor would he have to wait long for his concerns to become reality.⁹

Despite serving as voting members of the Joint Military Commission responsible for maintenance of the peace, the North Vietnamese and Viet Cong openly violated the ceasefire agreement. Using force wherever necessary to accomplish political ends, Communist military activities focused on strategically important areas. One such area and the site of numerous ceasefire violations was the Mekong River which played a central role in the resupply of Cambodia and U.S. support of that government.** On 29 June 1973, Congress altered that role when it voted on the Case-Church Amendment, a measure to end military assistance to Cambodia. Unlike its predecessor, the Cooper-Church Amendment which had attempted to ban combat activity in Cambodia in 1970, this rider to a continuing funding resolution passed. It prohibited the United States, after 15 August 1973, from engaging in any combat activity in Indochina, especially air operations.*** Without U.S. combat air support to protect the overland lines of communication, the

---

*Some of Tran Van Tra's statements are based on highly questionable sources as evidenced by his use of a quote from a report issued on 6 April 73 by the Committee to Denounce War Crimes in Vietnam, a U.S. antiwar group. He writes: "In the 2-month period between 28 January and 28 March 1973, the Saigon administration violated the Paris Agreement more than 70,000 times, including 19,770 landgrabbing operations, 23 artillery shellings, 3,375 bombings and strafings of liberated areas, and 21,075 police operations in areas under their control." *B2 Theatre*, pp. 18-19.

**In 1970, a coup replaced Prince Norodom Sihanouk, an avowed neutralist, with Lon Nol, who openly professed his alliance with the United States, which then immediately recognized the new Cambodian government and began aiding it in its struggle with Communist insurgents. For more information on Cambodia, see Chapter 7.

***In response to the American incursion into Cambodia in 1970, Senator Frank F. Church, a Democrat from Idaho, and Senator John Sherman Cooper, a Republican from Kentucky, cosponsored an amendment to the Foreign Military Sales Act which would have prohibited the use of American troops and advisors in Cambodia and outlawed direct air support of Cambodian forces. It passed the Senate but failed in the House and when finally passed on 29 December 1970 as part of the Defense Appropriations Bill, it only barred the introduction of U.S. ground troops in Laos and Thailand. Two years later, Senator Church and Senator Clifford P. Case, a Republican from New Jersey, combined forces to sponsor a bipartisan measure bearing their names. Its passage in June 1973 reflected the growing disenchantment of Congress with even minimal American involvement in Asian combat. In December 1973, Congress passed yet another ban on combat activity in Southeast Asia. This one, a part of the foreign aid bill, forbade the use of any funds for military operations in or over Vietnam, Laos, or Cambodia. Col Harry G. Summers, Jr., *Vietnam Almanac* (New York: Facts On File Publications, 1985), pp. 132-133; "Senate OKs Another War Curb," *Facts On File* (1973), p. 498; and "Foreign Aid Authorized," *Facts On File* (1973), p. 1078.

Mekong River supply link became even more important, representing Cambodia's best chance for survival. North Vietnam, recognizing the strategic value of this border area, already had begun offensive operations to harass the civilian population and disrupt daily activities. The U.S. Navy in its segment of an April 1973 Defense Attache Office report described the effects of the Communists' ceasefire violations in this region of South Vietnam:

> In the area of the Tan Chau Naval Base there are now no civilians. Because of the daily artillery attacks of the North Vietnamese communists the civilian populace has relocated to Chau Doc and Long Xuyen. . . . Since the beginning of the recent attacks (approx. 1 month) over one hundred civilians have been killed and hundreds wounded. ICCS inspection teams have visited the sites of the atrocities, but for fear of being rocketed themselves disappear after a short visit.[10]

In the face of diplomatic agreements to the contrary, including a second ceasefire signed by the United States and North Vietnam on 13 June 1973, the war between North and South Vietnam continued. The North Vietnamese shifted the emphasis from battlefield engagements to logistics. Part of North Vietnam's plan was to deprive the South Vietnamese and Cambodian forces of their supplies while at the same time reinforcing its positions and, when able, stockpiling supplies for future actions.

Military and political control of the countryside in western South Vietnam and eastern Cambodia made it possible for North Vietnam to modify its warfighting methods while still continuing to develop its long-range strategy. In prophetic testament to the changing tides of war and the shift in North Vietnam's peacetime battlefield tactics the authors of the U.S. Navy's portion of the April 1973 DAO Report wrote: "The decision of the enemy to control the "Blue Water" Mekong River as well as establish Hong Ngu as an entry point to Vietnam makes for a determined enemy."[11]

There was no "peace" in sight as conditions in South Vietnam seemed to indicate that no one really wanted the Paris Accords to work. Despite the uncertain combat conditions and the numerous ceasefire violations, the Marine Corps adhered to the terms of the Accords. It terminated the Vietnamese Marine Corps Advisors Program, thereby reducing its presence to a handful of officers in the reorganized Defense Attache Office, Saigon, and a Marine Security Guard company. A Commander Naval Force Vietnam message, 13 March 1973, said in part: "The Marine Advisory Unit, NAVADVGRP, MACV will be disestablished effective 29 Mar 73 . . . . With the disestablishment of the Marine Advisory Unit, follow-on technical and material support to the Vietnamese Marine Corps will be coordinated by the VNMC Logistics Support Branch, Navy Division, Defense Attache Office, Saigon."[12]

The U.S. Department of Defense (DOD) appointed Major General John E. Murray, USA, an expert logistician, to head the DAO and serve in the capacity of defense attache. An Army officer who had begun his career as a private in July 1941, Major General Murray quickly discovered that defense attache duty in Saigon in 1973 would differ significantly from the norm. As the senior American military officer in South Vietnam, he would work with the Ambassador, but report to the Secretary of Defense. The Ambassador only had direct authority over the defense attache in the area of public affairs and media matters. A briefing on his mission responsibilities provided him with his clearest indication of the drastic changes underway in Vietnam: "One of the things I was told my assignment entailed was not to lose any more American lives. And number two, I was told to get the hell out of there in one year."[13] America was leaving South Vietnam and Major General Murray had been chosen to complete Vietnamization with a staff of 50 military men. Of the 50 assigned to the DAO, only four were Marines. In fact, within two months of DAO's founding, the entire American military complement in South Vietnam totalled less than 250 men, a far cry from the peak total of 543,400 in April 1969.[14]

With such a minimal presence in Vietnam, the United States had difficulty influencing events. This situation most affected the enforcement of Article 8. More than any other part of the Paris Accords, Article 8 (MIA Accountability) depended on good faith and cooperation.[15] Mutual trust and confidence, already in short supply, became even scarcer when discussion focused on the accountability of personnel missing in action. An international point of humanitarian concern, MIA accountability, quickly became the most serious Peace Accords issue. The Communists not only failed to cooperate in resolving the status of Americans and others missing in action, but also actively obstructed United States and South Vietnamese efforts to do so. On 15 December 1973, in a rice paddy 15 miles southwest of Saigon, the Communists ambushed an American-South Vietnamese team searching (as permitted by the agreements) for the bodies of missing Americans.* Fatalities included one U.S. Army officer, Captain Richard Morgan Rees, of Kent, Ohio, and one South Vietnamese pilot.[16] In addition to the several injured South Vietnamese, the ambush wounded four American servicemen including Army First Lieutenant Ben C. Elfrink. The seemingly mild, official U.S. reaction to this unwarranted killing of one of its military officers (unarmed) on a JMC-sanctioned, MIA recovery mission reflected the American public's growing detachment from Southeast Asian affairs. Americans had begun to view Indochinese events as South Vietnam's problems. Besides registering a protest with the ICCS and North Vietnam, the United States did little else. A few days later, a *Des Moines Tribune* editorial, entitled "Murder in Vietnam," captured the relationship between the "non-action" and the subtle changes underway in America: ". . . giving up searching for American servicemen would be sad but not as sad as running the risk of more incidents which might give some U.S. military men a reason to take 'necessary measures.' Surely the military establishment, the administration, and Congress have learned not to walk into that mess again."[17]

In Vietnam, the DAO had already begun its analysis of the ambush in an attempt to discern the Communists' purpose and intent. In a "back channel" message to the Pentagon, Major General Murray offered his conclusions: "The enemy's hostility toward JCRC operations has been clearly demonstrated in the ambush. . . . All search operations are subject to enemy intervention . . . we see no definite change in the enemy's attitude. . . ." The only change that did occur was for the worse. In June 1974, the North Vietnamese and the Provisional Revolutionary Government (PRG) broke off all negotiations on MIAs by refusing to meet with the United States and South Vietnamese representatives.[18]

The PRG, having already (May 1974) stopped negotiating with the South Vietnamese on matters mandated by the Paris Accords, merely concluded the masquerade by supporting the North Vietnamese on

Photo courtesy of LtCol George E. Strickland, USMC (Ret)
LtCol George E. "Jody" Strickland, chief of the DAO VNMC Logistics Support Branch which helped supply the Vietnamese Marine Corps, poses in MR 1 with the commander of 4th Battalion, 147 Brigade, VNMC, LtCol Tran Ngoc Toan, shown here as a major.

the MIA issue and jointly they ended all negotiations. Ceasefire meant "less fire," but little else without consultation, cooperation, and some form of negotiations.

The NVA Marshals in the South

Immediately after the signing of the Accords, at the beginning of the ceasefire, there was a noticeable decline in the level of combat activity throughout South Vietnam.** This was cause for considerable optimism in Washington and elsewhere. Yet, the abatement in violence was merely a sign that the NVA had subscribed to new methods. Even though the Communists' tactics had changed, their strategy had not.

---

*Lieutenant Colonel Edward A. "Tony" Grimm, Plans Officer, USSAG, Thailand, from April 1974 until April 1975, remembered that "The lasting impact of the enemy ambush . . . was that Ambassador Graham Martin ordered a halt to any future JCRC operations in RVN. From then on the JCRC had to rely on . . . broadcasts and leaflets encouraging Vietnamese villagers to free their hamlets from the spirits of dead Americans." LtCol Edward A. Grimm, Comments on draft ms, 28Nov88 (Comment File, MCHC).

**U.S. Congressional records reveal that ARVN soldiers killed dropped from 28,000 in 1972 to 13,500 in 1973. On the last day of December 1974, when the statisticians compiled the totals for the year, a new trend became readily apparent, war had again supplanted peace. ARVN troops killed in action in 1974 were 30,000. *Senate Report Vietnam*, p. 1, and *House Report Vietnam*, p. 45.

North Vietnamese Army Photo

North Vietnamese Army soldiers build the Truong Son highway in western South Vietnam. Vietnamese Marines reported the activity in 1973, but RVN troops couldn't stop it.

North Vietnam's objective was still the conquest of South Vietnam, and the planned lull in fighting allowed it to refit and reinforce its units, reconstruct its lines of communication, and replenish its supplies in the south. During the early stages of this marshalling period, the NVA continued to maintain a military presence in South Vietnam and to apply pressure to the Army of the Republic of Vietnam through localized small unit actions. While the North Vietnamese participated in these disruptive activities, the American public remained largely uninformed; Vietnam was no longer front-page news.

By May of 1974, U.S. analysts agreed that Hanoi planned to continue its buildup in the south, and, in a matter of a few months, would have enough troops to conduct a major offensive. At year's end, the strength increase of the North Vietnamese forces in South Vietnam was so dramatic that some experts predicted an imminent attack.[19]

Although aware of the North Vietnamese Army's preparations and its size, American analysts still believed that if any large-scale attack occurred, it would fail. By basing their forecast on the command and control inflexibility displayed by the North Vietnamese in both the 1968 Tet Offensive and the 1972 Easter Offensive and the expectation of effective air support, the analysts erred. Lieutenant Colonel George E. "Jody" Strickland, who served in Saigon at the DAO as the Chief, Vietnamese Marine Corps Logistic Support Branch, Navy Division (Chief, VNMC LSB), from June 1973 until June 1974, offered his candid recollection of this evaluation: "The dichotomous assessment of an imminent NVA attack on one hand and the forecast of its failure on the other had obvious detrimental influences." Lieutenant Colonel Strickland related that despite the prediction of failure most Americans and South Vietnamese still vigorously prepared for the anticipated enemy offensive, including the Vietnamese Marine Corps (VNMC) which reacted by ". . . building up supplies, hardening defenses, and expanding reconnaissance and offensive operations in MR 1."[20] Yet others refused even to consider the possible consequences of an NVA success. The American Embassy,

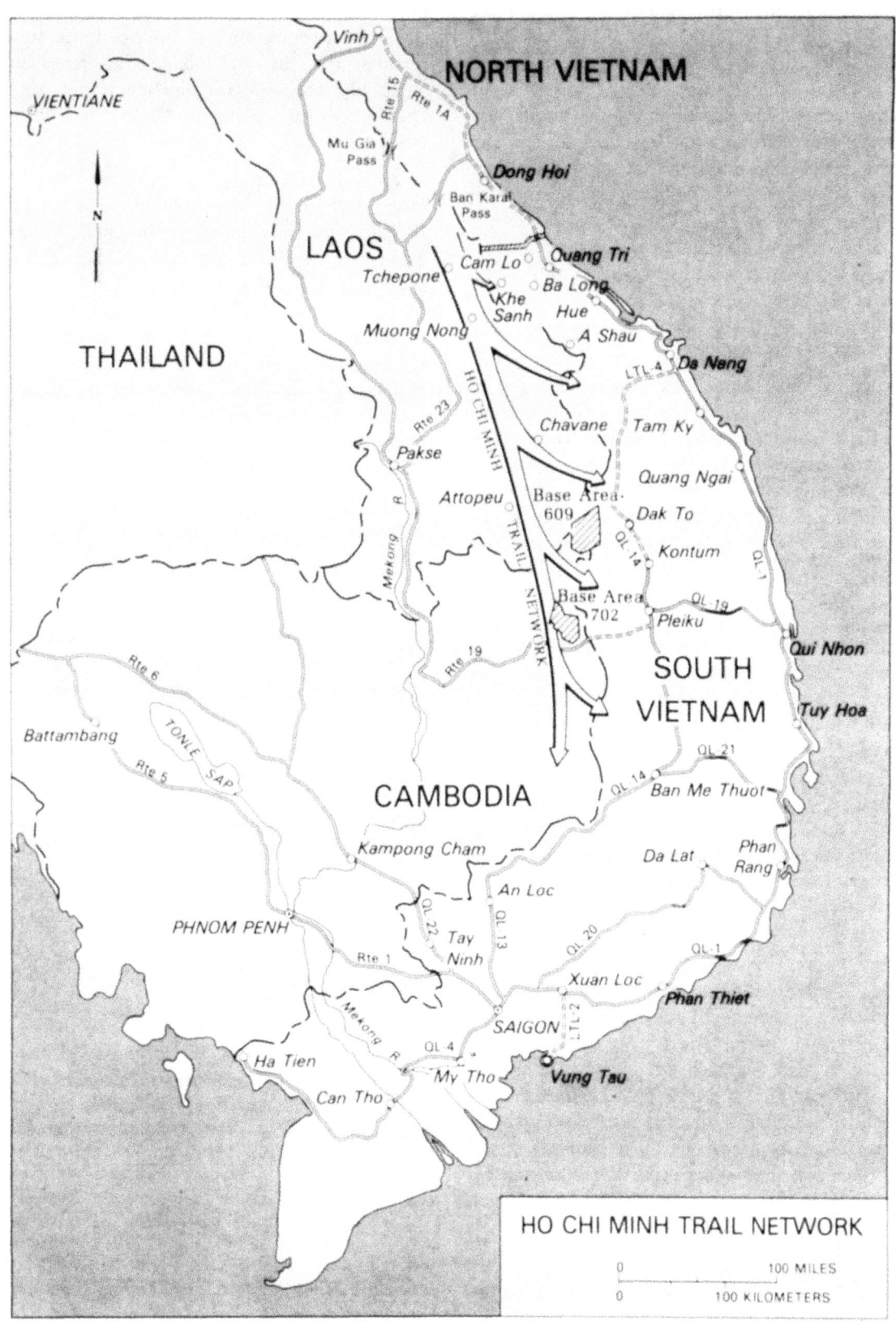

a bastion of optimism throughout this period, reacted to the forecast by agreeing to a reduction in the size of its security force and by refusing to acknowledge the need for contingency evacuation plans. The conflicting opinions on the extent of the North Vietnamese Army's progress and its offensive capability persisted until the bitter end. Fourteen years later, Strickland proffered his opinion of the consequences of this argument, stating: "Conflicting GVN [Government of Vietnam] decisions at the start of the 1975 NVA offensive were rooted in the disastrous prediction of NVA failure."[21]

The failure never occurred because of exhaustive efforts by the North Vietnamese to remedy longstanding deficiencies in command and control. Developing new lines of communication became their "peacetime" mission and evidence of significant new construction reflected the priority attached to it. Beginning, not by coincidence, with the ceasefire and immediate freedom from U.S. air interdiction, the Communists built or improved a road network that ran from North Vietnam through the western reaches of the three northernmost regions in South Vietnam. East-west spurs from the main highway ran into the A Shau and Que Son valleys in the northern part of South Vietnam and into the Central Highlands. Aerial photographs in December 1974 revealed the extent of these improvements.* In western Thua Thien Province, a mere trail two years prior had become a hard-surface, all-weather road. Formerly a trek to South Vietnam on foot consumed 70 days, but now North Vietnamese Army trucks could carry a battalion from North Vietnam to Military Region 3 in less than three weeks. With NVA troops riding instead of walking a majority of the distance, the number of casualties from fatigue, malaria, and other diseases significantly decreased.[22]

Yet without a sufficient supply of petroleum products, the Communists' road network meant little. North Vietnam could not sustain a major offensive in South Vietnam without a guaranteed source of fuel. To satisfy this need and properly complement their improved LOCs, the NVA constructed an oil pipeline from North Vietnam extending almost to Phuoc Long Province in South Vietnam. The length of pipeline in South Vietnam totalled 280 miles, of which about 270 were constructed after, and in violation of, the ceasefire.[23] General Van Tien Dung boasted of this accomplishment: "Alongside the strategic road to the east of Tuong Song range was a 5,000-kilometer-long oil pipeline which ran from Quang Tri through the Tay Nguyen and on to Loc Ninh...."[24]

With the opening of the pipeline, the NVA no longer had to rely for petroleum, oil and lubricant (POL) on barrels laboriously man-handled into position and cached in the countryside. In addition to the supplies of petroleum which it was able to store in South Vietnam, the NVA by January of 1975 had stockpiled an estimated 65,000 tons of ammunition. One estimate projected that this amount of ammunition could support an operation of the intensity of the 1972 Easter Offensive for at least one year. The Communists now possessed sufficient fuel to put these "bullets" to good use. [25]

By enhancing the means of transport which allowed an increase in the frequency of replenishment, the North Vietnamese Army almost doubled the number of artillery pieces and quadrupled the number of tanks it had in South Vietnam. Between January 1973 and January 1975, the enemy increased the number of artillery weapons in the South from 225 to an estimated 400. In armored firepower, the NVA expanded its force from an estimated 150 to approximately 600 100mm gun tanks including Soviet-built T-54s and Chinese Type 59s. Ominously indicating their intentions, the North Vietnamese also augmented their combat power by increasing the number of antiaircraft artillery (AAA) regiments in South Vietnam from 13 to 23. This threat included four battalions of the SA-2 surface-to-air missile, which they deployed in the northern part of South Vietnam, just below the demilitarized zone, from Khe Sanh to Dong Ha. In addition to the SA-2s, the NVA emplaced radar-directed 85mm and 100mm AAA guns in Military Region 1. The North Vietnamese also reintroduced sizeable quantities of the SA-7 (Grail), a man-transportable, shoulder-fired, heat-seeking missile which complemented its improved antiaircraft capability.[26] Because of the higher altitude potential of this antiaircraft system, it became increasingly more hazardous and difficult for the South Vietnamese to fly close air support missions, particularly in the northern provinces. Lieutenant Colonel Strickland recalled that during his tour (June 1973-74), "VNAF [South Vietnamese Air Force] close air support for the Vietnamese Marine Corps was virtually zero."[27] With

---

*Lieutenant Colonel Strickland stated that the road's discovery was reported by VNMC LSB personnel as early as August 1973 at which time airborne hand-held photos were provided to the DAO, VNMC, and HQMC. Strickland Comments.

Marine Corps Historical Collection

LtCol Anthony Lukeman, pictured later as a lieutenant general, replaced LtCol Strickland in 1974 as chief of the VNMC LSB. In that year he was concerned over severe cuts in funds for the Vietnamese Marines.

almost no interdiction from the air, the NVA wasted little time in exploiting this window of opportunity. The North Vietnamese Army's combat troops in South Vietnam, judged at the end of 1973 to be in excess of 149,000, grew in the next 12 months to over 185,000. Additionally 107,000 support personnel stationed in South Vietnam assisted the frontline troops by keeping the lines of communication open. Besides these regular soldiers, unofficial reports in January of 1975 placed 45,000 guerrillas in the Republic of South Vietnam.[28]

At first cautious, especially in the months immediately following the ceasefire, the North Vietnamese soon pursued their activities with impunity as the South Vietnamese showed themselves ineffectual in stopping the build-up. By its own admission, the North Vietnamese Politburo, which directed the military activities in South Vietnam, kept a weather-eye cocked toward the United States to gauge the reaction to each of its moves. They needed no reminder that a powerful U.S. Seventh Fleet in the South China Sea and an equally powerful U.S. Seventh Air Force based in Thailand were disconcertingly close. Yet what they did not see and hear, especially in the South Vietnamese skies, reassured them and encouraged much bolder actions in the days ahead.[29]

During Fiscal Years (FY) 1974 and 1975, the U.S. Congress slashed budget line items providing military aid to South Vietnam. Although not cut entirely, the funding equaled only 50 percent of the administration's recommended level. During FY 1973 the United States spent approximately $2.2 billion in military aid to South Vietnam. In FY 1974, the total dropped to $1.1 billion. Finally, in FY 1975, the figure fell to $700 million, a trend that was not misread in Hanoi. As General Dung very candidly phrased it, "Thieu [President Nguyen Van Thieu of South Vietnam] was forced to fight a poor man's war."[30] Perhaps more distressing, as far as the recipients of the military aid were concerned, was the fact that by 1975 the dollars spent for certain items were buying only half as many goods as they had in 1973. For example, POL costs were up by 100 percent, the cost of one round of 105mm ammunition had increased from 18 to 35 dollars, and the cost of providing 13.5 million individual rations exceeded 22 million dollars. Considering the steady reduction in funding and the almost universal increase in prices, the South Vietnamese in 1975 could buy only about an eighth as much defense for the dollar as they had in 1973.[31]

In June 1974, just before the start of FY 1975, Lieutenant Colonel Anthony Lukeman replaced Lieutenant Colonel Strickland as Chief, VNMC LSB. Almost immediately he began to notice the effects of the reduced funding, less than a third the size of the 1973 budget. In September, in a letter to HQMC, he penned his concerns:

> Briefly, the current level means grounding a significant part of the VNAF [South Vietnamese Air Force], cutting back on the capabilities of the VNN [South Vietnamese Navy], and running unacceptable risks in the stock levels of ammunition, POL, and medical supplies. I am concerned it will mean, in the long run, decreased morale, because replacement of uniforms and individual equipment will start to suffer about a year from now, and the dollars spent on meat supplements to the basic rice diet will be cut way back. At this point, the planners have concentrated (understandably) most of their attention on "shoot, move, and communicate" but have lost in the buzz words a feel for the man who will be doing those things.[32]

The South Vietnamese attempted to adjust to the decreased funding and rising costs, but each of these adjustments had the effect of placing them in a more disadvantageous position relative to the strengthened North Vietnamese forces. The tempo of operations of all services, most particularly the Air Force, was cut back to conserve fuel. The expenditure rate of munitions also dropped. Interdiction fire was all but halted. The decreased financial support forced the South Vietnamese to consider cutting costs in all areas of defense including the abandonment of outposts and fire bases in outlying regions.

The overall impact of the budget reduction on the allocation of military monies was readily apparent. In FY 1975 at the $700 million level all of the funded appropriations were spent on consumables. There was nothing left over for procurement of equipment to replace combat and operational losses on the one-for-one basis permitted by the Paris Accords. Handcuffed by a lack of funds, the South Vietnamese could derive little comfort from an agreement which authorized both sides to resupply selectively as losses occurred.[33]

In an effort to increase South Vietnam's purchasing power while complying with restrictions imposed by the Accords, the U.S. reduced the number of civilian contract maintenance personnel in South Vietnam. These U.S. civilians provided highly technical assistance to the South Vietnamese in the areas of management, maintenance, and supply. The reduction in the availability of their critical skills had an immediate and debilitating effect on the overall readiness of the Vietnamese Armed Forces. Technical expertise and training, an important element in successful combat service support, became a critical factor in the highly complicated task of maintaining reliable aircraft. The Vietnamese tried to shoulder more of the burden in this area, but as expected, they suffered severely from lack of experience. It required several years to develop the skills necessary to manage a field as complex as aviation maintenance, and that time did not exist.[34]

In an oversight hearing to develop the FY 1975 budget, the Subcommittee of the Committee on Appropriations of the House of Representatives discussed the merits of Fiscal Year 1975 military assistance to Vietnam. A comparison of raw statistics relating to ar-

The UH-1 helicopter, shown here, could carry a flight crew and 12 soldiers. The South Vietnamese operated 861 UH-1s; helicopters totaled more than 40 percent of RVN aircraft.
Department of Defense Photo (USMC) A801616

Photo courtesy of BGen William A. Bloomer, USMC (Ret)

An EA-6B Prowler cruises near ships of the Seventh Fleet providing electronic countermeasures support to the Navy-Marine Corps team. These aircraft of VMCJ-1 would fly from the USS Coral Sea *around the clock in support of Operation Frequent Wind.*

tillery reveals how misleading the numbers game really was. In total numbers of artillery pieces, the South Vietnamese were down from 1,600 at the time of the ceasefire to 1,200 in January of 1975. On paper this still presented a distinct advantage for the South Vietnamese when compared to the estimated 400 tubes the North Vietnamese operated in South Vietnam. If the comparison ended there, the South Vietnamese enjoyed an imposing three-to-one edge over the NVA. Yet the characteristics of the weapons presented a vastly different picture. The North Vietnamese were equipped with 85, 100, 122, and 130mm guns, all of which could fire faster with a longer range than their South Vietnamese counterparts. The ARVN, meanwhile, possessed primarily 105mm and 155mm howitzers. They augmented this array of weapons with 80 175mm guns, the only ones with enough range to fire counterbattery, while all of the enemy's artillery possessed this capability. Compounding this problem was the fact that the ARVN by this time was fighting a basically static war from fixed positions, budget reductions having limited their ability to conduct prudent clearing and counter-offensive operations. In contrast the NVA enjoyed relatively unrestricted freedom of movement. With the ability to mass its weapons at the time and place of its choosing, the NVA gained a significant edge. To neutralize the NVA advantage, the ARVN used air support, which often during times of critical need was not available, and when on station, usually ineffective.[35]

The question surrounding the reliability of air support arose from the combined effects of funding cutbacks and enhanced North Vietnamese AAA capability. This combination had a detrimental impact on the readiness and effectiveness of the South Vietnamese Air Force (VNAF). The VNAF numbered some 62,000 men and was subdivided into six air divisions with bases at Da Nang, Pleiku, Bien Hoa, Tan Son Nhut, Binh Thuy, and Can Tho. At the time of the ceasefire, South Vietnam operated 2,075 aircraft with Article 7 of the Accords allowing a one-for-one replacement of lost aircraft. More importantly, the VNAF composition reflected a serious degradation in firepower and the ability to suppress the enemy's air defense system. The South Vietnamese strike force consisted of 388 attack aircraft (79 A-1s, 248 A-37s, 11 AC-47s, and 50 AC-119s) and 143 F-5A/B fighters. In 1972 it added two squadrons (32 aircraft) of C-130As to its arsenal, significantly modernizing its transport fleet of 56 C-7s, 14 C-47s, 16 C-119s, and 19 C-123s. Still, the bulk of the VNAF, over 44 per cent, consisted of helicopters: 861 UH-1s and 70 CH-47s. Thus this seemingly impressive figure of 2,075 aircraft quickly translated into only 391 jet-propelled fighter and attack aircraft and no electronic warfare planes capable of neutralizing the enemy's highly effective, mobile air defense system.[36]

The North Vietnamese had used extensive numbers of radars to build a very deadly air defense network centered around three closely integrated weapon systems. As General William W. Momyer, a former commander of the Seventh Air Force, later wrote: "The air defense in North Vietnam was a thoroughly integrated combination of radars, AAA, SAMS, and MiGs. It was Soviet in design and operation."[37] This combination of high speed aircraft (MiGs), antiaircraft artillery, surface-to-air missiles (SAMs) like the SA-2, and numerous radar sites posed a serious threat to allied air superiority. To insure the primacy of allied air power, this enemy challenge had to be met with increasingly more sophisticated American weapons systems and antiair procedures. Before the ceasefire, these methods included jamming enemy radars using electronic counter-measure (ECM) aircraft such as the Air Force EB-66 and the Marine Corps EA-6A, high speed avoidance maneuvering (possible with low-flying, very maneuverable, tactical fighters—F-4s, A-4s, and A-7s), sophisticated detection devices installed on specific aircraft (code-named Wild Weasel) to detect, harass, and destroy SAM sites, and introduction of antiradiation missiles, precision-guided munitions (PGMs, such as laser-guided "smart bombs"), and chaff bombs (full of metallic strips used to confuse NVA radars attempting target identification).[38]

Although most of the Communist air defense system remained in place in North Vietnam, some of it appeared near the demilitarized zone (DMZ) in 1972. When North Vietnam launched the Easter Offensive in April 1972 it deployed SA-2s, radars, and a hand-held weapon, the SA-7, in support of its army. The presence of this modernized, mobile, ground air defense system in South Vietnam had immediate consequences for the United States and significant long-term effects for the VNAF: "No longer was it feasible to operate below 10,000 feet without using countermeasures."[39] The presence of the SA-7 with its heat-seeking missile meant that "low and slow" aerial delivery of munitions was unsafe and, as such, outdated. The alternative was to fly higher where the results were much less predictable. The SA-7, in effect, had removed a third of South Vietnam's attack aircraft from the battlefield as the Soviet-built weapon virtually "put some aircraft such as the A-1 out of business."[40]

In 1972, the United States countered this NVA move with new ECM and anti-SAM tactics including more sophisticated chaff delivery, flares to confuse the SA-7, and introduction of a new jamming aircraft, the Marine Corps' EA-6B Prowler. As successful and necessary as these measures proved to be, the United States, bound by the terms of the 1973 Paris Accords, had no choice but to remove its aircraft and highly technical weapon systems from South Vietnam. Overnight, the VNAF arsenal lost its means of suppressing the enemy's ground air defenses. The United States had bequeathed the South Vietnamese Armed Forces an air-ground team absent its most essential element, air supremacy. General Momyer succinctly summarized, "The contest for air superiority is the most important contest of all, for no other operation can be sustained if this battle is lost. To win it, [one] must have the best equipment, the best tactics, the freedom to use them, and the best pilots."[41] The South Vietnamese Air Force had none of these. Possibly worse, it had no all-weather attack aircraft like the A-6A Intruder, no navigational bombing punch in the form of F-4 Phantoms equipped with special electronic equipment (Loran), and no B-52s. Instead, out of necessity, the VNAF relied on the belief that, when needed, U.S. air power, technological aid, and money would be forthcoming. This belief would persist until the bitter end. Former Commandant of the Vietnamese Marine Corps and a member of the Joint General Staff (JGS), Lieutenant General Le Nguyen Khang, expressed the psychological and emotional importance of that faith: "We needed only one American plane to come in and drop one bomb to let the North Vietnamese know we were still getting strong U.S. support. We felt at that time (1975) if we could get one plane or a little bit of air support the war might change."[42]

Compounding their strategic problems were tactical and logistical problems. By 1 January 1975, the South Vietnamese had suffered the loss of 370 aircraft as a result of operational training and combat. None of these aircraft was ever replaced. The South Vietnamese simply could not afford replacement aircraft. Additionally, 224 aircraft were placed in flyable storage because the spare parts and petroleum products needed to keep them flying could not be funded within the constraints of the new $700 million U.S. budget package. The 1,481 operational aircraft in the South Vietnamese inventory on 1 January 1975 reflected a two-year attrition of nearly 25 percent. The debilitating effect of unreplaced aircraft losses and an imposing NVA antiaircraft threat had combined to produce a South Vietnamese Air Force simply incapable of neutralizing the North Vietnamese firepower advantage.[43]

With South Vietnam's air force nearly impotent, the navy represented a potential alternative. The U.S. Navy had provided gunfire support for ground operations prior to the ceasefire and many South Vietnamese military leaders expected the same level of firepower from the Vietnamese Navy (VNN). The concept of a navy to serve the coastal nation of Vietnam began with the French, but "During the years from 1954 to 1959, the Navy section of the Military Assistance Advisory Group, Vietnam worked to develop a viable navy for South Vietnam."44 Its efforts produced a Vietnamese Navy which within 15 years was capable of manning 672 amphibious ships and craft, 20 mine warfare vessels, 56 service craft, and over 240 junks. Composed of 42,000 men, the VNN in April 1975 consisted of a naval staff with Vice Admiral Chung Tan Cang as its chief of naval operations, a sea force headed by Captain Nyugen Xuan Son, and amphibious forces commanded by Commodore Hoang Co Minh. This navy operated on rivers, along the coast, and at sea using everything from destroyer escorts to patrol craft. Sixteen coastal radars, also manned by the Vietnamese Navy, assisted them in monitoring NVA coastal activity and supporting approximately 400 sea force vessels responsible for stopping resupply by sea. Within months of the U.S. Navy's departure, the coastal radars failed for want of parts and proper maintenance. Lacking the technical expertise to keep its radars operating, the VNN lost its best means of locating and interdicting North Vietnamese infiltrators. The Vietnamese Navy's other mission, supporting ground operations, fared little better.

The Vietnamese Marine Corps (VNMC), which for political reasons had been made a separate service in 1965, complained often about the VNN's inability to provide naval gunfire support. Accustomed to the U.S. Navy's version of firepower, this supporting arm suffered severely under the much smaller Vietnamese Navy. The VNN failed to provide the Vietnamese Marines with much needed, integrated, and coordinated naval bombardment. Captain Nguyen Xuan Son related that the VNMC often complained that it was not receiving enough gunfire support. It had been conditioned by the U.S. Navy, which upon request, would provide up to 1,000 rounds a day. Having experienced that type of firepower, the VNN maximum of 100 to 200 rounds a day fell far short of the Marines' needs and expectations. Captain Son described the navy's dilemma, "we had to explain to the Marines and to the JGS that our ships had only one gun, one 5-inch barrel, or the maximum which was two 3-inch barrels, and if we lined up five ships then we had five barrels and they could not fire all day."45

Although many of the weaknesses of the Vietnamese Armed Forces can be attributed to problems of inflation, cutting of funding, shortages, inferior equipment, broken promises, and North Vietnamese subterfuge, South Vietnam was not entirely blameless. Army Colonel Richard I. McMahon, a member of the Defense Attache staff during this period, later wrote that the South Vietnamese required:

> ... [a] formidable military force at their side ... [the] South Vietnamese commanders had little reason to believe they could stand on their own.... Although the departure of the American military was the major reason for this lack of confidence it was not the only one. Combat performance of the South Vietnamese Army was not good and its commanders knew it.46

Other factors, including corruption and poor senior officer leadership contributed to the eventual collapse of the Saigon government. As enemy pressure intensified, these cracks in the armor began to surface, especially on the battlefield.

In the late fall of 1973, the Communists began to increase direct military pressure on the ARVN forces. In November, the NVA launched a division-size offensive in Quang Duc Province, located on the Cambodian border just south of Darlac Province. The attack in the southernmost province of Military Region 2 resulted in the heaviest fighting since the ceasefire. Between December 1973 and February 1974, the NVA attacked and seized several South Vietnamese outposts in the remote border areas, including Tong Le Chan in western Military Region 3. During the spring and summer of 1974, fighting flared throughout South Vietnam.47

In the early morning hours of 17 May 1974, elements of the *2d Regiment, 3d NVA Division* launched a heavy attack against Phu Cat Airbase in Binh Dinh Province, Military Region 2. The objective was to neutralize the base in preparation for a general offensive throughout the province. After suffering initial setbacks, the 108th and 263d Regional Force Battalions counterattacked, driving the NVA forces from the vicinity of the base. The *NVA 16th Antiaircraft Battalion* and the *2d Battalion, 2d Regiment* of the *3d NVA Division* were rendered ineffective for combat as a result.48

On 10 August 1974, elements of the ARVN 22d Division opened a counteroffensive against the *3d NVA Division* guarding the entrance to the An Lao Valley in northern Binh Dinh Province. Combat operations in the valley, a Communist stronghold, represented some of the typical problems the ARVN experienced during this period of fiscal austerity. Due to budgeting considerations, the South Vietnamese Joint General Staff was forced during the operation to restrict the use of artillery and air support. Elsewhere in Military Region 2, the ARVN's 82d Ranger Battalion withstood a month-long siege in Camp Plei Me in southern Pleiku Province. Against the unrelenting pressure of the *48th* and *64th NVA Regiments*, the Rangers held out from 4 August until relieved by elements of the ARVN 53d Regiment on 2 September 1974.[49]

Between 27 and 30 September 1974, NVA forces drove ARVN defenders off Mo Tau Mountain. From this vantage point, the North Vietnamese artillery could command Phu Bai Airfield, the major government airstrip north of Hai Van Pass, located in Military Region 1. The NVA immediately brought up its guns and cleared the airstrip by fire. The mountain complex was occupied by four NVA battalions, which were finally dislodged by elements of the ARVN 1st Division and 15th Ranger Group on 11 December.[50]

During the first week of December, heavy fighting erupted in Military Region 4 when Communist forces launched attacks in both the northern and southern portions of the Mekong Delta. The major threat was the *5th NVA Division* whose regiments, refitted in Cambodia, were moving into Kien Tuong Province (just south of the Parrot's Beak region where a peninsula of Cambodian territory pokes a nose into South Vietnam). To parry the Communist incursion, the 9th ARVN Division engaged the NVA as they first entered the Cambodian border region.[51]

While major unit fighting was taking place in Military Regions 1 and 4, an equally ominous event occurred that December in Military Region 2. The NVA's *968th Division*, which had been operating in southern Laos for several years, moved en masse into the Central Highlands. This marked the first time since the Cease-fire Agreement that an entire NVA division had entered the south as a unit. During this period Military Region 3 had remained relatively quiet. Yet as the year came to an end, NVA units were closing in on Song Be, the capital of Phuoc Long Province. As the sun set on the last day of 1974, its shadows foretold more than just the impending arrival of a new year in the Republic of Vietnam.[52]

By the end of 1974, the North Vietnamese had wrested the initiative from the thinly spread and overcommitted ARVN Divisions. The Joint General Staff had no uncommitted reserve. Its strategic reserve, the Airborne Division and the Marine Division, were already deployed to Military Region 1. As early as 1973 when the United States installed an Army general as the head of its newly formed Defense Attache Office, Americans began to recognize the seriousness of the situation. General Murray recalled, "I was shocked to discover that they had no general reserve. All thirteen of their divisions were fully committed. We had left them without a general reserve."[53] The need for a reserve and the strategic value it offered as a means to buy time and avert forced withdrawal or even defeat would become readily apparent in 1975. It would not be a good year for the South Vietnamese. Time was running out.

A Division of Marines

Following the Easter Offensive of 1972, the South Vietnamese Marine Division remained in the northernmost part of Military Region 1. It faced three North Vietnamese divisions in defensive positions to the north and west. The division's assigned area of operations (AO) encompassed over 1,600 square miles of diverse terrain. Bounded on the north by the Thach Han River, the AO stretched south to the vicinity of Phong Dien. The South China Sea was the eastern boundary while to the west the foothills of the mountainous Hai Lang forest west of Route 1 marked the extent of the Marines' responsibility. The division headquarters was located in Huong Dien, a village northeast of Hue in the coastal lowlands of Thua Thien Province. Numerous units of the division's supporting organizations, among them the amphibious support battalion and the motor transport company, were based in Hue.[54] The Vietnamese Marine Corps' headquarters remained in Saigon at 15 Le Thanh Ton in the old French Commando Compound. This location also contained the Americans' VNMC Logistic Support Branch, DAO. Thus Lieutenant Colonels Strickland and then Lukeman maintained an office in the same building as the VNMC chief of staff, Colonel Le Dinh Que. Besides a division rear headquarters, the VNMC operated a training center, ranges, and a hospital complex at Song Than (10 miles northeast of Saigon, near Bien Hoa off Highway 1 at Di An); training facilities and a supply section at Thu Duc; and a training base at Vung Tau.* Opened on 8 September 1972 and occupying part of the former 1st U.S. Army Division encampment, Song Than also housed the VNMC's recruit depot and a company of LVTs, a few of which regularly trained at Vung Tau.[55]

The Marine Division was one of the best divisions in the South Vietnamese Armed Forces. Until Decem-

---

*Unlike the USMC, the Vietnamese Marine Corps as a separate service had its own medical battalion. Another unusual arrangement provided for the existence of two chiefs of staff. To assist him in his duties as division commander and commandant, General Lan had established a second billet at Huong Dien into which he continuously rotated officers junior to Colonel Que, the chief of staff at division headquarters in Saigon. Strickland Comments.

Entrance to VNMC Training Center and Song Than base camp on the outskirts of Saigon.
Photo courtesy of LtCol George E. Strickland, USMC (Ret)

ber of 1974 when the newly formed 468th Brigade* was added, the division consisted of three Marine Brigades: the 147th, the 258th, and 369th and supporting units. It was reinforced by the 1st ARVN Armored Brigade, the 15th Ranger Group, and eight Regional Force battalions. Brigadier General Bui The Lan, Commandant of the Vietnamese Marine Corps** and a graduate of both the U.S. Marine Corps Amphibious Warfare School and Command and Staff College, personally commanded the Marine Division. Lan also had operational control of the 2d Airborne Brigade. Additionally, the Marines maintained 12 joint Marine and Popular Force platoons living in assigned villages and hamlets within the AO, a variation of the earlier U.S. Marine Corps Combined Action Program in MR 1. Concentrated in the hamlets surrounding Huong Dien, these platoons provided additional security for the division command post.[56]

---

*Originally, before the shifting of units began, the brigade designation corresponded to the battalions in that organization, e.g. battalions 1, 4, and 7 constituted the 147th Brigade. Strickland Comments.

**On 4 May 1972, President Thieu appointed the commandant of the VNMC, Lieutenant General Le Nguyen Khang to the Joint General Staff as assistant for operations. The next day, Colonel Lan, the division commander, became acting Commandant (CMC) of the Vietnamese Marine Corps. On 1 June 1972, exactly eighteen years after receiving his commission as a second lieutenant, Bui The Lan pinned on his stars. At that moment, Brigadier General Lan officially became CMC, but he began his new role while maintaining tactical command of the division. LtCol G. H. Turley and Capt M. R. Wells, "Easter Invasion," reprinted in *The Marines in Vietnam, 1954-1973, An Anthology and Annotated Bibliography* (Washington: MCHC, 1985), p. 190; "VNMC/MAU HistSum."

While deployed in MR 1, the Marine Division remained part of the RVNAF General Purpose Strategic Force. Controlled and directed by the Joint General Staff, rather than by Lieutenant General Ngo Quang Troung, the MR 1 commander, the Marine Division received its orders from Saigon. The JGS believed that when the NVA began their general offensive, the major thrust would come from the north. Apparently, this military assumption was sufficient reason for Saigon to maintain direct control of the strategically placed Marine Division. Despite this awkward command arrangement, General Lan and General Troung established and maintained an amicable working relationship.[57]

To prepare for the expected offensive, General Lan personally directed the construction of a formidable, in-depth defense throughout the division's AO. For each crew-served weapon there were three alternate fall-back positions. All were bunkered, stockpiled with 14 days of ammunition, and well-camouflaged. These were the best protected, best concealed positions that Lieutenant Colonel Strickland had seen in his four tours in Vietnam.[58]

The construction of the observation post and forward command post bunkers was unique. General Lan insisted that these critical command and control facilities be able to withstand a direct hit by a 130mm artillery shell. Several candidate structures were tested by command-detonated, captured 130mm shells placed directly on top of the bunkers. Through this process of trial and error, the VNMC built a bunker

Photo courtesy of LtCol George E. Strickland, USMC (Ret)
In front of the 369th Brigade command bunker inside the Citadel at Quang Tri City are LtCol George E. Strickland and brigade commander, LtCol Luong. Bunkers were stockpiled with 14 days of ammunition.

that satisifed General Lan. The final product was remarkably simple, but effective. The process of construction consisted of digging a hole, erecting within it a pyramid of pierced steel planking, and then compacting four feet of earth over the pyramid. The bunker, designed to accommodate three Marines— one standing and two sitting, plus their two PRC-25 radios—adequately withstood the 130mm detonation test. The unanswered question remained—could troops survive a similar explosion and a direct hit? General Lan solicited volunteers to find out, and three men agreed to enter the bunker and remain there during a second detonation. When the smoke had cleared, the bunker was still there. How had the troops fared? When asked for his comments on the experience, one of the Marines replied, "Very loud." With these fortifications complete, General Lan felt confident that he and his subordinates could exercise effective command and control, even under the most intense attacks.[59]

Of all the weapons at his disposal, General Lan took particular, almost personal care of his antitank missile launchers that fired the TOW (Tube-launched Optically-tracked Wire-guided) missile. The Viet-

Vietnamese Marine Commandant BGen Bui The Lan, right, and his chief of staff, Col Le Dinh Que, discuss VNMC matters with LtCol Strickland, chief of the VNMC LSB.
Photo courtesy of LtCol George E. Strickland, USMC (Ret)

namese Marines were among the first to employ the TOW in combat. In the Easter Offensive of 1972, they achieved 57 kills of NVA armored vehicles out of a total of 72 missiles fired. Serious about its use, General Lan's Marine Division possessed 12 TOW systems despite an authorization for only nine. General Lan's concept of employment was to attach some of the weapons to his battalions deployed in the enemy's likely avenues of approach. The remainder he kept under his personal control for operational use as a mobile reserve to reinforce the action at its hottest spots.

The VNMC displayed a remarkable ingenuity in developing its total TOW capability, particularly the mobile part. General Lan was not satisfied with the standard M-151 jeep as a prime mover for the TOW system. With the weapon and a two-man crew, there was not enough space remaining in the jeep to carry more than two missiles. Also, General Lan did not like the idea of carrying spares in a trailer towed behind a vehicle. Displaying as much resourcefulness here as they had in developing the bunker, the South Vietnamese Marines solved the problem. Instead of using the standard M151, General Lan mounted the TOW system on the M170 ambulance jeep. This vehicle had a longer bed than the M151, and it could easily accommodate the launcher and its crew. Spare missiles were carried by welding special racks on either side of the vehicle. General Lan produced a mobile TOW system capable of carrying crew, launcher, and seven missiles all in the same vehicle.

General Lan felt so strongly about the TOW that if he discovered anyone abusing this prized possession, he took immediate remedial and punitive action. Such an incident occurred during one of his daily visits to the forward deployed battalions. General Lan, upon learning that one of his supplymen was using a TOW battery as a source of current for the light in his tent, called for the battalion supply officer and the battalion commander. Nonjudicial punishment proceedings were conducted on the spot. He fined the clerk, the supply officer, and the battalion commander the cost of the battery, $900. Additionally, the battalion commander received one week confinement at hard labor. This incident took place in early 1974, when TOW components were in short supply.

With their TOWs and their in-depth defense, the Vietnamese Marines did not fear an NVA land attack. One of the two concerns that Lieutenant Colonel Strickland observed as keenly critical to the VNMC centered around the practice of laterally shifting forces (General Lan's other major concern was VNAF close

Photo courtesy of LtCol George E. Strickland, USMC (Ret)
Col Le Dinh Que, at left, the VNMC chief of staff, discusses with LtCol Strickland the transfer of a platoon of LVTP-5s to Military Region 1. The vehicles became obsolete as budget cuts and high petroleum prices combined to make their operation too costly.

air support). Too clearly, the VNMC had seen the rout of the 3d ARVN Division during the Easter Offensive where the division, in the midst of shifting units, had been caught by the NVA with its guard down. Commonplace throughout the war, the lateral shifting of units between highlands and lowlands addressed not tactics, but morale. The average South Vietnamese truly believed that the highlands and not the lowlands were infested with malaria-bearing mosquitoes. These inherited beliefs forced commanders to shift units in order to maintain morale.* General Lan knew that the NVA were familiar with this routine. Certain they would try to capitalize on it, General Lan devised a plan to overcome this weakness. All lateral shifts of Marine battalions were conducted under a cloak of secrecy with no advance warning. They were executed no differently than a surprise attack.[60]

In 1973 the South Vietnamese Marine Corps provided the country another type of surprise, a technological one. Just six months after signing the Peace Accords, the VNMC displayed for the first time its "new" LVTP-5. The big amphibian tractors that rumbled through the streets of Saigon in July 1973 dur-

---

*Eventually, medical research proved that the malaria did originate in the highlands and not the lowlands as originally thought.

Marine Corps Historical Collection

Members of the newly formed 468th Brigade undergo training at Song Than base camp. Originally a three-brigade division, at the direction of the Joint General Staff, the VNMC added a fourth brigade in December 1974, meant to be fully operational by April 1975.

ing South Vietnam's Armed Forces Day parade caused quite a stir.* Several of the attaches of the foreign embassies in Saigon wanted to know what new weapon the VNMC had acquired for its arsenal. They might not have been as impressed had they known the rest of the story. The LVTP-5 was an outdated piece of equipment. The USMC advisor's turnover file in 1972 stated: "The LVTP-5 is a 20 year old vehicle designed for a maximum 10 year usage. It has a gasoline engine, is a fire hazard and gets 2-4 miles to a gallon. Spare parts are almost non-existent. Many parts are no longer manufactured."[61] The spare parts shortage was so severe that the amphibian tractors were literally towed to the parade starting point. Apparently, the Joint General Staff was as impressed by the event as the spectators. Shortly after the parade, they ordered the transfer of four LVTP-5s from the VNMC's Amphibian Tractor Company at Song Than to Military Region 1. In addition to this deployment, the Vietnamese Marines kept a small detachment of LVTPs at the training base at Vung Tau.

Operational use of the LVT brought about a closer association between the Taiwanese and South Vietnamese Marine Corps. The Chinese not only operated the LVTP-5, but maintained it as well. More importantly, the Taiwanese Logistic Command designed and tooled a supply system to manufacture spare parts unique to the LVTs. Lieutenant Colonel Strickland, through the U.S. Marine advisors on Taiwan, gained approval from the Commandant of the Chinese Marine Corps to supply spare parts for amphibian tractors to the VNMC on a contract basis. Furthermore, Lieutenant Colonel Strickland escorted the commanding officer of the VNMC Amphibian Tractor Company to Taiwan, where he learned shortcuts in LVT maintenance. The net result of these initiatives, despite supply shortages, was a significant increase in 1974 in the number of amtracs operationally ready for combat.[62]

The defensive mission and posture of the division did not prevent General Lan from conducting a very aggressive program of reconnaissance of NVA-occupied territory. Long-range reconnaissance companies regu-

---

*The procurement of 31 LVTP-5s had been arranged under a project known as Enhance Plus, a program established to strengthen the VNAF and make Vietnamization a success. The delivery of these vehicles to the VNMC on 8 November 1972 resulted in the formation of an amphibian tractor company at Song Than Base Camp. Their arrival predated the Peace Accords and therefore did not violate the prohibition on the introduction of new weapons. VNMC/MAU HistSum.

larly were sent north to the Rock Pile and into the western reaches of Quang Tri Province around Khe Sanh. All the Marines selected for these elite reconnaissance companies were handpicked by Colonel Tri, the Assistant Commandant of the VNMC. One of these platoons obtained an excellent hand-held camera shot of the SAM-2 sites around Khe Sanh. These patrols also provided the information which ultimately led the VNMC to conclude that a NVA division headquarters was located in Lang Vei, the old Special Forces outpost near Khe Sanh. Intelligence gathering was a two-way proposition as the NVA occasionally reminded the Vietnamese Marines by sending a reconnaissance flight over their AO. Expecting the Vietnamese Air Force (VNAF) to intercept these violators of South Vietnamese air space, General Lan became increasingly disconcerted when the VNAF failed to even challenge the NVA intruders. It seemed that even when the agonizing process of requesting tactical air support from battalion to brigade to division to Military Region 1 headquarters in Da Nang provided a timely contact, the Vietnamese Air Force still did not respond.* To Generals Truong and Lan, and their troops as well, who had become accustomed to and reliant upon timely tactical air support (formerly provided by the U.S.) this absence was an ominous portent. Lieutenant Colonel Strickland noted that this issue more than any other preyed on General Lan's mind and colored his outlook for peace in Southeast Asia.[63]

Following the signing of the Cease-fire Agreement, enemy ground activity in the Marine's AO consisted of monthly, sporadic mortar shellings, small but sharp firefights, and isolated ground attacks. Both sides spent considerable time and effort in firing propaganda barrages across the relatively fixed defensive lines. Major artillery or ground attacks were rare, but in early September enemy activity throughout the AO increased significantly. The tempo reached a peak just a few days before the major NVA thrust against Mo Tau Mountain, slightly to the south. On 21 September 1974, the Communists launched a battalion-sized ground attack against the 8th VNMC Battalion. The preceding day, the Marines had observed a 30-truck enemy convoy moving toward a possible assembly area. At approximately 1930, an observation post reported seeing what appeared to be helicopter lights approaching the vicinity of the suspected staging area. Based upon these reports, the Marines redeployed the supporting artillery to positions from which the 8th Battalion could receive more firepower. The enemy opened the engagement by directing approximately 5,500 rounds of mixed artillery and mortar rounds at the VNMC 8th Battalion positions. They followed the preparatory fires with a ground attack. The VNMC stopped the NVA infantry battalion in its tracks; after taking heavy casualties, the enemy withdrew. Many of the North Vietnamese casualties (247 KIA reported) resulted from artillery fire readjusted from ground observation posts. Approximately 300 rounds of 4.2-inch mortar fire from the ARVN armored brigade hit the advancing enemy with resounding accuracy. Effective small arms fire combined with the expenditure of over 50,000 M-60 machine gun rounds helped turn the planned NVA offensive into a VNMC victory.[64]

Following the engagement, enemy activity fell off, except for periodic mortar attacks against various VNMC positions. The remainder of 1974 was marked by light, sporadic NVA activity. Poor mobility caused by seasonal rains further contributed to the low level of activity. In December of 1974 the JGS, in an effort to reconstitute a mobile strategic reserve, directed the VNMC to form a fourth brigade and have it fully operational by the end of April 1975. The 14th, 16th, and 18th VNMC Battalions comprised the newly designated organization, the 468th Marine Brigade. Upon completion of its training, the 468th (formed and initially trained in Military Region 1) moved south to the Song Than Base Camp near Saigon. During the months immediately prior and subsequent to this event, the remainder of the Vietnamese Marine Corps enjoyed the relative "calm before the storm."[65]

On 13 December 1974 in a letter to HQMC, Lieutenant Colonel Lukeman prophetically wrote: ". . . The VNMC is getting a good rest from heavy fighting. They will need it in the spring . . . ."[66]

---

*The VNMC had no Direct Air Support Center (DASC) or the associated tactical air control infrastructure and its accompanying tactical air request and air direction radio networks.

CHAPTER 2
The United States Presence in Southeast Asia

*The Forces in Thailand—The Forces Afloat—The III Marine Amphibious Force
Americans Ashore—The Marines in Vietnam*

The signing of the Paris Accords in January 1973 reduced the size and significantly altered the structure of U.S. forces in Southeast Asia even though the majority of Americans had already been withdrawn from South Vietnam. Government statistics reflected less than 25,000 American servicemen in South Vietnam on New Year's Eve 1972, consisting of 13,800 soldiers, 1,500 sailors, 7,600 airmen, 100 Coast Guardsmen, and 1,200 Marines.[1]

The remaining field advisors and support units were removed from South Vietnam by the end of March 1973. On 29 March 1973, the United States officially disestablished Military Assistance Command, Vietnam (MACV), and opened the Defense Attache Office, Saigon. Its members assumed most of MACV's advisory duties and continued to the best of their ability to perform these functions with a significantly smaller staff. The Commander U.S. Naval Forces Vietnam Quarterly Summary graphically depicted the depth and significance of the reduction of forces in its chronology's highlights:

> 29 March—All USN/USMC personnel (with exception DAO/Embassy personnel) departed RVN. Military personnel remaining in country: Captain R. F. Stadler, Jr., USN, Chief Navy Division; Captain L. Young, USN, Chief VNN Logistic Support Division; Captain C. E. Cuson, USN, Chief Supply Section; Lieutenant Colonel W. D. Fillmore, USMC, Chief VNMC Logistic Support Division; Captain C. N. Conger, USNR, ALUSNA; Captain E. H. Belton, CEC, USN, Director of Construction; Colonel W. B. Fleming, USMC, Chief, Plans and Liaison Branch, Operations and Plans Division; Commander L. D. Bullard, USN, Staff Plans Officer, Plans Section, Plans and Liaison Branch, Operations and Plans Division; Major R. F. Johnson, USMC, Operations Staff Officer, Readiness Section, Operations and Training Branch, Operations and Plans Division. Additionally, there are 156 USMC spaces in the Embassy Security Detachment, Saigon. 29 March strength was 143.[2]

These changes in force size and function necessitated a restructuring of the American organization in Southeast Asia. Besides advisory duties, the U.S. charged the Defense Attache Office, Saigon, with supervision of the military assistance program permitted by the Paris agreements and shifted coordination and management of military operations to a new joint headquarters at Nakhon Phanom in Thailand. By August of 1973, the U.S. combat presence in Southeast Asia consisted of Seventh Air Force units in Thailand and Seventh Fleet elements in the off-shore waters bordering the Indochinese Peninsula.[3]

The Forces in Thailand

During the war, the number of U.S. forces in the Kingdom of Thailand had grown in direct proportion to the number of forces committed to South Vietnam. A complex of air bases had been built to support the U.S. effort in all of Southeast Asia. The principal U.S. component in Thailand, the Seventh Air Force, operated from the Royal Thai Air Force bases at Takhli, Utapao, Korat, Ubon, Udorn, and Nakhom Phanom. Seventh Air Force headquarters was at Nakhom Phanom, in extreme northeastern Thailand.

The withdrawal of U.S. forces from South Vietnam

Recruiting poster displays the slogan from which Nam Phong's nickname was derived. At its peak, the "Rose Garden" served as home to nearly 3,000 Marines.
Marine Corps Historical Collection

THE UNITED STATES PRESENCE IN SOUTHEAST ASIA

Department of Defense Photo (USMC) A26873

Aerial view of Nam Phong, Thailand, looking from the southeast to the northwest. In the left center of the photo is the parking apron housing the Task Force Delta aircraft.

did not cause a proportionate reduction of tactical air forces based in Thailand. The North Vietnamese Easter Offensive of 1972 justified the retention of sizeable numbers of tactical aircraft in the theater, and even resulted in a temporary increase in the number of Thailand-based tactical airplanes.

During the Easter Offensive, Marine Aircraft Group 15 (MAG-15) deployed to Da Nang on 9 April 1972 as a three-squadron fighter/attack group, Task Force Delta. It was moved to Nam Phong, Thailand, on 15 June.[4] Ironically known as the "Rose Garden," Nam Phong was nothing more than a Royal Thai training base with an airstrip. Its nickname borrowed from the Marine Corps advertising slogan, "We don't promise you a rose garden." Nam Phong was christened by the first Marines of MAG-15 to arrive. They knew immediately what the recruiter meant by that phrase when they set their eyes upon the barrenness of the base and realized the bleak existence that awaited them and their soon-to-arrive reinforcements, All Weather Attack Squadron 533 (VMA[AW]-533).* Yet there was little time to concern themselves with accommodations as moments after their arrival, the first strike mission was launched against NVA targets in South Vietnam. Besides, with Marine expeditionary equipment and Seabees' help, Nam Phong was transformed into a fully operational airfield, eventually possessing many of the comforts of home, including showers.[5]

During Task Force Delta's stay at the "Rose Garden,"

---

*MAG-15, originally configured as a three-squadron fighter/attack group, was comprised of the Iwakuni-based VMFA-115 "Silver Eagles" and VMFA-232 "Red Devils" plus the Kaneohe Bay-based VMFA-212 "Lancers." When the group relocated to Nam Phong, VMFA-212 returned to Hawaii, and was replaced by MAG-15's VMA(AW)-533 "Hawks." The fighter/attack squadrons flew the McDonnell Douglas F-4 Phantom with VMFA-115 employing 12 F-4Bs, VMFA-232 15 F-4Js, and VMFA-212 11 F-4Js. VMA(AW)-533 arrived at Nam Phong on 20 June 1972 with 12 A-6As. By the end of June this organization, called Task Force Delta and commanded by Brigadier General Andrew W. O'Donnell, also operated four CH-46D Sea Knights belonging to H&MS-36 and four KC-130F Hercules aerial refuelers from VMGR-152.

its aircraft flew air support missions under the operational control of the Air Force. On 15 August 1973, the United States officially halted all combat air operations in Southeast Asia and the Marine Corps began the final phase of its withdrawal from Nam Phong. Manned by more than 3,000 Marines at its height in early July 1972, Task Force Delta gradually decreased in size until the mount-out boxes were once again nailed shut and the last Marines departed Nam Phong on 21 September 1973. The task force's aerial refuelers and helicopters returned to Okinawa and MAG-15 returned to Marine Corps Air Station, Iwakuni.[6]

During MAG-15's assignment to Thailand, the Joint Chiefs of Staff (JCS) approved a new command structure in Southeast Asia. In November 1972, the JCS authorized the creation of a multi-service, integrated headquarters to be located at Nakhon Phanom, Thailand. The approved concept directed the new organization, upon inception, to assume many of the duties then performed by U.S. Military Assistance Command, Vietnam and replace Seventh Air Force as the manager of aviation assets and the air war in Southeast Asia. In February 1973, the Seventh Air Force, located in Saigon, ceased to exist as a separate headquarters. Its commander, General John W. Vogt, Jr., USAF, received orders directing him to transfer to Nakhon Phanom and assume command of the newly created, combined headquarters. Its shortened title, USSAG/Seventh Air Force (an acronym for United States Support Activities Group/Seventh Air Force) soon became known, due to the sensitivities surrounding the combat role of the Seventh Air Force, as just USSAG. General Vogt, USSAG's new commander, also had been MACV's deputy commander since its reorganization on 29 June 1972. In that position, he had been fully responsible for all combat air operations in Southeast Asia, making him the obvious choice for the new billet in Thailand. In addition to the air war, General Vogt assumed responsibility for all military matters not exclusively pertaining to Thailand. Mili-

Aerial view of isolated Nam Phong Air Base, the "Rose Garden," as seen during an approach to Runway 36. Task Force Delta flight line and encampment are on the left side of the north runway, most of it constructed after the Marine Corps' arrival in June 1972.

Marine Corps Historical Collection

An F-4 Phantom and A-6 Intruder of the Marine Corps, and an Air Force F-4, conduct electronic, Loran-assisted bombing over Cambodia. The U.S. set up a Loran transmitter site in Phnom Penh to provide close air support to the Cambodian government troops.

Photo courtesy of VMA(AW)-533

tary affairs pertinent only to the Royal Thai Government would continue to be handled by the commander of U.S. Military Assistance Command, Thailand (ComUSMACThai).[7]

The Joint Chiefs of Staff designated the Commander-in-Chief, Pacific (CinCPac), Admiral Noel A. M. Gayler, as operational commander of USSAG, but authorized General Vogt as USSAG/Seventh Air Force's commander to exercise control over all Thailand-based aircraft with the exception of Strategic Air Command and Pacific Air Traffic Management Agency units, B-52s and C-130s, respectively. Despite this restriction, USSAG served as tactical manager of the air war until it ended in 1973. Besides Vogt, JCS transferred many other members of MACV's staff to Thailand to fill the nearly 600 authorized billets at USSAG headquarters. General Vogt moved to Nakhon Phanom on 15 February and assumed his new duties while retaining his former title and functions. Those functions officially ceased on 29 March when MACV was disestablished at 1900 Saigon time. At that moment, the commander of USSAG/Seventh Air Force added to his list of duties oversight of all military and intelligence activities in Southeast Asia and operational command of the Defense Attache Office, Saigon. Control of this organization, occupying MACV's old offices, did not extend to defense attache matters, but it did cover security assistance planning, intelligence collection and analysis, and interfacing with regional military commanders, both American and Vietnamese, as well as the Vietnamese Joint General Staff (JGS).[8]

The JCS had created the USSAG/Seventh Air Force headquarters to ensure that there would not be a joint command void in Southeast Asia as a result of compliance with the Vietnam cease-fire agreements. The United States felt that the Defense Attache Office, Saigon, could not perform the joint command task and still abide by the spirit of the Accords. As a consequence, USSAG acquired most of MACV's combat-related functions including air contingency planning. Shortly thereafter, Congress mandated a cessation to combat air operations in Southeast Asia (15 August 1973) and USSAG adjusted to the change by shifting its emphasis from combat to preparations for other air contingencies. Planning for the possible evacuation of U.S. citizens from Indochina, in particular Cambodia, began to occupy an ever increasing amount of USSAG's time. In addition to this demanding task, its commander still retained responsibility for a diverse range of Southeast Asian operations. One member of the staff, Lieutenant Colonel Edward A. Grimm, recalled, "USSAG had a lot of other 'irons in the fire' including a vast array of different contingency plans—

the reintroduction of U.S. forces into Southeast Asia, rescue of any POWs found, and coordination of numerous monitoring and intelligence-gathering operations."[9]

Following the cease-fire in Vietnam in January 1973 and the bombing halt in all of Southeast Asia eight months later, the U.S. Air Force withdrew its augmenting units from Thailand. Some went to the Philippines where they were placed under the operational control of the Commander Thirteenth Air Force, Major General Leroy Manor, who in 1970, when a brigadier general, had been the air commander during the unsuccessful raid to liberate U.S. prisoners of war at Son Tay.* General Manor commanded all Air Force units in the Southeast Asia area of operations, except in those instances when a unit was committed to Thailand to support USSAG. For that specific period, the commander USSAG/Seventh Air Force exercised control.[10]

The units comprising the Seventh Air Force provided the same conventional capabilities that the rest of the United States tactical air arsenal possessed. Heavy ordnance and the ability to deliver it on a continuous basis was the province of the 307th Strategic Wing and its B-52 heavy bombers and KC-135 tanker aircraft stationed at Utapao. Sharing this seven-year-old, picturesque base (south of Bangkok near the Gulf of Thailand) was the 374th Tactical Airlift Wing. It flew the cargo workhorse of Southeast Asia, the C-130 Hercules. Keeping separate company, the tactical fighters of the 347th and 388th Tactical Fighter Wings (TFW) called Korat Air Base in central Thailand home. Equipped with the oldest fighter in the Air Force, the F-4 Phantom, the 388th shared the field with the newest fighters, the F-111s of the 347th which included the 428th and 429th Tactical Fighter Squadrons.** Additionally, an attack aircraft, the A-7 Corsair II of the 34th Tactical Fighter Squadron, used Korat as "homeplate." The 432d Tactical Fighter Wing located at Udorn Air Base in north-central Thailand also flew the F-4 Phantom.

The remaining units of the Seventh Air Force, specifically the 56th Special Operations Wing (SOW), and the 3d Aerospace Rescue and Recovery Group (ARRG), were based at Nakhon Phanom Air Base. During most of the war, the 56th SOW had been engaged primarily in covert operations. One of the wing's squadrons, the 21st Special Operations Squadron (SOS) or "Knives," flew CH-53C helicopters specially fitted with two 750-gallon gas tanks for extended range.*** Collocated at Nakhon Phanom with the 21st SOS and an integral part of the 56th SOW was the 23rd Tactical Air Support Squadron (TASS). The 23rd's pilots flew OV-10 Bronco aircraft, callsign "Nail." Some of the Broncos, "Pave Nails," were equipped with laser designators which enabled them to fix targets for laser-guided weapons.**** The Air Force also used these aircraft to locate downed airmen, especially in bad weather or at night. The 23d TASS was one of the largest squadrons in any air force, numbering 65 aircraft compared to a Marine Corps squadron of 12 to 18 planes. The third component of the 56th SOW, the 16th Special Operations Squadron, called Korat homebase and operated the AC-130 "Spectre" gunships.***** In July 1974, the USAF administratively transferred the 16th SOS from the 56th SOW to the 388th TFW, but its location remained the same.

The 3d ARRG, a Military Airlift Command unit, had two squadrons under its control. One, the 40th Aerospace Rescue and Recovery Squadron (ARRS), flew the HH-53, commonly known as the "Jolly Green Giant"; these helicopters were homebased at Nakhon Phanom.[11] The other member of this group flew HC-130 Hercules aircraft and bore the title 56th Aerospace Rescue and Recovery Squadron (ARRS). The HC-130s were used to perform a dual mission: in-flight refueling of the HH-53 helicopters and coordination of rescue operations from a command console in the

---

*A tactical success, the raiders found no POWs at Son Tay. For more on the Son Tay operation, see Earl H. Tilford, Jr., *Search and Rescue in Southeast Asia, 1961-1975* (Washington: Office of Air Force History, 1980).

**The F-111 bomber designed and built by General Dynamics in the mid-1960s was never given a name designation. In recent years, it has been called the Aardvark. Nalty Comments.

***Lieutenant Colonel Edward A. Grimm recalled that the CH-53Cs had 750-gallon ferry tanks which USSAG had identified as extremely vulnerable to small arms fire. He said, "An attempt was made by ComUSSAG during the summer of 1974 to 'foam' the tanks with Eagle Pull in mind. PacAF turned down the request." Grimm Comments. The former commander of USSAG, General Vogt, was PacAF commander until 30 June 1974 and General Louis L. Wilson, Jr. replaced him on 1 July.

****A means of accuracy enhancement, the laser-designator illuminated the target with a laser beam which the bomb then followed to its mark if released within a specified time window or "basket." If delayed too long, the lock would be broken and the bomb would not home on the target. Nalty comments.

*****One of the Spectre models, the AC-130E was armed with 20mm guns, a 40mm gun, and a 105mm howitzer. The U.S. Air Force called this gun system Pave Aegis. Jack S. Ballard, *The United States Air Force in Southeast Asia: Development and Employment of Fixed-Wing Gunships, 1962-1972* (Washington: Office of Air Force History, 1982), pp. 172-174.

aircraft. The 56th's HC-130s, dubbed "King Birds," acquired their name from the squadron's callsign, "King," and they, like the AC-130's of the 16th SOS, had Korat as their temporary nesting place.[12]

The 3d ARRG operated the Joint Rescue Coordination Center at Nakhon Phanom. Known as "Joker," it coordinated the activities of both the rescue aircraft and their supporting escorts. The units required to perform this type of operation were known as a Rescort Package.

Crews and aircraft for the Rescort Package usually came from the 40th ARRS, the 56th ARRS, the 23d TASS, and the 34th Tactical Fighter Squadron. The HC-130s coordinated the operation and refueled the HH-53s, who performed the actual pick-up of the downed crewmembers. In addition to the "Jolly Greens," the "King Birds" also controlled the OV-10s, serving as on-scene tactical support for use against any enemy targets near the rescue site which threatened or intimidated the slow, low-flying, rescue helicopters.[13] The Rescort operation was so well developed that a simulator installed at Udorn trained all newly arriving pilots on Rescort procedures, further enhancing the chances for mission success.

One of the units which redeployed from Korat AB, Thailand, to Clark Air Force Base, Philippines, was the 7th Air Command and Control Squadron. Even though the squadron moved in May 1974, its crews stood ready to return to Utapao, Thailand, at a moment's notice.[14] The squadron's aircraft, EC-130Es, modified to operate as airborne command centers, had served in Southeast Asia since the unit's formation at Tan Son Nhut Air Base, South Vietnam, in September 1965. Each Hercules was specially configured to allow for insertion of an airconditioned command and control capsule containing communications equipment, operator stations, and display boards. Designed to function during major operations as an airborne battlefield command and control center (ABCCC), the 7th ACCS, call sign "Cricket," performed that mission on a round-the-clock basis by always having a minimum of two aircraft on station. Carrying a battle staff of 12, "Cricket's" crew consisted of a director known as an airborne mission commander (AMC) and three sections: a five-man operations section, a two-man intelligence team, and a four-man communications unit. The aircraft contained 20 air-to-air and air-to-ground radios linking the command and control team to the outside world via 24 radio antennas. Despite all this state-of-the-art electronics equipment, the aircraft lacked a radar capable of identifying all targets in its vicinity. This type of equipment would have provided the battle staff with a real-time picture of the airborne elements it hoped to command and control. Without it, the AMC had to rely exclusively on the plane's sophisticated communications equipment and other aircraft radio calls for situation updates and display information. *Aviation Week & Space Technology* editor Benjamin M. Elson aptly summarized the consequences of this shortcoming: "Since the EC-130E does not carry search or track radar, the battle staff cannot provide positive control or insure separation of aircraft in a combat zone."[15]

The Forces Afloat

During the period January to July 1973, as Operation End Sweep (the removal of mines from North Vietnam's harbors required by the Paris Peace Accords) progressed, the North Vietnamese were reminded daily that the U.S. Seventh Fleet still controlled the South China Sea. In the months following the completion of the minesweeping operation, the Seventh Fleet may have been out of sight, but it was never far from the minds of the North Vietnamese leaders.[16]

The Seventh Fleet, largest of the deployed fleets of the United States, operated in an area bounded by the Mariana Islands on the east, by the Arabian Sea on the west, the Sea of Okhotsk to the North, and Australia to the south.[17] In addition to approximately 60 ships, the Seventh Fleet contained a Marine amphibious task force of varying size, consisting of ground, aviation, and support elements, a carrier air wing, and all the crews necessary to man and operate this force. All totaled it comprised a force of 60,000 sailors and Marines and more than 500 aircraft of all types.

Task Force 72 was responsible for antisubmarine warfare and served as the eyes and ears of the Seventh Fleet. Charged with search, reconnaissance, and surveillance, specially-equipped aircraft of this task force operated from Japan, the Philippines, and Guam.

While the fleet depended upon bases for refit and upkeep, as well as stores and supplies of all kinds, its range was extended by the mobile logistic support units of Task Force 73. The oilers, ammunition ships, stores ships, and ships that combined two or more of these capabilities were a vital part of the Seventh Fleet. The fast combat support ship (AOE) became the most valued supply support vessel in the Seventh Fleet because of its enormous capacity to carry critical stores. It carried more fuel than the largest fleet oiler and more ammunition than the largest ammunition ship. The combat stores ship with its refrigerated food

Three of the four major helicopters of the Marine amphibious unit are shown in this Seventh Fleet picture. In the foreground on the left is a CH-46 Sea Knight and to the right of it is the AH-1J Cobra. Two UH-1E Hueys sit on the port side of the flight deck.

stocks, aviation supplies, and general provisions was always a welcome sight to sailors and Marines long at sea.

The Seventh Fleet's submarine force was Task Force 74, while cruisers and destroyers made up Task Force 75. Both of these task forces maintained a high tempo of operations.

The amphibious force, Task Force 76, and the Fleet Marines of Task Force 79 were inseparable partners of over-the-horizon power projection.* Task Force 76 was usually composed of one amphibious squadron of eight ships ready to conduct sea-based operations upon call. The task force command ship function was performed by the amphibious force command ship USS *Blue Ridge* (LCC 19) or a flag-configured dock landing platform (LPD). The remaining seven ships of the force were divided into two amphibious ready groups: four ships in Alpha, three ships in Bravo. Normally, Amphibious Ready Group (ARG) Alpha consisted of an amphibious assault ship (LPH), a dock landing ship (LSD), and a tank landing ship (LST). The Bravo ARG usually was comprised of a LPD, an amphibious cargo ship (LKA), and either a LSD or LST. Task Force 79 provided the landing teams for the amphibious ready groups. When not at sea, the Amphibious Force, Seventh Fleet shared Okinawa with the Landing Force, Seventh Fleet as a base of operations.

The main striking force of the Seventh Fleet was its carrier aircraft, the fighting edge of Task Force 77. When the situation dictated, the Seventh Fleet drew on other task forces for the supporting ships and aircraft needed to form carrier task groups. Roving the seas in company with Task Force 72 units, elements of Task Force 77 patrolled as far west as the Persian Gulf, south to Australia, north to the Sea of Japan, east to the Marianas, and everything in between including the South China Sea and the Gulf of Thailand.

The magnificent base at Subic Bay, Republic of the Philippines, provided needed repairs, supplies, and recreation facilities for the Seventh Fleet. Yokosuka and Guam followed in order of importance as bases for the fleet. Some support was also available at Singapore and Sasebo. Aircraft of the fleet were based at Cubi Point

---

*An operation conducted at sea out of sight and danger of enemy ground fire, but within close enough range to deliver force, project power, and, if necessary, make a forced entry by surface or air.

Photo courtesy of BGen William A. Bloomer, USMC (Ret)
An RF-4 of VMCJ-1 lands on board the USS Midway *(CVA 41). One of the many Marine Corps supporting units then serving in the U.S. Seventh Fleet, VMCJ-1 and its aircraft possessed both aerial reconnaissance and electronic counter-measures capabilities.*

(part of the Subic Bay complex), Kadena on Okinawa, and at Misawa and Atsugi on the island of Honshu, Japan. Although the bases were not subordinate to the Commander, Seventh Fleet, base commanders were required to give priority support to the fleet and fleet aircraft.

Most of the ships and aircraft of the Seventh Fleet were detached from the California-based First Fleet for periods of six months, but one attack carrier, the USS *Midway* (CVA 41), two cruisers, including the flagship USS *Oklahoma* (CLG 6), a destroyer squadron, and two combat stores ships were home-ported in Japan. A submarine, the USS *Grayback*, and a tactical air support squadron called the Philippines home, while a reconnaissance squadron based its planes at the naval air station on Guam.[19]

In an emergency, the Seventh Fleet could be augmented by other units. In March and April of 1975, just such an emergency occurred when the Seventh Fleet was forced to concentrate its ships in the coastal waters near Saigon, ready for any eventuality. By the end of April, when evacuation of U.S. nationals was imminent, the Seventh Fleet realized the benefits of augmentation. The task force's size reflected the fact that it had been reinforced by a full carrier task group and an amphibious squadron.

The III Marine Amphibious Force

During the 1973-1975 Paris Peace Accords "ceasefire," the Marine Corps had three Marine amphibious forces within its Fleet Marine Force structure. Two of them, I MAF and II MAF, were based in the continental United States while the third was in Japan. The III Marine Amphibious Force (III MAF) maintained its headquarters on Okinawa. The Commanding General, III MAF was also the commander of the landing force of the Seventh Fleet, Task Force 79. As commander III MAF, the units subordinate to him were the 3d Marine Division, the 1st Marine Aircraft Wing (1st MAW), and the 3d Force Service Regiment.* Additionally, when wearing his Seventh Fleet "hat," the commanding general controlled the two deployed Marine landing forces with Amphibious Ready Groups Alpha and Bravo.

With most of its air units at Iwakuni, collocated with the Japanese Maritime Self-Defense Force and U.S. Navy patrol squadrons, the Marine Corps regularly had to rotate units out of Iwakuni in order to avoid overcrowding. As a result, normally two of the wing's five fixed-wing tactical squadrons were deployed for training, one to Naval Air Station Cubi Point, and the other to the Naval Air Facility Naha, Okinawa.[20]

---

*The 1st MAW's home base was Marine Corps Air Station, Iwakuni, Japan. In addition to its basic headquarters and support and control groups, the wing was comprised of three aircraft groups, an aerial refueling and transport squadron (VMGR), and a composite reconnaissance squadron (VMCJ). With the exception of Marine Aircraft Group 36 (helicopters and OV-10s), VMGR-152, and Marine Air Support Squadron 2, which were based at Marine Corps Air Station, Futema, Okinawa, all of the wing's subordinate elements were at Iwakuni. In March of 1976, the spelling of Futema was changed by the Japanese to its present form of Futenma. 1st MAW ComdC, 1Jan-30Jun73.

Photo courtesy of Capt Edwin W. Besch, USMC (Ret)
A-4 belonging to VMA-211 of MAG-12 sits in revetment at Bien Hoa, awaiting maintenance. MAG-12 departed Bien Hoa at the end of January 1973 in conformance with the recently signed Paris Accords.

The problem of space was somewhat relieved when in May 1972 some wing units deployed to Vietnam to meet the threat of invading North Vietnamese troops. Marine Aircraft Group 12, whose attack squadrons flew the A-4E Skyhawk, was sent to Bien Hoa Air Base, 16 miles northeast of Saigon, where it remained for almost a year, while Marine Aircraft Group 15 deployed to Da Nang.[21] On 29 January 1973, the "Tomcats" of Marine Attack Squadron 311 (VMA-311) and the "Wake Island Avengers" of VMA-211 began leaving Bien Hoa. Piloting KC-130Fs based on Okinawa, the air crews of VMGR-152 assisted MAG-12 in transporting its gear back to Iwakuni. By day's end on 30 January, all of VMA-211's aircraft had landed at the joint-use airfield on the southern end of Honshu island. VMA-311's retrograde progressed almost as fast and on 31 January its last aircraft returned to Iwakuni. When that A-4E touched down on runway 01, it marked the conclusion of a tour of duty in South Vietnam for "311" which spanned eight years and included 54,625 combat sorties.*[22] Seven months earlier, MAG-15 had departed South Vietnam, but instead of returning to Japan, it redeployed to Nam Phong, Thailand, to continue the air war. After 16 months of combat operations in Southeast Asia, the 1st MAW commander, Major General Frank C. Lang, directed MAG-15 to cease all activities and depart Thailand. Upon receiving the order, the three squadrons at the Rose Garden redeployed. On 31 August VMFA-115 went to Naha and the following day VMFA-232 departed for Cubi Point. While those two units mapped out a training schedule, Major Ronald E. Merrihew and his squadron, VMA (AW)-533, flew back to Iwakuni. Shortly after his flight of eight A-6s touched down on the Iwakuni runway on the last day of August 1973, the MAG-15 commander, Colonel Darrel E. Bjorklund, administratively and operationally returned control of the "Hawks" to MAG-12. Three weeks later, on 21 September, Marine Air Base Squadron 15 (MABS-15) officially returned control of the Royal Thai Air Force Base, Nam Phong, to the Royal Thai Government and departed, ending another chapter in a long history of advanced base operations.[23]

Between Commandant of the Marine Corps (CMC) General Robert E. Cushman's visit to Iwakuni on 29 and 30 September 1973 and the end of September 1974, the wing underwent several more organizational changes. On 14 October 1973, MAG-12 transferred control of VMCJ-1 back to MAG-15, and in August 1974, CMC administratively transferred VMA-311 to MAG-32. On 29 August in a ceremony at MCAS Beaufort, South Carolina, VMA-324, an A-4M squadron, was officially redesignated VMA-311. The Marine Corps balanced MAG-12's loss by replacing the "Tomcats" with VMA-513, the first AV-8A Harrier squadron to deploy overseas. The "Nightmares" joined MAG-12 on 1 September 1974.[24]

Based at Futema, approximately 500 miles south of Iwakuni, MAG-36 was one of the largest aircraft groups in the Marine Corps. It consisted of five helicopter squadrons and an OV-10 Bronco-equipped observation squadron. In addition to these units, MAG-36 administratively controlled VMGR-152, which received its operational orders directly from the wing commander via his G-3 and the Air Transportation Control Officer (ATCO). One of the group's transport helicopter squadrons was always assigned as a component of the 31st Marine Amphibious Unit (MAU) on board Amphibious Ready Group Alpha ships. The assigned unit actually was a composite squadron, usually either Marine Medium Helicopter Squadron 164 (HMM-164) or the "White Knights" of HMM-165, both flying CH-46Ds augmented by detachments of CH-53Ds from the "Heavy Haulers" of Marine Heavy Helicopter Squadron 462 (HMH-462); UH-1E Hueys of Marine Light Helicopter Squadron 367 (HML-367), call sign "Scarface"; and AH-1J Cobras of the "Gunfighters" of Marine Attack Helicopter Squadron 369 (HMA-369).[25]

The combat service support element of III MAF, the 3d Force Service Regiment (FSR) was based at Camp Foster, Okinawa. The regiment was at reduced strength, reflecting the cutback in personnel immedi-

---

*First Lieutenant Charles G. Reed flew the squadron's 50,000th combat sortie on 29 August 1972. VMA-311 ComdC, 1Jul-31Dec72.

KC-130Fs of VMGR-152's four-plane detachment assigned to support Task Force Delta await maintenance on the Nam Phong flight line. During the bombing of Cambodia, VMGR-152 aircraft provided aerial refueling support by flying a four-plane formation in a racetrack pattern over Tonle Sap, using the Angkor Wat ruins as a rendezvous point with Marine F-4s laden with bombs and enroute from Nam Phong to Phnom Penh.

ately following the war, but remained organized as a typical FSR with a headquarters and service battalion, supply battalion, and a maintenance battalion. Task-organized, logistical support units of the 3d FSR supported the two landing forces embarked in amphibious shipping.

The ground combat element of the MAF, the 3d Marine Division, was also located on the island of Okinawa. One of its regiments, the 3d Marines, was detached and stationed at Marine Corps Air Station, Kaneohe Bay, Hawaii, as the ground combat element of the separate 1st Brigade. The brigade's air element, MAG-24, consisted of three fighter squadrons, three helicopter squadrons, an observation squadron, and a support squadron. Units from the 3d Marine Division combat support and combat service support organizations normally attached to a regiment to constitute a regimental landing team were, in the case of the 3d Marines, attached to the 1st Marine Brigade. For example, Company A of the 3d Shore Party Battalion was assigned to the 1st Brigade. Since the 3d Marine Division was minus one of its regiments, the separate battalions of the division were each minus one company.*

*A division without all its regimental landing teams is referred to as a division "minus", written (-), but since the 3d Marine Division had organizations normally organic to Force Troops, FMFPac, attached to it, e.g., the 3d Tank Battalion and the 1st Amphibian Tractor Battalion, it was also a division reinforced (Rein). So the 3d Marine Division was a division (-) (Rein). For simplicity, it will be referred to as the 3d Marine Division.

The 3d Marine Division's elements were housed within five separate camps on the island of Okinawa. The division headquarters and headquarters battalion were at Camp Courtney overlooking scenic Kin Bay on the eastern shore. The division's artillery regiment, the 12th Marines, was located at Camp Hague, just south of Courtney. The 3d Reconnaissance Battalion was on the western side of the island at Onna Point. The largest camp on the island, Camp Hansen, sandwiched between Kin Bay and the Kin River, was home to the 4th Marines and most of the separate battalions of the division. Situated on the northeast coast of Okinawa adjacent to Ora Wan Bay was Camp Schwab, where the division billeted the 9th Marines, the 1st Amphibian Tractor Battalion, and the 3d Motor Transport Battalion.

After its return from Vietnam in 1969, the 3d Marine Division maintained and improved its combat-ready posture to fulfill its mission as a "force in readiness" in the Western Pacific. Primary emphasis was placed on providing well-trained battalion landing teams to the III MAF for deployment as the ground combat elements of the Seventh Fleet amphibious ready groups. One BLT of the division always was assigned as the air contingency BLT, prepared for quick deployment on board Air Force or Marine aircraft to accomplish contingency missions within the Seventh Fleet's area of operations.[26]

By 1974, the 3d Marine Division had gained as much stability as could be expected for an organiza-

Marine Corps Historical Collection

VMFA-232 F-4s undergo maintenance in preparation for a bombing flight in support of the Lon Nol government. VMFA-232 later redeployed from Nam Phong to Cubi Point.

VMA(AW)-533 A-6 awaits arming on a Nam Phong Air Base taxiway prior to a bombing mission against the Cambodian Khmer Rouge. The squadron, commanded by Maj Ronald E. Merrihew, departed the Rose Garden for Iwakuni on 31 August 1973.

Marine Corps Historical Center

THE UNITED STATES PRESENCE IN SOUTHEAST ASIA

Marine Corps Historical Collection

An aerial view shows the Task Force Delta headquarters and the mess hall at Nam Phong, Thailand. Task Force Delta ceased air support of the Lon Nol government in Cambodia in August 1973 as a result of a Congressional ban on flight operations in Southeast Asia.

A CH-46D of a H&MS-36 detachment parked on the ramp at the Nam Phong Air Base. These helicopters, which used the call sign "Green Bug," provided sea and air rescue support to Task Force Delta and the base. During its tour at the Rose Garden, the detachment flew 2,356 hours and 2,956 sorties, of which 80 were active SAR missions.

Marine Corps Historical Collection

Embarkation was significant in the rapid deployment of Marine helicopter squadrons in MAU turnovers. Pictured is a salute to HMA-369 S-4, Capt Charles A. Dittmar, top right.

tion whose members served only one-year tours of duty. To simplify personnel assignments, the 4th Marines was charged with the ARG Alpha commitment, and the 9th Marines was tasked with providing Marines for ARG Bravo.

Amphibious Ready Group Alpha, with the helicopter-equipped 31st MAU embarked, was capable of conducting sea-based, over-the-horizon, forced, surface, and vertical amphibious entry anywhere in the Western Pacific area. Amphibious Ready Group Bravo was configured to perform a forced, surface, amphibious entry in the same region. The combat efficiency of the embarked BLTs was maintained by conducting amphibious landings, training, and exercises at Camp Fuji, Japan, in the Republic of the Philippines, and on Okinawa.[27]

To meet these commitments, III MAF had to institute a system of controlled personnel inputs for the infantry battalions and the combat support and service support platoons, the units constituting every new BLT. Beginning in 1973, these changes resulted in a four-phased BLT Readiness Program [Input, Predeployment Training, Deployment, and Postdeployment]. The building of an organization, normally from zero strength, took place during the 60-day input phase. During this period, individual combat and physical skills were stressed, and by the end of the input cycle the battalion was at 100 percent of its manning level, the maximum strength authorized. At any given time, there was one and occasionally two battalions in the input cycle. This meant that the Commanding General, III MAF sometimes had four, and usually had five, of his six infantry battalions ready for contingencies and deployment.*

As the date for the opening of Expo 76 (Japanese exposition and World's Fair built on land in northern Okinawa near the Marine Corps' training area) ap-

---

*The status of battalions and BLTs as of 31 December 1973 was: 1stBn, 4th Marines—Input Phase; BLT 2/4—Deployment Phase; BLT 3/4—Deployment Phase; 1st Bn, 9th Marines—Post-Deployment Phase; 2d Bn, 9th Marines—Input Phase; and 3d Bn, 9th Marines—Predeployment Phase.

THE UNITED STATES PRESENCE IN SOUTHEAST ASIA

Marine Corps Historical Collection

The 3d Tank Battalion, here leading the column of M-48 tanks in a combat review at Camp Hansen, was one of the many units housed at this largest Marine camp on Okinawa.

Forming up for a predeployment inspection at Camp Hansen, Okinawa, are the ground combat and combat service support elements of the 31st Marine Amphibious Unit. After 1973, all units before deploying would undergo a four-phased BLT readiness program.

Marine Corps Historical Collection

Photo courtesy of LtCol George E. Strickland, USMC (Ret)
LtCol Strickland and VNMC LtCol Luong observe NVA positions across the Thach Han River near Quang Tri. Later, in 1975, the 258th Brigade was deployed on the southern bank of the river, west of the city.

proached, training for the III MAF elements on Okinawa became more difficult. The Japanese government had imposed more stringent regulations to ensure the safety and success of Expo and adherence to these rules forced the Marine Corps to restrict its training on Okinawa. As a result, Korean practice areas and the Zambales training area in the Philippines came to be used more extensively for III MAF exercises, as did the live firing ranges and maneuver areas located at Camp Fuji, Honshu, Japan, and Subic Bay and Zambales in the Philippines. Ranges in South Korea provided excellent practice areas for deployed BLTs, amphibian tractor and reconnaissance units, and forward air control parties.[28]

Despite the restrictions and the additional expense of long-distance exercises, III MAF did not suffer from the experience. The situation on Okinawa and the requirement to train elsewhere produced some beneficial results. To get to the other training areas, considerable embarkation planning had to be done, both for air and sea movement, and as a consequence the III MAF agencies responsible for moving Marines and their equipment perfected the techniques to an exceptional degree.

Americans Ashore

The deactivation of MACV and the creation of USSAG obligated the Marine Corps to provide two officers for the new joint staff in Nakhon Phanom. Both staff billets were in J-3, the operations directorate. The first officers assigned were Colonel George T. Balzer, chief of the Operations and Plans Division, and one of his assistants, Major John J. Carty, a plans action officer. In May of 1973, Major Horace W. Baker relieved Major Carty and a month later Colonel Edward J. Bronars replaced Colonel Balzer. The following year, in April, Major Edward A. "Tony" Grimm replaced Major Baker. The official title of his billet was Eagle Pull Action Officer, Surface Plans Division, J-3, USSAG, In June 1974, Colonel James P. Connolly II arrived in Nakhon Phanom as Colonel Bronars' replacement for the designated Marine Corps billet. Instead, because of questions over seniority at this joint command headquarters, the USSAG chief of staff assigned Colonel Connolly to a different position, chief of the Ground Operations Branch.[29]

With USSAG located in Thailand, over 400 nautical miles from Saigon, the DAO, charged with attache duties, logistics and supply functions, intelligence collection and analysis, and technical support and contracts, became the administrative heir to MACV. Having inherited several of its predecessor's functions, the DAO conducted business and maintained its offices in the former MACV compound, adjacent to Tan Son Nhut Air Base, in the northwestern suburbs of Saigon.

When the DAO was established, the protocols of the Paris Accords limited it to a staff of no more than 50 military and 1,200 U.S. civilian personnel. In addition, the Accords stipulated that there could be no more than 4,900 Department of Defense contractors in South Vietnam. The majority of the DAO personnel worked on the military assistance program, but most of the contact with Vietnamese military personnel was by contractors. There was, however, an exception to this arrangement—the VNMC Logistic Support Branch, at 15 Le Thanh Ton in Saigon consisting of a chief (a Marine Corps officer) and five American civilians. Two of the five men had prior service in the Marine Corps: Jerry Edwards, a Marine Corps captain in WW II, who served as the staff's deputy, and Master Gunnery Sergeant Charles C. Gorman, USMC (Ret), a former supply chief, who used his expertise in the role of supply advisor. All five of them maintained daily contact with their Vietnamese Marine Corps counterparts, often conducting on-site visits, a rare occurrence for American civilians working at the DAO.[30]

When the ceasefire agreement was signed, it was understood that the civilian DAO employees would be phased out by the end of January 1975, and that

Photo courtesy of MajGen John E. Murray, USA (Ret)

The occasion for this gathering of Marine Corps officers was a 1974 liaison visit by LtGen Wallace H. Robinson, Commanding General, Defense Logistics Agency, to the Defense Attache Office, Saigon to discuss logistical support to the South Vietnamese Armed Forces.

the number of civilian contractors would be reduced to 500 soon thereafter. In June of 1974, in addition to the 50 military personnel, there were approximately 860 civilians in the DAO and 2,500 DOD-sponsored contractor personnel still in South Vietnam. Two interrelated events shelved the implementation of the final planned reduction: ceasefire violations and deficiencies in the technical training program. NVA and VC noncompliance with the Paris Accords presented a problem that could only be offset by enhanced South Vietnamese readiness. The training of South Vietnamese personnel to achieve the necessary skills progressed at a much slower rate than originally anticipated and resulted in them not being prepared to replace the civilian contractors who performed vital support functions. As the tempo of combat operations increased, this situation worsened with the contractors spending more and more time maintaining equipment and less time training their South Vietnamese counterparts.[31] During the course of the "Vietnamization" program, the United States implemented Project Seven Hundred Million under which an additional $700 million worth of sophisticated military equipment was to be provided to the South Vietnamese during the 30 days immediately following the ceasefire. Unfortunately, in planning this project, too little emphasis apparently was given to providing the training needed to make the South Vietnamese self-sufficient in technical fields such as electronics, major aircraft inspection and overhaul, and supply facility and port management. Existing plans called for the reduction of contractor personnel to about 1,100 in the second quarter of Fiscal Year 1975, but it became clear to both the United States and South Vietnam that this support could not be reduced any further and probably needed to be increased. Meeting the original goal of elimination of all contract personnel by 1976 quickly fell into the category of "too hard." Both sides realized by the end of 1974 that American technical support might be needed for an indefinite period.[32]

The Marines in Vietnam

Upon establishment of the Defense Attache Office, Saigon, the Marine Corps received three military billets. The first of these bore a strong resemblance to the former military position of Chief of the Marine Advisory Unit. The new position carried the title Chief, VNMC Logistics Support Branch, Navy Division DAO, and Lieutenant Colonel Walter D. Fillmore served as the first. Later that year (1973) Lieutenant Colonel George E. Strickland reported to the DAO to assume the duties of the departing Lieutenant Colonel Fillmore. In June of 1974, Lieutenant Colonel Anthony Lukeman relieved him. The primary responsibility of each of these officers was to ensure that the South Vietnamese Marine Corps received an uninterrupted flow of supplies and equipment.[33]

Fillmore, then Strickland, and later Lukeman and the five American civilians who worked in the Logistics Support Branch were not subject to the rigid travel restrictions imposed on most of the DAO personnel. Exempt from this impediment, they made frequent trips to Military Region 1 (Huong Dien, Hue, Phu Bai, and Da Nang) and to other VNMC locations including Vung Tau and Song Than. This kind of contact enabled them to provide "personalized, direct, field support" to the Vietnamese Marine Corps. Lieutenant Colonel Strickland recalled, "Most of my tour was spent living with the Vietnamese Marine Corps in a bunker. While in Saigon, I maintained a billet at the Brinks Hotel, three blocks from my office. All of the U.S. civilians [LSB staff] lived in Vietnamese housing close to VNMC headquarters."*[34]

The senior Marine in the DAO then was Colonel Nicholas M. Trapnell, Jr., chief of the Plans and Liaison Branch, Operations and Plans Division. Responsible for planning and liaison on matters relating to support of South Vietnam's military, Colonel Trapnell assumed those duties in April of 1973 from his predecessor, Colonel William B. Fleming. Colonel Paul L. Siegmund relieved Trapnell a year later and departed South Vietnam in March 1975. Colonel Eugene R. "Pat" Howard reported to the DAO in January 1975 as Siegmund's replacement. Colonel Trapnell recalled, "I arrived late March 1973 and had a brief overlap with Colonel Bill Fleming. March 28 was the 'Magic Date' by which all military advisors had to be 'out of country.' "[35]

During the summer of 1973, Lieutenant Colonel Charles A. Barstow assumed the third Marine Corps billet in the DAO. Lieutenant Colonel Barstow became the readiness deputy of the Operations and Plans Division, replacing Major Joseph F. Nardo who a few months earlier, in April, had relieved Major Richard F. Johnson. In September 1974, Lieutenant Colonel William E. McKinstry undertook those tasks.

A fourth Marine officer was assigned to a billet created as a result of the ceasefire agreement: Liaison Officer, Four Power Joint Military Commission, RVN. Major Larry D. Richards joined the Four Power Joint Military Commission in 1973 as one of the U.S. representatives tasked with liaison duties. He was subsequently replaced by Major Jaime Sabater, Jr., whose planned but never effected relief was Major Richard H. Esau, Jr.[36]

In 1974, the number of Marine officers in South Vietnam increased by one when Captain Anthony A. Wood transferred from the Joint Casualty Resolution Center (JCRC) in Nakhon Phanom to Saigon. His official title was Operations Officer (Forward, South Vietnam), JCRC. In February 1975, he joined the Special Planning Group at the DAO headed by Colonel Pat Howard. Colonel Howard, an aviator, had been tasked by Major General Homer D. Smith, USA, the Defense Attache, with the additional, but secret, responsibility of discreetly planning for an evacuation of Saigon.** (Ambassador Graham Martin had refused to entertain any discussion of such an eventuality.) Lieutenant Colonel Strickland observed, "Both Majors Diffee and Bergen of Company E, MSG Bn (Marine Security Guard Battalion) worked continuously on an American Embassy security and evacuation plan in spite of Ambassador Martin's refusal to foresee its importance. They made a superb effort to be prepared."[37]

Company E of the Marine Security Guard Battalion, commanded by Major Gerald E. Diffee until 15 September 1973 when Major Daniel F. Bergen relieved him, represented the largest group of Marines in Southeast Asia following the signing of the Paris Peace Accords. It was charged with the responsibility of providing security for the United States Embassy in Saigon and consulates in Da Nang, Nha Trang, and Bien Hoa. Company E was organized into a headquarters and three platoons. Two platoons accounted for the interior and exterior guards at the embassy and the consulate detachments, while the third platoon

---

*Five American civilians worked in the VNMC Logistics Support Branch. Two members of the staff, the deputy chief of VNMC Logistics Support Branch and the branch's supply advisor, were former Marines. Terry Edwards, a Marine captain in World War II, served as the second in command, while Charles C. Gorman, Master Gunnery Sergeant, USMC (Ret), and a former supply chief, lived up to his own supply motto, "A supply shack is only a sorting place. The supplies belong in the field with the troops." Strickland comments.

**Colonel Trapnell stated that "The planning that led to the creation of the Special Planning Group began in the DAO under General Murray approximately six months prior to his departure on around September 1973" and that concurrent planning was already underway at USSAG. Trapnell Comments.

provided security for Ambassador Graham Martin's residence. The average strength of the company was five officers and 143 enlisted Marines.[38] The Embassy Marines in Saigon began to settle into a less demanding routine during the waning months of 1973. By 1974, the situation in South Vietnam appeared to be sufficiently stable to warrant reduction of the strength of Company E and by 23 April 1974, the Exterior Guard had absorbed the Ambassador's Residence Platoon. On 20 May 1974, the Interior Guard Platoon was redesignated the Marine Detachment, Saigon, and placed under control of the Hong Kong-based regional company, Company C, of the Marine Security Guard Battalion. On 17 June 1974, Captain James H. Kean, the Executive Officer of Company C, arrived in Saigon to complete the reassignment of the Interior Guard Platoon and coordinate the pending transfer of the consulate detachments. Additionally, Captain Kean traveled to the American Consulate at Can Tho to begin planning for the activation of a security detachment there. On 30 June 1974, Major Daniel F. Bergen, the commanding officer of Company E, deactivated it and transferred to Company C the remaining 90 enlisted Marines who comprised the Embassy Exterior Guard Platoon and the detachments at Da Nang, Nha Trang, and Bien Hoa.

Master Sergeant Juan J. Valdez became the noncommissioned officer-in-charge of the newly created Embassy Detachment in Saigon. Staff Sergeant Roger F. Painter, the senior Marine at Nha Trang; Staff Sergeant Walter W. Sparks, in charge at Da Nang; and Staff Sergeant Michael K. Sullivan, the detachment chief at Bien Hoa (subsequently relieved by Gunnery Sergeant Robert W. Schlager), all understood that their primary mission was to protect the American consulates and their classified material. Each detachment trained regularly to improve its readiness and enhance security of its consulate.

On 16 July 1974, Captain Kean, a major selectee, relieved Major Donald L. Evans as the Commanding Officer, Company C, Marine Security Guard Battalion, Hong Kong. Two months later, the company's new commander oversaw the activation of the Marine security guard detachment at Can Tho, the first ever in that city. On that day, 23 September 1974, he placed Staff Sergeant Boyette S. Hasty in charge of the Can Tho Marines. Located in the capital of Phong Dinh Province this detachment would never celebrate its first anniversary of existence.[39]

While the events in South Vietnam led to a false sense of security in late 1973 and early 1974, the war continued at an undiminished pace in Cambodia. For Gunnery Sergeant Clarence D. McClenahan and his 11-man detachment at the U.S. Embassy in Phnom Penh, a continuous series of alerts and quick responses to these crises was the order of the day. As the situation became worse, there was talk of an evacuation; talk evolved to preparation and waiting, but no evacuation.[40]

Thus, American forces in Thailand, forces afloat, and forces ashore were prepared for any eventuality, but predominately they were preoccupied with training and the seemingly unavoidable evacuation of Cambodia. Few Americans possessed the ability to foresee the events in Southeast Asia and what challenges awaited them. The Marine Detachment at Da Nang would be the first to gain that insight.

CHAPTER 3
Contingency Planning

The Plan for Cambodia—Vietnam

The Government of Thailand hosted the majority of American troops (35,000) in Southeast Asia after the last military unit left South Vietnam on 29 March 1973.[1] Accordingly, events in Thailand had a significant impact on American military contingencies in Southeast Asia, especially in Cambodia, its neighbor to the east. Considering the magnitude of the effect social and political factors had on military decisions in Southeast Asia, Thailand in 1973 demands examination.

In November 1971, a group of military and civilian leaders, headed by Premier Thanom Kittikachorn* and Interior Minister General Praphas Charusathien, effected a bloodless coup promising "not to change any existing institutions 'beyond necessity.' " By June of 1973, the council had abolished the constitution drawn up in 1968, dissolved parliament, disbanded the cabinet, and established martial law. In addition, it pledged to continue Thailand's anti-Communist and pro-American foreign policy.[2]

Students dissatisfied by this turn of events protested, staging numerous demonstrations in Bangkok. The student leaders demanded a new constitution and immediate replacement of the military dictatorship with a duly elected democratic government. The critics of the new regime contended that the dictatorship had created more problems than it had solved, and in particular pointed to the state of the economy. The validity of this charge was readily apparent; the economy had worsened and many of Thailand's problems stemmed from its economic woes, especially its high unemployment.[3] The students attributed the extensive joblessness to the government's inefficency and corruption. Still, despite the overwhelming argument against the government, the students and protesters lacked a dramatic issue to catalyze their movement. Events outside Thailand seemed to answer that need when American military operations and Thai politics collided over the use of force in Cambodia.

The issue of whether the United States military should be allowed to use Royal Thai bases to support the besieged government in Phnom Penh, Cambodia, quickly became the hottest topic in Thai political circles. U.S. air operations from bases in Thailand against the Khmer Communist offensive began at the end of March 1973 and by June the students had organized substantial public support against the American military involvement in Cambodia. On 20 June they held a massive protest rally in Bangkok. This upheaval in Thailand coincided with the U.S. Congress' passage of the Case-Church amendment cutting off all funding for combat operations in Southeast Asia effective 45 days after the start of the new fiscal year. As a result the U.S. Air Force and Marine Corps ceased bombing on 15 August and returned the Royal Thai Air Force Base at Nam Phong to the Thai government on 21 September, and then stood by and watched the students overthrow the military dictatorship on 14 October 1973. King Phumiphol Aduldet immediately appointed Sanya Thammasak as Kittikachorn's successor, the first civilian premier since 1953.[4]

The overthrow of the military government precipitated an immediate but previously scheduled withdrawal of major U.S. elements from Thailand and a reduction in military assistance funds. It also finalized a reorganization of forces in Southeast Asia, begun with the signing of the Paris Peace Accords and consummated by a U.S.-Thai Accord in August of 1973. The joint U.S.-Thai agreement was negotiated as a result of the recently displayed Thai nationalism and a growing need to realign Thailand's diplomatic affairs to adjust to the reduced American military presence confronting the Communist governments in Southeast Asia. Nearly surrounded by Communist governments and faced with an inevitable regional realignment, Thailand had to display an awareness of its changing security needs and a sensitivity to North Vietnam's interests. Thailand's new military arrangement with the United States sent a message to its neighbors that it controlled its own destiny and although its intentions were peaceful it would not

---

*Kittikachorn formerly held the title of field marshal and on 10 August 1966 had participated with the Ambassador to Thailand, Graham Martin, in a ceremony to dedicate the recently completed airfield at Utapao. The new base was built largely with U.S. funds to avoid having American military aircraft use the runways at the Bangkok commercial airport.

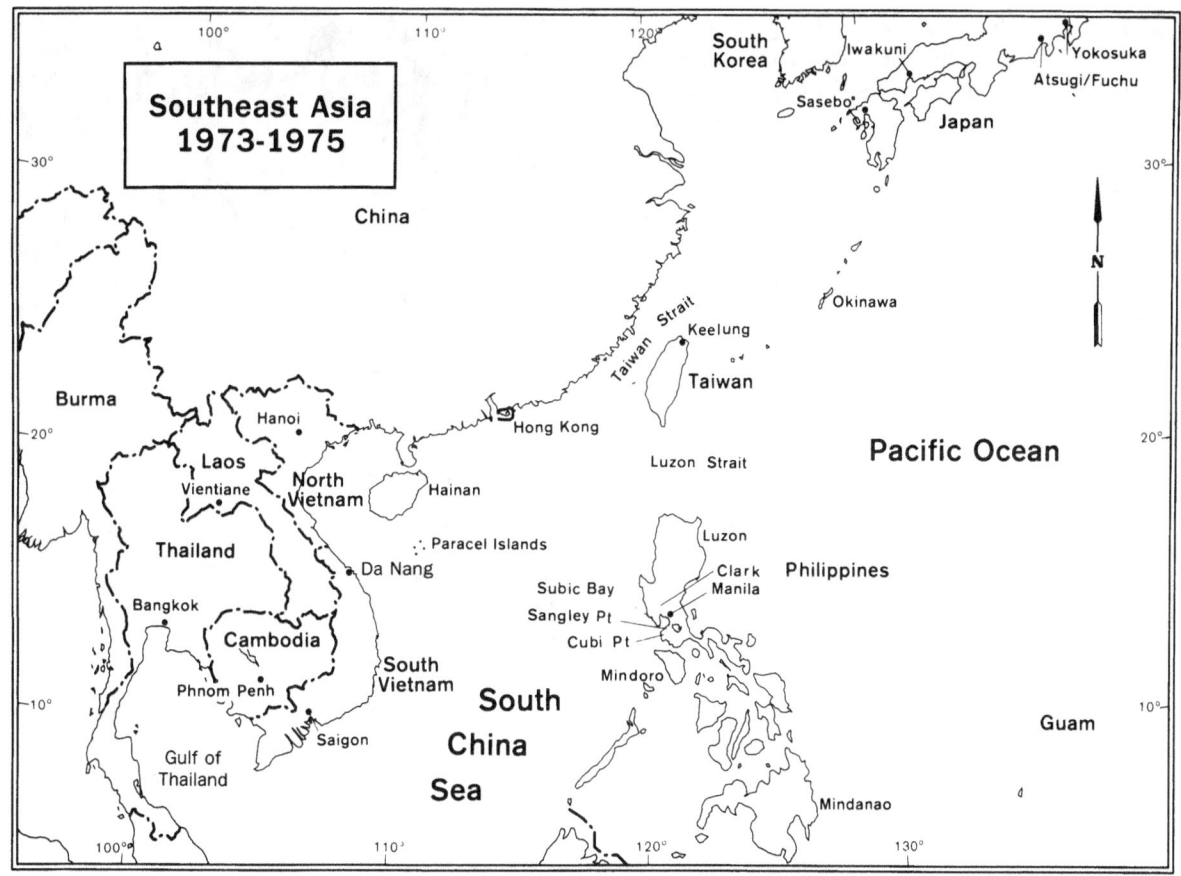

Map adapted from Edward J. Marolda and Oscar P. Fitzgerald, *The United States Navy and the Vietnam Conflict, From Military Assistance to Combat*, vol. II (Washington: U.S. Naval Historical Center, 1986)

tolerate intervention by anyone in Thai affairs. In accommodating the new government's diplomatic needs, the agreement confirmed the restructuring of the U.S. presence in Thailand and reshaped its command relationships. The end result was the return of the Military Assistance Command, Thailand (MACThai), to its pre-Vietnam function of overseeing logistics, administration, and liaison while the United States Support Activities Group/Seventh Air Force (USSAG) headquarters assumed the role of coordinating and supervising military activities of mutual interest to America's Southeast Asian allies. Thailand accepted America's explanation that USSAG was a temporary, nonpermanent organization that would be removed as soon as the transition to peace had been completed. General John W. Vogt, Jr., headed the joint command at Nakhon Phanom Royal Thai Air Force Base, and although responsibile for the air war in Cambodia, avoided any overt action that could be interpreted as a sign that the United States planned to expand hostilities using Thailand as a base of operations. This restriction even included dropping the well known Seventh Air Force's name from USSAG's title. With a 15 August ban on combat flights staring him in the face, General Vogt, with less than a month left on his tour of duty, had little choice but to begin planning for post-combat contingencies.[5]

The U.S. Air Force and its commander in Southeast Asia were now obligated to effect a transition to a training and standby alert status. Overnight, this became the major function of all Air Force units in Thailand. General Vogt oversaw the initial phase of this evolution while at the same time serving as coordinator of operational air requirements in Southeast Asia. Less than a month later, however, General Timothy F. O'Keefe, USAF, a native of Brooklyn and a well-respected combat veteran, succeeded him. General O'Keefe assumed command of a headquarters without a combat role but still responsible for air contingencies in the region, including possible reentry into South Vietnam or evacuation of Americans from Southeast Asia, particularly war-torn Cambodia. Political instability in Thailand and increased combat losses by America's allies in Cambodia served to make General O'Keefe's new job difficult and USSAG's future role uncertain.[6]

All of these events in Thailand converged in late 1973 to make military contingency planning for Cambodia a highly elusive and confusing proposition. It made all planning circumspect, complicated, and unusually dependent on variables beyond the control of USSAG and the American military. This translated into a realization that any planned military activity involving Southeast Asia might have to originate beyond the confines of the Indochina Peninsula and the next best option was the Gulf of Thailand. This, in turn, necessitated an increased and heavy dependence on Pacific naval forces for the possible implementation and execution of any such contingency plan.

The Plan for Cambodia

On 13 April 1973, Admiral Noel A.M. Gayler, USN, Commander-in-Chief Pacific (CinCPac), tasked General Vogt with responsibility for both the planning and execution of any emergency evacuation of American citizens from Cambodia. The planned evacuation would be codenamed Operation Eagle Pull.[7] The Commander, U.S. Military Assistance Command, Thailand (ComUSMACThai), was thereby relieved of this responsibility with the justification being that MACThai had already begun the process of dismantling its operational command post. One only had to look at events in Southeast Asia to know the more compelling and immediate reason was the imminent collapse of the Cambodian government.

CinCPac's message assigning General Vogt the evacuation responsibility reflected the sense of urgency prevailing in Pacific Command Headquarters in Hawaii over the developments in Cambodia. The message also specified that pending preparation and approval of USSAG's plan, Major General Andrew J. Evans, Jr., USAF, should be prepared to execute his (MACThai) command's plan.[8] This was little more than a concept envisioning three options: (1) evacuation by commercial air; (2) evacuation by military fixed wing; or (3) evacuation using Thailand-based Air Force helicopters. If required, U.S. Air Force Security Police already in Thailand would defend the landing zones, and the U.S. Army's Hawaii-based 25th Infantry Division would serve as a back-up. Pressured by the knowledge that battlefield events could precipitate an immediate evacuation of Cambodia, General Vogt's planners at USSAG Headquarters (Nakhon Phanom, Thailand) reacted almost immediately to the new assignment. Within two weeks, they released a message detailing their initial concept of operations, and not surprisingly it duplicated the MACThai plan.[9] Not satisfied with the initial concept and uncertain when

Department of Defense Photo (USMC) A558063
MajGen Michael P. Ryan, Commanding General, III MAF, learned in early April 1973 that senior Pacific commanders wished to use Marines as part of the evacuation security force. He ordered 31st MAU to provide a reinforced rifle company for Operation Eagle Pull.

they would have to activate it, USSAG strategists continued to develop, refine, and update the evacuation plan.[10]

Marines participated in the process from the outset. The message that directed USSAG to plan for an emergency evacuation from Cambodia also set forth a requirement for a reinforced company of Marines to be on call and available to USSAG for ground security purposes. In this role, they would supplant the Air Force units, designated as MACThai's landing zone security forces.[11]

From theory to realization, this change wound its way through the Pacific Fleet chain of command and arrived by message as an order to Major General Michael P. Ryan to provide a reinforced rifle company from his command, the III Marine Amphibious Force (III MAF). On 15 April 1973, he assigned this responsibility to the 31st MAU, which was ashore at Subic Bay. At that moment, the helicopter squadron assigned to Colonel Thomas J. Stevens (the MAU commander) and the ships designated to carry his MAU were already involved in minesweeping operations off

CONTINGENCY PLANNING

North Vietnam. Despite this shortfall in air assets, the MAU was prepared to conduct a company-size evacuation operation using Air Force helicopters.[12]

Additionally, General Ryan ordered the contingency battalion of the 3d Marine Division to serve as a backup force. Shortly thereafter, on 20 April 1973, the MAU was relieved of its evacuation responsibilities in favor of the air contingency battalion landing team (ACBLT), which then became the primary source for the special ground security mission in Cambodia.[13]

General Vogt assigned responsiblity for Eagle Pull planning to the Surface Operations and Plans Division within USSAG, which then designated Major Horace W. Baker the principal action officer. The senior Marine officers at USSAG, having recognized the necessity for rapid reaction to evacuation requirements, advocated the use of deployed Marine forces. As a result of their influence, the role of Marine forces changed from alternate to primary.[14]

With the developing sophistication of the plan came the realization that external and peripheral political, diplomatic, and humanitarian factors could not be ignored. Certainly they would complicate execution of the plan, but inattention to these matters would guarantee failure and portend fatal consequences. Wisely, Major Baker and the Surface Operations and Plans Division incorporated these factors into USSAG's planning.[15]

General Vogt's initial concept, like General Evans', entailed three options. Two involved evacuation from Phnom Penh's Pochentong Airfield by fixed-wing aircraft, while the third envisioned the use of helicopters from the same site. The first choice called for the evacuation of all designated persons from Phnom Penh by commercial planes, with the Ambassador controlling the operation. The second involved fixed-wing military aircraft transporting evacuees from Pochentong, with ComUSSAG in control.[16]

General Vogt correctly and prudently assumed that the U.S. colors at the Embassy would not be struck until the eleventh hour of the Khmer Republic had passed. Similarly, he presumed that the airfield at Pochentong (14 kilometers west of the city) would not be usable by then. Anticipating loss of the airfield at a critical hour, USSAG then concentrated on the third option, exclusive use of helicopters.[17]

In studying the details for a helicopter evacuation, two questions loomed larger than the rest. What was the total number of evacuees and where would they be located? This information represented the most critical factor and the one upon which all other decisions hinged. It not only would determine the number of helicopters required, but also the number of landing zones and their location. Additionally, it would dictate the size of the force required to protect those zones.

The time and distance factors related to this operation mandated use of the minimum essential number of security troops. This number would be predicated on helicopter availability rather than tac-

Massed colors of the regiments and separate battalions of the 3d Marine Division lead off a combat review at Camp Hansen, Okinawa. These are some of the troops USSAG planners decided to use as ground security forces if they had sufficient warning time.

Marine Corps Historical Collection

tical integrity of the required ground units.[18] The amount of warning time was yet another unknown factor in the equation to determine what sized force could be used. General Vogt knew he would have to conduct the evacuation on short notice, regardless of other commitments. With sufficient warning time, i.e., 24 hours or more, other forces would also be available, but in the spring of 1973 there was little promise of a day's warning.

USSAG planners recognized that the nearest infantry units capable of serving as security forces were III MAF Marines stationed on Okinawa. Given sufficient warning time, units from Okinawa could be airlifted to Thailand. In the event of insufficient warning time, Seventh Air Force security forces would have to suffice despite the fact that USSAG planners considered this a high-risk, last-resort option.

Helicopter availability loomed as the largest unanswered question confronting the planners. The Seventh Air Force had some helicopters in Southeast Asia as did the Marine Corps, but the distances involved dictated the use of heavy helicopters. The medium load CH-46 helicopters did not possess the required capacity nor the range to complete this mission successfully. Only a heavy helicopter could carry enough fuel for the extended distance and still have room to carry the payload. At this time, in early 1973, all of the Marine Corps' heavy lift helicopters were committed to Operation End Sweep, minesweeping operations in Haiphong Harbor. Consequently, USSAG envisioned for its initial concept of operations the use of Air Force helicopters and, time permitting, Marine security forces located on Okinawa.[19]

The Seventh Air Force's 21st Special Operations Squadron (21st SOS), equipped with CH-53 aircraft, and the 40th Aerospace Rescue and Recovery Squadron (40th ARRS), equipped with HH-53s, would provide the airlift support. Basically identical helicopters, the HH-53 differed from the CH-53 in that a rescue hoist, jettisonable auxiliary fuel tanks, and a refueling probe had been added to enable the HH-53 to conduct its mission of search and rescue. In the spring of 1973, combat veterans manned both squadrons, but with the passage of time many of these airmen were replaced by less experienced pilots.[20]

The antiaircraft capabilities of the Khmer Communists posed a serious threat to all aircraft, especially the helicopters. Similiarly, the American security forces once in their assigned zones could be subjected to Communist artillery and mortar fire. With these factors in mind, a detailed air support plan was developed along with stringent rules of engagement.[21]

Operational control of the forces committed to the evacuation rested with General Vogt, USSAG Commander, but would be exercised through a mission commander in a specially equipped C-130 airborne battle command and control center (ABCCC), which would orbit at some distance from Phnom Penh. Meanwhile control of tactical aircraft operating over the landing zones and along the helicopter approach and retirement routes would be handled by the tactical air coordinator airborne, TAC(A), in an OV-10 aircraft. Control of the helicopters was assigned to a separate helicopter direction center (HDC) in an additional C-130. The Seventh Air Force had enough planes to relieve this aircraft on station, thereby providing continuous round-the-clock control of the operation. The commander of the landing zone/security forces also would come under the Commanding General, USSAG, via communications with the orbiting ABCCC.[22]

With each passing week during the spring of 1973, the number of potential evacuees grew. The original estimate of 200 to 300 increased to 600-700 by the end of May 1973, a phenomenon directly related to the success of the Khmer Rouge offensive. Noting this, USSAG increased the number of landing zones, which in turn necessitated an enlargement of the security force. In June, III MAF received orders to provide a second reinforced rifle company and a command group to support the operation. This responsibility fell to the 3d Marine Division. From June 1973 until execution of the operation, a battalion of the division always had two companies on call for Operation Eagle Pull. The command group operated independently, preparing for every conceivable eventuality, but sometimes events overcame plans as they did in 1973.[23]

In July, without warning, General Vogt received a message from CinCPac to execute Operation Eagle Pull. As Major Baker was increduously absorbing the text of the message in preparation for placing the evacuation plan into effect, he received a phone call from the CinCPac Command Center, "Disregard the message!" The staff at CinCPac had been so sure that the evacuation would take place that they had prepared an "execute" message and, inexplicably, it had been released. A further touch of irony was added by the coincidental presence of the CinCPac action officer in Thailand. He had arrived at USSAG Headquarters to attend a previously scheduled planning conference

Department of Defense Photo (USMC) A708034
Col Edward J. Bronars, pictured here as a lieutenant general, served as USSAG's Chief of Surface Operations and Plans Division in 1973-74. In August of 1973, he chaired the first in a series of joint planning conferences held at Nakhon Phanom, Thailand.

which, after the excitement had subsided, did take place on 4 July 1973 in a rather anticlimactic atmosphere.[24]

Helicopter availability remained a major point of concern for CinCPac. The number of available Air Force helicopters combined with the highest estimate of evacuees required an excessive number of round-trip flights. As a consequence it prolonged the exposure to enemy ground fire and represented an unnecessary risk. The estimated duration of the operation, 48 hours, was unacceptable, and more helicopters had to be located or the number of evacuees had to be reduced. Fortunately, minesweeping operations off North Vietnam were rapidly approaching conclusion and amphibious assault ships and their embarked helicopters would be available by 1 August. The assignment of naval forces to the operation would not only double the number of available helicopters, but also would halve the distance from launch point to destination. This would significantly reduce the duration of the mission.[25]

On 30 July, upon completion of Operation End Sweep, the 31st MAU was reconstituted. Its helicopter organization was reconfigured to accommodate a maximum number of CH-53s on board the USS *Tripoli* (LPH 10). Consisting of 13 CH-53s, 4 CH-46s, 2 "Hueys," and 4 "Cobras," the new helicopter composition of the MAU became known as the "Eagle Pull mix". The reorganization of the MAU provided significantly enhanced flexibility to the planners. At this point though, the only MAU units incorporated in the operational plan were the helicopters.[26]

During the period 3-5 August 1973, the first series of planning conferences involving representatives of III MAF and USSAG convened at General Vogt's headquarters in Nakhon Phanom. The initial conference had as its goal coordination of III MAF's participation. Those present included the 31st MAU's new commander, Colonel David M. Twomey; the commanding officer of the 9th Marines and designated commander of the ground security forces, Colonel Stephen G. Olmstead; the III MAF Eagle Pull liaison

Col Stephen G. Olmstead, pictured here as a lieutenant general, commanded the 9th Marines and was the designated commander of the ground security forces for Operation Eagle Pull. Although Phnom Penh was not evacuated during his tour, Col Olmstead made several inspections of the Cambodian capital.
Marine Corps Historical Collection

Department of Defense Photo (USMC) 012144985
Col David M. Twomey, pictured here as a lieutenant general, commanded the 31st MAU from 26 July 1973 to 16 February 1974. The 31st MAU Marines assumed the tasks of ground security forces for Operation Eagle Pull in August of 1973 and never relinquished them.

officer, Major James B. Hicks; representatives from Seventh Fleet's Amphibious Ready Group Alpha, and key officers from participating Air Force units. Colonel Edward J. Bronars, USMC, the USSAG's Chief of Surface Operations and Plans Division, chaired the conference.

As part of the conference schedule, Colonel Olmstead and selected Marine officers visited Phnom Penh on 4 August and sighted the designated landing zones. While in Phnom Penh, Colonel Olmstead participated with the Embassy staff in a command post exercise. The Marines who remained at Nakhon Phanom helped develop helicopter coordination schedules, procedures for the rescue of downed helicopters, approach and retirement lanes, and a plan for emergency resupply of committed forces.

After Colonel Olmstead and his party returned to Nakhon Phanom on 5 August, Colonel Twomey, Lieutenant Colonel Arthur B. Colbert, and key MAU officers visited Phnom Penh for a similar reconnaissance. During these two visits, valuable liaison was established among the Marines, the Embassy staff, and the Military Equipment Delivery Team, Cambodia (MEDTC), headed by Brigadier General John R. Cleland, Jr., USA. The members of MEDTC were responsible for organizing, supervising, and controlling the Phnom Penh evacuation and, of particular importance, the selection of prospective helicopter landing zones.[27]

The landing zones were approved by the charge d'affaires in Phnom Penh, William K. Enders, based upon the recommendations of the MEDTC. The population concentrations in the city heavily influenced the recommended locations of the various landing zones. The number of zones reflected the planning assumption that chaos and confusion would render land transportation unusable.

The inability to improve prospective landing zones for helicopters limited the number of sites. Several athletic fields were potential landing zones, but light towers surrounding them made night use unsafe. This eliminated five of eight proposed landing zones including ones at the colosseum and at the university both of which initially were considered primary sites. Of those remaining, Landing Zone (LZ) B was adjacent to the Presidential Palace, while LZs C and H were the ones nearest to the American Embassy. The Embassy LZ, LZ C, was near the river bed, dry in winter and spring due to the absence of rainfall and completely surrounded by barbed wire. LZ H, added to the list in 1974, was a soccer field slightly removed from the river, bordered on three sides by apartment buildings; LZs D1 and D2 were alternate zones, each with a rated capacity of one aircraft per zone, to be used only if there were no means of getting evacuees to the primary zones.[28]

Subsequent conferences involving III MAF and 31st MAU representatives occurred with greater frequency as the situation in Cambodia worsened. During each conference, the Marines significantly refined and updated plans, including the addition of two options involving the employment of 31st MAU elements. The most important accomplishment was the integration of both the MAU's helicopter and ground elements into the plan. As a result, the final plan listed five courses of action for the helicopter evacuation option, Option III.

One common factor in all five alternatives was the source of the landing force command element, the 3d Marine Division. With the two most likely alternatives involving the 31st MAU, it seemed logical that the command element should originate from within the

CONTINGENCY PLANNING

Photo courtesy of Col Peter F. Angle, USMC (Ret)

The hazards to helicopter flight in University LZ, above, particularly from the light towers surrounding the soccer field and track, and in Colosseum LZ, below, also from its tall light towers and its frequent use as a military vehicle staging area, caused the planners to discard them as a primary sites once consideration was given to night evacuation. The Colosseum had been designated a primary zone in 1973. All zones were approved by the Embassy.

Photo courtesy of Col Peter F. Angle, USMC (Ret)

Aerial view of Landing Zone Hotel shows the soccer field shielded from the east bank of the Mekong River by an apartment building. Other side of the river is Khmer Rouge territory.

division. The 31st MAU could not provide the command element since the commander of USSAG had stipulated that the commander of the ground security force had to be prepositioned at USSAG Headquarters at least 72 hours prior to the start of the operation. His presence in Nakhon Phanom, the commander of USSAG felt, would allow the Marine commander to participate in last-minute planning and liaison. In essence, the argument was that the command element from Okinawa was always available to meet this requirement, but because of ship rotations and weather, the MAU command element was not.[29]*

---

*Colonel John F. Roche III, the commanding officer of 31st MAU as of June 1974, provided an insightful recollection: "The conclusion that a command element from the MAU would not be available at USSAG headquarters 72 hours prior to the operation because of ship movements and weather simply was not logical. Were the MAU not able to provide this element, it probably would not have been able to execute the operation for the same reasons. Beyond that the state of communications among the concerned headquarters was such that real-time interactions were possible and did take place throughout the planning period. I protested this arrangement vigorously until it was reaffirmed by CG, III MAF. Although this portion of history is accurate as a record, knowledgeable military planners will question its validity." Roche Comments.

Other significant conference accomplishments pertained to logistics and communications. An emergency resupply of CH-53 parts was arranged, in effect a lateral shift of Air Force parts. The parts would be delivered to Utapao Air Base, Thailand, where they would then be picked up by a sea-based MAU helicopter. In the area of communications, USSAG assigned a block of frequencies to the landing force for its internal use, and sent it a draft copy of the communications plan. Through these efforts the Marine commanders gained valuable insight into the USSAG communications procedures, especially those involving the Air Mission Commander in the orbiting C-130. In addition the Marines gained a comprehensive understanding of what would be a complex operation.

The consensus at the joint command headquarters in Nakhon Phanom was that it would not receive the order to evacuate until the last possible moment. By that time, the ground situation would have deteriorated to the point that the helicopter landing zones would be the only available egress points and they would be available only if they could be secured by ground forces. To complicate and compound the question of when, the attitude at the Embassy in Phnom

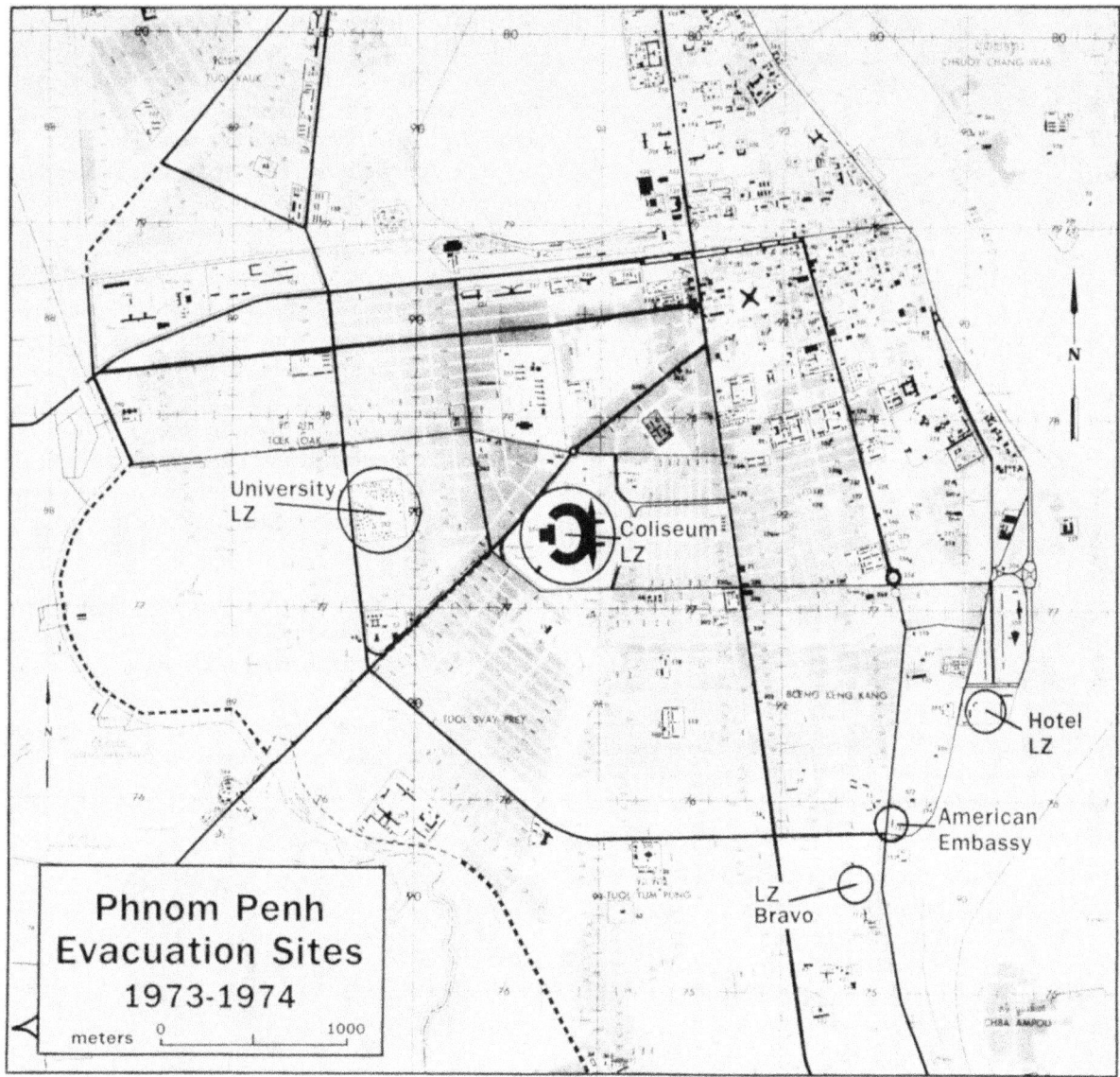

Phnom Penh Evacuation Sites 1973-1974

Penh fluctuated almost daily from "never go" to "maybe tomorrow."[30]

After the August 1973 conference, the major question that remained was when to go, because the planners had decided method and means; evacuation would be by air, either fixed-wing or helicopter. These were further divided into five options by helicopter and two by fixed-wing. The helicopter choices involved primarily Marine aircraft from the MAU while the fixed-wing course projected use of either commercial or Air Force aircraft.

On 10 August 1973, the 31st MAU/Amphibious Ready Group (ARG) reached its designated holding area in the Gulf of Thailand with an assigned 12-hour response time. (Assuming a 20-knot speed, the ARG could remain somewhere within a 240 mile arc of the launch point.) Three days later, USSAG issued Operation Plan 1-73 for Operation Eagle Pull. It reflected the decisions arrived at by the joint planning conference. The next day, the 31st MAU issued Operation Order 2-73 detailing its role in support of USSAG. On 16 August, General Vogt additionally tasked the 31st MAU with preparations for possible evacuation of the three MEDTC personnel from the Ream/Kompong Som area. To accomplish this mission, the MAU issued Operation Order 3-73. All of the elements of the real-life drama were now in place, and it was time to wait.[31]

Within three weeks, a crisis of a different sort confronted the Eagle Pull planners. On 8 September,

Department of Defense Photo (USMC) 051222434
Col John F. Roche III relieved Col Douglas T. Kane as commanding officer of 31st MAU on 13 July 1974. Col Roche and staff developed helicopter employment and landing tables (HEALT) for the MAU's CH-53s.

while steaming between Okinawa and Subic Bay, the USS *Tripoli*, the LPH assigned to Amphibious Ready Group Alpha (ARG Alpha), suffered a major engineering casualty and had to be towed to Subic. The effect of the loss was clear, but before a solution could be devised, USS *Duluth*, an LPD with the same group, developed its own engineering difficulties.[32]

Almost immediately, ARG Alpha formulated and obtained approval for a plan which would at least temporarily fix the problem. The USS *Coral Sea* (CVA 43), and subsequently the USS *Hancock* (CVA 19), were designated as standby LPHs. In addition, the USS *Vancouver* (LPD 2), an LPD with ARG Bravo, was assigned as standby for the *Duluth*. In the event of evacuation operations, the MAU elements normally on board *Tripoli* and *Duluth* would embark immediately in the *Coral Sea/Hancock* and *Vancouver*, respectively. All of these planning changes were made in light of the then-prevailing requirement to remain no more than 96 hours steaming time from the waters off Kompong Som. The MAU/ARG had to be able to restructure itself to meet this requirement.[33]

After extensive work at the Ship Repair Facility (SRF) in Subic Bay, the *Tripoli* came back on line on 28 September. The plans then remained unchanged until 26 January 1974, when the 31st MAU received orders to provide support for Option II of the evacuation plan, a military fixed-wing airlift of evacuees. The effort entailed landing a 90-man security force at Pochentong Airfield to assist in the evacuation.

By the time these modifications took effect, the outlook for the Lon Nol Government had changed from outright pessimism to guarded optimism. The 1974 Khmer Communist dry season offensive was not as successful as had been expected. The Communists had pushed hard during January, but the government forces were holding their own. In February, there was a noticeable decline in the intensity of the Khmer offensive. The feeling of optimism grew, and the newfound confidence was reflected in significantly relaxed evacuation response times. The clearest indication

Col Sydney H. "Tom" Batchelder, commanding officer of 3d Service Battalion, 3d Marine Division relieved Col Olmstead as commander of the Eagle Pull landing force during the summer of 1974. Col Batchelder made several liaison trips to Nakhon Phanom and Phnom Penh in the remaining months of the year.
Department of Defense Photo (USMC) IC31404

Marine Corps Historical Collection
The 1974-75 Eagle Pull command group is seen during one of its many liaison trips to Cambodia and Thailand. At center is ground security force commander Col Sydney H. Batchelder, flanked at right by LtCol Curtis G. Lawson and, left, by Maj George L. Cates.

came on 17 June 1974 when the MAU reverted to a composite helicopter squadron using medium helicopters (CH-46s) in place of its "heavy Eagle Pull mix"(CH-53s). This change occurred as HMM-164 relieved HMH-462.[34]

To add to the rapidly changing scene, a complete turnover of Marine Corps personnel participating in Eagle Pull planning and operations took place during spring and summer of 1974. Colonel Sydney H. "Tom" Batchelder, Jr., Commanding Officer, 3d Service Battalion, 3d Marine Division, was assigned the additional duty of commander of the Eagle Pull landing force in relief of Colonel Olmstead. Colonel John F. Roche III relieved Colonel Douglas T. Kane on 13 July 1974 as commander of the unit containing the security forces, the 31st MAU.*

Within III MAF Headquarters, staff changes affecting the planning of the Cambodian operation also took place, including the replacement of Major Hicks by Major George L. Cates as the Eagle Pull planner in the G-3 section. The annual rotation of officers actually began in March 1974, earlier than the usual summer changeover period, when Major Edward A. "Tony" Grimm relieved Major Baker, the key action officer at USSAG Headquarters. Grimm's early assignment afforded him the opportunity to become well versed in the plans and ready to brief the summer arrivals, including the new members of the III MAF staff.[35]

During the period July through December 1974, the recently assigned key personnel made several important liaison visits to Nakhon Phanom and Phnom Penh. As a result of their trips, the first three Eagle Pull options were further refined. An additional concept was even explored, whereby the evacuation would be conducted by loading the evacuees in ships and sailing them down the Mekong River. It was rejected as being too risky. In December 1974, Lieutenant Colonel Curtis G. Lawson relieved Lieutenant Colonel Glenn J. Shaver, Jr., as the 3d Marine Division air officer, a position which involved the all important additional duty as air liaison officer for the command element.[36]

Between September 1973 and December 1974, six major Eagle Pull planning conferences took place at USSAG Headquarters. As a result, the plan was further improved, but essentially it varied little from the one first issued in August 1973.**

---

*Colonel Kane, in turn, on 16 February 1974 had relieved Colonel David M. Twomey, who had assumed command on 26 July 1973 from the acting CO, Lieutenant Colonel Ronald L. Owen, the interim replacement (3-25 July 1973) for the departing commander, Colonel Thomas J. Stevens. 31st MAU ComdCs, 1Jan-31Dec73, 1Jan-31Dec74, and 1Jan-31May75.

**Colonel Roche noted that the plan to employ the CH-53 was developed by his staff in late 1974 and "provided for lifts from decks on which the MAU's elements were then located." Roche Comments.

Vietnam

Since the summer of 1972, when ships carrying the 9th Marine Amphibious Brigade had stood off the coast of Military Region 1 waiting to evacuate, if necessary, Americans then under fire, specific plans for evacuation of Americans had lain dormant. General contingency plans did exist. The Pacific Command had a plan for every possible contingency, including emergency evacuation of Americans. Characterized as "outline plans," they conveyed in a very general sense a concept for operations and logistical support and a sketch of command relationships, but no specifics. In keeping with the stated policy surrounding these plans, detailed items would be filled in as the particular situation warranted.[37]

As conditions in South Vietnam normalized following the implementation of the Paris Accords, the prospects of conducting an emergency evacuation of civilians from South Vietnam became less likely. With each day of relative stability in 1973, the sense of urgency to design specific plans waned. This complacency persisted until a few weeks after Gerald R. Ford assumed the American presidency in August 1974.

Beginning in September 1974 enemy activity intensified and the situation in South Vietnam, particularly in Military Region 1, the area immediately south of the Demilitarized Zone, began to deteriorate dramatically. Both Vice Admiral George P. Steele, the Seventh Fleet commander, and Major General Herman G. Poggemeyer, who had succeeded Major General Ryan as the commanding general of III MAF, became concerned about this turn of events.[38]* Almost daily they received information reporting the results of the fighting in South Vietnam and recognized the possibility that with very little advance warning the forces under their command could be tasked to conduct an emergency evacuation of Americans from MR 1. With the permission of the American Embassy, Saigon, and concurrence of Admiral Steele, General Poggemeyer sent his G-3, Colonel John M. Johnson, Jr., to South Vietnam, in particular to Da Nang for an on-the-scene liaison visit.[39] Admiral Steele remembered that his efforts to obtain the voluminous detailed information necessary to conduct an evacua-

---

*Admiral Steele recounted years later that his staff was far from complacent about evacuation matters and that his first concerns surfaced soon after assuming command of the Seventh Fleet in July 1973. He visited Saigon in late August 1973 to survey the situation and left with "no doubt in my mind that Vietnam would be lost during my Seventh Fleet command tour." Steele Comments.

Marine Corps Historical Collection

During the summer of 1974 LtCol Gene A. Deegan, pictured here as a major general, commanded BLT 2/9, the landing force of Amphibious Ready Group Bravo.

tion had been thwarted by Ambassador Graham A. Martin, whose permission had to be obtained before any American could enter South Vietnam. Admiral Steele recalled, "Ambassador Martin actually blocked me from sending people in" and argued that by planning an evacuation "we [the United States] would create the very fall of Vietnam that he was there to prevent." The authorization by the Ambassador (after numerous requests by Admiral Steele) to receive a planner from III MAF reflected the first change in his position and a growing concern by the Embassy staff that serious military problems did exist.[40]

While in Da Nang, Colonel Johnson reviewed emergency evacuation plans with the American Consul-General. Colonel Johnson discovered alarming news—the plans such as they were, were very sketchy and not up-to-date. The North Vietnamese offensive had placed such pressure on the South Vietnamese that, in Colonel Johnson's opinion, a concerted attack by the Communists might result in a debacle at Da Nang and thereby necessitate an emergency evacuation of the area. He reported his conclusions to Vice Admiral Steele who concurred in the findings and reported them up the chain of command, resulting in a proper sense of urgency. Johnson's report only served to confirm the admiral's worst fears: "We were certain that in spite of the Ambassador's assurances that he had adequate plans, the in-country plans were totally inadequate. We had a major job ahead of us." In preparing for this eventuality, Admiral Steele made a personal trip in the fall of 1974 to meet with the new defense attache, Major General Homer D. Smith, Jr., USA, and the Ambassador. Although he received from General Smith what he described as "fine help which later proved crucial," his meeting with the Ambassador proved far less conclusive as he parted with Martin's final words ringing in his ears, "Do not worry, Admiral, I will initiate the evacuation in good time. I understand the necessity for doing so."[41]

With his mission completed, Colonel Johnson returned to Okinawa. With him he carried a "bootleg copy" of the consul-general's evacuation plan. This document proved to be of some help, but it had minimal impact on the formulation of detailed III MAF plans.[42] III MAF would have to wait to see what the Commander, Seventh Fleet had decided, which in all probability would be reflected in his as-yet unpublished South Vietnam evacuation plan. Admiral Steele, in turn, was waiting for the publication of a plan by either Pacific Fleet, commanded by Admiral Maurice F. Weisner, or USSAG. The command relationships for this eventuality were not clear. Admiral Steele believed that for an evacuation operation, the Seventh Fleet should remain under his, and not General O'Keefe's operational control, but Admiral Gayler, CinCPac, decided that Commander, USSAG should control the evacuation and that the Seventh Fleet would provide support.* With this decision in hand, General O'Keefe, General Vogt's relief as USSAG commander, published his evacuation plan in October 1974, codenamed Talon Vise. The Seventh Fleet's plan for evacuation of Military Region 1 was then issued and codenamed Gallant Journey, subsequently retitled Fortress Journey. Admiral Steele immediately requested the designation of an amphibious objective area (AOA).[42]

The next important step in this planning evolution was the clarification of command relationships. While this complex and sensitive process was occurring, the III MAF planners, using a draft copy of the USSAG plan also acquired by Colonel Johnson, began preparing for III MAF involvement. They designated Lieutenant Colonel James L. Cunningham, III MAF plans officer, coordinator of evacuation operations. His staff developed a concept plan and quickly disseminated a draft copy to the subordinate MAF commands.[44]

With Amphibious Ready Group (ARG) Alpha, the 4th Marines, and elements of MAG-36 already committed to Eagle Pull, any amphibious forces needed for this operation would have to come from ARG Bravo. The ARG's landing force at this time consisted of a battalion landing team from the 9th Marines, BLT 2/9, commanded by Lieutenant Colonel Gene A. Deegan. Due to be relieved by Lieutenant Colonel Royce Lynn Bond's BLT 1/9, BLT 2/9 would relinquish its responsibilities in the ARG on 6 October 1974.[45]

In anticipation of the commitment of ARG Bravo and its landing force, III MAF planners went to Camp Schwab to brief Lieutenant Colonel Bond and his staff on the situation in Military Region 1 of South Vietnam. Based on the information gathered by Colonel Johnson plus intelligence gathered from local sources, the briefing provided both timely and accurate insight to a battalion commander deploying in less than a week.[46]

From this and the available draft documentation, Lieutenant Colonel Bond and his S-3, Major Ronald J. Gruenberg, were able to outline a plan for the possible evacuation of Americans from South Vietnam. In this manner, the BLT readied itself for the order to evacuate, should it come. Higher headquarters needed only to designate time and place.[47]

The essential points of this plan called for the major evacuation to be centered in the Da Nang area, and to be either a pier-side or an across-the-beach evacuation. The battalion would provide the ground security force and planned to use it to establish blocking positions inland, as well as provide security for the evacuation sites.[48]

Shortly after the Camp Schwab conference, the Seventh Fleet sent out a planning evacuation format to standardize procedures. It duplicated the III MAF and Task Force 76 plans, thereby eliminating the need for additional preparation, but also pointing up the likelihood that this concept of operations, developed by the Marines in the fall and winter of 1974-75, would serve as the standard for all subsequent efforts. The initiative III MAF planners had demonstrated in fill-

---

*Admiral Steele recounted his consternation over this arrangement: "I still do not understand Admiral Gayler's decision to place Commander USSAG in control of the evacuation. Only a tiny fraction of USSAG's assets could be used while the operation would have to be run almost totally by the Navy and Marine Corps. However, once this decision was made by CinCPac, we did our best to support it." Steele Comments.

ing this void, despite the absence of specific published guidance, enabled senior commands to speed their own planning process. Thus the plans for evacuation of South Vietnam were set, and only time and events would determine if the participants were properly prepared to execute them.[49]

CHAPTER 4
The Fleet Marines Are Readied

*The Air Contingency BLTs—The Eagle Pull Command Element
The 31st MAU—The Other Contingency*

In the six major planning conferences held in the 15 months between the cessation of combat air support in Southeast Asia and December 1974, III MAF liaison officers and USSAG Eagle Pull action officers developed and refined a highly sophisticated plan to evacuate Americans from Cambodia. After each conference, the Marine attendees would return to III MAF Headquarters at Camp Courtney on Okinawa and proceed to revise as necessary their plans and orders for Operation Eagle Pull. These revisions focused on the heliborne option, known as Option III of the basic evacuation plan. This option required several landing sites because of the anticipated number of refugees, whose estimated numbers varied from day to day. Since the Marine Corps possessed most of the heavy helicopters in Southeast Asia, III MAF was naturally sensitive to any talks involving their use.

As these discussions at Nakhon Phanom progressed, agreement centered on the employment of sea-borne helicopters over fixed-wing aircraft or land-based helicopters, thereby allotting the Marine Corps a proportionally larger role in Operation Eagle Pull. In his capacity as liaison officer to the joint planning headquarters in Nakhon Phanom, Major George L. Cates, III MAF's Eagle Pull planner, had to make sure that plans for the MAF's tasking matched its capabilities. By intensifying its readiness training, III MAF took a giant step toward increasing its capabilities. In light of these changes, the 4th and 9th Marines began holding evacuation training classes, making evacuation preparation the order of the day in III MAF.

The Air Contingency BLTs

In the first evacuation contingency plan of early 1973, the U.S. Army's 25th Infantry Division in Hawaii was assigned as the primary security force. Shortly after the decision, CinCPac planners realized that an interim, alternate force might be necessary if an evacuation of Cambodia were ordered without warning. To fulfill this requirement, CinCPac tasked III MAF to provide one company of Marines on a full-time standby basis. The evacuation security force contingency would rotate from company to company within III MAF, but if employed, the rifle company would fall under the operational control of Commander, USSAG from its arrival at the designated assembly point until the conclusion of the operation.[1]

On 15 April 1973, Major General Michael P. Ryan, III MAF commander, ordered the 31st MAU to provide the reinforced rifle company from its ground combat element, 1st Battalion, 4th Marines. A standing III MAF operation order directed the 31st MAU to develop and maintain the capability of conducting company-size evacuation operations. III MAF provided the 31st MAU with very specific guidance as to the organization of the reinforced rifle company. It directed that besides a headquarters detachment, the command element would include medical and communication elements, a flamethrower section, a 81mm mortar section, and a 106mm recoilless rifle section. The rifle company would also be supported by a sizeable logistics support element. The complexity of the

Maj George L. Cates, pictured here as a brigadier general, assumed the duties of Eagle Pull planner in the III MAF G-3 section during the summer of 1974.
Marine Corps Historical Collection

reinforced rifle company meant that more than just a routine mission was expected for this evacuation.

Operational and political considerations in Southeast Asia and the Western Pacific dictated that the unit providing ground security for the Cambodian refugee extraction would have to be airlifted to Phnom Penh. Then if circumstances required, the rifle company would become the advance echelon of a larger security force. Equipment and supplies included trucks, jeeps, even an ambulance jeep, and seven days of ammunition, again an indicator of the level of combat anticipated. General Ryan tasked the 3d Marine Division to provide as a backup, an identically structured and equipped rifle company.[2]

On 17 April 1973, Colonel Thomas "TJ" Stevens, the commanding officer of the 31st MAU, reported to the Commanding General, III MAF that the designated company had completed a mount-out exercise. Having demonstrated its readiness, Stevens stated that his company was immediately deployable.[3] General Ryan, in turn, notified Lieutenant General Louis H. Wilson, Jr., the commanding general of Fleet Marine Force, Pacific (FMFPac), and Vice Admiral George P. Steele, commander of the Seventh Fleet, that the designated companies from BLT 1/4 and the 3d Marine Division's air contingency battalion landing team, 2d Battalion, 9th Marines, commanded by Lieutenant Colonel Charles E. Parker, were ready to deploy. On 20 April, General Ryan directed a change of principal players, Company G (reinforced) from BLT 2/9 would now be the primary ground security force to support USSAG, and Company B (reinforced) from BLT 1/4 would assume the back-up role. The entire 31st MAU remained on notice to be prepared to support the operation.[4]

This was the first of several instances during the 1973 to 1975 period that the MAF commanding general was faced with a dilemma. Given the uncertainty of the situation, he had to decide whether to divide his ready force to meet the initial requirement, opening the possibility of piecemeal commitment, or leave the forward force intact, and use another force to make the first contact. As indicated by his directive to Colonel Stevens on 20 April, General Ryan opted for the second choice.

On 26 June 1973, USSAG made General Ryan's choice slightly more difficult. It upped the ante by requesting the commitment of a second rifle company and a command group to augment the Operation Eagle Pull ground security force. To accommodate the growing estimate of evacuees, General John W. Vogt, Jr., had added another helicopter landing zone, thereby necessitating additional forces to secure it. Again, General Ryan handed the task to the air contingency battalion—2d Battalion, 9th Marines—now commanded by Lieutenant Colonel Robert M. Stauffer. Stauffer designated Companies F and G as the Eagle Pull forces.[5]

As far as the Okinawa-based air contingency battalion was concerned, the assumption of Eagle Pull responsibilities did not alter its normal readiness posture. Two of its reinforced rifle companies and a command group were placed in an increased alert and deployability status. The command group, consisting of a security force commander and his small staff of an air liaison officer (ALO) and two communication officers, were on call at all times. The air contingency battalion, a rotational assignment among the 3d Marine Division's six infantry battalions, was drilled more extensively and more often in air movement exercises. Battalions assumed this mission during the post-deployment phase of their life cycles. Regularly scheduled loading drills and joint air movement and transportability exercises with the Air Force not only tested the battalions, but, equally important, they also improved the efficiency of the division's embarkation and movement control agencies. Starting with command post training drills and culminating in air-ground field exercises, the 3d Marine Division's infantry battalions and the 1st Marine Aircraft Wing's squadrons became increasingly proficient in emergency evacuation procedures.

The 3d Marine Division held Eagle Pull practice sessions on a monthly basis. Each drill involved all of the III MAF units required to function in the final operation: the designated companies and command group; the motor transport elements taking the security force to Kadena; and the embarkation units controlling the movement to Kadena.

From an operational point of view, the planners' gravest concern was the movement of the forces from their base camps to Kadena. It was difficult from a transportation aspect; many alerts, oddly, took place on weekends when motor transport personnel were on liberty and Okinawa highway traffic was in a snarl. In terms of operational security, 400 fully armed Marines could not move on Okinawa without being noticed, even when transported by air, because that many helicopters landing at Kadena at short, regular intervals was a highly conspicuous event.

On 28 September 1973, a typical Eagle Pull drill was conducted at the direction of Colonel Alexander S. Ruggiero, the 3d Marine Division G-3. He randomly asked individual Marines under what circumstances they would fire their weapons. Ruggiero concluded that the Marines in Companies F and G were well schooled in the rules of engagement, but also determined that some Marines knew not enough and others too much about the pending operation: ". . . Co G['s] . . . men gave the overall impression of being quite bewildered by the whole thing . . . . Co F, knew a little too much as they identified the country."*6

With the passage of time and subsequent drills, the functioning of the entire apparatus became smoother. The air contingency BLTs were ready to go, dedicated drivers from the 3d and 9th Motor Transport Battalions knew exactly where to go, and the control agencies knew how to move the air contingency BLTs in the shortest amount of time.7

When the dry season in Cambodia began in 1975, the air contingency BLT was the 2nd Battalion, 9th Marines under the command of Lieutenant Colonel Gene A. Deegan. In early January of that year, BLT 2/9 increased its alert status. Lieutenant Colonel Deegan recalled his designated Eagle Pull rifle companies, Company G, commanded by Captain James H. Davis, and Company H, commanded by Captain James L. Jones, Jr., from the Northern Training Area where they had been undergoing post-deployment training. As the month progressed and the Khmer Rouge pressed ever closer to Phnom Penh, the evacuation reaction time was decreased from 16 to 3 hours. Lieutenant Colonel Deegan and his S-3, Major Barry J. Murphy, became daily visitors at the division and MAF headquarters. Major General Kenneth J. Houghton, who had succeeded Major General Fred E. Haynes, Jr., as commanding general of the 3d Marine Division, almost daily presided over briefings of the designated Eagle Pull commanders. These changes foretold what everyone knew, that actual operations would soon supplant training as the priority of the day.

---

*Colonel Ruggiero also concluded from his inspection that each driver in the convoy needed to know through which gate to enter Kadena, because the convoy commander did not have time to wait until all the trucks had been loaded before beginning the movement (Maj Henry C. Stackpole memo to CO, 9th Mar, Subj: Eagle Pull, dtd 29Sept73, p. 1, Eagle Pull File). He also commented, years later, that the continuous rotation of companies to the Eagle Pull contingency made the maintenance of secrecy even more difficult, but the paramount concern during early training centered around the dense traffic on the roads to Kadena. Ruggiero Comments.

Photo courtesy of Col Peter F. Angle, USMC (Ret)
Col Stephen G. Olmstead, ground security force commander, stands outside his quarters in Phnom Penh.

The Eagle Pull Command Element

On 30 June 1973, four days after the requirement materialized for an overall ground commander, known as the Ground Security Force (GSF) Commander, General Ryan selected Colonel Stephen G. Olmstead, the commanding officer of the 9th Marines, to serve in that capacity. One of Colonel Olmstead's first duties involved a trip to Hawaii to brief Admiral Gayler at CinCPac and General Wilson at FMFPac on the concept and scheme of maneuver for Operation Eagle Pull. In August 1973 he went to Nakhon Phanom to participate in the initial planning conference between the USSAG staff and III MAF Marines. Returning to Okinawa, he formed his command element, which included Major Peter F. Angle (air liaison officer) and two communicators. Then throughout the fall and early winter, the command element stood ready to fly to Nakhon Phanom should the need arise for a final liaison with the USSAG commander before starting the actual evacuation. The 1974 dry season was less than a month old when the call came.

Photo courtesy of Col Peter F. Angle, USMC (Ret)

Ground security force commander Col Olmstead views Pochentong airfield during his January-February 1974 visit. The airfield was the only way out other than by river convoy.

The ground security force air liaison officer, Maj Peter F. Angle, photographed Embassy LZ during his January-February 1974 visit. The landing zone, 100 meters from the Embassy in Phnom Penh, could accommodate two CH-53s and was fenced by barbed wire.

Photo courtesy of Col Peter F. Angle, USMC (Ret)

LtCol Curtis G. Lawson, pictured here as a colonel, became the 3d Marine Division air officer in December 1974. An additional duty of this billet was to serve as air liaison officer for the Eagle Pull command element.

In response to increased pressure from Khmer forces around the city of Phnom Penh, General Timothy F. O'Keefe (ComUSSAG) requested that Colonel Olmstead and his command element deploy to Nakhon Phanom. Evacuation appeared imminent. The III MAF commander, Major General Herman Poggemeyer, Jr., who replaced General Ryan on 31 December 1973, in his semi-annual history reported, "Colonel Olmstead, the designated GSF Commander, deployed to Southeast Asia with the Regimental ALO and two radio operators on 23 January 1974 in an increased readiness posture. The group returned to Camp Schwab on 16 February 1974."[8]

Colonel Olmstead's notification of his impending departure came during a 9th Marines mess night when Major General Fred E. Haynes, Jr., 3d Marine Division commander, pulled him aside and said, "The bell has rung and you have been called down there." The next morning Colonel Olmstead and his party left Kadena on a T-39 aircraft for Nakhon Phanom via Cubi Point, Republic of the Philippines. Even though the deployment turned out to be a false alarm the Marines used the opportunity to visit Phnom Penh. On this visit, they spent three days in the Cambodian capital, visiting LZs, checking movement routes, and photographing anything deemed important to the operation. When Colonel Olmstead and Major Angle returned to Utapao, the GSF commander met with and debriefed Colonel Twomey, the MAU commander, who had flown from the command ship to Thailand to learn first hand about the latest developments in Cambodia. Before departing Utapao, Colonel Olmstead made two more visits to Phnom Penh and on the last trip as on the first one his air liaison officer, Major Angle, accompanied him. They rechecked the security of the landing zones and took additional photographs. By this time, Colonel Olmstead and Major Angle noticed a decrease in the military activity in and around the Cambodian capital and correctly surmised that the government forces had regained the initiative. After the initial attacks which the government forces parried, the Khmer Rouge offensive stalled. Little over a month after the command element's return to Okinawa, the 1974 dry season ended and so did the immediate urgency surrounding Operation Eagle Pull. With the coming of summer and the usual heavy turnover of senior commanders in III MAF, Colonel Sydney H. "Tom" Batchelder, Jr., relieved Colonel Olmstead as GSF commander in May 1974. He also assumed command of the 3d Service Battalion on 28 May 1974.[9]

Batchelder selected as his air officer Lieutenant Colonel Glenn J. Shaver, Jr., the division air officer and a former commanding officer of a CH-53 squadron. Colonel Batchelder and his command element repeated the same round of liaison visits to Nakhon Phanom and Phnom Penh during the late summer and fall of 1974. In November of 1974, Lieutenant Colonel Curtis G. Lawson replaced Lieutenant Colonel Shaver as the air officer.

During an earlier tour, Lieutenant Colonel Lawson, an A-6 pilot, had been shot down over North Vietnam and subsequently rescued by a "Jolly Green Giant" of the 37th Aerospace Rescue and Recovery Squadron (ARRS) flying from Da Nang.[10] Coincidentally, one of the 37th ARRS' detachments, redesignated the 40th ARRS in March 1968, had since moved to Nakhon Phanom, the home of USSAG.* Another recent arrival at Nakhon Phanom was USSAG's new commander, Lieutenant General John J. Burns, USAF. On 1 September 1974, the same day he pinned on

---

*On 16 January 1967, Detachment 2, 37th ARRS was organized and assigned to Udorn, Thailand, to rescue downed pilots in Laos and North Vietnam. In March 1968 the Air Force redesignated it the 40th ARRS and on 21 July 1971 moved the squadron to Nakhon Phanom.

his third star, General Burns replaced General O'Keefe. Besides Burns' distinguished combat record as a veteran of 340 air missions in three wars, he also had participated in a major Cold War battle. During the 1958 confrontation with China over Formosa and the ensuing crisis, he and his entire squadron deployed to Okinawa to await further orders and combat if required. Those orders never came but those that did arrive in 1974 sent a well prepared and experienced General Burns into a similar crisis environment.[11]

In early December Lieutenant Colonel Lawson visited Nakhon Phanom in order to obtain a briefing from General Burns' staff on the state of the pending crisis in Cambodia. Conducting this visit shortly after joining the division, Lawson gained valuable insight into the command structure and USSAG's plan for the evacuation mission. By mid-December 1974, the new, fully briefed, Marine Corps Eagle Pull command element needed only two more things: the order to go and the 31st MAU.

The 31st MAU

Before the 31st MAU finally received the order to "go," it spent 25 months in training and waiting. Battalions joined the MAU and in many cases rejoined it before the call to evacuate finally came. Although only one battalion actually received the order to execute, all contributed. Those two years of waiting encompassed endless days of repetition, but also many hours of anticipation, concern, and preparation. It was during those hours that the Marines of the 31st MAU wrote all but the final chapter of the history of Operation Eagle Pull beginning in the spring of 1973.

During the period 17 April 1973 to 20 July 1973, the 31st MAU maintained Lieutenant Colonel Floyd A. Karker, Jr.'s BLT 1/4 on standby as a backup force for Eagle Pull. Even though the original requirement stated the need for only one company as an additional security force, all of Lieutenant Colonel Karker's companies were assigned a landing zone in Phnom Penh.[12] The MAU was ashore at the base camp at Subic Bay. The amphibious ships that normally carried it and its assigned helicopter squadron, Lieutenant Colonel Arthur B. Colbert's HMM-165, were involved in Operation Endsweep, a mine clearing mission being carried out in North Vietnamese waters as per the Paris Accords.

On 21 July 1973, with its ships and helicopter squadron inbound to Subic, the MAU was alerted for possible commitment to Operation Eagle Pull. Purely a precautionary measure, the alert's purpose was to ensure that General Vogt (ComUSSAG) had enough helicopters available. Five days later, General Ryan on orders from CinCPac directed Major General Frank C. Lang, the Commanding General, 1st MAW, to "flight

The soccer field at the university in Phnom Penh was one of the original primary landing zones. CH-53 pilots of 31st MAU, known as the "Eagle Pull Mix," expected to use this LZ, Embassy LZ, or Colosseum LZ during late 1973 or early 1974, but Phnom Penh held.

Photo courtesy of Col Peter F. Angle, USMC (Ret)

ferry" (administratively move) "not less than twelve CH-53s" from MCAS Futema to Cubi Point for transfer to the USS *New Orleans* (LPH 11) where they would be used as substitutes for HMM-165's CH-46s. The CH-53s were to be configured for extended range operations, equipped with the ALE-29 flare dispensers to counter heat-seeking missiles, and armed, clear signs that this was no drill. For the first time, the MAU's aviation element would be composed of the "Eagle Pull mix" (13 CH-53s, 4 CH-46s, 4 AH-1Js, and 2 UH-1Es).

Immediately upon assuming command of Task Group 79.4 (CTG 79.4/31st MAU), Colonel Twomey received orders to arrive, within the constraints of the response time, off the coast of Kampong Som (a Cambodian port on the Gulf of Thailand), and once there to conduct BLT training in preparation for the ground security force evacuation mission. Furthermore, his orders directed him to stand ready to assume the duties of the senior ground force commander for Operation Eagle Pull. By 31 July, the MAU was reconstituted and embarked on ARG Alpha shipping in Subic Bay, with orders to maintain a 70-hour reaction time to the Gulf of Thailand and a position off the coast of Cambodia.[13]

Just prior to the MAU's departure on 6 August 1973, Colonel Twomey and other members of the 31st MAU attended the first joint Eagle Pull planning conference hosted by the USSAG commander. Upon the group's return from the meeting in Nakhon Phanom, the amphibious ready group, with the MAU embarked, sortied from Subic Bay. Four days later, ARG Alpha/31st MAU reached its assigned holding area in the Gulf of Thailand and assumed a 12-hour alert posture. This positioning allowed the amphibious ready group/MAU a half-day to rendezvous at the prospective helicopter launch sites off Kampong Som. Seventy-two hours later, General Vogt issued his operational plan for Eagle Pull, and the next day, 14 August 1973, Colonel Twomey issued Operation Order 2-73 (Eagle Pull) in support of the ComUSSAG plan. On 26 August, General Vogt also ordered the 31st MAU to prepare for the evacuation of the Military Equipment Delivery Team (MEDTC) personnel from the Ream/Kampong Som area.[14]

Upon notification of their pending participation in Operation Eagle Pull, BLT 1/4 and HMM-165, the 31st MAU's subordinate elements, started detailed planning for the operation. In addition, they began to reorganize their training to make it conform more to the unusual mission, the evacuation of civilians. The BLT conducted embarkation drills and the squadron tested the helicopter launch and recovery schedule. By the end of August, the 31st MAU was ready.[15]

Having an original relief date of 1 August, the BLT and its medium helicopter squadron began to experience, towards the end of August, personnel rotation problems. They would continue to occur as long as the MAU remained on station without relief. On 30 August, the personnel problem was solved, in part, when the MAU transferred the Marines scheduled for stateside return to the USS *Blue Ridge* (LCC 19).

The USS *Blue Ridge*, destined for Okinawa, carried these Marines to Okinawa where the division processed and returned them by plane to the United States. Besides the confusion created by the departure of these transferees, the 31st MAU also underwent other personnel changes. Lieutenant Colonel Bertram A. Maas arrived and exchanged positions with Lieutenant Colonel Ronald L. Owen, the executive officer. The following day, the *Blue Ridge* completed the transfer by highlining Lieutenant Colonel Owen and another key and experienced officer, Major Jerome T. Paull (the MAU S-2), to the USNS *Tuluga* (AO 62), for further transport to Subic Bay, Republic of Philippines, and then home.[16]

Its tour more than complete (in fact a month overdue), BLT 1/4 and its senior commands, ARG Alpha and 31st MAU, upon receipt of new orders on 30 August, sailed for Okinawa to effect a BLT turnover. ARG Alpha plotted a course for White Beach while maintaining a 120-hour (five-day) reaction time to the Gulf of Thailand and its required Eagle Pull position off Kompong Som.[17] The relief of BLT 1/4 was accomplished on 7 September when Battalion Landing Team 1/9 under the command of Lieutenant Colonel Larry R. Gaboury assumed the role as the ground combat element in the 31st MAU. Lieutenant Colonel Colbert's HMM-165 remained as the MAU's aviation element. During the transition period, Major Angelo A. Fernandez reported on board as the new 31st MAU operations officer. The turnover was accomplished smoothly, maintaining a seven-day response time (relaxed from the five-day response posture) to Kampong Som. The 120-hour reaction time was reassumed during the transit to Subic Bay during which, on 8 September, the USS *Tripoli* lost use of its propulsion system and had to be towed to port. The problem was fixed during the next three weeks while the MAU, ashore, prepared for Operation Pagasa II, a combined landing exercise with the Philippine Marines.

The entire 31st MAU did not take part in Operation Pagasa II, but its ground element, under the operational control of the 9th Marine Amphibious Brigade (as of 30 September 1973), participated as the landing force. Colonel Twomey assumed command of Regimental Landing Team 4 and controlled it during the exercise, which began on 29 September but ended prematurely, five days later, because of typhoon conditions.[18]

Faced on 3 October 1973 with the termination of Pagasa II and the imminent arrival of another dry season, the 31st MAU reassumed operational control of its subordinate units and reconstituted its aviation element using an "Eagle Pull helicopter mix." The MAU loaded the medium helicopters normally assigned to it, eight CH-46s and two UH-1Es, on the USS *Denver* (LPD 9) and sent them back to Okinawa.

Because of a shortage of amphibious assault ships (LPHs) in the Pacific fleet (only three for five squadrons), the LPHs operated on a rotation schedule not in synchronization with the amphibious squadron relief cycle. In October, in Subic Bay, the USS *Okinawa* (LPH 3) replaced the USS *Tripoli* (LPH 10). In order to complete the exchange of responsibilities, the two ships had to conduct a major housekeeping maneuver, a transfer of all embarked MAU elements. The move was completed smoothly with minimum disruption to the amphibious ready group's itinerary.[19]

During November 1973, the major training accomplished by the MAU was a helicopter landing exercise, HeloLEx 1-73. In it, ARG Alpha and the 31st MAU rehearsed one of the landing plans for Operation Eagle Pull. The aviation element flew 150 Marines into three landing zones. These troops constituted the ground security force while the 120 Marines already in position in the LZs played the role of civilian evacuees. The MAU then evacuated the Marine "civilians" to the primary receiving ship, *Okinawa*, to test and evaluate the effectiveness of its shipboard procedures for handling and medically treating evacuees. The MAU satisfied its exercise objectives: no significant problems were encountered in command, control, coordination, or the evacuation process.

On 24 November, ARG Alpha, with the 31st MAU embarked, sailed for Taiwan and its scheduled port visits. While enroute, the amphibious ready group encountered high winds and heavy seas. One of its ships, the USS *Tuscaloosa* (LST 1187, a tank landing ship), suffered damage to her bow doors, which as a result needed repair or replacement. The *Tuscaloosa* and the ARG proceeded directly to Kaohsiung, Taiwan. Once there, the *Tuscaloosa* transferred all its MAU units to the amphibious transport dock ship, the USS *Duluth* (LPD 6), and then waited for a replacement. With the *Tuscaloosa* out of commission, another tank landing ship, the USS *Barbour County* (LST 1195), detached from ARG Bravo and sailed for Kaohsiung. Upon its arrival, the *Tuscaloosa* immediately fired up its boilers and headed south for Subic Bay and major repairs.

On 30 November, five days after LST 1187's departure, the entire ARG/MAU weighed anchor in Kaohsiung and set course for Okinawa where it effected a planned swap of MAU units. BLT 2/4 assumed BLT 1/9's duties as the MAU's ground combat element while HMH-462 replaced HMM-165 as the aviation component, thereby accomplishing the final turnover of 1973.[20]

Completing this evolution in the first days of December, the 31st MAU welcomed Lieutenant Colonel Carl E. Mundy, Jr., the commander of BLT 2/4, and Lieutenant Colonel Steven R. Foulger, the commanding officer of HMH-462, on board by immediately getting underway for Subic Bay. While enroute, the MAU staff completed final planning for the impending exercises which they conducted in the Philippines near Subic. The first of these began on 5 December in the Zambales training area. By evening on that first Wednesday of December, the MAU had finished HeloLEx 2-73, a dress rehearsal for the Eagle Pull helicopter option. During the next two days, the 31st MAU completed an amphibious assault exercise, ZAMEx 2-73. Also staged in the Zambales training area, it tested the BLT landing and withdrawal plan. After completing this test of the MAU's readiness, the ARG returned to Subic on Friday evening, 7 December.

The following Sunday morning, Colonel Twomey and Lieutenant Colonels Mundy and Foulger departed Cubi Point Naval Air Station for a three day Eagle Pull planning conference. Besides an important meeting with representatives of General O'Keefe's USSAG staff and Colonel Olmstead (GSF commander), the visit included a trip to Phnom Penh where the Marines saw first-hand the proposed landing zones and assembly areas. On 12 December, Colonel Twomey and a fully briefed and well prepared staff returned to Subic and ARG Alpha. A little over a week later, the ARG got underway for liberty ports in Hong Kong and Taiwan with rumors circulating that the MAU would never get to use its training, because the evacuation response time would be lengthened so much that the MAU's presence in the Gulf of Thailand would

Photo courtesy of Col Peter F. Angle, USMC (Ret)
This area of Pochentong airfield would have to be secured if CinCPac decided to use the airfield as an evacuation site. The idea, later scrapped, was the most complicated of the many evacuation options considered from July of 1973 until April of 1974.

no longer be required.[21] For those who had envisioned reaping the benefits, extended liberty in exotic ports, the change in assignment arrived too late. It happened on 9 January 1974, after the amphibious ready group, by then enroute to Subic, had left its Taiwanese ports-of-call. On that second Wednesday of the new year, CinCPac ordered ARG Alpha/31st MAU to assume a 96-hour (four-day) response time for the Eagle Pull contingency.

Eight days later, increased enemy activity in Cambodia required 31st MAU/ARG Alpha to assume a 72-hour Eagle Pull response posture. On 20 January, Pacific command headquarters ordered 31st MAU/ARG Alpha to the Gulf of Thailand. By that evening, all units were underway, arriving in the Gulf on 23 January 1974. Although the crisis in Phnom Penh stabilized the next day, resulting in a relaxation of the response time for other Eagle Pull units, the MAU and ARG remained on station in the Gulf of Thailand, awaiting reassessment of the situation and further word.

On the 26th, III MAF tasked 31st MAU to prepare to provide support for the fixed-wing military airlift, Option II of the Eagle Pull contingency plan. To fulfill the requirements of this task, the MAU would have to land a 90-man ground security force at Pochentong Airfield (on the outskirts of Phnom Penh). The plan called for this force to secure the airfield and assist in the evacuation of civilian personnel. On 30 January, Colonel Twomey and Colonel Olmstead met at Utapao and discussed the military situation in Cambodia and the new manpower demands. The very next day, on 1 February, the 31st MAU/ARG Alpha incorporated into its flight training schedule rehearsal of the helicopter option (III) of the Eagle Pull evacuation plan.[22]

During the course of this training evolution, Admiral Gayler, CinCPac, ordered the task force on 2 February to assume a five-hour response posture for possible Eagle Pull activity. This change in orders came as a result of the enemy's newly gained advantage, which allowed them to attack and fire upon Phnom Penh. In order to neutralize this capability, Eagle Pull planners decided that the operation might have to be conducted after sunset. As a consequence, the 31st MAU intensified night helicopter operations during the 3 to 8 February period. In the midst of this training, on 5 February, the commander of the Seventh Fleet, Admiral Steele, recommended to CinCPac that because of the problems normally encountered in night-time evacuation operations, Eagle Pull be executed only during daylight hours. CinCPac concurred.

With a decrease in the enemy threat, Admiral Gayler, on 9 February, directed the 31st MAU/ARG Alpha to relax its response time to 72 hours, and sail to Subic Bay for turnover of ARG Alpha shipping. At Subic Bay, the changeover was accomplished on 14 and 15 February. The ships of Amphibious Squadron 5, amphibious cargo ship *Mobile* (LKA 115), dock landing ship *Mount Vernon* (LSD 39), and the tank landing ship *Barbour County* (LST 1195), were relieved by Amphibious Squadron 7's ships, amphibious cargo ship *St. Louis* (LKA 116), dock landing ship, *Fort Fisher* (LSD 40), and tank landing ship *Bristol County* (LST 1189). The *Okinawa* (LPH 3) remained as the ARG's amphibious assault ship. Additionally, Colonel Douglas T. Kane relieved Colonel Twomey as the commanding officer of the 31st MAU on 16 February 1974.

On 22 February, as a result of the stabilization of the situation in and around Phnom Penh, the 31st MAU/ARG Alpha's Eagle Pull response time was relaxed to 96 hours. As the situation in Cambodia continued to improve, the reaction time changed accordingly, and on 1 March, CinCPac assigned a response time of 120 hours.[23]

On 16 March, III MAF notified the 31st MAU that the possibility existed of a compromise of Eagle Pull, but also added that it considered the likelihood remote. Two weeks later, the 31st MAU and its units reembarked in ARG Alpha shipping and departed for Okinawa where BLT 2/4 and its logistic support unit (LSU) disembarked. III MAF returned operational control of these units to the 4th Marines, and the next day detached Battalion Landing Team 1/4, commanded by Lieutenant Colonel Charles E. Davis, Jr., and its LSU. Under the operational control of the 31st MAU, BLT 1/4 began the loading of its gear on the waiting ships of ARG Alpha. The 120-hour (five-day) response time to Kompong Som was further relaxed to 132 hours during this period in order to allow the MAU sufficient time to conduct the BLT/LSU replacement.

Less than a week after the switch, the 31st MAU/ARG Alpha departed Okinawa in two formations. On 5 April, elements of the 31st MAU embarked in the *Okinawa* (LPH 3) arrived in Subic Bay, and unloaded cargo in preparation for an LPH turnover. The rest of the MAU, in the remainder of ARG Alpha shipping, began its visits to Taiwanese ports. By the evening of the 6th, the LPH swap was complete and the 31st MAU's LPH units were on board a new amphibious assault ship, the USS *New Orleans* (LPH 11).[24]

On 23 May, in view of the fact that the military and political situation in Cambodia appeared more stable, CinCPac authorized the 31st MAU to further relax the response time for Eagle Pull to 168 hours (one week). Meanwhile, 31st MAU received approval to send two representatives in June on an orientation visit to Nakhon Phanom and Phnom Penh.

Although this visit was important, one situation far overshadowed it, looming larger with each passing day. The CH-53s had been on board ship almost continuously for over a year. Regardless of maintenance efficiency, continuous, long-term exposure to salt air causes aircraft structural materials to corrode at a faster than normal rate. The overriding need to remedy this problem combined with stable conditions in Cambodia precipitated a decision to exchange helicopter squadrons. Major General Herman Poggemeyer, Jr., the Commanding General, III MAF ordered the replacement of HMH-462, thereby returning the MAU to a standard helicopter inventory. To accomplish this, the *New Orleans* sailed to Okinawa where on 20 June, HMM-164 replaced HMH-462. The *New Orleans*, with the new helicopter squadron embarked, departed for Subic Bay, arriving there on 22 June 1974. During the helicopter turnover, the other ships of ARG Alpha remained at Subic Bay until relieved by Amphibious Squadron 3. The *Fort Fisher*, *St. Louis*, and *Bristol County* were relieved by dock landing ship *Monticello* (LSD 35), amphibious landing ship *Tulare* (LKA 112), and tank landing ships *Fresno* (LST 1182) and *San Bernardino* (LST 1189).[25]

This exchange ushered in two months of training which coincided with a calm period in Cambodia and the rainy season. On 13 August, a turnover of the MAU's ground combat element occurred when Lieutenant Colonel Edwin J. Godfrey's Battalion Landing Team 3/4 relieved BLT 1/4. HMM-164, on board the *New Orleans*, remained in place. During the replacement period, the reaction time to Kompong Som coastal waters continued to be 168 hours.

Less than three weeks later, the 2d Battalion, 4th Marines, commanded by Lieutenant Colonel George P. Slade, began its predeployment training on Okinawa in order to meet a scheduled departure date of 12 December 1974. There was evidence that during the coming dry season, the Communist forces would make an all-out effort to crush the Cambodian Army and destroy the Republic, thus increasing the probability that the evacuation would take place while BLT 2/4 was afloat. Lieutenant Colonel Slade adjusted his training accordingly; emergency evacuation became the byword of his battalion. The CH-53s of HMH-462, commanded by Lieutenant Colonel James L. Bolton and also scheduled for deployment in December, be-

THE FLEET MARINES ARE READIED

came frequent visitors to Camp Hansen and the surrounding Central Training Area, as Slade's battalion and Bolton's squadron perfected their teamwork. During November, two full-scale emergency evacuation exercises were conducted, one at Camp Hansen and the other at an abandoned World War II Japanese airfield on the Yomitan Peninsula of Okinawa. During the battalion's preparation period, 31st MAU/ARG Alpha continued its deployment, maintaining a relatively relaxed response time of 168 hours.[26]

On 16 December 1974, when the ships of ARG Alpha entered Buckner Bay to disembark BLT 3/4, BLT 2/4 stood ready, prepared to conduct an emergency evacuation if so ordered. After the exchange of BLTs, ARG Alpha headed south, eight days before Christmas. A few miles away, at MCAS Futema, HMH-462 was making its final preparations for the long flight to Cubi Point where it would stand by, available for employment should the situation suddenly change.

The Other Contingency

While the focus of attention and planning was on Eagle Pull, the 4th Marines, MAG-36, and the 9th Marines, except for periods of airborne contingency BLT assignment, appeared to be left out of the mainstream of activities. This situation changed when Colonel Johnson returned from his visit to South Vietnam in September of 1974. When he reported that no real plans existed to evacuate South Vietnam, especially the northern half, it became obvious that III MAF would have to begin preparing on its own for that possibility. Since the 31st MAU/ARG Alpha was already dedicated to Eagle Pull, any amphibious force involvement in an evacuation from South Vietnam would have to be planned and executed around BLT/ARG Bravo, the 9th Marines contingency group.

Shortly after Colonel Johnson's briefing on the situation in South Vietnam, Colonel Jack D. Rowley, the commanding officer of the 9th Marines, ordered his staff to develop a command post exercise (CPX) so the regiment and its deploying battalions could become familiar with the special emergency evacuation requirements and the situation in MR 1. Under the staff supervision of the regimental executive officer, Lieutenant Colonel Robert L. Wise, Major Burrel H. Landes, the regimental operations officer, prepared the plans. Even before Major Landes and his S-3 section began their efforts to write an operation order, the regimental S-2, First Lieutenant Thomas W. Kinsell,

This sign in English, "Drive Safely," along the Mekong in Phnom Penh in 1973-1975, seemed to apply to Americans charged with planning the safe evacuation of officials from the capital city of a country where U.S. influence and responsibilities could not be ignored.

Photo courtesy of Col Peter F. Angle, USMC (Ret)

prepared a general and special situation report for wide dissemination. While still preserving the secrecy of the actual mission, the brief more than adequately met all the requirements of the mission. This scenario or a derivative and the resultant operational plan were used on four occasions by the 9th Marines between November 1974 and April 1975 to test the ability of the regiment to respond to an emergency evacuation.[27]

The "CPX 3-75 Scenario," based on Vietnam, provided a realistic portrayal of the situation there, and as events would bear out, made Lieutenant Kinsell's situation brief a blueprint for history. Its accuracy on political events did not concern the Marines nearly as much as its depiction of the changing face of weaponry available to the enemy.[27] Intelligence sources indicated that the North Vietnamese Army had, and the Khmer Rouge were suspected of having, some of the same types of antiaircraft weapons which had played havoc with the Israeli Air Force during the Yom Kippur War in 1973. On 5 October 1974 in response to this expected threat, Major General Norman W. Gourley, Commanding General, 1st Marine Aircraft Wing, established the 1st MAW Tactical Evaluation Board. He appointed his assistant wing commander, Brigadier General Richard E. Carey, as the senior member of the board. The other members were the 1st MAW G-2 and G-3 officers, all of the 1st MAW group commanders, and representatives of the 3d Marine Division. The purpose of the board was to determine what changes were required and what innovations could be incorporated into Marine air/ground tactics to reduce the risk to aircraft when exposed to sophisticated surface-to-air missiles and antiaircraft weapons.[28]

General Carey convened the first meeting of the board at wing headquarters in Iwakuni, Japan, on 26 October 1974. He opened the meeting by announcing that he was confident U.S. technology could counter any advantages that enemy antiaircraft systems enjoyed at that moment. General Carey added, however, that this belief was of little comfort to him, in view of the fact that new technology was not yet operational. At present, there were contingencies that WestPac Marines had to be prepared to face, and the probability that other agencies would be of assistance was remote. This was to be a "self-help program all the way." As a result of the two days of meetings, the board concluded that the best way to combat weapons, which required visual acquisition before the weapon locked on the target, was to make the acquisition process as difficult as possible. This could be done by flying more missions in darkness and inclement weather. This would require a shift in training emphasis, in turn creating some safety problems. The environmental impact also had to be considered; nighttime noise abatement plans were in effect in the vicinity of several of the air stations in Japan. The board decided that the risks in the training shift were more than offset by the potential improvement in the tactical proficiency of the wing's pilots. At the conclusion of the meeting, General Carey told the 3d Marine Division representative to tell Major General Kenneth J. Houghton that the wing would still provide the same level of support, but the division should be prepared to see more air support at night because night operations would be less costly in countering enemy antiaircraft defenses.[29]

By December 1974, the division and wing, particularly MAG-36, had reoriented their training schedules to cover the full spectrum of night training and had increased its frequency. This reorientation was none too soon.

PART II
SOUTH VIETNAM

CHAPTER 5
The North Vietnamese Winter-Spring Offensive, 1974-75: The Mortal Blow

The Collapse of the Central Highlands—Defeat in Military Region 1—A Wasted Division

By the end of 1974, the balance of ground combat power in South Vietnam had clearly shifted in favor of the North Vietnamese Army. In spite of this advantage, the North Vietnamese leadership still harbored some doubts as to their ability to conquer the South rapidly. The ruling Politburo of North Vietnam met in Hanoi from 18 December 1974 until 8 January 1975 for the purpose of resolving the timetable for the conquest of South Vietnam. Hanoi apparently also had its own "hawks and doves." General Van Tien Dung, chief of staff of the North Vietnamese Army, counselled that the possibility of a resumption of American bombing could not be disregarded. This issue was discounted as not insurmountable and depending on United States reaction, possibly not even a concern.

The Collapse of the Central Highlands

On 13 December 1974 at Don Luan where Interprovincial Route 1A intersects Route 13, the *301st NVA Corps* undertook a campaign to capture Phuoc Long, a province in MR 3 bounded on the north by Cambodia. This offensive marked the beginning of North Vietnam's new strategy of attacking not only to destroy the Republic of Vietnam Armed Forces, but to capture populated areas as well. To accomplish its objective of seizing the provincial capital of Phuoc Long City, tucked between the Be River and Ba Ra Mountain, 75 miles northeast of Saigon, the NVA employed its recently formed *3d Division*, *7th Division*, a tank battalion, an artillery regiment, an antiaircraft regiment, and local force and sapper units. The Communists planned to use these forces to effect its new strategy of capturing populated areas by striking a city's center first and then in the resultant confusion and chaos, destroying from within its defensive perimeter. General Dung, who had employed this style of fighting with much success against the French in 1952, said: "We sent our troops in, avoiding enemy positions in the outer perimeter . . . and unexpectedly struck right in town, wiping out the nerve

North Vietnamese Army soldiers capture Phuoc Long (Song Be) City, capital of Phuoc Long Province. On 6 January 1975, after the loss of more than 3,000 troops, the defenders of Phuoc Long surrendered, making it the first province since 1954 to fall to Communists.

Marine Corps Historical Collection

THE NORTH VIETNAMESE WINTER-SPRING OFFENSIVE, 1974-75: THE MORTAL BLOW

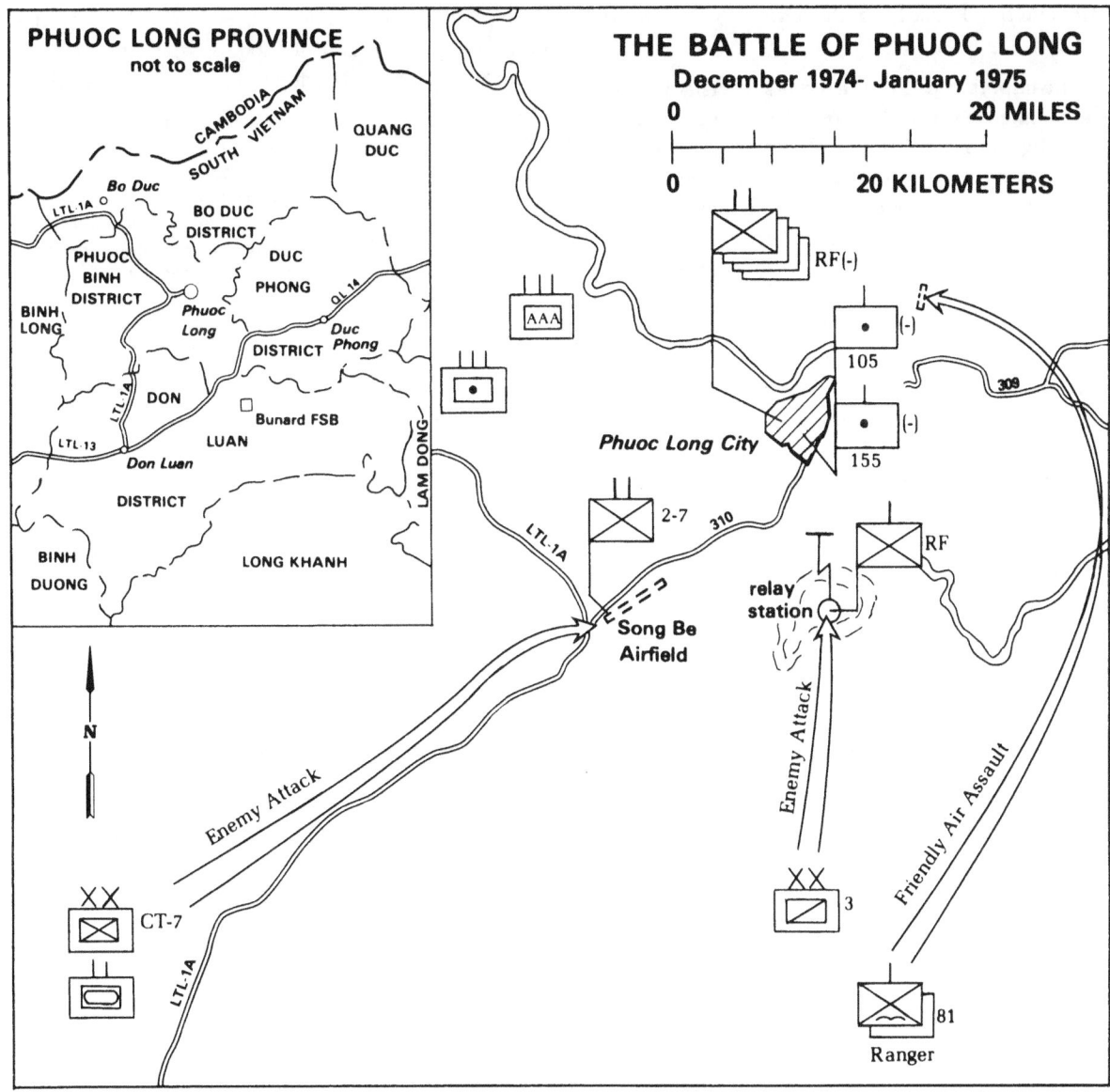

Map adapted from Gen Cao Van Vien, *The Final Collapse* (Washington: U.S. Army Center of Military History, 1983)

center of the enemy command, taking the town in one day and only then sending the troops out to destroy the perimeter outposts. We called these tactics the 'paratroop' tactics or the 'blooming lotus.'" The NVA would use a variation of the "blooming lotus" to capture Phuoc Long Province and upon that success build a battle plan that would know no defeat.[1]

North Vietnam's tactics in the Phuoc Long campaign involved isolating each garrison, attacking it, and through massive shelling and sheer numbers, overrunning it. By this process, which lasted less than three weeks, the NVA captured Duc Phong, Bo Duc, Bunard Fire Support Base, Don Luan, and, with the fall of Phuoc Long City on 6 January, the province. Phuoc Long became the first province since 1954 to fall intact into the hands of Hanoi's forces, and its capture exposed the VNAF's gravest weakness, the absence of an uncommitted reserve. For the South Vietnamese, it meant not only the strategic loss of territory in an area of intense North Vietnamese infiltration, but the loss of more than 3,000 soldiers including nearly half of the 250 members whom the elite 81st Ranger Group committed to the battle. At 0900 on 5 January, in a desperate attempt to save the besieged capital, the JGS inserted by helicopter these veterans of the 1972 South Vietnamese victory at An Loc, chosen for the mission because of their ability to fight behind enemy lines. The NVA tanks proved an unfair match and 39 hours after entering Phuoc Long, the Rangers withdrew from the city.

The importance of the victory was overshadowed by the manner in which the North Vietnamese achieved it. Using supporting arms and sappers to create confusion, chaos, and communication problems behind ARVN lines and in the headquarters area, the NVA destroyed any semblance of orderly resistance. The North Vietnamese then simply overwhelmed the disorganized defenders. To insure completeness of victory, the enemy neutralized RVN air support and destroyed defensive structures. Phuoc Long offered the NVA a blueprint for future operations and also served as an indicator of South Vietnam's battlefield prowess. The bitter end did not really begin at this isolated capital, but a growing cloud of doubt and discomfort did originate here, portending that, without some major changes in strategy, South Vietnam and its armed forces would suffer grave consequences. As General Cao Van Vien stated: "Psychologically and politically, the loss of Phuoc Long, the first provincial capital of South Vietnam permanently seized by the Communists, came as a shock to the population and the armed forces. The apparent total indifference with which the United States and other non-Communist countries regarded this tragic loss reinforced the doubt the Vietnamese people held concerning the viability of the Paris Agreement."[2] One experienced historian of the Vietnam War called Phuoc Long "a significant battle in terms of its influence on South Vietnamese morale and as the prelude to the events of 1975."[3]

This victory, followed by a weak South Vietnamese counterattack, strengthened the belief of the "hawks" in Hanoi that the balance of power in the South had shifted conclusively in their favor. Furthermore, the failure of the United States to intervene in the conflict made it easier to infer that America's willingness to support the South Vietnamese had waned. Based on this assumption, the North Vietnamese Politburo made plans to plunge ahead with maximum force. Before concluding its conference in January 1975, the Politburo adopted a two-year plan which aimed for a complete and final victory over the South. Initially, attacks would be directed toward My Tho in the Mekong Delta; Ban Me Thuot and Tuy Hoa in the center of the country; and Hue and Da Nang in the north. The objective was to seize the cities, and in the process, smash the ARVN.[4]

As the North Vietnamese Army staged its forces for the attack, it faced, in addition to the Vietnamese Navy and Air Force, a South Vietnamese Army ground force of approximately 192,000 soldiers and Marines. The South Vietnamese forces were disposed as follows:

—in Military Region 1, five divisions: the Marine, Airborne, 1st, 2d, and 3d ARVN Divisions; the 1st Armored Brigade; and four Ranger Groups, the 11th, 12th, 14th, and 15th, comprising 11 Ranger Battalions.

—in Military Region 2, two divisions: the 22d, and 23d; the 2d Armored Brigade; and seven Ranger Groups, the 4th, 6th, 21st, 22d, 23d, 24th, and 25th, comprising 17 Ranger Battalions.

—in Military Region 3, three divisions: the 5th (which had lost one of its regiments during the fighting in Phuoc Long Province), 18th, and 25th; the 3d Armored Brigade; and five Ranger Groups, the 7th (under direct operational control of the JGS), 31st, 32d, 33d, and 81st, comprising 18 Ranger Battalions.

—in Military Region 4, three divisions, the 7th, 9th, and 21st; and the 4th Armored Brigade. There were no Ranger units deployed in MR 4.*[5]

To oppose these forces in 1973 North Vietnam mustered 14 infantry divisions and 62 separate regiments for an estimated total of 149,000 to 167,000. By the war's end there were 18 NVA divisions, or approximately 185,000 to 200,000 frontline troops.**

General Dung's assessment of the VNAF's situation and the NVA victory at Phuoc Long helped him overcome objections by conservative members of the Polit-

---

*Normally assigned to the Saigon area, the 4th and 6th Ranger Groups were deployed along Highway 1 in Binh Dinh under the operational control of MR 2. *Vietnam From Ceasefire to Capitulation*, p.73.

**Sources vary as to how many divisions and Communist soldiers were actually in South Vietnam at any given time. The January 1973 figures are taken from the official Defense Attache Office reports and *The Final Collapse*. Sources also vary as to how many NVA divisions actually began the final assault on Saigon. Official records stated that the Communists "massed up to 16 divisions in MR 3 and had deployed forces for a three-pronged attack against Saigon" (DOA *Final Assessment*, p. 1-15; see also *From Ceasefire to Capitulation*, p. 176). Another source, *Fall of the South*, in its caption for a map showing the final offensive against Saigon said that General Dung "called for the simultaneous assault on Saigon's defenses by eighteen Main Force Divisions." That same map also detailed 19 divisions while the book's index listed under "North Vietnamese Military Units" 15 NVA divisions (*Fall of the South*, p. 140). The former chief of staff of the South Vietnamese Armed Forces, General Cao Van Vien, stated that "the total enemy force around Bien Hoa and Saigon during the last days amounted to fifteen NVA infantry divisions augmented and supported by a sapper division, an artillery division, some armor brigades, and SAM antiaircraft units" (*Final Collapse*, p. 129). General Dung purposely avoids discussing specifics concerning divisions and instead includes in the final assault forces: the NVA *1st Army Corps*, NVA *2d Army Corps*, NVA *3d Army Corps*, and the *232d Tactical Force*. *Spring Victory*, pp. 212-231.

NVA troops advance on Ban Me Thuot in a coordinated three-division assault. As a result of the swiftness of the 10 March attack, some Americans were taken prisoner and struggled to survive under grueling circumstances until their release in November of 1975.

buro to a major offensive in the South and dictated his strategy. The main attack would be directed against the weakest link in the South Vietnamese Army's defensive chain, Military Region 2. Commanded by Major General Pham Van Phu, the Central Highlands represented the Achilles heel of the South Vietnamese armor, the most thinly defended area in all of South Vietnam. Furthermore, the South Vietnamese had concentrated their forces in the northern portion of the region, in the vicinity of Pleiku and Kontum. Therefore, General Dung decided to strike first at Ban Me Thuot, a city in Darlac Province in the southern part of the region. He codenamed the battle plan "Campaign 275."[6]

At the beginning of 1975, the North Vietnamese had two divisions and two independent regiments in MR 2. During the month of January, they moved the headquarters and two regiments of the *968th NVA Division* (one of the "new divisions" created in September 1968, hence the 968 designation) from southern Laos into the Duc Co area of Pleiku Province. In mid-February, North Vietnam deployed the *316th NVA Division* to Darlac Province. The *316th Division*, one of the organizations in North Vietnam's strategic reserve, moved by truck from the Thanh Hoa area of North Vietnam through Quang Tri Province (via the new all-weather road network) to Military Region 2 for a rendezvous with the other divisions committed to the impending coordinated assault on Ban Me Thuot. Eventually, the members of this division would combine forces with the *10th NVA Division* and the *320th NVA Division*, also enroute to objectives in Darlac Province, to defeat the defenders of this strategic region.[7]

In preparation for such an assault, the North Vietnamese, between January 1973 and January 1975, increased their strategic reserve from two to seven divisions (not including the *968th Division*). This significant enlargement indicated both the NVA's offensive intentions and their planned means of execution. They would use their lines of communication to exploit the advantage they held over the ARVN—possession of a large, mobile force in reserve. During the same period, North Vietnam completed a road network in the area, prepositioned supplies in abundant quantities, and established command posts. In addition, most of the troops committed to this campaign were familiar with the battlefield and many of them

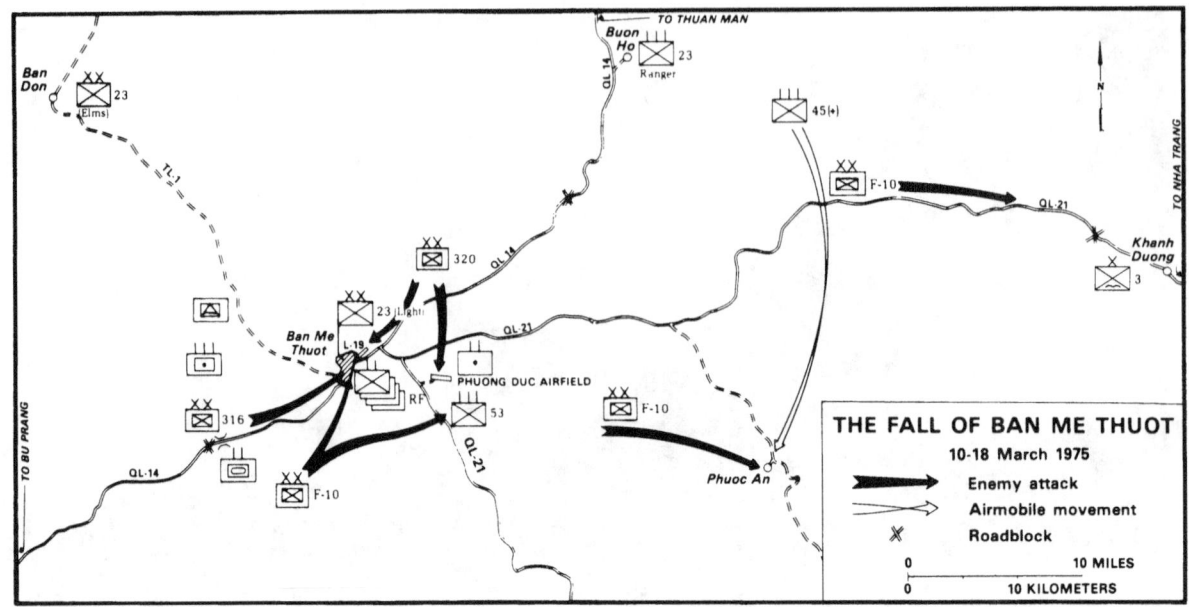

Map adapted from Gen Cao Van Vien, *The Final Collapse* (Washington: U.S. Army Center of Military History, 1983)

had considerable combat experience. A comparison of the North Vietnamese Army units with those of the South Vietnamese in MR 2 revealed that in firepower the forces were about equal. However, on what was to become the first field of battle in Darlac Province, the ratio of North Vietnamese infantry to South Vietnamese riflemen was six to one. In heavy artillery, the NVA enjoyed a two-to-one advantage. Of even greater significance was the longer range capability of the NVA guns. In numbers of tanks and armored vehicles the opposing sides were almost equal.[8]

The North Vietnamese launched a series of attacks in the northern and extreme southern portions of MR 2 beginning on 1 March when the *968th Division* struck RVN outposts west of Pleiku. On 4 March the Communists closed the Mang Yang Pass on National Highway 19 connecting Pleiku Province to Binh Dinh Province and the coast, and shortly after that attacked and damaged two bridges on National Highway 21 which provided access from the coast to the Central Highlands via Ban Me Thuot, the Darlac Province capital. On 9 March, the *9th Regiment* of the *320th Division* severed Ban Me Thuot's final link to the outside world and its source of possible reinforcements, National Highway 14 running north to Pleiku. These events marked the beginning of Campaign 275, Dung's plan to seize the Central Highlands by exploiting the ARVN decision to concentrate its soldiers in the Pleiku-Kontum area while leaving Ban Me Thuot thinly defended.[9]

At 0200 on 10 March, the *10th* and *316th Divisions* struck Ban Me Thuot. The *320th Division* augment-ed the attack on the city by assaulting the L-19 and Phuong Duc airfields. As at Song Be (Be River), the enemy employed the element of surprise and coordinated supporting arms to confuse, demoralize, and defeat the defenders. The NVA employed intense artillery fire and predeployed sappers to eliminate preselected targets and create havoc and confusion within the ARVN's command structure and its rear areas. At the same time it sent infantry supported by tanks into the city and captured strategic locations.[10]

The attack was a complete success, and the North Vietnamese quickly overran the city, defended by the 53d Regiment of the ARVN 23d Division and Regional and Popular Force units composed primarily of Montagnards.* The II Corps commander, General Pham

---

*In his book, *The Fall of Saigon*, David Butler described a published news story about the collapse of Ban Me Thuot's defenses. He wrote: ". . . partisans of an old Montagnard separatist group called FULRO (*Front Unifie pour la Liberation des Races Opprimees*) guided the attacking Communist troops to the approaches to Ban Me Thuot and joined with them in the fighting" (*Fall of Saigon*, pp. 80-81). A Vietnamese Marine Corps battalion commander captured by the Communists in Saigon on 30 April and subsequently placed in a Communist "re-education" camp recently confirmed this story. Lieutenant Colonel Tran Ngoc Toan (former commander of 4th Battalion, 147th Brigade, VNMC) said: "While in prison in North Vietnam, I had occasion to meet a Montagnard chief who told me that in a top secret meeting with an envoy of Hanoi's Politburo held in the jungle near the juncture of South Vietnam, Cambodia and Laos, the Communists promised self-government for the Montagnards in return for cooperation in defeating the ARVN in Miltary Region 2. He said that after leading the NVA tanks into Ban Me Thuot which helped conclude that battle in a victory for the Communists, the North Vietnamese immediately took him prisoner." Toan Comments.

Thousands of civilian and military vehicles, targets for shelling, clog Interprovincial Route 7B near Cheo Reo, the Phu Bon provincial capital. This poorly organized and led strategic retreat from the Central Highlands cost II Corps 75 percent of its 20,000-man strength.

Van Phu, ordered first one regiment and then another of the ARVN 23d Division to launch helicopter-borne counterattacks. The North Vietnamese anticipated this move and antiaircraft units were displaced forward in trail of the attacking tanks and infantry. Many of the troop-laden South Vietnamese helicopters were blasted from the sky. Those troops that did make it into the landing zones found themselves in a cone of fire delivered by five North Vietnamese artillery battalions. Once on the ground they ran headlong into a crowd of panicked, fleeing refugees who turned out to be their dependents. At this point, discipline broke down as many of the soldiers deserted their units and started to search for family members. As a result of this chaos, the fight was never a close one. By 18 March, the defeat of the 23d Division was complete.[11]

While the fighting at Ban Me Thuot was in its final days, a momentous conference took place at Cam Ranh. On 14 March, President Thieu flew there to confer with the II Corps commander, General Pham Van Phu. Thieu told General Phu, the man who had sworn to fight to the last in the Central Highlands, about his plan to defend a truncated South Vietnam. Thieu ordered Phu to abandon the highlands and form a defensive perimeter around the populated areas in the coastal lowlands to include Ban Me Thout. His first priority would be to retake the Darlac capital. Phu, a former prisoner of war as a result of the French surrender at Dien Bien Phu, showed no signs of enthusiasm for recapturing Ban Me Thout or in carrying out the ordered redeployment. Instead, he negotiated and pleaded with President Thieu for the promotion of a Ranger colonel named Pham Van Tat. The reason for this became obvious the next day at Pleiku when the II Corps commander directed the new one-star and his own chief of staff, Colonel Le Khac Ly, to effect the withdrawal. Before General Phu and his entire II Corps staff retired by helicopter from Pleiku to Nha Trang, he told Colonel Ly, " 'We will plan to retake Ban Me Thout from there [Nha Trang].' " Just prior to boarding the helicopter, Phu ordered his deputy for operations, Brigadier General Tran Van Cam, to remain behind as well.[12]

With Highways 14 and 19 out of Pleiku blocked, Phu's plan called for his corps to make its retreat over long abandoned Interprovincial Route 7B using the element of surprise (General Dung's staff had briefed him that this highway was unusable and therefore not an option should the ARVN try to escape from the Communists' planned encirclement). Despite this advantage, Phu also knew that Route 7B had a number of unusable bridges, some of which were actually missing, and that the final portion of the 135-mile trek would be over terrain which contained numerous land mines. Still Phu believed this was the best choice and he planned to assign the Popular and Regional Force (PF and RF) units holding positions at Pleiku and responsibility for screening the convoy's movement along the escape route. The II Corps commander expected that this action would provide his soldiers enough time to reach the coast. Unfortunately (and possibly on purpose), no one told the PF and RF about the evacuation and consequently they did not cover a withdrawal of which they had no knowledge. General

Phu's last-minute decision to leave behind Brigadier General Cam with vague instructions to "oversee" the withdrawal left Cam confused and angry. Unwilling to share command with newly promoted Pham Van Tat, General Cam jumped on a helicopter and flew to Tuy Hoa, virtually leaving the chief of staff in charge. When Colonel Ly inquired about Brigadier General Tat's whereabouts, he was told that Tat was rounding up Rangers at Kontum and that Ly was to proceed with the evacuation as planned with the 20th Combat Engineer Group leading and General Tat's Ranger Groups guarding the rear. Ly knew that once the withdrawal had begun, he would have little hope of concealing it from the NVA. By day's end on 16 March, the first day of the strategic retreat, the North Vietnamese knew full well the ARVN's intentions, and by the time the lead elements of the South Vietnamese column reached Cheo Reo (Phu Bon's province capital) on the evening of 18 March, the Communists responded with their own surprise. Units of the *320th Division* began shelling the stalled column: rockets, mortars, and artillery fire rained down on the evacuating South Vietnamese. The II Corps engineers' unfinished bridge over the Ea Pa River, east of Cheo Reo, had halted the convoy which by now stretched back past the intersection of Route 7B and Highway 14, almost as far as Pleiku. In order to avoid disaster, Colonel Ly walked through the crowd and the line of jammed vehicles to the command post in Cheo Reo (Hau Bon). He arrived just in time to deploy the 23d Ranger Group at Ban Bleik Pass, a strategic point just west of the capital. The Rangers stopped the NVA's ground attack on the column's flank and while they held the critical pass, the engineers finished the bridge and Colonel Ly and the battalion commanders got the convoy moving again. That marked the end of the good news as General Phu then ordered Ly to depart Cheo Reo by helicopter. As one writer observed: "From the nineteenth, what leadership there was came from individual battalion and group commanders who led whatever nearby troops would still obey orders."[13]

NVA General Dung was flabbergasted by the turn of events, and his own words best describe his reaction: "But now if a whole main force army corps was fleeing at full tilt . . . then why? On whose orders? Had our two thunderbolts striking in the southern Tay Nguyen shaken the enemy troops so badly? . . . This was another very big strategic mistake on their part. If the order to pull the Second Army Corps out had been issued by the central government in Saigon, then the matter had surpassed the bounds of this campaign and had reached strategic proportions."[14]

General Phu was issuing his forces a death sentence, and General Dung was agreeing to serve as the executioner. Dung ordered all of his available forces to close on Route 7B for he planned not just defeat, but annihilation.

Annihilation began on 21 March as the *320th Division* overran the 23d Ranger Group at Cheo Reo and cut the convoy in half, trapping more than 160,000 civilians; the 4th and 25th Ranger Groups; and the survivors of the 23d Rangers. Phu ordered General Tat and the rear guard to escape overland through the jungle. Of the original 7,000 Rangers, 900 actually made it to Nha Trang, the new location of II Corps headquarters. During the retreat, II Corps lost 75 percent of its 20,000-troop strength and of the 5,000 soldiers remaining, none was ready to fight, let alone implement Thieu's plan to retake Ban Me Thout! The flood of evacuees, including thousands of dependents who had clogged the roads and slowed the withdrawal to a chaotic crawl, ended in desperation at Tuy Hoa as approximately 60,000 battered, starving people sought food, water, and refuge where none existed. "One of the most poorly executed withdrawals in the war, and certainly the most tragic, had ended."[15]

Given only two days to prepare for what amounted to a massive withdrawal phased over four days, this retreat quickly turned into a rout as one senior leader after another disappeared from the scene of the action. By the third day, 18 March, the last hope for disciplined leadership, organizational control, and any hope of success disappeared with the unscheduled departure of the officer leading the convoy, Colonel Ly. Relentlessly, the Communists pursued this wounded, headless creature. The retreating, slow-moving ARVN column, hampered by the restrictive terrain and masses of civilians, soon became hopelessly disorganized and incapable of retreating in any kind of military manner. The North Vietnamese chased the South Vietnamese to the coast and in the process captured thousands of troops and tons of equipment which ARVN soldiers abandoned in their haste to escape. Improperly and ineptly executed, the withdrawal touched off a series of reactions which ultimately led to the general collapse of the northern and central regions. One author later wrote of the debacle, "The retreat from the highlands was the most drastic change on the Vietnamese military map in twenty years. In less than ten days, it yielded six entire provinces, a

THE NORTH VIETNAMESE WINTER-SPRING OFFENSIVE, 1974-75: THE MORTAL BLOW

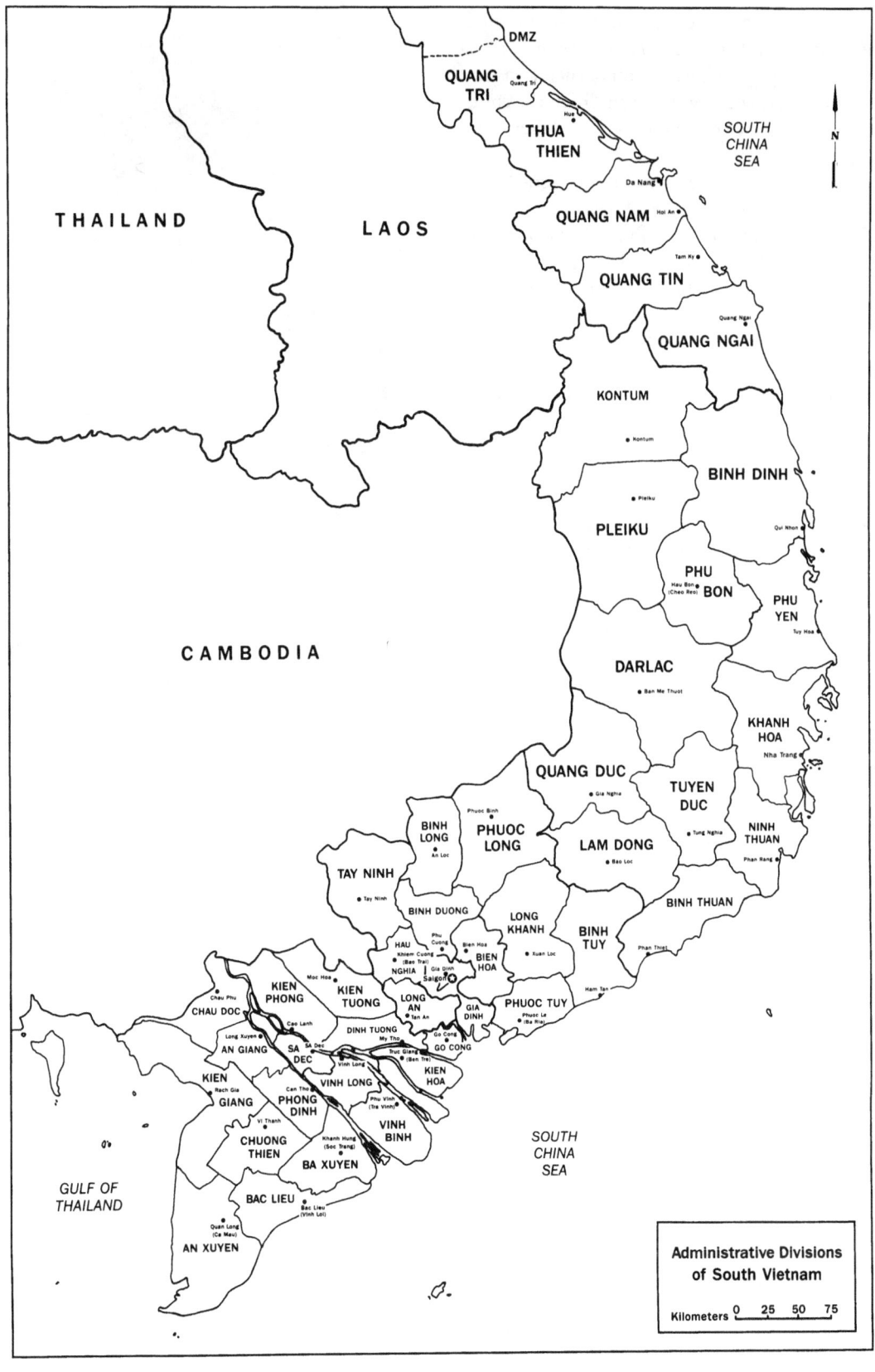

Administrative Divisions of South Vietnam

full infantry division, the equivalent of another division of Rangers, and tens of thousands more militia and support troops, along with most of their arms and equipment. It also cost Nguyen Van Thieu the confidence of his military commanders, his soldiers, and his people."[16]

The North Vietnamese Army moved quickly to capitalize on this opportunity. A few ARVN units, notably the 22d Division in Binh Dinh Province and the 3d Airborne Brigade in Khanh Hoa, resisted the aggressors, but otherwise the Communist drive to the coast met with little resistance. South Vietnam had been effectively cut in two. With II Corps' demise, the Communists shifted their attention to Military Region 1 where they hoped to continue their successes.

Defeat in Military Region 1

In early 1975, military activity in MR 1 was relatively light because seasonal rains had precluded major combat operations. Fighting began in January and focused on the high ground south and southwest of Hue—hills over which both armies had fought fiercely since late August 1974. The South Vietnamese finally regained most of this key terrain by mid-January and in the process inflicted heavy casualties on elements of one North Vietnamese Army division and its supporting independent regiments.

In late January, collected intelligence revealed to the South Vietnamese that major offensive preparations were underway as North Vietnamese armor units rolled out vehicles in ever increasing numbers for what appeared to be major maintenance repairs and overhaul. Additionally, South Vietnamese intelligence sources detected new armor parks, artillery positions, and maintenance areas. While these preparations were underway, sporadic fighting continued throughout the region.

After losing the high ground overlooking Highway 1, south of Hue, to South Vietnamese counterattacks in the first weeks of 1975, the North Vietnamese Army moved more units into the area. Activity during February entailed a series of sharp, but inconclusive engagements southwest of Da Nang. In Quang Ngai Province, the North Vietnamese Army and Viet Cong units continued the pattern of low-level attacks which had characterized military operations in the province starting in mid-1974. Spoiling actions by the 2d ARVN Division and Ranger forces succeeded in holding in place elements of the *52d NVA Brigade*, which had attempted at one point to move southward into Binh Dinh Province. Then came March and the disaster in

Department of Defense Photo (USMC) A800720
LtGen Ngo Quang Truong, MR 1 commander, stands at his headquarters forward-located in Hue. Between 12-17 March Gen Truong argued against transfer of the airborne division from MR 1, but to no avail.

the Central Highlands, which allowed the Communists to turn their full attention to the northern part of South Vietnam, Military Region 1.[17]

On 8 March, major fighting erupted when Communist forces attacked and occupied some 15 hamlets in southern Quang Tri and northern Thua Thien Provinces. Well over 100,000 of the inhabitants chose to become refugees by fleeing south to Hue.* At the same time in southern Military Region 1, the *2d NVA Division* and *52d Brigade* attacked and overran the district capitals at Hau Duc and Tien Phuoc and threatened the Quang Tin provincial capital of Tam Ky.

On 12 March, with mounting pressure in Military Region 1 and increasing apprehension over the defense of Saigon, President Thieu ordered the MR 1 commander, Lieutenant General Ngo Quang Truong, to release the Airborne Division for deployment from the Da Nang area to Saigon. At the same time, he ordered Lieutenant General Truong to give top priority within MR 1 to the defense of Da Nang. Truong strongly op-

---

*Vietnamese Marine Lieutenant Colonel Tran Ngoc Toan recently recalled the South Vietnamese response to this attack: "These hamlets were retaken by the VNMC and a detached ARVN tank unit on 10 March 1975. Tons of weapons and equipment were captured and 100 NVA soldiers were taken prisoner." Tran Ngoc Toan Comments.

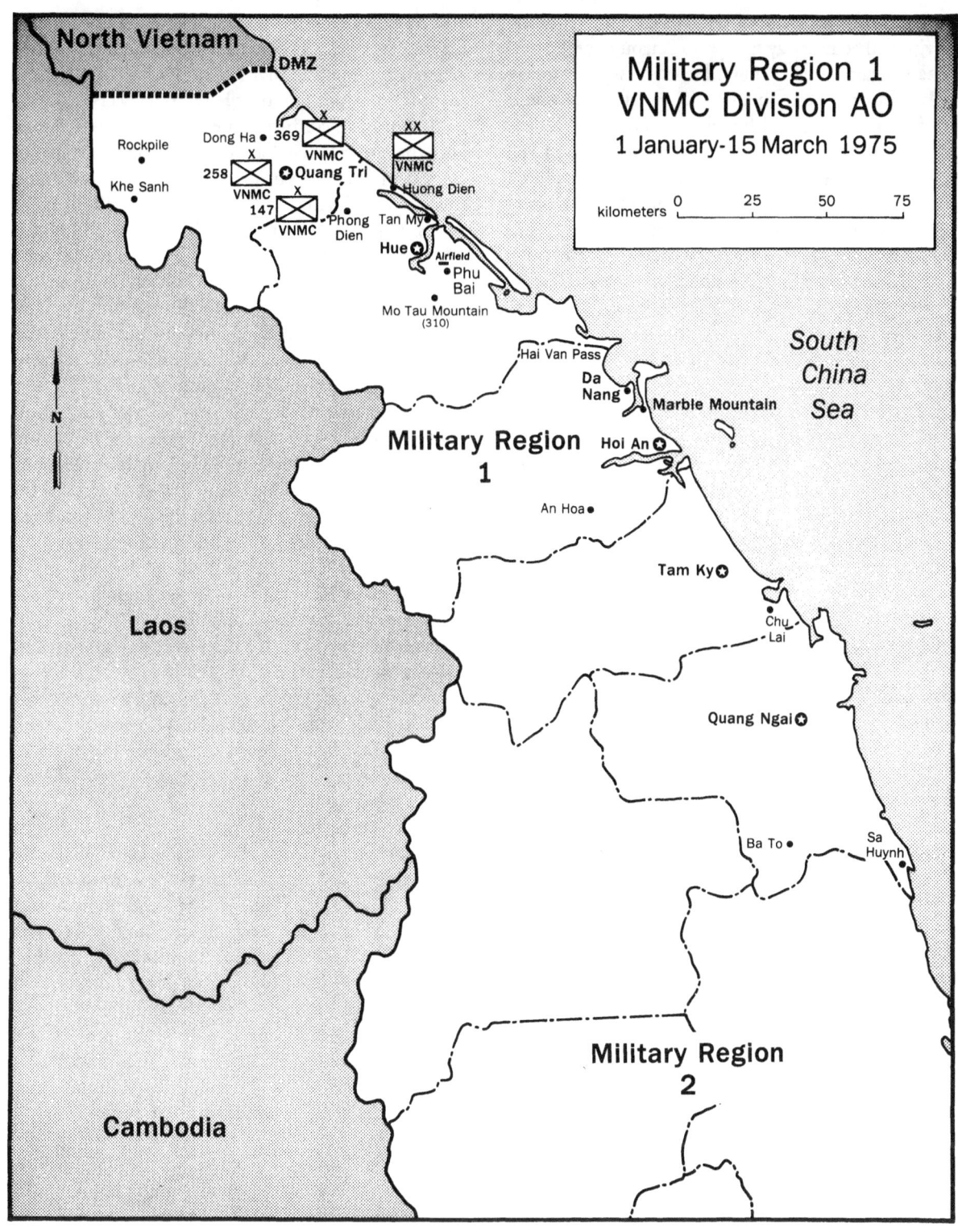

posed the president's decision to remove the Airborne Division. The next day he flew to Saigon to argue personally against such a move, but to no avail, gaining only a four-day postponement. The withdrawal would begin on 17 March, although two days later Thieu, after another personal request by Truong, authorized the 1st Airborne Brigade (the last brigade scheduled for redeployment to Saigon) to remain at Da Nang on the condition it not be committed to combat and the defense of MR 1. To replace the departing units, Thieu ordered the newly formed Vietnamese Marine Corps brigade to deploy to MR 1. Brigade 468 (composed of only two battalions—the 14th and 16th) of the VNMC Division arrived in Da Nang a few days later.[18]

Also at the 13 March meeting, Thieu directed the new III Corps commander, Lieutenant General Nguyen Van Toan, to withdraw his forces from An Loc and employ them in MR 3 wherever they were needed most. Both of these decisions represented serious blows to the morale of the RVNAF: the brigade's withdrawal because it ripped out the very heart of Troung's defenses, and the An Loc retreat because it reversed perhaps the ARVN's greatest victory. In June of 1972, the Communists ended a 95-day siege of this provincial capital when, in defeat, their forces withdrew to bases in Cambodia. The ARVN's shining moment in achieving a battlefield success at Binh Long's capital, just 65 miles north of Saigon, was made possible during the Easter Offensive by something dramatically absent in 1975—U.S. air support. Marine Corps A-4s and Air Force B-52s had helped to end the siege by continuously bombing the enemy concentrations around An Loc.[19] In March 1975 while Thieu attempted to redress the absence of a strategic reserve and the need for additional support, General Dung boasted: "The United States appears completely impotent, and even if they increased their aid they would not be able to rescue their puppets from the impending collapse."*[20]

Events would prove Dung correct, but neither South Vietnam nor the United States nor even General Truong expected what soon followed. To compensate for the loss of the airborne brigades, General Truong ordered the Marine Division to plan for a redeployment from its position near Hue to the Da Nang area. In the midst of confusion over the defensive strategy and the growing civilian panic, Communist forces crossed the Thach Han River, attacked and occupied the ruins of Quang Tri City. The South Vietnamese forces resisted and then fell back. The date, 19 March 1975, marked the beginning of the end for Military Region 1 and northern South Vietnam. The Government of South Vietnam (GVN) in the ensuing days concentrated its efforts on establishing a defensive perimeter around Hue. At 1800 on 24 March, Lieutenant General Truong decided to abandon Hue and evacuate as many troops as possible along a narrow coastal sandspit east of Highway 1, where they could move without restriction until reaching the evacuation column north of Hai Van Pass. The effort proved futile, and as panic grew, the withdrawal, compounded by North Vietnamese Army pressure, became a rout. This left, as the last line of defense, Da Nang.[21]

The massive influx of civilian refugees into the Da Nang area precipitated a breakdown in law and order. Attempts to establish a defensive perimeter around the city met with little success, and on 30 March, that former bastion of American firepower fell to the Communists. Da Nang, by now in total chaos, collapsed without a shot being fired. The aggressors from North Vietnam literally walked into the city and found planes, tanks, guns, and equipment; all serviceable and yet abandoned.

Responsibility for this disaster would be laid at the doorstep of President Thieu. The catastrophic chain of events leading to the surrender of Da Nang resulted directly from the decision to abandon Military Region 2 and the ill-advised withdrawal of the Airborne Division from Military Region 1. Subsequent efforts to adjust defenses in the face of increased Communist pressure destroyed confidence and morale, and worse yet, caused panic among the civilian populace. This, in turn, led to a total collapse within the country, handing the Communists a stunning victory at minimal cost.

The North Vietnamese plans and preparations that produced the successful offensive of the 1975 dry season were fully underway by 1974. The only modification to the plan and one which came as a complete surprise was the length of the operation. It was originally planned for both the 1975 and 1976 dry seasons. On 31 March, the North Vietnamese Politburo met

---

*Commenting on the issue of American assistance and aid, Lieutenant Colonel Edward A. Grimm recalled his Indochina experiences just prior to General Dung's boasts: "A particularly disheartening spectacle to all U.S. personnel present was the arrival in Saigon in the fall of 1974 of several U.S. Congressional delegations (CODELs) allegedly on fact-finding trips but who were actually and vociferously pre-decided against any further assistance to our allies. Both Major Jaime Sabater and myself were specifically assigned and prepared to brief members of these CODELs but we were repeatedly rebuffed. The CODELs sought and received briefings from the enemy and ostensibly 'neutral groups' instead." Grimm Comments.

Marine Corps Historical Collection

Abandoned vehicles on Highway 1 attest to the quickness with which the defense of Da Nang collapsed. President Thieu's decision to withdraw the airborne division from MR 1 precipitated panic among inhabitants and led to loss of this region in less than 12 days.

and decided to accelerate that timetable by one year to take advantage of their unexpectedly swift successes and the half-dozen weeks before the onset of the next monsoon season: "From this moment the final decisive battle of our army and people has begun; its aim is to complete the people's national democratic revolution in the South . . . ."22

Reaching this point of success so far ahead of schedule astounded even General Dung, whose troops had been preparing almost continuously for three months to ensure that they would begin the first phase of the campaign with the element of surprise and overwhelming odds on their side. The results were incredible. The South Vietnamese Armed Forces (RVNAF) had suffered a catastrophic defeat in MR 1. In the debacle, the 1st, 2d, and 3d Divisions were lost as identifiable military units, along with the territorial and Ranger forces. The RVNAF managed to extract some 16,000 troops, including 4,000 Marines from Military Region 1, but nearly all of the heavy equipment was left behind. Thus an unbroken series of defeats closed the final chapter on the region which once served as home to the U.S. Marines stationed in South Vietnam:

19 March — Quang Tri City and Province abandoned as the general retreat from Military Region 1 begins.

24 March — Quang Nai and Tam Ky fall.
25 March — Hue and Hoi An fall.
26 March — Chu Lai falls.
30 March — Da Nang falls.23

A Wasted Division

Since 1973, the Vietnamese Marine Corps Division had remained in a relatively unchanged defensive posture. In early 1975, the division was in defensive positions along the northernmost line in Military Region 1: VNMC Brigade 258 was on the south bank of the Thach Han River just south and west of Quang Tri City; Brigade 369 was defending a line running east from Quang Tri City to the coast; and Brigade 147 was in the southernmost part of Quang Tri Province defending the western approach to Highway 1 and the coast (It was located south of the My Chanh River and west of My Chanh). Additionally, during January 1975, the Marine Corps began outfitting a new brigade, the 468th.

As of 12 February, the division's mission was to defend Quang Tri and Thua Thien Provinces, to delay any enemy advances, and if forced to withdraw, then to defend Hue. On 12 March, when the Airborne Division was unexpectedly ordered to deploy from Da Nang to Saigon, the Corps Commander, General

Photo courtesy of MajGen John E. Murray, USA (Ret)

Despite the prohibition against military advisors, U.S. and South Vietnamese forces worked closely together. Seen here are LtGen Truong, MajGen Murray, LtGen Khang, Capt (Mrs.) Strickland and LtCol Strickland, and Gen Lan, receiving an award from Gen Murray.

Truong, was told that the defense of Da Nang had now become the top military priority in MR 1. He immediately communicated this change in strategy to General Lan, informing him to anticipate immediate movement of the Marine Division into positions vacated by the departing airborne units and assumption of primary responsibility for the defense of Da Nang. Within hours of the decision to withdraw the airborne units from Military Region 1, the Vietnamese Marine Corps, following Truong's orders, redeployed its forces, removing both of its brigades from Quang Tri. It shifted Brigade 147 south from My Chanh to Phong Dien where it straddled Highway 1 on an arcing line from the 4th Battalion, west and south of the city, to the 7th Battalion on the east side. General Lan ordered the 369th Brigade to move to a position north and west of Da Nang and directed the 258th Brigade to deploy south of Da Nang where it could cover the city's exposed southern flank. Additionally, the newest Marine brigade, the 468th, had been designated by the JGS as replacements for the departing Airborne Division. At the same time Truong's forces were shifting, the Communists launched heavy attacks against the recently arrived defenders of Phong Dien, the 4th and 5th battalions of the 147th Brigade. With no reserve available, General Lan ordered the brigade to delay the North Vietnamese Army and then fall back on Hue.[24]

By 17 March, the 258th Brigade had deployed to Da Nang and replaced the already departed 2nd Airborne Brigade. The next day, General Lan moved the division command post from Huong Dien, Thua Thien Province to Marble Mountain Airfield, southeast of Da Nang. This placed both Truong's I Corps Headquarters located at Da Nang Airfield and Lan's command post within miles of each other.

Even though the defense of Da Nang had become their primary mission, the Marines, on 20 March, were ordered to defend at all costs their positions north of Hue. That same day, VNAF C-130s delivered the 468th Brigade to Da Nang and its Marines deployed to defensive positions from the northern end of the Hai Van Pass along Highway 1 to Phuoc Tong. While this was underway, the 147th prepared for its task. To accomplish its mission the 147th Brigade had been task-organized into four infantry battalions, an artillery battalion, and various supporting units. Days earlier in anticipation of heavy fighting, division headquarters

THE NORTH VIETNAMESE WINTER-SPRING OFFENSIVE, 1974-75: THE MORTAL BLOW

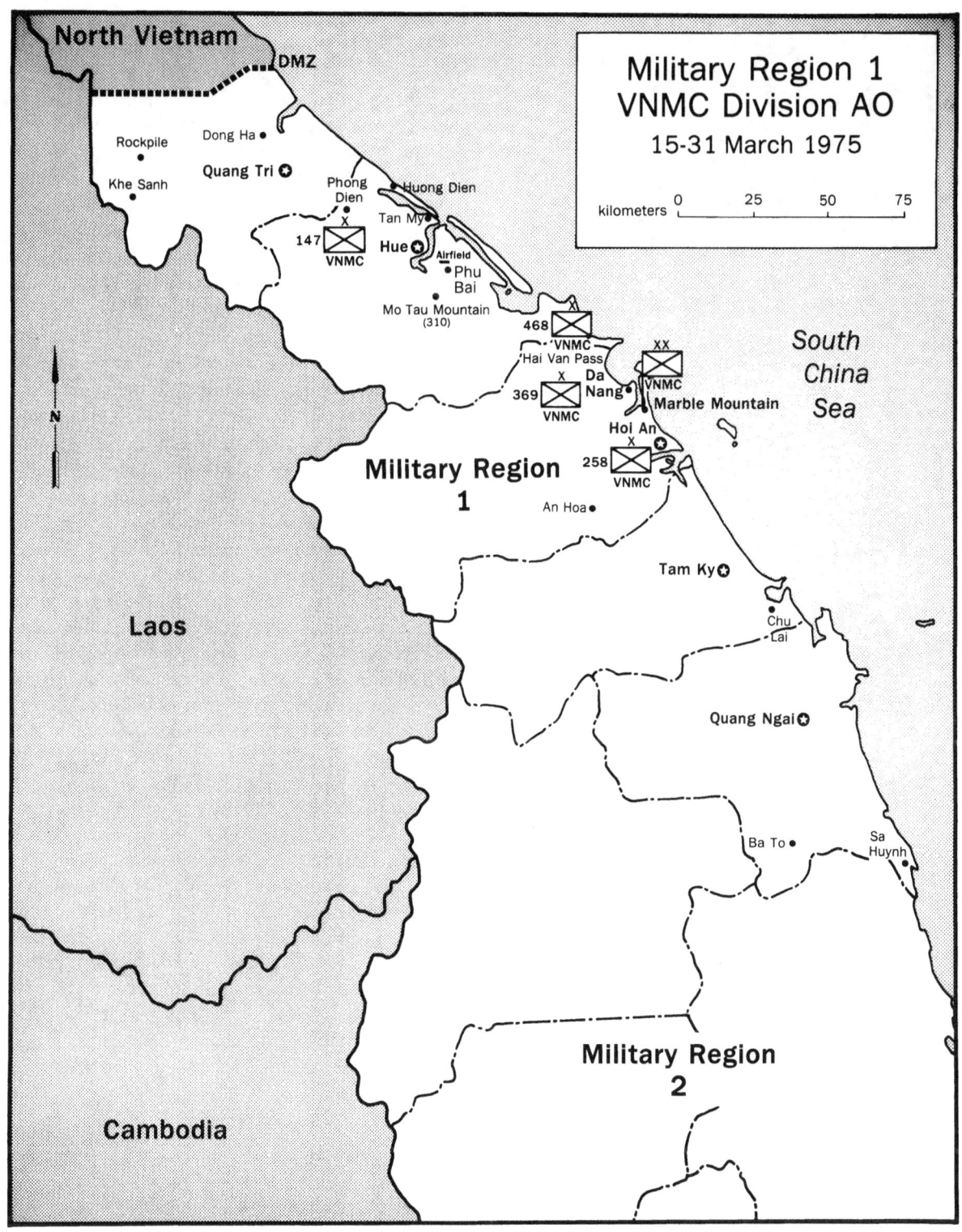

VNMC Commandant MajGen Bui The Lan addresses his division. In March 1975 he lost over half of the division during the evacuation of Military Region 1.

had reinforced the 147th Brigade with the 3d Battalion of the 258th Brigade.* With an overall fighting strength of 3,000, the 147th prepared materially and psychologically to execute to the letter the order to defend. Two days later, this order was countermanded, and the 147th was instead ordered to move southeastward to the coastline at Tan My where the Vietnamese Navy was expected to load and move it to Da Nang. On 23 March, the confused and concerned Marines executed their new orders and made their way southward to the beach, knowing that the brigade's fate now rested solely in the hands of the Vietnamese Navy.[25]

Characteristic of the almost total breakdown in coordination among the South Vietnamese forces, the Navy was not informed of this development until long after the Marines had left their positions. The Navy tried to effect the rendezvous, but arrived behind schedule with too few landing craft and failed to extract the stranded Marines. The few boats that got to the area could not beach because of submerged sand bars and only those Marines who were strong swimmers eventually made it to South Vietnamese ships.

When it became clear to the Marines that their newly acquired position was indefensible and that they would not be evacuated, they destroyed their crew-served weapons, and, in the case of the TOW missile launchers, dumped them into the surf. Less than 20 percent of the 147th Brigade made it to Da Nang. The remainder died in the beach area or were captured without ever having had a chance to fight in a major battle.[26]

Typical of the individual effects of this failed operation were the experiences of Vietnamese Marine Corps Lieutenant Colonel Tran Ngoc Toan, the commanding officer of 4th Battalion, 147th Brigade. During the retrograde operation, Lieutenant Colonel Toan's battalion, as well as the other battalions, could not reach the few LCMs which had made it as far as the sand bar, still hundreds of yards from the shoreline. He related, "One company swam out to the sand bar and climbed on board. This included the brigade commander. Sandwiched between 130mm artillery in Hue and the advancing NVA regiments, my battalion was decimated." In the next week Toan and approximately 450 Marines from the 147th made it overland to Da Nang.** They evaded capture and escaped to the southern end of the peninsula where Catholic residents of a small fishing village transported them in their boats to Da Nang. By the time they arrived there on 2 April, the city was already in the hands of the NVA. They immediately shed their uniforms and donned civilian garb, placing their pistols in the back of their pants and small hand grenades in their shirt pockets. Slipping out of the city, Toan said, "they walked, paid truck drivers for rides, and hitchiked their way down Highway 1 to Vung Tau, arriving two weeks later."[27]

The 258th and 369th Brigades fared little better. With each passing day, the area around Da Nang became more and more crowded, clogged with refugees attempting to escape the onrushing North Vietnamese, unimpeded by fighting forces.

---

*According to Lieutenant Colonel Tran Ngoc Toan, the commander of the 4th Battalion of the 147th Brigade, by the middle of March the four brigades operationally controlled the following battalions: 147th—3d, 4th, 5th, and 7th; 258th—1st and 8th; 369th—2d, 6th, and 9th; and 468th—14th, 16th, and 18th. The 18th Battalion consisted of a headquarters and two infantry companies. Toan Comments.

**Toan related: "The other battalion commanders, 3d, 5th, and 7th, were captured around Hue city and moved to Dong Ha, later Khe Sanh." Toan Comments.

Marine Corps Historical Collection

The VNMC memorial in Saigon was dedicated to the thousands of Marines who died fighting to defend the Republic of South Vietnam. VNMC Brigades 147, 268, and 369, deployed far from their Saigon headquarters to Quang Tri and Thua Thien provinces, would never be allowed to stand and fight the invading NVA units which captured MR 1.

By 27 March, the estimate of refugees in the Da Nang area exceeded one million. Locally raised units of the ARVN disintegrated when the soldiers gave first priority to the welfare of their families. Social order completely disappeared, broken down by fear and chaos. It soon became quite obvious to everyone that a coordinated defense of Da Nang was impossible. The only major units maintaining tactical integrity were the 258th and 369th Brigades. On 28 March these Marines were ordered to fall back to the city. All heavy equipment had to be abandoned and approximately 5,500 Marines reached their objective. The surviving Marines futilely attempted to defend Da Nang, but that short-lived effort ended two days later when approximately 4,000 of them boarded evacuation ships.*[28]

As an eyewitness to the loss of South Vietnam's second largest city, General Lan represented an excellent source of information on what had happened in MR 1.** In the days following Lan's evacuation from Marble Moutain, he met with Lieutenant Colonel Anthony Lukeman (Chief, VNMC Logistics Support Branch, DAO) at his headquarters at Vung Tau to discuss the re-equipping of his remaining Marines. During this conversation, General Lan shared with Lukeman his experiences in I Corps and his assessment of what went wrong.

Lan stressed six military aspects of the withdrawal which, though intrinsically linked to politics, were, in his mind, the overriding factors in determining the outcome of the strategic retreat. First and foremost was the decision to withdraw from prepared positions in Quang Tri and Thua Thien Provinces without contact with the enemy. The second factor was the impact of the sudden reversal of a critical strategy: deciding to

---

*There were conflicting reports as to the conduct and behavior of the heavily armed Marines during Da Nang's final hours. The Marines were no longer a cohesive fighting unit, but had disintegrated into small armed groups. See for example Alan Dawson, *55 Days, The Fall of South Vietnam* (Englewood Cliffs, New Jersey: Prentice-Hall, Inc., 1977), pp. 186-87.

**General Lan was rescued from a beach near Monkey Mountain early on the morning of 29 March by a South Vietnamese Navy boat. *Fall of the South*, pp. 80-81.

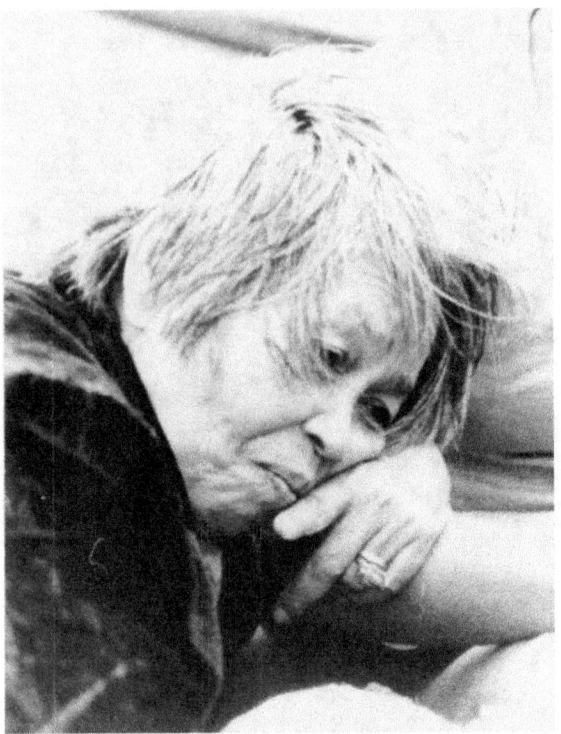

Marine Corps Historical Collection

This woman is one of the many thousands of refugees who fled Da Nang on 29 and 30 March. These South Vietnamese lost everything after the government transferred the airborne division from MR 1 and withdrew the Marine Division from Quang Tri Province.

withdraw immediately after having ordered the same units to "Defend at all costs" positions north of Hue. Both of these political decisions had an adverse effect on morale and fighting spirit. Further, the clogging of the avenues of retreat by fleeing refugees hampered Marine tactical maneuverability. "Tactical movement during the withdrawal was impossible," related General Lan. The dissolution of other fighting units within the area also influenced the attempt to defend Da Nang. It caused considerable degradation of fighting strength and military discipline and adversely affected the confidence of the fighting defenders: "When troops from those units (those located near their home and family) were ordered to withdraw, their homes were forfeited and their families became refugees. They deserted their military units and joined their families as refugees." (Lieutenant Colonel Lukeman noted that the Marines did not have the same problem as most had been recruited from another part of South Vietnam, primarily Military Region 3). Another significant aspect was the absence of coordination and control of the military arms, as evidenced by the Vietnamese Navy's attempt to rescue the Marines defending Hue. The last items of importance and the overall determining factors in the enemy's success were tactics and timing. The North Vietnamese demonstrated opportunism and efficacy: "[The enemy] attacked with rockets and artillery against populated areas and then at Da Nang, employed tanks on three axis lightly supported by infantry. Civilian panic, additional military desertions, and increased difficulty of movement in the rear followed."[29] The resulting chaos and absence of military control during the evacuation of Da Nang underlined the accuracy and the gravity of General Lan's observations.*

During the two-week period that Military Region 1 came apart at the seams, the United States took notice and decided to take action. At first the U.S. moved slowly, but in a matter of days it was expending maximum effort to address this sudden and unexpected calamity. The Marines of the III Marine Amphibious Force were the first to experience the effects of this reaction. Located in the region and having prepared contingency plans for the evacuation of Americans from Southeast Asia, III MAF had anticipated a call, but not quite this soon nor from this country. The command had been concentrating its efforts on Eagle Pull with its sights set on the almost inevitable evacuation of Cambodia. The events in South Vietnam quickly rewrote the script and seemed to indicate that the III Marine Amphibious Force might have to double load its gun and do so without delay!

---

*Recently, Lieutenant Colonel Toan offered his opinion of the cause of some of the undisciplined behavior in Da Nang at the end of March 1975. He attributed a large part of it to the confusion surrounding when and how the forces defending Da Nang would be evacuated. He said that late in the day on 28 March, General Lan phoned I Corps headquarters at Da Nang and when he got no answer, he knew that everyone had left and the Marines were on their own. At this point, the Navy offered the only means of retreat and at 0600 the next day, they conducted an evacuation at the beach near Marble Mountain. At this time, word was passed to the remaining South Vietnamese Marine units to make their way to Marble Mountain for another pickup scheduled for later that day at 1500. Information about the planned evacuation spread to other military units in Da Nang, and those soldiers who learned of it realized that if they had any hope of escaping capture, they too needed to move to the beach. As a consequence, chaos and disorder erupted, and the Navy was forced to cancel the second evacuation. Shooting and violence ensued as all those unevacuated Marines and soldiers desperately sought a way out of the surrounded city. Toan Comments.

CHAPTER 6
The Evacuation of South Vietnam's Northern Provinces

*The Amphibious Evacuation RVN Support Group — Initial Operations in Vietnamese Waters
Military Sealift Command Operations — Meeting the Needs*

The North Vietnamese spring offensive launched in March 1975 enjoyed a level of success far beyond its commander's greatest expectations. The utter collapse of resistance in the Central Highlands, with the flight of thousands of soldiers and civilians to the sea, followed immediately by a rout of the South Vietnamese forces in Military Region 1 came suddenly and unexpectedly. The ensuing chaos reflected the low morale and the rapidly deteriorating confidence of the South Vietnamese people in their government and its decisions. The United States reacted to these events by providing humanitarian assistance to those South Vietnamese fleeing the Communist onslaught. This assistance took the form of rescuing refugees at sea and transporting them to areas still under South Vietnam's control. America's military involvement, including the use of Major General Carl W. Hoffman's III Marine Amphibious Force, began on 25 March 1975.[1]

The Amphibious Evacuation RVN Support Group

The swiftness with which the situation in South Vietnam changed and the resultant need for American Marines to assist in evacuation operations posed some unique and challenging problems for General Hoffman and his staff. First, the amphibious ships that III MAF needed, known as ARG Bravo, were not readily available. Second, the battalion that his staff wanted to send was a thousand miles to the north on the main island of Japan. The battalion landing team of ARG Bravo, Lieutenant Colonel Robert E. Loehe's reinforced 3d Battalion, 9th Marines and its supporting units, already had deployed to Camp Fuji, Japan, for training. Dependent on ARG Bravo ships for transportation, BLT 3/9's mobility was severely limited by its ships' movements. The Navy, anticipating that the battalion would stay on the island of Honshu for two to three weeks of scheduled training, sent two of the three ships in the amphibious ready group south to Subic Bay for routine maintenance. When events unexpectedly went from bad to worse in South Vietnam, BLT 3/9 suddenly faced a dilemma: how to get to the scene of the action? With the *Frederick* (LST 1184) and the *Durham* (LKA 114) in Subic Bay, the battalion had at its disposal in Yokosuka harbor only one ship, the *Dubuque* (LPD 8), and diplomatic sensitivities made even its use questionable. An agreement between the United States and Japan precluded the deployment of military units from Japan directly to combat in Southeast Asia. Considering all these factors, General Hoffman made the decision to use Okinawa-based Marines instead of BLT 3/9.

On 25 March 1975, the 1st Battalion, 4th Marines received the warning order to support possible evacuation operations from Da Nang.* The battalion, commanded by Lieutenant Colonel Charles E. Hester, was located at its customary cantonment on Okinawa, Camp Hansen. It had all but completed its predeployment training in preparation for its scheduled relief in May of Lieutenant Colonel George P. Slade's 2nd Battalion, 4th Marines.

BLT 2/4, the landing force of the 31st Marine Amphibious Unit (31st MAU) which Colonel John F. Roche III commanded, was already on board ships of Amphibious Ready Group Alpha. It had deployed to the Gulf of Thailand on 28 February in anticipation of the impending order to execute Operation Eagle Pull, the evacuation of Phnom Penh.[2]

Its relief, the 1st Battalion, 4th Marines, possessed considerable leadership experience in its senior officers and senior NCOs, almost all of whom were veterans of combat in Southeast Asia. They led an extremely well-motivated group of junior officers and Marines, all anxious to join the action. The warning order on 25 March represented that opportunity, but before the battalion could actually effect the order, it was modified.

---

*Lieutenant Colonel Walter J. Wood, who as a captain commanded Company D, 1st Battalion, 4th Marines during this period, recalled the events surrounding the issuance of the warning order. He stated that when the battalion was alerted on 25 March 1975, the battalion commander immediately called a meeting around 0900 which lasted less than a half-hour: "I was instructed that my company would be helilifted to White Beach at around 1400 for embarkation aboard the USS *Blue Ridge*. During this brief, my company's mission was described to me . . . we were to embark aboard the *Blue Ridge* for immediate departure to Da Nang where we would reinforce U.S. facilities. We did embark on 25 March but for reasons never explained to me or since forgotten, the *Blue Ridge* did not get underway for Vietnam until 27 March." Wood Comments.

Department of Defense Photo (USN) K107687

Company D and elements of Headquarters and Service Company march down the pier at White Beach, Okinawa, on 25 March 1975, to embark in USS Blue Ridge *(LCC 19). These Marines, as members of the Amphibious Evacuation RVN Support Group, spent the next 13 days at sea recovering refugees evacuating northern South Vietnam.*

On 27 March, General Hoffman, who at the end of 1974 replaced Major General Herman Poggemeyer, Jr., as III MAF commander, activated the 33d Marine Amphibious Unit and assigned Lieutenant Colonel Hester's 1st Battalion, 4th Marines as its ground combat element. The MAU, led initially by the commanding officer of the 4th Marines, Colonel Alfred M. Gray, received the mission of supporting the evacuation of American citizens and other designated evacuees from Da Nang. The MAU headquarters and Company D, 1st Battalion, 4th Marines went on board the amphibious command ship, USS *Blue Ridge* (LCC 19), while it was moored at White Beach, Okinawa. As soon as the command group was embarked, Rear Admiral Donald E. Whitmire's (Commander Task Force 76) flagship departed for South Vietnam. The remainder of the battalion awaited the arrival of the amphibious transport dock ship, *Dubuque*, which along with the other two ships in ARG Bravo had been directed to assist in evacuation operations. *Durham* and *Frederick*, still in Subic Bay, were ordered to proceed directly to South Vietnamese coastal waters.[3]

The following day, Lieutenant Colonel James P. Kizer's Marine Medium Helicopter Squadron 165 (HMM-165) was attached to the MAU as its aviation component. The assignment of this squadron posed the MAU an additional problem. The squadron's helicopters were distributed throughout WestPac; most were located at Futema, but some were operating out of Cubi Point Naval Air Station in the Philippines. Additionally, the task force did not contain a ship specially configured for an aviation unit. As a result, HMM-165 was initially split into four separate detachments and divided among the available ships: the largest group of helicopters, seven CH-46s, was placed on board the *Dubuque*, a smaller detachment (two UH-1Es) went on board the *Blue Ridge*, and single helicopter (CH-46) detachments joined both the *Durham* and the *Frederick*.

Upon initial receipt of the warning order, Lieutenant Colonel Hester perceived his mission as the establishment and protection of evacuation sites in the Da Nang area. A mission of this magnitude would involve the majority of units in a task-organized battalion landing team. However, on 30 March, Easter Sunday 1975, as the remaining elements of BLT 1/4 boarded the *Dubuque*, events in South Vietnam significantly changed the complexion of the operation.

Da Nang fell into the hands of enemy forces, altering all plans to evacuate that region. The task force received new orders to sail instead to Qui Nhon and Nha Trang.

Once there, the new plan called for the battalion to aid and assist in the humanitarian evacuation of the area. The Marines of the 1st Battalion, 4th Marines would then assume responsibility for the internal security of the ships assisting the refugees. The new directive describing this role, although somewhat confusing, had an undeniable effect on the organization and make-up of the battalion. Rather than a BLT, all that would be required was a small battalion command group and the rifle companies organic to the battalion. Thus BLT 1/4 would deploy as a "light" battalion, specifically tailored for the task at hand. Most of the Headquarters and Service Company of the battalion as well as the normally attached units would remain behind. The amphibian tractor platoon carrying the battalion's 106mm recoilless rifle platoon, already on board the *Dubuque*, was unloaded. The 81mm mortar platoon, which had assembled at the Camp Hansen helicopter landing zone, found out only moments after its arrival that it had become a last-minute "cut" from the troop list. The frenetic and seemingly chaotic pace of the embarkation reflected, if nothing else, the battalion's flexibility, a trait it would exhibit time and time again in the ensuing weeks. If this event appeared confusing and haphazard to the participants, imagine the wonderment and disbelief of the spectators. The S-3 of the 9th Marines, one of those watching that Easter morning while the *Dubuque* laid to off Okinawa in Ora Wan Bay, related his observations:

> On my way to the Officers Mess that Sunday morning, I paused to watch as 1/4's 106s were loaded into LVTP-7s and then the LVTs splashed into the water and swam out to the *Dubuque*. After a leisurely brunch, I left the Mess about 90 minutes later and headed for the regimental command post. As I walked along the road bordering the bay, to my astonishment I observed the same LVTs swimming away from the *Dubuque* still fully loaded. They were heading for the LVT loading ramp at the foot of their tractor park and the *Dubuque* was getting underway, headed in the direction of White Beach. I immediately quickened my pace, curious to find out the latest change and the reason for the return of 1/4's heavy gear.[4]

During that Sunday afternoon, on 30 March, the *Dubuque* got underway from White Beach, Okinawa for Vietnamese waters. The *Dubuque* carried the battalion command group; Companies A, B, and C; and HMM-165(-) (seven CH-46s). Also on board were elements reinforcing the 1st Battalion, 4th Marines: First Lieutenant Joseph J. Streitz's detachment from the Military Police Company, 3d Marine Division; a platoon from the 3d Engineer Battalion led by Second Lieutenant Paul Melshen; the 3d Counterintelligence Team (3d CIT), commanded by Captain Charles J. Bushey; and the 17th Interrogator-Translator Team (17th ITT) commanded by Chief Warrant Officer Allen F. Kent.[5]

On 31 March, the 33d MAU was redesignated the Amphibious Evacuation RVN Support Group to emphasize the humanitarian nature of the mission. Colonel Dan C. Alexander, the Chief of Staff, 9th MAB, became its commander. The renamed group was assigned task designator 79.9, thereby consummating a major shift in plans to accommodate the rapidly changing situation in South Vietnam.[6]

Originally, Colonel Alfred Gray had been ordered to remain at Okinawa and reconstitute a new 33d MAU to be built around Lieutenant Colonel Lynn Bond's BLT 1/9, the airborne contingency BLT, and Lieutenant Colonel Herbert M. Fix's HMH-463. Fix's squadron was already embarked on the USS *Hancock* (CVA 19), outward bound from Pearl Harbor, steaming hard for the Western Pacific. Due to the fact that the rapidly changing situation in South Vietnam could make plans instantly obsolete, this idea never matured beyond its formative stage.

Overcome by events and the exigencies of the moment, the original plan was scrapped and replaced with the one calling for a shipboard security force. The modified concept received its initiation under Major General Kenneth J. Houghton, the 3d Marine Division commander, who also had observed the embarkation and departure of Colonel Alexander's force. General Houghton expressed the desire that this force—on the verge of a new and unique mission—make the best use of its company grade and lower leadership echelons.

Success, however, did not come without proper planning and to serve that end, on 31 March 1975, Joint Operations Order 76.8/79.9 was published. Although Task Force 76 retained its task designator, Admiral Whitmire activated the 76.8 designator to distinguish those involved in the special evacuation operation from the rest of his forces. Admiral Whitmire, himself, took command of Task Group 76.8. The order he and Colonel Alexander issued covered the group's anticipated activities and directed the placement of Marine rifle companies, describing their command relationships.[7] One company would be placed on each of the four amphibious ships and serve under the operational control of the ship's commanding officer. Its mission would be to provide internal security for the ship and to assist in evacuee processing and administration.

Initial Operations in Vietnamese Waters

On 2 April 1975, the *Frederick* and the *Durham* joined the *Blue Ridge* and the *Dubuque* off the coast of Nha Trang. That same day, the Joint Chiefs of Staff authorized the embarkation of Marine security forces on board Military Sealift Command (MSC) ships for purposes of security and assistance in refugee processing.*[8]

At the time of issuance of the authority to embark Marines on MSC ships, the Navy/Marine Corps force was preparing to use Colonel Alexander's Marines on Navy ships in the recovery and evacuation of refugees fleeing South Vietnam's coastal cities. Soon they would have to shift gears to respond to the newest directive, but for the immediate future, the Marines of the 1st Battalion, 4th Marines prepared themselves for evacuation duty on the amphibious ready group's ships.**

---

*Admiral Steele recalled that this decision was not reached without considerable effort after most in authority, other than those in the Western Pacific, had overlooked the disorder embarking evacuees could wreak on an unguarded MSC ship: "I immediately objected to the continued operational control by the MSC command of these ships in a combat zone and strongly recommended that Marines be embarked. It was not until after horror stories began to come from the civilian masters about what was happening on these ships, and many urgent recommendations on the part of Seventh Fleet and CinCPacFlt, plus actual seizure of a ship by onboard evacuees, that the Joint Chiefs of Staff finally responded." Steele Comments.

**Major Carl A. Shaver, the operations officer for BLT 1/4, remembered in detail the events of 2 April 1975 when, while underway, Lieutenant Colonel Hester and he hosted an operational meeting of the battalion staff members embarked on the *Dubuque*. His recollections reveal the embarked Marines' perspective on the ongoing events: "It was the general consensus of everyone present that the refugee evacuation assignment was only an intermediary mission. Obviously with all the men, money, and materials that had been poured into the war effort, it was inconceivable that the U.S. would stand idly by and allow the South Vietnamese government to lose significant amounts of real estate. Additionally, with the daily buildup of shipping and Marine combat capabilities in the area it was reasonable to assume that any immediately available Marine units could become involved in an offensive effort. Finally after approximately two hours it was time to terminate the meeting and allow various attendees to board Mike boats for transport to the ships to which they had been assigned. I closed the meeting by reminding everyone of the requirement to be innovative and creative, in executing a refugee evacuation mission of such large magnitude and one with no realistic existing precedent." Shaver Comments.

Labeled as Security Forces "Alpha" through "Delta," which matched their Marine Corps' designations, the rifle companies were distributed as follows:

Security Force "A" (Captain Harry Jensen, Jr.), *Durham*
Security Force "B" (Captain Robert T. Hickinbotham), *Frederick*
Security Force "C" (Captain Maurice O. V. Green), *Dubuque*
Security Force "D" (Captain Walter J. Wood), *Blue Ridge*

The Marine companies were reinforced by special evacuation teams including detachments of MP's, engineers, counterintelligence personnel, and interrogator-translators. Each attachment had a specific mission: the military policemen provided expertise in crowd control, searching procedures, and the movement of refugees once on board ship; the engineers aided in demolitions location and destruction; the counterintelligence personnel provided expertise on how to counter any sabotage and single out individuals suspected of being terrorists; and the Vietnamese interrogator-translator enabled communication with the refugees and, if necessary or desired, interviews.***

Once on board their assigned ships, the company commanders met with their respective ship's captains and formulated a plan for the embarkation, searching, and moving of refugees, and for the overall security of the ship. Each plan had unique characteristics, specifically tailored to fit the peculiarities of the ship. The threat of sabotage was very real and therefore these plans were in detail—specifying restricted areas on the ship, refugee billeting areas, screen and search areas, and movement routes. These detailed plans encompassed all of the varied methods of embarking evacuees.

Marines and sailors hastily trained to prepare for the anticipated mass of humanity. Crowd control, evacuation procedures, and a Vietnamese orientation course occupied the Marines' time on board ship. Counterintelligence personnel briefed Marines in the problems of identifying and neutralizing saboteurs. The interrogator-translator team gave a quick Vietnamese language orientation course. Key Navy and Marine Corps officers and senior enlisted men made walk-throughs of the evacuation chain. The versatile printing section on board the *Blue Ridge* reproduced thousands of signs in Vietnamese composed by the 17th

---

***Major James E. Livingston, operations officer for the Amphibious Evacuation RVN Support Group, recently recalled: "The engineers during the RVN Evacuation Force operations were utilized to conduct metal screening of Vietnamese for weapons and explosives. They utilized these (crude but effective) detectors very effectively in support of the 1st Battalion, 4th Marines detachments charged with ship security." Livingston Comments.

ITT. Captain Bushey's counterintelligence team prepared a simplified instruction card for the small unit leader that included basic Vietnamese phrases and human relations oriented "do's and don'ts." Preparation for this event was a total effort.[9]

On 3 April, the task force lay off Nha Trang. At this point, Colonel Alexander sent two UH-1Es aloft as a means of visually reconnoitering the coastline for refugees. He flew in the lead "chopper." The sight that greeted the airborne observers was incredible. Literally thousands of boats of every description loaded to the gunnels with refugees, were headed out to sea. Refugees on the larger craft were packed like sardines in numbers staggering the imagination. Keeping a safe distance from the shore, the airborne Hueys could see the semi-destroyed towns of Qui Nhon and Nha Trang where isolated fires dotted the landscape. The stage was set for a massive movement of panicked and fear-stricken refugees toward the ships that symbolized the last vestiges of freedom and a promise for safe haven, their most immediate need.

The next day, the *Durham*, with Security Force "A" on board, received the first group of refugees while off the coast of Cam Ranh Bay. They came slowly at first; cold, hungry, and fearful. Their numbers then rapidly increased until a priority for receiving craft had to be relayed to the refugee flotilla by interpreters. The process of evacuation, with some initial rough spots, went smoothly enough and the *Durham* took on board almost 4,000 Vietnamese. Next the *Frederick* and the *Dubuque* made preparations to receive refugees. *Frederick* pulled in relatively close to the port of Cam Ranh Bay, and its Marines and sailors watched intently as the South Vietnamese naval base fell before their eyes. After the North Vietnamese Army's tanks rolled over their opposition, they began firing at the South Vietnamese Swift boats.* The proximity of these tanks, visible to everyone on the ship, justified a quick withdrawal and a temporary cessation of evacuation operations. Meanwhile, *Dubuque* began accepting refugees into her well deck. One unusual sidelight of this effort was gleaned from interviews with the evacuees. In preparation to receive the refugees, the *Dubuque*, an LPD, ballasted down (filled with water) to provide a water access by which the small craft could enter the ship's well and navigate all the way to the loading ramp. The refugees mistakenly interpreted the ballasting down as the slow sinking of the ship and naturally were reluctant to leave their overcrowded but otherwise seaworthy vessel for one that was "sinking."[10]

At this point in the operation, the task force received a message that impacted both on the operations at hand and the long-term mission of the security force. It learned of the Joint Chiefs of Staff decision to place Marine security forces on board Military Sealift Command (MSC) ships. The Marines of the Amphibious Evacuation RVN Support Group, already involved in the Navy's evacuation effort, had been chosen to assist the MSC ships, besieged with more refugees than they could handle. One of the primary considerations of the Joint Chiefs of Staff, and a commitment they could not ignore, Cambodia, still held first priority for the Seventh Fleet and III MAF. Worse yet, new developments in and around Saigon did not bode well for the continued life of the Vietnamese government. This alarming development meant Seventh Fleet amphibious shipping might be needed to respond to two events simultaneously. The decision to release the task force from refugee operations and move the Marine security force to MSC ships reflected senior military commanders' recognition of the dilemma facing American forces in the Western Pacific in early April 1975.

As the battlefront conditions worsened for America's allies in South Vietnam and Cambodia, it became painfully obvious that the United States was faced with innumerable uncertainties and too few solutions. Events in the Western Pacific were converging at breakneck speed, producing a seemingly unavoidable crisis. Clearly, the United States was taking decisive action to deal with the crisis, but it was impossible to determine if those steps would be enough.

Recognizing this state of affairs, the commanding general of III MAF, General Hoffman, prepared for the worst-case situation. Having only six infantry battalions available, with one, 2d Battalion, 4th Marines, already committed to Operation Eagle Pull, he decided to increase the number of battalions available for deployment by relieving, as soon as possible, the 1st Battalion, 4th Marines of its ship security duties. Once replaced by another contingent of Marines, the battalion would be reorganized and redesignated BLT 1/4.

---

*Designed by the Louisiana-based Stewart Seacraft Company, the United States sent 84 Swift boats to South Vietnam prior to 1967 to augment the VNN's Coastal Surveillance Force. These 50-foot craft armed with .50-caliber machine guns and an 81 millimeter mortar could attain speeds in excess of 20 knots. Edward J. Marolda and G. Wesley Pryce III, *A Short History of the United States Navy and the Southeast Asian Conflict, 1950-1975* (Washington: Navy Historical Division, 1984), p. 46.

Pioneer Commander *awaits refugees in the South China Sea during April 1975. Sister ship,* Pioneer Contender, *received a Marine security detachment on the night of 4 April.*

As a result of this decision, General Houghton ordered the 3d Marine Division to constitute a series of specially configured ships' security detachments to replace the 1st Battalion, 4th Marines.[11]

General Houghton published a letter of instruction to his division in which he designated specific regiments and certain battalions to form these detachments and prepare them for deployment. Fourteen days would pass before they would be activated and ordered to replace the Amphibious Evacuation RVN Support Group. In the intervening two weeks, the 1st battalion, 4th Marines continued as the evacuation security force. During that delay, the decision to move the Marines to Military Sealift Command ships was implemented.

On the evening of 4 April, the security force received its first call for assistance from an MSC ship. Company B on board the *Frederick* received orders to place a reinforced Marine rifle platoon on board a distressed Military Sealift Command ship, the SS *Pioneer Contender*. The platoon, commanded by Second Lieutenant Robert E. Lee, Jr., was assigned this difficult task with minimum notice in less than ideal conditions. The SS *Pioneer Contender*, fully loaded with refugees and steaming south from Cam Ranh Bay enroute to Phu Quoc island, had no prior notice either.

Having started its journey in Da Nang where it embarked thousands of panic-stricken refugees from that devastated city, the *Pioneer Contender* never established control of its passengers. The ship's captain, fearful of a complete breakdown in order and discipline, sent out a call for assistance. His urgent request translated into Lieutenant Lee's orders to prepare to disembark.

As night settled over the coast of South Vietnam, Lieutenant Lee and his platoon, reinforced with one interpreter, a machine gun squad, and two corpsmen, went over the side of the *Frederick* and down the wet net. For most of these young Marines, this was their introduction to amphibious-related operations, made more memorable by the seemingly tiny LCM-6, bobbing and pitching in seas so wild that all refugee operations had been cancelled. From this start, there followed a harrowing ride in complete darkness and swelling seas to a slightly, but only slightly, more stable platform, the *Pioneer Contender*. Lieutenant Lee and his men, each laden with 50 pounds of equipment and consumables, made a precarious ascent up a jury-rigged Jacob's ladder suspended from the leeward side of the ship's stern. Following this feat, the Marines struggled to the ship's superstructure, totally oblivious to the teeming mass of refugees, nearly invisible in the dark. After a quick orientation by the ship's

THE EVACUATION OF SOUTH VIETNAM'S NORTHERN PROVINCES

Department of Defense Photo (USN) K107611

In the background is the USNS Greenville Victory *which was hijacked for a change of course to the mainland by disgruntled refugees who were actually deserters from MR 1. In the foreground is an LCM-8 from USS* Durham *used to ferry evacuees between MSC ships.*

master, Lieutenant Lee surveyed the situation and in a classic understatement, reported to the task force commander, "7,000 on board, everything under control." There were in fact almost 16,000 on board and insufficient food and water to sustain them. Many of the refugees were armed and the threat of a hijacking very real. The day before, under similar circumstances, armed refugees, most of them former military men, seized control of the USNS *Greenville Victory* and ordered its captain under penalty of death to alter its course and take them to the mainland. After steering a direct course for Vung Tau, the mutiny ended when the hostile passengers disembarked allowing the hostage captain to regain control of his ship. The *Greenville Victory's* hijacking reminded everyone of the dangers inherent in transporting refugees and what fate could befall a complacent commander.[12]

The *Pioneer Contender's* journey had begun nearly a week earlier when it picked up its first refugees in the Da Nang area. On 29 March, it sailed from that port but continued to pluck people from the sea as it made its way south along the coast. Its destination, Phu Quoc (a small island off the west coast of South Vietnam in the Gulf of Thailand), had been chosen by the Saigon government as the best location to receive and house evacuees from Military Regions 1 and 2.

A Marine from 1st Battalion, 4th Marines on board the SS Pioneer Contender *comforts a Vietnamese baby. The ship made two visits to Da Nang Harbor to pick up refugees between 29 and 31 March 1975, and after the second visit it sailed to Phu Quoc Island.*

Marine Corps Historical Collection

Department of Defense Photo (USMC) 10420075
A young refugee from MR 1 is befriended by a Marine of BLT 1/4, a member of Amphibious Evacuation RVN Support Group. Many BLT Marines went on board MSC ships during Operation Fortress Journey.

Phu Quoc's only claim to fame was that it was the home of a *nuc mam* (sauce made from fermented fish) factory. The government did not want the evacuees unloaded near any of the southern population centers for fear of touching off a panic.

Once established on board the *Pioneer Contender*, after a dramatic night arrival, Lieutenant Lee turned his attention to getting his vessel's refugees to Phu Quoc without any casualties. Lee's platoon of Marines would accomplish this objective by maintaining good order on the ship through a disciplined display of force. Throughout the trip south, the proper mix of strength and confidence calmed the passengers, enabling the Marines to control them despite numerous challenges, not the least of which was the wretched living conditions, typified by the ankle-deep human waste running over the decks.[13]

Time and time again, Lieutenant Lee and his Marines went forward to distribute food and water at locations predesignated by their interpreter. The Marines literally risked their lives each time they did this, because many of the refugees were starving and desperate. Just for one feeding, distribution throughout the ship was an all-day evolution, consequently causing many to fear that supplies would run out before their turn arrived. One incident pointed up the danger involved in the daily feeding routine. On that occasion, a group of Marines simply delivering the daily ration, was overwhelmed by the crush of refugees, instantly placing them in danger of being killed or seriously injured. A young Marine, Private First Class Charles P. Vidaurri, from his position in the superstructure, observed the commotion in the restless crowd and immediately delivered a burst of M-60 machine gun fire over their heads. This enabled the Marines on deck to restore order quickly and then finish distributing the day's food and water allocation. As each day seemingly grew longer in the hot sun, Lieutenant Lee used ever increasing amounts of warning fire to maintain order. He took the precaution of arming himself with a shotgun and told his platoon sergeant, Staff Sergeant Earle Livermore, a veteran of the Vietnam War, to do likewise. These precautions helped avoid the use of deadly force and the journey to Phu Quoc was completed without a casualty.[14]

Military Sealift Command Operations

Lieutenant Lee's deployment on board the SS *Pioneer Contender* marked a shift in operational priorities. The next day, 5 April, all embarkation of refugees on Navy ships ceased. (The amphibs did not get involved in evacuee transport again until the helicopter evacuations of Phnom Penh and Saigon.) The Navy ships now were free to maneuver as necessary. The restored mobility enhanced their participation in the evacuation by allowing them to locate additional refugees adrift at sea.

In this capacity, aircraft of HMM-165 conducted daily reconnaissance flights. At first, these flights covered only the Qui Nhon, Nha Trang, and Cam Ranh Bay areas, but eventually they ranged as far south as Vung Tau. Each flight observed the same thing—thousands of Vietnamese fleeing by boat from their homeland. On the coast, the North Vietnamese blitzkrieg was forcing those in its path to flee hastily, and as a result the seaborne evacuation could not keep pace with the flood of refugees. Recovery of these evacuees by the Military Sealift Command ships began off the coast of Cam Ranh Bay and within three days had moved south to Phan Rang and then Phan Thiet. Thus in less than a week, the evacuation effort had become one of scheduling and coordination: matching available Marine security forces with the numerous requests for protection made by commercial ships laden with starving and armed refugees.

This new use of Marines—as specially tailored, reinforced, platoon-sized security forces for Military Sealift Command's ships—required new planning. Each of the four rifle companies was broken down into three "security forces," task organized with support from the weapons platoon, medical section, engineers, military police, and interpreters. Two additional security detachments were formed out of various headquarters elements, as backups should they be needed. Various attached personnel—doctors, counterintelligence specialists, and some interpreters—were kept in a central pool to be used in general support. This security force structure was supported by ships of Task Group 76.8 and the helicopters of HMM-165. Each "force" was prepared to mount out with enough supplies to last a week.

In addition to the modifications in this force, the Navy reorganized Amphibious Ready Group Bravo. The reconstituted ARG Bravo consisted of the attack carrier, *Hancock* (CVA 19), the *Durham*, and the *Frederick*. The carrier *Hancock*, reconfigured as an LPH, served as its embarked squadron's (HMH-463) flight deck. The amphibious ready group, strengthened by the addition of the helicopter platform, prepared to embark Colonel Gray's 33d MAU. In anticipation of this reorganization, the *Durham* and *Frederick* transferred their embarked rifle companies to the *Dubuque*. This had to be done at sea in order to make room for the 33d MAU and still maintain the tactical integrity of the Amphibious Evacuation RVN Support Group. Crossdecking became a way of life for the Marines of the 1st Battalion, 4th Marines. Some made as many as four ship changes in a week, usually on a moment's notice.[15]

On 5 April, the evacuation flotilla positioned itself off the coast of Phan Rang. The 1st Platoon of Com-

Vietnamese refugees scramble down a cargo net to a barge manned by men of the 1st Battalion, 4th Marines who served as a specially tailored security force. In the foreground is tiny Pawnee, *which played a role throughout the evacuation of northern South Vietnam.*

Department of Defense Photo (USN) 1162058

The desolation of Phu Quoc island is reflected in this scene of the site selected to deposit thousands of MR 1 refugees. The island was known for its production of nuc mam *sauce.*

pany D led by Second Lieutenant Charles K. "Kenneth" Curcio was placed on board the SS *Transcolorado* (MSC ship) which was already loaded with approximately 8,000 refugees. Following embarkation of the Marines, the ship weighed anchor for Phu Quoc. Just before it got underway, the *Durham*, which had continued to pick up refugees as the amphibious force sailed southward along the coast, transferred its 3,500 people to the *Transcolorado*. This was only one of the many unstable, transient conditions.[16]

Almost overnight, control of the original task organization became decentralized. The success of the operation now depended upon the young platoon commanders' leadership skills and their Marines' expertise and judgement in the controlled application of force in crisis situations. Exercising restraint under some very adverse conditions, the Marine security forces achieved their goal despite the fact that they were on board ships scattered over a 500-mile area, from Phan Rang to Phu Quoc Island.

The organization of this task group, TG 79.9, was predicated on flexibility. In the space of 10 days, the task group's squadron, HMM-165, conducted numerous crossdecking troop lifts, provided airborne reconnaissance of the Vietnamese coast, and resupplied refugees with food and medicine. HMM-165 also performed "separate missions," including locating a C-5A flight recorder belonging to a U.S. Air Force transport which had crashed on takeoff from Saigon on 4 April while carrying hundreds of Vietnamese orphans and their American escorts.[17] A post-evacuation Air Force summary reported, "Early on the morning of 5 April, a crew member on the *Durham* heard the "Mayday" signal .... Directed to the vicinity of the signal, a Marine helicopter from the *Blue Ridge* spotted the recorder floating in the water and notified the *Reasoner* which had a swimmer on board."[18]

Also during this period, the helicopter squadron's staff began to draft detailed timetables to use in the event of the evacuation of Saigon. The maintenance problems inherent in a squadron consisting of four separate detachments conducting around-the-clock operations did not prevent Lieutenant Colonel Kizer's HMM-165 from maintaining a 100-percent availability rate throughout the dangerous and demanding ten-day period. Yet despite having every helicopter available, the task group soon discovered that its resources were stretched to the limit and it could not handle the seemingly endless supply of refugees.[19]

Its ability to evacuate the fleeing South Vietnamese was further confounded by the threat posed by the advancing North Vietnamese Army and the indecision of the South Vietnamese government. As one of the participants, Captain Charles J. Bushey, related in a letter to his wife, "I overheard one radio call late this afternoon asking Saigon where they wanted the refugees taken. Would you believe Saigon said they did not know where they could be taken?"[20]

Operating off the coast of Vietnam, the task force eventually deployed to the vicinity of Phu Quoc as evacuation efforts off Phan Rang and Phan Thiet ceased with the renewed North Vietnamese onslaught. The island of Phu Quoc offered the task group a new challenge. The group's arrival there coincided with the arrival of the Military Sealift Command's refugees.[21]

The events which had occurred earlier on board the *Pioneer Contender* overshadowed a less dramatic, but still important incident at Phu Quoc. No one there would take responsibility for unloading the refugees for fear they would riot and possibly kill South Vietnamese already on the island. Out of necessity, the Amphibious Evacuation RVN Support Group became heavily involved in this phase of the refugee operation, providing protection and an orderly transition. Marine security forces were on several Military Sealift Command ships in the harbor, and in each instance, Marine lieutenants led the reinforced rifle platoons protecting these vessels. They had full responsibility for their embarked refugee's welfare and that security extended to getting them safely to the island. This required maintaining close control of the evacuees until every last one of them had reached Phu Quoc.

Despite the apparent dangers involved in this task, the clearing of a ship represented a far easier challenge than the initial securing of a vessel. Each Marine unit

Three of the thousands of MR 1 refugees evacuated during the first 10 days of April 1975. Marines of BLT 1/4 and sailors of ARG Bravo conducted Operation Fortress Journey which lifted evacuees from the sea to MSC ships which then took them to Phu Quoc island.

Marine Corps Historical Collection

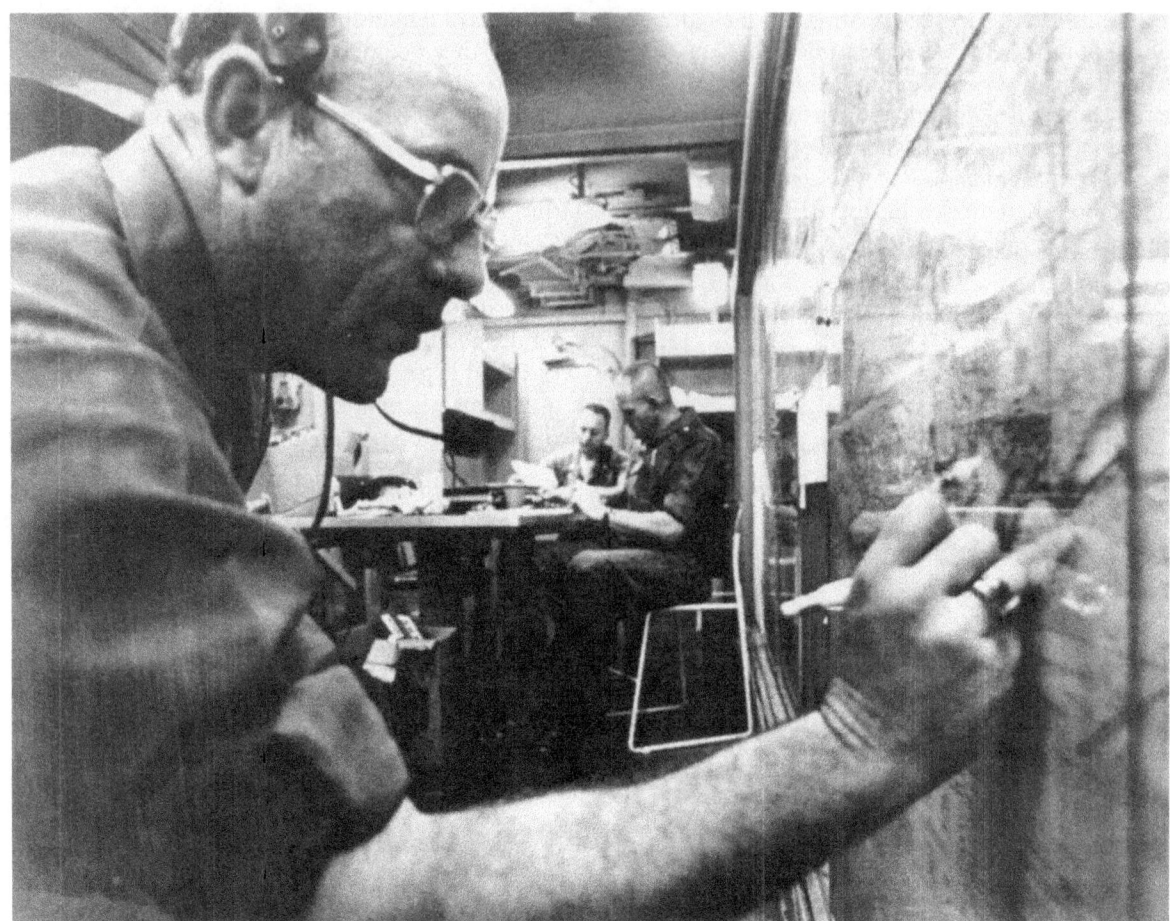

Photo courtesy of Col Carl A. Shaver, USMC

The staff of Amphibious Evacuation RVN Support Group lays plans for Operation Fortress Journey. Seated at rear are the commanding officer, LtCol Charles E. Hester, right, and the operations officer, Maj Carl A. Shaver, of the 1st Battalion, 4th Marines.

began its mission by entering a hostile environment with no prior intelligence or reconnaissance, always facing thousands of armed and starving people. Immediately after boarding, the Marines had to secure the ship's vital areas, establish law and order, and then and only then, could they begin the humanitarian work. While the *Pioneer Contender* was an extreme case, all the MSC ships with refugees on board were in distress. Each security force entered its respective ship prepared for combat with the armed refugees already on board. The expected deadly confrontation between the Marines and the evacuees never materialized, but the ever-present threat constantly demanded the security force's attention. In order to preserve human life and avoid major casualties, a delicate balance had to be established quickly through a prompt and solid show of force, tempered by good judgement and restraint. The first few hours on board each ship were the most critical and, as a consequence, the platoon commanders relied heavily on the expertise of the interrogator-translators. These highly trained Marines were responsible for communicating to the refugees the Marines' purpose. Having accomplished this, the interpreters then identified refugee leaders who could provide information on the internal situation, status of food, medical attention required, and potential troublemakers. Armed with this knowledge, the Marines then could respond more effectively to the evacuees.

The chaotic state of affairs in which the Marines of the Amphibious Evacuation RVN Support Group often found themselves was best reflected in Captain Bushey's diary entry of early April: "The scene here is tragic. There are thousands of people fleeing before the North Vietnamese. Many are being picked up by boat but as they are being evacuated, they have no place to go. As an example many have been fleeing since Hue fell weeks ago. First to Da Nang, then to Nha Trang, and finally Cam Ranh and Phan Rang. Some of the areas south of here are already in enemy hands. Only Saigon and some areas in the Delta are open. But the South Vietnamese do not want the refugees to come to Saigon. In fact at 2030 tonight, there are probably over 50,000 people on various ships with no place to go."[22]

Meeting the Needs

To assist the South Vietnamese government in resolving this crisis and mitigating somewhat the chaos, the United States had called upon the task force to provide for the needs of the thousands of starving refugees under its care. Food and medical attention were the most obvious areas and the Navy responded by providing large quantities of supplies which it had gathered from all over the Western Pacific. One of the most readily available supply sources was ARG Alpha, relatively nearby in the Gulf of Thailand and despite preparations for the impending evacuation of Cambodia, this force readily assisted in the massive effort to relieve the evacuees' suffering.[23]

Getting provisions into the hands of the Marine security force was one thing, distributing them to the refugees was quite another. Interpreters would announce the serving of meals and their designated distribution points. Armed Marines delivered the food to these locations where refugee leaders then helped distribute it. The sheer weight of numbers continued to present a problem, but this system relieved some of the pressure and, more importantly, made control of the crowds easier and food distribution safer because Marines were able to fulfill their role as security guards instead of acting as food servers.

Medical attention was another critical requirement. Each security force assigned to a ship had its own Navy corpsman. These overworked Samaritans were soon overwhelmed by the scale of the medical problems. To assist them, the doctors attached to the task group from 3d Medical Battalion were quickly pressed into service. Carrying as many medical supplies as could be spared, these doctors ran a traveling MedCap (Medical Civic Action Program) dispensing medical care while rotating between ships. They were confronted with every sort of medical problem; many refugees were simply beyond help, but most benefited significantly from this medical attention. Two Navy doctors, Lieutenant Richard Williams and Lieutenant John Oakland, worked around-the-clock, yielding eventually to exhaustion, but not before they had reduced substantially the amount of suffering.

Improvement of sanitary conditions was one of the major tasks undertaken by the doctors. Using Marines to assist them, the doctors organized the Vietnamese into clean-up squads. To rid the ship of filth and human waste, the Marines supervised the South Vietnamese and when the refugees had completed their part of the task, the Marines used the high-pressure, high-capacity waterhoses to blast the waste from the ship's deck.

There were many demonstrations of ingenuity, creativity, and compassion in dealing with the refugees. In one case, on board the *American Challenger*, the security force commander, Second Lieutenant Joe Flores, Jr., organized the South Vietnamese Army soldiers into a clean-up force. Using cooperation as a ticket off the ship, he was able to create an enthusiastic response. (In truth, all the refugees would get off the ship, but they did not know when or where, and as a consequence Flores could use this issue as leverage.)[24]

The total humanitarian and security effort of the task force involved the evacuation, control, and processing of well over 30,000 refugees. Operating from a command center set up on board the *Dubuque*, Major Carl A. Shaver, the battalion operations officer, coordinated and controlled all commitments involving the 1st Battalion, 4th Marines. Logistical support was a mammoth task of coordination handled by Captain William Harley, the S-4, who seemed equally adept at finding supplies, arranging transport of those supplies, and in anticipating new demands. One of his men, Lance Corporal Ricardo Carmona, an ammunition technician, literally lived in the well of the *Dubuque*. He remained on board throughout the operation, continuously breaking out supplies to support the evacuation.

HMM-165's noteworthy aviation support throughout this operation also was the result of a team effort. Despite the adverse effects from saltwater corrosion and high usage, the Marine maintenance crews and Navy supply clerks combined forces to achieve a remarkable record, no helicopters down for parts or maintenance.* Incredible under any circumstances, this achievement can only be attributed to closely coordinated teamwork. At the conclusion of this phase of the evacuation, when all of the refugees had finally

---

*Marine Corps aviation squadrons are supported chiefly by the Navy Supply System, from which they obtain their spare parts.

been unloaded at Phu Quoc, everyone in the task force knew that the challenge had been met and that they had taken part in a truly "all hands effort."[25]

With its work done at Phu Quoc, the task force returned on 10 April to the vicinity of Vung Tau where refugees were still arriving by boat. At this time, Colonel Alexander, formerly 9th MAB's chief of staff and most recently commander of the Marine security force (TG 79.9), reassumed his duties with Brigadier General Richard E. Carey's brigade and returned command of TG 79.9 to Lieutenant Colonel Hester. Evacuation operations then became the sole responsibility of Hester's 1st Battalion, 4th Marines.

As Lieutenant Colonel Hester prepared to assume command of the Amphibious Evacuation RVN Support Group, the news from Phnom Penh turned from bad to worse as friendly forces lost another battle to the Communists. Once again, events in that city dominated the minds of every military planner and operator. Barring another miracle, the Government of Cambodia faced certain defeat. Operation Eagle Pull would not be postponed again.

PART III
OPERATION EAGLE PULL

CHAPTER 7

The Evacuation of Phnom Penh

The Khmer Rouge—The Khmer Communists' Last Dry Season Offensive—The Marines Move into Position Final Preparations Ashore—Final Preparations at Sea—The Execution of Eagle Pull

---

The Khmer Rouge

Throughout the years of major United States involvement in South Vietnam, Cambodia was officially neutral. The nonbelligerent status was, however, a one-sided affair. Cambodian territory served as a vital link in the Ho Chi Minh Trail. Not surprisingly, Cambodia also became a convenient haven for North Vietnamese and Viet Cong (NVA/VC) forces worn out from the fighting in South Vietnam. Of particular importance to the North Vietnamese as sanctuary areas were the regions to the immediate west and northwest of Saigon. No change in these arrangements occurred until March of 1970 when a pro-Western coalition under the leadership of then-Marshal Lon Nol mounted a successful coup against the "neutralist" Prince Norodom Sihanouk. Marshal Lon Nol's coup created the Khmer Republic. The following month, U.S. and South Vietnamese forces launched an offensive into Cambodia, with the limited objective of destroying the NVA/VC sanctuaries. They focused their efforts in the Parrot's Beak region, the easternmost area of Cambodia that juts into the heart of southern South Vietnam, at its easternmost point only 50 kilometers from Saigon. As a fringe benefit, the offensive served to bolster the fledgling government in Phnom Penh. Struggling against an internal, Communist-dominated insurgency, Lon Nol's government welcomed such assistance.

The NVA forces, despite their longstanding differences with the Cambodians, supported the insurgent movement, and regardless of their ethnic differences, which occasionally erupted into open warfare, the North Vietnamese aided and even trained Cambodian cadres in North Vietnam. These cadres later joined those already in Cambodia. Their numbers grew to 60,000 hard-core guerrillas. Although their ranks contained a number of smaller factions, they collectively came to be known as the Khmer Rouge or Khmer Communists. Supplied with weapons from Communist China and the Soviet Union, the Khmer Communists for the most part lived off the land.[1]

During the first three years of its existence, the Army of the Khmer Republic was an ill-equipped band of soldiers. The Air Force and the Navy proved themselves to be the republic's elite forces. Yet despite its lack of equipment and funds, the Cambodian Army, called the FANK (Force Armee Nationale Khmer), was able, with U.S. air support, to hold at bay the better-trained, and initially better-equipped, Khmer Communists.[2]

The five-year conflict in Cambodia, like the war in South Vietnam, took its cues from the Southeast Asian weather. The southwest monsoon season annually inundated the lowlands adjacent to the government population centers, thereby effectively precluding or at least limiting any offensive action from June through December. During the dry season, January to June, virtually the same scenario occurred each year. At the start of each calendar year, the Khmer Rouge attacked the government enclaves, interdicted the lines of communication and attempted to draw sufficient Cambodian government forces from Phnom Penh in order to strike a mortal blow before the onset of another monsoon season. Neither side gained a clear upper hand during the first years of dry season fighting. Equilibrium was maintained in this see-saw battle of seasons by the American presence. U.S. air support provided the difference between victory and defeat for the Khmer Republic. It initially bought time for the government troops to improve their combat capabilities, particularly the government troops' fire-support coordination. American air support also allowed the Khmer Rouge time to improve, particularly in the area of coordinated offensive actions. Hampered by the confusion attendant to an army composed of diverse factions, the insurgents remedied their deficiencies through trial and error. As each new rainy season began, it became increasingly more difficult to ignore the ominous, inescapable fact that the Communists were gradually gaining control of the river and road network. As each new dry season came to a close, the noose around Phnom Penh shrunk ever tighter.[3]

To address this issue, the U.S. Congress sent a fact-finding commission to Cambodia in April 1973 to determine if continued American aid was warranted. Two of the Congressional staff members who made the trip, James G. Lowenstein and Richard M. Moose, authored the report to the chairman of the Subcommittee on

Photo courtesy of Col Peter F. Angle, USMC (Ret)

Various types of transport aircraft are parked on the ramp of Pochentong airfield while a UH-1 helicopter approaches the airfield. Pochentong was the heart of the resupply effort which sustained Phnom Penh when the Khmer Rouge laid siege to the city in 1973.

U.S. Security Agreements and Commitments Abroad, Senator Stuart Symington of Missouri. In it they stated that "the immediate concern of U.S. officials [in Cambodia] was simply to find a way to insure the government's survival and . . . to achieve that immediate objective the United States had greatly increased U.S. air operations in support of Cambodian government forces . . . ." Moose and Lowenstein contended that the fighting would not stop because there was ". . . no indication that the Khmer insurgents . . . and their North Vietnamese supporters were interested in a cease-fire" and even if they did ". . . eventually agree to a cease-fire they [would] insist on a role in the government, a cessation of U.S. air operations and either tacit or formal acquiescence to continued North Vietnamese transit of Cambodia in support of their forces in South Vietnam." These words sent arrows through the hopes of those who had been seeking to arrange a truce in Cambodia similar to the one concluded at Paris for the war in South Vietnam. Cambodia represented a key piece in the Nixon-Kissinger attempt to bring peace to Southeast Asia. The Moose and Lowenstein conclusion would have far-reaching consequences: "Thus, in the last analysis the key to a cease-fire may be Phnom Penh's willingness to accord the insurgents a role in the government. If the military situation should continue to deteriorate, however, Lon Nol and his colleagues may have no choice but to accept a cease-fire on whatever terms their opponents set."[4]

On 29 June 1973, two months after the senators received the report, Congress placed a rider on the 1974 budget bill requiring a halt to combat air operations in Southeast Asia. The Case-Church Amendment would prove the staff report's assessments correct: without U.S. air support the Cambodian government could not survive and if Cambodia ceased its struggle with the Communists, South Vietnam would face its worst fear, North Vietnamese troops on its flank with no U.S. air support. In the words of the South Vietnamese military and civilian officials with whom Lowenstein and Moose talked, ". . . if this possibility [Cambodia out of the war] were to materialize, South Vietnam would be faced with a serious if not untenable situation on its western flank." Few suspected at the time of the conversation that nothing but a total cease-fire in Cambodia would remove U.S. combat aircraft from Indochina. They were wrong. The Case-Church Amendment and subsequent Congressional appropriations bills removed U.S. combat aircraft from Southeast Asia, permanently.[5]

On 15 August 1973, the day the congressionally mandated halt to air support went into effect, the Cambodian government forces began a slide into oblivion. With each new day of fighting, the struggle became increasingly more violent. The already heavily congested population centers overflowed with new refugees fleeing the advancing Communists. The insurgents held over 80 percent of the countryside, but controlled only 35 percent of the population.

Interdicting the highways, the Khmer Rouge eventually controlled all but two of them. The fact that only two reliable routes of supply into Phnom Penh remained—by air into Pochentong airfield or by ship or barge via the Mekong River and the South China Sea—meant the life of the Khmer Republic hung in the balance. In jeopardy were the government-controlled province capitals which were being resupplied by the numerous "fly anything, anywhere, anytime" airlines operating from Pochentong Airport. Flying supplies in Bird Air Company aircraft (a U.S. contract airline) through Pochentong not only added considerable cost to the supply process, but also significantly reduced the probability of delivery. Under these difficult conditions, the continued survival of the outlying towns was doubtful and, at best, extremely tentative. Day-to-day existence now depended upon Phnom Penh's air and river resupply system.[6]

Thus, almost by default, the Mekong River, always a significant part of Cambodia, took on even greater importance. Navigable year round by coastal steamer and barge from Phnom Penh to the South China Sea, the river became the country's lifeline. As the Communists strenghtened their hold on the overland lines of communication, including the LOC linking Phnom Penh with the country's only seaport, Kompong Som, and with aviation support becoming more costly and inconsistent, the Mekong River became the only practical means of supplying the government forces and feeding the swollen population centers. Even rice grown in western Cambodia was supplied to Phnom Penh by way of the Mekong. Because the Communists controlled the highways, the Cambodians first shipped the rice to Thailand where it was loaded on ships bound for Phnom Penh.[7]

At least weekly in the South Vietnamese port of Vung Tau, Mekong convoys formed for the journey to the Cambodian capital. They were comprised of chartered coastal steamers and barges, laden with military supplies and civilian cargo of every variety. After a usually peaceful two-day journey through South Vietnam, they were met at the Cambodian border by Khmer Navy escort craft for the hazardous final day's steam to Phnom Penh. The FANK lacked the manpower to secure the 62 miles of riverbank stretching from the South Vietnamese border to Phnom Penh. It did, however, possess enough strength to provide sufficient strongpoints and fire bases along this dangerous portion of the waterway to enable them to deny the Khmer Rouge easy access to key chokepoints around river islands and narrows. The Cambodian Army reinforced this coverage with interlocking artillery fire.[8]

During the monsoon season the convoys were rarely threatened. The rains would inundate the foliaged river banks where the Khmer Rouge units always built their gun emplacements. As a consequence the flooding effectively neutralized the Communists' 12.7mm machine guns and rocket-propelled grenade launchers (RPGs) for nearly six months out of the year.

The Communist dry season operations of 1973 were successful in periodically interdicting the lines of communication into Phnom Penh. For a short period, all supply routes were cut. In order to continue to block these lines, the Khmer Rouge had to mass its forces, and whenever the Communists did, they usually suffered heavy casualties. FANK counterattacks using U.S. close air support (until August 1973), effectively neutralized the massed Communist forces. Whether the same Khmer Rouge tactic of massing its forces would have worked in 1974 remains a matter of conjecture. The Communists in 1974 altered their tactics. Instead of concentrating their forces in an effort to break or block the lines of communication into Phnom Penh, the Khmer Rouge attempted to terrorize the capital with artillery fire and 107mm rockets, principally the latter. It appeared for a while that these attacks by fire against the civilian population would succeed. But once again the Cambodian Government confounded the experts and the capital held.[9]

That dry season came to a close in June 1974 with the Khmer Rouge still maintaining a tight stranglehold on Phnom Penh, but without a victory. By not attempting to block the river in 1974, the Khmer Rouge gave the Lon Nol government at least another year's longevity. An inference could be made that because of the mauling the Khmer Rouge units received during the 1973 campaign, their manpower resources were insufficient to mount an offensive on the same scale in 1974. Regardless of the reason, the Cambodian republic had weathered another storm and the symbol of its strength, Phnom Penh, still housed the American Embassy and its staff.

The Khmer Communists' Last Dry Season Offensive

The Khmer Rouge opened their 1975 offensive on the last day of 1974. The Lon Nol government had expected a resumption of hostilities sometime in January of 1975 and the Communists did not disappoint them. The Khmer Rouge attack on 31 December seemed to be right on schedule. It immediately ex-

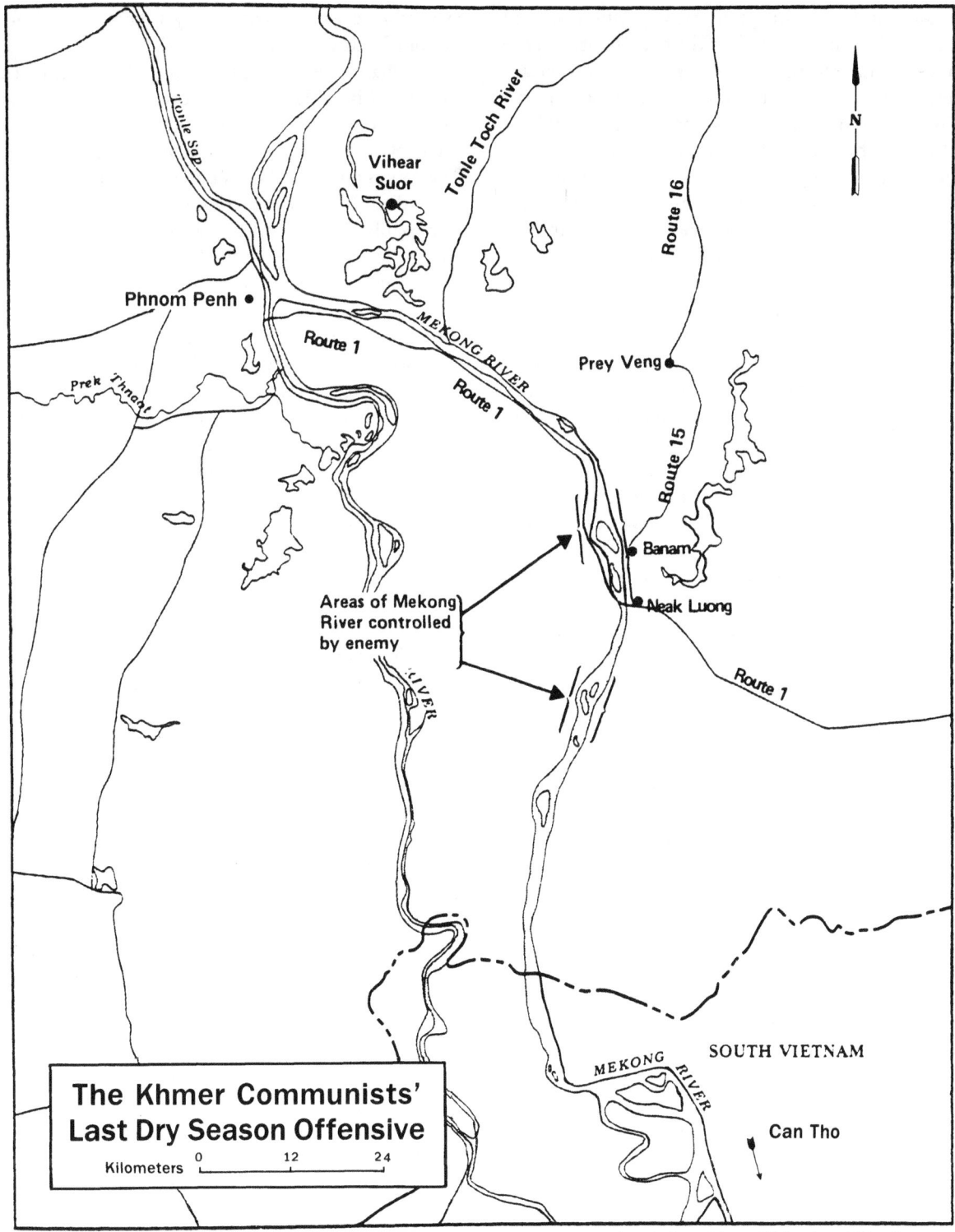

erted pressure on the government positions in and around Phnom Penh, and on the cities located in the surrounding provinces. At first glance, the attack seemed to indicate that nothing had changed in the Communist plan. Capture of the capital was still the ultimate objective and all offensive efforts centered around that purpose. Then gradually over the next few days subtle changes began to emerge. As combat activity intensified, government outposts guarding the Mekong River supply line also came under fire.

On 12 January, the Communists attacked Neak Loung, strategically the most critical outpost, located 38 miles downriver from Phnom Penh. Fighting escalated in the battle for the town, for its loss would seriously jeopardize and possibly end resupply by river.[10]

The vital convoys using the Mekong to transit from South Vietnam to Phnom Penh quickly began to feel the effects of the escalation. They suffered from ever-increasing amounts of ground fire directed at them from the riverbanks. During the third week of January, two small convoys reached Phnom Penh. The ships had suffered considerable damage from insurgent fire received during the 62-mile trip from the Vietnamese border to the capital. On 27 January, two tankers and five ammunition barges made it to the docks of Phnom Penh. These ships, the only ones of a 16-vessel convoy to survive the deadly fire incurred during their journey up the Mekong, bore battle scars attesting to the feat. Their superstructures and hulls displayed marks caused by rockets, bullets, and shells.

While the river outposts and convoys endured this harassment, the Communists subjected Phnom Penh and its vital Pochentong Airfield to rocket and artillery fire. Although the volume was considerably less than that experienced during the 1974 offensive, it seemed to confirm that once again a frontal assault on Phnom Penh would serve as the centerpiece of the 1975 offensive. Gradually, the Lon Nol government realized that this assessment was incorrect. The Communists had intentionally reduced the amount of artillery and rocket fire directed at Phnom Penh. The Khmer Rouge had aimed its latest offensive not at the capital, but instead at its supply lines. Specifically, the Communists had decided to attack the convoys which carried 80 percent of the city's supplies. Siege warfare had returned.

To the government forces a siege did not seem to offer a serious threat because since the short-lived Communist interdiction of 1973, at least three river convoys had always reached the Cambodian capital in any one-month period. Unfortunately, the government experts were wrong. The convoy which limped into Phnom Penh on 27 January would be its last.

Less than a week later, the Khmer Rouge inflicted the mortal blow. Returning empty to South Vietnam from Phnom Penh, a convoy of supply ships struck a minefield, sown days earlier by Cambodian insurgents. The explosions ripped the ships apart creating a scene of death and destruction which literally made the river impassable. Thus 46 miles from Phnom Penh, in the vicinity of Phu My where the Mekong narrows to gain its strength before a long journey to the sea, a weakened and hungry Khmer Republic suffered a casualty from which it would not recover. The Communists had ended resupply by convoy.[11]

The laying of mines across a river in and of itself could not have ended convoy resupply. Minesweeping offered an excellent means by which to counter this threat and eliminate the potentially damaging effects of a blockade. Yet in this instance Cambodia became the exception, not the rule, because sweeping the Mekong of mines presented the Cambodian Navy with a formidable task. Normally a complex and dangerous maneuver, Communist control of the riverbanks made minesweeping nearly impossible and, at best, very costly. The Republic's navy did possess a limited ability to sweep minefields, but the Khmer Rouge's use of command-detonated mines significantly reduced that marginal capability. The method of sweep used to eliminate these type mines entailed dragging the river's shallow water near its banks. This action would expose the command wires, allowing them to be severed. Once the wires were cut then the mine could be disarmed. In order to conduct this type of minesweeping operation, it was necessary to have control of the areas adjacent to the river. Without it, the minesweeping forces risked the prospect of being blown out of the water or captured. Neither option was a tactically sound alternative. Left with few choices, the government forces discontinued minesweeping operations. This decision guaranteed the convoy operators an extremely hazardous and nearly impossible journey. The sunken supply ships at Phu My stood as a stark testament to the futility of trying to run the blockade.

The ensuing government attempts to reopen the river only served to diminish its forces and were too little, too late. The isolated garrisons throughout the countryside, already seriously undermanned, suffered additional losses when many of their men were redeployed and ordered to join the battle to keep the Mekong open. Not only did these actions weaken the garrisons, but the force constituted to conduct the counterattack was so meager that its attack did not even disrupt the Communists' defenses, let alone overrun them.

On 17 February, the Cambodian Government gave up its effort to reopen the Mekong supply line to Phnom Penh. By the end of the month, the government forces controlled only a small segment of the river. The rebels held all of the Mekong except for a small area in the vicinity of Banam, and the adjoining naval base at Neak Loung, a major military facility and strongpoint, less than 40 miles south of the capital. Daily, these two outposts, now isolated, felt the pressure, enduring repeated attacks from the insurgent forces.[12]

With Phnom Penh under siege, the Khmer Rouge stepped up its attacks. On 5 March, the rebels for the first time effectively used artillery to attack Pochentong Airfield. Until then, they had missed their mark, but on this day their artillery barrage hit and slightly damaged an American aircraft. The plane had just completed ferrying rice in from South Vietnam, providing the Cambodians with a much needed resupply of food. Ten days later, the FANK recaptured the town of Toul Leap, northwest of Phnom Penh. While under their control, the Communists had used Toul Leap as a location from which to shell Pochentong Airfield. Its recapture, if only temporarily, ended the shelling. During the remainder of March, the Khmer Communists continued to increase the pressure on Phnom Penh, particularly in the sectors north and west of the city. These attacks again placed the airfield in jeopardy, which allowed the rebels to interdict by fire the daily supply flights.

Government forces tried but could not stop this new phase of shelling. Consequently, the Communists fired at the exposed airdrome almost at will. On 22 March, they fired rockets at two American supply planes forcing the Embassy to announce the following day that the airlift of supplies would cease until the military situation around the airport improved. Apparently recognizing the conflict of objectives contained in this announcement, the United States resumed the airlift two days later. Instead of improving the situation, the 48-hour suspension of flight activity had had the opposite effect. The Khmer Rouge, instead of waiting for the government forces to follow the American advice and counterattack, went on the offensive. Rather than fall back, they instead made significant ground gains in the vital northwest sector near Pochentong Airfield. The acquisition of this objective by the Communists took on added importance because of its strategic location. When last under their control, this vantage point had served as the location from which the rebels had mounted their most successful rocket attack on the airfield. It would again.[13]

Despite this fact and possibly because of it, the U.S. increased the number of daily airlifts to Phnom Penh. To avert final disaster and defeat due to a lack of supplies, the United States added three DC-8s to its fleet of C-130s. Bird Airways, a private company under contract to the American government, operated the C-130s and the airlift. The addition of three more aircraft enabled Bird Airways to double its daily flights from 10 to 20. By this means, the Cambodian Government's minimum daily resupply requirements were met.

The increased effort of the American airlift notwithstanding, it became painfully obvious to all concerned that if the Khmer Republic was to survive, the Mekong had to be opened. Resupply by air would not ensure success, because each flight encountered an ever-increasing volume of rocket and artillery fire, making the entire process too costly and extremely vulnerable. Any remaining vestiges of hope that the republic would weather another wet season ended on the first day of April 1975.[14]

On that Tuesday, the insurgents overran the only remaining government strongholds on the river, Banam and Neak Loung. Almost immediately the sagging morale of the government forces plummeted, knowing that the five enemy regiments previously engaged at Neak Loung were now free to attack them in Phnom Penh. As these units moved north towards the capital, the Cambodian Government simply waited for the inevitable while the American Embassy waited for the Marines, who themselves had been waiting since the first week of 1975.

The Marines Move into Position

Beginning on 6 January 1975, the United States had reacted swiftly to the Khmer Communist offensive. That Monday morning, CinCPac, Admiral Noel A. M. Gayler, via CinCPacFlt, Admiral Maurice F. Weisner, directed Commander Seventh Fleet, Vice Admiral George P. Steele, to place the 31st MAU/ARG Alpha in an increased state of readiness in anticipation of executing Operation Eagle Pull. Admiral Steele ordered the MAU and ARG Alpha to assume a 96-hour response time to the Gulf of Thailand and Kompong Som, Cambodia. The following day, Lieutenant Colonel James L. Bolton's HMH-462 was alerted for deployment to Subic Bay to replace Lieutenant

Photo courtesy of Capt Russell R. Thurman, USMC (Ret)
Col John F. Roche III, 31st MAU commanding officer, awaits orders to execute Operation Eagle Pull. The MAU ground combat element departed the Okinawa *on board HMH-462 helicopters at 0607 on 12 April to provide security for the Phnom Penh evacuation.*

Colonel Dwight R. Allen's HMM-164 on board the *Tripoli* (LPH-10). On 8 January, HMH-462's 16 CH-53s flew to Cubi Point adjacent to Subic Bay by way of Taiwan Air Force Base, Taiwan, from Marine Corps Air Station, Futema, Okinawa. The 31st MAU was reconfigured once again with a "dry season" mix of helicopters for the pending evacuation (heavy CH-53s, vice medium CH-46s, providing greater lift capability and range in the event of an evacuation). While the "heavy haulers" were enroute, BLT 2/4 moved back on board ship from the MAU camps at Subic. The 31st MAU/ARG Alpha was prepared to get underway should the situation in Cambodia deteriorate further, but with the *Okinawa* (LPH 3) inbound to relieve the *Tripoli* (LPH 10), the amphibious ready group remained at Subic. After completion of the turnover of LPHs on 28 January, ARG Alpha got underway immediately. The MAU's assignment was to respond to events in Cambodia and execute Operation Eagle Pull when directed. In order to accomplish this, the amphibious ready group with its embarked MAU had to operate within a 96-hour radius of Kompong Som. Underway and attempting to maintain the proper distance from Cambodia, *Okinawa* carried 14 CH-53s, 3 CH-46s, 4 AH-1Js, and 1 UH-1E from Marine Aircraft Group 36, all of them assigned to HMH-462.[15]

By the last week in January, Lieutenant General John J. Burns, USAF, Commanding General, USSAG, decided it was time to host another planning conference at his headquarters in Nakhon Phanom. Colonel Sydney H. Batchelder, Jr., the ground security force commander; Lieutenant Colonel Curtis G. Lawson, his air liaison officer; Colonel John F. Roche III, the MAU commander; and key members of the MAU staff attended the conference. In addition to these Marines, III MAF and 3d Division staffs sent representatives. With all of the key Eagle Pull commanders present, the conference allowed Colonel Roche and Colonel Batchelder, exercising overall operational control, the singular opportunity of discussing in detail the operation's timing, number of evacuees, use of landing zones, and the tactical situation in Phnom Penh. After an on-site reconnaissance of Phnom Penh, the Marines returned to their respective units except for Lieutenant Colonel John I. Hopkins who remained in Phnom Penh to assist on the Military Equipment Delivery Team, Cambodia, responsible for coordinating evacuation plans.*[16]

On 2 February, as the remainder of ARG Alpha steamed west toward the Gulf of Thailand, the *Peoria* (LST 1183) headed east, bound for the San Bernardino Strait and thence to the Trust Territory, Mariana Islands. Prior to its departure, members of BLT 2/4 went on board the *Peoria*. These elements included: Company E, commanded by Captain Matthew E. Broderick; the amphibian tractor platoon, led by Second Lieutenant Joseph C. Lotito; and elements of LSU 2/4. They were to participate in Operation Quick Jab II, a combined civic action-amphibious exercise on the island of Tinian during the period 9-15 February.[17]

The U.S. reaction to the Communists' mining of the Mekong placed the evacuation force in a higher state of responsiveness. On 6 February, Admiral Steele reduced the reaction time of the 31st MAU/ARG Alpha to 48 hours. The same day General Burns requested that the Eagle Pull command element report to his headquarters as soon as possible.

---

*Lieutenant Colonel Edward A. Grimm, the USSAG Plans Action Officer, recalled the normal routine at the end of each Eagle Pull planning conference: "The USSAG Eagle Pull action officer customarily took the new participants to Phnom Penh for an on-the-ground recon of the LZs and to meet embassy planners. The January 1975 on-site recon became particularly important as it included many who would become key players in the actual operation." Grimm Comments.

Colonel Batchelder's command group departed Kadena Air Force Base, Okinawa, at 0520 on 7 February on board a Navy T-39 aircraft, arriving at Nakhon Phanom at 1235 the same day. In addition to Colonel Batchelder and Lieutenant Colonel Lawson, the party included Major George L. Cates, III MAF liaison officer, and First Lieutenant James L. O'Neill, landing zone control team officer. The group brought with it PRC-75 and -77 radios and one piece of special equipment, a glide angle indicator light (GAIL). The GAIL was designed to enable helicopter pilots to land under conditions of reduced visiblity by adjusting their rate of descent and approach angle to a glide path indicated by the lights. The remainder of the command element, six Marine communicators carrying additional communications equipment, arrived at Nakhon Phanom on board a Marine KC-130 the next day. Shortly after arrival, an Air Force medic augmented the command element to provide a degree of medical assistance and expertise.[18]

While Batchelder's command element continued its preparations, the ARG, less the *Peoria*, began maneuvers off the coast of South Vietnam. On 20 February, the 31st MAU, with participating elements of BLT 2/4 and HMH-462, conducted HeliLEx 1-75. Designed to test HMH-462's ability to execute a helicopter employment and landing table (HEALT) specifically developed by Colonel Roche and his staff, this exercise produced excellent results and provided valuable experience. Based upon HMH-462's performance and its successful execution of the HEALT, the 31st MAU adopted the same helicopter employment and landing table for use in Operation Eagle Pull.[19]

Thinking that the Cambodian Government would at least weather the immediate crisis, the mining of the river, Admiral Steele relaxed the response time. On 22 February, he directed the Eagle Pull forces to assume a 96-hour posture. This permitted the amphibious ready group to return to Subic for minor repairs and replenishment and meet its LST, the *Peoria*.

The respite, however, was shortlived. In less than a week, as the fortunes of the Khmer Republic went from bad to worse, the response time was dramatically reduced. Effective 28 February, Amphibious Ready Group Alpha assumed a readiness posture of 24 hours which required a significant modification to its operating area, basically restricting it to the Gulf of Thailand. (These modified locations of the operating area acquired the acronym MODLOC.) For the ensuing 43 days, the Marines of the 31st MAU and the sailors of ARG Alpha became intimately familiar with the

Marine Corps Historical Collection

LtCol John I. Hopkins, pictured here as a major general, was in Phnom Penh from late January to April. He was a member of the Military Equipment Delivery Team Cambodia responsible for supporting and supplying the Cambodian government and its army.

term "MODLOC liberty" while the USSAG staff in Nakhon Phanom, when not preparing for the evacuation, pulled liberty in the "ville." Admiral Steele recalled his concerns with "MODLOC liberty": "It was a continuing worry to me that we had a MAU/ARG going in circles awaiting the execution of Eagle Pull. The amphibious ships were not designed to have so many active young men embarked for such a long time. The Marines needed exercise ashore whether that meant a liberty port or a training exercise. I kept pressing these considerations on all concerned."[20]

Although permitted liberty, the Marines in Nakhon Phanom found little time for recreation. They faced the demanding and time-consuming task of refining, in concert with their Air Force counterparts, the operational plans for both a helicopter and a fixed-wing evacuation of Phnom Penh. Although excellent in concept and thorough in preparation, the original plan lacked the details to make it completely current. During the draft stages as many as 18 separate courses of action were outlined for helicopter lifts alone. When these planners published USSAG/7AF OPlan 2-75 on 3 March, the helicopter courses of action had been reduced to four. The published plan for fixed-wing evacuation also listed four options. Both plans specified the use of three possible sources for ground security forces. Tactical air and fixed-wing airlift schedules listed the available ground forces: a 50-man Air Force security police detachment from the Seventh Air Force Security Police Squadron; two reinforced rifle companies from the 3d Division on Okinawa; or two reinforced rifle companies from 31st MAU. Helicopter planning factors were limited by the available assets: 12 Air Force CH/HH-53 aircraft at Nakhon Phanom and 16 Marine Corps CH-53 aircraft from the 31st MAU. In every scenario, the Marine command element, augmented by the Air Force Combat Control Team, was tasked to provide overall command and control of the activities at the evacuation sites.

At Nakhon Phanom, First Lieutenant O'Neil and Lieutenant Colonel Lawson conducted instructional training exercises for the Air Force helicopter crews in the use of the GAIL and standard night lighting and hand signals in the event night operations became a necessity. Additionally, the Marine officers in the command element visited Phnom Penh to confer with Embassy personnel and inspect designated landing zones.[21]

Two factors militated against the use of just one helicopter carrier and its 14 Marine helicopters and 12 land-based Air Force helicopters: First, the number of potential evacuees continually fluctuated. At

Col Batchelder and his command group at Ubon Air Base on 3 April, just prior to their insertion into Phnom Penh. They were the last to be evacuated from the city and rode to safety on Air Force HH-53s.
Photo courtesy of Col Curtis G. Lawson, USMC

times, the projected total exceeded the entire lift capability of the combined USAF/USMC helicopter inventory in Southeast Asia. Second, the contingency at first glance appeared to be a minimum time operation, but upon reexamination, the Eagle Pull command staff classified this assumption as fallacious. They decided that due to frequent and rapid changes in the tactical situation, the duration of the operation could not be determined. Despite unfavorable conditions and a lack of reinforcements, the Cambodians continued to hold the perimeter around Phnom Penh. With the United States determined to remain in Cambodia until the last possible minute, each day that the government forces successfully defended the capital guaranteed additional waiting time and another day on station for the relief force, 31st MAU/ARG Alpha. With the date of execution of the MAU's mission continuously being postponed, the need to create a helicopter-capable, relief/rotation force began to grow in importance. The concern centered around the fact that the only other ARG in the Western Pacific, ARG Bravo, did not possess a major helicopter platform.

On 16 March, as a result of these concerns, the Joint Chiefs of Staff directed that an aircraft carrier proceed to Subic Bay with a Marine heavy helicopter squadron embarked, and upon arrival, assume a 72-hour response posture for Operation Eagle Pull. The following day, CincPacFlt directed the *Hancock* (CVA 19) to unload sufficient Navy personnel and material to accommodate 16 Marine CH-53Ds and associated crewmen, supplies, and equipment, and proceed to Hawaii. Having unloaded the necessary equipment and men, *Hancock* departed Alameda, its homeport, on 18 March. Upon its arrival in Pearl Harbor on 23 March, *Hancock* received further guidance and more specific details on its new mission. Upon completion of the loading phase, the carrier received orders to sail as soon as feasible on or after 26 March at a speed of 20 knots with Subic as its destination.[22]

During *Hancock*'s 2,000-mile trip from the West Coast, Lieutenant General Louis H. Wilson, Jr., Commanding General, FMFPac, chose HMH-463, a heavy helicopter squadron of the 1st Marine Brigade, as the deploying unit. Commanded by Lieutenant Colonel Herbert M. Fix, the squadron embarked in the *Hancock* on 26 March and sailed for the Western Pacific. The wisdom of the decision to use the *Hancock* soon became apparent. At this point, the news from South Vietnam was progressively becoming worse with the latest reports revealing that the defense of the northern and central regions had collapsed. The ensuing chaos and panic had created a military and political crisis in South Vietnam, and as a result the available Western Pacific forces now had two contingencies with which to contend, possibly at the same time. With the *Hancock* steaming west and the situation in Vietnam deteriorating, Eagle Pull planners developed a fifth and final option for the fixed-wing plan.

Throughout the planning phase, the anticipated number and location of evacuees fluctuated. At one point in the planning cycle, 21 March, the Embassy forecast 3,600 refugees, a number far exceeding the original prediction of 400. In the event it became impossible or unfeasible to evacuate such a large number by helicopter, especially if the highly vulnerable Pochentong Airfield suddenly came under attack, an additional course of action had to be available. The fifth option, devised as a "worst case" version, served this purpose. It called for the use of fixed-wing, U.S. Air Force aircraft to effect the withdrawal. Under these circumstances, a ground security force large enough to secure the entire airfield would be needed. The extensiveness of the area to be secured would mandate the deployment of at least two battalions thereby making the event a multi-battalion operation. For this reason, on 26 March, the III MAF Commander, Major General Carl W. Hoffman, reactivated the 11th Marine Amphibious Brigade.[23]

General Hoffman selected Brigadier General Harold L. Coffman, Assistant Division Commander, 3d Marine Division, to be the commanding general of the 11th MAB. During December 1974, General Coffman had commanded the 9th MAB while participating in Operation Pagasa II in the Philippines. Upon being designated Commanding General, 11th MAB, he requested that several of the officers formerly assigned to his staff during that exercise be added to the newly constituted MAB's roster. The 3d Marine Division complied with General Coffman's request and temporarily transferred the designated officers to the 11th MAB. The newly assigned Marines quickly formed a planning staff, the nucleus of the new brigade. Staff agencies within the division headquarters readily provided administrative support to this nucleus of 10 officers.[24]

The planning for participation by the 11th MAB in the evacuation of Cambodia began immediately and the planners used the United States Support Activities Group/Seventh Air Force's Operation Plan 5060(C) as a blueprint. In the process, the MAB staff resolved the differences in assumptions, missions, and courses of action as they arose. The 11th MAB distributed its operational plan on 2 April as the combat activity in Cambodia reached a new level of intensity. To expedite matters and insure immediate delivery to prospective subordinates, the MAB issued the plan in message rather than standard, more formal, format.

As drafted, the planning concept contained a six-phase operation: Phase I—Movement to Ubon Air Force Base in Thailand on board Military Airlift Command aircraft; Phase II—Air assault movement to Pochentong on board Marine and U.S. Air Force C-130 aircraft; Phase III—Establishment of a defensive perimeter around Pochentong; Phase IV—Conduct of security and evacuation operations; Phase V—Withdrawal from Pochentong; and Phase VI—Return to home stations. The operation entailed the employment of Lieutenant Colonel Royce L. Bond's BLT 1/9, Lieutenant Colonel Robert E. Loehe's BLT 3/9, and forces from the 31st MAU (BLT 2/4 and HMH-462). The plan called for initial insertion of one BLT, 2/4, by HMH-462 helicopters in order to secure the runway at Pochentong. Immediately after the insertion, BLT 3/9, including its artillery battery, would be flown to Pochentong on board C-130 aircraft. The two battalions would then press outward establishing a security perimeter around the airfield complex. Evacuation operations would begin approximately 45 minutes after the initial landings. The helicopters would ferry evacuees from Phnom Penh to Pochentong to board C-130s for the flight to Thailand. An estimate of seven hours to evacuate and three hours to extract the security force made this operational plan a complex and involved process, requiring tactical Air Force aircraft on station over Pochentong and Phnom Penh. Additionally, the MAB's reserve, BLT 1/9, would be placed on call at Ubon Air Base, Thailand, for possible insertion should the situation dictate.

Precise timing was of the essence. Critical to the success of the entire plan was the air assault schedule developed by Major Martin J. Lenzini, the brigade air liaison officer, on loan from the 9th Marines. Major Lenzini, an A-4 pilot and former commanding officer of VMA-223, formulated a scheme of movement that meshed the flow of amphibious-based helicopters with a stream of fixed-wing transports. His objective was to achieve a maximum build-up of security forces at Pochentong in the shortest possible time. The complex, critical time-flow charts that he developed made this an exceptional plan.

Before the plan could be tested, its reason for im-

Department of Defense Photo (USMC) A50903
LtCol Royce L. Bond, commanding officer of BLT 1/9, right, attends a briefing with his executive officer, Maj Burrel H. Landes, Jr. BLT 1/9 served as the 11th MAB's reserve for the six-phase operation to evacuate Phnom Penh, cancelled three days after its 2 April inception.

plementation disappeared. Within two days, the perceived requirement for a major operation involving the 11th MAB had passed. Two factors weighed heavily in the decision to deactivate the 11th Marine Amphibious Brigade. First, the estimate of persons to be evacuated was decreasing daily. The aircraft resupplying the government forces had begun to speed this process by transporting increasing numbers of refugees on their outbound legs. The second reason hinged on the anticipated arrival of the *Hancock* and HMH-463. With the carrier and its embarked squadron only three days steaming time from the Gulf of Thailand, the addition of 16 transport helicopters now seemed a certainty, and so without a mission, the 11th MAB had no military purpose. Effective 0001 5 April 1975, CG III MAF deactivated it.[25]

Three days earlier on 2 April, in response to the further deterioration of the Cambodian government's defenses around Phnom Penh, Ambassador John Gunther Dean had requested the insertion of the Operation Eagle Pull command element into Phnom Penh. The following day, Colonel Batchelder and his group flew into Pochentong airfield. On 4 April, the United States brought in additional C-130s to speed the fixed-wing evacuation process. Simultaneously, the MAU/ARG Alpha assumed a six-hour response posture. During the week of 4 to 10 April, the additional flights extracted hundreds of Cambodians, former employees of the American Embassy. This massive removal of Embassy personnel left a staff of only 50 people to manage both daily business and the evacuation. On the positive side, it decreased the estimate of Cambodians awaiting evacuation to a much more manageable level and nearly eliminated the likelihood of using anything other than the helicopter option.[26]

As the Embassy, the Marines ashore, and the MAU prepared for that option, events in neighboring Vietnam forced ARG Bravo, on 9 April, to sail from Phu Quoc back to Vung Tau. Included in the amphibious ready group were *Durham*, *Frederick*, *Dubuque*, and the latest addition to the Western Pacific evacuation forces, the *Hancock*. Vung Tau, a peninsula in southern South Vietnam near Saigon, looked like it might become the site of the next major evacuation as thousands of South Vietnamese fleeing the Communist offensive took refuge there. Colonel Alfred M. Gray commanded the combat forces (the 33d MAU) designated to provide security should ARG Bravo be forced to conduct evacuation operations. The *Hancock*, the ship designated to support the evacuation of Cambodia using HMH-463, also carried other units of the 33d MAU including elements of Lieutenant Colonel Bond's BLT 1/9. Additionally, while in Subic, the *Hancock* had taken on board additional helicopters, CH-46s, UH-1Es, and AH-1Js, ferried to Subic by the USS *Midway* (CVA 41) expressly for the purpose of augmenting HMH-463 and 33d MAU.*[27]

On 10 April, in order to resolve the conflict in mission, CinCPacFlt detached the *Hancock* and HMH-463 from 33d MAU/ARG Bravo and passed operational control to 31st MAU/ARG Alpha. Late the following day, on 11 April 1975, the carrier rendezvoused with ARG Alpha in the Gulf of Thailand. Despite its late arrival, less than 24 hours before H-Hour, HMH-463 was ready for action.[28]

From the moment it left Pearl Harbor, the squadron had begun preparing for the operation. In particular, it made modifications to the aircraft to counter the effectiveness of SA-7 surface-to-air missiles. Maintenance personnel installed the ALE-29 flare dispenser

---

*The *Midway* had been ordered to the area in response to the growing crisis in South Vietnam. Enroute from her homeport in Yokosuka, Japan, to Subic Bay, Republic of the Philippines, the *Midway*, as it steamed past Okinawa, embarked the helicopters designated for transfer to the *Hancock*. Stationed at Marine Corps Air Station Futema, they joined Detachment 101 of VMCJ-1 already on board the *Midway*. Under the command of Lieutenant Colonel William A. Bloomer, the detachment consisted of two RF-4s and three EA-6s.

Marine crew of HMH-463 prepares their CH-53 Sea Stallion for Operation Eagle Pull. Since intelligence reports had indicated the presence of SA-7 surface-to-air missiles in Southeast Asia, the heavy helicopter receives a coat of infrared low-reflective paint.

and gave each CH-53 a fresh coat of low infrared reflective paint. The ALE-29 fired flares whose heat would attract, or at least confuse, the homing device of the heat-seeking SA-7. Adding paint to the fuselage reduced the infrared signal transmitted by the helicopter, and likewise decreased the probability of a "lock-on." As an additional means of distraction, the gunners carried flare pistols to fire at incoming missiles.

Lieutenant Colonel Fix also decided to use the crew concept. A specific crew was assigned to each aircraft. It flew together anytime its aircraft was launched. In this way, it developed into a tightly knit group, each member familiar with the others' techniques and ways of operating.*[29]

Final Preparations Ashore

Before departing from USSAG Headquarters for Phnom Penh after having received a request from the Ambassador for their immediate presence, the members of Colonel Batchelder's command element completed their final stage of planning for Operation Eagle Pull. Upon their arrival at the Embassy on 3 April, they reviewed and incorporated last-minute changes to the Embassy plan and then began preparing for the actual evacuation. From the outset, beginning with an immediate audience with Ambassador John Gunther Dean, Colonel Batchelder and his command element integrated themselves into the daily routine. They joined the in-country team and assisted it in the execution of the fixed-wing portion of the evacuation which began their second day in Cambodia. Many of the Embassy personnel had departed on earlier evacuation flights leaving a serious gap in the staff and the Marines quickly filled these positions paying particular attention to evacuation-related responsibilities. Lieutenant Colonel Lawson took charge of the evacuation operation at Pochentong Airfield. Coordinating the movement and manifesting of refugees at the airfield, Lawson's crew of Marines were subjected to 80 to 90 rounds of incoming fire a day. The Khmer Rouge treated the command element and one of its

---

*Brigadier General Richard E. Carey, the 9th MAB commander, recalled that "in spite of the detailed combat preparations of the unit [HMH-463] I was required on the night before the evacuation to certify in writing to Rear Admiral Whitmire that the squadron was combat ready and was capable of performing the mission." Carey Comments.

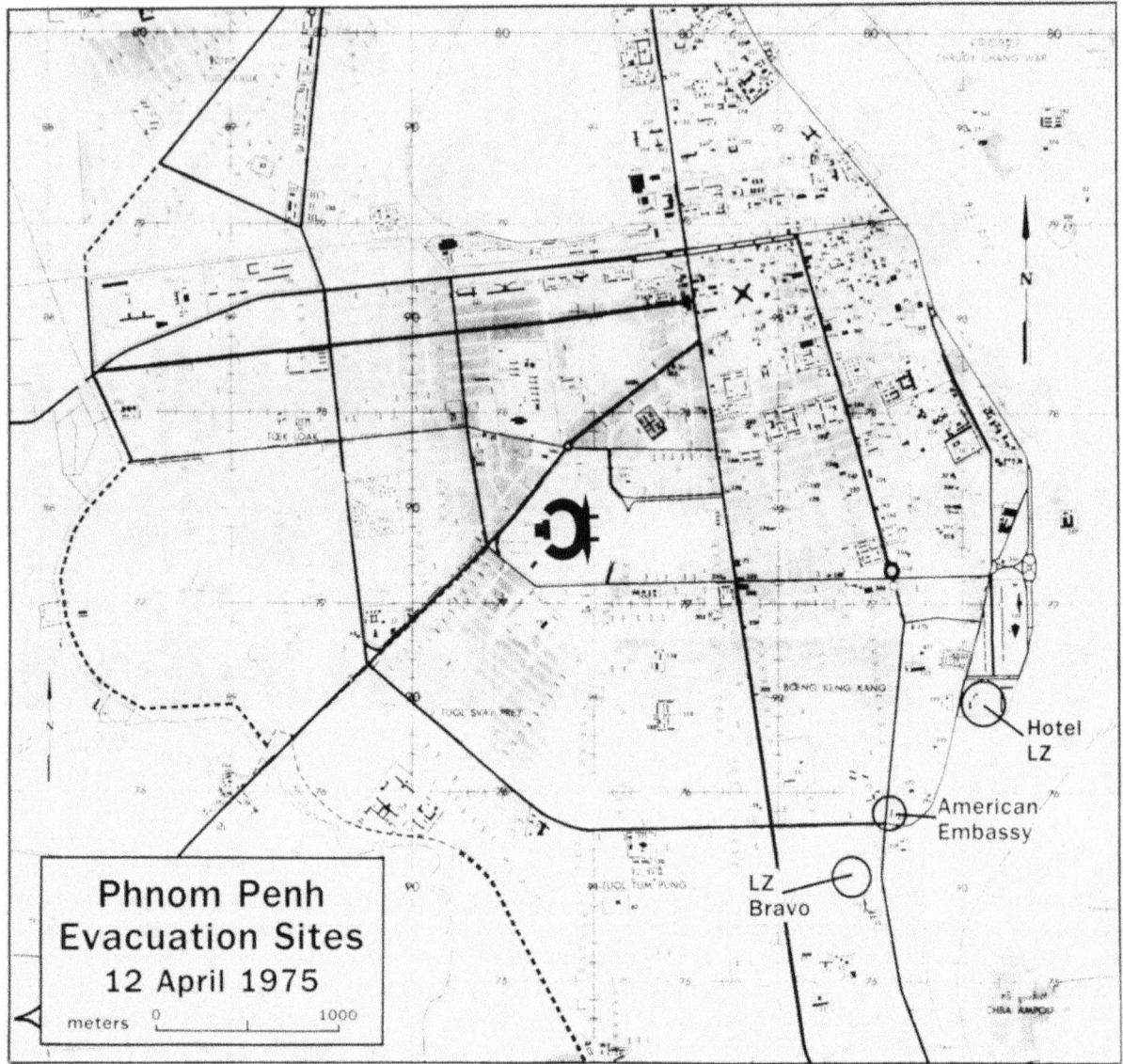

Phnom Penh Evacuation Sites 12 April 1975

members, upon arrival, to a taste of what their short sojourn in Cambodia would be like. The Communists offered Corporal James R. Osgood, Jr., a special welcome, a preview of the daily artillery bombardment he would endure while in Phnom Penh. As the last member of the command element to exit the Bird Air C-130 after an uneventful landing at Pochentong, Corporal Osgood witnessed close-up one of the incoming rounds as it landed between him and a bunker, his new home. Slightly distracted and somewhat surprised, he made it to safe haven without further incident.

Routinely, the rebels would fire 105mm and 107mm shells directly at the airfield, and whenever an aircraft materialized they would crank up the volume. Despite this treatment, all the incoming fire did not seem to bother Lawson's airfield Marines, especially Private First Class Daniel N. Catania. One of five radio operators, Catania proved unflappable under fire, providing continuous communication service. As the only American capable of speaking French, Private First Class Catania also passed instructions and directions to the evacuees, most of whom spoke no English.[30]

In the ensuing seven days, the week just prior to the helicopter extraction, Lieutenant Colonel Lawson's team processed through Pochentong more than 750 Cambodians. As a result of the very close relationship that developed between members of the command element and the Embassy staff, they encountered no problems in completing last-minute refinements and

Marine Corps Historical Collection

Acting Cambodian President Saukham Khoy arrives on the Okinawa. *President Lon Nol had left on 1 April after receiving an "invitation to vacation" with the Indonesian president.*

modifications to the plans for notification, assembly, and transportation of evacuees.

With each passing day, the situation at the airfield became less tenable. The Communists continued to press their attacks all around the city and with the insurgent reinforcements arriving from Neak Loung, the balance of combat power began to shift. The rebels controlled, uncontested, the eastern side of the Mekong, and by 10 April they so inundated the airfield with artillery fire that the United States ceased all fixed-wing evacuation operations.

With this option eliminated, site selection for helicopter landing zones dominated the command group's planning meetings. Acknowledging Communist control of the east bank of the Mekong River, the planners decided not to use the zone closest to the Embassy because of its proximity to the river. These LZs were situated on the Mekong's west bank. Instead, they selected, as a single landing site, Landing Zone Hotel, a soccer field about 900 meters northeast of the Embassy. Masked from the river by a row of apartment buildings, this LZ could not be interdicted by direct fire weapons, making it the safest location and thereby the best choice.

The Embassy personnel prepared to depart on 11 April, but instead delayed one more day. The decision to wait assumed as accurate and reliable the estimated arrival time of the *Hancock*. With its presence, the Marine Corps would have available HMH-463. Until this point, the planners had assumed only one Marine Corps squadron would be available and expected to employ an equal number of Air Force helicopters to have sufficient lift capability. The *Hancock's* arrival allowed a modification to this scheme of maneuver and consisted of using HMH-463 in the initial insertion and extraction phase while keeping the Air Force "53s" in reserve. In addition the Air Force helicopters could be employed as sea and air rescue. Planned use of these additional CH-53s also included adding them to the flow as necessary, and recovery of the command element.[31]

On the morning of 12 April, each member of the Embassy staff and the command element prepared for his specific evacuation task. At 0730, Ambassador

Photo courtesy of Capt Russell R. Thurman, USMC (Ret)

The Marine Security Guard Detachment from the American Embassy in Phnom Penh gathers after its evacuation to the USS Okinawa. *On 12 April, HMH-462 CH-53 helicopters removed the Marines led by GySgt Clarence D. McClenahan, standing third from left.*

Dean notified the acting Cambodian chief of state, Prime Minister Long Boret, and other Cambodian leaders including Sirik Matak, that the Americans would officially leave the country within the next few hours and inquired if any desired evacuation. All declined except for Saukham Khoy, successor to Lon Nol as president of the republic, who left without telling his fellow leaders.*[32]

The Ambassador then alerted designated Embassy personnel to marshal the preassigned groups. At this time, the command element proceeded to its station,

the landing zone. Each of the 10 members of the command group drove a vehicle to the landing zone. They parked them so as to block access to the zone from any part of the city, and then disabled them. The disabling process had to be done quickly and pulling the distributor cap was easy but rendering the tires unusable was not an easy task. Some way had to be found to flatten the tires without drawing attention by shooting them out. Major George L. Cates found the proverbial needle in a haystack when he located six valve stem extractors, seemingly the entire supply in all of Phnom Penh. Their value so exceeded their worth that Major Cates kept them in a plastic bag suspended from a chain around his neck until the moment of issue, Saturday, 12 April 1975. The vehicle which Major Cates drove had been designated as exempt from destruction, because of its accessory equipment. It was a pickup truck rigged with a winch and cable. It would serve as a means to remove from the landing zone any helicopter crippled by either enemy fire or a mechanical malfunction.[33]

The Embassy's Marine security guards, led by Gun-

---

*The Khmer Rouge executed both Long Boret and Sirik Matak within the next two weeks. On 20 April, the Communists physically removed Sirik Matak from the French Embassy where he had sought refuge, purposefully disclaiming it as French territory. Lon Nol, who with the help of Sirik Matak (his deputy prime minister), had overthrown Prince Norodom Sihanouk in March 1970, already had departed Cambodia. Under the guise of an invitation from Indonesian President Suharto to vacation with him on Bali, the ailing Lon Nol left Pochentong Airport at five minutes after noon on Tuesday, 1 April, with his party of 29, thereby escaping the Khmer Rouge bloodbath which followed the government's capitulation on 17 April. *Without Honor*, pp. 198-199 and 265-276.

THE EVACUATION OF PHNOM PENH

Marine Corps Historical Collection

Aerial shot catches three Marine CH-53D aircraft in LZ Hotel during Operation Eagle Pull. The last helicopter to leave arrived on the Okinawa *at 1214 on 12 April with Ambassador John Gunther Dean.*

nery Sergeant Clarence D. McClenahan, assisted the drivers in disabling the remaining vehicles which blocked off the southern accesses to the zone. This left only one road open for traffic, the highway leading directly from the Embassy to the airfield. With the zone's access secured by the vehicles, the command element turned to the next task at hand, setting up communications and laying out marking panels. Almost immediately, they established radio contact with "Cricket," the airborne command and control aircraft, and then they contacted "King Bird," the 56th ARRS HC-130 used to control the helicopters. Lieutenant Colonel Lawson provided "King" a landing zone brief and requested that he relay it to the incoming helicopters. By 0830, everything was in place awaiting the first elements of the 2d Battalion, 4th Marines whose similar preparations at sea would now merge with those ashore.[34]

Final Preparations at Sea

While the situation deteriorated in Cambodia, the 31st MAU continued its preparations at sea. The 3d of April, the day the command element landed at Phnom Penh, 31st MAU/ARG Alpha recorded its 34th consecutive day at sea. On station in the Gulf of Thailand during this entire period, the Marines and sailors of ARG Alpha expected to execute their mission each succeeding day. Despite the fact that each day ended without results, the anticipation of putting into practice their acquired skills kept the Marines' and sailors' morale high.

Teamwork and coordination would become the intrinsic elements of mission success or failure, and particularly in the aviation maintenance effort. The Navy supply system had to provide the necessary parts, and maintenance personnel had to install them properly or the number of available heavy helicopters would drop below the critical level. Should this occur, either the mission would have to be scrapped or Air Force helicopters would have to be substituted. By prestaging

LtCol George P. Slade, commanding officer of BLT 2/4, studies a map of Phnom Penh in preparation for Operation Eagle Pull. BLT 2/4 pacticipated in both Eagle Pull and Frequent Wind, providing security for evacuation of both capitals, Phnom Penh and Saigon.

Photo courtesy of Capt Russell R. Thurman, USMC (Ret)

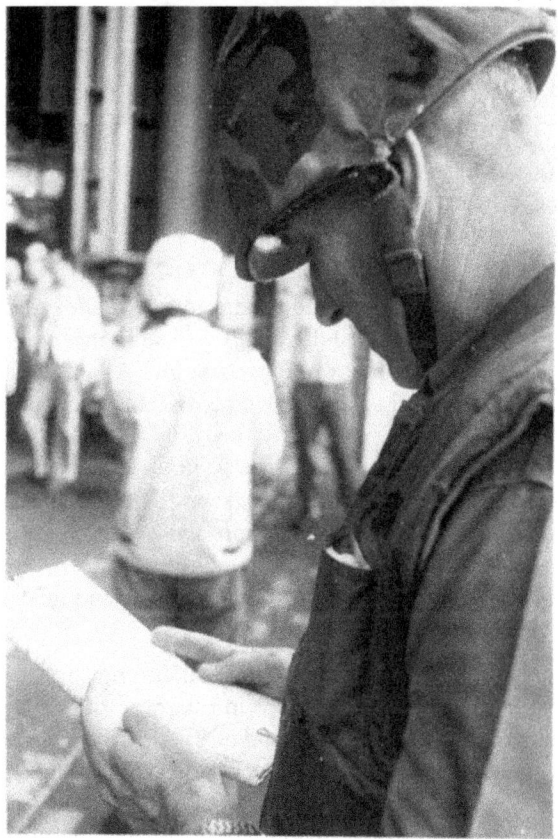

Department of Defense Photo (USMC) 07760875

Capt Thomas A. Keene, Commanding Officer, Company F, 2d Battalion, 4th Marines, briefs his men before embarking in HMH-462 helicopters to launch Operation Eagle Pull in Cambodia. Capt Keene and his Marines were located on the Okinawa *along with Company H, commanded by Capt Steven R. Bland.*

aircraft parts at Utapao Air Base for pick-up by ship's helicopters, the Navy assured vital spares needed to maintain the Marine CH-53s in top operating condition.[35]

This spirit of preparation and teamwork spilled over into other areas as well. Especially evident in the junior officers, this willingness to prepare for every eventuality manifested itself in the daily training programs which the officers, along with their NCOs, conducted. During these sessions, the small unit leaders disseminated enough information to keep the Marines appraised of the tactical situation and aware of their operational status. This continuous two-way exchange went a long way toward sustaining morale and maintaining an edge.[36]

The constant flow of information also meant continually changing data which in turn necessitated alterations in the final guidance. The helicopter employment and landing tables (HEALTS), developed months earlier by the joint effort of the squadron and battalion staffs, facilitated incorporation of last-minute changes and provided the ARG with much needed flexibility. This plan enabled the MAU to deliver to the operational area several different heliteam configurations. The MAU commander commented years later that "the planning considerations concerning helicopter flow and unit integrity . . . were integral to the plan even prior to the allocation of CH-53 assets during February."[37]

To sustain this flexibility meant quickly acquiring and disseminating the most up-to-date data available. Colonel Roche's numerous liaison visits to Nakhon Phanom provided him an opportunity to access a source of this knowledge. At USSAG Headquarters, an abundance of intelligence, particularly photo coverage of the landing zones, existed. Colonel Roche considered this the most-current and best-prepared information on the tactical situation in Cambodia. As a result, every unit commander, including the fire team leaders, received a detailed briefing on his specific landing zone and the lay of the land around it. In addition, for each course of action, the Marines rehearsed their procedures for both helicopter embarkation and their sector defense deployment. It seemed that no detail escaped inspection or rehearsal and as a consequence, this well-drilled group of Marines represented an assault unit properly prepared to perform an operation requiring precise timing and movement. At the MAU and battalion staff level, the commander and his staff discussed anticipated problems and worse-case situations with the expectation that nothing would be overlooked. Finally, this team effort would be put to the test.[38]

Beginning 7 April, the 31st MAU went to a one-hour readiness posture, which meant by 0400 each day, all heliteams had to be assembled in their assigned area, fully outfitted and ready to go. At this time, staged ammunition marked with a team's number was broken out for issue. Pending the signal to execute, the flight crews and heliteams waited and the actual issuance of ammunition was placed on hold.[39]

On the afternoon of 11 April, the MAU received the order to execute Operation Eagle Pull. General Burns established L-Hour as 0900 the following morning. The option selected involved the use of a single landing site, Landing Zone Hotel. At 1930, 11 April on the *Okinawa*, Colonel Roche called a meeting of his subordinate commanders. For the final time, the MAU S-3, Major James R. Brown, Jr., briefed the selected plan of action.[40]

The use of Landing Zone Hotel would require a 360-man security force. To balance the principle of

THE EVACUATION OF PHNOM PENH

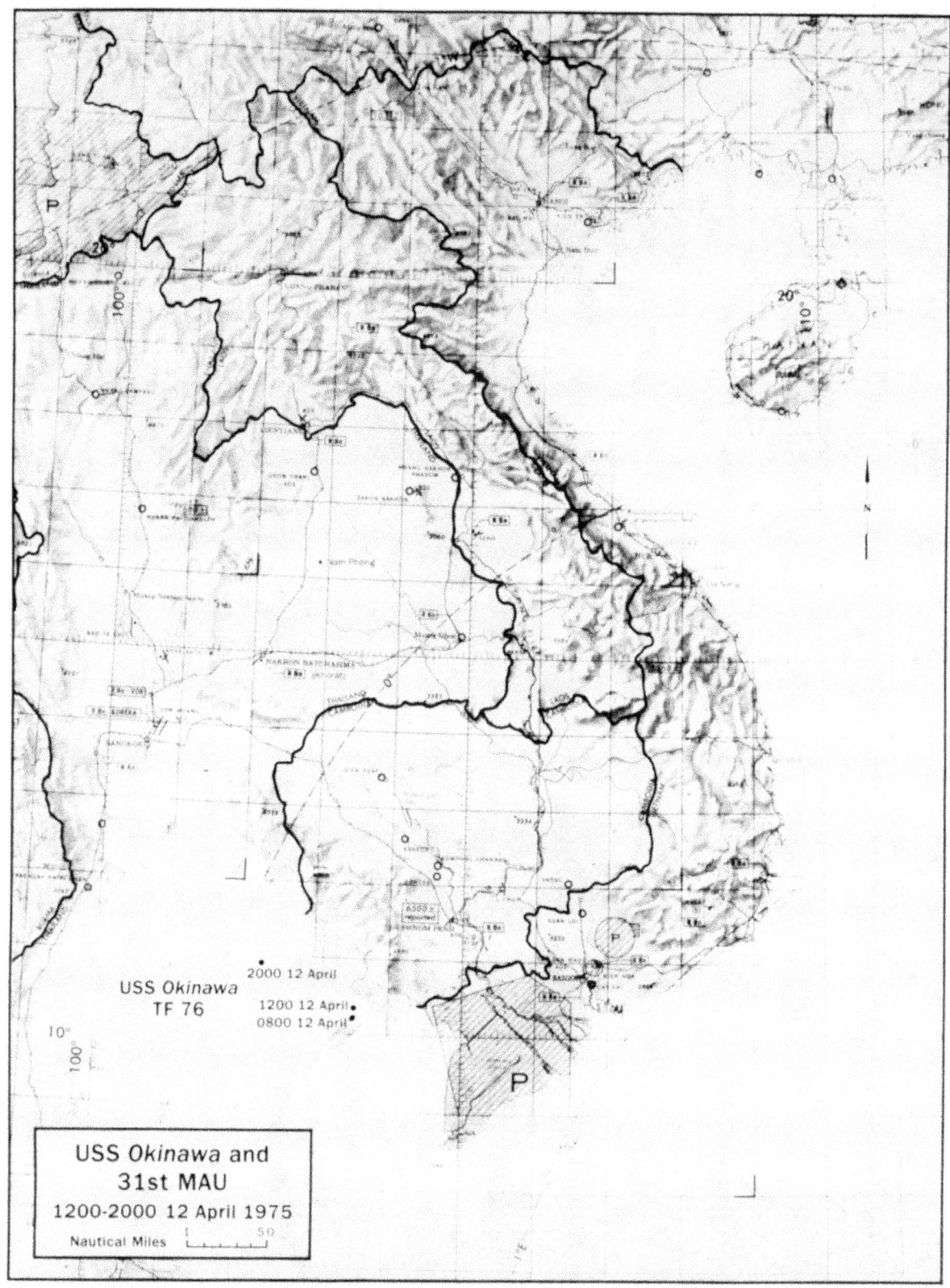

Map adapted from U.S. Air Force, *USAF Global Navigation and Planning Chart, Southeast Asia.* (10 June 1959); hatched areas and other land notations are a part of the original map.

Photo courtesy of Capt Russell R. Thurman, USMC (Ret)

Heliteams from BLT 2/4 on the portside elevator of USS Okinawa *are lifted to the flight deck where they will embark in CH-53s from HMH-462 for Operation Eagle Pull.*

A Marine helicopter gunner views Phnom Penh. The first helicopter from HMH-462 departed the USS Okinawa *at 0607 on 12 April, beginning Operation Eagle Pull.*

Department of Defense Photo (USMC) A150857

Department of Defense Photo (USMC) A150858
Landing Zone Hotel comes alive with activity as Operation Eagle Pull begins. BLT 2/4 Marines reposition as CH-53Ds from HMH-463 touch down to begin the extraction.

unit integrity with available deck space, the spread load of BLT 2/4, and the helicopter flow schedule, a compromise would have to be made. Whereas two rifle companies would satisfy the troop strength, it would be necessary because of the need for additional machine guns and mortars to commit elements of three companies. With this factor in mind, Lieutenant Colonel George P. Slade, BLT 2/4 commander, designated as the landing force elements: Company F commanded by Captain Thomas A. Keene and Company H commanded by Captain Steven R. Bland, both located on board the *Okinawa*, and Company G, commanded by Captain William R. Melton, positioned on board the *Vancouver* (LPD 2).

In view of the limited time available to integrate HMH-463 into the planned helicopter flow, 9th MAB Commander General Carey made the decision to use the existing helicopter employment schedule.* This meant that HMH-462 would insert the landing force and extract the evacuees, and HMH-463, following in trail, would extract the landing force after all of the refugees had been rescued. The planned elapsed time from beginning until the extraction of the last landing force element would be two and one-half hours.[41]

The Execution of Eagle Pull

Shortly after 0600 on 12 April 1975, 12 CH-53s from HMH-462 launched from the deck of the *Okinawa* and ascended to their orbit stations above the task group. At 10-minute intervals, the helicopters returned to the deck of the *Okinawa* for loading. Elements of Companies F and H, and the command group embarked from the *Okinawa* while elements of Company G boarded their helicopters on the *Vancouver*. During the loading of 360 Marines and corpsmen, each helicopter topped off its fuel tanks and then waited for its turn to launch. The HMH-462 birds strictly adhered to the sequence set forth in the flow schedule. Once airborne, they formed up in divisons of three looking to those on deck like a swarm of bees ready to enter the beehive. They continued to orbit the ship awaiting their turn to depart for Phnom Penh. After the initial division left on its 130-mile journey to the

---

*Colonel Roche stated, "Although General Carey may have made the decision noted here concerning the integration of HMH-463 into the helicopter employment schedule, that decision was not communicated to me. In the event, that was a decision which I made unilaterally on the recommendation of my staff and the respective helicopter squadron commanders." Roche Comments.

Marine Corps Historical Collection

Marines from BLT 2/4 deploy to take up defensive positions around Landing Zone Hotel, a soccer field in an apartment complex on the Mekong River's west bank in Phnom Penh.

CH-53Ds touch down in Landing Zone Hotel. As soon as they land they begin extracting ground security forces from BLT 2/4 because all of the evacuees have been rescued.

Photo courtesy of LtCol William R. Melton, USMC

Cambodian capital, each succeeding one followed at 10-minute intervals. The first helicopters crossed the coast-line north of Kompong Som, penetrating Cambodian airspace at 0743, proceeding along a track parallel to Route 4.*

Their flight path took them to the final checkpoint, Point Oscar, approximately 30 miles from the capital. It marked the holding area for the final approach to Phnom Penh and while inbound to Point Oscar, the pilots announced their arrival by checking in with "King."** After the first division of helicopters checked in with the airborne HC-130, "King" instructed them to proceed directly to the landing zone, ahead of schedule. Upon completing this transmission, he then radioed the leader of the division, Lieutenant Colonel Bolton (commanding officer of HMH-462), to switch frequency and contact landing zone control, Phnom Penh. At the other end of the new frequency, Lieutenant Colonel Lawson and his landing zone control team waited for their first call. Bolton's helicopter with Colonel Roche (the MAU commander) embarked, touched down in Landing Zone Hotel at 0854. The troops quickly debarked and sprinted to their assigned sectors in the perimeter. Lieutenant Colonel Slade, the battalion commander, immediately reported to Colonel Batchelder, the senior ground force commander. At the same time, his air liaison officer, Captain Kermit C. Corcoran, assumed the duties of landing zone controller.[42]

Large crowds of Cambodians confronted the Marines, but for the most part they came out of curiosity and not to interfere. Having established the perimeter defense, the Marines began the process of moving the crowds back in order to keep the landing zone clear. The teams of Marines designated for evacuee control then began moving their groups to the awaiting helicopters. Once loaded, the HMH-462 helicopters launched for the return flight to the Gulf of Thailand and the waiting ships of ARG Alpha. In the event no evacuees materialized for loading, then that helicopter took off and entered a holding pattern over the zone. This became necessary in order to ensure that succeeding waves of security forces could enter the zone on schedule, thereby guaranteeing a proper build-up of the perimeter defense. With only enough room in the zone for three CH-53s, flights arriving after the initial build-up had to be held at Point Oscar, even though the delay put them beyond their scheduled estimated time of arrival. This decision ensured minimum congestion in the zone and allowed the controller the flexibility of calling in helicopters as passengers appeared. The ability to anticipate allowed everyone more time to adjust to the situation in Phnom Penh. The American Embassy did not officially close until 0945, nearly an hour after the first helicopters landed. As evacuees from the Embassy arrived at the zone, the controller called in the orbiting helicopters, loaded them, launched them back to the ship, requested reliefs from Oscar, and began again the same process. Continuing like clockwork, this operation moved every available evacuee, but almost disappointingly the numbers were far less than anticipated.[43]

The last diplomatic report just prior to D-Day had indicated 590 evacuees, 146 Americans and 444 third-country nationals. HMH-462 actually removed 287, of which 84 were U.S. citizens and the rest, 203, foreign nationals. On the morning of the scheduled extraction, Ambassador Dean's note to key Cambodian officials advising them to be at the Embassy by 0930 ready to leave produced a stinging reply from Sirik Matak, a former prime minister and a driving force behind the formation of the Khmer Republic. He explained to Ambassador Dean that not only would he not leave with him ". . . but mark it well that, if I shall die here on the spot in my country that I love, it is too bad because we are all born and must die one day. I have committed this mistake of believing in you, the Americans."[44]

The paucity of evacuees did not affect the press coverage. Colonel Roche remembered an Associated Press photographer who pestered him the entire time, repeatedly asking what would happen next. The colonel finally stopped, turned to him, and said, "If I knew that, I probably would not have come in the first place."[45]

Twenty-five minutes after the last three HMH-462 helicopters left Oscar for Phnom Penh, Lieutenant Colonel Fix, the commander of HMH-463, launched the first of his four three-helicopter divisions, and a

---

*In accordance with the War Powers Act, a message with Flash precedence was sent to President Ford through the JCS notifying him of the precise penetration time.

**One of the Air Force helicopter pilots in Thailand at that time, a member of the 40th ARRS who participated in the initial hour of the evacuation, then-Major John F. Guilmartin, Jr., remembered one of the "King Bird's" other contributions that day: " 'King' was controlled by 'Joker,' the 3d Aerospace and Recovery Group at Nakhon Phanom. In this operation, the formally prescribed USAF communication channels became saturated and the 'King-Joker' link served General Burns and his staff as the primary source of information." Guilmartin Comments.

Department of Defense Photo (USMC) A332339

Marines from Company F, 2d Battalion, 4th Marines protect the perimeter of Landing Zone Hotel. The zone was not selected until summer 1974, but served its purpose as no enemy fire reached it until just prior to the departure of the last Marine commanders.

section of two as backups. As expected, the controllers held these aircraft at Oscar approximately 30 minutes beyond their sheduled estimated time of arrival. Upon confirmation by the Embassy that the last citizens, including Ambassador Dean and the acting president of the Khmer Republic, Saukham Khoy, had safely boarded a HMH-462 helicopter, the squadron aircraft began extracting the landing force. At approximately 1050, 107mm rocket fire began impacting in the vicinity of Landing Zone Hotel. Less than 10 minutes later, the zone also received some 82mm mortar fire. As soon as the enemy initiated its rocket and mortar attack, the controllers in the zone notified the Air Force forward air controllers (FACs) flying overhead in 23d Air Support Squadron OV-10s. The FACs immediately made low passes over the east bank of the Mekong, but could not spot any fire coming from known enemy positions in that location. At 1059, the last element of BLT 2/4 left the zone and 16 minutes later, two Air Force HH-53s from the 40th Aerospace Rescue and Recovery Squadron (ARRS), as scheduled, extracted Colonel Batchelder and his command element. As they departed the zone, the helicopters

HMH-462 Marine sits in a CH-53D at the end of his Phnom Penh evacuation mission. Sgt Ervin E. Breyette, Jr., leans against his .50-caliber machine gun and watches evacuees disembark on the USS Okinawa.

Photo courtesy of Capt Russell R. Thurman, USMC (Ret)

Air Force HH-53 crews from 21st SOS celebrate the successful finish of Operation Eagle Pull. Air Force helicopters extracted Col Sydney H. Batchelder and his command group.

received fire.* Captain Melton, the Company G commander, recalled the extraction of his ground security forces:

> I had passed the word to my company to pull in the perimeter; that we were leaving. I expected no problems, but there was a lot of noise from the helicopters. As Company G began embarking I saw Lieutenant Colonel Slade near the last helicopter. He motioned to me and I ran over to him. He asked me how things were going and I said fine. He nodded his approval and said I should get back to my company and make sure that I had everybody. I ran to the one remaining helicopter to be loaded and stood at the tailgate and watched the platoon sergeant count his people on board. I stood in dismay as the sergeant's eyes grew wide in disbelief and horror. He turned toward me and indicated by mouthing his words and using two fingers that he was missing two Marines. I motioned to the platoon commander and the platoon sergeant to follow me. We ran around the long building on the edge of the soccer field (the LZ) to the entrance gate the platoon had been guarding. We saw two Marines standing in their original positions, almost catatonic. They probably had not moved since being first posted there and they had not heard the order to move out. I ran up to one and slapped him on the shoulder and yelled at them that we were leaving. When they both turned around and saw that the sector was completely void of Marines, their faces whitened in shock and dismay and they then turned and sprinted full speed to the waiting helicopter.[46]

Removal of the ground security force came none too soon because as the last helicopter lifted off Landing Zone Hotel, several rounds found their mark. The Khmer Communists had finally hit the center of the zone, but fortunately for the command element and the Air Force pilots they did so nine minutes too late.

Neither the Marines nor any of the other participants sustained casualties. The *Okinawa* eventually berthed all of the extracted citizens, and in the process of removing them from Cambodia no American, not the Marines on the ground nor the tactical aircraft airborne, fired a shot in anger. The two Air Force HH-53s from the 40th ARRS sustained the only combat damage of the operation. Small arms fire during the final extraction caused minimal damage to the first aircraft, but a 12.7mm heavy machine gun round hit the second chopper's tail rotor as it climbed out of the zone. Escorted by a third, backup HH-53, this Jolly Green Giant, despite severe vibrations, made it safely back to Ubon Air Base in Thailand.[47]

The last Marine helicopter to leave Cambodia landed on the *Okinawa* at 1215. At 1450, a HMH-462 bird with Ambassador John Gunther Dean and his party

---

*In his comments, Lieutenant Colonel Guilmartin related that these two HH-53s were commanded by First Lieutenant Donald Backlund and First Lieutenant Philip Pacini who received credit from the USAF for "Combat Support Missions" vice "Combat Missions." Guilmartin Comments.

U.S. Ambassador to Cambodia John Gunther Dean steps off an HMH-462 CH-53 at Utapao. He arrived in Thailand on the afternoon of the day he departed from Phnom Penh.

on board launched from the *Okinawa*. They requested clearance to Utapao Air Base, the military airfield closest to Ambassador Dean's new destination, Bangkok, Thailand. The next day, Sunday, 13 April, the remaining 270 refugees flew to Utapao on HMH-462's Sea Stallions. When the last of these aircraft returned to the *Okinawa*, Amphibious Ready Group Alpha set course for the next crisis area, the South China Sea and South Vietnam, where it intended to rendezvous with Task Group 76.[48]

PART IV
ENDING AN ALLIANCE

CHAPTER 8
The Other Contingency

Marine Security Guard Detachment, Da Nang—Military Region 2: Nha Trang—III MAF and the NVA Onslaught 9th MAB and Task Force 76—The Brigade

---

Sun Tzu, the great Chinese philosopher on warfare, wrote in 500 BC: "Generally, in war the best policy is to take a state intact; to ruin it is inferior to this."[1]

As the final events unfolded in Cambodia, many experts wondered if the same fate awaited South Vietnam. The disaster which befell Military Region 1 had come as a surprise to many including the Ford administration and Ambassador Martin who was in North Carolina recuperating from dental surgery when the Communists' spring offensive began. Even the consul general for Da Nang, Albert A. Francis, did not expect the unraveling which followed Ban Me Thuot. The swiftness of the subsequent events required his early return from Washington where he had been undergoing treatment for a thyroid problem. His arrival in Saigon on 22 March was followed closely by Martin's. The Ambassador was welcomed back by his staff at 0300, 28 March, after a long flight from Andrews Air Force base on Air Force One. Two days later, the NVA entered Da Nang, completing its conquest of all five northern provinces and precipitating a mass exodus of the panicked population.[2]

Few had planned for such a debacle and the chaotic panic which ensued. Most of the South Vietnamese leadership, including President Thieu, thought the Vietnamese Armed Forces (RVNAF) could successfully defend at least the MR 1 coastal region: Hue, Da Nang, and Chu Lai.

Lieutenant Colonel Charles A. Barstow, a member of the DAO staff in 1973-74, in a personal letter to former Commandant General Wallace M. Greene, Jr., captured the essence of South Vietnam's post-Accords military strategy: conserve resources and whenever possible use artillery and air.* The Vietnamese seemed to emphasize an avoidance of engagements with the enemy, a husbanding of forces and military equipment, all in anticipation of the big battle during which, at just the right moment, they would strike a fatal blow and defeat the enemy. The "right time" never arrived, but it scarcely mattered. Without a reserve division to move around the battlefield as necessary, any South Vietnamese strategy was suspect.

As a result of the events in the Central Highlands, and the need to implement his plan to save a truncated South Vietnam, Thieu ordered the withdrawal of the Airborne Division from MR 1. This fateful decision set in motion an uncontrolled retreat from northern South Vietnam and the collapse of MR 1 occurred without even a struggle. Both the decision and the subsequent collapse were directly attributable to the South Vietnamese Armed Forces' most glaring weakness, the absence of a strategic reserve. This serious shortfall, identified in 1973 by Major General John E. Murray, USA, forced Thieu's hand and in the end precipitated irreversible problems that possibly could have been avoided had they been addressed when the Defense Attache first raised his concerns. In his letter to General Greene, Lieutenant Colonel Barstow wrote: "I am concerned over the deployment of troops and units. The Marine and Airborne Divisions, the country's two most reliable and well-trained, are deployed in static positions in Quang Tri and Thua Thien Provinces. Any breakthrough in Hue would mean no significant reserve once the two best are overrun."[3]

The decision to use the Airborne Division to solve the strategic reserve problem contained a very important, but false assumption: defense of I Corps had no relationship to the people living there. I Corps Chief of Staff, Colonel Dang, said, "This [withdrawal of the Airborne Division] had three bad effects. It reduced our fighting strength; it reduced the morale of our troops; and it hurt the morale of the population. It upset the balance of forces."[4]

The population trusted the forces that had guarded them since the cease-fire in 1973, including the Marine brigades north of Hue. When these units redeployed, the Vietnamese voted with their feet on the wisdom of this strategy by beginning a mass exodus to Da Nang. According to ARVN I Corps officers, ". . .

---

*Lieutenant Colonel Barstow wrote, "My initial impression, General, is that we are still suffering from the 'Whiz Kids.' The [South Vietnamese] Army has been fed too much sophisticated equipment without being properly trained as to its employment and maintenance. . . . Further, it appears we have taught the Vietnamese to rely entirely on artillery and air support, as they seldom close with the enemy." Barstow ltr.

the departure of the Marine Division from the northern provinces [caused] the civilian population . . . to panic and evacuate en masse Quang Tri and Hue."[5]

Those ARVN soldiers who did not desert to assist their fleeing families, but instead chose to stand and fight, were overrun. The troops who somehow managed to escape capture then joined the crazed mob attempting to leave Da Nang on anything that floated. Chaos ruled the streets of Da Nang Easter weekend 1975 as military deserters armed with their combat weapons attempted to dictate the terms of their departure. Before the weekend ended some of the most disciplined members of the armed forces would use their weapons against their countrymen in order to gain passage from Da Nang. Eventually, many of these same weapons would be confiscated by American Marines.

Marine Security Guard Detachment, Da Nang

During the confusion and chaos caused by the collapse of the defensive perimeter surrounding Da Nang, six Marine security guards stationed at the consulate played a major part in the successful removal of Americans from the besieged area. Staff Sergeant Walter W. Sparks, the noncommissioned officer-in-charge of the detachment, and his five noncommissioned officers, although primarily responsibile for the safety and well-being of Consul General Francis, moved quickly to provide the consulate staff its support. The five NCOs at the Da Nang consulate who assisted Staff Sergeant Sparks in this task were: Sergeant Venoy L. Rogers; Sergeant Lazaro Arriola; Sergeant William S. Spruce III; and Corporals Leonard A. Forseth and Ronald W. Anderson.[6]

To accomplish the evacuation, the Da Nang Marines had to contend with the bedlam outside the consulate, while attending to the business at hand inside. One of the detachment's gravest concerns was the ever-present threat of uncontrolled crowds, mobs of deserters, and criminals prowling the streets. As a consequence, the Marine security guards spent their final days in Da Nang in the consulate rather than the Marine House. In the opinion of Staff Sergeant Sparks, they needed to protect the consul general and the consulate and not worry about the rest of the compound: "I moved the Marines . . . . The consulate was not getting attacked but there were crowds of people, trying to come in and get tickets."[7] The tickets were for an air and sea evacuation the consulate had set up for past and present employees. This somewhat orderly affair rapidly deteriorated when the rioting, or what Sergeant Sparks called the "cowboys riding" began. He said, "all [the soldiers] were looting, robbing, and killing people."[8] This problem intensified as more and more ARVN soldiers entered the city either as deserters or stragglers. The deserters had left their units in the heat of battle, many to search for their families. All were armed, desperate, and extremely dangerous.

Messages received by the Marine Corps Command Center in Washington during the last week of March 1975 graphically depicted the difficulties that Staff Sergeant Sparks faced in Da Nang. One on the 27th from the Navy's Pacific headquarters stated, "The [South Vietnamese] Marine Brigade remains the only viable combat force in MR 1. The 1st Infantry Division and the Ranger groups have broken up and are moving more as mobs. Chu Lai fell on 26 March. Public order is breaking down, an atmosphere of panic has begun to spread."[9] Another said in part, "City overflowing with refugees and soldiers. Absence of policemen. Immediate threat is internal, i.e., mob violence."[10]

Having moved the Marines into the consulate on Saturday, 22 March, Staff Sergeant Sparks immediately began destroying all classified records. Four days later, on Wednesday the 26th, Consul General Francis asked Ambassador Martin to consider a helicopter extraction of his 50 people, including the Marines, should the "streets of the city become impassable because of the refugee panic."[11]

The Marine detachment continued to do what Staff Sergeant Sparks saw as its primary duty: destruction of classified material and protection of the consulate and its staff. He assigned one Marine to shred classified documents, and a second to burn them. He posted two Marines as guards at the vehicle gate and permanently secured the pedestrian gate. The sixth Marine joined the staff in the consul general's office. His mission was twofold: security and administrative assistance.

Despite the efforts of the consulate staff and the Marines, considerable confusion and chaos existed at the consulate during the final days of March 1975. Sergeant Sparks placed a large part of the blame for this squarely on the shoulders of members of the American community who refused to leave Da Nang until the last possible moment: "They kept thinking maybe the tide would turn and everything would turn up rosy."[12] The consul general could strongly encourage people to leave, but he could not force them to do so. Many waited, expecting to get on the last flight from the

Da Nang Airfield or better still, on the requested helicopter lift. Staff Sergeant Sparks even said to some of them, "What are you still doing here? Get out of here!" But they would reply, " 'You're here.' To which I said, 'Yes, partner, but maybe there ain't going to be room on the helicopter that I'm leaving on.' "[13]

The helicopter option would never materialize because the day after Chu Lai fell, General Burns, the overall operational area commander, learned that the anticipated helicopter lift from Nha Trang was impossible because "Eagle Pull assets on hand now are not adequate to permit this."[14] As the fixed-wing evacuation limped on, nearly overwhelmed by the sea of refugees, U.S. Secretary of State Henry A. Kissinger sought the assistance of the Military Sealift Command (MSC). The request to use MSC ships to evacuate U.S. citizens and other designated civilian refugees was initiated at 0529 on 27 March. Unfortunately, the earliest estimated time of arrival of any of these ships in the area was the afternoon of 28 March. Until then, the airfield would serve as the only exit for the Americans in Da Nang. Later in the day on 27 March that door slammed shut after crowds of refugees started mobbing aircraft landing at Da Nang.

The panic actually began when waiting Vietnamese spontaneously rushed a World Airways plane loading for a scheduled departure of 0900. After that incident, the crowd could not be controlled and smaller aircraft, like the C-47, were diverted to the helicopter airfield nearby. Located east of the Da Nang airport, Marble Mountain, which earlier in the war had served as home to some of the 1st Marine Aircraft Wing's helicopter squadrons, possessed a relatively short runway, but offered a luxury the Da Nang airport no longer had, security from the crazed crowds. At 1029 on 28 March, because of the chaos, the Saigon government suspended all airlift flights into Da Nang. Sergeant Sparks remembered a creeping sense of finality: "I was talking to the Air America guy who runs the terminal out there and he wasn't panicked. At least on the radio, he was calm. He said, 'It's all over. We can't get them out anymore; the planes won't land.' "[15]

Fortunately for those Americans who at that moment were waiting at the airport for the next flight, and for Consul General Francis, who was at the airfield checking on the airlift, a CH-47 from Marble Mountain whisked them away before the crowds could react. Later in the day, Francis returned to the consulate in another helicopter, and after some discussion gave the order for all Americans to leave Da Nang. At 2000 that Thursday evening, he halted all U.S.-controlled flights except those from Marble Mountain. Francis had the few Americans still remaining at the Da Nang airport moved back to town so that they could be evacuated with his remaining staff.

The plan called for a pick-up by an Air America helicopter at the International Commission of Control and Supervision's landing zone. Staff Sergeant Sparks said, "We [those to be evacuated] drove down there, this was about 1830, we got to the LZ and it was very calm and quiet there."[16] The staff, the Marines, and the remaining Americans (Consul General Francis and a few other officials had decided to postpone their departure*) stayed at the LZ until they received word that there would be no more helicopter flights because the pilots had used up all their fuel and the Vietnamese would not give them any more. By then it was 2100 and the remaining Americans reassembled at Francis' house where they realized, in discussing their options, that the only way out was by tugboat and barge. At 0130 on 29 March (Friday), Consul General Francis requested that Alaska Barge and Transport Company use one of its tugs to push a small barge to the dock in front of the consulate and place another slightly larger one in the open water where it would be visible to the Vietnamese. They were to be in place by 0330. This they hoped would assure the South Vietnamese soldiers guarding the pier that they too had an alternate means of escape, thereby precluding the need for seizure or destruction of the barge docked near the consulate.[17]

Less than two hours later, everyone, including the Marines, American civilians, and the Vietnamese staff, left the consul general's house and climbed into the back of a Vietnamese garbage truck (which was covered) and rode a half mile to the dock. Sergeant Sparks described the horror of what happened next: "We got off the truck and helped the people on this barge. That . . . was one of the most tragic things I have seen in my life, and I have been in combat a few times . . . . Women and old people were throwing their babies to that barge for people to catch, and they were missing and falling in the water. Old people crawling up this rope, trying to get to the barge and

---

*Consul General Francis eventually escaped Da Nang shortly after midnight on 30 March by swimming from a beach near Monkey Mountain to a South Vietnamese Navy patrol craft. He had remained behind on 29 March to continue to oversee an ad hoc airlift operation at Marble Mountain. (*Fall of the South*, p. 80). Several other Americans who had remained behind escaped Da Nang on board the *Oseola*, an Alaska Barge and Transport Company tug captained by a New Zealander. *Fall of Saigon*, p. 171.

Department of Defense Photo (USMC) 7712975

Equipment of the Alaska Barge and Transport Company was used to evacuate the consulate at Da Nang. Marines of the consulate security guard spent six hours on 29 March unloading a similar barge tied to the Pioneer Contender, *underway for Cam Ranh Bay.*

falling off, and then the barge would come back and crush them."[18]

Despite the fact that South Vietnamese were shooting other South Vietnamese in boats in the harbor, that the barge was overloaded, and that the tug was straining and groaning to push it, the Americans made it to the harbor just as the *Pioneer Contender* arrived in port, at 0800 29 March. The Americans immediately boarded the ship and the Marines prepared to assist the crew in unloading the barge. That task would eventually consume almost 10 hours.

Staff Sergeant Sparks experienced a certain amount of surprise upon learning in his initial inquiry that, ". . . the captain of the *Pioneer Contender* did not know he was coming for refugees. He thought they were coming for vehicles, American vehicles." The Marines quickly agreed to the captain's request for assistance in disarming the refugees and in controlling the mass of humanity, a task that did not end until they reached Cam Ranh Bay. The situation on board the barge quickly spun out of control as other refugees in small boats approached the ship and disgorged their panicked cargo onto the barge, making loading of the ship extremely hazardous and very time consuming.[19]

To expedite the process, the barge was lashed to the side of the ship which allowed the *Pioneer Contender* to reach the open sea while continuing to board refugees. Sparks said: "We started loading these people on . . . . They would not behave themselves, they would not sit down, they would not relax. They wouldn't help themselves. I saw a Vietnamese major stomping on babies to get up the ladder instead of trying to help his people. Fathers pushing their own wives and children out of the way. The old people being crushed and small babies being crushed. [For the individual Marine] . . . it became a question of risking your life."[20]

With the waves crashing the barge against the side of the ship and under fire from desperate South Vietnamese whose small boats could not catch the swiftly departing ship, Sergeant Spruce and Corporal Forseth passed babies up the ladder and assisted the elderly off the barge. When the barge was finally unloaded, Staff Sergeant Sparks, Sergeant Arriola, Sergeant Rogers, and Corporal Anderson inspected it for bodies. In addition to more than two dozen corpses, they found an elderly man with a broken leg and what later turned out to be his wife crumbled up in a heap. After assisting them on the ship, they cut loose the barge and the *Pioneer Contender* increased its speed and headed for Cam Ranh Bay. It arrived there at noon on Easter Sunday, 30 March 1975.[21]

Despite numerous pleas from the ship's master and Staff Sergeant Sparks, and the word that some Americans were still on a barge in Da Nang Harbor, the American Embassy would not allow the Da Nang security guard detachment to accompany the *Pioneer Con-*

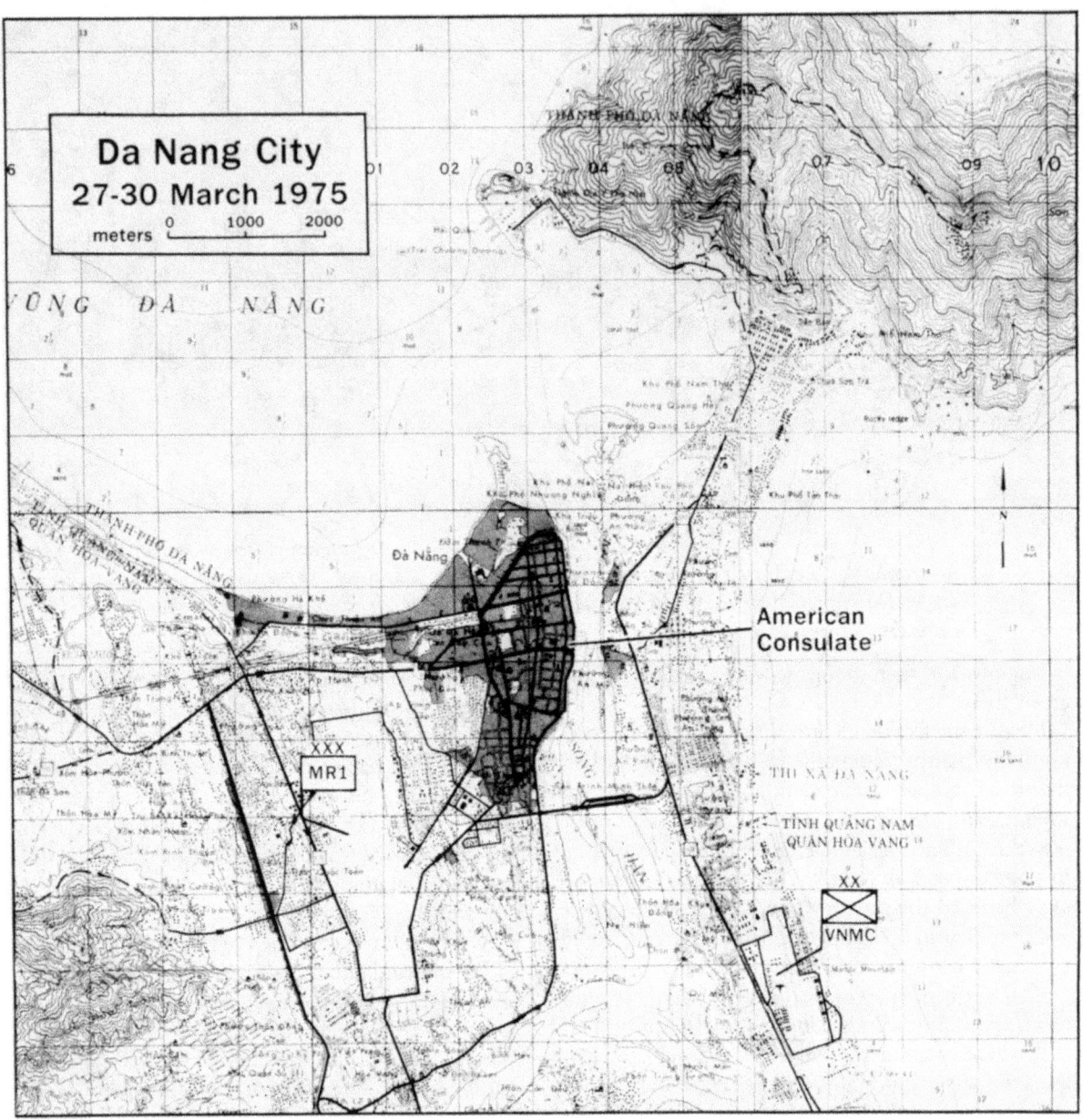

tender on its return trip to Da Nang. Reports and radio communications with the Americans on the barge indicated that members of the Vietnamese armed forces had control of the barges and were shooting anyone who seemed a threat to their safe rescue. To an undetermined extent, their conduct during the last few days of March included rape, looting, and murder. Military discipline generally had disappeared; in many instances it had become every man for himself.[22]

The final act of these desperados was to commandeer one of the MSC ships, the *Greenville Victory*. Seizing this sister ship of the *Pioneer Contender*, the mutineers forced the captain to sail the ship to Vung Tau and not the destination the Saigon Government had selected for its MR 1 refugees, Phu Quoc Island. Eventually, thanks to the Seventh Fleet commander, the Vietnamese peacefully returned control of the ship to the master but not before it dropped anchor off Vung Tau whereupon they departed. Admiral Steele helped ensure a peaceful conclusion to this incident by opting to "place a cruiser on one side of that ship and a destroyer on the other, with their guns trained on it."[23]

Considering the uncertain effect six American Marines might have had under the circumstances existing on the *Greenville Victory*, the decision not to allow them to escort additional refugees appeared to have substantial merit. Without another opportunity to return to the consulate, the history of the Marine Security Guard Detachment, Da Nang officially ended at 0330, 28 March 1975. The evacuation of Da Nang ceased at 1930 on Easter Sunday. The National Military Command Center reported, "As of 301130Z, Military Sealift Command has suspended evacuation operations because of unsafe conditions. SS *Pioneer Contender* and three tugs departed Da Nang at 301130Z." Actually the *American Challenger* was still picking up any refugees who could escape by small craft on the first of April. At this time the estimate of refugees evacuated from Da Nang by sea stood at approximately 70,000.[24]

While the last remnants of the Vietnamese Marine Corps' defenders of Da Nang attempted to escape by sea from the advancing North Vietnamese Army, the U.S. Marines being loaded in ARG Bravo shipping in Buckner Bay, Okinawa, still thought that Da Nang was their destination. As the 1st Battalion, 4th Marines embarked on the *Dubuque*, word of Da Nang's capture altered the battalion's orders and in effect changed its organization and mission. This occurred in a matter of six hours on Easter Sunday morning, 30 March, via messages from the JCS to Admiral Whitmire and from him to III MAF and 33d MAU. The change placed Colonel Alexander in charge of a force whose duties would entail maintaining order and discipline on evacuation shipping. With the change in orders, the Marines who left Buckner Bay that Easter Sunday eventually received the official title of Amphibious Evacuation RVN Support Group as a result of the nature of their mission—to render assistance and support to the Republic of Vietnam in the rescue and relocation of its refugees. Bound for the coastal region between Qui Nhon and Nha Trang, the amphibious ready group arrived off the coast of Khanh Hoa Province on 2 April 1975, just in time to start rescuing the evacuees of Nha Trang and the thousands of refugees from Military Region 2.*[25]

Military Region 2: Nha Trang

Having forced the South Vietnamese to effect disastrous withdrawals from Pleiku and Kontum earlier in the month, the North Vietnamese Army remained relatively inactive until the end of March. All of that changed when the Communists focused their energies on Binh Dinh Province and its defenders, the ARVN 22d Division. The initial pressure on the 22d came from the highlands, but after Quang Ngai Province fell on 27 March, the Communist forces there turned their attention south to Binh Dinh and Qui Nhon. The resultant effect pitted the 22d Division against a force more than double its original size. At this point, amidst the confusion created by sappers attacking its rear area, the division chose to withdraw to Qui Nhon rather than stand and fight. By the end of March, the retreating 22d Division had but one goal, evacuation by sea.[26]

Nha Trang was in no better shape. An attempt to defend it ended when the 3d Airborne Brigade, in a blocking position astride Highway 21, was outflanked. The survivors withdrew to the city down Route 21. Nha Trang was by this time near self-induced chaos, and with the unannounced desertion of its defense by senior commanders who fled by helicopter, "everyone ran."[27]

As April began, with the exception of the two southeastern provinces of II Corps (Ninh Thuan and Binh Thuan), the Communists were in control of all of Military Regions 1 and 2. Military efforts to anticipate events in MR 2 fell short as the NVA raced to the coast. An intelligence report on the 1st of April predicted the collapse of Nha Trang within the next two to seven days. That same day Admiral Gayler directed that a helicopter-capable ship move within one mile of Nha Trang for possible rescue operations. Neither message would have any value by the time it reached the addressee.[28]

The date of Gayler's message and the date of the intelligence report, 1 April 1975, was a day Nha Trang's Consul General Moncrieff Spear and the Marines guarding him would not soon forget. For that Tuesday morning, the sounds of NVA artillery awakened them. Although still many miles from Nha Trang, the Communists were informing the Americans that they would arrive in Nha Trang well before the intelligence experts' prediction of "two to seven days." Based on the sound of the concussions, it appeared that the forecast should have indicated hours instead of days. Staff Sergeant Roger F. Painter and his five Marines knew that the distant enemy fire meant the city would be under siege before day's end, and in all probability they would have to evacuate in the next day or two. After a phone conversation with the Embassy, Consul General Spear relayed to the Marines

---

*For more information on the Amphibious Evacuation RVN Support Group's operations, see Chapter 6.

Marine Corps Historical Collection

Fishing boats rest peacefully in water near Nha Trang prior to the catastrophic collapse of MR 2 and the closing of the American consulate in the city on 1 April 1975. Anything that floated, including tires, was used by thousands of Vietnamese fleeing the NVA.

his new instructions—to leave Nha Trang immediately. In the confusion of their unexpectedly sudden departure, the Marines left their health and pay records behind. To retrieve them, Staff Sergeant Painter sent Sergeant Michael A. McCormick, his assistant noncommissioned officer-in-charge, back to the consulate. When McCormick returned to the airfield less than an hour later, he noticed that his bag, left with those of the other Marines, was gone. Incredulously, he realized that Painter, and the other members of the detachment, Corporals Robert L. Anderson, John G. Moya, Levorn L. Brown, and Jimmie D. Sneed, had left without him. Later, he discovered that they, along with the consul general and the other Nha Trang-based Americans, had flown to Saigon. Sergeant McCormick quickly found another American in the same lonely situation who said that an Air America helicopter was presently inbound to Nha Trang. The Air America helicopter only had enough fuel to fly them to Cam Ranh Bay whereupon it refueled and then flew on to Saigon. McCormick recalled, "I will never forget the anger, fear, and then relief I experienced that day. I was very fortunate to escape Nha Trang. The enemy was everywhere." Subsequently, Sergeant McCormick learned that Staff Sergeant Painter had no choice that day but to leave when he did because of the consul general's orders.*[29]

As an epilogue, the Nha Trang Marines spent more than three weeks in Saigon before they moved to the Marine Security Guard Headquarters in Manila. During their interlude in Saigon, Lance Corporal Darwin D. Judge arrived in South Vietnam as an Embassy Guard replacement on 24 April. The NCOIC of the Embassy Detachment, Master Sergeant Juan J. Valdez, assigned Sergeant McCormick the responsibility of orienting and acquainting Judge with his new surroundings. A few days after McCormick and the Nha Trang Marines left, Judge, along with Corporal Charles McMahon, Jr., was transferred to the DAO Compound to augment the security force guarding that installation.[30]

III MAF and the NVA Onslaught

For the two weeks preceding the fall of Nha Trang, III MAF Headquarters had been attempting to complete its preparations for a number of contingencies.

---

*Sergeant McCormick recalled years later that the Nha Trang Marines did not simply "cut and run." They were prepared to stay as long as necessary, but were never given the opportunity. McCormick Comments.

The major ones were interrelated and dealt with the potential evacuation missions in Cambodia and South Vietnam. The knowledge that these evacuations might occur simultaneously was futher complicated by the lack of reliable information on the number of refugees requiring transportation. How to evacuate the South Vietnamese refugees whose estimated numbers varied significantly from day to day monopolized the discussions at MAF headquarters during the first part of April. A daily evaluation of the war in South Vietnam offered little hope for a cancellation of the requirement to support this contingency. In fact, the early April reports of military setbacks in South Vietnam led III MAF to activate three MAUs, and for a few days, even two MABs. Both alarming and disconcerting was the news from South Vietnam on 3 April that the Vietnamese Armed Forces had abandoned the cities of Qui Nhon, Nha Trang, and Dalat, giving the NVA control of most of MR 2.[31]

Indeed, 3 April produced a number of historically important events. On that Thursday, Brigadier General

An AH-1J Cobra lands on board the Okinawa. *Cobras from HMA-369 were operationally assigned to HMH-462 after USS* Midway *embarked them on 3 April while enroute to Subic Bay in the Philippines.*
Department of Defense Photo (USMC) A150964

Harold L. Coffman, the commanding general of the newly created 11th MAB, departed for Nakhon Phanom, Thailand; Admiral Steele, the Seventh Fleet commander, released a message detailing his plan for the evacuation of South Vietnam's Military Regions 3 and 4; MABLEx 2-75, originally a MAF exercise scheduled for 21 April to 3 May, was officially cancelled; and *Midway*, ordered on short notice to the South China Sea via Okinawa, embarked MAG-36's HML-367(-)(Rein) and 11 UH-1Es, HMA-369(-)(Rein) and 4 AH-1Js, and 14 CH-46Ds belonging to HMM-164 and H&MS-36. Admiral Gayler's intelligence report for that day stated, "The situation continues to deteriorate rapidly. The Communists are expected to take the remainder of MR 2 before the end of the week. Their final attack toward the capital could occur in as few as seven days. Forces are in position with three more divisions enroute from North Vietnam."[32]

Combat was light for the first few days of April as Communist divisions consolidated their victories and began preparations for the push to Saigon. Those divisions from MR 1 and MR 2 moved south while those in MR 4 moved north and east. They would join forces in MR 3 since recently captured equipment and a newly built road network facilitated rapid movement. Additionally, the North Vietnamese redeployed their antiaircraft artillery and surface-to-air missiles, especially the portable SA-7 Grail, to the area. The CinCPac's report of 2 April confirmed this: "Bien Hoa lies within a confirmed SA-7 operating area and will probably be the first base at which the enemy will deny air operations."[33]

The next day Admiral Steele also addressed the enemy's presence in Saigon when he issued Operational Plan 1-75. Sent to all subordinate units, the 3 April message stated: "Bien Hoa is already within range of 130mm artillery as well as 122mm rockets . . . . The airfield also lies within a confirmed SA-7 operating area. Tan Son Nhut . . . is only 8km south of a known SA-7 operating area, and is adjacent to targets of known high interest to the enemy. An extensive SA-7 operating area parallels the Saigon River corridor running between Saigon and Vung Tau."[34]

It appeared that the immediate capture of Saigon through the use of armor and infantry supported by extensive antiaircraft cover could occur momentarily. The NVA's final offensive was close at hand. An intelligence report issued at the same time as Admiral Steele's message revealed similar findings. It summarized: "A GVN enclave around Saigon could encom-

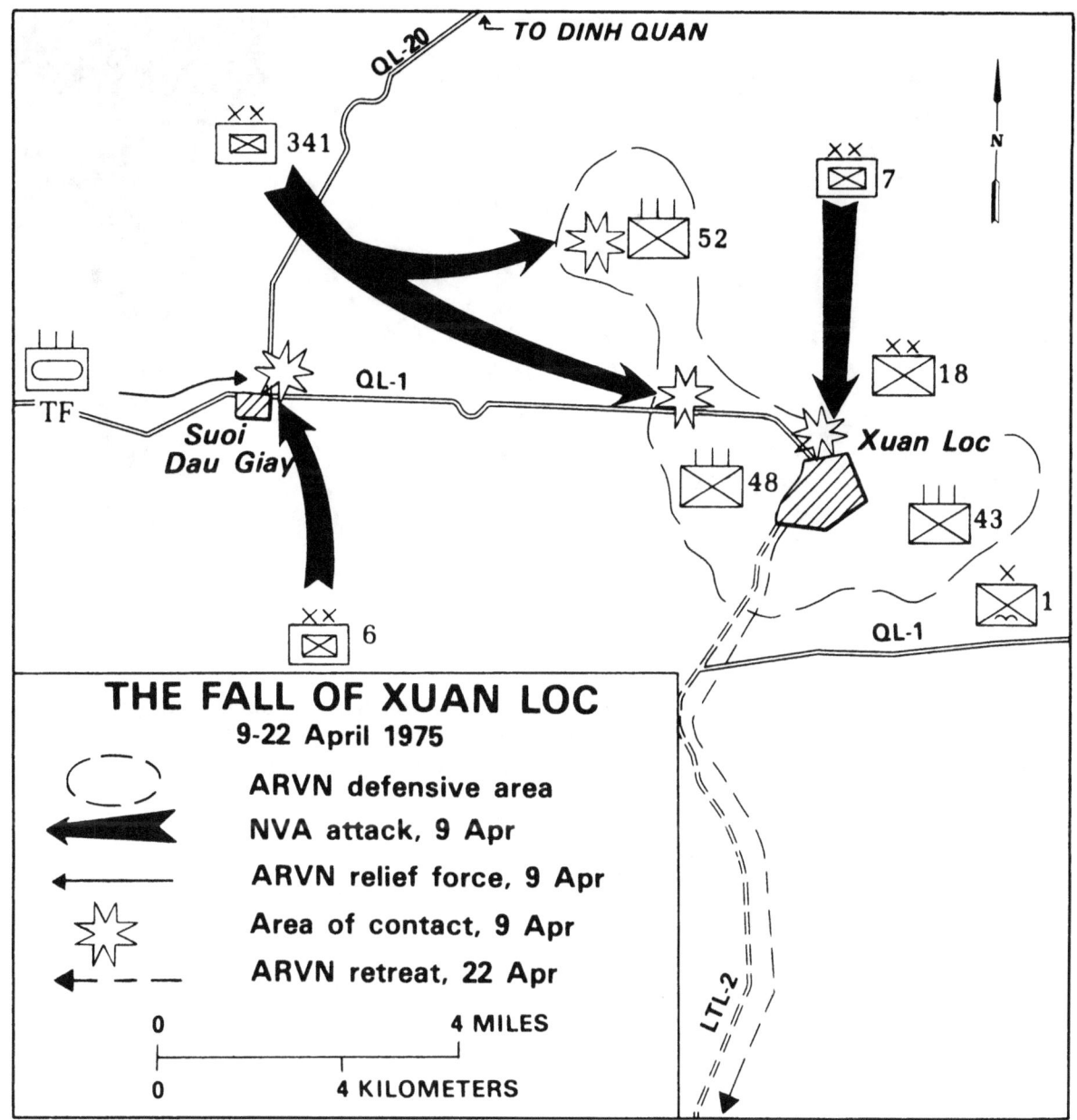

Map adapted from Gen Cao Van Vien, *The Final Collapse* (Washington, U.S. Army Center of Military History, 1983)

pass the Saigon-Gia Dinh area with a refugee-swollen population of more than four million civilians defended by remnants of three plus ARVN divisions.... The NVA are expected to concentrate on destruction of ARVN combat forces rather than continue a slow war of attrition around an isolated capital enclave."[35]

Although demoralized, the ARVN attempted to regroup and reorganize in preparation for the Communists' next strike. Soldiers evacuated from MR 1 and MR 2 formed new units, which when subsequently committed to combat, proved marginally effective. Unfortunately, these units represented 40 percent of South Vietnam's combat power. As a consequence, when the fighting resumed, the ARVN soldiers truly ready for battle constituted a force numerically inferior to the enemy's.

The renewal of fighting and combat activity in Tay Ninh Province quickly revealed this truth. A massive combined arms attack eliminated the ARVN from the area west of the Van Co Dong River. The NVA then launched heavy attacks against ARVN positions along Route 1 and Route 22 in the eastern portion of the region. Fighting soon shifted to Xuan Loc, the capital of Long Khanh Province.

Department of Defense Photo (USMC) A150931

U.S. Seventh Fleet ships steam in formation in the South China Sea. These ships would support Task Force 76 and its embarked 9th MAB Marines during most of April 1975.

On 9 April, the *341st NVA Division* attacked the forces defending Xuan Loc (the 18th ARVN Division). The Communists wanted to gain control of Highway 1, the main access route into the Bien Hoa/Saigon area. The South Vietnamese quickly moved to reinforce Xuan Loc and thwart the latest and most crucial Communist offensive. The ARVN soldiers, commanded by Brigadier General Le Minh Dao, counterattacked on 10 April and retook a considerable amount of the city they had lost the day before. The next day, they repulsed an attack by the *165th Regiment* of the *7th NVA Division* and regiments from the *341st Division* and the *6th NVA Division*. This victory by the 18th ARVN renewed hopes that possibly the NVA's spring offensive could be halted and Saigon saved. If the Communist onslaught could be stopped then the 9th MAB and its units would be able to concentrate on other contingencies and maybe even undertake the cancelled MAF exercise.[36]

9th MAB and Task Force 76

During South Vietnam's series of defeats in late March and early April and before the ARVN's successful counterattack at Xuan Loc, the U.S. Marine Corps assembled a fighting force capable of aiding that republic once again. The centerpiece of that organization was the 9th Marine Amphibious Brigade (9th MAB). Eventually, it would comprise over 6,000 Marines and Navy corpsmen, 80-plus helicopters of various types, and vehicles, supplies, and other equipment normally associated with amphibious operations. Together with the Navy's amphibious ready group, the 9th MAB Marines would be capable of supporting airlift, sealift, or helicopter evacuation operations, either afloat or ashore.

On 26 March 1975, the Commanding General of III MAF, Major General Carl W. Hoffman, reactivated the 9th Marine Amphibious Brigade, to participate in a landing exercise in the Philippines, MABLEx 2-75. It had been in the planning stage for 18 months. The order to activate 9th MAB addressed the exercise at hand, but it also referenced recent events on the Indochina peninsula. Not intentionally designed as such, the MABLEx served as an excellent explanation for the movement of units to the South China Sea.

The Navy supported this exercise by providing the amphibious ships to move these units. Except for exercises or actual operations, amphibious squadrons in the Pacific performed a one-for-one replacement with one squadron of ships leaving station as soon as the relieving squadron arrived from San Diego, homeport for these ships.

The relief of a squadron normally took a day, maybe two, long enough to transfer the landing forces from the outbound to the inbound ships. Built into this long-term schedule was an extended overlap, usually occurring every two years. In those years, the exchange of duties occupied a two- to three-week period which in turn provided enough ships to conduct a major landing exercise, sometimes involving as many as four battalions. The spring of 1975 happened to be one of those overlap periods. Consequently, in order to provide the Seventh Fleet and III MAF with the means to conduct MABLEx 2-75, CinCPac approved a rotation schedule which doubled the number of amphibious ships in the Western Pacific.[37]

The Marine units that in 1975 planned to join forces to perform the exercise as the 9th MAB were, in late March, still dispersed throughout the Western Pacific. Shortly, events in Southeast Asia would force an early rendezvous. The fighting edge of this Navy-Marine Corps team, the 31st MAU, was already embarked in Amphibious Ready Group Alpha ships, on station in the Gulf of Thailand. The 31st MAU consisted of Battalion Landing Team 2/4 (BLT 2/4), Marine Heavy Helicopter Squadron 462 (HMH-462), and Logistic Support Unit 2/4 (LSU 2/4). The MAU had been floating and waiting for nearly two months, expecting on any day to receive orders to evacuate Phnom Penh, the besieged capital of Cambodia.

Other units which eventually would become part of the 9th MAB kept pace by continuing to follow their monthly training schedules. The unit assigned as the landing force for ARG Bravo shipping, BLT 3/9, even deployed to mainland Japan to complete its planned readiness requirements. BLT 3/9 and its logistic support unit, LSU 3/9, went ashore at Camp Fuji, Japan, to conduct routine, infantry training. Two of the four remaining infantry battalions on Okinawa—1st Battalion, 9th Marines and 1st Battalion, 4th Marines—served as the primary and backup air contingency battalions. Supporting them and conducting training of their own on Okinawa were Marine Medium Helicopter Squadron 165 (HMM-165) and Marine Light Helicopter Squadron 367 (HML-367). At the same time, 3,000 miles to the east at Marine Corps Air Station Kaneohe, Hawaii, another helicopter squadron, Ma-

USS Duluth *(LPD 6) of Amphibious Squadron 5 sits off the coast of South Vietnam after its recent arrival from San Diego. The ship was quickly deployed to assist in the operations carried out in the South China Sea during the last two weeks of April 1975.*
Photo courtesy of Capt James D. Tregurtha, USN (Ret)

rine Heavy Helicopter Squadron 463 (HMH-463), prepared to join the contingency operations in the South China Sea. The *Hancock*, homeported in Alameda, had not been included in the MABLEx. While enroute to Pearl Harbor, it received instructions to load HMH-463 and carry it to Southeast Asia.

Naval forces scheduled to participate in MABLEx 2-75 and also available for any contingency that might arise in that area of the Pacific were either undergoing repairs or completing pre-exercise preparations (for more specific details see the chart below). In addition, the Air Force in the Pacific could support, if requested, 9th MAB's exercise or, if required, any Western Pacific operation by employing its aircraft and airmen stationed at bases throughout Thailand: Utapao, Korat, Ubon, Udorn, or Nakhon Phanom.

As originally planned, MABLEx 2-75 included the use of an entire MAF, but the commitment on 28 February of the 31st MAU and ARG Alpha to an indefinite deployment in the Gulf of Thailand (possible evacuation of Phnom Penh) altered that plan. It made necessary a reduction in the size of the exercise force, from a MAF to a MAB.[38]

The Brigade

General Hoffman chose the assistant commander of the 1st Marine Aircraft Wing, Brigadier General Richard E. Carey, to command the 9th MAB. General Carey, an aviator, had a previous combat tour in Vietnam as the commanding officer of VMFA-115 from 5

Marine Corps Historical Collection

BGen Richard E. Carey, pictured here as a lieutenant general, assumed command of the 9th Marine Amphibious Brigade on 26 March 1975. Gen Carey enlisted in the Marine Corps in 1945 and served in the Korean War at Inchon and the Chosin Reservoir before his designation as a naval aviator in 1953.

October 1967 to 16 January 1968. His new command would take him back to Vietnam, this time not as an F-4 pilot, but as the commander of an evacuation force.*[39]

Within 48 hours of the reactivation of the 9th MAB, the South Vietnamese situation had deteriorated to such a degree that modifications had to be made to the newly completed plans. The rapidly changing state of affairs in Southeast Asia had begun to affect 9th MAB planning and even its assembly. These events had the greatest impact on courses of action involving Military Regions 1 and 2. The Marines had been chosen to help evacuate their fellow citizens from northern South Vietnam. Operation Gallant Journey, later redesignated Fortress Journey, attempted to move Americans and some of the general populace, including the Viet-

---

Naval Ship Disposition, March 1975

—ARG Alpha, consisting of the amphibious assault ship *Okinawa* (LPH 3), the amphibious transport dock *Vancouver* (LPD 2), and the tank landing ship *Peoria* (LST 1183), was on station in the Gulf of Thailand.

—ARG Bravo, composed of *Dubuque* (LPD 8), the amphibious cargo ship *Durham* (LKA 114), and the tank landing ship *Frederick* (LST 1184), was undergoing in-port repairs. The *Dubuque* was at Yokosuka while the *Durham* and *Frederick* were alongside the pier at Subic Bay.

—The amphibious command ship *Blue Ridge* (LCC 19) was in port at White Beach, Okinawa.

—Amphibious Squadron 5, containing the *Denver* (LPD 9), *Duluth* (LPD 6), *Anchorage* (LSD 36), *Mount Vernon* (LSD 39), *Mobile* (LKA 115), *Barbour County* (LST 1195), and *Tuscaloosa* (LST 1187), was preparing to get underway for its impending Westpac tour.

---

*In his previous tour in South Vietnam, General Carey also had served as the 1st MAW's operations officer during the 1968 Tet Offensive and the siege of Khe Sanh. During Tet, he participated in the planning for air support and resupply at Khe Sanh, providing him with multi-service, large-scale, operational experience in South Vietnam. Carey Comments.

Before-and-after pictures show USS Hancock *(CVA 19), assigned to Task Force 76 just prior to Eagle Pull and carrying HMH-463, having shed most of its air wing, right. Most of the fixed-wing aircraft, above, were flown to Cubi Point during the middle of April.*

namese military, from the overrun northern provinces to safe haven in the south. This had to be done using Marines currently available in the 9th MAB. For the Navy, it signalled a call to immediate action. ARG Bravo quickly embarked the Marines of BLT 1/4 in Ora Wan Bay, Okinawa, and made a hasty departure for South Vietnam to assist in the evacuation of the northern region.[40]

At the same time (during the last week of March 1975), General Hoffman sent the primary MAB staff to the South China Sea to join Admiral Whitmire and Task Force 76. These Marines would serve as control headquarters (a defacto 9th MAB forward headquarters) for BLT 1/4, soon to have its mission changed to ships' security guards. The Navy used the BLT 1/4 Marines to maintain law and order on refugee ships. Colonel Dan C. Alexander, while still retaining his position as Chief of Staff, 9th MAB, also was charged with the responsibility of overseeing these Marines. They would be known as the Amphibious Evacuation RVN Support Group (see Chapter 6).[41]

The Chief of Staff, 9th MAB and his core of officers were normally collocated with the commander of Task Force 76, the commander of amphibious forces in the Seventh Fleet, where they functioned as a headquarters with representatives from each operational area. For contingencies and exercises, the full brigade staff was activated by drawing previously designated officers from III MAF, 3d Marine Division, and 1st Marine Aircraft Wing, and integrating them into the original nucleus to form the tactical MAB headquarters. Ground combat, aviation combat, and service support forces were then attached to the brigade as mission or operational requirements dictated.

When General Carey arrived at III MAF Headquarters at Camp Courtney, Okinawa, on 3 April, he found only a handful of officers there. The *Blue Ridge*, with the MAB's nucleus staff officers already embarked, had left Okinawa for Subic Bay and the South China Sea. As soon as the advance staff reported on board, it began preparing for the evacuation of Military Regions 1 and 2.

After determining the whereabouts of his forward staff, General Carey conferred with General Hoffman. Both agreed that the MAB commander should consolidate his headquarters and join Admiral Whitmire and the task force as soon as possible. Carey decided to join the *Blue Ridge* at Subic Bay where the reconstituted amphibious ready group was forming.

General Carey alerted his remaining staff members to prepare for immediate movement to Subic Bay and further transit to a rendezvous with Task Force 76. On 4 April, General Carey flew to Subic Bay, accompanied by Colonel Alfred M. Gray, commanding officer of the 4th Marines, and the MAB's augment staff. The augmented officers normally worked in the headquarters of the 4th and 12th Marines and the 1st Marine Aircraft Wing, while Colonel Gray also held the position of commanding officer designate of the 33d MAU, the landing force assigned to ARG Bravo.[42]

III MAF's liaison officer in Subic Bay, Major Robert M. Reed, quickly arranged for office spaces for the brigade staff at the Subic Bay Marine Barracks. III MAF and 1st MAW Headquarters temporarily provided personnel on a rotational basis to augment the Marine Barracks office, which spent extensive time and effort supporting the numerous Marine units training in the Philippines and operating from Subic Bay. The brigade planners used this office space to begin planning for the real thing, setting aside their MABLEx plans, preparing for the upcoming emergency and a rendezvous in the South China Sea with Task Force 76.[43]

On 7 April, III MAF activated the 33d MAU and its attached elements. It consisted of BLT 1/9, commanded by Lieutenant Colonel Royce L. Bond, and the battalion's logistical mainstay, Major Donald O. Coughlin's LSU 1/9. Already on alert at Subic, having been flown there on 5 April by the USAF Military Airlift Command (MAC), BLT 1/9 was ready for the word to move out. In a round-the-clock shuttle, the Air Force delivered all of the battalion's attached elements, even the assault amphibian tractor platoon. It unloaded the final elements at the Cubi Point Naval Air Station (situated adjacent to and across the bay from the naval base at Subic Bay) just 27 hours after the initial alert. Perhaps the most difficult part of this movement actually occurred on the ground, on Okinawa.

While Marines readied the assault amphibians for movement to Kadena, Air Force C-5 "Galaxys" prepared to fly to Okinawa to pick them up. By noon on 6 April, 9th Motor Transport Battalion's flat bed "low-boys," loaded with eleven tractors, began their trek from Camp Schwab. They had a 1600 rendezvous at Kadena with the world's largest transport aircraft. Lieutenant Colonel Joseph F. Molineaux, Jr., commanding officer of the 1st Amphibian Tractor Battalion, led the convoy. Even though he would not make the trip south with his tractor platoon, he had decided to at least go part of the way with his "tractor rats."*

By 1430, as the convoy passed through Ishikawa on the narrow, two-lane, east coast highway, the Okinawa Sunday traffic was literally backed up for miles. The low-boy drivers had their hands full contending with daring Okinawa drivers. These daredevils would dart in and out, dodging among the evenly spaced Marine vehicles, and challenging the oncoming, northbound traffic. Despite these intrusions, the tractors arrived at Kadena on time.[44]

Within two days of BLT 1/9's landing at Cubi, the heightened activity at the MAU camp and the airfield subsided. Its disappearance marked the successful conclusion of the hectic job of reconstituting Amphibious Ready Group Bravo. Likewise, the *Hancock's* (CVA 19) arrival meshed perfectly with the *Midway's* (CVA 41)

---

*Lieutenant Colonel Molineaux had assumed command of "1st Tracs" six months earlier, 8 October 1974. This organization claimed the distinction of being the longest continually deployed unit in the Marine Corps. "1st Tracs" had shipped out of San Diego in August 1950 with the 1st Marine Division.

USS Okinawa *is seen underway with the 16 CH-53D helicopters of HMH-462 embarked. Having just been used for Operation Eagle Pull on 12 April, the helicopters underwent maintenance and repair while at sea in preparation for Operation Frequent Wind.*

appearance. Carrying numerous helicopters which had flown on board the carrier as it steamed past Okinawa, the *Midway*, both to observers in Subic and to its own crewmembers, looked unusual with its fixed-wing flight deck covered with rotary-wing aircraft. In order to move these MAG-36 helicopters from the *Midway* to the *Hancock*, which already had HMH-463 on board, deck space had to be found. To accomplish this, *Hancock* sent its fixed-wing contingent ashore. The planes flew from the ship to their new home, NAS Cubi Point. This evolution transformed, in looks at least, the *Hancock* from a carrier to a helicopter landing ship. With the embarkation of the 33d MAU, ARG Bravo stood ready ready to sail. Shortly before the completion of this transfer, the rest of ARG Bravo (the *Dubuque*, *Durham*, and *Frederick*) sailed into Subic, returning from a shortened evacuation stint off the coast of South Vietnam's northern provinces.

On 9 April, the MAB staff, 33d MAU, and ARG Bravo (*Hancock, Durham, Frederick,* and *Dubuque*) departed Subic Bay for Vung Tau, Republic of Vietnam. At this time, the helicopter squadron on the *Hancock*, HMH-463, and the one on *Dubuque*, HMM-165, were placed under the operational control of 33d MAU. The following day, General Carey requested that HMH-463 be reassigned to 31st MAU to assist in Operation Eagle Pull. At the same instant this was done, Admiral Whitmire transferred operational control of the *Hancock* to ARG Alpha. With HMH-463 on board, the *Hancock*'s new mission was to assist in the evacuation of Phnom Penh.

On 11 April, General Carey rendezvoused with Admiral Whitmire and the amphibious task force commander's flagship, the *Blue Ridge*. Finally, two weeks after 9th MAB's reactivation, General Carey caught up with his forward headquarters and merged it with the staff accompanying him. Carey and the full staff immediately began to plan and prepare for the evacuation of South Vietnam, initially called Operation Talon Vise. However, within a week the secret name would be reported "compromised," forcing the assignment of a new codename, Frequent Wind.[45]

Having been alerted on 6 April to react to the new contingency in Southeast Asia, the second BLT of the MAB, BLT 3/9, still at Camp Fuji, Japan, moved from there overland to the Naval Air Facility, Atsugi. In Atsugi, BLT 3/9 boarded Marine KC-130s for a two-hour flight to Okinawa. Once on Okinawa, the Marines embarked in the ships of Amphibious Squadron 5, which had just arrived from California. Aware that his normally assigned shipping was either already off the coast of South Vietnam or preparing to head there, this otherwise cumbersome method of "getting to the action" did much to assuage the land-locked, marooned feeling of BLT 3/9's commander, Lieutenant Colonel Robert E. Loehe.

The movement was accomplished in its entirety by using aircraft from Lieutenant Colonel Jerry L. Shelton's Marine Aerial Refueling Squadron (VMGR) 152. The entire evolution was completed in less than 72 hours. Due to cargo configuration and weight limitations, the amphibian tractor and tank platoons were left at Camp Fuji. They would eventually embark in the *Anchorage*, which had been ordered to proceed independently to Numazu, Japan. Of the event, Lieutenant Colonel Shelton said, "Operations went around the clock with minimum ground time, allowing time for fuel and crew changes only."[46]

While BLT 3/9 was in transit from Atsugi, the 35th MAU, to be commanded by Colonel Hans G. Edebohls, was forming at Camp Schwab. Personnel from 9th Marines Headquarters formed the new MAU's skeleton staff. The 35th MAU consisted of Lieutenant Colonel Loehe's BLT 3/9, Lieutenant Colonel James R. Gentry's HML-367, and Major Fred L. Jones' LSU 3/9. Once embarked in Amphibious Squadron 5's ships, now designated ARG Charlie, the MAU would join 9th MAB and support its operations off the coast of South Vietnam. At least, that was the plan.[47]

The inclusion of the 35th MAU created an unusual organization, a brigade with three MAUs. This organization reflected the uncertainty prevalent in WestPac at the time. No one could predict if or when an evacuation might be necessary, or even if the inbound ships of Amphibious Squadron 5 would arrive in time. Each MAU formed as amphibious ships became available.[48]

To meet both the Cambodian and South Vietnamese emergencies and still maintain mobility, the Pacific command ordered the formation of three MAUs, each assigned to a different amphibious ready group, under the 9th MAB. The brigade thereby possessed the ability to control all these forces with a single headquarters.

On 12 April, the Marines of the 31st MAU and its command element carried out a model emergency evacuation of Phnom Penh. By noon, with Operation Eagle Pull complete, South Vietnam remained the only contingency. The following day, the 31st MAU reported to 9th Brigade for planning and operations. For all practical purposes the 9th MAB was formed, and with the exception of the 35th MAU which was scheduled to arrive within 10 days, was ready for operations.[49]

CHAPTER 9

Planning the Evacuation

Brigade Planning and Liaison—The Restructured 9th Marine Amphibious Brigade—The Concept Additional Forces, Plans, and Liaison—DAO Planning: The SPG and Project Alamo

---

Brigade Planning and Liaison

South Vietnam in April 1975 offered few opportunities for U.S. Marine planners to control and direct events precipitated by North Vietnam's highly successful invasion. The absence of a strong U.S. military presence in Southeast Asia only compounded this already complicated crisis situation. In the Pacific command, operational forces belonged either to the Seventh Fleet or USSAG/Seventh Air Force, and if any jurisdictional disputes arose, CinCPac would have the final word. The Seventh Fleet's amphibious force included the Navy amphibious task force, Task Force 76 (TF 76); the 9th MAB, designated Task Group 79.1 (TG 79.1); and the MAB's parent organization, III Marine Amphibious Force, Task Force 79 (TF 79).

American Marines in South Vietnam in 1975 came under the jurisdictional control of two persons, the Defense Attache or the Ambassador. The Marines guarding American facilities took their orders from Ambassador Graham A. Martin while those at the DAO received their directions from General Homer D. Smith, Jr., USA, the Defense Attache. As early as February, General Smith had instructed Colonel Eugene R. "Pat" Howard, the senior Marine in South Vietnam and a DAO staff member, to begin planning for the evacuation of Saigon. Both General Smith and Colonel Howard knew that ultimately the final decisions concerning the evacuation would come to rest with the senior military officer in the Pacific, Admiral Gayler. Unless the final evacuation occurred without military support, it would be at a minimum an air and naval event.

To oversee and control such an event, CinCPac, the overall commander in the Pacific theater of operations, designated Lieutenant General John J. Burns, the commander of USSAG, to be his coordinating authority for any emergency evacuations conducted in Southeast Asia. Already the tactical commander of all U.S. forces assigned to Thailand, this additional duty placed General Burns in the position of controlling any evacuation force once that unit entered the Indochinese peninsula. This meant that the 9th Marine Amphibious Brigade while afloat served under the amphibious force commander and the Commander, Seventh Fleet, but once ashore belonged to General Burns.[1]

The geographic point marking the change in operational control from the Seventh Fleet to USSAG was the Southeast Asian coastline. Once past that imaginary line, the units were deemed "feet dry" having left their "feet wet" status at the water's edge. Thus the Commanding General, 9th Marine Amphibious Brigade, Brigadier General Richard E. Carey, operated within a dual command structure, although most of the time the Seventh Fleet exercised control over his forces.[2]

General Burns' decision on 5 April 1975 to employ Marines of Task Force 79 as a ground security force and Marine helicopters to evacuate South Vietnam actually began the 9th MAB's compressed planning phase. Prior to this, the evacuation options included only the use of either commercial air transports or sealift or the employment of military transport aircraft or sealift. These options anticipated the use of only limited numbers of ground forces, if any, in South Vietnam. After the collapse of Da Nang, however, General Burns realized that he needed some additional alternatives.[3]

Adding Marine helicopters and ground forces to the plan signified an escalation in requirements. It caused III MAF and the 9th MAB to mobilize their forces, and with the assistance of the Navy amphibious ready groups, to relocate off the coast of South Vietnam. Planning for the use of helicopters in such a large evacuation assumed that the maximum number of helicopters would be available to launch if execution became necessary.

On 5 April 1975, there was only one amphibious assault ship, USS *Okinawa* (LPH 3), in the Western Pacific. The attack carrier USS *Hancock* (CVA 19) had been summoned from the West Coast and was due to arrive off the coast of South Vietnam in the next few days. The *Midway* (CVA 41), homeported in Yokosuka, Japan, also was available.[4]

As the month of April progressed, other changes took place and were reflected in new directives received by the brigade from General Burns' headquarters. Most were amplifying instructions pertaining to the original courses of action, while others simply defined

Department of Defense Photo (USMC) A151000

BGen Richard E. Carey is pictured on the bridge of the attack aircraft carrier USS Hancock *while visiting with BLT 1/9 and HMH-463. Gen Carey, the 9th MAB commander, served on the* Hancock *many years earlier as a corporal in its Marine detachment.*

USS Okinawa *with HMH-462 aircraft embarked steams along the coast of South Vietnam on 18 April 1975. At that date* Okinawa *had been at sea almost continuously since February 1975 and therefore often was underway with only three of its four boilers working.*

Department of Defense Photo (USMC) A150855

in more detail the helicopter alternative. Through its "feet wet" chain of command, the 9th MAB received additional instructions from the Navy. These directives for the most part were complementary to USSAG's; however, they did contain additional taskings. The brigade headquarters became in effect a conduit for melding the various plans of the dual chain of command. The 9th MAB staff, in particular the G-3 section, under the direction of Lieutenant Colonel Robert D. White, was required to examine every minute aspect of the operation, ensuring that the parallel planning cogs did in fact mesh. Where they did not, the brigade assisted in rectifying the differences.[5]

Many of the conflicts arose from the changing assumptions caused by the highly volatile situation in South Vietnam. With the North Vietnamese controlling the action and dictating the tactics, little could really be done in selecting a single best course of action. As a consequence it was necessary for the brigade to develop detailed plans for each course of action, making no assumptions which would place the lives of the evacuees in jeopardy. Thus, USSAG and the 9th MAB had to develop a definitive and comprehensive plan covering a wide range of alternatives which minimized the risk for confusion or conflicts for the participants.

This spectrum of alternatives ranged from the insertion of a handful of small security teams onto rooftop landing zones in Saigon to an amphibious landing on the Vung Tau Peninsula. The latter option required the landing force to secure a major marshalling/evacuation area. Plans for these potential missions had to take into account the requirement to provide landing forces for security of the landing zones. Finally, the idea of providing helicopters for all of these options in addition to the Marines serving as security for the Military Sealift Command ships meant that by committing the 9th MAB to this operation, III MAF would have limited numbers available for any additional commitments.

After its arrival off Vung Tau on 10 April, one of the 9th MAB's first orders of business was to make contact with officials in the U.S. Embassy and the DAO in Saigon. At the same time, III MAF sent a liaison team to Saigon via Nakhon Phanom (USSAG Headquarters) to gather planning information. The next day this team briefed the MAB staff on the situation in Saigon. Before the MAF team left the ship on 10 April to return to Nakhon Phanom, General Carey asked them to inquire as to the possibility of the 9th MAB staff visiting Saigon and conducting a personal

Marine Corps Historical Collection

Col Alfred M. Gray, pictured as Commandant of the Marine Corps, commanded 33d MAU in early April. When the 9th MAB was restructured on 18 April, he assumed command of Regimental Landing Team 4.

reconnaissance of potential evacuation sites. Upon gaining approval of this mission, the 9th MAB sent a delegation of air and ground officers to Saigon on 12 April.[6]

Having spent the entire day in Saigon, the delegation returned to the *Blue Ridge* and reported to General Carey that the primary evacuation sites most likely would be either the DAO/Air America Compound, the Newport Pier, or Vung Tau Peninsula. The officers brought back schematics and photographs of these facilities. Further the group related the concerns that Ambassador Martin had manifested during their visit to the Embassy. In no uncertain terms, he had conveyed to the Marines that he would not tolerate any outward sign of intent to depart the country because he felt it would become a self-fulfilling prophecy. The Ambassador believed an overt vote of no confidence could even speed the inexorable movement toward collapse. Hence, all planning and related evacuation activities would have to be conducted discreetly, while for the purpose of appearance, business would continue as usual, or seem to, for U.S. officials in South Vietnam.

In order to gain a better personal understanding of the situation and visually integrate this new information into his planning, General Carey visited South Vietnam. The major purpose of his trip on 13 April was reconnaissance. In the helicopter, he took with him the 33d MAU commander, Colonel Alfred M. Gray. During his stay, he talked with the Defense Attache, General Smith, and the CinCPac Saigon representative, Rear Admiral Hugh G. Benton, USN. General Carey also visited the Embassy and was given a very short but formal audience with Ambassador Martin. The Ambassador tactfully avoided any detailed discussion of the impending evacuation, merely explaining that all operations would be conducted from the DAO where General Smith would coordinate and that Martin's plan called for him to leave the Embassy with a small group of Marines at a time to be determined by him. Years later, General Carey recalled that meeting with Ambassador Martin: "During our discussion he instructed me to coordinate through my appropriate military channels for detailed evacuation information. The visit was cold, non-productive and appeared to be an irritant to the ambassador."[7]

General Carey's other stops on 13 April included the DAO/Air America Compound, Tan Son Nhut Airfield, the Newport Pier, and various LZ's throughout Saigon. While enroute to and from Saigon, he reconnoitered the Vung Tau Peninsula. Although relatively short, this trip provided the MAB commander a first-hand view of the Saigon situation and valuable information for future decision-making.[8]

The Restructured 9th Marine Amphibious Brigade

General Carey's trip to Saigon and the 9th MAB's liaison efforts coincided with the slowing of the North Vietnamese Army's advance toward Saigon. As General Van Tien Dung, the Chief of Staff of the North Vietnamese Army later noted, the army's campaign headquarters became concerned that the offensive might bog down and miss its opportunity to capture Saigon before the end of April:

> We worried in particular about the 10th Division, which still was in the Cam Ranh area and still faced enemy troops along their route into Eastern Nam Bo. With the long difficult road they had to travel, we did not know if they would be able to get down within the appointed time period.[9]

By 15 April, with the North Vietnamese offensive stalled and the 18th ARVN Division successfully defending Xuan Loc and Highway 1's eastern entrance to Saigon, the tactical situation in South Vietnam stabilized, giving the impression that the new defensive perimeter had successfully checked the enemy's advance. In truth, the Communists had outrun their supply lines, but the United States did not know that. As a result, Task Force 76 requested and received permission to return to Subic Bay for much-needed repairs. The evacuation of refugees by Navy vessels had been suspended and activity on Military Sealift Command shipping was at a lull. Moving away from the South Vietnamese coast at this time was a calculated, but necessary risk. With the brigade returning to Subic Bay, General Hoffman decided to reorganize the 9th MAB.[10]

On 17 April, General Hoffman directed that the 9th MAB combine its ground units into a regimental landing team and its squadrons into a provisional air group. To this organization would be added a brigade logistic support group (BLSG). That evening, shortly after arriving in Subic, the task force received news that the NVA had renewed its offensive. Orders to get underway accompanied that update. On 18 April, the III MAF commander flew down to Subic to see his restructured brigade leave for South Vietnam. Colonel Wylie W. Taylor, the commanding officer of the 9th Marines, accompanied him on the trip. General Hoffman had assigned him to the brigade as its deputy commander. Colonel Taylor was to head the advance command element of the 9th MAB, scheduled to fly to Saigon to be the on-the-scene "eyes and ears" of the brigade.[11]

General Carey believed such an arrangement was essential for coordination and mission success. He also decided that the brigade would be better served if they had a representative in Nakhon Phanom on General Burns' staff.* He chose his plans officer, Major Richard K. Young, to fill the role of liaison between USSAG and 9th MAB. On 18 April as the aircraft carrying General Hoffman, Colonel Taylor, and the advance command element from Okinawa taxied up to the Cubi Point passenger terminal, another aircraft 1,200 miles to the west landed at Nakhon Phanom. Stepping onto the tarmac, one of its passengers, Major "Keith" Young began a two-week stay at USSAG Headquarters during which he continuously passed information to General Carey via the DAO Compound and the *Blue Ridge*.[12]

---

*Due to difficulty in pronouncing its name correctly, most visitors to Nakhon Phanom called it NKP, the letters emitted in Morse code by the airfield's main navigational aid, its TACAN. Each TACAN had its own set of identifying letters which distinguished it from all others in the region and when collocated with an airfield described that airport as well.

As Major Young settled into his new surroundings in northern Thailand, Colonel John M. Johnson, Jr., the III MAF G-3, briefed Colonel Taylor and his four-man advance command element in Subic. The next morning, they departed Cubi Point with the DAO as their destination. An unexpected change at Tan Son Nhut ended the command party's day (19 April) not in Saigon but in Nakhon Phanom where they joined Major Young and Lieutenant Colonel James L. Cunningham, the III MAF, G-3 Plans Officer, all of them in Thailand for the same purpose: liaison with USSAG Headquarters. In addition to Colonel Taylor, the aircraft's manifest included: Lieutenant Colonel Donald J. Verdon, communications officer; Major David E. Cox, air liaison officer; Captain Raymond J. McManus, explosive ordnance specialist; and Master Sergeant William East, explosive ordnance specialist.

While in Nakhon Phanom, Colonel Taylor and his team received a comprehensive after-action brief on Operation Eagle Pull delivered by its ground security force commander, Marine Colonel Sydney H. Batchelder, Jr. After extensive meetings with USSAG's staff, lasting until lunchtime on the 20th, the advance command element boarded another plane and returned to Saigon, leaving Major Young behind to begin his liaison duties.[13]

Young's presence at USSAG Headquarters helped alleviate the confusion over jargon and procedure peculiar to each service, and also fulfilled the joint operational requirement for each participating branch to provide a liaison officer. Throughout his tour at Nakhon Phanom, Major Young answered numerous questions concerning size of units, equipment carried, and capabilities. This type of face-to-face contact was almost as critical as the presence of an advance command element in the DAO Compound.

On 21 April, the morning following his Sunday afternoon arrival in Saigon, Colonel Taylor established the 9th MAB forward headquarters in the DAO Evacuation Control Center (ECC) and remained there until the bitter end. His command element's presence at the "Pentagon East" facilitated the critical communications link between General Carey and Major Young.[14] As these events unfolded in Thailand and South Vietnam, General Carey and his brigade continued to adjust to the reorganization. Task Force 76 headed back to its station off the South Vietnamese coast near the Vung Tau Peninsula. While enroute the

BGen Richard E. Carey hosts one of many planning sessions over Saigon contingencies conducted on board the USS Blue Ridge *(LCC 19). Seated to Gen Carey's right, from left, are LtCol Royce L. Bond, Col Frank G. McLenon, and Col Alfred M. Gray.*
Department of Defense Photo (USMC A150913

9th MAB staff began to modify the evacuation plan to reflect the recent organizational changes. In addition to ordering the brigade's reconfiguration, III MAF decided to reorganize its shipboard security forces. To accomplish this, the MAF attached a newly created ship security group to the 9th MAB, the Amphibious Evacuation Security Force (AESF). This unit replaced the 1st Battalion, 4th Marines as the Navy and Military Sealift Command's shipboard security contingent. The AESF was composed of a control group drawn from the headquarters staff of the 9th Marines and 10 72-man detachments representing various commands within the 3d Marine Division.

Weeks prior to the AESF's activation, the 3d Marine Division Commander, Major General Kenneth J. Houghton, anticipating this requirement, issued a letter of instruction which directed division units to supply him with a list of highly qualified Marines capable of carrying out this potentially dangerous and demanding security task. Upon receiving the word to activate this force, General Houghton instructed his division units to provide the previously designated Marines for transshipment to the Philippines and the South China Sea. At this point, the 1st Marine Aircraft Wing directed Marine Aerial Refueler Squadron 152 to respond to this short-fused, logistical requirement. In a round-the-clock shuttle on 17 April, the Marine KC-130s of "Ichi Go Ni" (152) moved the newly formed security force a thousand miles south to the "PI" (Philippine Islands).[15]

The restructured brigade consisted of three major elements: Regimental Landing Team 4 commanded by Colonel Alfred M. Gray, Provisional Marine Air Group 39 with Colonel Frank G. McLenon as its commander, and the Brigade Logistic Support Group headed by Colonel Hans G. Edebohls. BLT 1/9 led by Lieutenant Colonel Royce L. Bond, BLT 2/4 commanded by Lieutenant Colonel George P. Slade, and BLT 3/9 with Lieutenant Colonel Robert E. Loehe as its commander made up the ground combat elements of the regimental landing team. The shipboard, combat-ready, flying units were HMH-462, HMH-463, and HMM-165. Lieutenant Colonels James L. Bolton, Herbert M. Fix, and James P. Kizer were the respective commanders. In addition, HML-367, commanded by Lieutenant Colonel James R. Gentry, belonged to Provisional MAG-39, but its headquarters remained at Subic. Colonel McClenon assigned HML-367's aircraft to the other squadrons within ProvMAG-39 as he did the "Cobras" of HMA-369. The logistics support group was composed of LSUs 1/9, 2/4, and 3/9.

Major Donald O. Coughlin, Major James A. Gallagher, and Major Fred L. Jones commanded these individual units, respectively. Major David A. Quinlan served as the officer in charge of the newly attached unit, the Amphibious Evacuation Security Force.[16]

On 19 April, the 9th MAB arrived in South Vietnamese waters. As he had during the brigade's earlier afloat period, General Carey immediately reported to the task force commander for operational matters. Prepared and anxious for action, the 9th MAB had suffered little from the interruption. On 20 April, it published Operation Order 2-75, its plan for Operation Frequent Wind.[17] The same day the brigade published its order, Colonel Alfred M. Gray, commanding Regimental Landing Team 4 (RLT-4/CTU 79.1.2), issued the regiment's operational plan. Major James E. Livingston, the regimental operations officer, and his staff's collocation and close coordination with the brigade aided both headquarters in producing plans with detailed annexes in a highly compressed time period.

Close cooperation between the brigade and regimental staff also assisted in relieving some of the communications backlog on the *Blue Ridge*. Delays still occurred because of the large number of staffs using the communications facilities. The various organizations participating in the operation were so widely dispersed that the majority of the orders issued by the various headquarters had to be transmitted in message format. It therefore became essential for the brigade and its subordinate units to implement procedures to minimize or eliminate duplication of communications. The ability to pass instructions and changes without delay faced a crucial test as each command element intensified its dissemination efforts.[18]

The Concept

With the communications system nearly overloaded from the exchange of information needed to make last-minute adjustments to the concept of operations, the collection of accurate raw data became critical to the 9th MAB's final planning efforts. Thus the advance command element in Saigon undertook as one of its primary functions, the gathering of intelligence and its analysis. It had to update continuously the information on the evacuation sites, collate it, interpret it, and then transmit it to the appropriate commands. The breadth of the possible evacuation sites and their varied contingencies made this a requisite step. The potential evacuation sites included all of the following:

Newport Pier—This facility was situated adjacent to the Long Binh Bridge on the Saigon

Department of Defense Photo (USMC) A150969

This aerial photo of Saigon and the Newport Pier shows why planners considered using the river as a means of evacuating the South Vietnamese capital. The lightning-quick success of the NVA encirclement made this option unusable by the last week of April 1975.

riverfront. It featured four deep-water berths and a number of ramps and landings for assorted tugs and smaller craft. Parking lots provided nine CH-53 landing spots. Newport was envisioned as a large-scale evacuation site accommodating up to 100,000 evacuees by waterborne means. At a minimum, one battalion would be needed to secure the pier. In addition to special security force detachments to search and screen the evacuees and provide security for the ships, an undetermined number of rifle platoons would be needed to accompany the evacuation ships on the perilous ride down the Saigon River to the South China Sea. Insertion of the landing force could be by helicopter or by ships using the Saigon River. Extraction was equally flexible, thereby making this option viable until the last possible moment.

DAO/Air America Complex—Situated adjacent to Tan Son Nhut Air Base, this complex was considered the primary site should evacuation become necessary. With a little preparation, numerous landing zones could be made available in the DAO Compound, the Annex, and across the highway on the Air America apron. At least two infantry battalions would be needed to secure this area, and if the scope of the operation were broadened to include security for fixed-wing evacuation flights out of Tan Son Nhut, then as many as three battalions would be required. The DAO Compound was divided into roughly two separate areas, one called the Alamo and the other the Annex. The Alamo housed the main headquarters and the Evacuation Command Center. The Annex consisted primarily of the Exchange, the bowling alley, a swimming pool, and a gymnasium.

Can Tho—The concept for this region involved a movement up the Bassac River to Can Tho, about 50 miles southwest of Saigon, to evacuate as many as 2,000 people. To support this plan, the MAB was prepared to insert secu-

Marine Corps Historical Collection

Company E, Marine Security Guard Battalion forms in the American Embassy parking lot which for Operation Frequent Wind was designated as an evacuation site. The tree in the center of the photo was felled on 29 April to permit CH-53 helicopters to land.

The Vung Tau Light stands out as a prominent landmark signalling the end of the Vung Tau Peninsula and, for many, the end of a way of life. Serious consideration was given by U.S. commanders to conducting a MAB-size amphibious landing at this site.

Department of Defense Photo (USMC) 7718975

rity forces either by helicopter or by waterborne means.

Saigon Rooftops—This entailed assembling evacuees for preliminary extraction at approximately one dozen locations throughout Saigon. Helicopters would then transport them to the DAO/Air America Complex for further processing and marshaling. Fireteam-sized elements were envisioned for rooftop security and to serve as landing zone control teams.

U.S. Embassy—With only one rooftop landing zone restricted to a single CH-46 or smaller aircraft, the Embassy was never seriously considered as a mass evacuation site. The maximum extraction total for this location was estimated at no more than 100 people. The possibility of using an additional landing zone existed, but only if a large tree and some lesser obstacles could be removed from the area adjacent to the courtyard parking lot.

Vung Tau—The largest of all the possible evacuation sites, Vung Tau, plagued the planners from the first day. Hundreds of thousands of refugees, as well as the remnants of the South Vietnamese Army and Marine Corps had retreated to the Vung Tau Peninsula by mid-April. Many had hopes of being sealifted from there to safe haven. For this reason, consideration was given to a MAB-sized amphibious landing to secure both the airfield and the port facilities in order to develop a major marshaling and evacuation center. The estimated size of the force necessary to accomplish this ranged from one battalion landing team to the entire brigade. To commit a brigade-sized force to the Vung Tau alternative meant more than just a temporary fix or an emergency evacuation. It meant a full-scale commitment of logistical and personnel assets. With the added confusion each new day brought, this complicated alternative became a planner's nightmare and more of an enigma than a solution. It truly offered more problems than it solved.[19]

The majority of the landing sites provided access only via helicopter and as a consequence most of the joint planning focused on making the brigade's helicopter flow plan (movement schedule) mesh with USSAG's operational plan. The forward extension of USSAG's Headquarters, the airborne battlefield command and control center, would control the helicopters in and out of the landing zone once they went "feet dry" (over land). Until that point they would be under the control of the Navy and thus the two schedules had to be integrated.

The coordinated flow schedule had to support a scheme of maneuver ashore that would include insertion of the landing force, emergency evacuation of the civilians, and extraction of the security force with enough inherent flexibility to encompass all of the potential sites and the use of any or all of the available flight decks. Additionally, the final schedule had to be one that could be controlled "feet dry" by the airborne controller and "feet wet" by the helicopter direction center (HDC) on the *Okinawa*. After achieving this, the planners faced another problem, clarification of L-Hour. To the Marines it meant the landing time in the zone, while to the Air Force it signified mission launch time. The former definition was used in the evacuation from Cambodia. For this operation, L-Hour was defined as the time the first helicopter should touch down in the landing zone.[20]

Another matter of concern, the weather, represented a significant variable that the 9th MAB commander could ill afford to ignore. Predictions called for periods of inclement weather with ceilings of less than 1,000 feet and reduced visibility. Since the time of the operation was unpredictable, night operations also had to be included in the planning. The resultant scheme of maneuver anticipated performing the mission day or night, and under instrument conditions if necessary. There would be difficulties and operational limitations: no approved helicopter letdown (a tested and approved approach to a landing site for other than visual conditions), limited navigational aids, suspect air defense network, and a makeshift air control system. Even the threat of a tropical storm did not alter the MAB's plan or the timing of its release. This did not mean that higher headquarters was without reservations about the wisdom of attempting an evacuation at night or under instrument conditions. They had reservations, but General Carey believed that if weather conditions permitted takeoff, the Marine helicopter pilots could finish the job.

In evaluating aircraft availability, the staff closely monitored the daily reports and confidently noted that despite an extended period at sea, the Marine maintenance crews, with the support of the Navy supply system, had consistently attained high operational ready rates. Yet variances in the average cycle rate for helicopters in their round trips between ship and shore

A Marine CH-53 navigates to Saigon by following the Saigon River towards its source. Most deadly obstacle to safe flight was local weather which could not be controlled nor predicted.

had caused a problem in creating a workable refueling schedule. The planners determined that if in their calculations they limited changes in the ships' location in the South China Sea, cycle rate variances would be eliminated, and they could obtain a realistic estimate for turnaround time. To accomplish this, the planners averaged the sum of the anticipated, modified locations and arrived at a point of origin which when combined with the assumed use of the farthest evacuation site (DAO Complex) produced a cycle rate of 90 minutes. With this factor in hand, the planners knew the fueling limits of their helicopters and then devised a viable refueling plan. With this issue resolved, the staff turned its attention to the next critical element, deck availability. The potentially large number of evacuees dictated the use of the largest helicopter in the Marine Corps inventory, the CH-53. By using all the helicopter-capable ships in the task force, the planners could count on 30 CH-53 landing spots. This became even more complicated when additional options were added to the original plan, requiring in each change more security forces or at least a new combination of forces.[21]

As a result of these changes, the increased number of security forces had to be distributed among the amphibious ships. Even though separated, they still would have to maintain as much tactical unit integrity as possible with the expectation that prior to L-Hour, extensive crossdecking and repositioning would reunite them. The amount of movement in the crossdecking phase would depend on the option selected. The option also would determine the number of helicopters needed.

Additional Forces, Plans, and Liaison

In addition to the movement of HMH-463 from Hawaii on board the *Hancock*, CinCPac also tasked USSAG to provide transport helicopters, both HH-53s, the rescue version, and CH-53s. General Burns directed the 3d Aerospace Rescue and Recovery Group to send to the *Midway* two HH-53s, call sign "Jolly," and also the 56th Special Operations Wing to provide eight CH-53s. Upon their arrival at Utapao, Air Force Colonel Loyd J. Anders, Jr., USSAG/Seventh Air Force's representative for the mission (executive agent), assumed responsibility for these aircraft. The following day, 20 April 1975, Colonel Anders sent the Air Force helicopters on to the *Midway*. Two of the CH-53s, call sign "Knife," aborted that morning and the 40th Aerospace Rescue and Recovery Squadron (40th ARRS), which had spares airborne (HH-53s), replaced them with two HH-53s, making the *Midway* complement six CH-53s and four HH-53s.[22]

Two days later the 21st Special Operations Squadron (21st SOS) flew two CH-53s to the carrier to replace two of the four HH-53s. The CH-53, a special operations helicopter, was a better choice in this situation, because without the rescue equipment that the HH-53 rescue helicopter carried, the CH-53 could transport more troops. The real problem with the Air Force helicopters on board the *Midway* was that their blades did not fold as did the Navy-Marine Corps version, and as a consequence these 10 helicopters ate up all of the carrier's deck space. Thus, the *Midway*'s Air Force contingent was limited to 10 helicopters.

The detachment consisted of eight CH-53s and two HH-53s with Major John F. Guilmartin, Jr., as the ranking officer.* These aircraft augmented the 16 CH-53s of HMH-462 on board the *Okinawa* and a like number of the same aircraft of HMH-463 on board the *Hancock*. In addition to these heavy haulers, the task force also possessed 27 medium transport helicopters, CH-46Ds. Based on their current availability rate, it was reasonable to assume that 40 "53s" and 24 "46s" would be ready to embark two battalions of Marines (1,680 men). Helicopter employment and assault landing tables were developed accordingly.[23]

While Marine planners developed helicopter flow tables, General Burn's USSAG staff created a detailed air plan. The Marine Corps resolved the only major question in the plan, a lack of escort helicopters, by providing Cobra gunships. Additionally, the Navy's carrier aircraft would be on alert and available for an immediate air strike if needed. With regard to the use of tactical air, General Carey decided that a strong show of force, using fixed-wing aircraft capable of delivering suppressive fire as needed, would deter enemy rockets and artillery from firing upon the landing zones and at the helicopters.

This idea of combining tactical air for a massive show of force gained instant and unanimous approval. Immediately, CinCPac approved plans to integrate the entire tactical structure of Seventh Air Force with the Navy's carrier air wings. The Seventh Fleet agreed to commit all available aircraft from the USS *Enterprise* (CVAN 65) and the USS *Coral Sea* (CV 43) for round-the-clock air support. Included in the Air Force inventory were AC-130 "Spectre" gunships, aircraft specially equipped for night strike and suppression missions. This combined show of force and the air umbrella it represented provided the planners with the best possible countermeasure to the enemy's most significant threat, a belt of antiaircraft weapons guarding the helicopter approach corridors to Saigon. The planners thought that the heavy fire coverage might even deter the daytime use of the SA-7, and the cover of darkness would tend to favor the helicopter rather than the enemy's line-of-sight gunners. To avoid or minimize the effect of small arms fire, the approach called for an altitude of 6,500 feet with the egress route restricted to 5,500 feet.

As events began to unfold and liaison with Saigon became a daily occurrence, certain things became clear. First, that the DAO/Air America complex would probably be the primary evacuation site, and second, that the insertion force would have to be tailored to the existing conditions in and around the complex. General Carey knew that the force had to be large enough to provide adequate security, but not so large that extraction would create even greater problems. With this in mind, the commanding general of the brigade announced four planning options.

The first alternative provided for the introduction of a battalion-sized security force into the DAO compound to meet any hostile threat and provide crowd control and security for a large group of evacuees. Insertion and extraction would be by helicopter, using as landing zones the PX parking lot, the softball field, the tennis court, and the north and south parking lots. All the other alternatives were derivatives of this basic plan.

The second choice envisioned similar security conditions and called for the insertion of an additional battalion command group and one company into the Air America complex, capable of expanding to a full battalion if necessary. The third option involved only two companies and a battalion command group. They would occupy the DAO compound and use the landing zones in the Alamo, expecting little threat and extraction of only a few evacuees. The last option foresaw a totally permissive environment and no need for a landing force.[24]

Regardless of which alternative the evacuation force selected, communications would play a key part in the

---

*The CH-53s of 21st SOS from Nakhon Phanom replaced the original two rescue helicopters flown by the 40th ARRS squadron commander, Lieutenant Colonel Joseph McMonigle, and his wingman. They rotated back to Nakhon Phanom, leaving only two HH-53s on board the *Midway*, the backup helicopters. When McMonigle's flight returned to Nakhon Phanom, he left behind the lead pilot of the original flight of airborne spares, Major John F. Guilmartin, Jr., USAF. By virtue of his commander's departure and his field-grade rank, Major Guilmartin became the senior Air Force helicopter pilot on the *Midway*. Guilmartin Comments.

operation's success or failure. Long before the final options were developed, members of General Burns' staff addressed the critical area of communications. Early in February 1975, communicators wrote a plan which, when modified by fragmentary orders, supported any emergency operation to evacuate civilians from Southeast Asia. With this already in his possession, Commander, USSAG only had to make minor adjustments.

The planned nets, assigned frequencies, and call signs were combined with frequency and circuit designators. Married with the organizational structure, they produced a master radio plan. By entering it into a computer, the planners then gained the flexibility they needed to accommodate any last-minute changes. By this means, a fragmentary order could be issued designating what nets to activate and what steps to follow, which in turn allowed the plan to support any of the potential organizations. The computerized communication plan smoothly incorporated the changes precipitated by the brigade's reorganization on 17 April, avoiding a time-consuming rewrite of the original plan.[25]

Restructuring of the brigade aided the planners in their final concern—logistics. Activation of the 9th Marine Amphibious Brigade Logistic Support Group on 19 April created a headquarters element and three logistic support units, capable of providing highly specialized logistical support. Everyone in the task force quickly realized the value of this type of supply support as they faced seemingly endless numbers of starving, destitute refugees.[26]

Supply matters took on an added meaning as the task force attempted to provide for thousands of unplanned additions to its ranks. Faced with the threat of a hostile group of evacuees much like those encountered during the evacuation of Da Nang, the 9th MAB staff also had to develop some appropriate rules of conduct to guarantee protection of its own people while still avoiding injury to those it sought to help.

The 9th MAB adopted rules of engagement which restricted but did not restrain the Marines' application of force. To achieve this, the brigade wrote rules which directed the commander to use the minimum amount of force, and empowered him, if the situation dictated, to increase it. With the adoption and

Sitting adjacent to the Defense Attache Office in northwest Saigon was Tan Son Nhut Air Base, the most important airport in South Vietnam and the primary site for evacuation. Parked between the revetments are Vietnamese Air Force C-130As which were used, in addition to transport and evacuation missions, as platforms for delivering BLU-82 bombs.

Department of Defense Photo (USMC) A150968

PLANNING THE EVACUATION

An overhead view of the DAO compound with the Air America terminal across the street to the west, at left. Large building at center is DAO offices, formerly MACV headquarters.

inclusion of these rules of engagement, the 9th Marine Amphibious Brigade concluded its evacuation planning. With a blueprint in hand, everyone's attention refocused on the events in South Vietnam as the brigade staff calculated when they might expect to execute Operation Frequent Wind.[27]

DAO Planning: The SPG and Project Alamo

During April 1975, while Task Force 76 maneuvered its ships off the coast of South Vietnam and 9th MAB prepared for the evacuation, the Defense Attache Office in Saigon maintained an incredibly busy schedule. One group in particular had been sustaining, since its formation in late February, a furious planning pace. Known as the SPG or Special Planning Group, it consisted of Colonel Eugene R. "Pat" Howard, the senior member; Major Jaime Sabater, Jr., a representative to the Four-Power Joint Military Commission; Captain Anthony A. Wood, the Joint Casualty Resolution Center's deputy for operations in South Vietnam; and Army Captain George Petry, a member of the Joint Casualty Resolution Center.

Years later Captain Wood recalled his mission: "We had to devise a plan to fortify and reinforce the Compound to hold 10,000 people for 10 days should the situation dictate that in order to accomplish evacuation. Immediately I called it Alamo because it seemed obvious that was what we were doing and the name stuck." Project Alamo included the fortification of the compound for the purpose of safely evacuating from Saigon all Americans and "third country nationals."[28]

General Smith designated his deputy defense attache, Brigadier General Richard M. Baughn, USAF, as the person responsible for all matters relating to evacuation. To assist General Baughn in coordination of the overall evacuation, General Smith created three other groups and integrated them into the process. For overall command and control, he established the Evacuation Control Center (ECC) and located it in the old MACV bunker, and for processing of the anticipated high numbers of evacuees, he organized the Evacuation Processing Center (EPC) which eventually settled on the DAO Annex as its processing site. As a source of counsel and a conduit for information exchange, he formed the evacuation council whose meetings Captain Wood and approximately 30 other members of the Defense Attache Office attended.

Almost all of General Smith's staff participated in more than one aspect of the evacuation process due to the compressed timeframe and the complexity of the mission. The innumerable tasks undertaken by Lieutenant Colonel William E. McKinstry, operations staff officer in the Readiness Section, Operations and

Training Branch, Operations and Plans Division, DAO, and Lieutenant Colonel Anthony Lukeman, Chief, VNMC Logistics Support Branch, Navy Division, DAO, during April 1975, reflected the magnitude of the events transpiring in South Vietnam. Lieutenant Colonel Lukeman spent most of his daylight hours in April in Vung Tau refitting and resupplying the Vietnamese Marine units evacuated from Da Nang. In the evenings he would spell Lieutenant Colonel McKinstry in the Evacuation Control Center. That was how he spent his last 30 days in South Vietnam, splitting the 24-hour days equally between the VNMC in Vung Tau and the ECC at the DAO. Sometime in between he might catch a few hours of sleep and something to eat. At the same time, Lieutenant Colonel McKinstry almost lived in the ECC. Responsible for controlling the waiting evacuees, McKinstry worked hand-in-glove with the processing center and maintained close contact with the planning group and the evacuation council. Both of these officers also supported the 9th MAB's advance command element and its daily visitors who would fly from the task force to the DAO on Air America helicopters, spend the day, and then return at night. Most importantly, all of the Marines at the "Alamo" dedicated many hours to assisting the Special Planning Group in its mission.[29]

The SPG viewed the evacuation from Saigon as a three-phase operation, dealing first with the daily removal of selected candidates, especially those South Vietnamese who because of their previous activity or occupation could die at the hands of their would-be captors. The Communist execution of South Vietnamese Air America workers in Ban Me Thuot, after the NVA victory in March, intensified this concern. The DAO soon added Americans working on various agency staffs and similarly employed citizens of other nations to this fixed-wing commercial aircraft extract.

The second phase of the evacuation concerned the surface and air movement of potential candidates from the city of Saigon and the American Embassy to the DAO Compound. Upon completion of this movement, the third and final phase of the operation would begin, the massive air evacuation of all of the remaining personnel occupying the DAO installation.

The SPG and its members focused on the second phase of the evacuation with its primary emphasis on resupply, reinforcement, and retrograde. Major Sabater undertook the task of fortifying the perimeter and reinforcing the DAO's security contingent while Captain Wood concentrated on resupply, surface and air evacuation of the city, and the most important part of that movement, identification of the evacuation candidates.

From the outset, Colonel Howard, Major Sabater, Captain Wood, and the other planners made three assumptions: the NVA would not interfere with the U.S. effort to fulfill its treaty and moral obligations, removing other nations' citizens from Saigon; the greatest threat would come from the collapsing city and the South Vietnamese; and the South Vietnamese Air Force would remain loyal to the end and defend Tan Son Nhut Air Base and its adjoining installation, the DAO Compound. Aware of the debacle at Da Nang, the SPG knew that the dynamics of a dying city would preclude normal ground transportation and operations. As a consequence, they would need an alternative which could be communicated and controlled under the worst conditions.[30]

The SPG undertook as one of its first tasks the improvement of communications. General Smith arranged for the delivery of a U.S. satellite communications unit from California, one of only four in the world (all American-owned). Capable of communicating with any installation worldwide, it enabled the Special Planning Group to talk to Travis AFB in California and rearrange flights and flight loads to accommodate its supply and logistical needs.

The DAO used these flights and other aircraft carrying military supplies for the ARVN to remove its personnel designated for evacuation in the "thinning out" process ordered by General Smith. To further reduce the excessive American and other nationalities population (one estimate placed the number at 13,000), the Defense Attache Office encouraged all Americans residing in South Vietnam to leave as soon as possible. General Smith added emphasis to this request by cancelling the exchange privileges of retired American veterans living in Saigon. In addition, in early April, the United States authorized the acceptance of South Vietnamese orphans, especially those of mixed blood. One of the supply flights, a C-5A carrying 105mm howitzers for the beleaguered ARVN, was tapped to support this transfer of children known as Operation Baby Lift. For this particular flight, the DAO sought volunteers to accompany the children, and 37 women from the DAO staff willingly offered their services. Although in consonance with the gradual drawdown of the office's civilian workforce, the reassignment of these DAO members meant a substantial reduction in expertise, experience, and energy.

Shortly after takeoff, the C-5A experienced an explosive decompression during which the rear doors blew off the aircraft, severing the flight control cables to the tail section. The crippled "Galaxy" crashed while attempting an emergency landing on Tan Son Nhut's runway 25L. USSAG reported to the JCS the pilot's valiant attempt to control the aircraft using only power and ailerons: "At approximately 2,000 feet, pilot saw that rate of descent was too fast and that with a frozen slab he could not reduce it. He applied full power but descent was not halted before impact with the ground. Few, if any, survived on lower deck while most on upper deck survived." This disaster, which counted only 176 survivors out of 314 passengers and only one from the original 37 escort volunteers, ended Operation Baby Lift and seriously affected the morale of the SPG and the remaining DAO staff.[31]

Within days of this accident, which occurred on 4 April, small groups of curious onlookers began to gather outside the large American installation, approaching in size the Pentagon itself, and known as "Pentagon East." The SPG recognized this activity as the first signs of a city starting to question its chances for survival and exploring the alternatives. In the next two weeks, these symptoms of decay accelerated to action as mothers started tossing their babies over the fence to other South Vietnamese standing in the processing lines, and the DAO began what Captain Wood called "The mobile catch-a-baby drill."[32]

Many of the Vietnamese in the processing line at the DAO Annex were wives of Americans who worked in South Vietnam or had remained behind after their husbands' military tours of duty ended. Most of these women had never been officially registered, and now in a panicked state, they anxiously attempted to clear bureaucratic hurdles overnight. Captain Wood years later noted that by this time, the compound had started to look nasty because "We just did not have enough people to tend to the abandoned children, process the thousands of evacuees, maintain security, and carry out the daily functions which included keeping the facility clean. The bowling alley had been converted into a nursery and many C-141 flights carried pallets of Enfamil and tons of diapers."[33]

In the midst of this growing unrest outside the gate, General Baughn decided the time had come to reinforce the DAO's security force and sent a message to that effect, requesting additional security guards. Upon seeing this official declaration of evacuation and security needs, the Ambassador directed the deputy defense attache to leave the country. As a result, future decisions concerning preparations of the DAO Compound for evacuation and security were kept secret from everyone save General Smith and his immediate evacuation planners. Captain Wood remembered the consequences: "From that moment forward everything to do with the evacuation went secret ('black') and the SPG went into deep cover."[34]

The SPG's efforts soon took form as they used agency reports, taxi records, and some organizational assistance to collect data on the numbers and whereabouts of "third country nationals" in South Vietnam. Using these numbers, the group placed dots on a map of Saigon and then on top of those numbers superimposed private club membership records to arrive at a reasonably accurate picture of the locations from which these individuals would need to be evacuated. Applying that information along with the scant records of Americans still living in Saigon, Captain Wood was able to design both pickup points and surface evacuation routes to get these people to the "Alamo." He named these eight routes after pioneer trails in the American West. Names like Colorado, Oregon, Chisolm, Santa Fe, and Texas became part of the surface evacuation vocabulary. Captain Wood's choice of nomenclature for the surface routes prompted his fellow officers to dub him the "Wagonmaster," and for the duration of the operation that was his call sign.[35]

To determine if evacuation routes, checkpoints, and plans met their needs, the planners required reliable data on the status of the evacuation population. Acquisition and update of this information posed a serious problem for the SPG because its normal sources were rapidly disappearing as agencies reduced their operations and limited services. Understaffed, with their infrastructure melting away, most organizations provided little or no help to the SPG in its effort to maintain an accurate picture of Saigon's American and other foreign nationals population. Recognizing these problems and using flight records of daily departures, the SPG determined the probable numbers needing surface evacuation would not exceed 5,000 and planned their logistics support with that goal in mind.

From this point, everything rested solely on support, both from American volunteers in Saigon and the supply system. The plan called for the use of DAO buses and 40 American Fords (former DAO vehicles) painted and equipped with blue police lights (flown in from California) to replicate perfectly the cars of Saigon's security police force. The black and white DAO buses escorted by the fake police cars would move through Saigon over the designated western-named trails and pick up all foreign nationals, Americans, and specified South Vietnamese who in the final hours had

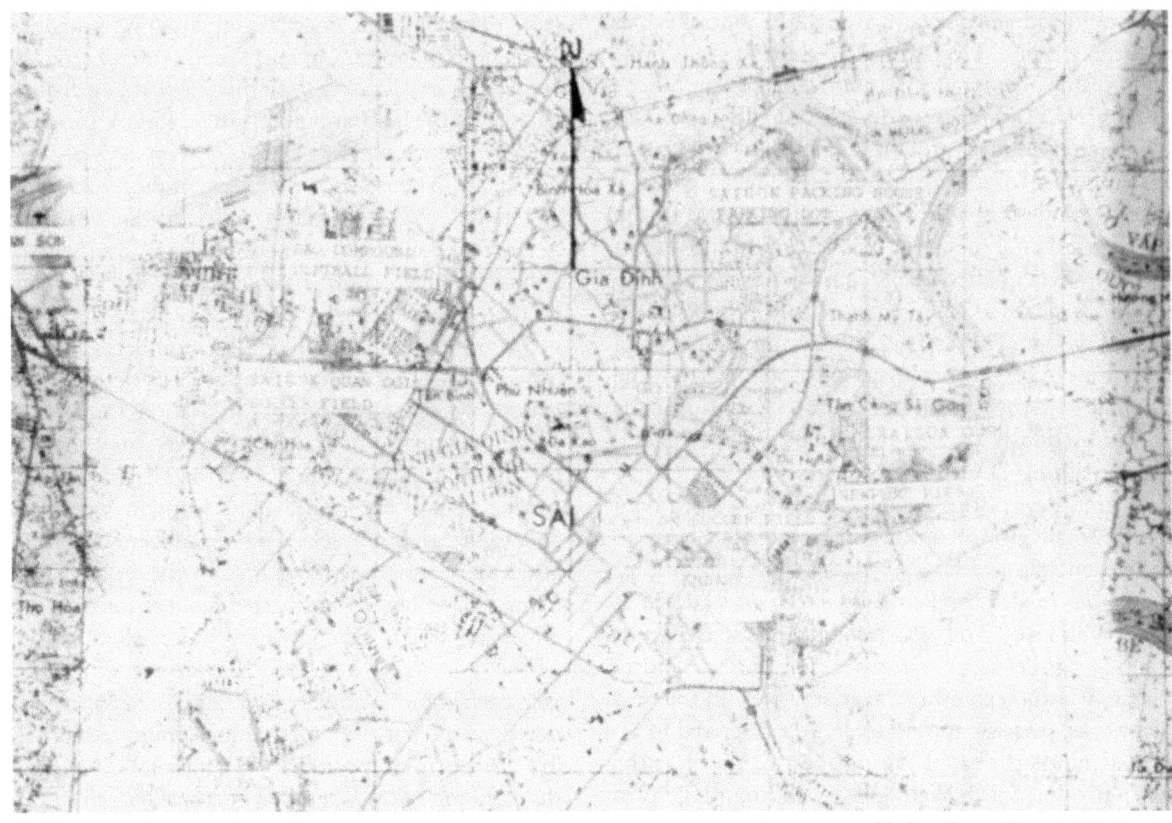

Marine Corps Historical Collection

This map of Saigon was used by 9th MAB to depict potential evacuation sites. Note distance from the Embassy to the DAO compound which had to be traversed by vehicles or CIA helicopters. Capt Wood and the SPG were responsible for planning that movement.

been unable to make it to the DAO. Failing pickup by this means, these evacuees would make their way to the rooftops of the way stations (specifically chosen because they could be defended), and gain access either by stairs or via ladders built and installed by volunteers.* Once on the roof, Air America helicopters would extract and deposit these evacuees at the compound. The planners assumed that the ground transportation portion of this plan would only work for one or two cycles before the deception was discovered and then they would have to depend exclusively on the Air America helicopters to rescue any stragglers. Captain Wood recently stated: "The surface evacuation plan for Saigon was based on planning and bluff, mostly bluff."[36]

One of the reasons the bluff worked was because of the contributions of 40 or so American civilians, men and women whose average age was 48 with the oldest 62. They volunteered their services to the SPG and ably assisted in the surface evacuation phase. An individual who played a key role in this operation was William D. "Bill" Austin, area auditor for the U.S. Agency for International Development (USAID). This very senior American official not only volunteered to drive a bus through the dangerous Saigon streets, but willingly agreed to help Captain Wood prepare the other drivers. These men and women trained at night under cover of DAO buildings designated by the SPG for the secret evacuation preparations. Each night one or two volunteers would get to sit in the seat, start the black and white civilian bus, and move it back and forth in place. In addition, other volunteers quietly bulletproofed and equipped the buses for evacuation by placing wire meshing in the windows, flak jackets along the sides below the window line, and PRC-25 radios on board. The plan called for these same buses to be staged throughout the city at designated way stations and billet pick-up points prior to the actual surface movement. Lastly, the guides, who would sit

---
*Captain Wood designated 12 locations as primary sites and 18 as secondary pickup points.

in the right-hand seat of the fake national police cars, driven by former South Vietnamese employees, had to be trained and oriented for this extremely dangerous mission. Employees of Pacific Architect and Engineers (a company contracted by DAO to design and build structures) volunteered for this mission which involved learning the eight surface routes so well that they could almost perform the task blindfolded. In addition to this contribution, members of this company also made possible, through the construction and installation of folding ladders, access to rooftops of buildings selected as way stations, which possessed excellent sites for helicopter landing pads but lacked a way to reach the roof itself.[37]

The last element of preparation involved what Captain Wood termed night "kamikaze runs" necessitated by the road blocks randomly imposed by the national police on various sections of the city of Saigon. Each night the police would close a different sector, and the SPG constantly had to know the status of Santa Fe, Oregon, Texas, and the other five routes. Personal observation was the only solution. Consequently, each night, beginning around mid-April, either Major Sabater, Captain Wood, or Army Captain George Petry would grab an automatic weapon, jump in a jeep driven by a Marine and ride the streets of Saigon.[38]

For the remaining days in April, these activities and preparations intensified as did efforts to improve the DAO Compound's defenses. To enhance security there, the Embassy moved some of its Marines to Tan Son Nhut shortly after General Carey's visit in mid-April. Major Sabater further solidified the perimeter by rigging petroleum barrels so that they could be exploded into a wall of flames should any group attempt to overrun the compound. Major Sabater also trained a small "militia" to use in the event of an "extreme emergency."[39]

While immersed in these time-intensive tasks of preparation, Major Sabater, Captain Wood, and Captain Petry experienced an unwelcome interruption. Colonel Howard had been notified that a C-141 carrying approximately $13 million in bills of varying denominations was inbound to Tan Son Nhut. Requested by Ambassador Martin as a final payment to his South Vietnamese employees, the cash had to be picked up by some responsible person. The three officers grabbed their automatic weapons and personally drove a borrowed bread truck to Tan Son Nhut where they met a C-141 on the runway with its jet engines still turning. They proceeded to unload crate after crate of American greenbacks into the truck, stacking it from the floor to the ceiling. Once loaded they returned to the DAO and unloaded their cargo in a secure building.* After losing precious time, Sabater, Wood, and Petry returned to their SPG duties and the planning of the evacuation.[40]

As the last weekend in April 1975 began, the DAO and the 9th MAB concluded their planning efforts. With the DAO ready and the plan for Operation Frequent Wind approved, everyone simply waited for the Ambassador's request to evacuate.

---

*Many of these same officers helped to burn approximately eight million of these dollars during the afternoon and evening of 29 April, but a full accounting of the undelivered money was never completed. Wood intvw.

CHAPTER 10

The Final Days

*The AESF—Xuan Loc Remembered
Saigon and the Final Preparation Pieces—Consulate Marines*

With the battle for Xuan Loc in Long Khanh Province (40 miles east and north of Saigon) entering its second week, General Van Tien Dung, commander of the NVA's Spring Offensive, evaluated his options. The 18th ARVN Division and other Vietnamese Armed Forces maintained a tenuous hold on Xuan Loc. NVA forces already had intercepted an ARVN armor task force attempting to reach the besieged 18th Division. The South Vietnamese, however, still held and blocked the North Vietnamese advance to Bien Hoa and Saigon. To avoid a stalemate, Dung decided to enlarge the battle area and outflank the South Vietnamese while intensifying the bombardment of the strategic RVN airbase at Bien Hoa. With a significant escalation in pressure, General Dung hoped to turn the tide of battle and get his stalled offensive back on schedule. He had to leave Xuan Loc behind and move on to Bien Hoa if he was going to meet Hanoi's goal of capturing Saigon before the end of April.

As the fighting for the capital of Long Khanh expanded, politicians in Saigon renewed their calls for President Thieu to step aside and allow a candidate more acceptable to the Communists to take power. This political maneuvering only served to make for further insecurity among the people. Increasingly unruly crowds began to gather each day outside the DAO Compound and watch their countrymen line up inside for processing, while flight after flight of commercial and military aircraft departed Tan Son Nhut, loaded with evacuees. This growing threat to security eventually forced the Ambassador to authorize the transfer of a squad of Marines to the DAO Compound. The "Pentagon East" welcomed this addition to its undermanned security force, a handful of retired South Vietnamese soldiers.

With the crowds outside the gate growing larger and more menacing while the DAO began what Captain Anthony A. Wood described as the "mobile catch-a-baby drill," the Special Planning Group accelerated its efforts. The fortification of the compound had to keep pace with the evacuation of South Vietnamese or the U.S. installation would be overrun by citizens seeking refuge. From this moment on, panicked refugees would represent the gravest threat to security and to the evacuations. Marines would fill this need for security.

The AESF

On 17 April, the III MAF Commander, Major General Carl W. Hoffman, activated a new security force to replace the Marines of the 1st Battalion, 4th Marines serving as members of the Amphibious Evacuation RVN Support Group. The Amphibious Evacuation Support Force (AESF) was comprised of Marines assigned from the 4th Marines, 9th Marines, 12th Marines, 3d Engineer Battalion, 7th Communication Battalion, 3d Service Battalion, Headquarters Battalion, 3d Tank Battalion, and the 1st Amphibian Tractor Battalion. The specially selected Marines of these units initially were formed into 10 72-man detachments, comprised of a 12-man headquarters detachment, and three 20-man sections (two squads of nine men each plus a two-man section headquarters).

To command these detachments, Major General Kenneth J. Houghton, the commanding general of the 3d Marine Division, chose Major David A. Quinlan, the 9th Marines operations officer. At the moment General Houghton made that decision, Major Quinlan was, by coincidence, conducting 9th Marines business at the combined headquarters of III MAF and 3d Marine Division. In an office on the second floor of the Camp Courtney headquarters building on Okinawa, Major Quinlan was completely unaware of the activity on the first floor. Not until he returned to neighboring Camp Schwab did he learn of the division's efforts to locate him.

As he entered Camp Schwab, he noticed a flurry of activity around the regimental command post, including a CH-46 sitting in the LZ with its blades idling. Stopping to observe, Major Quinlan spotted the 9th Marines executive officer, Lieutenant Colonel Robert Wise, who greeted him with very few but important words:

> The [waiting] helicopter is for you. Your gear is on the bird. Marty [Major Martin J. Lenzini, 9th Marines air liaison officer] has packed for you. You are the commander of the ships' guards. Get going![1]

After receiving his .45 automatic and a box of ammunition from Lieutenant Colonel Wise, Major Quin-

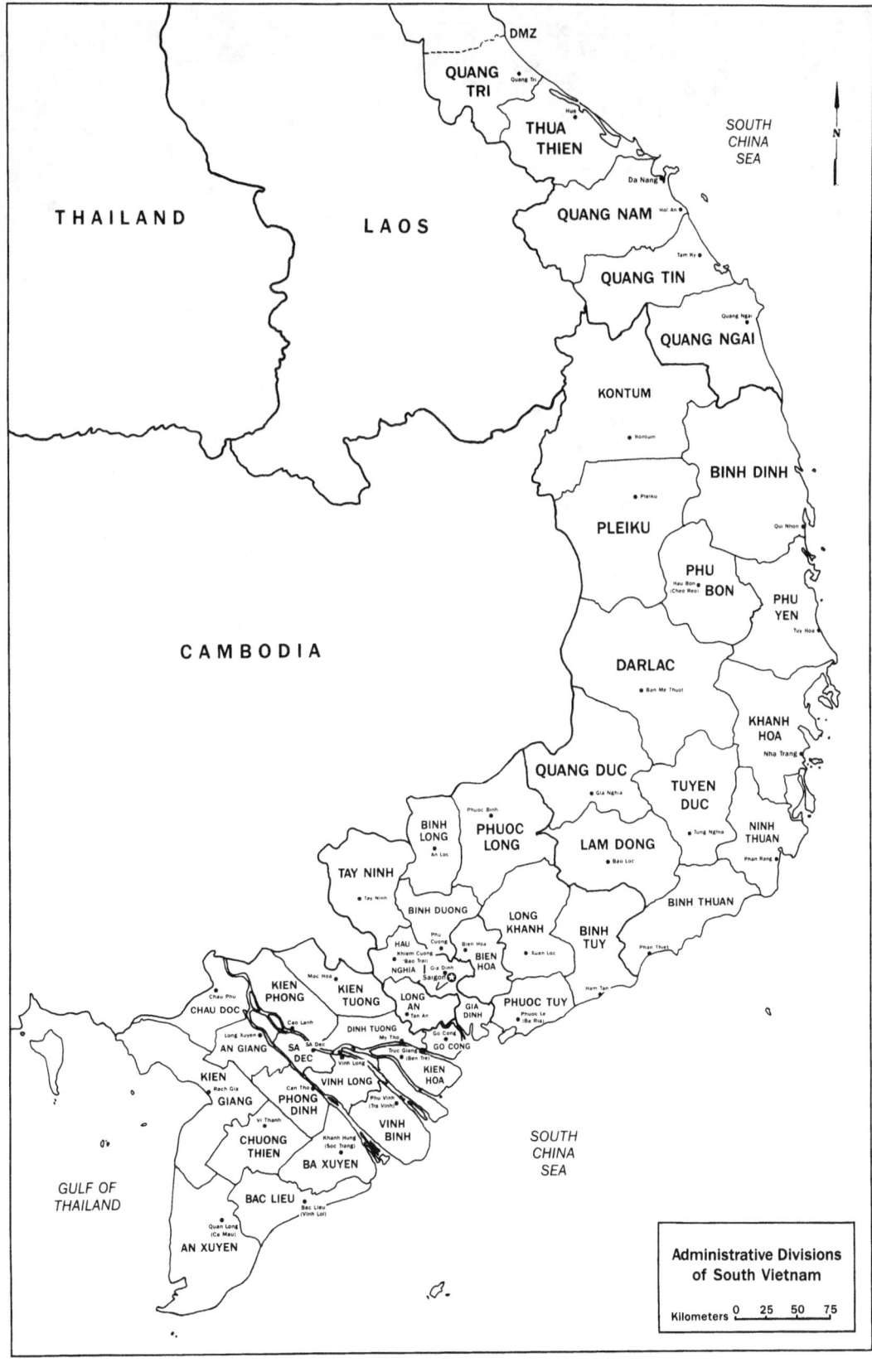

Marine Corps Historical Collection

The Amphibious Evacuation Security Force Commander, Maj David A. Quinlan, and his detachment commanders and staff gather for a post-operational debrief. The AESF deployed to Subic Bay on board KC-130Fs of VMGR-152 on 17-18 April 1975.

lan buckled on his web gear and dashed for the helicopter. Already on board were his newly assigned executive officer, First Lieutenant Thomas W. Kinsell, and two radio operators. After the short flight to Futema, the new AESF commander stepped off the CH-46 and walked to the passenger terminal where the mission's significance instantly became clear. There stood Major General Houghton who greeted Major Quinlan with a reminder—the AESF represented the 3d Marine Division. Major Quinlan recalled what General Houghton said that day: "The AESF is a microcosm of the division. Use my call sign, 'Constitution,' lest anyone forget who you are."[2]

After meeting with General Houghton, Major Quinlan inspected his troops. Later that day, 17 April, the control group and two of the detachments boarded KC-130s. In the ensuing 24 hours, Marine Aerial Refueler Transport Squadron 152 and six of its KC-130 tankers (reconfigured as cargo aircraft) used 21 sorties to transship Quinlan and his detachments to the Philippines. Once there, the Marines of the AESF made their way to the Subic pier by whatever means of rolling stock they could beg, borrow, or procure. Major Quinlan recalled: "Lieutenant Kinsell singlehandedly coordinated the arriving detachments' transportation from Cubi Point to the Lower MAU Camp, and then across Subic Bay to the *Dubuque*. By phone, by radio, and sometimes in person, Lieutenant Kinsell was able to mesh a chain of trucks, jeeps, buses, and landing craft into an orderly flow enabling all of the detachments to get on board the *Dubuque*."[3]

Time was critical because as Marines of the 1st Battalion, 4th Marines exited the *Dubuque's* "Mike" boats on 18 April, AESF Marines moved to occupy their places. Only hours after arriving in port, the Marines of 1st Battalion, 4th Marines ended their shipboard security role.

Having assumed command of the Amphibious Evacuation RVN Support Group only the week before from Colonel Dan C. Alexander, whose duties as 9th MAB chief of staff negated a dual role, Lieutenant Colonel Charles E. Hester disembarked his battalion from the *Dubuque* on Friday, 18 April. Actually, the first troops from Quinlan's AESF already had arrived. The previous evening, Captain Richard L. Reuter and his Detachment Echo accompanied by Captain Richard

R. Page and his Detachment Foxtrot landed along with the control group. Without even unpacking, the detachments deployed the next morning (18 April). They departed Cubi Point on Navy C-2 "Greyhounds" destined for the *Coral Sea* (CVA 43). From the *Coral Sea*, they transferred to the guided missile frigate *Gridley* (DLG 21), which took Reuter and his detachment to their Military Sealift Command (MSC) ship, the USNS *Sergeant Kimbro*, and Page and his Marines to their MSC ship, the USNS *Greenville Victory*.[4]

That Friday, after seeing off Captains Reuter and Page, Major Quinlan made his way to the *Blue Ridge* where he met with the commanding general of the 9th MAB, Brigadier General Richard E. Carey. General Carey advised Major Quinlan that the *Dubuque* would serve as his command post, and stressed the need for rapid embarkation of his forces in anticipation of immediate orders to get underway. Major Quinlan assured General Carey that his detachments would embark on the *Dubuque* as quickly as possible after their arrival from Okinawa.

The AESF commander next met with his predecessor, Lieutenant Colonel Hester, and his staff. Quinlan received an invaluable briefing from them on their experiences and the unusual requirements involved in this type of mission. Major Quinlan later related, "Lieutenant Colonel Hester's staff told us that the best way to prepare rice for thousands of people was to place the rice in large barrels, connect a hose to the ship's steam line, and hit the rice with a blast of the ship's superheated steam, and in a matter of seconds, you had hot, cooked rice ready to eat."[5]

This simple expedient provided quick nourishment for the starving evacuees and possibly prevented deadly riots over the distribution of food. Additionally, Hester and Colonel Alfred M. Gray, commander of the newly activated Regimental Landing Team 4, advised General Carey to assign the majority of his military police, interrogator-translators, and counter-intelligence people to the AESF. This advice also proved invaluable.

General Carey's decision to include all of these specialists in the AESF, especially the interrogator-translators, paid dividends throughout the deployment. Nothing, not even the show of deadly force, meant more than the ability to understand and communicate with the refugees. Captain Cyril V. Moyher, the India detachment commander, said, "Without the translators, we would have never been able to pick out the leaders and communicate to them our intentions

USS Dubuque *(LPD 8) steams toward Vung Tau and the South Vietnamese coastal waters. The* Dubuque *served successively as the headquarters ship for 1st Battalion, 4th Marines during Operation Fortress Journey; for the Amphibious Evacuation RVN Support Group; and for the Amphibious Evacuation Security Force during Operation Frequent Wind.*

Marine Corps Historical Collection

so they could in turn inform the rest of the refugees."[6]

Shortly after noon on 18 April, as these specialists and the AESF started to arrive at the Cubi Point airfield, it became obvious to senior American commanders that the South Vietnamese would lose the battle for Xuan Loc. To prepare for the consequences, Admiral Gayler ordered Admiral Whitmire and Task Force 76 to return to the waters off Vung Tau. The first ships weighed anchor at 1600, long before the last of Quinlan's detachments was scheduled to arrive from Okinawa. Knowing this, Major Quinlan went to the *Dubuque's* commanding officer, Captain Roy W. McLain, USN, and asked him to delay the ship's departure until 2130. Captain McLain agreed, and Quinlan immediately dispatched First Lieutenant Kinsell to the Cubi Point Airfield with instructions to meet the last detachment and personally escort it to the *Dubuque* so as to arrive no later than the new departure time.

Unaware of the events taking place in Subic in preparation for their arrival, Captain David A. Garcia and his detachment, Victor, began at 0600 what would become an extremely hectic and demanding day. By 1300, he had mustered his Marines in front of the 9th Marines' headquarters for what seemed an interminably long truck ride to Marine Corps Air Station Futema and an awaiting "Ichi Go Ni" (VMGR-152) KC-130. After a two-and-one-half hour flight in the Hercules, which began its taxi just as Captain Garcia buckled the two halves of his seat belt together, the detachment landed at Cubi Point. While Captain Garica unhooked his seat belt, the ramp and cargo door opened the plane's innards to the pitch-black, tropical night. Suddenly, Garcia and everyone on board beheld a strange sight, a Marine standing on the ramp signalling double time. Before anyone could react to this "apparition," it started heaving gear off the back of the plane. To expedite the transition, First Lieutenant Kinsell, without the approval or knowledge of the aircraft's loadmaster, had begun throwing Garcia's Marines' gear to an awaiting ground crew. Kinsell's unusual conduct moved everyone to rapid action and ignited a chain of events which gained speed as Garcia spied his welcoming committee: Generals Houghton and Coffman, and Colonel Wylie W. Taylor. Their presence and words of encouragement only served to underline the importance of the mission and added urgency to the detachment's impending rendezvous with the task force. Detachment Victor, Captain Garcia, and First Lieutenant Kinsell "enjoyed" a quick ride to the MAU camp landing ramp where their waterborne taxi, a "Mike" boat, shuttled them to their ship, already underway. Finally, after chasing the *Dubuque* across Subic Bay, they entered its well at 2200.[7]

As the *Dubuque* passed Grande Island outbound to the South China Sea, eight of 10 of the AESF's detachments and all of its attached personnel settled into their new quarters. Included in the group of attached units were: two doctors, Navy Lieutenants Ken Andrus and John Oakland; the 3d Counter-Intelligence Team led by Captain Charles J. Bushey (who would later become the executive/operations officer); a 26-man military police detachment from the 3d Marine Division MP company, with First Lieutenant Joseph J. Streitz in charge; the 17th Interrogator-Translator Team led by Chief Warrant Officer Allen F. Kent; and Lance Corporal Ricardo Carmona, on loan from BLT 1/4 because he knew better than anyone else the disposition of the *Dubuque's* stock of ammunition. Major Quinlan used the nearly five days of voyage to organize and school his Marines. Ordered to provide 14 54-man detachments vice the initial 10 72-man ones, Major Quinlan formed Kilo, Mike, Quebec, and Romeo detachments from the Marines still on the *Dubuque*. Marine first lieutenants commanded each of the new detachments.*[8]

While enroute to South Vietnam, the AESF began its preparations for the impending security mission: "Training was conducted for embarked detachments in key Vietnamese language phrases, conduct of evacuation operations, rules of engagement, security of vital shipboard spaces, and riot and crowd control to include use of 150 psi hoses."[9] Additional training in the use of the M60 machine gun, the M79 grenade launcher, and the M72 LAW (light antitank weapon) took place after the AESF commander received word that senior commanders seriously entertained the idea of inserting four detachments of his force onto ships docked at the Newport Pier. This option would involve the insertion of 200 Marines into an extremely hostile environment for a dangerous trip down the Saigon River. During this time, the Marines would provide order among thousands of refugees on noncombatant MSC ships which might come under enemy attack.

To carry out this mission and the necessary training, Major Quinlan needed combat arms. Captain McLain,

---

*A *Coral Sea* helicopter flew a section of Foxtrot Detachment from the *Greenville Victory* to the *Dubuque* in support of this reorganization. On 27 April a contingent of 28 Marines led by First Lieutenant David A. Kratochvil went on board the *Barbour County* (LST 1195), thereby constituting a 15th detachment. AESF ComdC.

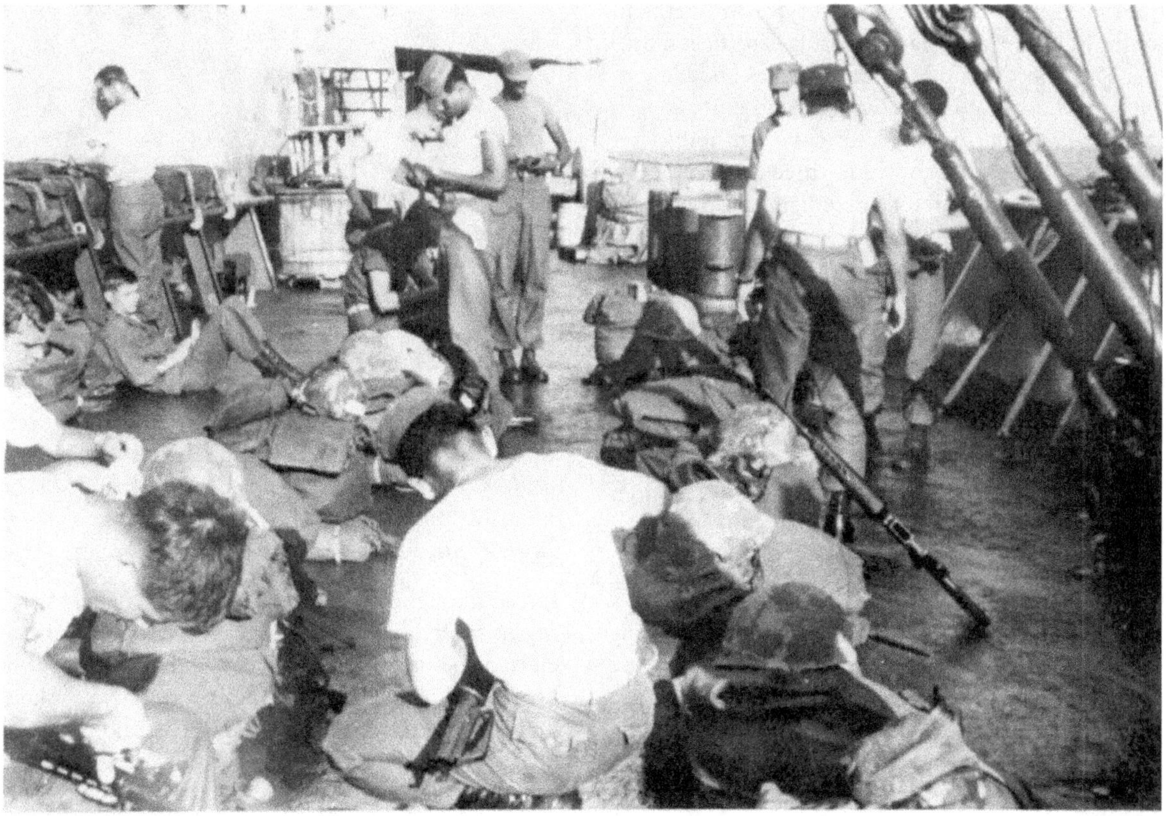

Marine Corps Historical Collection

Marines of Detachment Sierra (HqBn, 3d MarDiv) prepare for inspection on board USNS Sgt Andrew Miller *off the coast of Vietnam in the vicinity of Vung Tau. The detachment, commanded by Capt Edward R. Palmquist, Jr., went on board the ship on 22 April.*

the *Dubuque's* captain, provided a short-term answer when he authorized the AESF commander to use the shipboard complement of weapons. For a permanent solution to this problem, Major Quinlan sent a message to General Carey requesting additional weapons for his deploying detachments. At the same time, he sought permission to break open the *Dubuque's* supply of ammunition.

On 22 April, the AESF commander deployed three detachments to MSC ships: Sierra Detachment to the USNS *Sergeant Andrew Miller*, Victor on the SS *Pioneer Contender*, and Papa on board the SS *Green Port*. The next day, the reorganization and formation of detachments Kilo, Mike, Romeo, and Quebec became official, and the following day, Captain Cyril V. Moyher took India Detachment on board the SS *Pioneer Commander*. At the same time, Captain Robert D. Amos took the Marines of Tango to the SS *Green Forest*.[10]

By the time these transfers were complete, the *Dubuque* and the MSC ships' logs recorded their posi-

The American Challenger, *guarded by Marines of the Amphibious Evacuation Security Force, rides high in the South China Sea while it awaits Vietnamese refugees. The AESF November Detachment Commander, Capt Michael T. Mallick, took his Marines on board this Military Sealift Command ship on 25 April 1975.*

Marine Corps Historical Collection

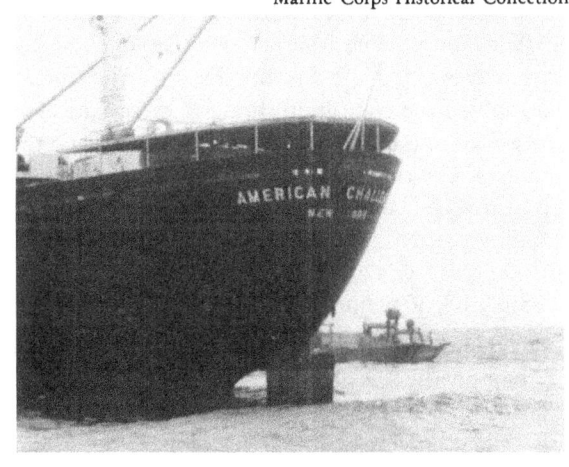

tion as 15 miles off the coast of South Vietnam, southeast of the Vung Tau Peninsula. The next morning, 25 April, Captain Michael T. Mallick and November Detachment left the *Dubuque* and embarked in the SS *American Challenger*. Twenty-four hours later their new ship moved to within three miles of South Vietnam, off Long Hai, to load refugees shuttled from the beach in Vietnamese landing craft. Major Quinlan recalled, "This was the first of many instances when our commodore really responded to our needs. Thinking that the *American Challenger* was too far from the task group without protection and close enough to the shore to take fire, I requested a destroyer escort for the ship carrying my Marines." In response, Captain James D. Tregurtha, Commander Task Group 76.5, ordered the *John Paul Jones* (DDG 32) to join immediately with the *American Challenger*.[11]

To ensure the cooperation and communication desired by Captain Tregurtha, Major Quinlan or a member of his staff preceded each of the transferring detachments to the MSC ship. They met with the ship's master and explained the desired relationship between him and the Marine detachment commander and the rules of engagement that guided the Marines in their shipboard security duties. From 22 to 27 April, the remainder of the detachments, Kilo, Quebec, and Romeo, provided security and working parties for the small boats conducting logistical and administrative runs between the MSC ships and the *Dubuque*. First Lieutenant Johnnie Johnson, the Romeo Detachment commander, oversaw this exchange of logistical stores, including the transfer of "C" rations, which served as the major source of nourishment for the Marines who slept on the decks of the MSC ships they guarded.

On the evening of 27 April, thinking his work done, Johnson retired to his "bed" on the *Dubuque*. His sleep was shortlived as he was awakened by a one-hour alert "to assume evacuation stations." For Johnson, this meant overseeing the Seventh Fleet Service Force's resupply of the evacuation ships, an event critical to the welfare and safety of both the participants and the refugees. The replenishment of ships' stores translated into a 12-hour task using a continuous chain of working parties drawn from the *Dubuque's* detachments. This feat marked only the beginning of an incredibly hectic period of resupply.[12]

By the time Lieutenant Johnson received the order to resupply the Seventh Fleet ships in preparation for the anticipated arrival of thousands of more refugees, his fellow officers and Major Quinlan's AESF was

Department of Defense Photo (USMC) 7712175
A pontoon causeway from the Tuscaloosa *is maneuvered into position alongside one of the MSC ships designated to take refugees by LCM-6s from the* Durham. *The pontoons were used as a platform where refugees could be screened before boarding MSC ships.*

spread throughout the South China Sea, already assisting in the rescue of thousands of evacuees who had elected the open sea and starvation over Communist hospitality. On 28 April, the disposition of Major Quinlan's forces read more like a cruise novel than a military operation, as most of his detachments were on civilian-run Military Sealift Command ships. Only 12 days earlier, all of these Marines had been on Okinawa. Yet by Monday, 28 April, almost every one of them had shared in the danger and frustration of handling refugees, eyewitnesses to incredible displays, in turn, of courage and cowardice.

Essentially, however, the Marines of the AESF waited for the final act in Vietnam's tragic history and the expected onslaught of refugees that would surely follow. As Captain Charles J. Bushey, the executive officer of the AESF, recorded in his diary: "So far nothing has happened although I expect all of that to change very quickly and on very short notice. Everyone is ready as they are going to be. We have sent some more detachments of about 54 people to the MSC ships to provide security. Now all they do is wait."[13]

Captain Reuter's Echo Detachment, because it was one of the first to deploy, had endured the frustration of waiting the longest. Since 19 April, the Marines on board the USNS *Sergeant Kimbro* had anticipated their first refugees. Ten days passed before, on 28 April, a "Da Nang-Saigon" ferry, escorted by a Navy ship, transferred 150 South Vietnamese to the *Sergeant Kimbro*. Captain Reuter recalled, "The group was comprised of upper-class professional people, including doctors, lawyers, nurses, a province chief, the

THE FINAL DAYS

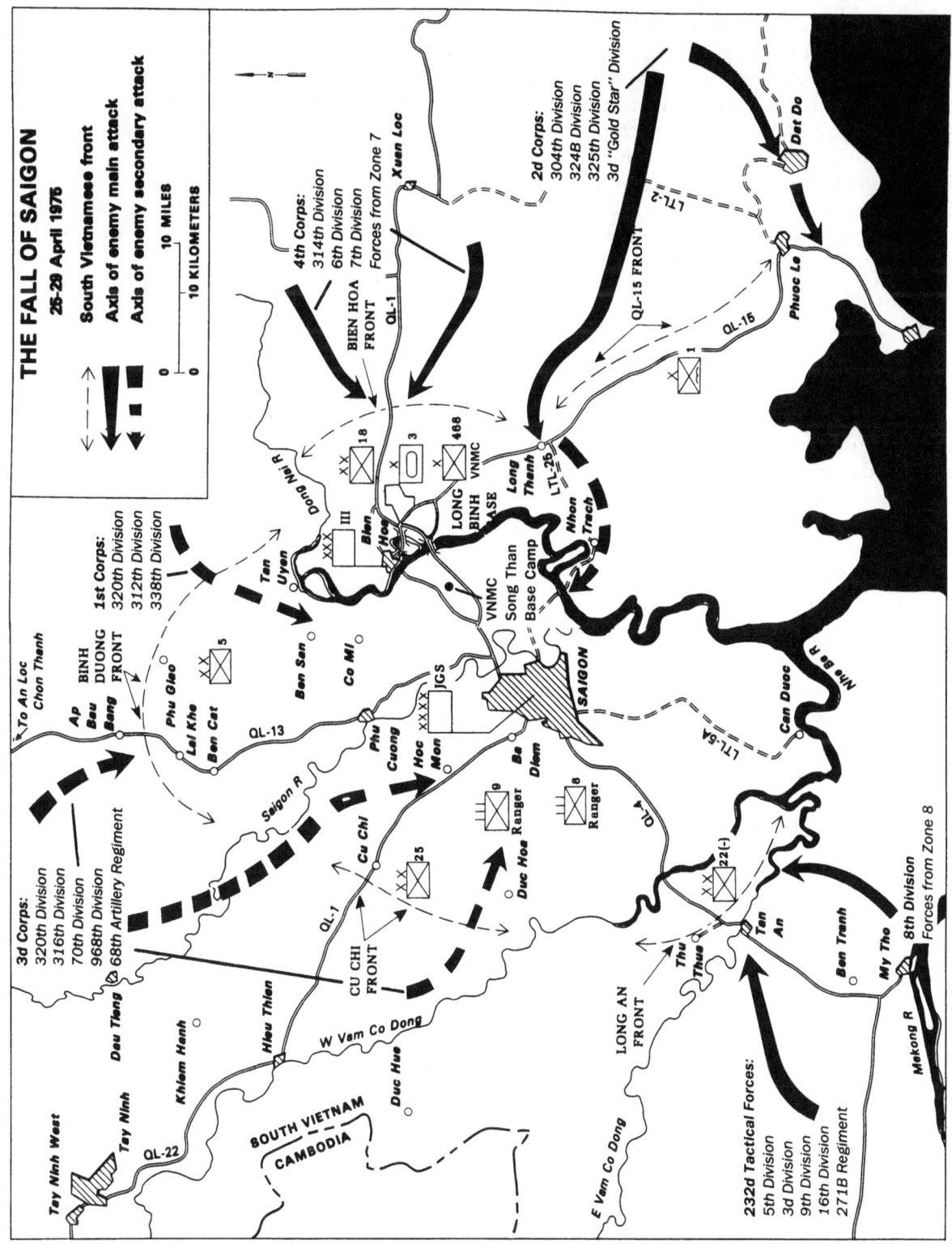

Map adapted from Gen Cao Van Vien, *The Final Collapse* (Washington: U.S. Army Center of Military History, 1983)

mayor of Vung Tau, a newspaper owner, professors, and college students. The group had paid 50 million piasters for the boat and intended to sail to Singapore and sell the boat there." After berthing this group of evacuees, Detachment Echo began an around-the-clock routine which did not cease until it finally discharged its passengers. Within 24 hours of Echo Detachment's introduction to refugee-related functions, every AESF detachment was inundated with evacuees. The delay had been supplanted by non-stop activity.[14]

Xuan Loc Remembered

The mid-April decision to reorganize the brigade and activate the AESF occurred during a 48-hour lull in the battle for Xuan Loc. Described in many newspaper reports as the "killing ground," this deadly battle entered its second week on Wednesday, 16 April, as both sides fought for what each had deemed critically necessary objectives. The ferocity of the fighting reflected the need by the ARVN for a battlefield victory and the NVA obsession with the capture of Saigon before the end of April.

With authorization from Hanoi to delay the final offensive for a week to allow his supply lines and other units to catch up, General Dung chose to modify his plan and bypass the Long Khanh provincial capital. Instead of continuing frontal assaults, he decided to neutralize Xuan Loc by outflanking the city's defenses, attacking only the perimeter. He planned to leave elements of three units (*341st, 6th,* and *7th NVA Divisions*) behind while moving the majority of his forces westward, thereby resuming the offensive against Bien Hoa and Saigon. According to Dung: "We advised that once the enemy amassed troops to save Xuan Loc, we need not concentrate our forces and continue attacking them head on. We would shift our forces to strike counterattacking units in the outer perimeter, where they had insufficient defense works and were not in close coordination with each other . . . ."[15]

After the short respite, the NVA pursued its new strategy and on 17 April, after several unsuccessful assaults, it overran the 48th Regiment of the 18th ARVN Division which had been guarding the western edge of the city. With the earlier loss of the 52nd Regiment, which had been defending the intersection of Highways 1 and 20; the diminishing number of resupply and evacuation helicopters; and the collapse of the city's western flank, the 18th ARVN Division and the 1st Airborne Brigade faced encirclement.

To avoid losing these forces, the JGS authorized III Corps to order Brigadier General Le Minh Dao, the division commander, to evacuate Xuan Loc. On the evening of 20 April, the 18th ARVN Division, 1st Airborne Brigade, and Regional and Popular Force elements conducted a successful withdrawal from Xuan Loc, retreating south toward Ba Ria, along Interprovincial Route 2. Overshadowing the military consequences of this withdrawal were the political consequences.

The following day, President Thieu resigned and, accompanied by his family, flew to Taiwan.* Vice President Tran Van Huong, the president's constitutional successor, replaced Thieu. His term lasted a week. On 27 April, with Saigon surrounded by Dung's forces (*232d Tactical Force* interdicting Highway 4 on the Long An Front; *3d NVA Corps* dominating Route 1 on the Cu Chi Front; *1st NVA Corps* controlling Highway 13 on the Binh Duong Front; *2d NVA Corps* dominating the QL-15 Front and targeting Long Thanh and Ba Ria; and the *4th NVA Corps* on the main axis of attack controlling the eastern approach to Saigon, the Bien Hoa Front), the National Assembly designated General Duong Van "Big" Minh to replace Tran Van Huong as President of the Republic of Vietnam.[16]

On the evening of 28 April, with Saigon nearly surrounded, General Minh took the oath of office. If he harbored any doubts about whether or not Saigon and its beleaguered ARVN defenders could protect the city from the impending Communist onslaught, the sound of exploding bombs quickly removed them. For within minutes of the ceremony, a flight of captured South Vietnamese A-37s bombed Tan Son Nhut. This attack and an early morning rocket attack, which had occurred the day before, marked the first time in five years that the citizens of Saigon had experienced enemy hostilities. The sudden conclusion to the city's five-year "peace" convinced the new leaders of the republic that they had but two choices: negotiate or capitulate.[17]

---

*Plagued by repeated calls to resign, President Thieu had continued to refuse to turn over the government and had become a most unpopular leader. Since his decision in March to withdraw the Airborne Brigade from MR 1, his political support had evaporated. The most visible manifestation of Thieu's fall from favor occurred on 8 April when a disgruntled VNAF F-5 pilot, Lieutenant Nguyen Thanh Trung, attacked the presidential residence, dropping two of his four bombs. This F-5 pilot would subsequently train a handful of NVA pilots to fly A-37s the NVA had captured earlier in the war. In late April those same Communists led an aerial attack on Saigon. *Fall of the South* and *Spring Victory*.

Before dawn on the next day, at 0358, the Communists launched another rocket attack. They directed this one at Tan Son Nhut, sending a reminder to General Minh that they had no intentions of negotiating a settlement. The deadly rocket barrage marked the beginning of the final offensive. Two of the first rockets slammed into a checkpoint just outside the DAO's main gate, killing instantly the two Marines manning it. Corporal Charles McMahon, Jr., of Woburn, Massachusetts, and Lance Corporal Darwin D. Judge of Marshalltown, Iowa, became the first two casualties of Operation Frequent Wind and the last two Marines to die on the ground in South Vietnam. At the airfield itself, confusion reigned as three Air Force C-130s, part of the just resumed fixed-wing evacuation, attempted to depart Tan Son Nhut and escape the enemy fire. General Smith temporarily halted the evacuation and called the Ambassador.[18]

Shortly after the attack, many South Vietnamese pilots, following orders from their superiors, departed Tan Son Nhut for safe haven in Thailand. Leaving the airfield in haste, a number of them jettisoned bombs and external fuel tanks on the runway. With the airfield littered with debris and abandoned equipment and aircraft threatened by roving bands of ARVN soldiers. General Smith encouraged Ambassador Martin to cancel the fixed-wing evacuation scheduled for that day. The Ambassador then made a personal visit to General Smith's headquarters to assess the damage. General Smith recently recalled that meeting: "Ambassador Martin actually came out to my headquarters and received a briefing from the USAF officers who had come over from the airfield. It was after this briefing that he decided to fall off his position to continue the fixed-wing evacuation and so he informed the Secretary of State from my headquarters immediately thereafter. This set in motion officially the rotary-wing evacuation."[19]

After his meeting with General Smith, Ambassador Martin returned to the Embassy and made his decision. When the Ambassador picked up the secure phone in his office and called Secretary of State Kissinger, he officially relinquished control of the evacuation of South Vietnam. In less than 20 minues, it became a military operation. At 1051 29 April 1975, USSAG passed the word to execute Frequent Wind's Option IV.[20]

Sun Tzu, the great Chinese warrior and philosopher, had preached to his military disciples: "The worst policy is to attack cities. Attack cities when there

VNAF C-130 burns from hit by NVA rocket on 29 April. The assault forced Ambassador Martin to halt, then cancel, fixed-wing evacuation and take Frequent Wind Option IV.
Department of Defense Photo (USMC)A150966

Marine Corps Historical Collection

Maj James E. Livingston, seen here as a brigadier general, served as operations officer for Col Alfred M. Gray's RLT-4. Maj Livingston spent many hours at the DAO refining the regiment's scheme of maneuver.

is no alternative." General Dung proved to be a good disciple. The NVA never attacked the city of Saigon because less than 24 hours after USSAG sent the execute message, the president of South Vietnam, General Minh, told his soldiers to lay down their arms. On 30 April 1975, the Republic of Vietnam ceased to exist.[21]

Saigon and the Final Preparation Pieces

As the final events leading up to the collapse unfolded, Colonel Taylor and his Advance Command Element (9th MAB forward headquarters) attempted to integrate their efforts into those of the DAO's Special Planning Group. Beginning their work the same day the 18th ARVN Division left Xuan Loc, every member of the team knew they had only a little time left in which to prepare for the final evacuation. They were aided in their efforts by various members of the 9th MAB, RLT 4, ProvMAG-39, and BLSG staffs. Individuals from these headquarters shuttled between the task force and the DAO almost daily, serving as an important link between the *Blue Ridge* and the 9th MAB forward headquarters. As a result of these liaison visits, Major John A. Murray, the RLT S-4, was able to develop a very sophisticated air plan while the operations officer, Major James E. Livingston, fine-tuned Colonel Alfred M. Gray's plan for RLT 4 to secure the DAO Compound for evacuation. This team

Members of 1stLt Bruce P. Thompson-Bowers' platoon arrive at the DAO, Saigon. The 3d Platoon of Company C, BLT 1/9 departed the Okinawa *in civilian clothes to avoid an overt breach of the Paris Accords, despite the imminent collapse of the Saigon Government.*

Marine Corps Historical Collection

effort greatly enhanced the DAO's careful preparations and underscored the difficulty and the value of the 9th MAB's reorganization. As Major Livingston later recalled, "One of the key lessons that evolved from Operation Frequent Wind was the concept of compositing. This process was accomplished while all units (three MAUs) were at sea. Numerous liaison trips by personnel aboard the *Blue Ridge* using Air America helicopters resolved issues" that arose between the reconfigured 9th MAB and the other commands. A force had been composed at sea to handle the impending emergency on land, and the ensuing liaison made everyone aware of its capabilities, its limitations, and the criticality of good communications.[22]

With command arrangements in Saigon complicated and Ambassador Graham Martin attempting to maintain a professional facade at the Embassy of "business as usual," these visits took on added weight. The need to give the appearance that America was not quitting and running from South Vietnam meant that visitors to Saigon had to keep a low profile during the day. The night, however, belonged to the 9th MAB, its forward headquarters, and the DAO's evacuation planners.

There was one exception to this rule, the DAO. By 21 April evacuation flights were departing every halfhour fully loaded. Each evening as the National Police enforced the curfew and closed the city, the arrival of new evacuees ceased and with the normal lag effect, it usually did not resume until 1000 the next day. To ensure that there were always enough passengers to process and fill the precious spaces that left Tan Son Nhut, the evacuation processing center and Lieutenant Colonel McKinstry had to keep between 200 and 600 South Vietnamese in the compound every night. As the numbers increased, sanitation and security became problems. Even though the crowds were, as McKinstry said, "well-behaved and friendly," they roamed the installation essentially uncontrolled because, by this time, the DAO was seriously undermanned. On 21 April the DAO sent a message to Washington requesting permission to insert a platoon of Marines into the DAO. Four days later, Air America helicopters transported a platoon of Marines, dressed in civilian clothes and carrying their combat gear, from the *Hancock* to Tan Son Nhut.* Just before noon that Friday, 25 April, First Lieutenant Bruce P. Thompson-Bowers and the 3d Platoon of Company C, 1st Battalion, 9th Marines became the DAO's security force, joining Colonel Taylor and the Advance Command Element as augmenting members of the "Pentagon East."[23]

Arriving at the compound the day the DAO requested additional security, the Advance Command Element immediately recognized that a great deal of preparation had already been accomplished, but efforts to make the area suitable for helicopter operations had barely started. By late evening on 21 April, the 9th MAB forward headquarters had inspected all of the proposed landing zones. Engineering efforts to improve the zones began immediately and, within days, Colonel Taylor's group had clearly marked all of the LZs. These activities, including the placing of wind socks and luminescent markings on 13 preselected rooftops designated as American evacuee assembly points, were always conducted between sunset and sunrise to avoid panicking the citizens of Saigon. At the DAO compound, itself, the SPG and the 9th MAB Marines made the necessary improvements to enable an initial wave of 12 CH-53s to land. Throughout the slow and seemingly tedious landing zone repair period, the 9th MAB, RLT 4, and ProvMag staffs all visited the DAO compound. They inspected the progress and reported the results to their respective commanders.[23]

On Monday morning, 21 April, Lieutenant Colonel Donald J. "Duffy" Verdon, the Advance Command Element's communications officer, began his first full day at the DAO by obtaining a comprehensive briefing on the compound's communications facilities. After a physical inspection of the assets of the Evacuation Control Center, he decided that the existing equipment, with some minor additions—mainly one receiver-transmitter and the placement of an antenna on the compound's water tank, would suffice. The 9th MAB immediately transferred his additional requirements, including a contingent of support personnel and their equipment, to the DAO. The introduction of troops and equipment continued (final count, 18) until the DAO's communications facilities could simultaneously sustain three landing zone control parties. Specifically, each party could communicate from each zone on high, very high, and ultrahigh frequency. Almost on a daily basis during the 9th MAB forward headquarter's stay in the "Alamo," the communications-electronics officer, the 9th MAB communications officer, and his counterpart in RLT 4, all visited the Compound and exchanged ideas and information in order to achieve the highest state of communications readiness.[25]

On 25 April, the Advance Command Element air

---

*Once inside the confines of the DAO, these Marines donned their gear and assumed their security duties.

Photo courtesy of Capt Anthony A. Wood, USMC (Ret)

The Defense Attache Office, Saigon, on 30 April 1975, shows the effects of 9th MAB's thermite charges. Thanks to the efforts of Capt McManus and MSgt East, the one-time U.S. headquarters, made of concrete and reinforced steel, has literally melted and shrunk.

liaison officer, Major David E. Cox, conducted a readiness briefing for the commanding general of the 9th MAB, his principal staff, the RLT 4 staff, and the staff of ProvMAG-39. Included in the meeting on board the *Blue Ridge* was a 35mm slide presentation of the DAO landing zones, obstacles to flight, aerial checkpoints, and the ingress/egress route from the task force to Saigon. At the conclusion of the session, General Carey gave Major Cox a copy of the plan for the employment of the landing force at the DAO/Air America complex. Major Cox then departed for Saigon where he conveyed those intentions to the Defense Attache, General Smith. During his meeting with the Defense Attache, Major Cox highlighted General Carey's plans for helicopter operations, landing zone organization, and evacuee processing.[26]

On that same day, the landing zones were declared ready for use. Each zone bore distinctive markings colored with luminescent paint and known as CH-53 "footprints." Taken from the CH-53 NATOPS Flight Manual, they were placed to provide maximum rotor tip clearance. In cases where the zone could not be painted, iron rods were installed. Sometime just prior to L-hour, members of the Advance Command Element would attach standard Marine Corps marking panels to the rods. Communications remained the only unfinished major area as Lieutenant Colonel Verdon continued his preparations. During this period, he also provided technical assistance and support to the Special Planning Group, responsible for controlling the surface evacuation of Saigon.[27]

In all respects, Colonel Taylor's team of experts supported by their counterparts on the 9th MAB and RLT 4 staffs greatly aided and enhanced the Special Planning Group in its last-minute preparations. Their presence eased some of the strain of an undermanned DAO staff attempting to conduct a massive fixed-wing evacuation while its own numbers decreased daily. When Ambassador Martin made that unavoidable phone call on the morning of 29 April, the DAO Compound stood ready to begin the helicopter evacuation of Saigon. Only one task remained.[24]

Before the Americans departed South Vietnam, all sensitive equipment and gear had to be demolished to preclude its capture by the North Vietnamese. Captain McManus and Master Sergeant East already had been assigned that mission: destruction of designated controlled areas within the DAO compound. As the two men set their explosives on the evening of 29 April, they undertook a historic task, elimination of

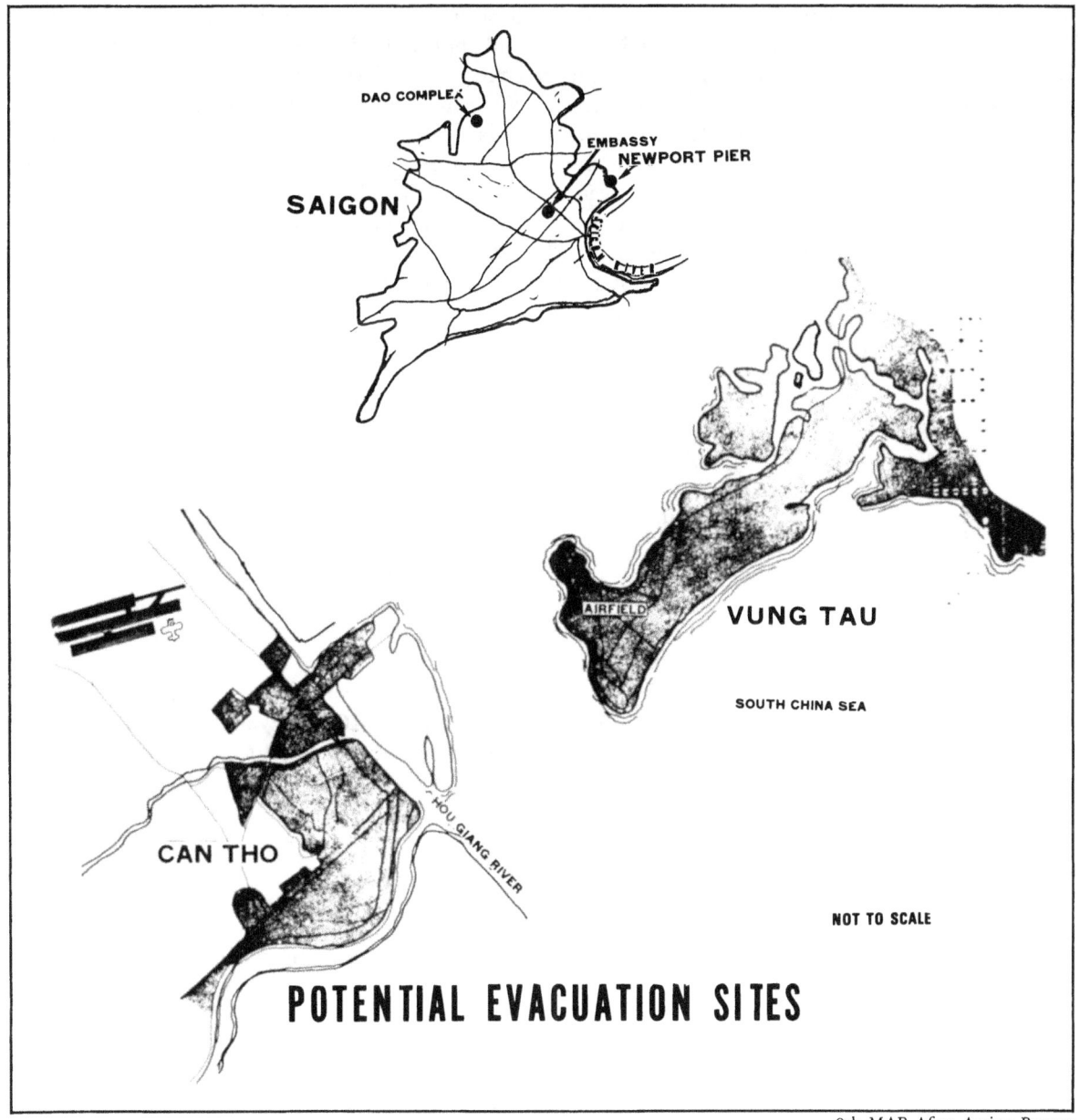

This 9th MAB post-operational summary map shows potential evacuation sites including Can Tho and its airport. Consul General Francis McNamara and SSgt Boyette S. Hasty explored the possibility of a fixed-wing evacuation, but quickly cancelled it when they learned there was no way to preclude being overrun by panicked South Vietnamese.

the last home to America's military in South Vietnam.[28]

Consulate Marines

As the pace of preparations for the Advance Command Element and the AESF accelerated with the fall of Xuan Loc, a cloud of uncertainty settled over the two remaining American consulates in South Vietnam. The loss of Xuan Loc, earlier counted as the only ARVN "victory," catapulted both the consulate at Bien Hoa and that at Can Tho into hectic preparations for what now appeared to be the inevitable.

With the eastern gateway to the nation's capital fully open, Bien Hoa stood as the only obstacle in the NVA's path to Saigon. This increased exposure made the American consulate highly vulnerable and as a consequence, Consul General Richard Peters directed his staff and the Marine detachment to begin preparations for the consulate's closure. Gunnery Sergeant Robert W. Schlager, the noncommissioned officer-in-charge of the detachment, ordered his Marines to assist the staff in this effort. During the three days preceding and following the end of the battle for Xuan Loc, the Marines in the Bien Hoa Detachment (Sergeant Ronald E. Duffy, Sergeant James M. Felber, Corporal Carlos R. Arraigna, Corporal Gary N. Lindholm, and Lance Corporal Dean M. Kinzie) either destroyed or transferred to Washington every piece of sensitive gear and all classified documents. On 24 April, Consul General Peters, his staff, and the Marine detachment closed the consulate and returned to Saigon. Due to confusion and uncertainty over how the war would end, the Consul's staff closed and locked the facility, but left the American flag flying. A few days later, when it became obvious that there would be no negotiated settlement, the consul general's deputy, Charles Lahiguera, and two of the detachment's Marines returned to Bien Hoa and properly retired the colors. This event and the Bien Hoa detachment's incorporation into the Marine Security Guard, Saigon, officially ended its history, leaving only one American consulate in South Vietnam. As of 29 April 1975, a detachment of Marines still guarded the Can Tho consulate.

The first people to know that the evacuation of that consulate had begun were not the Ambassador or even the consul general, but the Marines in the AESF. The final supply preparations orchestrated by the AESF's supply officer, Lieutenant Johnnie Johnson, barely had ended when two helicopters appeared on the horizon that Tuesday morning, 29 April.[29]

In a matter of minutes, two Air America helicopters landed on the amphibious transport dock ship *Vancouver* (LPD 2) and discharged the first of Can Tho's evacuees. They included the bulk of the compound's CIA employees, and as far as the Navy knew, these refugees comprised the entire consulate staff at Can Tho. The Navy, using a landing craft, then transferred all of the Vietnamese refugees and one embassy official from the *Vancouver* to the *Pioneer Contender*. They chose the *Pioneer Contender* because with the *American Challenger* still unloading refugees at Phu Quoc island, the *Contender* was the only MSC ship in the area.

Later that evening, (actually 0200 on 30 April) Captain Garcia's security force would help load the rest of the Can Tho refugees including Consul General Francis McNamara, Can Tho's Marine Security Guard detachment headed by Staff Sergeant Boyette S. Hasty, and approximately 300 Vietnamese refugees (former consulate employees and their families). Among the Vietnamese group were Staff Sergeant Hasty's mother-in-law and brothers-in-law. He had married a South Vietnamese woman only days before his forced departure from Can Tho. Their surprising arrival on the *Pioneer Contender* culminated a series of strange events which had begun several days earlier. It started with the Can Tho Consulate's Marines' efforts to prepare for the expected evacuation.

Staff Sergeant Hasty and his five Marines, Sergeant John S. Moore [his assistant], Sergeant John W. Kirchner, Sergeant Terry D. Pate, Corporal Lee J. Johnson, and Corporal Lawrence B. Killens had prepared for over two weeks for the inevitable word "to evacuate the consulate."[30] What they had neither prepared for, nor anticipated, were the unusual circumstances which would confront them in their attempt to depart Can Tho. Staff Sergeant Hasty recounted, "At that time, we didn't know they (CIA) were pulling their own bug-out, and we were a little bit worried about them, but it finally dawned on us they were not coming back." He said the CIA staff also had commandeered two of the consul's four LCMs previously purchased from the Alaska Barge and Transport Company.[31]

Hasty had prepared the LCMs as an alternate means of escape should an air option suddenly disappear. In preparation, he had even equipped the LCMs with M60 machine guns. Days earlier, in anticipation of using fixed-wing as a means to evacuate Americans from Can Tho, the consul general and Staff Sergeant Hasty had gone to the Can Tho Airfield and asked the base commander if he could provide protection for an air evacuation. He replied, "No! You'll be overrun as soon as the first plane lands."[32]

With this option eliminated, they decided to use either the Air America helicopters or the LCMs. Thus when Saigon called at 1030 on 29 April and asked to talk with Mr. McNamara, neither the call nor the instructions surprised Staff Sergeant Hasty. The consul general told him, " 'Yes, we've received the word. We're to evacuate by helicopter immediately.' " That was not to be, as less than 30 minutes later Saigon called back and ordered them to send the helicopters to them—empty![33]

In relating this peculiar turn of events, Sergeant Hasty stated: "I was called back upstairs and the consul general told me that Saigon had called; Saigon needed our four helicopters to help them evacuate. So we sent our four helicopters up to Saigon. As it

An LCM-8 with a load of Marines awaits the order to move out. Boats similar to this one were used by the consulate staff and SSgt Hasty and his Marines to evacuate Can Tho.

turned out, all four did not get to Saigon because the CIA people in Can Tho got for sure one, and we're almost positive two, of the helicopters."³⁴

Now with the sea as the only available escape route, everyone climbed into the two LCMs. (They chose not to use a barge they also had purchased, because it would have slowed their speed of movement too much.) A further complication occurred, Hasty said, when the CIA officials left behind some of their local employees in the frantic effort to leave. He stated, "The CIA pulled out, leaving behind their three Filipino employees, some of their Vietnamese employees, and one American CIA agent, their communicator."³⁵ The AESF's report that the *Vancouver* picked up 68 Vietnamese refugees and one embassy official from Can Tho early on the 29th conflicted with Hasty's statement, and confirmed that the CIA agents must have taken a large number of their employees with them, but nonetheless their actions still left the consul general with serious problems.³⁶

As the last group of people boarded the LCMs, the Marines, and the consulate staff suddenly realized that none of them knew how to drive a LCM. Hasty said: "The consul general . . . a former naval officer was the only one that had any concept whatsoever. So the consul general, wearing the helmet we had given him as a souvenir, got behind the helm of the LCM, looked at it awhile, played with it awhile, and said, 'I can run it.' And he could."*³⁷

Clearing this hurdle, the "convoy" departed Can Tho for a 60-mile journey down the Basaac River through Viet Cong-NVA territory that save for a miracle could have been anyone's last trip. Just as they were entering the most hazardous part of the journey where the river narrows, the realization that disaster awaited them suddenly flooded their consciousness. Having already suffered through one firefight during which small boats manned by Viet Cong attacked, and without the air cover that the Embassy had promised in earlier discussions over what would happen should the consul and his staff need to conduct a waterborne evacuation, they found themselves in desperate need of help. Unbelievably, it arrived in the form of an intense downpour which obscured their presence from the enemy-infested shoreline. Staff Sergeant Hasty said: "Luckily, we did not take a round into the LCMs, because if we had it would have been like tossing a grenade into a garbage can. After that firefight, we figured we were going to be in for a hell of a time, or we would have to be awfully damn lucky to get out. It rained so heavy and so hard you couldn't see the banks of the river, and that is what saved us."³⁸

During the conversations in which air cover was discussed, the American Embassy, Saigon, also promised Consul General McNamara that a U.S. Navy ship would be waiting to pick him and his staff up as soon as they reached the coastline. Yet when the two LCMs and its passengers reached the mouth of the river at approximately 1900, they beheld an unnerving sight—empty ocean! As far as the eye could see, not a ship or vessel of any kind was on the horizon. Certain that, as Sergeant Hasty said, "We were on our own," they headed out to sea in their flat-bottomed boats.³⁹

Expecting to see a Navy ship at any moment, they chugged along while sending out "Maydays" every few minutes. For over six hours, they searched the seas for any sign of life and finally well into the seventh hour, one of the men spotted what appeared to be a ship's light. They headed in the direction of the light, firing clusters of flares at 20 minute intervals. Despite never receiving a radio response or a return signal, the Can Tho Marines and Consul General McNamara pursued the ship for an hour. Finally reaching it, they discovered as Staff Sergeant Hasty described, "They (the *Pioneer Contender*) were not expecting us, were not waiting for us. They just happened to be there."⁴⁰

The *Pioneer Contender* did not "just happen to be there." Instead, it had been sent there to pick up the Can Tho refugees; a task it had accomplished earlier that day (or so the ship's captain thought). The truth was that Captain Garcia's Marines had seen the flares and reported the sighting to the ship's crew, but the crew chose to disregard them, assuming the flashes to be ARVN fire on the shore. Reassured in the thought that they already had their consulate evacuees on board, they ignored such strange sightings.

Once on board the *Pioneer Contender*, Sergeant Hasty said that his men immediately began assisting the Victor Detachment Marines. "I just attached my Marines to the ship's Marines to assist in loading refugees." His stay on the *Pioneer Contender* was very short and after several transfers, he eventually reached a Navy ship.⁴¹

On 1 May, after first riding on a Japanese tugboat and then a Korean LST, he finally placed his feet on the deck of the *Blue Ridge*, ending three harrowing and tiresome days of fear and frustration, and the official history of the Marine Security Guard Can Tho.⁴²

---

*Records do not reflect who operated the second LCM and in the book, *The Fall of Saigon*, the author described them using two LCMs and a rice barge.

PART V
OPERATION FREQUENT WIND AND A NEW BEGINNING

CHAPTER 11
The Evacuation

9th MAB—The DAO Compound—The Embassy

On Monday morning, 28 April, Major James E. Livingston, RLT 4 operations officer, and Major Morris W. "Moose" Lutes, ProvMAG-39 executive officer, climbed on board an Air America helicopter bound for the DAO Compound. One of the numerous daily shuttles flown by Air America to enable the 9th MAB to conduct evacuation preparations at the DAO without exceeding the Paris Accords' limit of a maximum of 50 military personnel in South Vietnam, this flight carried Livingston and Lutes into Tan Son Nhut for a liaison visit with the DAO evacuation planners. Their mission that day included a review of the evacuation plan and a reconnaissance of the DAO, Air America Compound, the Embassy, and the Newport Pier area. Earlier in the week Lieutenant Colonel William E. McKinstry, the officer-in-charge of the Evacuation Control Center (located in his office in the DAO building), had accompanied Colonel Alfred M. Gray, Jr., the regimental commander, on a similar reconnaissance.[1]

Ambassador Graham A. Martin had instructed Major General Homer D. Smith, Jr., USA, that he did not want to exceed the "50" limit and as a consequence he expected every visitor to return to the task force no later than midnight each day. This restriction placed a tremendous burden on the Air America pilots who were tasked with providing transportation in the unfamiliar circumstances of night shipboard operations. Despite their lack of experience and expertise in landing on a ship at night, these pilots displayed remarkable skill and courage in safely delivering their passengers. Due to the high demand for outbound seats, on occasion visitors would be bumped from a flight and forced to remain overnight. On the evening of 28 April, a Vietnamese general and an Army colonel acquired the seats that Majors Livingston and Lutes planned to use to return to the *Blue Ridge*, forcing them to remain in the DAO Compound overnight. That evening, the NVA subjected Tan Son Nhut and the adjoining "Pentagon East" to a rocket attack, launching a series of events which ended with the decision the next morning to execute Operation Frequent Wind. Major Livingston, still in the compound as a result of his involuntary stay, talked by radio with his commander, Colonel Gray, and provided him a firsthand account of the situation in the DAO. He also made recommendations as to the size of the force necessary to secure the landing zones for the impending operation.[2]

Very early the next morning, approximately 0500 29 April, in a room behind an unmarked door, three officers met and discussed the preceding night's events. Having just returned from their individual trailers where they had stolen a couple of hours of sleep, these members of the Special Planning Group (SPG) concluded that today would be "the day." A few minutes

Capt Anthony A. Wood, seen here as a lieutenant colonel, helped devise the evacuation routes used to move third-country nationals from downtown Saigon to the DAO. Since he named the routes after western trails, fellow officers dubbed him the "Wagonmaster."
Photo courtesy of Col Anthony A. Wood, USMC

Photo courtesy of Capt Russell R. Thurman, USMC (Ret)
Members of the press evacuate Saigon on Marine CH-53s via the DAO compound. Many refused to board the DAO buses at the way stations and had to be reminded that Ambassador Martin had given the order for all Americans to leave South Vietnam.

later, Colonel Eugene R. "Pat" Howard, Jr., the officer General Smith had chosen to oversee all evacuation matters for the DAO, entered the building referred to as "the bunker" and confirmed their predictions. He said that he had just talked with the Defense Attache and received instructions to begin preparations to execute the surface evacuation of Saigon. Colonel Howard, Major Jaime Sabater, Jr., Captain George Petry, and Captain Anthony A. Wood reviewed their earlier activities, and noted that convoy buses had been prestaged throughout metropolitan Saigon at buildings designated as pick-up points, American civilians, fully trained to drive those buses, were standing by in town at the way stations, and the drivers of the fake national police cars along with their guides awaited only the word to depart.

Within two hours, Captain Wood, his driver—a Marine lance corporal, and his radio operator—a Marine sergeant, were "riding the trails" of Saigon, checking on Santa Fe, Oregon, Texas, and the rest of the routes. His presence as a coordinator in downtown Saigon facilitated communications and placed a member of the DAO staff at the scene of the action. The PRC-25 radios, used by the evacuees waiting on the rooftops for the arrival of the Air America helicopters, came in loud and clear as long as no large building blocked their line-of-sight transmission. As a result, Captain Wood depended on the Motorolas to monitor the progress of the convoys because they were the only radios which consistently worked in the built-up areas of the city. Captain Wood's presence in downtown Saigon on 29 April helped to enhance the effectiveness of the bluff, but more importantly, it permitted him to troubleshoot problems as they arose. This part of the plan worked so well that the DAO successfully cycled the convoys through Saigon—not the hoped for one time, but three times. As the "Wagonmaster" rode the streets of Saigon, monitoring the radio and checking on the progress of each trail, he encountered several incidents necessitating quick action. The first problem requiring attention occurred on the Santa Fe trail when a few members of the press refused to board the bus and Captain Wood had to remind them that the Ambassador had ordered all Americans to leave Saigon. After resolving this problem, the convoy's bus driver subsequently made a wrong turn and became lost in the crowded streets of downtown Saigon. Although unfamiliar with that part of the city, Captain Wood eventually got the convoy on the right road to Tan Son Nhut. The second happened on the Oregon trail when Captain Wood received a request to pick up the Ambassador's dog. The final and most difficult problem arose when the South Vietnamese guarding the main gate at Tan Son Nhut refused to

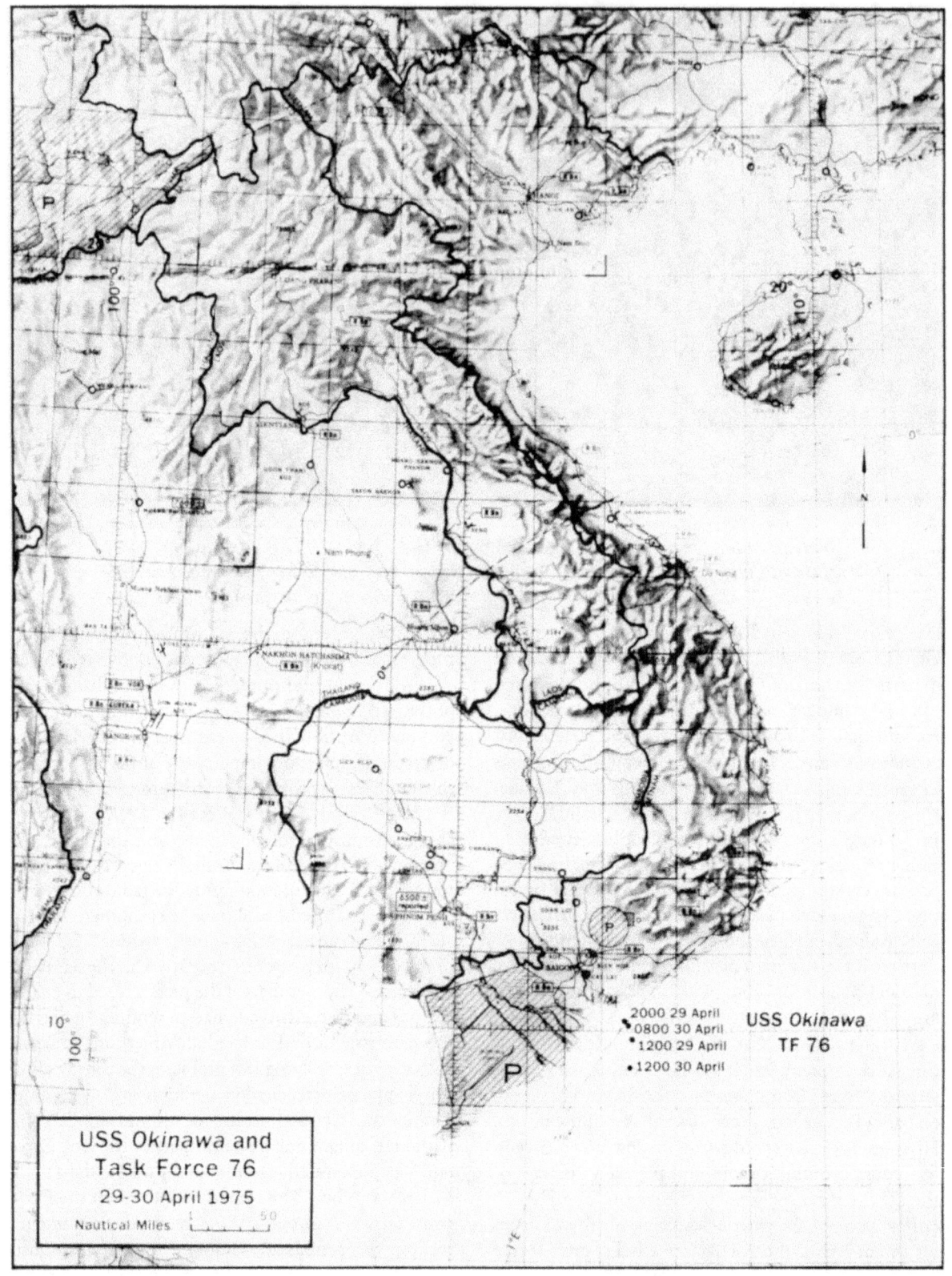

Map adapted from U.S. Air Force, *USAF Global Navigation and Planning Chart, Southeast Asia*, (10 June 1959); hatched areas and other land notations are a part of the original map.

allow the last convoy of buses into the DAO Compound. As this was happening, a firefight between two ARVN units broke out and caught the rearmost buses in the crossfire, disabling two of the vehicles. Eventually, Lieutenant Colonel McKinstry convinced the ARVN commander controlling the gates to permit the remaining buses to enter the compound. General Carey's threat to use the armed Cobras flying overhead probably played a large role in the ARVN commander's decision.* Shortly thereafter, the Air America helicopter pilots, who had been delayed by various problems of their own, completed the last pickups from the rooftop LZs. The "bluff" had worked—over-the-road evacuation of Saigon ended as the 9th MAB deployed its ground security force in the "Pentagon East."[3]

9th MAB

After floating off the coast of South Vietnam for over a week, the 9th MAB was more than ready for action. Every day since its arrival the task force had expected orders to begin the evacuation, but the only directives it received changed the response time. The first change arrived only hours before the 18th ARVN Division abandoned Xuan Loc. On that afternoon, Admiral Steele notified the MAB of CinCPac's desire to begin a six-hour alert stance before day's end.[4]

As the situation in South Vietnam, and especially Saigon, deteriorated, the standby reaction times decreased. On the night of the 27th, Admiral Steele directed the 9th MAB to be in a one-hour alert status before sunrise the next morning. Accomplishing this, the brigade waited. When it became apparent later in the day that action was unlikely, Admiral Steele authorized the MAB to relax its readiness to a six-hour standby condition. Within hours of this decision, he received word that Tan Son Nhut Airport had been attacked by enemy aircraft. Early evening, 28 April, a few hours after the Tan Son Nhut incident, Admiral Gayler (CinCPac) reduced the reaction time to one hour. At 0130, 9th MAB reported to Admiral Whitmire (CTF 76) and General Burns (USSAG/Seventh Air Force) that it was ready. Now, all awaited L-Hour.[5]

Despite prior arrangements, questions over L-Hour still created some confusion at this point in the operation. General Burns initially had defined L-Hour as the time that a helicopter would be launched for a given zone. To Marine pilots though, L-Hour meant the time a helicopter would land in a given zone. During the latter stages of planning, Admiral Whitmire requested a clarification of L-Hour. General Burns' staff responded that L-Hour was the time that the first helicopter touched down in the evacuation zone, a reversal of the original definition. Based on this change in L-Hour, it then became necessary for the planners to modify the helicopter flow schedule. Admiral Whitmire and General Carey, in a joint message to Admiral Steele and all the participants in the operation, issued a helicopter time schedule which reflected and complied with their understanding of USSAG's definition of L-Hour.[6]

Yet on the evening of 28 April in the USSAG (call sign "Blue Chip") command bunker, General Burns sent a messenger to the Marine Corps liaison desk manned by Lieutenant Colonel James L. Cunningham (III MAF plans officer) and Major Richard K. "Keith" Young (9th MAB operations officer), who were in Nakhon Phanom to assist the joint command in its coordination and control of the operation. The messenger informed Major Young that General Burns had a question about the definition of L-Hour and would like to see him. Major Young recalled his conversation with the USSAG commander: "He asked me how the 9th MAB defined L-Hour and I explained to him the Marine Corps used the time a helicopter landed in the zone as L-Hour and not the time it took off. He seemed surprised by the difference and could not understand why four hours would pass before the first elements of the security force landed in the zone."[7]

Adding to the confusion created by the difference between the Air Force and Marine Corps definitions of L-Hour** was the relationship between L-Hour and

---

*Captain Wood, in radio communication with the Ground Security Force, was asked by Colonel Gray if he could control a close air support mission and he replied, "I can see and I can control." An air strike was never delivered because the ARVN commander got what he was after—a way out of Saigon. Wood Comments.

**Years later, Admiral Steele proffered his assessment of the confusion over L-Hour. He said: "This deplorable mix-up over L-Hour never would have occurred, except for the subordination of the Seventh Fleet and the Seventh Fleet Marines to CG, USSAG. The *Blue Ridge* with Rear Admiral Whitmire and General Carey embarked was in close company with the *Oklahoma City*, my flagship. As the evacuation preparations began after execution, I had the *Oklahoma City* fall in astern of the *Blue Ridge* at 1,000 yards and transferred my flag to the *Blue Ridge*, which had better communications than the Seventh Fleet flagship. Early on the morning of 29 April, Rear Admiral Whitmire had called me on a secure voice radio requesting instructions on the execution. CinCPacFlt was saying one thing, and CG, USSAG was saying another. I instructed Whitmire to follow General Burns' direction and so informed CinCPacFlt. My reason for going over to *Blue Ridge* was simply to keep higher authority off Whitmire and Carey's back, particularly now that confusion had developed regarding L-Hour, and in view of the complicated chain of command that had been set up." Steele Comments.

Department of Defense Photo (USMC) A150967

While USSAG Headquarters tried to clarify L-Hours, reconnaissance aircraft spotted a North Vietnamese Army convoy, lower left, entering Saigon on the afternoon of 29 April. The next day, President Duong Van "Big" Minh ordered his soldiers to lay down their arms.

the one-hour alert posture. The alert signified that the forces had one hour to get into position before the start of the operation. Weeks earlier the brigade's air planners had computed 30 minutes as the flight time from the average ship's location to the farthest landing zone, the Defense Attache Office Compound, adjacent to Tan Son Nhut Airfield. Combining the 90 minutes needed for crossdecking operations with the 30 minutes of flight time automatically added two hours to the hour of standby time. Thus a one-hour response time meant that from the moment the order to begin was received until the first helicopter landed in Saigon three hours would elapse. This parameter had to be further modified by the Air Force's restrictions. USSAG/Seventh Air Force's operational order required that a fixed-wing aircraft be on station before any evacuation helicopter entered the city. For its support aircraft to achieve control of the target area and bring to bear maximum firepower, the Air Force required three hours preparation time to launch, refuel enroute, and arrive on station, which for a one-hour alert status translated into four hours, the amount of time between the word to begin and the earliest moment a Marine helicopter could land in the zone.

At the same time the 9th MAB was preparing for the helicopter evacuation which they had been expecting for the past three days, the Evacuation Control Center was preparing for a final and massive fixed-wing evacuation schedule. At 2000 on 28 April, it announced that the evacuation would resume at 2330. The plan, unrealistic in its expectations, called for 50 to 60 sorties to lift over 10,000 people. Shortly after midnight, the scheduled start time was slipped to 0330. Between 0300 and 0330 the first of the C-130s landed. Despite planning to carry refugees, each of these three aircraft, for some unexplained reason, carried a BLU-82 weapon.*

For obvious reasons, each bomb had to be carefully unloaded. Nearly one-half hour passed before the South Vietnamese completed the task. Minutes later the North Vietnamese Army delivered an unfriendly welcome to Option II of the evacuation plan (military fixed-wing airlift). Besides altering the alert posture of the 9th MAB, the ensuing artillery and rocket attack on the Tan Son Nhut Airfield, which began just before 0400, destroyed one C-130 and forced the other two to leave empty. Before their hasty departure, they picked up the crew of the destroyed Her-

---

*BLU-82 is a 15,000-pound bomb known "affectionately" as the "Daisy Cutter" because it is used to destroy vegetation in jungle areas selected for use as helicopter landing zones. BLU is the U.S. Air Force acronym for Bomb Live Unit. During the NVA Spring Offensive the VNAF had used BLU-82s as a poor man's substitute for the B-52, employing C-130s as the delivery platform. At the end of the battle for Xuan Loc, the VNAF dropped one of them on the *341st NVA Division's* headquarters.

cules, barely avoiding getting hit themselves. With debris jettisoned from scrambling VNAF aircraft scattered all over the airport's apron, taxiway, and runway, the rescheduled lift was temporarily suspended and eventually cancelled after the Ambassador's midmorning visit to General Smith's office.[8]

Thus in a matter of a few, short hours the fixed-wing airlift of Saigon evacuees ceased being even a remote possibility, and the helicopter became the only way out. It would be a few more hours until Ambassador Martin's painful decision translated into action.

By the morning of Tuesday, 29 April, everyone in the task force knew the status of the North Vietnamese offensive and the peril that Saigon faced, and wondered why the evacuation had not begun. Waiting for the word to "execute," the 9th MAB began the day just as it had the previous three days, very early, shortly after midnight. This day, however, was different.

LtCol George P. Slade, commander, 2d Battalion, 4th Marines waits for the signal to board the lead aircraft for Saigon. BLT 2/4 and the other Marines of 9th MAB spent many hours waiting, but knew after the morning rocket attack which had killed two Marine Security Guards, that the day, 29 April, was "the day."
Photo courtesy of Capt Russell R. Thurman, USMC (Ret)

In anticipation of a long day for his pilots, with a substantial part of it spent strapped in the helicopter, General Carey directed his aviators to assume a standby position on the flight deck; outside rather than inside their craft. After waiting in the vicinity of their respective helicopters from 0200 to almost 1100, the pilots stood down and went to lunch. Their break however was shortlived.[9]

At approximately the time the pilots started heading for chow, General Carey received an update from Colonel Wylie W. Taylor, his deputy in the DAO Compound. His call included "the information that two Marines were KIA as a result of the rocket attack."* An earlier call from Major Livingston to Colonel Gray also had informed the 9th MAB staff of the rocket attack and the death of Corporal McMahon and Lance Corporal Judge. Based on these two reports and recommendations from his deputy commander and his RLT 4 commander, General Carey decided that initially he would insert one battalion, Lieutenant Colonel George P. Slade's 2d Battalion, 4th Marines, into the DAO Compound and Annex. Then later, if necessary for crowd control and security, he would send a command group and a company from Lieutenant Colonel Royce L. Bond's 1st Battalion, 9th Marines into the Air America Compound.[10]

Finally, the waiting was over. Admiral Gayler directed USSAG/Seventh Air Force and Seventh Fleet to begin Frequent Wind Option IV at 1051 (Saigon time). With that announcement the evacuation of Saigon officially began.[11]

The DAO Compound

At 1215, the 9th MAB received General Burns' message directing them to "execute." For some unexplainable reason, dissemination of this message to the participating units had been delayed from 1052 until 1215.**[12] Captain William R. Melton, a company com-

---

*Colonel Taylor offered his opinion of this tragic loss: "This event had major influence at all levels, and I believe, really was the triggering event for Frequent Wind." Taylor Comments.

**On the morning of 29 April confusion still existed at USSAG headquarters over which definition of L-Hour the Navy-Marine Corps team was using, and attempts to clarify when crossdecking could begin and when the helicopters could depart delayed the execute message's official passage from Nakhon Phanom to the Seventh Fleet—and worse, clouded its intent. The misunderstanding between USSAG and the task force produced several postponements of L-Hour and as a result of this perceived problem, the Joint Chiefs of Staff commissioned a formal investigation team, headed by Major General John R. D. Cleland, Jr., USA, to determine exactly what took place during the execution of Operation Frequent Wind. The investigation team reached the conclusion that no abnormal delay occurred. Cleland Report.

Photo courtesy of Capt Russell R. Thurman, USMC (Ret)
Capt William R. Melton, commander of Company G, BLT 2/4, briefs his men. Capt Melton's Marines participated in both Eagle Pull and Frequent Wind.

mander in BLT 2/4, said, "An unsubstantiated rumor circulating among the ship's company and the Marines on the *Okinawa* was that the message somehow had gotten lost in the *Blue Ridge's* message center."[13]

The delay in passing the message coincided with the MAB's decision to break for lunch, and as a consequence, the pilots were in the ship's mess when the execute message arrived. Captain Kurt A. Schrader, a helicopter commander in HMH-462, related, "We had just stood down when the ship's captain came over the 1MC (public address system) and announced that the mission was a go but the message directing it had been lost by the *Blue Ridge's* communications center."[14] The sudden shift in direction initially caught everyone off guard, but within minutes the Marines and sailors had resumed their combat ready, prelaunch status. Since General Carey had not received the order to begin the operation until 1215, the landing of the first helicopter in the zone could not be expected until 1615 (based on the times contained in the operational order). All concerned deemed this expected time of arrival (ETA) unacceptable. As a consequence, the Seventh Fleet and the 9th MAB expedited their preparations, attempting to compress the four-hour package into less than three hours. Achieving this objective would nearly double the number of daylight hours available to the pilots.[15]

Regimental Landing Team 4 (RLT 4), commanded by Colonel Gray, wasted no time in readying itself for an immediate departure. Only days earlier, Colonel Gray had received orders to prepare to provide a security force in support of the C-141/C-130 airlift. Word to transfer that security force never came, only causing the Marines' anticipation to intensify. The signal to mount out meant anticipation would be supplanted by action.

Aware of the situation at the compound and familiar with the time-sensitive scheme of maneuver, General Carey began crossdecking operations the instant he received the execute order.[16] Each pilot rechecked his helicopter flow schedule, made last-minute, minor, but necessary changes, and transmitted them to the Helicopter Direction Center (HDC) on the *Okinawa*. Complicating all of this activity was a sky filled with South Vietnamese Air Force helicopters, looking for a place to land and disgorge their panic-stricken passengers.[17]

Following receipt of detailed information from the HDC on the *Okinawa*, Admiral Whitmire announced that L-Hour had changed again and would now be 1500. Despite this modification, due in large part to the continuing confusion over USSAG's understanding of L-Hour, Operation Frequent Wind was finally in motion.[18]

At this time, the brigade began the most critical aspect of pre-L-Hour operations: positioning the landing force. Gunnery Sergeant Russell R. Thurman, the 31st MAU public affairs specialist, recalled, "The most incredible thing that morning was the number of ships. Every direction that you looked all you could see were ships and more ships."[19]

The helicopter schedule took into consideration the number of ships and the distribution of helicopters. It called for the loaded and fueled helicopters to reposition themselves on the USS *Okinawa, Hancock, Dubuque, Denver, Duluth, Mobile, Peoria,* and *Vancouver*. This would be accomplished 30 minutes prior to the scheduled landing time in the zone. Essentially, it represented the same type of evolution employed at Phnom Penh, by the same squadrons: Lieutenant Colonel James L. Bolton's HMH-462 and Lieutenant Colonel Herbert M. Fix's HMH-463. Not by coincidence, they also carried the same Marines, BLT 2/4.[20]

To make the flight schedule work, the Marines had to redistribute vast amounts of men and equipment in order to achieve some semblance of pre-mission integrity. They had either, to launch fully loaded helicopters simultaneously from various ships for an overhead rendezvous and an integrated flight to Sai-

Amphibious and MSC ships deploy off Vung Tau awaiting the order to begin Frequent Wind. At the last minute, confusion occurred over the definition of L-Hour and as a consequence the ships did not receive the order to "execute" until 1215, 29 April 1975.

gon, or to launch them unloaded to hold at an air orbit point until they could be loaded. Once loaded, they would return to the formation and wait for the flight to depart. If prior to this, fuel consumption became a consideration, then that helicopter would hold on deck, and just before scheduled departure, it would load troops/equipment on that ship or the one designated. If neither of these alternatives offered the proper conditions, then the Marines were prepared to spot the helicopters on board a carrier or an assault ship and use it as a platform from which to embark and launch the first wave.[21]

In anticipation of this, BLT 2/4 had distributed its infantry, reconnaissance, and engineering units among the *Okinawa*, *Vancouver*, and the *Peoria*. They totalled 23 CH-53 loads.[22] The *Okinawa* housed more than half of them (twelve), while the *Vancouver* carried six and the *Peoria* five. None of the ships possessed enough space to load all of the heliteams at the same time. As a result, each helicopter picked up its passengers two hours before L-Hour and then moved as directed by HDC to deck space designated for refueling and launch. By doing this, the Marines assured themselves sufficient time to make L-Hour. In order to accomplish the complicated crossdecking maneuver with the limited space available, they had to use all of the task force's ships.[23]

Twelve CH-53s from HMH-462 comprised the first wave. Loaded with the BLT 2/4 command groups "A" and "B," and Company F and reinforced Company H, they departed the launch area 30 minutes prior to L-Hour in order to arrive in the DAO Compound at L-Hour, 1500. This wave actually landed at 1506.[24] The second wave of CH-53s consisted of 12 helicopters from HMH-463. They departed 15 minutes after the first wave and landed in the DAO Compound at 1515.

While the second wave waited for the order to begin crossdecking operations, the first wave completed its preparations by loading 10 heliteams from its ship, the *Okinawa*, and two from the *Peoria*. After the first wave completed its launch, the second wave picked up six heliteams from the *Vancouver*, three from *Peoria*, and two from *Okinawa*. HMH-463 accomplished this complex maneuver as planned, through redistribution of its assets. The squadron's crossdecking of two empty CH-53s provided a vivid illustration of the coordination required in launching a force of this size on time. Empty, they flew together to the *Peoria*. One loaded troops and moved to the *Mobile* while the other took on troops, refueled, and remained on the *Peoria*. The two then launched together for Saigon, making up a third wave.*[25]

Unintentionally complicating this evolution were

---

*The 10 USAF helicopters from *Midway* joined this wave to bring the total for all three waves in the first cycle to 36 CH/HH-53s.

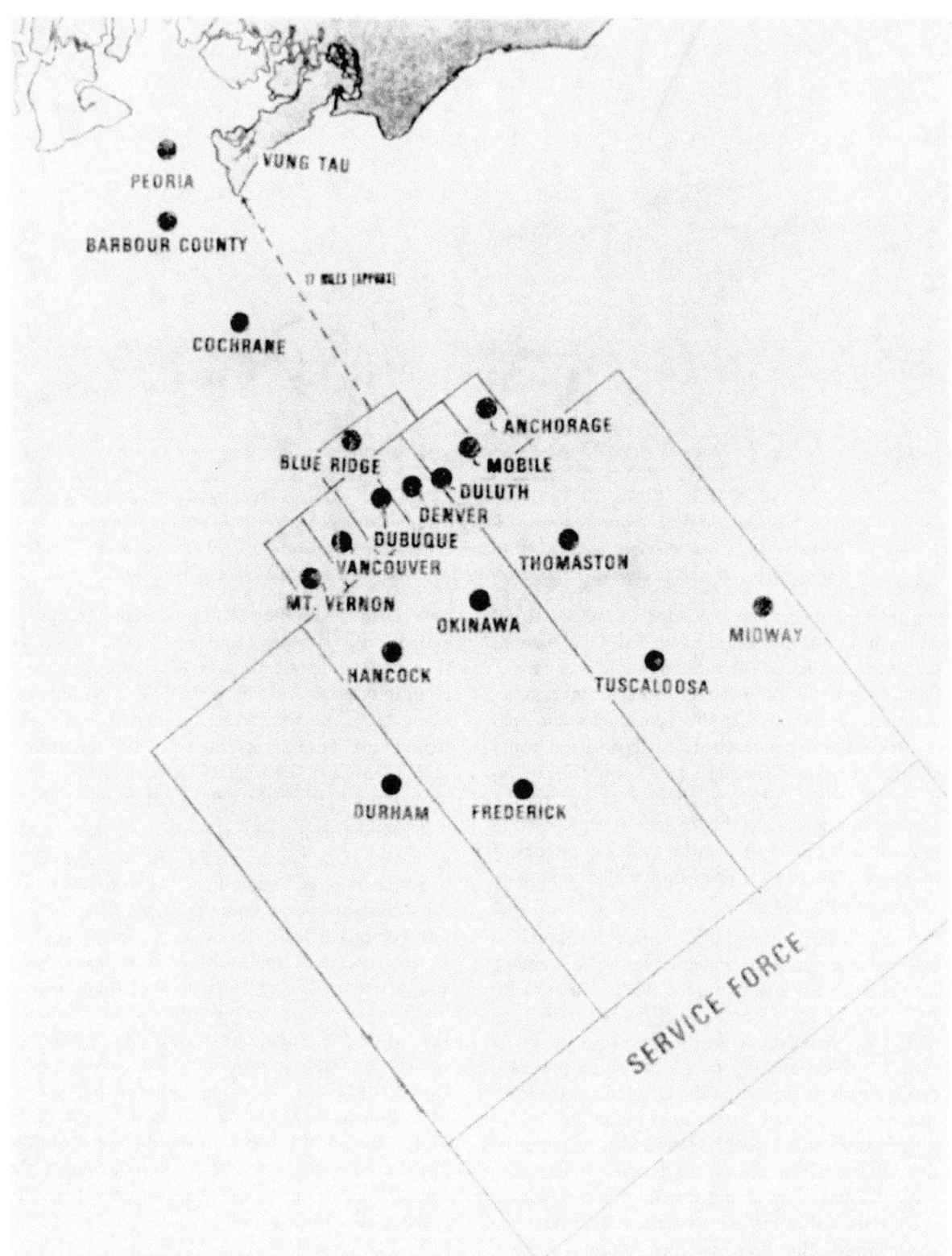

This diagram shows deployment of naval forces at the start of Operation Frequent Wind. Note that at 1500 on 29 April the Blue Ridge was approximately 17 miles from Vung Tau.

THE EVACUATION

the MAG-36 medium and light helicopters, now members of ProvMAG-39 and in position on the decks of the other ships in the task force. These helicopters, CH-46s, UH-1Es, and AH-1Js (Cobras) were an integral part of the pre-L-Hour preparations and could not be pushed aside or relocated to other deck space. They had to fit into the flow pattern because each one had a support or rescue role in the overall operation. Their missions included everything from sea and air rescue to carrying 15-man, quick-reaction "Sparrow Hawk" teams of Marines from Company A, 1st Battalion, 9th Marines.[26]

The 9th MAB planned to use two Sparrow Hawk teams, with each one on board a CH-46. These two CH-46s would then orbit along the evacuation route, positioned to assist any helicopter in distress. In the event that the NVA shot down a helicopter or a mechanical malfunction forced one to make an emergency landing in enemy-held territory, a Sparrow Hawk team stood ready to land and provide security. Its defensive perimeter would then enable a sea and air rescue (SAR) helicopter to pick up the crew. Besides this support, two CH-46s would provide medical evacuation capabilities while the Cobras would fly cover for the transport helicopters and, if possible, for anyone else who requested it. In addition, the Cobras could serve as Tactical Air Coordinators (Airborne) or Forward Air Controllers (Airborne). Another critical means of support would be provided by the UH-1Es, a command and control platform for General Carey, Colonel Gray, and Colonel Frank G. McLenon, the ProvMAG-39 commander. Thus, crossdecking for the initial transport waves would have to integrate the medium and light helicopters into the overall flow pattern, adding one more factor to the already complicated process.[27]

With all these helicopters in a relatively small airspace, control and safety became paramount considerations. The demanding and important task of safely controlling the skies over South Vietnam had to be shared by two Services, the Navy and the Air Force. Admiral Whitmire retained responsibility for air control over the water, or "feet wet," while General Burns as USSAG/Seventh Air Force commander (call sign

A 9th MAB "intel" picture numbers LZs 34 and 35 in the Annex and 36-38 in the Alamo. Alamo LZ 39 is outside the photo, top left; Air America terminal LZ 40 was not used.

Marine Corps Historical Collection

"Blue Chip") controlled all aircraft "feet dry," over land. The on-scene, local control rested with the airborne mission commander (AMC). For the first six hours of the operation, Colonel John J. Roosma, Jr., USAF, served as the AMC. Located in an airborne C-130 designated the Airborne Battlefield Command and Control Center (ABCCC), he answered to the radio call sign of "Cricket."[28]

The commanding officer of ProvMAG 39, Colonel McLenon, exercised control of his Marine aircraft through the Tactical Air Coordination Center (TACC) on board the *Blue Ridge*. The Helicopter Direction Center, on board the *Okinawa*, maintained aircraft spacing and routing. It also passed directions to aircraft outbound from Saigon, informing them which deck space was available for unloading and refueling and relaying any other pertinent landing data. In addition, Admiral Whitmire designated the *Okinawa* as the primary control for over-water helo operations, with *Hancock* as backup should the *Okinawa* suffer damage or equipment failure.[29]

The primary difference between TACC and HDC was that TACC controlled the tactical disposition of the helicopters and HDC controlled the helicopters as long as they were in the Navy's airspace. These areas of responsibility often overlapped and at times even merged. Under the conditions existing on the morning of 29 April 1975, the difference in control responsibilities of TACC and HDC at best seemed blurred, at worst redundant.

To address flight safety, the 9th MAB staff prescribed altitudes, routes, and checkpoints for the operation. To avert mid-air collisions, the planners chose altitudes which would not only provide separation of traffic but also a capability to see and avoid the enemy's SAM and SA-7 missile threat (6,500 feet for flights inbound to Saigon and 5,500 feet for those outbound from Saigon to the Navy ships). In addition, these altitudes were high enough to avoid small arms and artillery fire. To further reduce the missile threat, HMH-462 painted its helicopters with infrared paint. HMH-463 had already painted its helicopters, but HMH-462 did not have an opportunity to modify its CH-53s until after the evacuation of Phnom Penh (reports had indicated an absence of SAMs in Cambodia). Despite all the concern over these obvious threats, the weather still remained the gravest danger.

At the beginning of the operation, pilots in the first wave reported the weather as 2,000 feet scattered, 20,000 feet overcast with 15 miles visibility, except in haze over Saigon, where visibility decreased to one

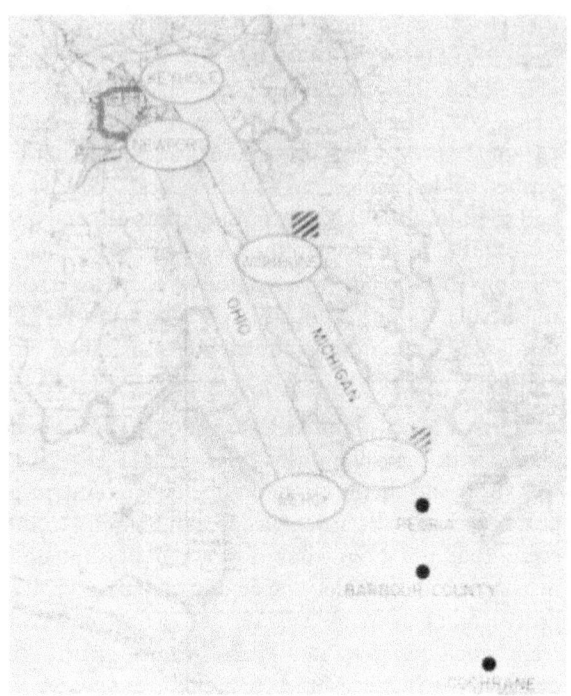

Marine Corps Historical Collection
This is one of the briefing maps used for Operation Frequent Wind. Along these routes were stationed two airborne CH-46s, each with a 15-man, quick-reaction force on board designated a "Sparrow Hawk" team.

mile. This meant that scattered clouds existed below their flight path while a solid layer of clouds more than two miles above their heads obscured the sun. Additionally, the curtain of haze, suspended over Saigon, so altered the diminished daylight that line of sight visibility was only a mile. The weather conditions would deteriorate as the operation continued. Captain Edward J. "Jim" Ritchie, flying a MAG-36 CH-46 from the *Hancock*, recalled his first sortie into Saigon at approximately 1830: "The sky was completely overcast, meeting the ground in the distance with the lights of the city and the burning buildings reflecting off it, giving one the sensation that you were seeing a strange movie about the Apocalypse."[30]

Although all these factors, including the enemy's proximity to Saigon, had to be considered, General Carey never hesitated in making his decision to insert a battalion of Marines into the DAO Compound. Despite the unknown variables of size of crowds, numbers of refugees, degree of crowd control, and South Vietnamese military reaction, General Carey believed this was the appropriate show of force. With the size of the security contingent decided and his preparations complete, General Carey boarded a UH-1E

Photo courtesy of LtCol William R. Melton, USMC

The first section of CH-53s approaches the DAO landing zones. At 1506 the first helicopters of HMH-462 touched down at the Alamo, officially beginning Operation Frequent Wind.

helicopter and at 1315 departed the *Blue Ridge* for the landing zone.[31]

At 1350, a section of Huey helicopters landed at the DAO Compound and discharged its passengers, General Carey and Colonel Gray. During their approach to the compound, they experienced a firsthand view of the enemy's firepower. The NVA was shelling nearby Tan Son Nhut Airport with ground, rocket, and artillery fire. Upon touching down after an uneventful but exciting flight, General Carey exited the lead helicopter followed by Colonel Gray from the second Huey. They quickly established an austere command post in preparation for the arrival of the Marine CH-53s and the ground security force.[32]

Proceeding by way of Point Hope, the initial checkpoint and the spot where the *Peoria* positioned itself to pick up any downed pilots, the first wave checked in with Air Force control. Upon contact with Cricket, the flight radioed its next checkpoint, Keyhole, and its destination, the DAO Compound. Just prior to passing Keyhole, Cricket directed Lieutenant Colonel Bolton and his squadron to switch to the landing zone controller's frequency. After an initial radio check, Bolton requested and obtained clearance into the zone for his flight, and the first wave started landing at 1506. At that moment, it was 0306 in Washington, the same day, 29 April 1975, and 2106, 28 April, at the CinCPac Command Center in Honolulu, Hawaii.

Greeted by the cheers of a crowd of American and South Vietnamese evacuees, the Marines of BLT 2/4 rushed to their assigned positions in the sector. They wasted no time in establishing a security zone to protect the 679 people in the compound who were waiting to board the helicopters. (The evacuees in the compound at 1500 represented only those who had been pre-staged for the initial lift. Subsequent refugees were organized as they arrived.) Years later, the Defense Attache, General Smith, described the crowd's mood: "The Vietnamese were undeniably sad and even apprehensive but throughout it all very calm. The Americans were also sad but perhaps for different reasons."[33]

After loading the first group of evacuees, the 12

Photo courtesy of Capt Russell R. Thurman, USMC (Ret)

First evacuees from the DAO compound are seen alighting from an HMH-463 Sea Stallion. HMH-463 helicopters made up the second wave of security forces to enter the compound.

Marines of BLT 2/4 guard the perimeter of the DAO Annex landing zones during the first hours of the evacuation of Saigon. LZs 34 and 35 were located here and all operations from the Annex were completed before sunset, which occurred at 1847 on 29 April.

Department of Defense Photo (USMC) A150965

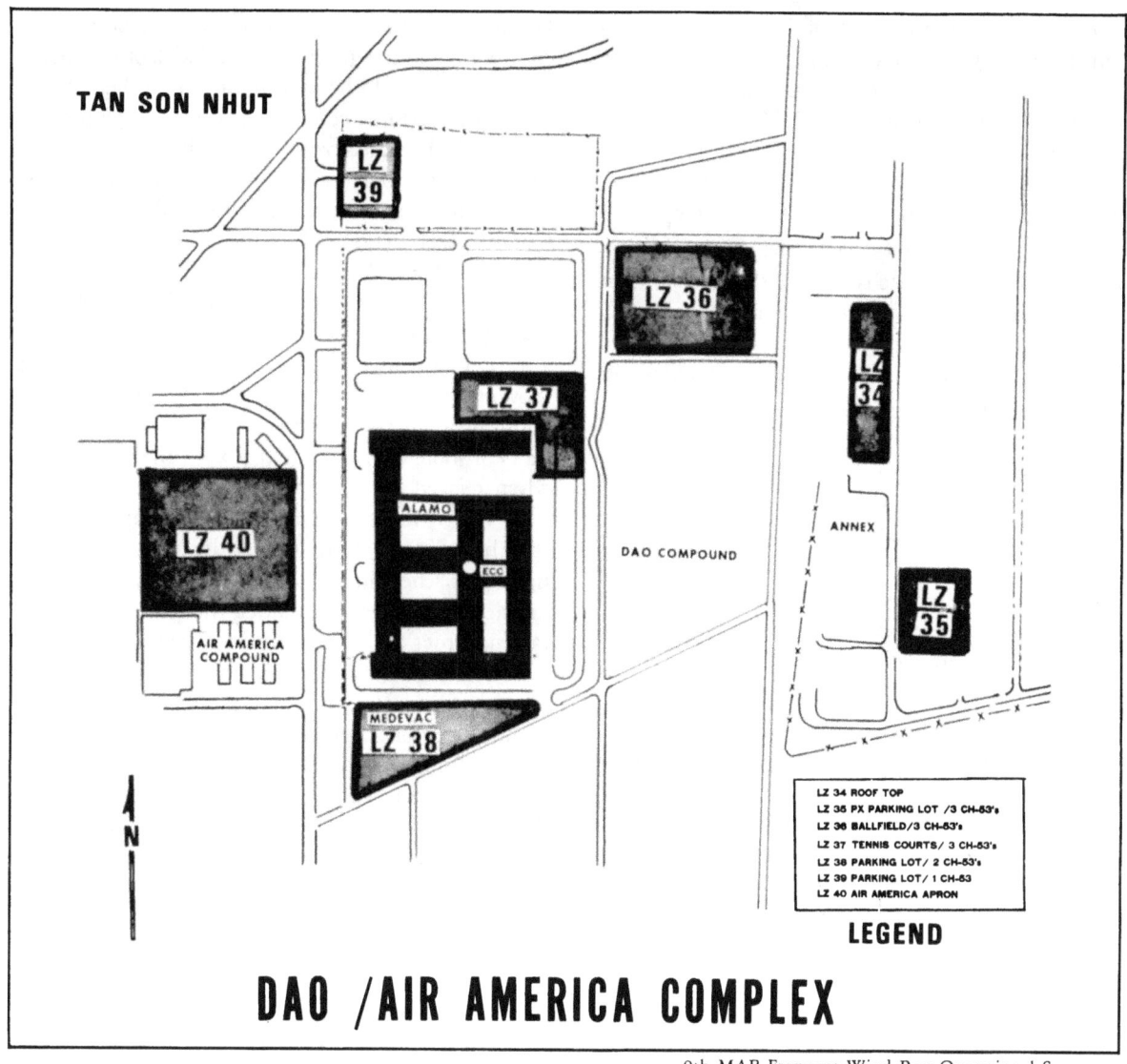

A map produced by the 9th MAB staff illustrates the layout of the DAO compound and the landing zones. Note locations of Air America terminal, Annex, and Alamo.

HMH-462 CH-53Ds left the compound and flew outbound via Newport Pier to the task force. In doing so, they attempted to maintain a visual separation of 1,000 feet from the inbound second wave. When the first wave reported "feet wet" at Point Mercy to the HDC controller on the *Okinawa*, its helicopter pilots received vectors to ships with enough deck space to accommodate them. Landing on these ships at 1540, they unloaded the first refugees delivered by Operation Frequent Wind.[34]

As the second wave loaded the next group of evacuees in the DAO Compound, Lieutenant Colonel Slade reinforced his positions with the newly arrived Marines from the second increment. The DAO Compound lent itself to easy access by air, but its configuration made security difficult. Slade's scheme of maneuver called for deployment of his "Alpha" command group, two rifle companies, and his 81mm mortar platoon around the DAO headquarters building (the Alamo) and its adjacent landing zones. The "Bravo" command group led by the BLT 2/4 executive officer, Major Thornton L. "Luke" Youngman, consisted of two rifle companies and the 106mm recoilless rifle platoon. It assumed responsibility for security of the DAO Annex and its adjoining landing zones.

Using an east-west axis which bisected the Alamo defensive perimeter, Lieutenant Colonel Slade had Captain Matthew E. Broderick deploy his Company

E Marines to the northern half of the zone while Captain Thomas A. Keene's Company F occupied the southern section. At the Annex, Captain William R. Melton moved his Company G Marines into the eastern section of a perimeter using a north-south axis. At the same time, Captain Steven R. Bland's Company H assumed control of the western sector.[35]

As the number of refugees decreased, so did the size of the zone. Despite continuous adjustments in the perimeter resulting from the reconsolidations, BLT 2/4 attempted to incorporate the existing defensive features of the compound, including the bunkers and barbed wire entanglements.[36]

Originally, General Carey had intended to deploy a command group and a company from BLT 1/9 to the Air America Compound as additional landing zone security. However, after assessing the relative security of the two areas in the DAO Compound and consulting with Colonel Gray on the apparent success of the South Vietnamese defensive stand at Tan Son Nhut Airport, he decided to cancel the BLT 1/9 security mission. To insure effective command and control, General Carey remained in the compound.[37]

The evacuation of the DAO Compound continued like clockwork. When a helicopter arrived, the guides moved the evacuees from the staging areas directly to the ramps. Bending down as they approached the swirling rotor blades, the refugees then climbed on board the waiting CH-53 as the guides returned to the assembly area.

Aircraft loads varied in size depending upon the type of helicopter used. Besides those flown by the Marine Corps, the Air Force (USAF had eight CH-53Cs and two HH-53s deployed on the *Midway*) supplied 10 from its nearby bases in Thailand. Each model's load capacity (a factor of its internal configuration), adjusted for fuel, determined the number of evacuees that a particular helicopter could carry on that sortie. The landing zone marshals had to keep these factors uppermost in their minds as they prepared each load. Once a decision as to the number of passengers had been made, the marshals would then communicate that information to the guides. When loads exceeded the planned limit of 50, signals between guides and marshals became especially critical. Complicating everyone's ability to communicate was the helicopters' deafening rotor blade noise and their electronic interference with hand-held radios. This interference severely limited the marshals' ability to relay such important information as the size of the evacuee population. This particular data provided the landing zone controllers and the guides a general idea of how many more flights would be required to move the remaining evacuees. To be certain that the correct numbers reached the intended party, the marshals and the landing zone controllers used a colored signal paddle system to communicate. In addition, the controllers (Alamo controllers handled landing zones 36, 37, 38, and 39 while the Annex controller covered LZs 34 and 35) advised the marshals of the number of inbound helicopters and their estimated time of arrival. They also used this link to pass information about troop movements including the status of the Sparrow Hawk teams as well as the progress of the evacuation. The news of more flights headed toward the compound, when relayed to the refugees, significantly lowered their anxiety levels. Oftentimes, these people thought they had already witnessed the departure of the last helicopter. The calming effect this reassuring news had on the refugees definitely aided the Marines in maintaining order and control in the staging area.

Unfortunately, coordination and control of the overall embarkation operation suffered from more serious communication problems. Direct communications with Admiral Whitmire and 9th MAB Rear were sporadic, at best, requiring a continuous relay by the ABCCC (airborne C-130 equipped with several types of radios). Added to the already heavy traffic, these relays served to create confusion on the radios. One of the first instances of using the ABCCC to pass information from the DAO Compound (9th MAB) to 9th MAB Rear occurred when the ABCCC (Cricket) radioed that General Carey had reported at 1350 that he was ashore and in radio contact with his prospective operational commander, General Burns.* About an hour before, the Annex and Alamo landing zone controllers had used the ABCCC to communicate their status, the weather, enemy activity, and landing zone conditions. Later in the operation, the controllers would have to repeat this unusual procedure in order to ensure that important data reached the commanders. The ABCCC eventually relayed to the task

---

*General Louis H. Wilson, Jr., FMFPac commander during Operation Frequent Wind, later remembered his concerns over the command relationship in USSAG's theater of operations. According to General Wilson, "There was no clear passage of command ashore, therefore the naval chain of command continued to act as though they were still in operational control. General Carey failed to officially report ashore or 'chop' to General Burns and a Marine has the responsibility once he has established his command post ashore to make a hard copy, reporting for operational control to his new commander." Wilson Comments.

Landing Zone 38 received some of the first CH-53s on 29 April. The accompanying picture is a view from the Alamo of the same landing zone, taken while Tan Son Nhut Air Base burned in the background.

Department of Defense Photo (USMC) A150960
Marine Corps Historical Collection

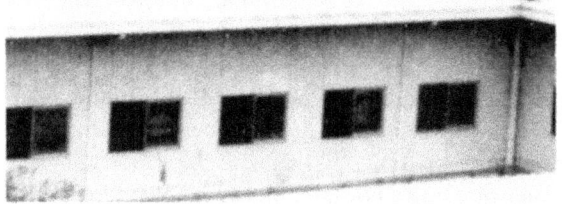

force the following types of information: the arrival of the security force, the number of evacuees extracted, the number remaining, and the status of the evacuation helicopters. Fortunately for all concerned, contact with the ABCCC remained satisfactory throughout the operation, with two nets always functioning.[38]

Despite the additional communication workload, Cricket and the landing zone controllers still performed their functions and deftly controlled air operations over South Vietnam. The ABCCC would pick up control of inbound aircraft as soon as they reached landfall, and then at checkpoint Keyhole, hand them off to the Alamo and Annex controllers. They in turn would direct the flight leaders to the first available zone. If no sites were available, the helicopters would orbit near Keyhole, though instances of holding were rare during daylight hours. With nightfall approaching and the security force consolidating its position, that changed. As the pilots and controllers adjusted to the darkness and the shrinking number of landing zones, holding became routine, normally lasting no longer than five minutes.

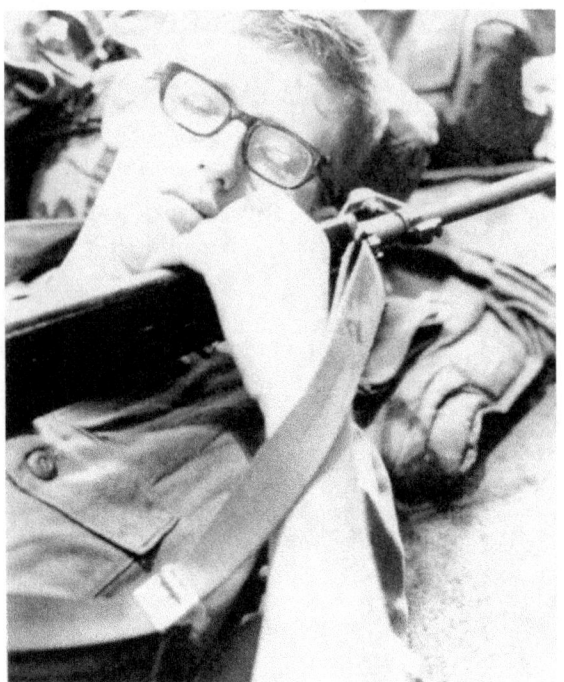

Photo courtesy of Capt Russell R. Thurman, USMC (Ret)
BLT 2/4 Marine sleeps on hangar deck of USS Okinawa *prior to the word to execute Operation Frequent Wind. Well into the evacuation at 2205, control of operational phases at the DAO compound shifted to BLT 2/4 as the landing zone control teams departed.*

Both during the day and at night, upon initial radio contact, the Alamo and Annex controllers would provide the inbound pilots with the latest winds and landing zone conditions including enemy fire and any unusual activity along their intended route of flight. Soon, even with the threat of deadly SAM missiles, darkness became the most important consideration, especially during the approach to the zone. The pilots could no longer see the landing area, and even worse, they had no way to distinguish nearby obstructions from the surrounding darkness.[39]

Existing lighting in LZs 36 and 37 at the Alamo, augmented by automobile headlights and portable lighting equipment, was enough to at least keep these two zones illuminated. For guidance into the zone the controllers initially used a strobe light, but its effectiveness was limited by the large number of fires and the flashes of tracer rounds and antiaircraft fire near the DAO Compound. Worse, the strobe light posed a threat to some of the Marines on the ground. Major David E. Cox and his team of controllers shared the rooftop of a DAO building with the strobe light, further exposing a position already highly vulnerable to attack. While the strobe flashed its welcoming beacon to inbound pilots, it also sent an invitation to snipers and enemy small arms. Consequently, the radio soon replaced the strobe as the method for terminal guidance. As a means of identification, flight leaders would turn on their landing lights in a set sequence of short flashes, to which Major Cox and the controllers would respond with radio-transmitted vectors to the landing zone. Major John F. Guilmartin, Jr., the senior Air Force pilot on the *Midway*, related his impressions of this process: "Major Cox and his people were very cool and professional. Their landing procedure worked like a champ."[40]

After arriving, and during the process of loading, the pilots would request clearance to depart. Unless crowded skies made it more judicious to hold on the ground, the helicopters were immediately granted permission to takeoff. Once clear of the zone, the pilots would switch to Cricket for vectors and the passing of extraction totals to General Carey. The ABCCC relayed the same totals to General Burns as well.* Each flight repeated this cycle while Major Cox and his controllers watched from their "box seats," atop the DAO building.

Throughout the period they controlled the air traffic at the compound, Major Cox and his team observed extensive enemy fire throughout Saigon including the artillery and rocket fire impacting at nearby Tan Son Nhut. Numerous South Vietnamese pilots attempted to escape by flying their aircraft off the Tan Son Nhut runway for a one-way flight to either Thailand or the sea and the waiting American fleet. Adding to the excitement of this spectacular show was the occasional round which would hit near the DAO Compound, but not close enough to damage the compound's buildings.** Numerous blazes, so intense

---

*Major Guilmartin offered his recollections of this phase of the operation: "This part of the system had broken down by dark and we were not even bothering to pass totals on to 'Cricket.' I can testify from personal observation that 'Cricket' had no evident command of the tactical situation." Guilmartin Comments.

**Captain Wood recalled years later the consequences of the shelling of the DAO Compound: "When I returned to the DAO that afternoon (29 April) with the last convoy, I discovered that my quarters (a trailer) had taken a direct hit and everything had burned. All I had left were the clothes on my back." Wood Comments. Major Guilmartin noted: "When we began our initial descent into the DAO Compound at around 1530 hours local, our radar homing and warning device was indicating the presence of three SA-2 batteries to the north and northeast of Tan Son Nhut, all of them within range. In commenting on the hostile fire I would note that . . . I and my crew saw a fair amount of fire and returned it. . . ." Guilmartin Comments.

that an hour's heavy rain did not diminish them, kept the controllers alert and aware of the ever-present danger of the advancing NVA. At 2205, one minute shy of seven hours after the first extraction helicopter had arrived, the controllers received word that their mission was complete.* At that point, they vacated the rooftop and proceeded to the DAO theater for extraction. Control of the remaining operation at the compound shifted to BLT 2/4.[41]

All during this operation and for the duration of Frequent Wind, BLT 3/9 stood ready to back up BLT 2/4, serving as the MAB and RLT 4 battalion in reserve. On board the USS *Denver* (LPD 9), Lieutenant Colonel Robert E. Loehe and his battalion were prepared for any contingency, even an amphibious landing on Vung Tau Peninsula. In addition to planning for an amphibious assault on the beaches of Vung Tau, BLT 3/9 also provided two platoons for Sparrow Hawk missions. Although not used or inserted ashore in South Vietnam, BLT 3/9's presence as a ready reserve provided General Carey and his staff with the all important reassurance that they had a guaranteed source of reinforcements.[42]

Another group of Marines who contributed, but did not see direct action were the EA-6 pilots of Marine Composite Reconnaissance Squadron One (VMCJ-1). To provide electronic countermeasure capabilities, the commanding officer, Lieutenant Colonel William A. "Art" Bloomer, temporarily assigned two aircraft and three crews from the *Midway* to the *Coral Sea* for Operation Frequent Wind. Lieutenant Colonel Bloomer stated: "I sent three pilots, two ECM operators, and 14 support personnel to *Coral Sea*. From the time the operation commenced on 29 April at about 1500 hours until 0600 on the morning of 30 April this small group of Marines kept jamming radar signals identified with the Firecan radar that controlled the 37mm air defense weapons of the NVA. Major Marty Brush [Major Martin C. Brush] led this small contingent to the Coral Sea . . . [and] . . . their round-the-clock effort flying from an unfamiliar carrier deck." Their support typified the unsung contributions of the thousands of American military men who together made the evacuation of the DAO Compound and the American Embassy possible.[43]

The Embassy

Soon after BLT 2/4 arrived at the DAO Compound, the American Embassy notified General Carey that over 2,000 people needed to be evacuated from the Embassy. This came as a complete surprise since no one had planned for a major evacuation from this location. With a landing zone that could only accommodate one CH-53 and a rooftop that would hold only one CH-46 on its landing pad, General Carey ordered an immediate adjustment in the helicopters' assigned priorities. Cricket, the ABCCC, immediately started directing helicopter traffic to either the compound or the Embassy, depending on the helicopter's size and the space available at the Embassy. Many of the *Hancock*'s 46s started launching approximately one hour before sunset to remove the ever growing crowd of Vietnamese refugees. This was to be the most demanding and time-consuming part of the entire operation.[44]

To provide additional security and assistance to the Marines already guarding the Embassy, General Carey removed three platoons (130 men) of BLT 2/4 from the DAO Compound and inserted them into the Embassy Compound between 1900 and 2100. These Marines assisted the Embassy guards in controlling the multiplying Vietnamese crowd. First Lieutenant John J. Martinoli, Jr., a forward air controller (FAC) from

This is an aerial view of the American Embassy in Saigon. The Embassy was never considered a primary helicopter evacuation site because it had a rooftop zone which could handle nothing bigger than a CH-46.
Marine Corps Historical Collection

---

*General Smith, the Defense Attache, remembered: "I departed with my staff shortly after 2000 hours. I recall that there were no evacuees subsequent to then." Smith Comments. At the other end of his trip on Air Force helicopters, General Smith was welcomed on board the *Midway* by Lieutenant Colonel William A. "Art" Bloomer, commanding officer of VMCJ-1. Lieutenant Colonel Bloomer related: "The Defense Attache in Saigon, Major General Homer D. Smith, Jr., USA, and his last remaining staff officers, including Lieutenant Colonels Anthony Lukeman and William McKinstry, were evacuated by Air Force helicopters to *Midway* where myself and the Marines of VMCJ-1 made them feel at home with the few remaining amenities." Bloomer Comments.

Photo courtesy of Capt Russell R. Thurman, USMC (Ret)

Members of Company G, 2d Battalion, 4th Marines return from Saigon to USS Vancouver *on 30 April. They had reinforced security at the Embassy during Operation Frequent Wind.*

BLT 1/9, joined them with his landing zone control team, bringing the total Marine complement at the Embassy to 171.[45]

This team assisted in the landing and loading of the CH-46s, the first of which touched down in the zone at about 1700. Additionally, CH-53s began landing in the small and very confined Embassy parking lot. Late that afternoon, Ambassador Martin had authorized the removal of a large tree which had been obstructing helicopter access to that area of the compound.*

---

*Opinions vary on the conduct at the Embassy on 29 April concerning preparations of the landing zone. General Smith offered his thoughts: "I wonder if the Ambassador was the authority for cutting down the Baobab tree in the Embassy courtyard. I believe it was otherwise and the tree was cut down in the morning or early afternoon and not necessarily by Marines." Smith Comments. Admiral Steele remembered it somewhat differently: "Ambassador Martin's unrealistic attitude towards the evacuation is exemplified in the delay in his personal authorization to cut down the tree in the Embassy compound that prevented helicopter access. Having failed to initiate the evacuation in a timely way so that the majority of evacuees could be taken from Tan Son Nhut Airfield as the plan envisioned, the Ambassador still was not taking those actions large and small necessary to facilitate matters." The Seventh Fleet commander added that he "had been urgently recommending that the evacuation occur two days earlier than it did because of the approach of North Vietnamese forces, and on the 27th the forecast of bad weather which could obstruct or prevent flight operations." Steele Comments.

The landing situation at the Embassy gradually deteriorated as daylight receded. The groups of Vietnamese in and around the Embassy grew in size and aggressiveness as their chances for escape diminished. Restricted deck space to load passengers, small landing zones, hostile fire, poor communications, and darkness did nothing to make the Marines' job any easier.[46]

Exactly the opposite situation existed at Tan Son Nhut. With the evacuation at the DAO Compound proceeding swiftly and flawlessly, General Carey decided at about 1730 to extract the 3d Platoon, Company C of BLT 1/9. Inserted on 25 April to assist the Marine Security Guard at the compound in maintaining security and control, the 3d Platoon, led by First Lieutenant Bruce P. Thompson-Bowers, had borne the brunt of the rocket and artillery fire directed at the compound on the evening of the 28th and the early morning of the 29th.[47] Yet despite the intensity of the attack Lieutenant Thompson-Bowers' platoon had suffered no casualties.

Mindful of the inherent dangers and the political and military implications of augmenting the American security force with additional Marines, the MAB had sought higher approval. As a consequence, the Joint Chiefs of Staff, with the Ambassador's expressed agreement, authorized the insertion of a platoon of

THE EVACUATION

Department of Defense Photo (USMC) A150961
Vietnamese board CH-53s in LZ 39, a parking lot. The 9th MAB extracted 395 Americans and 4,475 Vietnamese and third-country nationals, evacuating the last shortly after 2000.

Marines. Its safe evacuation on the evening of 29 April successfully concluded the effort to bolster DAO security.[48]

Shortly thereafter, General Carey directed that the remaining elements guarding the Annex be withdrawn (at 1930) to the Alamo where the last of the evacuees would await their flight. Once completed, the new defensive perimeter encompassed LZ 36 and the Alamo. Less than an hour later, the Marines at the DAO loaded their last group of evacuees, bringing the total evacuated to 395 Americans and 4,475 Vietnamese and third-country nationals.[49] Lieutenant Colonel Jim Bolton said it went so smoothly that his only concern was not enemy fire, but running into another helicopter.* He said, "I told all of my pilots to turn on their lights to help avoid a mid-air collision."[50]

At 2250, with the evacuation of the landing control teams from the Annex and Alamo completed, General Carey ordered the withdrawal of the ground security forces from the DAO Compound. Just after midnight (0030) on 30 April, thermite grenades, having been previously placed in selected buildings, ignited as two CH-53s left the DAO parking lot. These helicopters carried the last elements of BLT 2/4, including Captain McManus and Master Sergeant East, the EOD Marines.** Between the time of their departure and the Marines' arrival on *Okinawa* (at 0046), enemy fire directed at the DAO buildings more than doubled. The evacuation of personnel from the compound had lasted nine hours and involved over 50 Marine Corps and Air Force helicopters.[51]

Prior to leaving the DAO, General Carey talked on the phone with Ambassador Martin and learned that, for unknown reasons, the flow of helicopter traffic had ebbed. The general attempted, through various channels, to ascertain the reason for what amounted to only a trickle of helicopters arriving at the Embassy. Before relinquishing command of the compound forces to Colonel Gray, General Carey determined that if the flow of helicopters was reestablished, the evacuation could be completed in a relatively short time. To insure security at the Embassy until the conclusion of the evacuation, General Carey decided to use platoons from BLT 1/9 as ground security forces in reserve. At times, they were even sent aloft as heliteams with orders to reinforce the ground security force at the Embassy, but each time, at the last possible moment, they received word to return to the ship. (The last such incident occurred at 0530 on the 30th.)[52]

---

*Major Guilmartin, the Air Force HH-53 pilot on *Midway*, recalled: "I saw numerous '53s' running blacked-out and in order to be seen, I had my wingman, Captain Vernon Sheffield (the only other HH-53 helicopter commander involved in Frequent Wind), turn on, as I had, his top anti-collision lights while leaving the lower lights off so as to avoid an SA-7 lock-on." Guilmartin Comments.

**These Marines along with Major Sabater and Captain Petry spent many of their last hours in the DAO compound burning some of the 13 million dollars that had arrived earlier that month. Colonel Taylor said, "The EOD duo with the Advance Command Element also destroyed three barrels of money at the DAO Compound." Taylor Comments. Captain Wood recalled: "When I returned from Saigon with the last convoy around 1800, Major Sabater and Captain Petry were burning money as fast as they could shovel it onto the fire." Wood Comments.

With the Embassy's security high on his list of priorities and very much on his mind, General Carey departed the compound at 2250, leaving Colonel Gray in command of the withdrawal of the ground security force. When he arrived on the *Blue Ridge*, having made an intermediate stop on the *Midway*, General Carey wasted no time in attempting to discover why the sortie rate had decreased. Admiral Whitmire (CTF 76), out of concern for flight safety, had halted all flights to the Embassy. (The only flights arriving there during this period were ones which had been diverted from the DAO Compound for lack of passengers.) Pilots had been flying for over 12 hours, weather conditions had deteriorated, and lighting in the zone had become either poor or nonexistent. To make matters worse, there were reports that the Embassy was on fire. In fact, Embassy personnel were burning American money in a barrel next to the landing pad on top of the building. Additionally, navigation to Saigon had become even more difficult as a line of thunderstorms stood astride the flight path, and upon arrival, the pilots would often have to use their instruments to land. Considering all these factors, the commander of Task Force 76 thought a halt to flight operations was warranted, even though he had not consulted with General Carey.*[53]

With the Cobra helicopters acting as pathfinders, the pilots had been able to navigate under adverse conditions with success. Knowing this, General Carey believed that the flights could be continued safely. Captain Ritchie remembered the same thoughts, "We had flown so many sorties over the same route already that the weather was less a factor than finding a place to land once we got to the Embassy."[54]

Learning that serious consideration was being given to discontinuing all flights until first light, General Carey, a Marine aviator confident in the skills of his fellow pilots, felt that Saigon would be in the hands of the North Vietnamese by dawn. He knew that he had to press for immediate resumption of all helicopter flights to speed up the lift from the Embassy. He convincingly argued in favor of continuing flight operations and when Admiral Whitmire agreed, he promptly ordered the launch of Marine Corps CH-53s and additional CH-46s. In General Carey's words, "I was damned angry at his stopping my helos, and I made this point in no uncertain terms. Had I not had to return to the *Blue Ridge* it was my intention to go to the Embassy to straighten that mess out." The 9th MAB commander learned later that at approximately the same time he was having his discussion with Admiral Whitmire, Lieutenant General Louis H. Wilson, Jr., FMF Pacific commander, was addressing the same problem (halt in flight operations) in the CinCPac command center where he spent the evening of 28-29 April (Hawaii time) with Admiral Gayler, CinCPac.[55]

The command center had a landline hookup with Admiral Steele's immediate commander, Admiral Maurice F. Weisner (CinCPacFlt), located down the street in Pearl Harbor, and radio communications with Admiral Steele, the Seventh Fleet commander. It was from Admiral Steele that General Wilson learned that flight operations had been terminated for administrative restrictions on the maximum number of flight hours allowed in one 24-hour period. General Wil-

Evacuees ride a Marine CH-53 to another ship in the formation. Because of the tempo of operations and the number of refugees, most of them had to be repositioned from a tactical ship to a non-tactical vessel.

Photo courtesy of Capt Russell R. Thurman, USMC (Ret)

---

*The post-operational JCS investigation, conducted to determine why L-Hour was postponed and why there was a two-hour gap in flight operations (from 0100 to 0300 Saigon time on 30 April), confirmed that Admiral Whitmire made an independent decision to halt flight operations. The report stated: "Following the extraction of the GSF from the DAO Compound at 1612Z [0012 Saigon time] all H-53 helicopters were directed by CTF 76 to return to base for aircraft servicing and crew rest. Although instructions were given to continue evacuation of the Embassy with CH-46s, CTF 76 decided it was necessary to shut down for required maintenance checks which took the better part of an hour to complete." Cleland Report.

Last members of the ground security force arrive on board the Okinawa *after midnight on 30 April. BLT 2/4 Marines provided perimeter security at the DAO until the bitter end.*

son said, "I learned from the Seventh Fleet commander that the Marines had flown their maximum number of hours and therefore he was stopping flight operations." Upon receiving this word which essentially meant that the Marines in Saigon would not be recovered, at least until first light, General Wilson took immediate action. He informed Admirals Gayler and Weisner that he would prefer charges against any officer who ordered his Marine pilots to stop flying so long as there were Marines still on the ground in Saigon. General Wilson recalled, "If General Carey was damn angry, I was out of my mind. I told Admiral Gayler and Admiral Weisner on the phone, that there was no such thing as Marines not evacuating Marines. We do not understand that."⁵⁶

The Air Force, also over their crew day (i.e. having flown in excess of the 12 hours allowed in one day), did not resume the airlift. Their eight CH-53s and two HH-53s shut down after the final sortie from the DAO Compound and did not launch again. The resumption of flight operations caught many of the Marine CH-53 pilots by surprise. As Lieutenant Colonel Bolton said, "I was on my way to my quarters when I received word to standby for the possible launch of my squadron's aircraft."⁵⁷

By 0215, one CH-46 and one CH-53 were landing at the Embassy every 10 minutes. The Embassy at this point indicated that 19 more lifts would complete the evacuation.* As this number approached, General Carey notified Captain Gerald L. "Gerry" Berry, a HMM-165 pilot, that his CH-46 would extract Ambassador Martin. His instructions included the order to remain atop the Embassy building as long as necessary to load him. At 0458 on 30 April 1975 Captain Berry, in "Lady Ace 09," departed the Embassy helipad,

---

*Admiral Steele offered his recollections of the nearly endless supply of evacuees at the Embassy: "One thing not generally known is that Ambassador Martin was attempting to get large numbers of Vietnamese evacuated from the Embassy. It appeared to be a bottomless pit, and as our men and machines began to tire I began pressuring the Embassy to get all Americans and the Ambassador out. I did not want him captured. The number three man in the Embassy arrived on board the *Blue Ridge* and reported the Ambassador to be ill and exhausted. Through loyalty to our Vietnamese colleagues, he was going to keep that evacuation going indefinitely, and in my opinion, force it to keep going by not coming out himself." Steele Comments.

and Ambassador Martin bid farewell to South Vietnam. The American Embassy had officially closed its doors. Unofficially, a handful of American Marines still remained at the Embassy, waiting for their ride to freedom.[58]

Actually, the Ambassador's departure reflected more than the completion of the 19 lifts predicted necessary to finish the evacuation. It represented the results of a presidential order to Ambassador Martin, passed via a Marine CH-53 flown by Captain Jon M. Walters. At 0327, President Ford ordered that no more than 19 additional lifts would be flown and that Ambassador Martin would be on the last one. At 0430, General Carey received word that the 19-lift limit had been exceeded and he immediately relayed to his aircraft commanders, via the ABCCC, the order to extract all remaining Americans, and directed the Marine security force to take up positions on the rooftop, awaiting evacuation.[59]

After Berry's helicopter departed, the only thing that remained was to extract the Marines still guarding the Embassy. Major James H. Kean, the Officer-in-Charge of the Marine Security Guard, had with him a small contingent of Embassy and 9th MAB Marines. Within the next hour this force shrank to 11 Marines.

Upon Ambassador Martin's departure, Major Kean moved his Marines inside the embassy, barricaded the doors, and then moved up through the building until they occupied only the top floor. From this location, he had easy access to the helo landing pad. Dodging small arms fire and using riot control agents against people attempting to force their way to the rooftop, he and his 10 Marines boarded "Swift 2-2," a HMM-164 CH-46, the last American helicopter to leave South Vietnam. Checking his watch, Major Kean noted that it was seven minutes until eight, only 23 hours since the NCOIC of Marine Security Guard, Manila, had called him to relay a message from his wife in Hong Kong that she was pregnant. Only 32 minutes later on that unforgettable day, 30 April 1975, the 11 Marines exited "Swift 2-2" onto the deck of the *Okinawa* where Gunnery Sergeant Russell R. Thurman captured their weary faces on camera. Disembarking, many on board the *Okinawa*, Gunnery Sergeant Thurman included, wondered why so much time had elapsed between the arrival of the Ambassador's flight and Swift 2-2, well over two hours. Had someone forgotten these Marines were still at the Embassy? The answer is no. The intention was to remove the Ambassador while some security still remained at the Embassy, and then have other helicopters pick up the remaining Marines, but it appears that when Captain Berry's aircraft transmitted "Tiger is out," those helicopters still flying, including Captain Walters who was orbiting the Embassy at the time the Ambassador left, thought the mission was complete. This particular transmission had been the preplanned code to indicate when the Ambassador was on board a helicopter outbound to the task force. Having waited so long for his departure, this transmission caused some to conclude that he had departed as part of the last group

A CH-53 departs LZ 39 after depositing its security force. After the withdrawal of the last ground forces at 0030, 30 April, flight operations ceased for nearly two hours.

Department of Defense Photo (USMC) A150962

THE EVACUATION

to leave the Embassy. Captain Berry later explained that radio message: " 'Tiger—Tiger—Tiger' was the call to be made when the Ambassador was on board and on his way out of Saigon. It had absolutely nothing to do with the cessation of the operation. We had originally planned to bring the Ambassador out on the afternoon of the 29th."[60]

At this juncture, thinking the mission complete and the Ambassador safe, Captain Walters headed back to the *Okinawa*. Subsequent to his landing at approximately 0700, the command realized that Captain Walters did not have the remaining Marines on board.* Due to a misunderstanding and miscommunication, they were still at the Embassy. General Carey immediately recycled a CH-46, but by this time due to the ships' offshore movement, the time required to reach the Embassy exceeded 40 minutes.[61]

To the Marines waiting in Saigon, attempts by the South Vietnamese to reach the roof kept them busy and as a consequence, they did not notice the extended gap between the flights. Major Kean later stated that he and his Marines did not become alarmed because they knew that another CH-46 would arrive: "We never had a doubt that our fellow Marines would return and pick us up. They had been doing it all night long."[62]

For the immense size and complexity of this operation, there were few mistakes. Besides the nearly 5,000 people evacuated from the DAO compound, 978 U.S. and 1,120 third-country nationals were lifted from the Embassy.[63] Despite numerous phone calls and extensive efforts to ensure that all Americans, even deceased ones, were extracted, the bodies of Corporal McMahon and Lance Corporal Judge were left behind. Inexplicably, they had been left at the Seventh Day Adventist Hospital, nearby Tan Son Nhut. (In phone calls to the hospital on the afternoon of 29 April, the few remaining members of its staff reported that the deceased Marines' bodies had already been delivered to the task force. Senator Edward M. Kennedy of Massachusetts through diplomatic channels recovered them the following year.)[64] In addition, the Marine Corps suffered the loss of two aircraft. One of the two was an AH-1J Cobra, whose pilots, Captain John W. Bowman, Jr., and First Lieutenant David L. Androskaut, successfully made a night water ditching after the Cobra's engines flamed out from fuel starvation. Shortly after overflying the USS *Kirk* (DE 1087) while in search of the *Okinawa*, Captain Bowman noted that his altimeter read 900 feet and his fuel gauge 200 pounds. In the next instant, he found himself groping with an emergency autorotation to a dark, empty sea. Many agonizing moments after impact, Captain Bowman finally managed to unfasten his seat belt on the third attempt while his sinking helicopter filled with water. He recalled, "As I exited the helicopter in the dark, I had no idea which way was up, but I remembered that the helicopter must be sinking toward the bottom, so I swam in the opposite direction and just when I was about to doubt my decision, a sliver of moonlight bounced off the dangling legs of my co-pilot, suspended just above my head."[65] Soon after Bowman and his copilot linked up, a boat, launched from the *Kirk* after its officer of the day heard the helicopter's engines quit, picked them up.

The other aircraft's pilots were not as fortunate. A CH-46F from the *Hancock* flown by Captain William C. Nystul and First Lieutenant Michael J. Shea crashed into the sea on its approach to the ship after having flown a long and exhausting night sea and air rescue mission (SAR). Amazingly, the two enlisted crewmembers survived, but the bodies of the pilots were not recovered. The cause of the crash was never determined, but crew inexperience and unfamiliarity with the mission may have been factors.** Normally, ships carrying helicopters do not use a SAR helicopter. Instead they assume that all airborne helicopters are potential SAR aircraft during helicopter flight operations. The *Hancock*, accustomed to fixed-wing flight operations where an airborne SAR helicopter is mandatory, did not modify its procedures. However for an operation of this size, a designated rescue helicopter provided the task force with the capability of respond-

---

*Captain Berry recalled the incident somewhat differently. He stated, "When Lady Ace 09 brought the Ambassador out there were only two CH-46s still flying (Lady Ace 09 and wingman). This was because there was much confusion over flight time. When I landed on board the *Blue Ridge* and informed General Carey of the lack of aircraft he took immediate action with HDC on board the *Okinawa*—Lady Ace 09 and flight then returned to the Embassy and extracted most of the remaining Marines—as we were departing Swift 2-2 was approaching the Embassy for the final pick-up. The reason for the long delay between the Ambassador and the Marine pick-up is easy to figure out—only two aircraft flying from the 28 CH-46s and 30 plus CH-53s (CH-53s could not land on the roof.)" Berry Comments.

**Captain Berry recently related the flying backgrounds of this crew. He said, "Captain Nystul had just returned from Pensacola fixed-wing instructor duty and had about 20 hours of refamiliarization in the '46.' His co-pilot was First Lieutenant Shea, a CH-53 pilot, who had gotten approximately 25 CH-46 hours with us in Futema before deploying." Berry Comments.

Photos courtesy of Capt Russell R. Thurman, USMC (Ret)

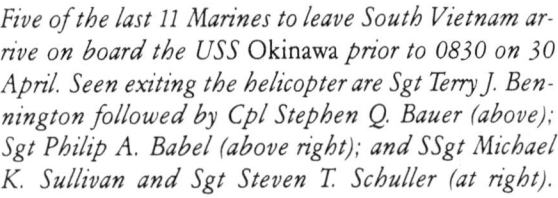

Five of the last 11 Marines to leave South Vietnam arrive on board the USS Okinawa *prior to 0830 on 30 April. Seen exiting the helicopter are Sgt Terry J. Bennington followed by Cpl Stephen Q. Bauer (above); Sgt Philip A. Babel (above right); and SSgt Michael K. Sullivan and Sgt Steven T. Schuller (at right).*

ing instantly to any airborne emergency and thus extended its options.[66]

Despite these losses, Operation Frequent Wind accomplished its purpose, the safe evacuation of American, Vietnamese, and third-country citizens from South Vietnam. It stands as the largest helicopter evacuation in history*. For the Marine Corps it meant 1,054 flight hours and 682 sorties, 34 of which be-

---

*Major General Norman W. Gourley, commanding general of the 1st Marine Aircraft Wing, later recounted his assessment of the operation. "I spent 36 years in the Marine Corps; fought WW II in Corsairs; the Korean War as a night fighter pilot flying F-7Fs and F-3Ds; and the Vietnam War flying F-4 Phantoms. I have seen and heard of combat air operations which required all the talent, guts, and nerve available. Never in the annals of flying, and I am including all U.S. combat air operations of any war, have a group of pilots performed so magnificently as the helicopter pilots who extracted those folks out of Saigon in late April, 1975. The term 'distinguished flying' fits each and every one. These young helicopter tigers did it all—long hours in the cockpit, night operations, terrible visibility and weather, being shot at—the bottom line being 'mission completed,' they did their job. It is indeed unfortunate that more recognition was not forthcoming to this group of Marine aviators." Gourley Comments. Colonel Edward Pelosky, USA, a member of the DAO staff evacuated to the *Vancouver*, offered his appraisal of the operation: "My hat is off to those individual planners and participants who got us out of Saigon. It was a deliberate exercise pulled off with precision, confidence, and the great skill of the aviators—a textbook version." Pelosky Comments.

longed to Captain Gerry Berry. He logged the most hours, 18.3, in a 20 hour period, which reflected the operation's intensity and complexity. For its effort, HMH-463 received the Marine Corps Aviation Association's (MCAA) General Keith B. McCutcheon Award as the 1975 Helicopter Squadron of the Year. In addition, the MCAA chose Lieutenant Colonel James L. Bolton (HMH-462's commanding officer) as the 1975 Aviator of the Year and recipient of the Alfred A. Cunningham Award. Captain John B. Heffernan, one of Bolton's pilots, recently recalled his thoughts at the conclusion of the operation: "I will never forget one minute of this incredible flying experience. I was lucky to be here." Surely, the 1,373 Americans and 5,595 non-American evacuees agreed that they too were lucky to be there, on American ships.[67]

Photo courtesy of Capt Russell R. Thurman, USMC (Ret)

Two Marine pilots were rescued from the sea at night after their Cobra crashed. Capt John W. Bowman, Jr., right, piloted the AH-1J, and 1stLt David L. Androskaut was co-pilot.

CHAPTER 12
Refugee Operations

A Link to Freedom: The Exodus and a New Beginning — Way Stations — Preparations: 1st Battalion, 4th Marines and the Task Force — Evacuation and Passage: Frequent Wind and the AESF's Final Chapter A Vietnamese City in Guam — The Final Link: Camp Pendleton

---

"Operation New Arrivals will commence Phasedown incrementally when directed about 15 September (75). As presently planned, refugees at Camp Pendleton, California will be reduced to approximately 6800 on or about 30 September 1975."[1] With those words Brigadier General Paul G. Graham published his final order in the final chapter of the Marine Corps' official involvement in the South Vietnamese refugee operation. He concluded this assignment by submitting an after action report to the Commandant of the Marine Corps in November 1975. It marked the completion of more than six months of refugee operations for the Marine Corps which began in March with Staff Sergeant Walter W. Sparks and his detachment assisting evacuees in Da Nang Harbor. Those 200 days consumed the lion's share of the daily lives of the Marines participating in the rescue and resettlement of Vietnamese refugees.

Sandwiched between the initial security force (the Amphibious Evacuation RVN Support Group) and General Graham's Refugee Receiving Center were the efforts of the Marine Security Guard Detachments in South Vietnam; the Amphibious Evacuation Security Force; 1st Battalion, 4th Marines; Marine Barracks Guam; MCAS El Toro; and Marines from various commands, primarily units located on the West Coast. Highly publicized, very visible, and extremely sensitive, this undertaking represented an event as complex, complicated, and expensive as a major battle, and in essence had many of the trappings of warfare. To say it was disruptive and changed America belies the magnitude of the event. The refugee story, especially the story of their resettlement, is the Vietnam War's living legacy. In effect, it symbolized the Marine Corps' final Vietnam battle; the bitter end to a bitter struggle, but as in the case of a bitter end of a rope, that same end can also be a beginning, a rescue line, and a link to freedom.

A Link to Freedom: The Exodus and a New Beginning

Admiral Steele's Seventh Fleet, including Admiral Whitmire's Task Force 76 and General Carey's 9th MAB, extracted more than 7,000 fleeing South Vietnamese, providing them a new beginning. In addition, Colonel Frank G. McLenon's Provisional Marine Aircraft Group 39's helicopters removed 395 U.S. citizens and 4,475 refugees from the DAO compound and 978 Americans and 1,120 evacuees from the American Embassy.* These numbers did not include the American security force or Embassy Marines. Using 34 CH-53s, 29 CH-46s, 8 AH-1Js, and 6 UH-1Es, the ProvMAG flew 682 sorties (360 at night) and 560 hours [CH-53, 314; CH-46, 206; AH-1J, 34; UH-1E, 6], while the 10 Military Sealift Command ships continued, along with some 45 Navy ships, to pick up refugees escaping from Vietnam in everything from helicopters to sampans. The count for this four-day period put the total at over 40,000 evacuated with a final estimate for the month of April of approximately 130,000.[2]

In applauding the success of this mission, the Commander-in-Chief, Pacific, Admiral Noel Gayler, said, "This was a tough one. The job was uncertain, unprecedented, dangerous beyond measure. It demanded the last ounce of endurance and fortitude and savvy, and you gave it that and more . . . The rescue was a tremendous and joint enterprise, under the most difficult conditions. Performance of all hands superb. Well Done."[3]

A successful rescue does not always mean a happy ending. Those rescued on 30 April and the thousands of others who left South Vietnam during April had to first reach safe haven before they could even think about freedom. The first link in this chain to freedom, the rescue, had to be joined to the next link, passage. For the majority of the Vietnamese evacuees, who had

---

*Evacuation numbers vary somewhat from those depicted by the 9th MAB Command Chronology. ProvMAG-39 reported: "Later in the day evacuation began at the U.S. Embassy. An estimated 1150 American citizens and over 6,000 Vietnamese and Third Country Nationals were evacuated." ProvMAG-39 ComdC. The JCS investigation of Operation Frequent Wind stated: "At approximately 1700, the evacuation of the U.S. Embassy began. During the period 18 CH-53 and 54 CH-46 sorties evacuated 2379 passengers of which 978 were U.S. citizens, 1228 were foreign nationals and 173 USMC personnel." In addition it provided slightly different figures for the DAO: "A total of 122 sorties were flown during the evacuation of the DAO with 6416 passengers lifted from that location. This total includes 395 U.S. citizens, 5205 foreign nationals, and 816 GSF personnel." Cleland Report.

Capt Robert D. Amos, Jr., commander of Detachment Tango (HqBn, 3d MarDiv), AESF, offers assistance to a Vietnamese Navy dependent as she boards the SS Green Forest.

been at sea for several days, survival had become their sole concern. Water, sustenance, and survival were less pressing matters for the South Vietnamese citizens evacuated by helicopter, but they represented only 10 percent of the 26-30 April refugee flotilla, later called "boat people." To them the ships of Task Force 76 represented a haven of hope and safety, and above all else a ticket to freedom. For those Vietnamese who had been evacuated earlier in April and by 30 April were already in Guam or the Philippines the means of exodus may have been different, but the results would be the same; most South Vietnamese evacuees' final stop would be a processing center stateside awaiting sponsorship by an American family or organization.

Many of the "boat people" as well as all of the refugees in the 29-30 April air evacuation ended their initial journey from South Vietnam on an American naval vessel. In order to place these refugees with those forces best prepared to handle them, the Navy transferred the majority of them to MSC ships. Purposely kept empty just prior to the beginning of Frequent Wind, these ships stood ready to receive the maximum number of evacuees. In fact, a post operation summary of MSC shipping revealed that just prior to the start of the major evacuation of Saigon, eight of the 12 MSC ships were empty while waiting with Task Force 76 ships in international waters off the coast of South Vietnam. The only other empty ship, the *Green Forest*, awaited its human cargo while at anchor off Con Son Island. On the evening of 30 April, the deluge began. Thousands of desperate South Vietnamese engulfed the MSC ships. To the Amphibious Evacuation Security Force Marines guarding these ships, the waves of approaching refugees meant the waiting was over. Their job had begun.

On 30 April, Major Quinlan, the Amphibious Evacuation Security Force commander, would report the following distribution of forces: Detachment Foxtrot and Captain Richard R. Page on the USNS *Greenville Victory*; Detachment India and Captain Cyril V. Moyher on *Pioneer Commander*; Detachment November and Captain Michael T. Mallick on the SS *American Challenger*; Detachment Papa and Captain Richard M. Jessie, Jr., on the SS *Green Port*; Detachment Sierra and Captain Edward R. Palmquist, Jr., on the USNS *Sergeant Andrew Miller*; Detachment Tango and Captain Robert D. Amos, Jr., on the *Green Forest*; Detachment Victor and Captain David A. Garcia on the *Pioneer Contender*; and Detachment Echo and Captain Richard L. Reuter on the USNS *Sergeant Truman Kimbro* (she already had 150 Vietnamese on board, delivered by a Navy ship on the 29th).[4] Within 24 hours, these largely empty ships would be enroute to Subic Bay with 39,824 refugees embarked. Within the next few days, the SS *Transcolorado* and the *American Racer* began embarking refugees. Initially without Marines, each ship, upon arrival in Subic, received a complement of security forces. Detachment Hotel and Captain William H. Hackett, Jr., transferred from the *Dubuque* on 4 May to the *Transcolorado*, and the next day, Detachment Mike and First Lieutenant Carl W. Fredericksen left the *Dubuque* and embarked in the *American Racer*. Another ship involved in the care and especially the feeding of the evacuees was the SS *Green Wave*, a cargo ship. At 0800 on 5 May, Detachment Uniform and Captain Steven A. Shepherd joined the *Green Wave*. Once loaded to capacity with refugees and with its Marines fully prepared for their security role, these three ships (*Transcolorado*, *American Racer*, and *Green Wave*) left Subic, bound for Guam.

One of the reasons for such a quick transfer of refugees and Marines in Subic was due to Filipino sensitivity and the arrival of a flotilla of Vietnamese Navy vessels fully loaded with thousands of refugees. Literally, there was no more room in Subic for them, and diplomatically, the Philippines Government had no more time for unprocessed aliens. During the period from 21-28 April, the United States had evacuated by airplane 42,910 people. Although the 170 Air Force C-130 and 134 C-141 sorties took some of these refugees to Guam, the majority landed and disembarked at Clark Air Force Base. The numbers of undocumented and therefore illegal immigrants so alarmed President Ferdinand Marcos (the U.S. had promised him that all transiting South Vietnamese would have passports and required documentation) that the Philippines Government informed the American Embassy in Manila that refugees could not remain in the Philippines any longer than 72 hours and that no armed

Capt Edward R. Palmquist, Jr., commander of Detachment Sierra, shouts to his men on the USNS Sergeant Andrew Miller. *Within 24 hours MSC ships loaded nearly 40,000 refugees.*
Department of Defense Photo (USMC) 7714875

Vietnamese refugees board an Air Force C-141 Starlifter at NAS Cubi Point, Philippines, passenger terminal. These evacuees were on their way to Guam and Operation New Life.

military personnel or vessels would be allowed to enter the country. Thus no Vietnamese vessel, naval or otherwise, would be allowed to enter Subic Bay, leaving the Vietnamese with only two choices, abandon ship or sail their vessels to Guam. The edict also meant that all other transiting refugees would have to minimize their stay in the Philippines, and in order to accomplish that, the processing procedure at "way stations" like Clark and Subic would have to be expedited.[5]

Way Stations

To help meet the demands of the Philippines Government by assisting in the task of streamlining refugee operations in the Philippines, the 1st Battalion, 4th Marines, after standing down as the Amphibious Evacuation RVN Support Group, reformed as a battalion and reentered the evacuation process. Eventually its mission would be to assist in the establishment of a refugee base camp—a way station to aid transiting refugees.

At approximately the same time Lieutenant Colonel Charles E. Hester's battalion began preparing to reenter evacuee operations, Ambassador Parker Borg notified the State Department, Ambassador Martin in Saigon, the Joint Chiefs of Staff, and Admiral Gayler, CinCPac, of the Philippines Government's displeasure with the refugee situation. Borg had become aware of the seriousness of the problem when he received a note from the Philippines Department of Foreign Affairs setting forth new guidelines for the Vietnamese refugees. It said: "No more than 200 evacuees shall be at the base at any one time. The evacuees shall depart from the base for a mother country within three days. The evacuees shall not go outside the base, and the length of time of this evacuation through the base shall be determined by the Philippines Government, taking into account the prevailing circumstances." The Ambassador agreed with Marcos' position, believing that the initial airlift had been organized poorly. He contended that "had evacuees been more carefully screened for eligibility and staged more quickly through the Philippines, the GOP [Government of the Philippines] action might have been avoided. However, see no choice now but to comply with GOP instruction." Ambassador Borg's first recommended course of action to resolve this potential threat to the harmony of Philippine-American relations entailed removing, as quickly as possible, the backlog of refu-

Department of Defense Photo (USMC) 1163039

Refugees are loaded into a C-141 Starlifter at NAS Cubi Point for the trip to Guam. The Philippines Government had given the U.S. only 72 hours to process these refugees.

Members of the AESF provide assistance as crewmen and dependents disembark from a Vietnamese Navy minesweeper at Subic Bay. Processing took place in the warehouse to the left and later the refugees were placed on board the USNS Sergeant Truman Kimbro.

Department of Defense Photo (USMC) 1163133

REFUGEE OPERATIONS

Grande Island sits just west of Cubi Point and was identified as an ideal location for a refugee camp. The island was the first way station for Vietnamese seeking a new life.

gees from Clark Air Base. He stipulated, "No more third country evacuees permitted to stage through U.S. bases in the Philippines until backlog cleared. Backlog of evacuees at Clark must be removed immediately."[6]

Fortunately, this diplomatic impasse occurred prior to 29 April and before Operation Frequent Wind and the mass exodus from South Vietnam. By that date, Air Force transport aircraft had moved the entire backlog from Clark to Guam where Marines from Marine Barracks, Guam (manning the Operation New Life receiving centers), welcomed them. Removal of the backlog addressed only the immediate problem and not the one troubling Ambassador Borg: how to minimize the stay of evacuees on Philippines soil so as not to exceed the 72-hour restriction. Since the majority of the next wave of refugees would arrive by ship, Borg decided to shift his focus from Clark to Subic Bay.

The ships carrying the evacuees to Guam would have to dock in Subic Bay for replenishment, and therefore it seemed logical to relocate the refugee center there. Ambassador Borg believed that this action would also reduce the delay involved in processing the evacuees. Considering the constraints set forth by the Philippines Government with regard to security and length of stay, the site for the center had to be near the water, highly secure, and limited in access. Nothing fit that description better than land surrounded by water, an island in Subic Bay. Two miles off the approach end of Runway 7 at Naval Air Station Cubi Point sits Grande Island. Normally used for recreational activities, it suddenly became the refugee housing and processing center. Temporary and functional by design, this initial check-in point would serve as a way station enroute to Guam, but first it had to be constructed, then stocked with stores and manned by personnel, and finally secured by forces. Starting from ground zero, all of this had to be accomplished

South Vietnamese Air Marshal Nguyen Cao Ky strolls the deck of the USS Midway. *He flew his personal helicopter to the ship shortly after noon on 29 April.*

Department of Defense Photo (USMC) A801612

Marines keep order among Vietnamese pilots on board the attack aircraft carrier USS Hancock (CVA 19). Many brought their entire crews as they fled from Saigon area bases.

VNAF helicopters approach the Midway from all directions. They are observing no specific traffic pattern and are creating a hazard to both the ship and other aircraft in flight.

Photo courtesy of BGen William A. Bloomer, USMC (Ret)

Photo courtesy of BGen William A. Bloomer, USMC (Ret)

A Cessna O-1 Bird Dog lands on the USS Midway *without benefit of a tailhook or barricade. The pilot, a Vietnamese major, brought with him his wife and five children.*

in less than 48 hours. Already, thousands of refugees were on board ships headed for Subic at near flank speed.

Although the numbers of evacuees on these ships far exceeded initial estimates, the total did not surprise the Navy and Marine Corps. They had anticipated the worst. On 22 April, Admiral Maurice F. Weisner, the commander of the Pacific Fleet, sent a message to Admiral Gayler requesting guidance on how to handle what he expected to be an onslaught of refugees attempting to board Navy ships from every type of craft imaginable. Additionally, he addressed the aspect of safe havens. He said: "Consider it likely that a substantial number of Vietnamese may attempt to flee the coast of South Vietnam in small craft and assorted boats . . . a number of them will approach USN and MSC ships and request refuge . . . . These personnel must also be considered in planning for safe haven, designation of which remains an urgent requirement. Request policy guidance in this matter."[7]

The Navy's Pacific headquarters then queried JCS as to what they should tell Admiral Weisner. Unfortunately, the response came in the form of a message on 27 April, and was of little help. It did not even mention the possibility of Vietnamese heliborne refugees. It only said, "Suggest such persons be delivered to Phu Quoc."[8]

The designation of Grande Island as the first stop to safe haven and the simultaneous establishment of Guam as another "way station" and a refugee receiving center went a long way toward addressing Admiral Weisner's concerns. The answer to his question of who should be granted permission to board American ships never came and eventually events made a response unnecessary. On 29 April, when the first Vietnamese helicopters (Air Marshal Nguyen Cao Ky flew his helicopter to *Midway* shortly after noon on 29 April) began landing on any floating platform they could find, authorized access became a mute issue. Unknowingly and certainly unintentionally, these Vietnamese helicopter refugees helped the Americans. They alerted and thereby prepared the crews for the imminent crisis that Admiral Weisner had anticipated, literally thousands of small craft overflowing with frantic Vietnamese seeking refuge. They tried to board the ships in any manner possible, but received an unexpected reception. Before any ship would permit entry, each refugee had to submit to a screening. Marines checked each one for weapons and once cleared, then permitted them to board. In this way, the Americans attempted to insure safe passage for all.

The helicopter problem reached crisis proportions when Vietnamese pilots started to cut in front of Marine helicopters on final approach to their respective ships while other Vietnamese pilots tried to land on barges filled with refugees. Although the numbers these helicopters carried were incidental, the hazards and difficulties they created were totally unanticipated and nearly impossible to handle. More than 30 empty Hueys went to intentional ocean graves at the hands of Navy crewmen attempting to keep the flight decks of their ships clear.

Although many unexpected events such as this occurred, it can be argued that the large number of evacuees was anticipated and predicted by Ambassador Graham Martin. On 23 April, in a message to the Secretary of State and Admiral Gayler, he estimated that the total number of evacuees for the entire operation could be as high as 200,000. Likewise, Rear Admiral Hugh G. Benton expected some problems as a result of the size of the potential evacuee population. Placed (on 5 April) in overall charge of the ongoing evacuation from South Vietnam as CinCPac's representative in Saigon, Admiral Benton predicted some problems with shipboard evacuation in the final days. He alerted Admiral Gayler in Hawaii by wiring on 23 April: "It is proposed that operational control of MSC shipping be passed to Commander Seventh Fleet early enough to permit an orderly turnover and provide continuity of operations. It is recommended that additional MSC personnel be assigned to Commander Seventh Fleet when MSC ships are chopped." (Chopped means the transfer of tactical control from one commander to another.)[9] According to the Seventh Fleet commander, this transfer of control never took place. Admiral Steele stated, "Operational control of Military Sealift Command was never passed to Commander Seventh Fleet as recommended by Rear Admiral Benton. In my opinion, this was a serious error. It was another instance of violation of the cardinal military principle, unity of command."[10]

The release of the message authorizing the refugee receiving center on Guam, the reorganization of the Amphibious Evacuation Security Force into 14 MSC shipboard detachments, and the use of 1st Battalion, 4th Marines to construct and outfit the Grande Island refugee camp indicated that the events of 29 April were not unanticipated, possibly just underestimated, especially in terms of magnitude and speed of occurence. The fact that these actions happened immediately after the release of the Weisner and Benton messages signalled a gathering consensus that additional preparations had to be made. The Philippines Government's diplomatic note provided the stimulus. These decisions, made none too soon, would have a far-reaching impact on the Marine Corps.

Marines would be affected in four different areas. It would touch first and foremost the 1st Battalion, 4th Marines. Additionally, the AESF would feel the impact as the group most directly involved in the handling of refugees. The third area affected would be Guam and its Marines, and the 3d Marines on Hawaii. Additionally, a contingent of Marines drawn from Camp Pendleton and Marine Corps Air Station El Toro would also become involved in the process. The links in the chain to freedom were forming and the Marine Corps would continue to play a major role in forging it.

Preparations: 1st Battalion, 4th Marines and the Task Force

When Admiral Donald B. Whitmire's Task Force 76, Major Quinlan, and the AESF sailed out of Subic Bay on 18 April leaving the 1st Battalion, 4th Marines behind, Lieutenant Colonel Hester felt certain his battalion had completed its contribution to the evacuation effort. Little did he know that before the month ended, he and his Marines would be key players in relieving what stood as a potential diplomatic roadblock to continued refugee operations. Lieutenant Colonel Hester reported: "1st Battalion, 4th Marines played a large role in the orderly processing of thousands of refugees through Grande Island, by providing manpower for movement of equipment, setting up of over 140 refugee tents and assisting in the overall control of the evacuees."[11] Just as importantly, the Marines assisted in the unloading of barges and shipping and provided security for all of these activities. Petty Officer First Class Paul Long recalled that, ". . . before the evacuees arrived, the Marines and Seabees worked around the clock, erecting hundreds of tents, building a chain-link fence, installing security lights and setting up nearly 200 toilets on the island."[12] The Headquarters and Service Company commander, Captain James P. Rigoulot, stated, "We averaged about 300 Marines a day working, pitching 140 tents, and setting up."[13]

As the numbers of South Vietnamese attempting to flee the country multiplied, other means of transport exceeded the use of the helicopter. Approximately 30,000 escaped on a Vietnamese Navy flotilla of gunboats, patrol boats, and other small craft.[14] The first refugees to reach Grande Island arrived well before the

Photo courtesy of Capt James D. Tregurtha, USN (Ret)
Tents to house refugees are erected on the softball field and golf course of Grande Island. The camp commander was Subic Bay executive officer Capt W. B. Moore, Jr., USN.

Vietnamese Navy's evacuees even left South Vietnam. These early visitors "called it 'Project New Life,' and during the height of the massive airlift, nearly 5,000 evacuees arrived on Grande Island at the mouth of Subic Bay . . . . Fifteen minutes after a tent was up it was occupied."[15] Until 28 April the South Vietnamese came by C-141 and C-130, but on that day Admiral Gayler in a message to the Air Force suspended all but C-130 flights which themselves were ended the following day when a Hercules incurred damage from artillery fire directed at Tan Son Nhut Airport. The admiral also addressed how he expected the refugees to get to their next destination: "MAC [Military Airlift Command] will arrange onward movement to Guam/Wake and other designated locations."[16] This would change significantly within the next 24 hours. The suspension of the fixed-wing airlift would mean the start of Frequent Wind and the helicopter evacuation of South Vietnam, followed by the RVN Navy's evacuees.

As soon as Tan Son Nhut Airport came under siege, first from a bombing attack by Communist-flown A-37s late on the afternoon of 28 April and then from a rocket barrage 10 hours later, South Vietnamese Air Force pilots started manning their planes and helicopters and flying them, along with their dependents, to U.S. Navy ships off the coast or to bases in Thailand. The *Blue Ridge* reported the landing of one of these craft, a VNAF CH-47, on its deck shortly after the aerial bombardment of Tan Son Nhut. It quoted the pilot and copilot, each of whom had brought along his wife and children, "Our crew was refueling at Tan Son Nhut when six A-37s commenced attack . . . . The only way out for South Vietnamese helo pilots was to head to sea and U.S. shipping." In the process of landing, the Vietnamese Chinook cut off the approach of an Air America helo attempting to land on the *Blue Ridge*.[17] This type of incident would become commonplace in the next 48 hours. These refugees, arriving by Vietnamese helicopter, and subsequent groups, arriving by small craft or carried by Marine helicopters, represented the gravest challenge to the evacuation

Photo courtesy of Capt James D. Tregurtha, USN (Ret)

A flotilla of Vietnamese Navy ships sits at anchor in Subic Bay. There was no more room on Grande Island for these refugees so they had to be loaded directly to MSC ships.

security force and the Navy. All of them had to be moved and as quickly as possible to ships prepared to house them. Once on board, they would then be transported as soon as possible to Grande Island for processing.

The Military Sealift Command's ships had been outfitted, manned, and equipped to handle large numbers of evacuees. Where to transfer them and how quickly became the key questions. Congress had just announced that day, 28 April, the refugees' final destination. House Democratic Whip John J. McFall stated that refugees located in four different areas of Asia would be brought to Camp Pendleton, California; Eglin Air Force Base, Florida; and Fort Chaffee, Arkansas. Also that day, Admiral Gayler notified the JCS and Seventh Fleet that it was time to begin the refugee air evacuation to Guam and the United States and that within 24-36 hours he expected a rate of 3,000 per day. With a destination finally in hand, the only thing that stood between the refugees and freedom was the Pacific Ocean. With the means available to navigate at least to the island of Guam, the next step for the refugees would be to find a way from the gray Navy ships to the blue MSC ships.[18]

Admiral Whitmire, the task force commander, had ordered that all of the amphibious ships with well decks (decks that can be opened to the sea and filled with water) be placed in a line landward of the helicopter platforms.* This meant the LSDs and LPDs would move their evacuees down to the well decks where they would board LCMs (Mike Boats) for a ride to one of the four MSC ships anchored eastward, seaward of the amphibs. Once a sealift ship was full, it would weigh anchor and make room for an empty one. In order to facilitate the transfer of refugees, the tank landing ships (LSTs) would float their causeway sections. With

---

*Captain James D. Tregurtha, USN, commander of Task Group 76.5, Surface Evacuation Forces, remembered: "We had to move the holding area farther out from the coast because of the possibility of attack by North Vietnamese PT boats and also to discourage the exodus of fishing boats and other craft to the Navy ships." Tregurtha Comments.

REFUGEE OPERATIONS

Department of Defense Photo (USMC) A801617
South Vietnamese pilot and his family walk with Marine across the USS Hancock's *flight deck. Entire families escaped by air and many flew to Thailand.*

these sections lashed to the belly of the ship next to the accommodation ladder, the Mike boats then would have a relatively safe place to dock and unload. This distribution of refugees to their temporary sea quarters ensured a minimum amount of passenger traffic on the decks of the helicopter platforms and achieved its primary goal of getting the Vietnamese to the available food, water, and medical supplies. This evolution was so important that a special situation report announced its start. Special Frequent Wind Execution Situation Report 018 issued at 1700 on 29 April stated, "Transfer of evacuees from USN to MSC shipping has commenced and proceeding smoothly."[19] Vice Admiral Steele, on board the *Oklahoma City* (CLG 5), having received this message from the *Blue Ridge* (Rear Admiral Whitmire's command ship), knew that things were proceeding as planned. To the casual observer, this did not seem to be the case because as far as the naked eye could see there was nothing but boats coming from the coastline, headed directly for the fleet. Each of these small Vietnamese vessels carried more passengers than it could safely hold and this represented only the first wave of those fleeing their homeland.

This picture of a Vietnamese pilot ditching his helicopter is testimony to the desperation that prevailed. As a result of the unexpected arrival of dozens of South Vietnamese helicopters on 29 April, many of the helicopter-capable ships had decks covered with aircraft.

Department of Defense Photo (USMC) 711643

As a result of this incredibly large armada of small craft, the efficient movement of refugees between ships became even more critical and meant the difference between control and chaos and even life and death. Indications of the onset of confusion were everywhere, but no where more so than in the skies overhead. On the *Dubuque* alone, five Vietnamese helicopters had made unauthorized landings.

To prevent the Vietnamese pilots' flagrant disregard of basic flight safety from endangering his ship and its crew and thereby impeding the evacuation process, Navy Captain Roy W. McLain, Jr., the *Dubuque*'s captain, established fire-fighting teams augmented by Marines from the AESF's detachments Quebec, Romeo, and Uniform. This mini-crash crew stood by ready to assist should one of these many, wildly gyrating helicopters crash on the *Dubuque*. The important contributions of these AESF Marines would be matched by their peers in detachments who now found themselves fully committed to assisting and controlling the arriving refugees.

Evacuation and Passage:
Frequent Wind and the AESF's Final Chapter

For First Lieutenant Joseph J. Rogish, Operation Frequent Wind began 29 April with a wake-up call and ended approximately 24 hours later with a night helicopter landing on the *Hancock*. After four frustrating days of arising at 0130 and waiting hours to learn of another postponement, the word to begin Operation Frequent Wind came as a most rewarding and welcome surprise. Yet even this event occurred in a convoluted manner, with first a cancellation then an immediate recall.

The unusual events surrounding this operation actually began two weeks earlier when Lieutenant Rogish's ship, the *Hancock*, left the formation as the task force prepared to depart Vietnamese coastal waters. The *Hancock*, with a different destination, quickly put many miles between it and the Subic-bound task force. The next day, the *Hancock* and its complement were enjoying a port call in Singapore.* Then just as quickly as liberty had begun, it was over. Admiral Steele had ordered the ship and its pilots back to the South China Sea.

---

*During the time the *Hancock* was in Singapore, the Vice President of the United States was attending Chiang-Kai Shek's funeral in Taipei, 15-17 April. The Ford administration took this opportunity to schedule a secret meeting between Vice President Nelson Rockefeller and the leader of the Vietnamese Senate, Tran Van Lan. No available records reveal whether the meeting was actually held or its contents.

Department of Defense Photo (USMC) 1162056
AESF Marines enforce a sanitization check for weapons among Vietnamese refugees on board the Green Port.

As Rogish said, "this did not make sense because just a few short days ago they had sent us to Singapore, telling us they would not need us because the South Vietnam government looked like it would be able to hold on."[20]

Back on station in the South China Sea, the *Hancock* received word on 29 April that the extraction force should be over the zone at 1200 local (time of receipt approximately 1130). Six hours later, Lieutenant Rogish received his next shock. Suddenly, without warning, the flight section in which he was flying was diverted to the American Embassy instead of the briefed pick-up point, the Defense Attache Office Compound. The next surprise followed immediately upon its heels. As the four "Lady Ace" CH-46s cleared the area, they radioed the Embassy that they had just departed with 100 evacuees on board. The staff "rogered" the Lady Ace call and replied that they still had 200 refugees awaiting extraction. Having listened to virtually the same transmission on their inbound leg, the HMM-165 pilots experienced first shock then anger. Lieutenant Rogish said, "We knew right then that in effect what they were doing was lying about the number of people they had to go which left us in the dark during most of the operation as to what we really had to move. Consequently, despite pilots

Vietnamese barges and sampans approach SS Sergeant Andrew Miller off Vung Tau. Marines from AESF Detachment Sierra, right foreground, guard the boarding platform.

taking back load after load, we never really knew what we had left to do."[21]

This meant that not only would 9th MAB helicopter pilots not know how many people still awaited rescue, but also neither would the receiving ships and their Marine security guards. With 257 Marines spread among eight MSC ships and the *Barbour County*, the AESF believed it was as ready as it could be, but never did it suspect the arrival of 30,000 refugees in 30 hours (the majority would arrive by sea). Certainly, no one, save possibly the Ambassador, expected more than 100 from the Embassy. U.S. Army Major General John R. D. Cleland's post-action investigation of Frequent Wind stated: "The evacuation at the U.S. Embassy was not a coordinated action. This resulted from the confusion as to the total number of evacuees to be transported which was never made clear, and the lack of the necessary command and control to properly accomplish evacuation requirements. The GSF had only scheduled a single helicopter lift from the Embassy, hence no plan existed for the large volume of evacuees assembled there. Inasmuch as the Embassy plan was for a minimum evacuation from that location, the execution of the unplanned lift became essentially a 'seat of the pants' operation."[22]

As a result of this "seat of the pants" operation, Lieutenant Rogish and every available CH-46 pilot continued making trips to the Embassy rooftop, while the AESF Marines screened and loaded the seemingly unlimited supply of refugees. As soon as they arrived on the MSC ships, the Marines processed the South Vietnamese and placed them in predesignated areas. In the case of the *Pioneer Commander*, India Detachment loaded 4,020 evacuees in little over 12 hours.[23]

The problems the *Pioneer Commander* and its Marines overcame during this phase of Frequent Wind typify the MSC and AESF's efforts. Captain Cyril V. Moyher, the detachment's commander, assisted by his NCO-in-charge, Gunnery Sergeant Robert Wicker, oversaw this difficult evolution. Captain Moyher related how it began: "At 1330 on 29 April 1975, the code word 'Deckhouse' was received over the MSC Broadcast Net. Deckhouse was the code word for us to depart our waiting position and head for the refugee pick-up point off the coast of Vietnam."[24] Shortly after this, the ship attached a causeway to its side and at about 1815 the evacuees started arriving in Mike boats. Despite the presence of numerous small fishing craft which appeared soon after the first Mike boat, the orderly processing of refugees from the Navy ships continued until about 2200. The commander of Task Group 76.5, Surface Evacuation Forces, Captain James D. Tregurtha, USN, credited predeployment preparations for the ease with which refugees were moved between ships.* He recently recalled, "One of the reasons refugee processing was handled fairly smoothly was that during predeployment workup and a MAU-size practice landing at Camp Pendleton, we had male and female volunteers from the amphibious base at Coronado act as refugees. They were bussed up to the landing zone where they were interrogated, identified, and accommodated on the ships."[25]

While Mike boats continued to deliver Vietnamese refugees to the *Pioneer Commander* well into the pre-dawn morning of the next day (Wednesday, 30 April), the last Mike boat in the first wave unloaded its passengers at 2200 and departed. This gap in traffic left, for the first time that day, the loading ramp/causeway unguarded and accessible. With its sides unprotected, the platform offered an opportunity which the circling Vietnamese vessels did not decline. Gunnery Sergeant Robert Wicker recalled what happened next:

> The departure of the Mike boats left the platform open on three sides, and the population on the platform increased from 8 Marines in a matter of minutes to 200, 500, 1,000 refugees and they were jumping on and off boats, passing kids and household effects until the platform was packed. With the mad scramble by the refugees driving the Marines back until they were pressed around the base of the accommodation ladder, it became impossible to process the air evacuees to which the Navy had given priority. The platform was slowly cleared after Marines were placed on the outer edges of the platform to keep the fishing boats away. Utilizing the Interrogator-Translator people and a Vietnamese priest we were able to get the crowd settled down.[26]

The work of loading the passengers from Mike boats continued until 0400 when the last of the refugees from the Navy ships boarded. At this point, the rush to occupy the platform began again, and this time order could not be restored. As a consequence, the ship hoisted its accommodation ladder with the Marines still on it, and this act finally made a impression. Gunnery Sergeant Wicker recalled, "The refugees were informed that we would leave them if they did not become orderly, quiet, and with as little confusion as possible start to board the ship."[27]

By sunrise, all of the refugees on the platform had been loaded and the *Pioneer Commander* then directed seven newly arrived vessels to nearby MSC ships. Still, the scene that Wednesday morning (30 April) was one of utter chaos with the sea crowded with abandoned fishing boats; some burning, some dead in the water, and some circling with their helms tied down and their motors running. Avoiding these dangerous shipping hazards, the *Pioneer Commander* weighed anchor and proceeded to the holding area. Once there, it waited for other ships to join it for the express purpose of forming a convoy for the voyage to Subic. The *Pioneer Commander* spent the next 20 hours embarking an additional 650 people, 200 of them from the *Greenville Victory*. After a health and sanitization check, Navy medical personnel gave the *Pioneer Commander*, the *Pioneer Contender* and the *American Challenger* medical clearance for a trip not to exceed five days. The first two ships in the convoy, *Pioneer Commander* and *Pioneer Contender*, pulled up their anchors at 0230 on 2 May and headed for Subic Bay at 21 knots.

Shortly before their departure the deluge of refugees peaked and then began to subside. During this period, the third ship in the convoy, the *American Challenger*, remained in the holding area and assisted the overcrowded *Greenville Victory* by relieving it of 3,000 Vietnamese refugees. Once loaded, the *American Challenger* set off in pursuit of the *Pioneer Commander* and *Pioneer Contender*.

Thirty-eight hours later, while approaching Subic Bay, the *Pioneer Commander* received word of a new destination, Guam. Less than two hours after that, while undergoing a night medical resupply by helicopter, the *Pioneer Commander* steamed out of Subic Bay and headed for Apra Harbor, Guam, leaving the *Pioneer Contender* behind. Meanwhile, the third ship to leave the holding area, the *American Challenger*, received its updated orders: proceed directly to Guam.

While *American Challenger*, *Pioneer Commander*, and *Pioneer Contender* headed for Subic, the MSC ships and their Marine security detachments wrestled with the most serious challenge still confronting them, disarming the remaining refugees. The combination of overcrowding, fatigue, and a never-ending stream of refugees, driven by a sense of finality or "no tomorrow," had created an extremely volatile situation. Stripping them of their weapons during the loading process

---

*Captain Tregurtha also credited the logistic planning when he added: "Success of the evacuation was also due to the setting of a goal prior to deployment that all ships would deploy with no 'CasReps' (disabled or non-functioning equipment). This was accomplished and the squadron transited to Vietnam and operated for over a month before the first 'CasRep' occurred. By then our job had been completed." Tregurtha Comments.

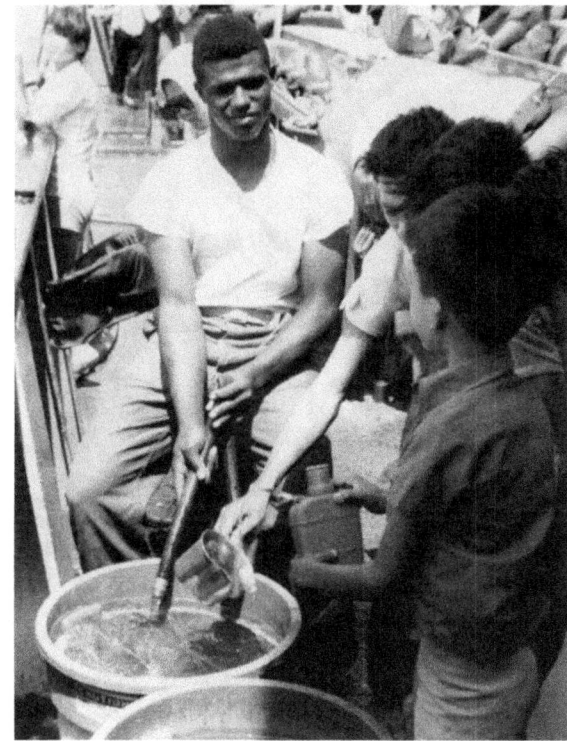

Department of Defense Photo (USMC) A801627
Marine LCpl M. R. Bishop of the AESF operates a water point for refugees on board the SS American Racer *enroute to Guam. This ship and the SS* Transcolorado *departed Subic Bay for the island of Guam on 5 May with more than 10,000 refugees between them.*

quickly became tedious and eventually dangerous, occasionally leading to physical confrontations.

In one instance, Captain Richard L. "Rick" Reuter, the Echo Detachment commander, barely averted a disastrous and catastrophic panic on board the *Sergeant Kimbro* when some Vietnamese physically resisted sanitization. Captain Reuter responded to this crisis by calling in a reaction force from the 3d Battalion, 9th Marines. The mere presence of these additional Marines, who had arrived by helicopter from the nearby task force, calmed the people enough to enable Reuter's men to reestablish control. In the case of many refugees, the overwhelming fear of being left behind to the mercy of the Commmunist invaders was intensified by the absence of food or water. Many of the refugees had seen neither of these necessities for more than four days.

Yet by 2300, 1 May, every evacuee, save a few hundred, had access to at least water, and by midmorning, 2 May, almost every evacuee had received some form of sustenance. By late morning that Friday (2 May), every MSC ship had reached capacity except the *Sergeant Kimbro* which continued to load refugees until the afternoon of the next day. By nightfall on 2 May, MSC ships had embarked nearly 40,000 refugees while a newly arrived Navy ship, the *Barbour County*, with a recently assigned detachment of Marines led by First Lieutenant David A. Kratchovil, had loaded an additional 958 evacuees. With all but a few of the AESF Marine detachments on MSC ships and the loading of Vietnamese refugees virtually complete, CinCPac transferred control of the AESF from General Carey to Rear Admiral Whitmire and his task force on 3 May. The admiral's mission would be to ensure the refugees' safe arrival in Guam.[28]

That night, as the *Pioneer Commander* and the *American Challenger* set course for Guam, the *Pioneer Contender*, which they had left behind, pulled alongside the pier at Grande Island and began unloading a third of its passengers. The transfer of these 2,000 Vietnamese coincided with the transfer of command of the AESF to Admiral Whitmire, and began its final phase of the evacuation. Six hours later, the *Pioneer Contender* and its AESF Detachment Victor departed for Guam, fully resupplied and carrying the remaining 4,000 refugees. Less than 36 hours later, on 5 May, the *Transcolorado* with Hotel Detachment embarked and the *American Racer* with Mike Detachment on board left the Philippines for Apra Harbor. Nearly exceeding capacity, the two ships counted more than 10,000 refugees. The *Greenville Victory*, *Sergeant Andrew Miller*, and *Green Forest*, because of overcrowding and unsanitary conditions, had to unload their passegers at Subic, as did the *Green Port*.

A Tango detachment squad leader, then-Sergeant J. C. Owens, recalled the unhealthy state of affairs on the *Green Forest* in 1975, "The most ridiculous and unsanitary condition was created when they hung the portable toilets over the ship's railing and the Vietnamese after using them threw the toilet paper through the holes. Before you knew it there was used toilet paper streaming from every part of the ship not to mention those pieces of paper that landed on our sleeping bags, laying on the ship's after deck. A more unhealthy situation could not have existed." These unsatisfactory living conditions caused the medical authorities to declare these four ships unfit for habitation until thoroughly cleaned. Once sanitary conditions were restored then and only then could refugees reboard these MSC ships (*Greenville Victory*, *Sergeant Andrew Miller*, *Green Forest*, and *Green Port*).[29]

Department of Defense Photo (USMC) 1163161

Men of Detachment Tango, AESF, help Vietnamese sailors and dependents up the gangway of SS Green Forest *at Subic. Overcrowding caused sanitation problems on MSC ships.*

Having sailed from Vung Tau to Subic Bay on board their own ships, members of the South Vietnamese Navy prepare to embark on board SS Green Forest *at Subic. The Philippines government would not let any refugees remain at Subic Bay more than 72 hours.*

Department of Defense Photo (USMC) 1163149

Department of Defense Photo (USMC) 1175628

Pioneer Commander *unloads its refugees at the pier in Apra Harbor, Guam, on 7 May 1975. Once all of the evacuees were clear of the ship, Capt Cyril V. Moyher led his Detachment India to their temporary quarters on Guam before returning to Okinawa on 10 May.*

As these events were unfolding, the *Pioneer Commander* and the *American Challenger* were racing toward Guam. The *Pioneer Commander* probably would have been the first MSC ship to deposit seaborne Vietnamese refugees on American soil except for an old naval tradition endowing the senior skipper in a convoy with the privilege of entering port first. The Commander of Marine Detachment November on board the *American Challenger*, Captain Michael T. Mallick, recently recalled that part of the journey: "Enroute to Guam, the *Pioneer Commander* was ordered to reduce speed so as to allow the *American Challenger* to reach Guam first, the reason being the skipper of the *Challenger* (Captain Bouchie) was senior. We arrived at 0115 on 7 May, deposited 5200 refugees on Guam and departed before dawn."[30]

The *Pioneer Commander* arrived in Guam at 0800 on 7 May and it too began unloading almost immediately. By noon every one of the refugees had left the ship, beginning the first of their many days on the island of Guam. For three of those days, the Marine contingent from the *Pioneer Commander*, India Detachment, would also remain on the island, at the Marine Barracks, Guam. At 0630, 10 May, these AESF Marines boarded a bus and rode to Andersen Air Force Base where a C-141 waited to fly them to Okinawa. Captain Moyher, the detachment commander, summed up the experience: "On the morning of 7 May we entered the harbor at Guam and discharged 4,678 evacuees. Prior to disembarking, the refugees presented the detachment with a set of lacquered 4 seasons plaques and a letter of thanks."[31]

By 7 May, the *American Racer*, accompanied by Mike Detachment and carrying most of the remaining Frequent Wind refugees (including those that the *Green Port* had unloaded on 5 May), was less than 24 hours from completing the mission Admiral Gayler had tasked Rear Admiral Whitmire with five days earlier: safe passage to Guam for all of the Frequent Wind evacuees. At approximately the same time that Wednesday afternoon, the AESF control group, detachments Quebec, Papa, and Romeo, 17th ITT, and MP personnel began screening, unloading, and processing the refugees on board 29 Vietnamese Navy ships which had escaped from South Vietnam. They attempted to ensure that these refugees spent as little time as possible in Subic in order to honor the wishes of the Philippines Government that no refugee remain in that country more than 72 hours. Major Quinlan reported, "This pierside operation involved processing the refugees, many of whom had to be disarmed, from ships ranging in size from gunboat to destroyer escort, then immediately embarking them on board waiting evacuation ships. In less than 24 hours over 20,000 people were unloaded, processed, and reembarked without incident. This herculean effort was directed by First Lieutenant Johnnie Johnson and Chief Warrant Officer Al Kent."[32]

On 8 May, the final phase started when the *Green Port* (carrying a new detachment, Kilo, which had replaced Papa on 5 May), and *Green Wave* (Detachment Uniform) left Subic Bay. These two ships, with 7,522 evacuees on board, preceded by one day the *Sergeant Andrew Miller's* (Detachment Sierra) departure with 3,200 refugees. Tango Detachment and the *Green Forest* joined these ships the next day when it boarded the last of the large groups of refugees (more than 4,000) and took them to Guam. Between the time the *American Challenger* deposited its load of evacuees at Guam and returned to Subic (7-10 May), the refugee camps on Guam had reached their capacity. No longer could Guam handle large groups, and consequently the *American Challenger* and its security detachment (November) were released from evacuation operations.* Eleven days later, after the remainder of his detachments, save one, had also been released, Major Quinlan and his command group departed Subic. They left behind one detachment (Foxtrot) on the *Greenville Victory*. Remaining for the exclusive purpose of assisting in any future refugee operations, they returned to Okinawa after six days of waiting without action. With Detachment Foxtrot's arrival on 27 May, the AESF's function, in effect, ceased. Two days prior to this, Admiral Whitmire had returned control of the AESF to III MAF. On 31 May 1975, Maj General Hoffman made the termination official by deactivating the unit.[33]

A Vietnamese City in Guam

On Guam the American Command prepared to receive the expected flood of refugees. On 23 April a message from Admiral Gayler to his representative on Guam read: "JCS has directed immediate implementation Vietnamese refugee support at Guam."[34] This, by no coincidence, came at the same time the Philippines Government notified the American Embassy in Manila that the refugees could not remain in the country. Guam, only three hours flight time by C-130 from Cubi, offered an excellent solution to the diplomatic dilemma.

Earlier notification and more preparation might have eliminated a series of problems on Guam, but the alarmingly large number of evacuees seemed to surprise Washington. Despite the short notice, Marine Barracks Guam jumped into Operation New Life with enthusiasm and energy. That alone would not be enough to overcome the absence of time to plan and prepare, forcing in many instances the barrack's 11 officers and 333 men simply to react. "Having received word that we could anticipate involvement in the refugee program on the morning of 23 April 1975, the first refugees arrived Camp Asan at 1820 hours on 24 April. Planning therefore was brief and simple."[35]

Colonel Gene M. "Jinx" McCain's first act, once having received notification of the operation, was to call a staff meeting. Just prior to it, he learned that Admiral Gayler had directed that the old Asan Hospital Annex, deserted since 1973, would be used as the site of the Vietnamese refugee center. Besides discussing this topic during the meeting, Colonel McCain detailed the initial responsibilities of his staff. He told them that he would serve as the commanding officer, Camp Asan, and that Lieutenant Colonel Charles W. Gobat would be his deputy. In addition, Captain Eugene R. Hardman and Captain Charles R. Provini became the Camp Asan executive and operations officers, respectively. First Lieutenant Ronald E. Spratt learned that he would fill the billet of camp supply officer.

That same day, immediately after the morning meeting, Captains Hardman and Provini, accompanied by Lieutenant Spratt, visited the site of the new refugee center. They found two years of rubble and hundreds of seabees furiously attempting to put the place in habitable condition. Immediately, they set to work devising a scheme that would enable them to accept their first arrivals in less than 24 hours. Categorizing their anticipated concerns into general management areas, they formed three working groups, each with three subsections. The first, administration, contained population control and accounting, locator system, and billeting assignments. The second, operations, oversaw processing (both in and out), an interpreter pool, and coordination/liaison. The third group, logistics, involved food services, supply, and sanitation.

For every organization and participant, the foremost

---

*Captain Mallick related: "The *American Challenger* with 27 members of November Detachment and myself proceeded to Subic where we were assigned to provide security for 27 Cambodian/Vietnamese ships." Mallick Comments.

Camp Asan awaits the arrival of its first refugees under Operation New Life. South Vietnamese and evacuees of other nationalities started arriving in Guam at 1820 on 24 April.

concern was meeting the incoming buses and obtaining a valid manifest. With this in hand, they then could assign billeting, plan meals, and organize linen/bedding issue. The task of refurbishing the old hospital annex in less than 24 hours presented a nearly impossible undertaking. Formidable as the job appeared, no other choices existed and the Marines and Seabees on Guam turned all their attention to meeting this deadline. When the first busloads of refugees arrived the next day, the Navy-Marine Corps team had four of the 15 barracks ready. The new occupants also found blankets, sleeping gear, and food awaiting them.

The initial buses took their passengers to Building 502 for processing and orientation. Next, the Marines showed the refugees their new living spaces with its dimensions and assignment based on the size of the family. From here, the new occupants moved to blanket issue after which the Marine hosts gave them the choice of either going to bed or to the messhall. At Building 548, hot rice and tea awaited their arrival. This process would be repeated thousands of times before Operation New Life ended and Camp Asan closed its doors. By the following day, 25 April, Camp Asan had a population of 5,000 people. On that Friday, the first departing group left Camp Asan for Andersen Air Force Base, and a flight from Guam to the United States. After that, a continuous flow of arrivals and departures became the routine.[36]

Colonel McCain later related that by the time the first refugees arrived at 1800 on 24 April, he had established a complete camp organization to provide full support including administration, billeting, baggage handling, messing, medical, transportation, clothing, and location of relatives. By 1130 on 26 April, the organization administratively processed 6,420 arrivals, adding them to the camp rolls. This effort involved not only the Marines on Guam but also their families as well. Marine wives assisted with the initial reception and processing of evacuees, including the collection and distribution of clothing and baby supplies.[37]

The first evacuees came to Guam via Air Force C-141s and C-130s. Landing at Andersen Air Force base, they soon found themselves at an increasingly more crowded Camp Asan. Despite the fact that each aircraft could only transport a hundred or so Vietnamese per sortie, Camp Asan quickly reached its capacity. Within less than 48 hours of the first arrival, Colonel McCain requested a 48-hour moratorium in order to give his Marines a chance to stabilize the situation in the camp and continue to upgrade the facilities. During the moratorium, only 17 new refugees entered the camp and more importantly at this juncture, Admiral Gayler decided to increase the number of camps and make Colonel McCain the overall commander of Naval Refugee Camps, Guam.

In his initial message establishing a refugee support

center, Admiral Gayler told Colonel McCain to expect an initial input of 10,000-13,000 with a rapid buildup to 50,000. He said, "The center's operation is expected to last a minimum of 90 days."[38] With these requirements in mind and after having surveyed the initial situation at Asan during the moratorium, Colonel McCain reported to the Commandant of the Marine Corps that he would need eight officers and 225 staff noncommissioned officers and enlisted men to accomplish this task. Little did he know then the volume and rate at which refugees would arrive, and that the operation would last double the forecasted minimum. Besides Marine Barracks, Guam's involvement, Colonel McCain enlisted the assistance of 10 men from Marine Detachment, USS *Proteus* (AS 19) (a submarine tender), as a working party to assist in establishing a refugee camp at Orote Point, Guam. He also obtained permission to assign one officer and 60 Marines from his Company C as a force to participate in the conversion of a local hotel into an evacuee billeting site.[39]

As Operation New Life unfolded, the Marines' involvement significantly expanded. Besides assisting in the opening of new camps, the Marines worked on the docks meeting the Military Sealift Command ships as they arrived; their efforts made the refugees' initial transition easier. From the unloading of the ships to the processing of the refugees, the Marines had one philosophy: as much as possible, make the evacuees feel at home. Captain Provini, who had witnessed refugee resettlement efforts in Vietnam in 1972, offered his advice based on the South Vietnamese Government's handling of the former Quang Tri residents. His experiences and ideas were instrumental in developing this "Welcome Home" philosophy. He pointed out that the refugees coming south after the fall of northern I Corps in 1972 received a very regimented welcome. The South Vietnamese Government officials placed them into holding areas for subsequent relocation and readmittance into society. The consequences of this were tragic; the refugees experienced confusion and fear. Eventually, they rebelled and this act provoked their countrymen into using force against them. As a result, these South Vietnamese felt like prisoners in their own country.[40]

Avoiding such aggressive behavior became the focus and intent of the Marines on Guam. The camp guards and staff made every effort to let the Vietnamese know that they could expect the best treatment possible. Upon arrival at Camp Asan, the Vietnamese departed their buses for their first event, a "welcome aboard" brief. At this initial meeting, and throughout their stay, chaplains always made their presence known by announcing that they, too, were available to assist and counsel anyone in need. Besides their well-timed human relations training, the Marines acted with one purpose, "to show compassion and consideration to the refugees." To further enhance their image and present a sharp appearance, the Marines at the refugee operation center always wore the uniform prescribed for the occasion. Those working at Camp Asan wore their modified blue uniform instead of combat gear, for two reasons. They hoped to provide a favorable first impression to the Vietnamese to reduce their anxieties, and they wanted to make them feel welcome in their new home. The Marines thought combat gear would remind the refugees too much of the war and the pain they had left behind.[41]

By presenting the appearance of a city with a friendly living environment, the Camp Asan Marines gained the confidence and trust of the new arrivals. Using this trust, they induced the refugees to form their own community structure and govern themselves. Once the refugees elected a mayor for their new "city," the Marines assumed advisory roles and became even less conspicuous. The elected official, "Tony" Lam, assumed the title of Vietnamese camp manager, and retained this function until transfer to the states on 23 July. Lam's departure signalled the end of the camp's outstanding internal command network. For three months (April 25-July 23), Lam and his organization virtually ran the Asan camp.[42]

Satisfied with the progress and developments at Camp Asan, Colonel McCain redeployed some of his Asan Marines to the satellite camps: Tokyu Hotel, Camp Socio, and J&G Construction Camp. Despite the move, their mission remained the same, "to organize, supervise, assist and take care of the refugee populations within these camps."[43]

Throughout this endeavor, Colonel McCain received his guidance for the conduct and running of the camp from Admiral Gayler's representative on Guam, Rear Admiral George F. Morrison. Admiral Morrison actively participated in the refugee operation and after an initial briefing of Colonel McCain and his staff on 23 April, he personally visited Camp Asan at least two more times. One of those times, on 9 May, Rear Admiral Morrison escorted the overall commander, Admiral Gayler (CinCPac), through Camp Asan.

Apparently satisfied with Colonel McCain's handling of the operation, Admiral Morrison changed Colonel McCain's title from Camp Coordinator of all

Orote Point, a former airfield, was the most isolated and most secure of the camps. When repatriates threatened violence, Capt Howard P. Shores III reminded them of Orote Point.

camps under Navy jurisdiction to Military Support Officer, New Life Guam, effective 1 August. His new mission responsibilities entailed coordinating with the Senior Civil Coordinator to provide necessary administrative, logistical, and operational support for the internal camp functioning. He also provided guidance to the Marines who were carrying out these functions. Colonel McCain insured above all else that they avoided law enforcement activities in the camps, maintaining as minimal a military presence as possible.

Just prior to Colonel McCain's redesignation, Rear Admiral Kent J. Carroll replaced Admiral Morrison as Commander, Naval Forces, Marianas (ComNavMar) and overall military coordinator for refugee operations. At about the same time, the newly designated Senior Civil Coordinator arrived. Julia Taft, the Director of the Interagency Task Force (IATF) for Indochina Refugees, had appointed retired Army Brigadier General James A. Herbert to head a team of representatives responsible for coordinating the processing and preparation of refugees for shipment to the United States. The Senior Civil Coordinator and the Military Support Officer soon would work closely together in solving the "repatriate" problem and bringing to a close the refugee operation on Guam.[44]

Colonel McCain's redesignation reflected the changing complexion of the camps' population. As each new group of refugees boarded a flight for the continental United States, the percentage of those remaining who desired to return to Vietnam increased. Known as "repatriates," the potential danger they represented, and their alarming threats, grew as they approached a majority.* As this problem intensified, the Marines had to take overt action to stem the growing threat of violence. Captain Howard P. Shores III, the commander of Camp Socio, before taking control of what later became the Socio repatriate camp, received only one instruction, "insure that the camp functions."[45]

To accomplish this security mission, Captain Shores had no choice but to deal directly with the leader of the repatriates, Colonel Quay (political leader) and his assistants, Captain Tam (political second in command) and Major Hai (administrative leader). Upon their initial meeting, Colonel Quay stated his position: "The only thing we want is to be able to repatriate to Vietnam and we will do anything including

---

*Recently, General Herbert explained the origin of the repatriates and the extent of the problem: "VNN ships were evacuated with crews. The crews never contacted their families, who remained in Vietnam. The same was true of some VNAF aircraft (C-130s which were flown to Thailand) crews whose families were in SVN. There were families sent out in the refugee stream whose (husbands) did not make it and were in SVN. Most of the repatriation group wished for family reunification, regardless of the cost. All of those who expressed a desire to leave were moved to Camp Asan, as other camps were closed out." General Herbert's task upon arriving in early August as the newly designated Senior Civil Coordinator "was to resettle about 6,000 refugees remaining on Guam, to assemble repatriates from Eglin, Indiantown, Chaffee, and Pendleton on Guam and care for them there until the 'repatriate problem' was solved." Herbert Comments.

Photo courtesy of BGen James A. Herbert, USA (Ret)
Repatriates, protesting the delay in their return to Vietnam, burned this barracks at Camp Asan. Most of the repatriates were peaceful and only sought reunion with the families they had left behind.

violence in order to accomplish this goal."[46] Captain Shores explained to Quay that he did not have the authority to repatriate them and, while he did have the responsibility of making their stay comfortable, his first priority was the safety and welfare of his Marines. He asked Quay not to interpret compassion as a sign of weakness and reminded him that the first person to break the rules would be sent to the isolated and more primitive Orote Point where tighter security restrictions could be imposed. Thanks in large part to the establishment of these ground rules, Camp Socio did not have one dangerous incident. The only overt activity took place on 30 July 1975, when eight repatriates shaved their heads in protest. They objected to Captain Tam's confinement at Orote Point for his part in the burning of a Camp Asan barracks.*[47]

Eventually, by the end of August, all of the Socio occupants had been moved to Camp Asan. The marginal sewage pumps at Socio inspired that decision when they malfunctioned two times in three days, spilling more than 8,000 gallons of raw sewage. These new occupants of Asan, 240 Vietnamese, still adamantly wanted to return to Vietnam despite a meeting with Brigadier General Herbert, who explained in detail the ramifications and dangers of repatriation.** Still, they insisted on returning to their homeland. Consequently, on 15 October, they and the other repatriates of Camp Asan boarded a Vietnamese vessel, the *Thuong Tin I*. At 1230 the next day the ship with its 1,546 repatriates departed for Vietnam.*** Two weeks later, Camp Asan closed. With its closure, Operation New Life ended, having lasted nearly four months longer than its original forecast of 90 days.[48]

The repatriates by far had represented the gravest challenge to the overall refugee operation. Their contentious behavior and threatening demands prompted command changes at other satellite camps in addition to Socio's. On 5 July because of repatriate problems, Colonel McCain assigned First Lieutenant Roger D. Gabelman as the commander of Camp J&G. He would remain there until two days after the transfer of that camp's repatriates to Camp Asan on 20 August. First Lieutenant Keith L. Johnson received word the day Gabelman transferred his camp occupants that effective 22 August he would become the commander of Tokyu Hotel. Although Tokyu Hotel did not house any repatriates, it had its own problems. It contained hundreds of third-country nationals who awaited an immigration judge's ruling on whether they qualified for American citizenship and benefits. On 10 September, he decided that they did not and ordered them deported. He ruled that the special law passed by Congress allowing the entry of Vietnamese refugees into the U.S. did not apply to them. Within two weeks of the order, all of the third-country nationals were

---

*General Herbert recently described that incident: "There were some 'hot heads' among the group of repatriates. They burned down a barracks and the group was told by me that we really did not care how many buildings were torched because the entire group would remain at Camp Asan until repatriation, with or without the comfort of a roof over their heads. There was no more violence." Herbert Comments.

**General Herbert mentioned his attempts to change the repatriates' decision: "As the Senior Civil Coordinator, I had numerous sessions with the repatriate leadership and explained the probable actions to be taken by the Hanoi folks if they returned. They were for the large part committed to their family members remaining in Vietnam, regardless of the warnings." Herbert Comments.

***The Senior Civil Coordinator explained his participation in this undertaking: "We developed the plan to fix up the *Thuong Tin I* ship, convert the freighter to passenger use, and send the repatriates back. I obtained authority to seize the *Thuong Tin I* and ComNavMar was instructed by CNO via CinCPacFlt to repair it as necessary and fit it out to carry the repatriates. This job was done rapidly and well, at a cost of $800,000, as I recall. On 16 October, with outstanding support from Rear Admiral Kent Carroll and the combined efforts of the Naval Ship Repair Facility, Marine Barracks Guam, Naval Logistics Center, and the IATF team, the *Thuong Tin I* set sail with 1,546 repatriates on board from Agana for Saigon." He added that he still had the text of a lawsuit in which he was sued for $3,000,000 for his part in the seizure of the ship. Herbert Comments.

Photo courtesy of BGen James A. Herbert, USA (Ret)

Thuong Tin I *gets underway for Vietnam on 16 October with 1,546 repatriates on board.*

returned to their native countries, leaving only a few hundred Vietnamese refugees. On 23 October, after having found sponsors for these last few evacuees, including the 123 who had elected to live on Guam, the Tokyu Hotel closed its doors.

Having successfully accomplished its refugee mission on Guam, the Marine Barracks Guam justly gave credit to the additional forces whose assistance Colonel McCain had needed as early as April when he employed Marines from the *Proteus*. Other units external to his battalion which Colonel McCain used during the course of the operation included Company E, 2d Battalion, 3d Marines, 1st Marine Brigade, who arrived on Guam for temporary duty on 5 July 1975, and Company F, 2d Battalion, 3d Marines, 1st Marine Brigade, who joined them on 24 July. These elements departed Guam for Hawaii on 23 September 1975.

The Marines from 1st Brigade and the Marine Barracks Guam combined forces in the final months to insure that no repatriate or disconsolate refugee harmed or endangered life or property. Considering the fact that the only reported casualties during the entire operation involved two auto-related deaths (a retired Army sergeant and a Marine off the *Proteus*), one would have to conclude that their efforts to protect life and property were extremely successful.

A South Vietnamese child enjoys an American favorite. Within days this child would be on her way to America and a new beginning at Camp Pendleton.
Photo courtesy of Capt James D. Tregurtha, USN (Ret)

Processing more than 100,000 refugees, including a one-day camp population high of 7,221 in Asan on 10 June, they expended thousands of hours and helped move the refugees one step closer to the final link in their chain to freedom.[49]

The Final Link: Camp Pendleton

When the base duty officer at Camp Pendleton answered the phone on Saturday, 26 April 1975, he was intrigued to hear the voice at the other end identify himself as the Headquarters Marine Corps Command Duty Officer. Even more intriguing was what he said next, could Camp Pendleton house and administer Vietnamese refugees? The Pendleton duty officer immediately passed the call to the chief of staff, Colonel Tullis J. Woodham, Jr., who, in turn, notified the base commander, Brigadier General Paul G. Graham.* The duty officer added that headquarters had said it would be very unlikely for Pendleton to be selected because it was a fully operational base, but just the same they still needed the answer to the feasibility question by midnight that day. This unexpected event would serve as General Graham's only advance warning that his base would be used as a refugee processing facility. Despite assurances to the contrary, the interagency task force created as a result of President Ford's appeal to Congress on 10 April to help the Vietnamese refugees, eventually chose Camp Pendleton as one of its three receiving and processing sites in the continental United States.

General Graham later recalled: "The first inkling I had of the possibility of establishing a refugee camp was about 1730 on Saturday afternoon on the 26th of April."[50] He related that after Colonel Tullis Woodham told him of the Headquarters Marine Corps inquiry, Graham told Woodham "we had better get together and talk it over with all the assistant chiefs of staff." He then "set up a meeting for seven o'clock that evening."[51] At that meeting, General Graham and the assistant chiefs of staff discussed whether Camp Pendleton could handle such a facility even though Headquarters had said it ". . . really did not have to worry about being selected as a refugee facility because of the size of the base and the amount of training we do here . . . ."[52] After exploring the various facets of such a possibility and viewing engineer studies and maps of the base, they decided that the northern section of the base at Camp Talega could handle a refugee center. General Graham stated, "after looking at all the aspects of Talega, we came to the conclusion that we probably could put a facility up there, but it would have to be a tent facility, under field conditions."[53] That evening General Graham informed Headquarters Marine Corps that Camp Pendleton could build a facility to handle 18,000 refugees, but under austere living conditions.

At 0720, shortly after arriving at work Monday, 28 April, General Graham received a call from his chief of staff. Colonel Woodham informed him that ". . . Pendleton had been selected as the reception center for the refugees."[54] From this point, the news only seemed to get worse as the chief of staff told his base commander that refugees were scheduled to start arriving anytime, and in fact some were already airborne. Indeed, the very refugees Colonel McCain's Marines had processed so quickly through Camp Asan were inbound to Marine Corps Air Station El Toro with a final destination of Camp Pendleton, California.

General Graham quickly moved to action, lining up support and translating his plans into productive results.** He first sought assistance from the 1st Marine Division, whose commander, Brigadier General William L. McCulloch, readily provided two engineer battalions. According to Graham, "We had 1,500 to 1,700 people here about ten o'clock that morning (28 April). We brought about 10 bulldozers in. We just lined them up track-to-track, went right down in an area, leveled it off, brought the graders in and turned to the 1st Force Service Regiment to get the tents."[55] After some frantic telephoning that morning, the base commander felt a little more comfortable knowing that either the Marine Corps Supply Depot, Barstow, or the General Services Administration in Ogden, Utah, would provide additional tents and supplies as soon as they were needed. General Graham said, "We knew that if we were receiving refugees as fast as this first group, that we would be one step ahead of disaster unless we got some outside assistance very quick-

---

*Colonel Woodham first contacted the staff. He stated: "General Graham was not notified immediately. I received the information in the early afternoon. I went directly to my office and attempted to make calls to key staff officers who could answer the basic question 'what if' and then told them to prepare for a meeting with the CG . . . ." Woodham Comments.

**Colonel Woodham related: "Initially, the major load rested on the shoulders of Colonel George A. 'Red' Merrill (assistant chief of staff for facilities) and Colonel Robert W. Calvert (assistant chief of staff for logistics and supply). At the JCS level the operation received support from Colonel Kenneth L. Robinson, Jr., and at the Headquarters level from Colonel Neil A. Nelson of the Installations and Logistics Division, HQMC." Woodham Comments.

Bulldozers prepare ground for the erection of hundreds of tents. Five hours before the official notification to establish a refugee camp at Pendleton, the first evacuees arrived.

ly."[56] They did receive this support and with it some well-timed local assistance. The combination made the center a success.

At the beginning, a favorable ending did not seem likely, especially after 800 bone-weary refugees arrived at El Toro at 0200 on 29 April, well before anyone expected them.* Confused, tired, scared, and disoriented after having flown for 14 hours, these refugees arrived in their new country in the middle of a pitch black night. Many responded to the unfamiliar surroundings by simply crying. Marines at El Toro helped them board Marine Corps buses for the relatively short ride to Camp Talega (less than 45 minutes). General Graham immediately placed them in the Camp Talega quonset huts, which had been constructed years earlier as additional housing for Marine Corps units assigned to Camp Pendleton. His decision to postpone the mandatory processing procedure until morning saved the refugees from further suffering and allowed them some much-needed sleep.

The irony of this eleventh-hour arrival and the extreme crush it placed on General Graham's forces was that the official authorization to perform resettlement duties did not arrive until after the first refugees had fallen asleep in their new home, the Camp Talega "hotel." At 0736 on 29 April, Headquarters Marine Corps sent a message to the commanding general of Camp Pendleton. It said, "Establish New Horizon Coordination Center and be prepared to provide billeting, messing, essential medical treatment, transportation, security, and camp administration for up to 18,000 evacuees."[57] The next day the final authority arrived: "This message confirms previous oral arrangements that you take action required to establish and operate the Camp Pendleton Refugee Processing Center."[58]

From this inauspicious beginning, Camp Pendleton more than sufficiently met the Joint Chiefs' original objective: "The Marine Corps will be tasked to receive, process, billet, and support 18,000 (eighteen thousand) RVN evacuees for a period of 90 days or more commencing about 29 April 1975."[59] To accomplish this, General Graham had to organize his forces, create a staff, and plan while still receiving more refugees each day.** Complicating this matter was the presence of a dual system of command that functioned under the auspices of the State Department, which had overall responsibility for the South Vietnamese

---

*Colonel Nicholas M. Trapnell, Jr., Chief of Staff, Marine Corps Air Station El Toro, had anticipated the refugees' arrival. He related that the reason the processing went so smoothly at 0200, 29 April, was because of his prior knowledge of the evacuation plans. He gained that understanding while serving in Vietnam on the DAO staff from 1973 to 1974. He stated, "I initiated preparations for the refugees more than a week before receiving word from HQMC and by then the planning and rehearsal were complete." Trapnell Comments.

**Colonel Woodham related General Graham's daily routine: "General Graham's schedule entailed arriving at Base headquarters at 0715, taking care of pressing base matters, then boarding the standby UH-1E and flying to the refugee camp headquarters where he would stay until 1700, and finally returning to Base to make decisions on matters that had arisen during the day. In inclement weather, he would ride in his sedan and usually arrive back around 2000. Oftentimes his staff would remain at work until 2300 or later." Colonel Woodham also described the inordinate importance the dimension of public relations assumed at staff headquarters when he said, "Refugee matters were constantly in the national news and as a consequence a TV was installed in my office to monitor day and night the media reports." Woodham Comments.

Marines prepare to build a new city at Camp Pendleton, California. Marines participating in Operation New Arrival erected nearly 1,100 tents to house Vietnamese refugees.

Department of Defense Photo (USMC) 8607499

This is an aerial view of BGen Graham's Vietnamese city. Each tent, weighing 360 pounds, required a minimum of 35 minutes for 10 men to erect it in this instant "urban area."

Department of Defense Photo (USMC) 8607508

Marine Corps Historical Collection

Coordinators welcome visitors to the "New Horizon Refugee Center." Mrs. Gerald Ford, flanked by BGen Paul G. Graham, military coordinator, and Nicholas G. Thorne, senior civil coordinator, greets Mr. Joseph Battaglia of the U.S. Catholic Conference.

A bus from Camp Pendleton loads newly arrived Vietnamese refugees at the air passenger terminal at Marine Corps Air Station, El Toro, California. Operation New Arrival would eventually process more than 50,000 refugees before its conclusion in November 1975.

Department of Defense Photo (USMC) 8809675

evacuee program. To fund this task, Congress had enacted the Indochina Migration and Refugee Assistance Act which authorized the expenditure of $455 million, to which President Ford had added $98 million more. Beneath this State Department and Congressional umbrella existed the dual chain of command.

General Graham served as the military coordinator while retaining his title of installation commander, and Nicholas G. Thorne (a lieutenant colonel in the Marine Corps Reserve) served as the civil coordinator. All matters of controversy had to be resolved by joint agreement. Fortunately, due to the personalities involved, this convoluted arrangement never became a problem. It could have very easily become a major stumbling block save for Graham's and Thorne's efforts to work together.

An example of the potential for command conflict occurred the day after the first load of refugees arrived. Although relatively insignificant, it pointed up the need to maintain liaison and unity of command. Pendleton officials said in their description of the event that the first aircraft arrived in the middle of the night (0200) with no prior notice and that no processing occurred until the next morning, while El Toro officers reported that the "First aircraft arrived Marine Corps Air Station El Toro approximately 1000 (local), processing smooth, no significant problems."[60] Why the two commands disagreed over this minor point cannot be explained, but it does illustrate the ease with which confusion and disagreements can occur. Add to that mixture the ingredient of multiple commanders, and the results could be confounding. In this particular operation, one more commander joined the chain of command when headquarters directed the commanding general of the 3d Marine Aircraft Wing to provide air support. In response, Major General William R. Quinn ordered Marine Aircraft Group 16 to ". . . provide helicopter support for Operation New Arrival to consist of one VIP configured CH-46 and one UH-1E on strip alert at MCAF Camp Pendleton from 0800-1700 daily, Monday through Friday, under the operational control of Marine Aircraft Group 16 Detachment." Fortunately, the addition of another commander did not alter the command structure or the spirit of cooperation.[61]

Despite the fairly complex chain of command and multiple commands involved, the Marines quickly and handily constructed seven camps in the Cristianitos-Camp Talega area and one camp in the San Onofre area. This exceeded the requirements contained in the original order which stated, "Construct five tent camps in the Camp Talega-Cristianitos Areas with the capability of billeting and feeding approximately 18,000 refugees; billet and feed approximately 4,000 more refugees in quonset huts in Camp Talega and San Onofre."[62] Ultimately, General Graham's Marines would erect more than 1,000 tents and process more than 50,000 refugees. The most difficult period would be the first week when the refugee population increased from 800 to 18,000 in five days. He explained some of the challenges: "A lot of people don't understand when you say you put up 1,100 tents. It has no impact on them. It's only when you tell them that a tent weighs 360 pounds and that it takes about ten men to unpackage it and to get all of the poles and all of the guide wires, and manhandle this thing and erect it; and it takes thirty, thirty-five minutes for a good crew to erect one tent."[63]

The sizeable cost involved in erecting and overseeing a city within a city also indicated the effort expended. The total operational cost of $15.5 million included necessities: refuse collection and disposal, $84,456; water, $28,497; sewage disposal, $58,761; and electricity, $62,146. In and of themselves, these statistics do not reveal the most significant factor, that the entire west coast Marine Corps organization participated in this operation. The carpenter shop alone, "used 216,000 board feet of lumber, 4,500 sheets of plywood and 2,850 pounds of nails."[64]

On 29 April, General Cushman stated that the Marine Corps' involvement and purpose in this operation was twofold: to establish a port of entry at MCAS El Toro and to create a refugee center at Camp Pendleton. The Marine Corps accomplished both goals within the first week of the operation. General Graham was instrumental in achieving the second goal by overseeing and coordinating the building and sustaining of the camps. Still, all refugee matters had to be coordinated with the Senior Civil Coordinator, Mr. Thorne, whose responsibilities included processing the evacuees and managing all of the participating civilian agencies. Both men set up their own internal organization which for General Graham eventually consisted of 77 officers and 1,205 Marines. Graham placed Colonel John F. Roche III in charge of this organization, entitled New Arrivals Military Coordination Center.

Within this structure, General Graham created an operations section which oversaw the movement of the refugee from El Toro to his new, albeit, temporary home. Additionally, it contained a security section

Department of Defense Photos (USMC) A357525 and A357508
Vietnamese children learn American ways fast. Both of the children, above and below, are assisted by members of Operation New Arrival at Camp Pendleton.

which provided for the safety of all occupants and camp workers, and various other support elements such as refugee affairs, communications, logistics, and medical.[65]

Once organized, this staffing structure functioned smoothly and efficiently. After Colonel George A. Merrill and Colonel Robert W. Calvert and the 1st and 7th Engineer Battalions, assisted by the 1st Shore Party Battalion, completed the camp construction on 4 May, it simply became a matter of improving and refining the product. Colonel Roche, the officer-in-charge, wrote: "The Herculean task of completing a camp of 18,000 people was accomplished in less than six days. The accommodations though Spartan at first, were continually expanded and improved, providing not only the necessities of life but also many comforts and amenities for the refugee population."[66]

The day after the completion of the last camp (on 5 May), the former Vice President of South Vietnam, Nguyen Cao Ky, arrived.* Four days later, the camp population peaked at 18,608,** and then the sense of urgency that had gripped the Marines since their last-minute notification, began to subside. It gradually turned into a daily routine of insuring that the refugees had everything they needed including a locally produced Vietnamese newspaper. The daily routine was somewhat altered on 30 June when the senior military coordinator retired from the Marine Corps, but General Graham quickly returned to his former position. On 2 July, the Marine Corps recalled him to active duty.[67]

The refugee center continued in operation well beyond the arrival of the last refugee in mid-July 1975. Between mid-May and the end of July, Mr. Thorne and his civilian organization found new homes and sponsors for 29,135 evacuees, in effect, freedom and a new

---

*Colonel Woodham related the events surrounding Vice President Ky's arrival and how Camp Pendleton had received detailed guidance from the State Department and Headquarters Marine Corps on how to behave. Despite specific instructions to all concerned to the contrary, Ky was still waited upon as though royalty and served his meal the first day of his arrival. Woodham said, "A Marine captain had made an independent moral decision that 'no vice-president' of an allied nation would have to stand in line for his food. He was immediately relieved and returned to his base." Unfortunately Colonel Woodham gained knowledge of this by watching the evening news. Upon calling the camp, Colonel Coffman, its commander, replied that the story was false. Shortly thereafter a return call from the camp revealed that the evening news report was indeed correct. Woodham Comments.

**Actually, the camp complex reached its maximum occupancy on 13 July at 20,048, but this came after an increase in the size of the original facilities. NewArr AAR.

Department of Defense Photo (USMC) A357523
Former South Vietnamese Vice President Ky enjoys the attention of the media. His presence and the nation's interest created a media challenge for BGen Graham and his staff.

beginning. Yet despite these relocations, Camp Pendleton still housed more than 18,000 Vietnamese and Cambodians*. By October, less than three months later, all but a few hundred refugees had been placed. In the final report, Colonel Roche stated, "On 31 October, the last eleven Thai Dam refugees departed and the Camp Pendleton portion of Operation 'New Arrivals' was completed—mission accomplished."[68]

By September, the New Arrival Task Force had become so organized that Colonel Roche issued a phasedown plan. In part, it said that phasedown would begin about 15 September and be conducted in increments. The plan projected 1 November as the closeout date for all refugee operations.[69] The camp officially closed on 15 November.

Certainly more than satisfied with the accomplishments of his Marines, General Graham noted in his summary of lessons learned that the paucity of available information on refugee operations and the dual chain of command caused him numerous problems

---

*Included in this total were a few hundred Cambodians evacuated during Operation Eagle Pull.

throughout the operation.** To eliminate this in the future, he encouraged the publication of a manual on

---

**General Graham in recent comments on this operation singled out two officers who contributed significantly to the success of this operation and he felt deserved recognition. He related that: "Colonel George A. Merrill was directly responsible for organizing and obtaining the logistical support for the refugee camps. For the first few critical weeks of the operation, he was instrumental in establishing the tent camps as well as the billeting, messing, and sanitation facilities and the myriad associated details. Without his efforts to ensure that these necessities were in place and functioning in an exceptionally short period of time, Operation New Arrival could have encountered major difficulties and the inevitable backlash of criticism from the national and world news media.

"Lieutenant Colonel Arthur P. Brill, Jr., found himself in the unique position of having to deal with the media. He was the Base Public Affairs Officer and a few days after the arrival of the refugees, it became obvious that the public affairs aspect of the operation would have a major impact on the image of the Marine Corps and the Administration. Well over 100 reporters from the major wire services, the press, television and radio, both national and international, descended on Camp Pendleton, clamoring for information on the refugees. It was equally obvious that I did not have the time to deal with them. I therefore assigned Lieutenant Colonel Brill to the camp on a full-time basis. His handling of the media was superb and it resulted in outstanding and positive news coverage throughout the operation." Graham Comments.

Department of Defense Photo (USMC) 8607521

One of thousands of satisfied customers, this Amerasian child is packed and ready to go. The Marines helped to introduce more than 50,000 refugees into American society.

this type of operation: "In any future operations of a like nature, . . . there must be a clearly defined chain of command with full authority and responsibility vested in a single individual."*⁷⁰

Ultimately, it came down to command and control and the results proved that nothing can supplant good organization and enthusiasm, especially when dealing with unfamiliar situations. General Graham underscored the knowledge and experience the Marine Corps had gained as a result of Operation New Arrival (whose name had been changed three times before this final choice) when he said, "We've refined that process a thousand-fold since then and we're not doing what we were doing in the early stages."⁷¹ The Marine Corps learned a lot about refugee operations over the course of six months and in the process, helped to move nearly 50,000 South Vietnamese and Cambodians into the mainstream of American society.**

---

*To date, no such manual has been published.

**The U.S. Marine Corps, constituting one-sixth of the nation's Naval Service members, in 1975 processed over one-third of the Indochina refugees in less than seven months.

PART VI
AFTER 'VIETNAM'

CHAPTER 13
Recovery of the SS *Mayaguez*

The Mayaguez *Crisis—The Initial Decisions—Assault Preparations—The First Assault Wave*
The Linkup—The Second Wave—The Retrograde—The Aftermath

While General Graham and his staff discussed expanding the refugee facility at Camp Pendleton, on 12 May 1975, the SS *Mayaguez* steamed off the coast of Cambodia, its crew not suspecting that they would become the center of world attention for the next five days. Nor did they realize that the approaching Cambodian gunboats intended to halt, board, and seize their ship.

The ship's captain, called a master, Charles T. Miller, recorded in the *Mayaguez's* log book what happened: "On May 12, 1975 at approximately 1410 hours the vessel was challenged by Cambodian gunboat P128. At 1420 hours reduced to maneuvering speed and gunboat fires antiaircraft machine guns across starboard bow.... 1435 [hours] vessel boarded by 7 armed men carrying AK 47s, shoulder held rocket launchers, and grenade launchers."[1]

The *Mayaguez* Crisis

When informed of the Cambodian action, President Ford decided on a quick response. He notified the Joint Chiefs of Staff of his desire to react to this piracy in the swiftest manner possible. Ron Nessen, the President's press secretary, said failure to release the crew and their vessel "would have the most serious consequences."[2] Symbolically, the seizure occurred exactly one month after the Marines of III MAF evacuated the last Americans from Cambodia. America seemed determined to avoid another "*Pueblo* crisis," even if it meant a military response.* Senator John Sparkman, chairman of the Senate Foreign Relations Committee, declared "We ought to go after it, . . . We should get that ship back . . . anyway that we can."[3]

Ultimately, the President elected to attempt to get the ship back by using his military option. Although a joint service operation and rescue, it would be the Marines of III MAF who would attempt to rescue the *Mayaguez's* crew and the *Mayaguez*, by employing two simultaneous and coordinated raids. The complexity and awkwardness of the command relationships in this joint military venture became further clouded by the lack of intelligence on the crew's whereabouts. For most of the crisis, no one in the joint chain of command knew with any certainty where the Cambodians had taken the crew and the absence of this information seriously affected all of the participants' decisions, and at times even obscured their objectives. It was, at a minimum, a very difficult situation, made worse at times by the confusing and complicated operational chain of command.[4]

At 1400 on 12 May, the *Mayaguez* and its crew were in international waters near the coast of the new Khmer Rouge "republic" (renamed Kampuchea by the victorious Communists). Despite the fact that the *Mayaguez* was well beyond Cambodia's territorial waters, within an hour it had been fired upon, boarded, and seized. Enroute from Hong Kong to Sattahip, Thailand, the *Mayaguez* and its crew ended their day not at the pier in Sattahip but at anchor near a Cambodian island called Poulo Wai, held against their will by armed Cambodians.[5]

The American Embassy in Jakarta, Indonesia, quickly relayed this fact to Washington and to the National Military Command Center at the Pentagon: "At 0830Z (1530 local), 12 May 1975, the Delta Exploration Company in Jakarta received a distress message from the SS *Mayaguez*, a US containership."[6] Within hours (some have argued too many hours), the United States began surveillance of the merchant ship using P-3 reconnaissance flights out of the Royal Thai Air Base at Utapao. This coverage continued for the duration of the incident, a result of the Joint Chiefs' decision to maintain contact with the ship's crew. However, from the moment of seizure until implementation of the JCS order nearly five hours elapsed. Most of the delay can be attributed to the time required to assess the situation and decide on an initial course of action. This took nearly three hours.

Immediately after reaching the decision, the JCS ordered via phone that air reconnaissance flights begin. The surveillance aircraft tracked the ship's movement during the next 12 hours, from the point of seizure near Poulo Wai Island to Koh Tang—Tang is Cambodian for island—where the ship's crew, as directed by the Cambodians, dropped anchor in 100 feet of water at about noon on Tuesday, 13 May. This

---
*The *Pueblo* was a U.S. Navy intelligence ship captured by the North Koreans in 1968.

238

anchorage, only a mile from Koh Tang, would become the focus of a good deal of diplomacy and military planning. Eventually, it would be the site of one of two raids conducted to rescue the crew. The other location would be the island off the ship's bow, the unknown and unfamiliar Koh Tang.*

The Initial Decisions

The Cambodian seizure of the *Mayaguez*, occurring just two weeks after the evacuation of Saigon, caught the U.S. by surprise. Distressed by this act of aggression, President Ford faced a difficult situation: how to negotiate with a country the United States did not recognize and one whose most recent military victory had forced America to close its Embassy and flee. Under these circumstances, it seemed to many that force would be the only means by which to effect a rescue of the crew. As a result, Washington placed U.S. forces in the Western Pacific on alert while the President attempted to secure the crew's release through diplomatic means.

The forces that had participated in Operation Frequent Wind two weeks earlier and the forces placed on alert for the recovery of the *Mayaguez* were one and the same. Despite the fact that his ships had scattered to various ports in the Pacific, Vice Admiral George P. Steele, the Seventh Fleet commander, knew that a military response to the *Mayaguez* contingency would involve the Seventh Fleet and its naval forces. Upon receiving orders from Admiral Noel A. M. Gayler, CinCPac, via his immediate superior, Admiral Maurice F. Weisner, CincPacFlt, to prepare to participate in the rescue of the container ship *Mayaguez*, Steele immediately notified his commanders to undertake whatever action necessary to ready their forces for a military response to the crisis. To expedite their preparations, Admiral Steele directed them to proceed immediately to the Gulf of Thailand, to the vicinity of Koh Tang, off the Cambodian coast. On 13 May, he ordered the ships nearest the crisis scene, the guided missile destroyer *Henry B. Wilson* (DDG 7), the escort destroyer *Harold E. Holt* (DE 1074), the stores ship *Vega* (AF 59), and the carrier *Coral Sea* (CVA 43) to proceed immediately to the waters off Kompong Som, Cambodia's main port.[7]

Admiral Gayler designated the Commander of United States Support Activities Group/Seventh Air Force, Lieutenant General John J. Burns, Jr., USAF, as the on-scene operational commander and the central coordinating authority. Marines returning to Okinawa and Japan with their respective amphibious ready groups, also received guidance from the Joint Chiefs of Staff. Passed via CinCPac, the orders directed them to reverse course and proceed to the Gulf of Thailand. Captain Edward J. "Jim" Ritchie, a "Lady Ace" CH-46 pilot returning to Futema, remembered that moment very vividly: "I was on the flight deck preflighting my helicopter for a flight when all of a sudden the ship made a hard port turn and reversed course. The turn was so sudden and severe that I had to grab hold of the helicopter to keep from falling. I later learned the reason for the quick change was the *Mayaguez*."[8] Within 24 hours, other ships and Marines in the Pacific received the word to get underway or deploy. One of these ships, *Midway* (CVA 41), was ordered to increase speed to 25 knots and anticipate action in the vicinity of Cambodia. Additionally, CinCPac directed the *Hancock* and its escorts to leave Subic Bay for the Gulf of Thailand.[9]

While the Seventh Fleet commander communicated his intentions to his subordinates, General Burns directed his staff to plan for the immediate rescue of the *Mayaguez's* 40-man crew.* He chose U.S. Air Force Colonel Loyd J. Anders, deputy commander for operations of the 56th Special Operations Wing, to head the operational task force, and instructed him to deploy to Utapao Air Base from Nakhon Phanom. In all likelihood the Joint Chiefs of Staff (JCS) and Pacific Air Force (PacAF) Headquarters chose Utapao, located on the southeastern coast of Thailand, because of its proximity to Koh Tang. General David C. Jones, in his capacity as acting chairman of the Joint Chiefs of Staff, ordered all of the Seventh Air Force's heavy helicopters to fly to Utapao. They included nine HH-53s (two others were kept on ground alert in Korat and three more were unflyable due to maintenance problems) and 10 CH-53s (four others were unavailable because they needed repairs). The "Jolly Greens" (HH-53s, nicknamed "Super Jolly" or "Jolly Green Giant") designated for redeployment to Utapao belonged to the 40th Aerospace Rescue and Recovery Squadron (40th ARRS) while the CH-53s, carrying the same

---

*Despite the surveillance flights, the operation's commanders never could pinpoint the crew's whereabouts.

*Admiral Steele recalled the consequences of the decision to react quickly: "The sad part of the *Mayaguez* evolution is that we had sufficient force coming up with the Seventh Fleet, after it had been turned around from the evacuation of Vietnam stand down, to seize Southern Cambodia. I begged for another day or two, rather than commit forces piecemeal as we did . . . . The idea that we could use U.S. Air Force air police and Air Force helicopters as an assault force appears to me as ridiculous today as it did then." Steele Comments.

nicknames and using the radio call sign "Knife," were owned by the 21st Special Operations Squadron (21st SOS).[10]

These helicopters departed Korat and Nakhon Phanom the evening of 13 May for Utapao. Seventh Air Force Headquarters ordered the 21st SOS CH-53s to transport the Nakhon Phanom base security police. General Burns intended to deploy these men as an early answer to the need for ground security should Admiral Gayler order him to immediately effect the rescue of the crew.

In General Burns' initial operations order issued a little after midnight on 14 May 1975, he directed the use of 125 Air Force Security Police as helicopter landing zone security stating, "The Airborne Mission Commander will establish contact with 7AF/TACC on the HF command net and control the mission as directed by ComUSSAG/7AF."*[11] Three hours later, after Admiral Gayler's chief of staff, Lieutenant General William G. Moore, Jr., USAF, talked to General Burns on the phone, Admiral Gayler amended General Burns' operating order by changing "USAF Security Police" to read "USMC GSF personnel," and adding "Command and control will be maintained by CinCPac who will be acting under direction from JCS (NMCC)."**[12]

During the initial hours of this crisis, because of the Marine Corps' continued involvement in post-evacuation and refugee-related operations, the combination of Air Force ground and air assets in Thailand represented the only option available to implement immediately an NMCC order to recover the SS *Mayaguez* and its crew. The first of the helicopters designated for this possible mission departed Korat at 1943 followed by a second flight which departed Nakhon Phanom at 2000. A half-hour later, Knife 01 and his wingmen in three CH-53s also launched from Nakhon Phanom. Shortly after takeoff, 40 miles west of the field, Knife 01-3 disappeared from departure control's radar screen. The 21st SOS helicopter had crashed, killing all on board. Its passengers, 18 air police and crew of five became the first casualties of the *Mayaguez* rescue operation.[13]

The two helicopters that Colonel Anders had stationed at Korat Air Base as search and air rescue attempted to assist at the crash scene, but once the pilots determined that no assistance was possible, they proceeded directly to Utapao and joined the others. With their arrival, the initial assault force consisted of 11 helicopters: six HH-53s and five CH-53s. The HH-53 or "Jolly Green" (call sign designator "JG") possessed an inflight refueling capability and the CH-53C or "Knife" (call sign designator "K"), the Air Force version of the Marine Corps' "Sea Stallion," carried external fuel tanks which extended its range capabilities. Considering the distance from Utapao to Koh Tang, range (based on weight and fuel consumption) would be a critical factor in deciding what forces to employ and where and by what means to deploy them.

By the time these helicopters arrived in Utapao, the President and his staff had decided to proceed with the military option with final authorization and the order to execute to be delivered from President Ford via JCS. Later that evening, sometime between 2355 on 13 May and 0255 the next day, General Burns phoned CinCPac's chief of staff, Lieutenant General William G. Moore, Jr., to discuss his options. In seeking a decision, he offered his recommendation: "I believe that the Marines are the preferred troops for this mission and if the two hours later time which they can make is acceptable, I recommend their use with a planned insertion time of 0050Z."[14]

Concurring with this recommendation, Admiral Gayler decided to use the Marines. He had already alerted Major General Carl W. Hoffman to expect orders on short notice which would call for his air contingency battalion landing team and its support elements to assist General Burns and USSAG forces in recovering the *Mayaguez*. General Hoffman had chosen Colonel John M. Johnson, the III MAF G-3, to command the task group, 79.9.*** It contained two separate elements known as task units. The infantry battalion, BLT 2/9, under the command of Lieutenant Colonel Randall W. Austin, bore the task unit designator 79.9.1, while the second element carried the designation 79.9.2. Major Raymond E. Porter, the battalion's executive officer, commanded this smaller force, comprised of Company D(-)(reinforced) of 1st Battalion, 4th Marines. With BLT 2/9 on Okinawa and Company D, 1st Battalion, 4th Marines in the MAU camp in Subic, getting the task group to the scene

---

*The Airborne Mission Commander or AMC's role included the responsibility of serving as the airborne on-scene coordinator. He would perform that function while aloft in an EC-130 known as an airborne battlefield command and control center or ABCCC.

**National Military Command Center (NMCC), located in the Pentagon, was responsible for coordinating and controlling military responses to international crises such as the illegal seizure of an American vessel on the high seas.

***Colonel John F. Roche III, the 31st MAU commander, mentioned that at the time of Colonel Johnson's selection to lead the rescue mission, Colonel Johnson was "unassigned awaiting change of station." Roche Comments.

of the action quickly became General Hoffman's top priority.[15]

When the 2d Battalion, 9th Marines received word that it had been chosen to deploy to Thailand, it was still in the training cycle. In fact at that precise moment, it was in the midst of a training exercise on northern Okinawa in the Central Training Area. Less than five hours later, by 0200 14 May, the battalion had arrived back at its Camp Schwab base, and along with its support elements had prepared to mount out, still uncertain of its destination. Just 15 minutes prior to its arrival at Camp Schwab, the battalion landing team's artillery elements had left for Kadena Airbase. In the ensuing three hours, all of the units attached to BLT 2/9 made their way to Kadena, with the last one arriving at 0545. The command element launched first at 0530, followed by the main body at 0615. They flew to Utapao on Air Force C-141s.[16]

While the preparations on Okinawa began to take shape, the Marines of Company D, 1st Battalion, 4th Marines completed the packing of their gear and at 0030 started to board an Air Force C-141 at the Naval Air Station Cubi Point. Led by Major Porter and their company commander, Captain Walter J. Wood, the Marines of Company D landed at Utapao at 0445, just as the first elements of BLT 2/9 started arriving at the Kadena passenger terminal. Accompanying the Marines from Subic on the flight to Thailand were 12 volunteers, six sailors from the *Duluth* and six civilians from the *Greenville Victory*, a Military Sealift Command ship, who had agreed to use their technical expertise to sail the *Mayaguez*.[17]

Upon their arrival in Utapao, Major Porter and the officers of Company D met with members of General Burns' staff. At this meeting, the staff informed them that their company of Marines would board the *Mayaguez* from Air Force helicopters. In addition, Major Porter and Company D learned that from this point on, they should consider themselves in a 30-minute standby status. Less than six hours later, at 1200, they boarded helicopters but remained on the ramp, waiting for word to launch. Two hours later, still sitting in the helicopters, they received orders to disembark. Major Porter later learned that General Burns had cancelled the mission for that day.* The US-SAG commander believed that insufficient time remained to complete the recovery before sunset and he had no desire to attempt it at night. Thus, the Marines continued in a standby status until 0200 the next day when the USSAG staff finally completed its plan for the recapture of the *Mayaguez*.[18]

Boarding the *Mayaguez* from Air Force helicopters would be no easy feat, and because of the variables involved, additional preparations would have to be made.** First, and foremost, Major Porter's command element had to deal with incompatibility factors. The *Mayaguez's* cargo consisted of containers which covered all of the main deck. Because of the weight of the HH/CH-53s and the distribution and stress characteristics of the aluminum containers, planners deemed a landing on the *Mayaguez* unsafe. Consequently, the Marines would have to jump or rappel from the helicopters onto the cargo, and then using some type of ramp or bridge, move from container to container until they could lower themselves onto the ship's deck. From there they would move quickly to secure the critical areas of the ship.

For almost 24 hours, this concept did not change. Admiral Weisner's initial orders to Admiral Steele at 1014 on 14 May did not foresee using Steele's ship, the *Holt*, as a boarding platform for the Marines. He reached this conclusion based on the assumption that the *Holt* would not arrive in the area until sometime after sunrise on 15 May. Later, on the evening of 14 May, when General Burns and his staff learned of the favorable change in the *Holt's* ETA, they decided to use it to board the *Mayaguez*. In the intervening period, Major Porter and his Marines continued to prepare for the boarding of the *Mayaguez* from Air Force helicopters.[19]

At 0730, the time the Task Group 79.9 commander, Colonel Johnson, arrived at Utapao—about three hours after Major Porter—Marines had their then-assigned task well in hand. At this point, Colonel Johnson learned that his mission to recover the *Mayaguez* would probably be expanded. It would include the requirement to "seize, occupy, and defend Koh Tang," and rescue and recover any crewmembers found there.[20]

While Colonel Johnson and his forces moved south to Thailand, the Navy repositioned its ships and recon-

---

*According to one account, President Ford did not issue the order to begin the operation until early morning on 15 May, 0345 Cambodian time: "At 4:45 [p.m., Eastern Daylight Savings Time, 14 May] . . . the President issued the orders for one Marine assault force to seize and hold Koh Tang, and for another Marine force . . . to board the *Mayaguez*." Roy Rowan, *The Four Days of Mayaguez* (New York: W. W. Norton & Co., 1975), p. 176.

**Admiral Steele revealed in his comments: "I suggested that the *Mayaguez* be covered with tear gas in order to subdue whoever was on board, even the crew could have been there, or some of them, and we did not want to endanger them." Steele Comments.

Members of Company F, 2d Battalion, 9th Marines assemble into heliteams at the joint operations airfield at Utapao, Thailand, on 14 May for insertion onto Koh Tang. They would have to wait 14 hours before the first real assault wave took off in eight Air Force helicopters bound for the small Cambodian island, 195 miles southeast of Utapao.

noitered the area with patrol planes from Task Force 72. At the same time, the Air Force launched its tactical aircraft. The fighter and attack planes had orders to prevent, if possible without endangering the crew, the Cambodians from moving the *Mayaguez* and/or its crew to the mainland, specifically, the port of Kompong Som. Shortly thereafter, less than two hours after Colonel Johnson's arrival, an Air Force F-4 pilot spotted a fishing vessel carrying what appeared to be Caucasians. At approximately 0900 on 14 May, the pilot attempted to stop the vessel as it sped toward the Cambodian coastline. He fired shots over its bow, but avoided any close shots for fear of hitting the passengers. His efforts met with no success as the boat ignored the warning shots and continued on its course toward Kompong Som. During this unusual and uncertain activity on the morning of 14 May, General Burns and his staff continued their planning sessions in an attempt to arrive at the best course of action to rescue the ship and its crew without any further loss of life. They worked with current, but oftentimes incomplete information.[21]

Assault Preparations

After Colonel Johnson and his command group arrived, the option to use Marines in the assault force to secure the island gained momentum. Obviously, once on Koh Tang, the Marines could provide ground security for the Air Force evacuation helicopters. Yet by the time Lieutenant Colonel Austin and his staff landed at 0945, the final decision to use Marines still had not been made. As Austin's individual Marine elements continued to land, Colonel Johnson briefed the battalion commander on the tactical situation and then waited for further word. At 1300, one hour before Austin's final elements reached Utapao on board a C-141, General Burns' staff passed the word to Colonel Johnson that the mission would definitely include rescue of the ship's crew. Staff members provided little additional information and no details on the crew's exact location. Colonel Johnson assigned Lieutenant Colonel Austin and BLT 2/9 responsibility for seizing Koh Tang and recovering the *Mayaguez's* crew. The task was simple to assign, but with a dearth of intelligence, extremely difficult to execute. According

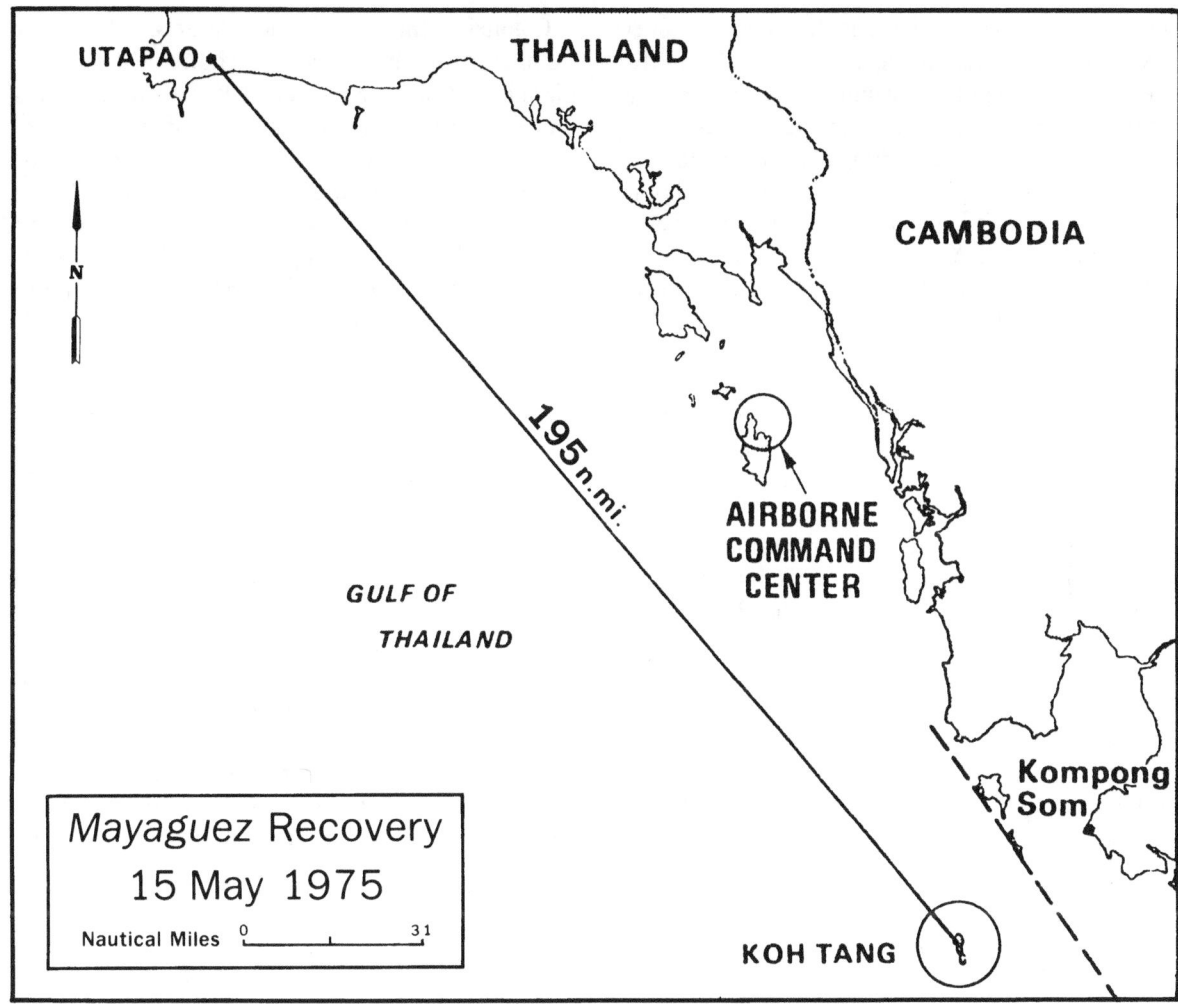

Map adapted from Urey W. Patrick,"The Mayaguez Operation, Final Report" (Washington: Center for Naval Analyses, 1977)

to the report of a later Congressional investigation, "Despite the availability of various assets and the apparent uncertainty concerning the location of the *Mayaguez* crew, little attempt appears to have been made to use photography or other means to verify reports or obtain additional information."*22

---

*Admiral Steele commented on the actions he took and those actions he requested which were denied: "As soon as the *Mayaguez* seizure had taken place and we were informed of military action to be taken to recover her, I turned [around] the *Coral Sea* task group which was enroute to the Coral Sea battle observance in Australia—they were about to enter Lombok Strait at the time. Shortly thereafter, we requested permission to fly reconnaissance flights in the area, and later, specifically over the island of Koh Tang. Despite repeated requests to do this, it was denied until so late that the reconnaissance flight's photographic results could not be processed in advance of the actual assault on the island. I think that this is another example of a disastrous attempt to micromanage, from distant headquarters with inadequately trained staff, large operations in which communications play so great a part." Steele Comments.

Austin's first decision dealt with this scarcity of intelligence and his need for additional information about the island and its terrain. This became a formidable task in itself as every possible source was sought and used, from Cambodian refugees in Thailand, to a former Cambodian naval officer, to an oil company employee familiar with the Cambodian coastal waters, all with little success. On top of this, no one possessed a tactical map of the island.23

In an attempt to fill the void, an Army U-21 took Lieutenant Colonel Austin, his S-3, and two other officers to Koh Tang, 195 miles from Utapao, for an airborne inspection of the island, but the Air Force restricted the flight's altitude to 6,000 feet. The Air Force imposed the restriction in order to avoid drawing undue attention to the flight or worse yet, enemy fire. This severe limitation became even more critical when it was discovered that the only photographic equipment available was a Marine's pocket camera.

During the overflight of Koh Tang, Lieutenant Colonel Austin saw open areas on opposite sides of the northern end of the island that could be used as landing zones. Here where the island significantly narrowed, the two potential sites, consisting of relatively flat terrain cut from the jungle, offered access by air and possible access by sea. Due to the island's extensive foliage, Lieutenant Colonel Austin had no other choice. He had to land his assault forces here, even though he knew almost nothing about the enemy.[24]

Meanwhile at Utapao, Colonel Johnson was experiencing similar frustrations in his attempts to gather intelligence. Much to his dismay, he was spending most of his time driving to USSAG/Seventh Air Force's forward headquarters on the other side of the base to either answer secure voice phone calls or questions from General Burn's staff. Neither the calls nor the questions contributed anything to his planning and intelligence-gathering efforts. Unfortunately, these interruptions continued into the early evening, long after Lieutenant Colonel Austin returned from his reconnaissance flight at 1500. Only the final planning conference at 1900 seemed to halt the interruptions, but nothing reduced the frustration caused by the physical separation of General Burns' staff's headquarters and Colonel Johnson's command post.[25]

Colonel Johnson, Colonel Anders, Lieutenant Colonel Austin, and Major Porter attended the 1900 planning session with General Burns' staff. At this meeting, they discussed and decided upon a final course of action. The plan entailed the use of eight helicopters inserting approximately 180 BLT 2/9 Marines onto Koh Tang's eastern and western zones with the first helicopter landing at 0542 on 15 May. Simultaneously, 57 Marines of Company D, 1st Battalion, 4th Marines and 11 volunteers (The Air Force amended the original composition of six sailors and six Military Sealift Command [MSC] personnel to two corpsmen, two Air Force explosive ordnance demolition specialists, one Army intelligence officer, and six MSC seamen) would board three helicopters and fly to the *Holt*. Company D's orders reflected the most recent change to the original plan for boarding the *Mayaguez*. Having learned that the destroyer escort *Holt* would arrive in the area in time, General Burns decided that the helicopters would not insert the Marines onto the container ship, but instead deliver them to the *Holt* which then would be used as a platform from which to board the *Mayaguez*. At a midnight meeting which Major Porter attended, General Burns' Utapao staff made some last-minute adjustments to the *Holt* rescue plan and then declared it complete.

This is the best reconnaissance picture of Koh Tong the commander of the 2d Battalion, 9th Marines could obtain. At right is the wing of the U-21 from which a glimpse of the island was captured as LtCol Randall W. Austin and his staff rode at 6,000-feet altitude.

Photo courtesy of Maj Charles D. Melson

With that done, Major Porter returned to the hangar, briefed Company D, and then led his *Mayaguez* insertion force to the waiting helicopters.[26]

The operational plan called for General Burns to exercise control of all aspects of the assault, including the Marines under Colonel Johnson's charge. Having decided to remain in Nakhon Phanom, General Burns' ability to maintain command and control of the planned activity in the Gulf of Thailand would depend almost exclusively on the actions of the airborne mission commander (AMC). That unnamed Air Force officer (no records reveal his name) would discharge his tactical duties from an airborne battlefield command and control center (ABCCC) located in a specially equipped EC-130. Normally, Colonel Johnson, the task group commander, would have been the on-scene commander, but due to the scarcity of helicopters, he opted to wait until the second wave for insertion. By waiting, he effectively relinquished control of his Marines to Lieutenant Colonel Austin and the airborne mission commander. Until he could land on Koh Tang, this command and control status would remain unchanged. Although concerned about this awkward arrangement and his absence from the first assault wave, Colonel Johnson expected, during what he thought would be a relatively short wait at Utapao, to be able to advise General Burns in Nakhon Phanom and through him influence the tactical situation on Koh Tang.[27] Unintentionally, General Burns increased Colonel Johnson's anxieties about the command structure when he stated that, "The Airborne Mission Commander in ABCCC will coordinate the strike activities and receive directions from ComUSSAG."[28]

"Receive directions" would soon become the operative words thanks in large part to the range and sophistication of the communications network which was used. General Burns and even the Joint Chiefs of Staff would be able to talk to the battlefield via the ABCCC. Unbelievably, Colonel Johnson, just 200 hundred miles away, could not. Eventually, oversaturation of the network's frequencies by various higher headquarters seeking insignificant or irrelevant information rendered this technologically sophisticated system of communication and control ineffective, further complicating Colonel Johnson's unenviable situation.

Yet with plans complete and ready for implementation, including the news that Navy tactical aircraft from the *Coral Sea* could provide additional on-scene close air support, the Marines concerned themselves with more important matters, the impending mission.

At 0230, already assembled, they boarded their assigned helicopters. All 11 helicopters took off from Utapao at 0415. Three HH-53s, using call signs "JG 11, 12, and 13," carried the boarding party for the *Mayaguez* while five CH-53s and three HH-53s flew the assault force to Koh Tang. The three helicopters carrying Major Porter's team dropped it onto the *Holt* between 0550 and 0625.[29]

The Air Force chose the HH-53 for this mission because of its functional characteristics, especially its refueling capability. An Air Force after action report pointed up the important differences: "The HH-53 is air refuelable, has 450 gallon foam-filled tip tanks, a tail mini-gun with armor plating, and two waist mini-guns. The CH-53 is not air refuelable, but has 650-gallon non-foam-filled tip tanks and two mini-guns, although no tail gun.*"[30] Thus the HH-53, with its refueling capability, could remain in the battle area indefinitely as long as it had access to a HC-130. In this operation, it would have access to fuel from a Lockheed Hercules using the call sign "King."

The First Assault Wave

To accomplish the transfer of the assault elements led by Captain Walter J. Wood to the *Holt*, the Air Force HH-53s, because of the size of the ship's helipad, placed only their front wheels on the ship's pad and hovered. Captain Wood described the process:

> The helicopters could only set down their nose wheels and basically hover. As they set down in this fashion, we all exited the helicopters through the starboard doorway. This entire process took approximately 15-20 minutes for three helicopters to disembark the boarding party.[31]

At the beginning of the operation, the *Holt* stood 12 miles northwest of the island. Once the helicopter pilots had safely debarked the boarding party, the *Holt* started moving very slowly in the direction of the *Mayaguez*. Everyone waited and watched as the Air Force saturated the captive ship with chemical agents.** Upon observing the last A-7 complete its bombing run, the *Holt* pulled alongside the *Mayaguez* and Major Porter's assault force prepared to board the ship.

Captain Wood described what happened next: "Once the boarding party was on board the *Holt*, I

---

*As noted earlier in the text in comments from Lieutenant Colonel Edward A. Grimm, USSAG had attempted unsuccessfully in 1974 to obtain permission to foam the CH-53's tip tanks. Grimm Comments.

**According to Admiral Steele, "The suggestion that the captive ship be saturated with 'chemical agents' was a Seventh Fleet idea." Steele Comments.

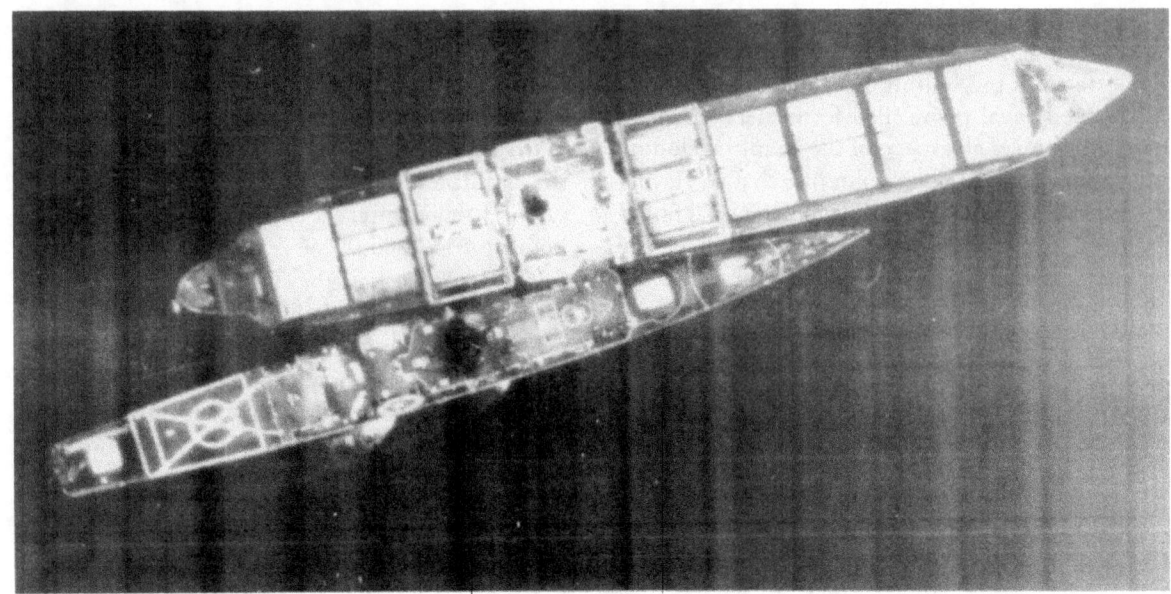

Department of Defense Photo (USMC) 711631

USS Harold E. Holt *maneuvers alongside SS* Mayaguez *to permit a boarding party from Company D, 1st Battalion, 4th Marines to seize the container ship. The Company D commander, Capt Walter J. Wood, and a squad leader, Cpl C. R. Coker, found themselves alone on the* Mayaguez *as backwash from the* Holt *pushed the two ships apart.*

met with Captain Petersen and the Executive Officer." In their discussion, they determined that the deck above *Holt's* main deck would match with the *Mayaguez's* main deck. Yet as the destroyer escort drew closer to the container ship, Captain Wood could see that both of the main decks were on the same level and so he quickly moved his boarding party down to the *Holt's* main deck. Just as they arrived there, the *Holt* slid alongside the container ship and the Company D commander told Corporal C. R. Coker, the leader of the squad designated to seize the bridge, to jump, and Captain Wood followed in trail. As they boarded, the squad leader took off for the bridge while Captain Wood proceeded aft to secure the squad's rear. As he turned around to determine the squad's progress, he beheld a most unusual sight, an empty ship save for one Marine corporal. Captain Wood remembered that eery occasion: "As I proceeded aft, I turned to my rear to view the progress of Coker's squad and the remainder of the boarding party who were supposed to secure the lines between *Holt* and *Mayaguez*. But much to my surprise I discovered that Coker and I were the only Marines on board the *Mayaguez*."[32]

Apparently the backwash created by the *Holt* coming alongside the *Mayaguez* had pushed the two ships apart just as the two Marines landed on the deck of the captive ship. Almost immediately sailors on the *Holt* threw lines to them and after considerable effort the two men lashed the ships together and the remaining members of the boarding party joined them. Company D in the ancient naval tradition, had boarded a vessel "known" to be held by armed defenders. The captain and the corporal had been on board for five minutes; the squad leader's watch read 0725 and not a shot had been fired.[33]

Once on board, using only hand signals (their gas masks precluded verbal communication), the Company D Marines moved deliberately but quickly to preassigned areas of the ship.* Securing the engine room before the Cambodians could disable the ship headed their list of priorities. This important task fell to Sergeant William J. Owens' squad which had to make its way through darkened passageways and ladderwells just to get to the gas-filled engine room. What

---

*Captain Wood recently explained how his Marines modified this procedure to accommodate the circumstances: "The boarding party was not limited to hand signals. When the line was thrown from *Holt* to *Mayaguez* and Coker and I were fumbling with it, using methods every Marine is taught during NBC training, I could communicate and ask for instructions from *Holt's* ship personnel as to how and where to secure the line. I simply lifted up my mask, shouted the question, replaced my mask, cleared it and breathed normally. For the first one to two hours above deck, this became standard practice on board the *Mayaguez*." Wood Comments.

Members of Company D, commanded by Capt Walter J. Wood, board Mayaguez. *Gas masks were worn because the ship was bombed with tear-gas cannisters by the Air Force.*

Marines await instructions after securing the Mayaguez, *which had no one on board, at 0822. The two civilians, at center, from the* Greenville Victory, *had volunteered to operate the ship and were flown to Utapao on an Air Force C-141 on the morning of 14 May.*

surprised Owen's squad, and the other squads as well, was not what they found in the engine room, but what they did not find. The ship was deserted! Having searched for booby traps and found none, the Marines declared the *Mayaguez* secure at 0822 on 15 May 1975.[34]

As the first helicopter started its descent to the *Holt*, a flight of eight Air Force helicopters in four sections approached Koh Tang.* The Air Force's after action report stated, "K 21 and K 22 were to insert their Marines on the western beach, while K 23 and 31 were to be the first into the eastern beach. The third wave, K 32 and JG 41, and the fourth wave, JG 42 and JG 43, were to follow up with insertions on the eastern beach."[35]

As the island came into full view at 0615, the pilots, based on the intelligence briefing they had received, still expected little or no opposition.** Initially, it appeared that they were right because as Knife 21 flew into the western zone with K 22 in trail, they received no enemy fire. Then as K 21 unloaded 21 Marines of Company G's 1st Platoon, including its commander, Second Lieutenant James McDaniel, "The enemy opened up on both helicopters with small arms, rockets, and mortars."[36]

With Knife 21 still in the zone, Knife 22 attempted to provide suppressive fire. Suffering the loss of an engine from the intense enemy fire, K 21 had no choice but to attempt a single engine takeoff. Successful in this effort despite additional damage to the transmission, K 21 barely cleared the treeline and eventually ditched in the ocean about a mile offshore. One of the helicopters from the third wave (K 32) rescued the crew, save for one member (Staff Sergeant Elwood Rumbaugh), who was lost at sea. After the aircraft commander of K 22 terminated his efforts to assist his wingman, and gave way to K 32, he returned to the western landing zone where he again encountered heavy fire, this time as early as 150 yards from the shoreline.[37]

During this approach, K 22 suffered severe damage including the loss of an engine and a ruptured fuel tank. Forced to abort its run because of the damage and subsequent fuel loss, Knife 22, carrying the assault company commander (Captain James H. Davis) made an emergency landing on the Thai coast, 125 miles northwest of Koh Tang and 85 miles east of Utapao. The SAR helos picked up the crew and passengers and transported them to Utapao.

Those aircraft entering the eastern zone received a no less hostile reception from the well-fortified Cambodian defenders. The first two helicopters into the eastern zone, Knife 23 and 31, encountered heavy enemy fire.***

While Knife 23 attempted to land on the eastern beach, his wingman, Knife 31, followed in trail. Both helicopters received intense fire, including automatic weapons and rocket propelled grenades (RPG). Suddenly, Knife 31's port fuel tank exploded, followed immediately by a second explosion, the result of an RPG. The round blew off a substantial portion of the cockpit, killing the copilot. K 31 crashed in the ocean about 55 meters from the island's eastern shoreline. In addition to the copilot, casualties included 10 Marines and two corpsmen killed. Five of the 10 Marine casualties initially survived the crash, but three subsequently died when they attempted to rush ashore. Enemy fire coming from the treeline, just inland of the shore, cut them down before they could reach the beach. Another Marine drowned attempting to swim to the open sea, while a fifth Marine, wounded, apparently died later near the downed helicopter. Thus only a few minutes after the first Marine had set foot

---

*Admiral Steele suggested in his comments that tactical employment of the Air Force helicopters may have been a factor in this operation: "My recollection is a bit dimmed by time, but I believe that the U.S. Air Force helicopters came in high over the island as was their normal practice, whereas Marine helicopters were trained to come in very low, and thus avoid enemy fire. I believe that this contributed to the disaster to the USAF helos that occurred." Steele Comments.

**According to First Lieutenant Terry L. Tonkin, the Marine forward air controller on this mission, the Air Force intelligence briefers told them to expect "18-20 Cambodian irregulars with families," yet a 12 May Defense Intelligence Report estimated 200 Khmer Communists with 82mm mortars, 75mm recoilless rifles, 30-caliber machine guns, and a B40 Rocket Propelled Grenade (RPG) launcher. According to Tonkin the Air Force had this report in its possession six hours before the assault began. He has always wondered why the Marines never received that briefing. Tonkin Comments. Lieutenant Colonel George E. "Jody" Strickland served at FMFPac Headquarters in Hawaii after his 1973-74 tour at the DAO in Saigon. He shared insight that he gained about what he called the "Washington/Nakhon Phanom high-tech command and control debacle." He said, "It is now clear that General Burns' staff did possess intelligence that was not provided to our Marines. Once again it appears that the proper 'clearances' were factors in denying our Marines intel. The 'Green Door' intel in General Burns' hands was never provided!" He cited as his source: FMFPac/PacAF Intel Conference. Strickland Comments.

***According to Marine Corps records, K 23 and K 31 were the first helicopters to attempt landings on Koh Tang. They began their approaches to the eastern zone at 0600, well before K 21, which landed at 0630 in the western zone. 2/9 Koh Tang Report.

Marine Corps Historical Collection

Downed CH-53s are visible in the eastern LZ at Koh Tang. At left is Knife 23, which carried 2dLt Michael A. Cicere and members of his platoon, who established defensive positions in the rocky ground to the left of the helicopter. At right is Knife 31, which was hit by an RPG round fired from the tree line at middle right. The destroyed Cambodian Swift boat, upper right, attests to the accuracy of Air Force A-7 bombing runs.

on Koh Tang, no less than nine Marines, two corpsmen, and an airman were dead.[38]

The survivors, afloat amongst the debris and flaming wreckage, opted to swim seaward and await rescue. These 10 Marines and three airmen lost most of their weapons and equipment in the crash. Two of them demonstrated exceptional initiative, resourcefulness, and courage. During the difficult swim, which lasted three and one-half hours, Private First Class Timothy W. Trebil, a fire team leader, continually encouraged and assisted others, especially the weaker swimmers. At the same time, First Lieutenant Terry L. Tonkin (the assault team's forward air controller), using an Air Force survival radio he had recovered from the crash, directed Air Force attack aircraft on bombing runs of enemy positions on the eastern half of the island. His contributions lasted until the *Wilson* plucked him and 12 other tired survivors from the sea almost four hours after they had escaped from the wreckage of Knife 31. The rescue by the *Wilson* gained added significance when the survivors discovered that the ship had happened upon them by chance. The *Wilson* had been proceeding to Koh Tang to provide naval gunfire support when a lookout spotted something floating in the water.[39]

Meanwhile, the first chopper into the eastern zone (K 23), suffered such extensive damage that it crash-landed at the water's edge. Without a moment's hesitation, the heliteam exited the aircraft and immediately set up a defensive perimeter. These Marines would be the first and last into this zone as the AMC decided to halt any further insertions. Thus, Second Lieutenant Michael A. Cicere and 20 Marines of his 3d Platoon, Company G, along with five aircrewmen, instantly became isolated, cut off from the rest of the assault forces. Wisely, the Air Force copilot, before exiting the wrecked CH-53, grabbed the emergency UHF radio. Once ashore, he used it to establish contact with the strike aircraft. With the crew and passengers of Knife 23 in a nearly untenable position, support of them suddenly became a priority. Recognizing the gravity of the situation, USSAG directed one of the *Holt* mission helicopters to effect a recovery. Jolly Green 13 made an unsuccessful attempt to rescue them at approximately 0815. Sitting on the beach for less than a minute, the HH-53 took automatic weapons fire from the treeline for the entire time. As they waited for the embattled Marines to move from their defensive perimeter to the helicopter, the pilots of JG 13 could see that only a matter of moments and

Marine Corps Historical Collection

An Air Force HH-53, JG 41, bears evidence of the resistance at Koh Tang. JG 41 made four attempts to enter the western zone and finally, on its fifth attempt, successfully unloaded 2dLt Richard H. Zales' 2d Platoon, Company G. By the end of the retrograde three of the original 14 helicopters were operational.

50 meters of beach stood between them and disaster. With recovery at this time an impossibility, Jolly Green 13 decided to abort its rescue attempt.

The four remaining helicopters in the first wave had only slightly better luck. One of these (JG 41), carrying Second Lieutenant Richard H. Zales' 2d Platoon, Company G, finally made it into the western zone at 0930 on its fifth attempt. Earlier, two other helicopters, Knife 32 and Jolly Green 42, had inserted their heliteams into that zone.*

The fourth helicopter in the first assault wave, JG 43, gave up trying to get into the site and unloaded its Marines far short of the zone. To make matters worse, this helicopter carried Lieutenant Colonel Austin, his staff, and the mortar section. Thus upon disembarking from the helicopter, they not only found themselves 1,000 to 1,200 meters southwest of the zone, but also separated from the main body.

The main body, now commanded by the Company G executive officer, First Lieutenant James D. Keith, the next senior officer present, had to expand its perimeter. While attempting to enlarge it under heavy enemy fire Lieutenant Keith also had to make contact with Austin and his 29 Marines. Besides Austin's group and Keith's 60 Marines, Second Lieutenant Cicere counted 20 Marines in the eastern zone, including one who had sustained wounds. The first wave of the assault force had numbered 180 when it left Utapao. It now stood at 109, plus five Air Force crewmembers, divided among three positions. Not until Second Lieutenant Zales and his 21 Marines landed (at 0930) would the total Marine Corps strength change, and then it would only increase to 131. These were less than ideal conditions from which to mount a raid, especially when facing a well fortified and entrenched enemy.[40]

Thus the assault forces found themselves divided into three groups, separated from their supporting elements, and without the planned buildup of fighting strength. Complicating this perilous situation was the fact that the command group was isolated, separated from the main body by hundreds of meters of rugged jungle.

Except for a man-made opening connecting the eastern half of the island's middle to the western section, heavy foliage covered every inch of the terrain. From a position south and west of this cut, the enemy directed multiple fire at the Marines in the western zone. To gain relief from this shelling, First Lieutenant Keith ordered one of his platoon commanders, Second Lieutenant McDaniel, to destroy the position. The absence of other officers in the zone made this mission even more critical; Keith could not afford to lose anyone, especially a platoon commander.

McDaniel led a reinforced squad against the Cambodians whose exact location was impossible to pinpoint because of the thick underbrush. While McDaniel and his squad attempted to identify the source of harassing automatic weapons fire, another group of Cambodians hit their flank from close range with grenades and small arms. As in the case of the initial attack, the source of this fire could not be pinpointed either because the ground level visibility extended no more than 15 feet. Surprised by the attack against the flank, McDaniel and five of his Marines sustained wounds, including Lance Corporal Ashton N. Looney of Albany, New York, who later died. In the ensuing moments, McDaniel and his patrol responded with an intense volume of fire directed at the enemy's concealed location. It forced the Cambodians to cease firing and retreat.[41]

Having witnessed the firefight and fearing an en-

---

*The number of Marines in the western zone at any set time cannot be pinpointed because official accounts vary. The description of Knife 32's insertion serves as an example of why this confusion exists. Air Force records state that Knife 32 unloaded 13 Marines, a 14th Marine was wounded and remained on board, and an Army language specialist refused to disembark. Marine Corps records reflect that 15 Marines disembarked. 2/9 Koh Tang Report. "Assault on Koh Tang," and CNA *Mayaguez* Report.

circlement of the now vulnerable squad, Lieutenant Keith decided it was time to pull them back. His decision came none too soon for almost within seconds of McDaniel's squad regaining cover within the zone's defenses, the Cambodians attacked the southern perimeter and McDaniel's Marines. The Marines of BLT 2/9 again repelled the Communists' thrust. Throughout the firefight, these Marines, who had never seen combat and who had had their training on Okinawa cut short by this mission, consistently performed with courage and self-control.* They repeatedly turned aside the enemy's attempts to overrun them. Most held a rank no higher than lance corporal.

Shortly after this incident, at approximately 0925, Lieutenant Keith finally established contact with the tactical air coordinator (airborne) (TAC[A]), flying in a holding pattern near the island, and asked for close air support. Using the battalion radio frequency, Keith discussed the possibilities. In the midst of this communication, Lieutenant Zales and his 21 Marines arrived. Keith immediately stopped talking to the airborne coordinator and told Lieutenant Zales to deploy his men on the besieged southern flank of the perimeter. Zales, ignoring the enemy fire, charged forward to his newly assigned piece of Koh Tang. Once Zales was in place, Keith resumed his conversation with the TAC(A) and personally orchestrated the Air Force strafing runs whose cannon fire kept the Cambodians at bay. Yet even with this close air support and Zales' added firepower, the Communists retained a tenacious grip on the zone. The Cambodians were so closely engaged with the Marines on the southern perimeter that the Air Force pilots did not dare drop their bombs for fear of hitting friendly lines. Literally, only meters separated the Marines from the Communists. Hand grenades vice bombs became the order of the day, but neither side could break the deadlock. For the Marines, additional forces offered the only solution to the stalemate. The buildup had to continue.[44]

This meant that the second wave had to be inserted and without delay. In the interim, neither Austin's group nor Cicere's could even consider moving from their defensive position without external support. As Lieutenant Colonel Austin said, "Our group of Marines was in serious straits because between us, we only had four rifles."[45]

The operational plan had anticipated the need for a rapid buildup of forces on the island and had specified that all of the available Air Force helicopters would be used for this express purpose, in theory an excellent idea, but in this instance difficult to implement because only a few of the transport helicopters were still operating. Of the eight helicopters in the first wave at Koh Tang, only one escaped undamaged. One had crashed at sea (Knife 21), two had crash landed on or near Koh Tang's eastern shore (Knife 23 and Knife 31), and another on Thailand's eastern shore (Knife 22). Three more (Knife 32, Jolly Green 41, and Jolly Green 42) had received such extensive damage that they were unflyable. The three helicopters used in the *Holt* insertion encountered no hostile fire and suffered no damage. However, one of the three, Jolly Green 13, subsequently suffered severe battle damage while attempting, after refueling with an HC-130, to rescue the crew and passengers of Knife 23, stranded on the eastern beach. After this aborted rescue attempt, JG 13 made an emergency landing at Rayong, Thailand, where it remained for the duration of the operation. Thus of the 11 helicopters initially used, only three remained operationally flyable (all HH-53s). These three (JG 11, 12, and 43) would be joined by two CH-53s used as SAR helicopters during the first insertion (Knife 51 and 52). Together, the five helicopters would have to move as many assault forces to Koh Tang as quickly as possible. Considering the fact that a round trip flight required more than four hours to complete, additional helicopters had to be found to ensure a sufficient buildup of forces.

But there were no more available. The Air Force arrived at a gloomy count: five grounded for mechanical reasons, a destroyed CH-53 which had crashed two days earlier 40 miles west of Nakhon Phanom while

---

*When chosen for this mission 2d Battalion, 9th Marines was in its predeployment training cycle, serving only as a backup to the air contingency battalion, BLT 1/9. The decision to send a battalion still in its combat training cycle was based in part on administrative matters. A majority of the Marines in BLT 1/9 had nearly reached the end of their year's tour on Okinawa and could not be extended except in case of an extreme emergency. Having sought such authorization and been denied, III MAF sent instead the Marines of 2d Battalion, 9th Marines.[42] Two of them, members of McDaniel's platoon, his radio operator, Lance Corporal Charles A. Giselbreth, and Private First Class Jerome N. Wemitt, helped hold the southern perimeter despite incurring serious wounds. Staff Sergeant Serefino Bernal, Jr., also demonstrated exceptional bravery while additionally providing much needed experience and seasoned leadership. During this critical period, Bernal (McDaniel's platoon sergeant), saw a Marine in trouble and without concern for his own life raced across open terrain, picked up the wounded Marine, and carried him to safety. After completing this deed, Staff Sergeant Bernal led a small group of Marines from their secure positions through enemy fire to a location where they provided cover for the withdrawing Marines of McDaniel's patrol.[43]

Capt Walter J. Wood, left, and his Company D Marines provide security for the Mayaguez as it sits at anchor a mile offshore from Koh Tang. At 1700, the security force was transferred to the USS Wilson as the Mayaguez bid farewell to its unexpected 72-hour ordeal.

enroute to Utapao, five CH-53s and three HH-53s lost in the first assault wave, and five helicopters operationally ready to fly. Thus only JG 11, JG 12, JG 43, K 51, and K 52 prepared for the impending mission, the insertion of the second assault wave.⁴⁶

The second wave took off at staggered times between 0900 and 1000. It carried elements of Captain Mykle E. Stahl's Company E and Captain James H. Davis' Company G. For Captain Davis, this would be his second attempt at landing on Koh Tang. The five helicopters in the second wave carried a total of 127 Marines. While enroute, the pilots received word from the ABCCC that the crew of the *Mayaguez* had been picked up by the *Wilson* and that the flight was to return to base. With the successful rescue of the ship's crew, there was no need to insert a second assault wave.

At approximately the same time the last elements of the assault wave left Utapao, the crew of the *Mayaguez* sighted the *Wilson* and began waving white flags. An airborne P-3 Orion reported to the destroyer that the approaching boat appeared to carry a number of Caucasians. Within minutes, at approximately 1015, a Thai fishing vessel pulled alongside the *Wilson* and unloaded its 40 passengers. Apparently, earlier air strikes which had sunk a number of Cambodian gunboats and sprayed the captors with tear gas had changed their minds about the best use of the hostages and instead of taking their captives to Kompong Som the morning of 15 May, they decided to release them along with some Thai fishermen they had been holding captive for five months. Within a few hours of Captain Charles T. Miller and his shipmates' arrival, the *Wilson* returned a somewhat harried but otherwise healthy crew to the *Sea Lanes* container ship. By 1700 the *Mayaguez*, manned by its own crewmembers and steaming under its own power, had no further need of assistance from the Department of Defense and transferred its security force, 15 members of the 1st Battalion, 4th Marines, to the *Wilson*. These Marines had remained on the *Mayaguez* to act as a security force after the conclusion of the early morning raid, but with the *Mayaguez* enroute to a new destination, Singapore, the ship's master, Captain Miller, felt reasonably certain he would no longer need their services.

The sudden change in plans caused by the crew's rescue translated into actions which altered the flight path of the second assault wave and almost cancelled

Marine Corps Historical Collection

SS Mayaguez *is towed away from Koh Tang by the USS* Harold E. Holt *(DE 1074). The Mayaguez crew was rescued shortly after this, at 1015, by the USS* Wilson. *The rescue caused JCS to cancel the operation and the insertion of the second assault wave until LtCol Austin insisted that additional forces were needed in order to secure his position.*

its insertion at Koh Tang. These changes resulted from orders passed to General Burns via the ABCCC from the highest authority. A Joint Chiefs of Staff message at 1155 confirmed the earlier communication which, in effect, recalled the flight.* It said, "Immediately cease all offensive operations against Khmer Republic related to seizure of Mayaguez."[47]

At approximately the same time Washington was deciding to cease all offensive activity, Lieutenant Colonel Austin was becoming concerned about the delay in the promised buildup of forces on Koh Tang. He contacted the ABCCC to inquire as to the whereabouts of his second assault wave. Upon learning it had been cancelled, he insisted that he still needed them to help secure the island and protect his position. Finally, Austin convinced the ABCCC and General Burns that the operation should not be terminated and that the second wave had to be landed on Koh Tang.** Upon receiving approval for insertion of additional Marines, the airborne mission commander ordered the five helicopters to reverse course and proceed as originally directed. Even though the ground security force commander eventually overcame this command and control problem, the damage had been done; the reinforcements' arrival would be delayed even longer than first feared.

The Linkup

To keep a bad situation from getting even worse, Lieutenant Colonel Austin had to link up with his main body, but without incurring additional casualties. To accomplish this, Lieutenant Keith and Lieutenant Colonel Austin worked up a plan over the radio. Correctly assuming that the Cambodians had no access to their frequency, Austin and Keith discussed their scheme of maneuver. Keith would attack through his perimeter using Zales' platoon to drive a wedge between the Cambodian forces, thereby enabling him to penetrate far enough to make contact with Austin.

Certainly there were risks involved in this plan, primarily the chance of a Cambodian counterattack, but something had to be done before Austin's group was overrun. In order to preclude an enemy counterattack and keep them off balance, Austin and Keith devised a method of using supporting fire from tactical aircraft and 81mm mortars. Not only would this prepare the area, it would also keep enemy heads down and delay any offensive they might have in mind. This maneuver appeared far less difficult than it actually was because the 81mm mortars were not with Lieutenant Keith. Instead, Lieutenant Colonel Austin's isolated group contained the mortar section. Bringing

---

*Admiral Steele recounted his thoughts on this arrangement: "This complicated, jury-rigged command arrangement and detailed management from the Joint Chiefs of Staff level endangered and nearly destroyed the forces on the island." Steele Comments.

**According to Captain Mykle E. Stahl, who was riding in the lead helicopter, the incident occurred differently. He related that when he noticed the helicopters change course, he went up to the cockpit and inquired as to what was happening. Upon learning they had reversed course, he insisted that his Marines had to land on Koh Tang. He said that after this conversation, the pilots resumed their original heading to the island. Lieutenant Colonel Mykle E. Stahl, unrecorded interview, 8Jun87.

the Air Force aircraft in on top of Austin's position would be relatively easy compared to controlling and directing the mortar section's rounds, because only a few meters separated the enemy's lines from Keith's. This job would rest solely with the 81mm mortar platoon leader, Second Lieutenant Joseph J. McMenamin, and with Lieutenant Colonel Austin.[48]

McMenamin, himself, would act as the forward observer. Leaving his mortars, he crawled to a small hill and took up a position where he could observe his rounds hitting. To prevent an errant round from striking Marines in Keith's perimeter, McMenamin fired his marking round seaward, thereby safely gauging his range and deflection. After calling in the adjustment, he ordered the next spotting round fired, but this time at the enemy. It hit dead center! The Marines were ready to begin their linkup offensive.[49]

Lieutenant Colonel Austin began the linkup preparations none too soon. The Cambodians were preparing to mount another attack against the southern perimeter. To repel this assault, Austin and Keith employed their fire support plan. It worked superbly, stopping the Cambodians in place. The plans' success and apparent simplicity only served to mask its problems and underlying complexity. Coordination of the air strikes required Keith to have communications with both the attack aircraft and the forward air controller (FAC). Unfortunately, the FAC, First Lieutenant Tonkin, and his UHF radios had been on Knife 31 which had been shot down shortly after 0600 that morning while attempting to land in the eastern zone. Without a FAC, and more importantly his radios, First Lieutenant Keith and the battalion's air liaison officer, Captain Barry Cassidy, had to improvise. To devise a workable communications system, they used the battalion's tactical frequency and their Very High Frequency radios to talk to the airborne mission commander (AMC) who in turn relayed the information to the aircraft flying close air support (A-7s and F-4s). Eventually, the AMC told the pilots to tune directly to the battalion's frequency. In this manner, one of the tactical aircraft pilots would become the TAC(A) as long as he had enough fuel to remain on station. With this always a consideration, these aircraft constantly arrived and departed after only a relatively short time because of their high rate of fuel consumption. Each time, the replacement had first to assess the sit-

BLT 2/9 command group, with LtCol Austin, debarks from Jolly Green 43 on the west coast of Koh Tang, south of the perimeter of Company G. It had to fight its way north through Khmer Rouge-controlled jungle to link up with the main body in the western zone.

Marine Corps Historical Collection

uation and then to familiarize himself with the tactical disposition of forces before he could safely direct an air strike. The Air Force improvised these tactical aircraft as "on-scene" and "search and rescue (SAR) on-scene" commanders. They used this method of control for more than nine hours. The on-scene commander's responsibilities changed continuously, 14 times with 10 different aircraft. Four turnovers alone occurred from about 0600 to 0700, the first and most critical hour of the assault phase.[50]

This extremely slow and frustrating process adversely affected Cassidy and Keith's plan. It forced Captain Cassidy and Lieutenant Keith to use a rather unorthodox method of calling in air strikes. Each time the TAC(A) changed, Lieutenant Keith, as a safety precaution, would verbally redraw the map of his position over the radio. Respecting the obvious opportunity for error inherent in such a procedure, he then had to use a trial-and-error method to set the parameters for each new series of air strikes. This always included the use of dummy runs before the pilots were cleared in "hot." It should be noted that Captain Cassidy was with the isolated command group and not with Lieutenant Keith and the main body. Although separated and unable to conduct face-to-face communications, Keith at the southern end of his lines, and Cassidy at the northern extreme of the command group's position, could simultaneously view the pilots' dummy runs. In this manner they could spot the runs and when both of them agreed that the Air Force A-7 had properly split their positions, they cleared the air strike for a "hot" run. Their successful efforts eventually resulted in the pilots laying down a strip of supporting fire which when combined with McMenamin's mortars forced the enemy to stay low and allowed the 2d Platoon to attack.[51]

Second Lieutenant Zales; Second Lieutenant Daniel J. Hoffman, the weapons platoon commander; and First Sergeant Lawrence L. Funk led the advance of the 2d Platoon, Company G in its attempt to break through to Austin. With the assault proceeding well, Lieutenant Zales did not suspect nor realize that a Cambodian squad had moved to outflank his platoon. The Communists intended to attack his exposed left (eastern) flank. Seeing this event unfolding from the vantage point he had used to spot mortar rounds, Second Lieutenant McMenamin decided to intercede in an effort to thwart the Cambodians. McMenamin and two lance corporals, Larry J. Branson and Robert L. Shelton, jumped up and charged across the open terrain which separated them from the enemy. Their sudden appearance so surprised the Communists that they turned and fled into the jungle. McMenamin's disruption of the enemy's counterattack allowed the 2d Platoon to continue its linkup operation. Zale's manuever ended successfully with the two forces joining at 1245.[52]

The Second Wave

Even though this action, and the majority of the activity took place on the southern perimeter, the Marines guarding the northern sector saw considerable fighting as well. Staff Sergeant Fofo T. Tuitele and Staff Sergeant Francis L. Burnett led these Marines, a combination of men from Company G's 2d and 3d Platoons. Knowing that enemy automatic weapons fire could severely limit their maneuverability, they decided to attack two bunkers held by the Cambodians. The success of their effort enabled them to gain a position from which they could neutralize with fire another Cambodian strongpoint. Despite all this activity and maneuvering, the enemy still held the upper hand and the tactical advantage.[53]

Fortunately, by this time the second wave had reversed course and was again enroute to Koh Tang. Although a decision had been made to reinforce the Marines already on the island, Colonel Johnson, the Marine task group commander (still in Utapao), did not participate in the process. Neither did he have any insight into what decisions had been made. CinCPac, in charge of the overall operation, relayed his decisions on matters such as these to his superiors, the Joint Chiefs of Staff, and to the "on-scene" operational commander, General Burns. (Actually, General Burns was in Nakhon Phanom, hundreds of miles from the scene of action.).* For some reason, Colonel Johnson never received word from General Burns' staff that the decision had been made to devote all future efforts to disengaging and recovering the combat forces on Koh Tang. In describing this event in his first situation report to JCS, Admiral Gayler said, "JCS directed immediate cessation of all offensive operations. Accordingly further strikes were diverted to support the extraction of the GSF from Koh Tang island . . . . Extraction of the 182 men that were put ashore is now the objective."[54]

Colonel Johnson thus found himself in the back-

---

*Admiral Steele severely criticized General Burns for his decision to remain in Nakhon Phanom: "It is quite clear that the 'on scene operational commander,' General Burns, was not 'on scene.' The man who should have been on scene unfortunately was still in Utapao without information. CinCPac was making tactical decisions. I think this was *Alice in Wonderland* at its worst." Steele Comments.

waters of the operation. His only link to Lieutenant Colonel Austin went via Nakhon Phanom (USSAG/Seventh Air Force) to the airborne C-130 directing operational traffic (ABCCC), and finally from the ABCCC to BLT 2/9. Likewise, replies went in reverse order via this convoluted means. Compounding this awkward method of communicating was the massive amount of radio traffic generated by other participants and senior commanders wanting to know what was happening. General Burns' deputy chief for operations, Colonel Robert R. Reed, succinctly described in his end-of-tour report the source of the extraneous radio traffic which adversely impacted on the mission and, in particular, on Colonel Johnson:

> The constant requests for detailed information to be furnished higher headquarters was a definite hindrance to both the *Mayaguez* and TV/FW (Talon Vise/Frequent Wind) operation. A secure conference line was opened for this purpose and remained open for the duration of each operation. This not only required extra personnel to man the circuits, but also unnecessarily divided the attention of the 7AF battle staff. . . . The *Mayaguez* and TV/FW were of national importance and had the highest level of interest; however even this is little justification for the headquarters to require tail numbers and call signs of each aircraft.[55]

Thus Colonel Johnson, hampered by these communications problems, would have minimum input to the critical choices made at this juncture. Despite the adverse and grave reports he received from the returning wounded, he had no choice but to face the fact that General Burns at his headquarters in Nakhon Phanom had tactical control of the assault mission through his airborne command center. Unless Colonel Johnson could get to Koh Tang, and with all of the available helicopters airborne this was highly unlikely, he would exert little influence over the remainder of the operation. The rest of the key decisions would be left to the Air Force and the Navy, but they would still have to be made based on the needs and demands of the battlefield commander, Lieutenant Colonel Austin. The second operational plan issued by General Burns' headquarters dated 14 May addressed just such an exception. Although predicated on the assumption that the designated ground security force commander, Colonel Johnson, would be on Koh Tang with his battalion commander (Lieutenant Colonel Austin) and he was not, General Burns' directive still applied: "Nothing in these authorities shall be construed as precluding a commander from using all means at his disposal to exercise the inherent right and responsibility to conduct operations for self-defense of his forces."[56]

Without question then, the ground commander's request for additional forces fell within the limits set forth. Whether anyone made a conscious decision not to employ covering fire to protect the requested reinforcements and the five helicopters delivering them to Koh Tang cannot be determined. What is known, however, is that none was provided, and for the second time in the same day, unescorted helicopters entered the western and even the eastern zone.

The difference between no suppressive air cover and some form of close air support could be the difference between success and failure, and ultimately, the difference between life and death. A vivid demonstration of this difference occurred just before the eighth helicopter (JG 41) in the first assault wave made "one more attempt" to land its Marines. An AC-130 gunship, equipped with 20mm and 40mm guns and a 105mm gun, received instructions to support JG 41's approach. In doing so he provided the first real suppressive fire at Koh Tang. The Air Force's official account of the assault recorded that, "An AC-130 gunship, call sign, Spectre 61, was then directed to attempt to pinpoint friendly and enemy positions while JG 41 held off the island."[57] The importance of this suppressive fire was underscored by the fact that this helicopter, Jolly Green 41, already had made four unsuccessful attempts to enter the zone, and not until its fifth effort with considerable covering fire from "Spectre 61" did it actually land in the zone. Even then, because the HH-53 lacked close-in, slow-moving air cover to detect and then suppress the enemy's fire (in this case Cambodian mortars), it achieved limited success. JG 41 could unload only 22 of its 27 combat Marines. According to the Air Force's operational report, "Spectre 61 went to Koh Tang island. Info was passed to Bingo Shoes 03 [BLT 2/9 command post] by Spectre. Spectre was then cleared by Crickett (AMC) and Bingo Shoes 03 to expend on position."[58] Due to the supporting fire of the AC-130, JG 41 delivered much-needed Marines to a depleted ground security force.

More importantly, by the airborne units coordinating their support with the friendly forces on the ground, they were able to deliver much more effective and infinitely safer suppressive fire. The effectiveness of this support would vary throughout the course of the day and eventually deteriorate by evening. Suppressive fires applied during the night extraction phase conditions would achieve far less results. Yet by this time, all involved recognized the importance of at least their application, emphasized by the fact that the Air Force thought them important enough to include in

At center is the area designated the eastern landing zone on Koh Tang. The hatched rectangle, also at center, is where it was believed that the Mayaguez crew had been taken. One of the CH-53s in the second assault wave, Knife 52, attempted unsuccessfully to land in the zone, incurring such severe damage that it was forced to make an emergency landing in Thailand.

their later situation reports: "Spectre gunship is working in support of GSF which is attempting to secure an area to be used as an HLZ on Koh Tang island."[59]

Unfortunately for the second wave of helicopters, the "Spectre" gunship departed Koh Tang shortly after JG 41, around 1000. As the second wave approached Koh Tang, the importance of providing covering fire with either close air support helicopters or other slow-moving aircraft became readily apparent. With the AC-130 gunship no longer in the area, the Cambodians confronted the arriving Americans with a barrage of antiaircraft fire. The single ship entering the eastern zone (Knife 52) was so badly damaged that it had to make an emergency landing on the coast of Thailand.*

Despite the resumed enemy fire, the other four helicopters (K 51, JG 11, JG 12, and JG 43) made it safely into the western zone and disembarked 100 Ma-

---
*Why K 52 attempted to land in the eastern zone is not explained by the Air Force's operational report.

rines, bringing the total on the island to 222 (during the operation the Air Force inserted 231 Marines and evacuated nine). This number fell far short of the planned buildup. Knife 52's failure to unload its 27 Marines from the second wave illustrated why Lieutenant Colonel Austin never received his full fighting force.[60]

From this point little would change save for the consolidating of positions. The important question now became whether to reinforce or extract the Marines on Koh Tang. One change which had occurred which would have a significant impact on the Marines on the ground by providing them better air support, involved the tactical air coordinator. By 1600 OV-10s had assumed the role of TAC(A), replacing the "fast movers." According to the Center for Naval Analysis report on the Koh Tang assault: "There was no dedicated airborne forward air controller (FAC) at Koh Tang until an OV-10 aircraft [Nail 68], arrived on the scene about 1600, some 10 hours after the assault had begun."**[61] For those on the ground the arrival of the Nail aircraft meant less radio chatter, more support, and as darkness rolled in, someone to spot the flashes of the enemy's weapons. These flashes, when once marked by the OV-10s, became aiming points for the AC-130 gunship on station. This change in controllers marked a turning point in the quality of airborne firepower available to the Marines on Koh Tang, because for the first time that day they had an airborne observer exclusively dedicated to providing accurate and timely close air support. The presence of the OV-10 also meant that an attack aircraft no longer had to fill the role of tactical air coordinator airborne and could instead return to its primary role of dropping bombs. The attack force welcomed this addition to its airborne arsenal. On-call strike capability would be a critical consideration in evaluating when to begin the evacuation.[62]

The Retrograde

Lieutenant Colonel Austin made it clear to everyone that once the decision was made to evacuate and the extraction of his forces had actually begun, it had to be completed quickly and without interruption. With one platoon still isolated on the eastern shore and no way for the rest of the Marines to link up with it, General Burns had to decide whether it was feasi-

---
**According to one of the 40th ARRS pilots in Utapao, Major John F. Guilmartin, Jr., "The pilot of Nail 68, Major Robert W. Undorf, allegedly was responsible for imposing order on an air battle which until his intervention had been less than coordinated and orderly." Guilmartin Comments.

ble to leave an isolated unit overnight and try to reinforce and resupply it. The USSAG commander knew that if he attempted to extract the platoon on the eastern beach, he had no choice but to evacuate all of them at one time. General Burns believed that he could resupply the western zone, and with this logistical support, the Marines could sustain themselves through the night. Even without an immediate resupply, the main body of 202 Marines could sustain a night attack, but Lieutenant Cicere's small force in the eastern zone, if not reinforced, could not. With this possibility facing him, General Burns ordered the second-wave helicopters (two HH-53s had remained in the area to perform SAR duties) to withdraw Second Lieutenant Cicere and his 20 Marines from Koh Tang. At approximately 1415, these "Jolly Greens" (JG 11 and JG 43) attempted to enter the eastern zone and, as all but one of their predecessors, failed. One of the two helicopters (Jolly Green 43) suffered extensive damage. Jolly Green 11 and King 24, the HC-130 used to refuel the HH-53s, escorted JG 43 to the *Coral Sea* (CVA 43), where it made an emergency landing at 1436. The *Coral Sea* repaired the HH-53 in record time and had it back in service by 1700. This maintenance miracle meant a 25-percent increase in the number of available helicopters, because by this time only four others remained operational. Even that many helicopters existed only because the newly repaired JG 44 had just arrived from Nakhon Phanom where it had been out of service since the beginning of the *Mayaguez* mission.* In addition to JG 44, JG 11, JG 12, and a CH-53, Knife 51, stood ready for further duty while Jolly Green 43 underwent repair. The importance of the rapid turnaround of JG 43 and the unexpected return to service of JG 44 significantly increased when the Air Force undertook yet another effort to rescue the Marines and airmen pinned down on Koh Tang's eastern beach.[63]

Even though JG 11 and 43 had failed to penetrate the eastern zone, General Burns still believed that rescue by air was possible. He knew, however, that it could not be accomplished without additional support. As a consequence, the Navy and Air Force decided to coordinate their efforts and together to attempt recovery of Lieutenant Cicere's platoon. In addition to the harassing fire from the Cambodians on the ground, the Marines were receiving fire from Cambodian gunboats just offshore. So while the *Coral Sea's* maintenance crew was completing its repairs on JG 43, the forces on the scene were preparing to undertake a joint withdrawal from the eastern zone. Despite the importance of the events about to occur on Koh Tang's eastern shore, no information was ever communicated by the AMC to the ground force commander, Lieutenant Colonel Austin. Between 1730 and 1800, the Navy, Air Force, and Marine Corps combined to perform a successful and casualty-free extraction of the Marines and airmen from the eastern zone. While the *Wilson's* gig, call sign "Black Velvet," provided close-in ship-to-shore suppressive fire using four mounted M-60 machine guns and immediate rescue capability, the OV-10 FAC, call sign "Nail 68," the air commander, called in F-4s and A-7s to neutralize enemy positions and cover Lieutenant Cicere's withdrawal. Even though the OV-10 and all aircraft in the vicinity, including Jolly Green 12 and Knife 51, strafed the Cambodians, Jolly Green 11 (the rescue bird) still took heavy fire. Due to the damage it incurred, Jolly Green 11 did not fly again.[64]

The Marines contributed to their own rescue by returning disciplined and effective ground fire which kept the helicopters' time in the zone to a minimum. Lieutenant Colonel Austin's operational summary reported that "The Marines made an orderly withdrawal, stopping to fire weapons every few feet. They were pursued by enemy forces who had obtained hand-grenade range on several occasions."[65] In forcing the Communists to respect their position even though they were withdrawing, the Marines made possible a successful recovery, evidenced by the fact that JG 11 landed on the *Coral Sea* with 25 passengers, 20 Marines and 5 air crewmen, only a few of whom had wounds, none incurred during the extraction.** Second Lieutenant Michael A. Cicere, commander of the 3d Platoon, Company G, related his recollection of this

---

*Major Guilmartin, who had flown the last flyable, rescue Super Jolly (who for the mission used the call sign JG 44) to Utapao late in the afternoon of 15 May, explained his understanding of how the Navy repaired JG 43's damaged fuel line, hit by a 50-caliber round: "The flight mechanic, Technical Sergeant Billy D. Willingham, assisted the Navy maintenance personnel who effected the repair by cutting out damaged line (one and one-quarter inch aluminum standpipe) with a hacksaw and put in its place a section of hose held together with radiator hose clamps. Certainly, not by the book, but despite concerns about fuel contamination by the pilots, it worked." Guilmartin Comments.

**In reference to injuries, Second Lieutenant Cicere recalled: "There were two personnel with us that were wounded: one a Marine (PFC Nichols, I believe) shot in the foot; the second, an Air Force crewman who was wounded in the arm and leg exiting the hulk of Knife 23 and dashing toward the tree line. He left the aircraft well after the Marines and the other Air Force personnel had disembarked the stricken helicopter after it was shot down." Cicere Comments.

Marine Corps Historical Collection

Marines board one of the five remaining Air Force helicopters for extraction from the fighting in the eastern zone of Koh Tang. The extraction was completed between 1730 and 1800 when 2dLt Michael A. Cicere and his 20 Marines were recovered by Jolly Green 11.

event: "The helicopter did not actually sit on the ground because the hulk of Knife 23 was sitting on the beach. Instead, the pilot skillfully hovered the helicopter several feet off the ground just north of the original beach LZ. It made the extraction difficult because the helicopter would see-saw up and down. Only a few Marines at a time could board the helicopter's rear ramp in this fashion as they timed their jumps to coincide with the downward motion of the aircraft."[66]

Besides being the first extraction from Koh Tang, it also represented the first successful entry into the eastern zone in nearly 12 hours. But it also had its costs. During the recovery, in addition to JG 11's flight-ending hit, the Air Force lost a second helicopter, JG 12, struck while checking for a wounded Marine. Earlier flights had reported seeing a Marine holding onto part of the wreckage of Knife 31. Jolly Green 12 tried to no avail to locate him, even lowering its rescue device, called a jungle penetrator, a plumb-bob-like affair on the end of the rescue hoist cable, to the wreckage. With no success and drawing lead like a shooting gallery target, Jolly Green 12 diverted to the *Coral Sea* with major battle damage and a wounded flight mechanic. This casualty left only three helicopters (JG 43, JG 44, and Knife 51) to evacuate more than 200 Marines still on Koh Tang![67]

Once the evacuation of the eastern zone had been completed, the Air Force began the recovery of the Marines in the western zone. To remove the assault forces from the western beach "required six helicopter loads and two hours to complete."[68]

Again as in the recovery from the eastern zone, the decision to remove all of the Marines from Koh Tang before day's end was never shared with Lieutenant Colonel Austin. Neither he nor his immediate superior, Colonel Johnson, was ever informed of General Burns' decision. Lieutenant Colonel Austin was still waiting for word on the proposed time of evacuation when he heard helicopters approaching the zone. Since it was past sunset, the ground force commander suspected a resupply, but quickly learned that the helicopters had orders to extract them. The Pacific Air Force Command history reported that the official decision to evacuate occurred at 1717 on 15 May 1975.[69] The Marines at Koh Tang recalled what happened after they spotted the first helicopter, "Shortly, thereafter, several additional helos appeared on the horizon and it was obvious a helo extraction of the main force was on."[70]

Despite having no prior warning, the Marines were ready to depart. They had already prepared for the moment by gathering their wounded into one area and devising a staggered withdrawal plan. This allowed them to reduce the zone without compromising its overall security. The phased withdrawal would permit Lieutenant Colonel Austin to shrink the zone after each lift and fortify the new perimeter before the next flight arrived. Unfortunately, in the darkness and the confusion caused by the deafening noise of the helicopter rotor blades mixing with the ugly chatter of enemy gunfire, all did not go as planned, but this fact would not be known until many hours after the last flight had landed. Lieutenant Colonel Austin recalled how the final two hours on Koh Tang began: "When the first helicopter approached the zone which was being marked by Marines with flashlights since by this time it was completely dark, it was met by a heavy volume of fire."[71]

During the next two hours, the gunners of the incoming HH-53s fired at the suspected Cambodian positions while the AC-130 used its 20mm and 40mm weapons against the flashes of the enemy's guns. At the same time, the Air Force F-4s and A-7s, directed by Nail 68 and Nail 69, two OV-10 FACs, conducted strafing runs in an effort to interdict the Communists and keep them from shooting at the recovery helicopters. The Spectre gunship reported, "We expended 200 rounds of 20mm HEI, 158 rounds of 40mm MEISH, and 87 rounds of 105mm HE at the target."[72]

With the Cambodians' attention diverted by this firepower, each helicopter would hover at the beach's edge with its nose pointed in the direction of safe haven, the sea, and load as many Marines as possible. The recovery helo would then take its load of Marines to one of the Navy ships standing off the coast of Koh Tang. Most of the Marines eventually disembarked on the *Coral Sea*, but 34 ended up on the *Holt*.

The third ship in the area, the destroyer *Wilson*, already had on board 10 Marines from BLT 2/9 (the Knife 31 survivors) and 15 from 1st Battalion, 4th Marines (*Mayaguez* security crew). With these 25 Marines on board, the *Wilson* stood by offshore as its gig assisted in the recovery of the 20 Marines and five airmen isolated on the eastern beach. After the *Wilson's* well-armed small boat, "Black Velvet," completed this support mission, it moved around the northern tip of the island to a position near the western shore. From its new location, "Black Velvet" laid down a band of suppressive fire in the area of Staff Sergeants Tuitele and Burnett's position, the western zone Marines' northern perimeter. Besides this assistance, earlier in the evening, the *Wilson* sank at least one and possibly two Cambodian gunboats which had been harassing the Marines and their air cover. In total, in support of the two extraction efforts, the *Wilson* fired 157 5-inch rounds and provided an alternative to helicopter extraction, evacuation by boat.[73] To the 10 Marines

A shell fired from the USS Henry B. Wilson *(DDG 7) explodes over a Koh Tang beach. The* Wilson *and its gig, "Black Velvet," and the USS* Holt *provided gunfire support to the Marines as they evacuated the western zone between 1830 and 2010 on 15 May.*

Marine Corps Historical Collection

Department of Defense (Air Force) 507-541

USS Henry B. Wilson *(DDG 7), seen off the coast of Koh Tang, rescued 13 survivors of Knife 31 and supported the retrograde from the island by expending 157 5-inch rounds.*

of BLT 2/9, the many contributions the *Wilson* made during the operation, which duly gained the ship noteworthy recognition, paled when placed alongside their rescue: "Crew and troops of single downed helo on northeast beach recovered by boat to USS *Wilson*."⁷⁴ The Seventh Fleet's commander, Admiral Steele, aptly summarized the Wilson's "other" contributions: "The *Henry B. Wilson* delivered naval gunfire on hostile positions ashore on Tang Island to assist Marines landed there. She even armed her gig and used it successfully to suppress and direct fire, aiding extraction of the Marines from the island."*⁷⁵

As the *Wilson's* gig moved to a position from which it could support the western zone, Knife 51 accompanied by Jolly Green 43 and 44 appeared. When Knife 51 landed at 1830 and loaded 41 Marines, the extraction of the western zone officially began. As K 51 headed to the *Coral Sea*, JG 43 landed and loaded 54 Marines. While JG 43 recovered on board the *Coral Sea*, JG 44 executed a quick turn-around by depositing its 34 Marines on the *Holt*, the nearest ship to Koh Tang. JG 44's shortened round-trip enabled it to extract the next-to-last load, 40 Marines, leaving 32 still on the island.**⁷⁶

The group of 32 Marines remaining on Koh Tang

---

*Admiral Steele shared his thoughts about the dearth of overall gunfire support. He commented: "Imagine the distress of the Seventh Fleet Commander, with an enormous force within 24 to 36 hours from the combat zone, to find that the *Henry Wilson's* gig was being used to suppress and direct fire, and aid extraction of the Marines from Koh Tang." Steele Comments.

**This number does not include the fatally wounded Lance Corporal Looney. As his body was still in the western zone, the total number that remained was 33, which when added to the number already extracted accounted for the 202 Marines still on Koh Tang at 1800, 15 May.

included Captain Davis and Gunnery Sergeant Lester A. McNemar. These two Marines had known for hours that once the retrograde began, their most serious challenge would be a Cambodian counterattack. Somehow they had to ensure that the Cambodians did not overrun their final defensive position. Even before Captain Davis and Gunnery Sergeant McNemar shrunk the perimeter for the last time, they received a taste of the peril they would face. Prior to Jolly Green 44's arrival, at which time it picked up the next-to-last load, the 72 Marines then in the zone experienced some harrowing moments.

In its official description of those critical minutes, the Air Force recorded: "Radio contact with the friendlies was lost, and no helicopters were immediately available to make pickups. Finally at approximately 1225Z (1925L), communication with the ground commander was reestablished, and he reported that he might be overrun in fifteen minutes. Two minutes later, he reemphasized the urgency of immediate evacuation."⁷⁷ In fact, it was reported that at this point Captain Davis said to the helicopter pilots, "Go for broke."⁷⁸ At this critical juncture, through luck and the good headwork of JG 44's pilot, things improved: "Within five minutes . . . JG 44 had returned from the USS *Holt* and had landed in the LZ, assisted by a strobe light set up by the Marines." Jolly Green 44's independent decision to go to the *Holt* had literally saved the day for the Marines remaining on the island.⁷⁹

Even though the immediate crisis had passed, the Cambodians now posed an even greater threat to Captain Davis and his small contingent of Marines: "Twenty-nine Marines were still under fire on the western beach and there were no helicopters immedi-

Department of Defense (Air Force) 111051

Knife 22 sits in a field on the eastern coast of Thailand as a Marine prepares to disable it permanently. Company G Commander Capt James H. Davis, who had been riding in this helicopter, returned to Koh Tang in the second assault wave and remained on the island until Knife 51 extracted the last 29 Marines.

ately available to make the pickup."*[80] Finally Knife 51 landed and began loading. Having loaded everyone save for themselves, Captain Davis, Gunnery Sergeant McNemar, and a Pararescueman or "PJ" on K 51, Technical Sergeant Wayne Fisk, combed the beach one last time for stragglers.** Finding none, they leaped onto the hovering HH-53 as it lifted off Koh Tang for the final time. It was 2010.[81] The much-awaited situation report stated, "Marines helo-lifted from Koh Tang island as of 151300Z [2000]."[82] The Navy's intelligence command in the Pacific reported to Admiral Gayler that "All U.S. personnel have been extracted from the island. Final extraction was by CH/HH-53 helicopter."[83] This intelligence report would later prove to be incorrect.

The Aftermath

The entire evacuation of the Marines in the western zone lasted less than two hours, all of it logged as night flight time by the pilots. Possibly because of the darkness and despite the efforts of Davis, McNemar, and such Marines as Sergeant Carl C. Andersen, platoon guide, 3d Platoon, Company E, and Lance Corporal John S. Standfast, squad leader, 3d Squad, 3d Platoon, Company E, mistakes still occurred. Standfast and his squad covered Company G's withdrawal during the reduction of the perimeter, and he then singlehandedly directed the pullback of his own squad. In the all important job of making sure none of the Marines were left behind in each zone reduction, Standfast received assistance from his platoon guide, Sergeant Andersen. Before withdrawing to the safety of the new perimeter, the two Marines would move forward to the old perimeter to ensure that no member of the company inadvertently had been left behind, each time checking every foxhole.[84]

Hours later, with the assault forces dispersed among three Navy ships, the Company E commander, Captain Mykle K. Stahl, discovered that three of his Marines were missing. The Marines checked all of the Navy ships, but could not locate Lance Corporal Joseph N. Hargrove, Private First Class Gary C. Hall, and Private Danny G. Marshall, members of the same machine gun team. Captain Stahl stated later, "As the evacuation terminated and it was determined that Hargrove, Hall, and Marshall were missing I inspected all the equipment to determine if any of the serialized

The western zone on Koh Tang is seen from the tail of one of the Air Force helicopters used to insert and recover Marines. During the confusion of the retrograde three Marines were left on the island: LCpl Joseph N. Hargrove, PFC Gary C. Hall, and Pvt Danny G. Marshall. In addition, the body of LCpl Ashton N. Looney was inadvertently left on this beach.
Department of Defense Photo (Air Force) 111056

---

*The variance between 29 and 32 (or 33) is explained in the next section.

**Major Guilmartin shared his knowledge of this "PJ." He related, "TSgt Wayne Fisk was a veteran of the Son Tay raid and normally would not have been on a CH-53, but present in Utapao the morning the first helicopters took off, he subsequently talked the aircraft commander, First Lieutenant Richard Brims, into accepting him as a crew member on Knife 51's second flight to Koh Tang." Guilmartin Comments.

weapons or other equipment belonging to any of the three were on board."[85] They were not. Subsequent to this, Lieutenant Colonel Austin learned that the body of Lance Corporal Ashton N. Looney, killed earlier in the day, had somehow also been left behind on Koh Tang. To further add to the confusion over accountability, the *Coral Sea* reported to Admiral Steele that the final helicopter, Knife 51, had offloaded 25 Marines. The Air Force reported 29.[86]

The Marines missing from Stahl's company were never recovered nor was their disappearance ever explained, other than noting the difficulty and confusion of conducting joint-service, night-retrograde operations under fire. A few of the factors that could have contributed to the machine gun team's disappearance are: enemy fire during the withdrawal; friendly ground fire during the reduction of the perimeter; friendly fire from the helicopter's miniguns, the AC-130, and the close air support aircraft; and battlefield disorientation. In all probability, these Marines suffered death at the hands of the enemy.

The final time they were seen was just after the next-to-last reestablishment of the perimeter defense. A post-action investigation revealed, "That upon determining Hall, Hargrove, and Marshall were ineffective as a machine gun team, Sergeant Andersen ordered them to move back to a new position which was located to the left of the position occupied by Captain James H. Davis . . . . Sergeant Andersen was the last member of the Marine force to see Hall, Hargrove, and Marshall and that the time was about 2000."[87] Throughout the retrograde action, extensive enemy fire, friendly ground fire and suppressive air fire were delivered. The Air Force pilots at Koh Tang during the final extraction observed that "From 1245Z-1300Z (1945-2000 local) random bursts of 50 Cal [were] fired in the direction of both aircraft. When Spectre 11 began suppressive fire to cover the ingress of the final helicopters the fire ceased."[88]

While BLT 2/9 attempted to determine if its Marines had been killed, and if not, their whereabouts, a message from the *Wilson* further confused the issue. Sent less than 24 hours after the operation ended, it said, " . . . possible PW camp on Koh Tang Island."[89] The Marine Corps' investigation into the disappearance of these Marines concluded in its final opinion, "That Hall, Hargrove, and Marshall could have been fatally wounded subsequent to the last time they were seen by Sergeant Andersen at about 2000 and the time when the final helicopter lifted off, since

Department of Defense Photo (USMC) A705991
1stLt Terry L. Tonkin, a forward air controller with BLT 2/9, receives a Purple Heart medal from MajGen Kenneth J. Houghton at Subic Bay. Lt Tonkin was a passenger in Knife 31, which was shot down approaching the eastern landing zone on Koh Tang. Lt Tonkin used a survival radio to call in A-7s as he swam to sea, where he and 12 others were picked up by the Wilson.

there was firing by both enemy forces and the Marines awaiting extraction from Koh Tang."[90]

The casualties involved in recovering the *Mayaguez* crew totalled: 11 Marines killed, 41 wounded, 3 missing (later declared dead); 2 Navy corpsmen killed and 2 wounded; and 2 airmen killed and 6 wounded.* This did not include the 18 passengers and five crew members of the CH-53 which crashed enroute to Utapao on 13 May.[91]

The BLT 2/9 Marines still at Utapao, some returned casualties, and the rest of the men who had waited in vain for insertion, immediately flew back to Okinawa on a C-141. The reason for their sudden departure was a formal protest lodged by the Thai Government

---

*In documenting the losses for an Air War College Faculty Paper, Doctor James E. Winkates included the Nakhon Phanom helicopter crash: "U.S. forces sustained 18 killed in action, fifty wounded, and twenty-three other personnel killed in a related helicopter crash." Dr. James E. Winkates, "Hostage Rescue in a Hostile Environment: Lessons Learned from Son Tay, *Mayaguez*, and Entebbe Missions," Air War College Faculty Paper (Maxwell AFB, Alabama, 1978), p. 4.

about the military methods the U.S. used in retaking the *Mayaguez*. Thailand refused to allow any further use of its bases for this purpose. Prime Minister Khukrit informed the American Charge D'Affaires, ". . . should the U.S. resort to military retaliation in regard to this matter . . . , the Thai government wants it to be a matter between America and Cambodia only. The Thai government does not want to be involved in it in any way whatsoever. And it does not and will not give permission for the United States to use any base in Thailand."[92] Due to the delay in receiving the formal protest, its timing did not interfere with the assault on Koh Tang. As a result of the Thai demands, the BLT 2/9 Marines at Utapao arrived on Okinawa well before the rest of their combat-tested battalion.

Meanwhile, the Marines who had participated in the *Mayaguez* operation went to Subic on Navy ships where the Marines of 1st Battalion, 4th Marines disembarked and rejoined their unit. From there, the Marines of BLT 2/9 returned to Okinawa by way of Kadena Airbase and an Air Force C-141. Once at Camp Schwab, the 2d Battalion, 9th Marines resumed its interrupted training which ironically included a test to see if it was ready for combat! General Hoffman deactivated Task Group 79.9 the day the battalion headquarters returned, 21 May 1975.[93]

In terms of the Navy's participation, Vice Admiral Steele said, "The May 1975 rescue of the container ship *Mayaguez* and the crew assisted by the USS *Harold E. Holt* (DE-1074) and the USS *Henry B. Wilson* (DDG-7) shows the readiness and flexibility of the ships."[94] Certainly, readiness and flexibility was also reflected in the Marine Corps' contribution to this operation. Immediately upon conclusion of the operation, General George S. Brown, Chairman of the Joint Chiefs of Staff, issued the following statement: "The success of the unique operation to recover the SS *Mayaguez* and her crew by the combined efforts of the Air Force, Navy, and Marine Corps represents an outstanding display of the versatility, dedication, and professional competence of all the participants."[95]

Despite these plaudits, the *Mayaguez* operation, from inception to completion, from planning to execution, contained flaws and failings. Planning, command and control, communications, and adherence to doctrine all suffered in some respect. The short-fuse nature of the contingency held the planners hostage to the clock. From the outset, planners never had adequate time to develop fully a conceptual plan, a problem which was then compounded by a lack of reliable intelligence. At this juncture, senior officers created command relationships among Services that placed an excessive reliance on long distance communications. Thus the entire operation became highly vulnerable to equipment failures and miscommunication. Admiral Steele offered his opinion of the rescue operation. He argued, "I insist that the short-fused nature of the contingency did not hold the planners hostage for time. I believe that our political leadership, starting with President Ford and Secretary [of State] Henry Kissinger, demanded from the military a speed of performance that it could not provide, and forces were committed piecemeal and pell mell, from different services with different doctrines, and [who are] unused to working with each other. There were too many cooks by far in this broth. Had the Seventh Fleet and its Marines been instructed to recover the *Mayaguez* and her crew, as simple as that, there probably would have been no loss of life, and the *Mayaguez* and her crew would have been recovered successfully, one or two days later."[96]

After the initial landings met with unexpected resistance and the inserted forces were unable to move, potential problems became real problems. Soon, they multiplied as three Services spontaneously attempted to apply dissimilar solutions to problems which required uniform and coordinated ones. Urey Patrick, an analyst for the Center for Naval Analyses, remarked on the lack of coordinated effort: "Of the 8 helicopters damaged or lost in the first wave, 6 were damaged or lost before there was any air or naval gunfire support."[97] Despite this, the Air Force still sent helicopters into the zone without sufficient covering fire and the Navy failed to provide gunfire support until 1600, nearly 10 hours after the first Marine landed on Koh Tang. One of the worst examples of faulure to communicate and coordinate was the indiscriminate delivery of ordnance without the ground force commander's consent or knowledge. The arrival of an unrequested and unwanted 15,000-pound bomb on the afternoon of 15 May highlighted the depth to which command responsibility had sunk. The battalion's after action report under the sub-title "Problem Areas and Lessons Learned" almost understated the seriousness of the event: "Not all ordnance delivery was cleared with the CO BLT 2/9. The most glaring example was the use of a 15,000-pound bomb dropped in mid-afternoon with absolutely no prior notice to or clearance from 2/9."[98]

Eventually, all three Services combined to effect a

successful withdrawal from the island, having earlier recovered the *Mayaguez* and its crew. The high cost of this mission in terms of men and equipment does not obscure the fact that it accomplished its purpose—to rescue the ship and its crew. Yet, it did so in an inefficient and even deadly manner, demonstrating the need for prior preparation for short-fuse responses to worldwide contingencies. The *Mayaguez* rescue operation highlighted the fact that to conduct a successful joint operation, units must first train jointly. In honor of those who paid the highest price for this knowledge, Koh Tang must be remembered.

Koh Tang will never be forgotten by those who participated, nor those other military forces in the Pacific who, because of the perceived need to respond quickly, could not get to the Gulf of Thailand in time. One of the many military units not in the Gulf but relatively close by and anxious to assist in the recovery of the *Mayaguez* was the seaborne force used in Operation Frequent Wind, the 9th MAB. The commander of that over-the-horizon assault force, Brigadier General Richard E. Carey, recently provided his thoughts on the *Mayaguez* mission. He wrote: "The *Mayaguez* Rescue was the most classic example of assured failure with Joint Operations to that time. Unfortunately, the lesson was not learned and the same mistakes were repeated in the Iranian Hostage Rescue operation (1980). Modern communications are wonderful but they also are deadly. The capability to talk over thousands of miles from the very highest levels to the frontline foxholes takes many of the important decisions out of the hands of the responsible commander, the man on the scene. In the final analysis, in the case of the *Mayaguez*, the lack of accurate intelligence resulted in faulty decisions. Decisions were driven by the desire to do something and to do it as quickly as possible. The National Image was at stake. Unfortunately, the frontline Marine was the recipient of the results of poor decision-making. Again, coordination was conducted by an isolated commander (USSAG) without the proper input from the field commander. To undertake a mission of this type from 195 miles away and with inadequate resources is naive and foolhardy. The results only reinforce my statements."[99]

CHAPTER 14
Epilogue

"He who knows when he can fight and when he cannot will be victorious." When Sun Tzu wrote those words more than two thousand years ago he succinctly presented a principle of warfare that still applies today and aptly describes the U.S. Marine Corps' experience in Vietnam. From the beginning, in 1954, with the assignment of the first Marine advisor, Lieutenant Colonel Victor J. Croizat, to the departure of the last Marine Corps officer to assist and advise the Vietnamese Marine Corps, Lieutenant Colonel Anthony Lukeman, the quality of the Corps' experience in Vietnam depended upon where and when it was allowed to fight.

The Marine Corps presence in Vietnam gradually escalated between 1954 and 1965. Its first sizeable increase occurred in April 1962 when the 1st Marine Aircraft Wing deployed a headquarters element, Marine Medium Helicopter Squadron 362 (HMM-362), and a sub-unit of Marine Air Base Squadron 16 (MABS-16) to Soc Trang. Within three years of their arrival, the 9th Marine Expeditionary Brigade landed at Red Beach 2, northwest of Da Nang. At 0903, 8 March 1965, 11 Marine amphibian tractors unloaded the first elements of BLT 3/9. The 9th MEB soon became the III Marine Amphibious Force (III MAF), eventually consisting of two reinforced divisions and a reinforced Marine aircraft wing.

By late summer 1965, the United States had established the command structure, which save for a few minor exceptions, would govern and control Marine Corps operations for the remainder of the war. III MAF came under the operational control of the commander of the U.S. Military Assistance Command, Vietnam (ComUSMACV). For logistical and administrative matters, the Marines remained under the Commanding General, Fleet Marine Force, Pacific (CGFMFPac). Under this arrangement, III MAF prosecuted the war until its departure in 1971.

The sizeable Marine Corps force in the Republic of Vietnam attained its highest strength in 1968 when it numbered nearly 86,000 Marines ashore, or more than one-fourth of the Corps' total strength. In that year, III MAF withstood the test of the North Vietnamese Army's best efforts at Hue City and Khe Sanh. By the end of the year, the Marines had assumed the offensive.

In 1969 the Marine command undertook its most ambitious operation, Dewey Canyon. The 9th Marines conducted a series of assaults against the North Vietnamese Army (NVA) in the Da Krong Valley and enemy Base Area 611, netting 1,600 enemy killed and more than 1,400 weapons captured.

By the end of 1969, the Marine Corps had begun to withdraw units as part of President Richard M. Nixon's plan of "Vietnamization," but continued the pacification efforts that Marines had emphasized since soon after their arrival at Da Nang. Dedicated to ridding the rural areas of Viet Cong, part of the effort included Marine Corps civic action and the imaginative combined action program which placed reinforced squads of Marines with South Vietnamese local militia units in the countryside. At the end of May 1971, the U.S. Marine Corps operational presence in South Vietnam ended.

For most Marines, it meant the last time Vietnam would be part of their active vocabulary. But for the Marines of the 9th Marine Amphibious Brigade on board ships in the Western Pacific, and the 1st Marine Aircraft Wing, at Iwakuni, Japan, and on Okinawa, the call to arms rang twice more, both times on an Easter weekend. The first was in 1972 when the NVA launched the "Easter Offensive," forcing the United States to deploy Marine Corps aircraft squadrons quickly from Iwakuni and Kaneohe Bay, Hawaii. The second and last time occurred in April 1975, when the NVA's "Spring Offensive" resulted in victory for the North.

During the months between the withdrawal of the last operational units and these two offensives, the Marine Corps advised and assisted the Vietnamese Marine Corps (VNMC). U.S. Marine advisors wore the Vietnamese Marine uniform and provided on-scene operational advice and assistance. After the signing of the Paris Peace Accords in January 1973, the Marine advisors were replaced by a single billet in the new Defense Attache Office with the title, Chief, VNMC Logistic Support Branch, Navy Division, DAO.

Three Marines would serve in this capacity before the final chapter of the Vietnamese Marine Corps came to a close. It met its end with two of its brigades, 147 and 468, deployed northeast of Saigon in blocking positions, while its headquarters element and an undersized battalion remained at Vung Tau. Only the officers and men of the headquarters unit escaped capture as they and their dependents evacuated by air in the last days of the republic. On 30 April 1975, after President Duong Van Minh surrendered to the Communists and ordered his soldiers to lay down their arms, the Vietnamese Marines marched from their positions near Long Binh to their base camp at Song Thon. After arriving there the battalion commanders and their men changed into civilian clothes and began to exit the base. As this was occurring, the invading NVA entered Song Than and rounded up the officers, taking them prisoner. The capture of these officers ended the proud history of the VNMC and for them it began a new life in North Vietnamese re-education camps, some of the same camps occupied earlier in the war by many of the 47 U.S. Marine Corps prisoners of war.

The war was costly to the U.S. Marine Corps. From 1965 through 1975, an estimated 730,000 men and women served in the Marine Corps; approximately 500,000 of that number served in Vietnam. The Marines sustained casualties of more than 13,000 killed in action and 88,630 wounded, nearly a third of all American casualties in the war.

Would a strategy of pacification as Marine commanders advocated early on, rather than a strategy of attrition as followed by ComUSMACV, have made for a different outcome? Was a direct amphibious assault against North Vietnam possible without leading to a larger conflagration? Could the United States have occupied Laos and Cambodia and cut the Ho Chi Minh Trail without bringing in China? Was there a way for civilian and military policymakers to have better explained the war to the American people? Should we have gone into Vietnam in the first place? These are the unresolved questions about America's longest war.

Notes

PART I
The United States Presence in the Western Pacific

CHAPTER 1
THE WAR GOES ON

Unless otherwise noted the material in this chapter is derived from: 9th MAB ComdC, May75; "Ending the War and Restoring Peace in Vietnam, Agreements and Protocols: Signed January 27, 1973," *United States Treaties and other International Agreements*, Vol 24, Part 1 (Washington: U.S. Department of State, 1973), pp. 4-64, hereafter "Ending the War"; General Van Tien Dung, *Our Great Spring Victory*, John Spragens, Jr., trans. (London: Monthly Review Press, 1977), hereafter *Spring Victory*; General Tran Van Tra, *Vietnam: History of the Bulwark B2 Theatre—Concluding the Thirty Years War*, vol. 5, Southeast Asia Report, No. 1247, 2Feb83, trans. by Joint Publications Research Service for Foreign Broadcast Information Service, hereafter *B2 Theatre*; U.S. House Subcommittee on Appropriations, *Oversight of Fiscal Year 1975 Military Assistance in Vietnam*, 94th Cong., 1st Sess., 1974, hereafter *House Report Vietnam*; U.S. Senate Committee on Foreign Relations, *A Staff Report, Vietnam: May 1974*, 93rd Cong., 2d Sess., 1974, hereafter *Senate Report Vietnam*; Defense Attache Office, Saigon, "Defense Attache Saigon: RVNAF Final Assessment Jan thru Apr FY 75," dtd 15Jun75, prepared by Col William E. LeGro, USA, hereafter "Final Assessment"; LtCol George E. Strickland intvw, 6May76, Tape 6171, (Oral HistColl, Marine Corps Historical Center, Washington, D.C.), hereafter Strickland intvw; Senior Marine Advisor, VNMC/Marine Advisory Unit Historical Summary dtd 22Mar73, hereafter VNMC/MAU HistSum. All U.S. Army documents unless otherwise indicated are held at the U.S. Army Center of Military History, Washington, D.C., hereafter CMH. All U.S. Navy documents unless otherwise indicated are held at the Operational Archives Branch, Navy Historical Division, Washington, D.C., hereafter OAB, NHD. All other documents and interviews unless otherwise noted are held at Marine Corps Historical Center (MCHC), Washington, D.C. Messages and After Action Reports are held in the Vietnam File (1973-75) at the MCHC, hereafter Vietnam File, 1973-75. Unless otherwise cited all comments on the draft manuscript are held in the Comment File, 1973-75, also at the MCHC, hereafter Comment File.

1. 9th MAB ComdC, May75.

Paris Peace Accords

2. "Ending the War," p. 4.
3. *Spring Victory*, pp. 9-10.
4. "Iran to Replace Canada on ICCS," *Facts on File*, Vol 33, No. 1709, p. 633; "Iran Assumes ICCS Duties," *Facts on File*, Vol 33, No. 1713, p. 717.
5. "Ending the War," p. 7.
6. *B2 Theatre*, p. 19.
7. Ibid., pp. 19-20.
8. Ibid., p. 20.
9. Jeffrey J. Clarke, *Advice and Support: The Final Years, 1965-73, The U.S. Army in Vietnam* (Washington: Center of Military History, 1988), pp. 491-492, hereafter *Advice and Support*.
10. U.S. Embassy, DAO NavDivHistRpt for Apr73, Tab E, Mekong Convoys, 7Jun73 (OAB, NHD).
11. Ibid.
12. ComNavForV msg to Commander, Naval Forces Vietnam, dtd 29Mar73 (OAB, NHD).
13. Stephen Weiss, Clark Dougan, David Fulghum, Denis Kennedy, and editors, *A War Remembered, The Vietnam Experience* (Boston: Boston Publishing Co., 1986), p. 144, hereafter *War Remembered*; MajGen John E. Murray, USA (Ret) intvw, 28Sept89, Memorandum for the Record (Vietnam File, 1973-75).
14. Directorate for Information, Operations, and Reports, *Department of Defense Selected Manpower Statistics, Fiscal Year 1983* (Washington: Department of Defense, 1984), p. 128.
15. "Ending the War," pp. 7-8.
16. Files of the U.S. Army Adjutant General Casualty Information Center (1961-81), National Archives and Records Service, Washington, D.C.; Philip A. McCombs, "U.S. Body Hunter Killed by VC," *Washington Post*, 16Dec73, pp. A1 and A32.
17. "Murder in Vietnam," *Des Moines Tribune*, 18Dec73, p. 10.
18. MajGen Murray, USA, msg to VAdm De Poix, USN, DIA, dtd 24Dec73 (Vietnam File, 1973-75).

The NVA Marshals in the South

19. LtCol William E. McKinstry intvw, 16Apr76, Tape No. 6170 (Oral HistColl, MCHC).
20. LtCol George E. Strickland, Comments on draft ms, 12Oct88 (Comment File), hereafter Strickland Comments.
21. Ibid.
22. *House Report Vietnam*, p. 9.
23. Ibid.
24. *Spring Victory*, p. 14.
25. *House Report Vietnam*, p. 10.
26. Ibid.; "Final Assessment."
27. Strickland Comments.
28. Ibid.; "Final Assessment."
29. *Spring Victory*, pp. 9, 19-20.
30. Ibid., p. 17.
31. *Senate Report Vietnam*, pp. 21-25; *Spring Victory*, pp. 17-18.
32. LtCol Anthony Lukeman ltr to Maj Robert E. Hamilton, dtd 11Sep74.
33. *House Report Vietnam*, p. 95.
34. Ibid., pp. 81-86.
35. *Senate Report Vietnam*, p. 6.
36. U.S. Air Force Directorate of Management Analysis, *Southeast Asia Review*, dtd 31May74, pp. 34-35; *Advice and Support*, pp. 458-461.

37. Gen William W. Momyer, USAF (Ret), *Airpower in Three Wars* (Washington: Department of the Air Force, 1978), p. 118, hereafter *Airpower*.
38. Kenneth P. Werrell, *Archie, Flak, AAA, and SAM: A Short Operational History of Ground-Based Air Defense* (Maxwell Air Force Base: Air University Press, 1988), pp. 107-109, hereafter *Air Defense*.
39. *Air Power*, p. 326.
40. *Air Defense*, p. 116.
41. *Air Power*, p. 337.
42. LtGen Le Nguyen Khang intvw, 30Sept75, pp. 77-78 (Oral HistColl, MCHC).
43. *House Report Vietnam*, pp. 95-98.
44. Edward J. Marolda and G. Wesley Pryce III, *A Short History of the United States Navy and the Southeast Asian Conflict, 1950-1975* (Washington: Navy Historical Division, 1984), p. 3.
45. Captain Nguyen Xuan Son intvw, 16Jul75, pp. 3-4 (OAB, NHD).
46. Col Richard McMahon, USA (Ret), "Saigon '75: The Inevitable Collapse," *The Retired Officer*, Apr85, pp. 18-22.
47. *House Report Vietnam*, p. 21; "Final Assessment."
48. *House Report Vietnam*, p. 119; "Final Assessment."
49. *House Report Vietnam*, p. 121; "Final Assessment."
50. *House Report Vietnam*, p. 117; "Final Assessment."
51. *House Report Vietnam*, p. 122; "Final Assessment."
52. *House Report Vietnam*, p. 13; "Final Assessment."
53. *War Remembered*, p. 144.

A Division of Marines

54. LtCol Anthony Lukeman intvw, 6May76, Tape 6169 (Oral HistColl, MCHC), hereafter Lukeman intvw.
55. Strickland Comments; VNMC/MAU HistSum.
56. DAO, Saigon, Qtr Rpt 30Jun74, Ch 8, pp. 8-1 to 8-4 (CMH).
57. Lukeman intvw.
58. Strickland intvw.
59. Ibid.
60. Strickland intvw.
61. VNMC/MAU HistSum.
62. Strickland intvw.
63. Ibid.
64. Intel Div, HQMC Fact Sheet on VNMC, Jan75, p. 4-1.
65. Ibid.
66. LtCol Anthony Lukeman ltr to Maj Robert E. Hamilton dtd 13Dec74.

CHAPTER 2
THE UNITED STATES PRESENCE IN SOUTHEAST ASIA

Unless otherwise noted the material in this chapter is derived from: 1st MAW ComdCs for 1Jan-30Jun72, 1Jul-31Dec72, 1Jan-30Jun73, 1Jul-31Dec73, and 1Jul-31Dec74, hereafter 1st MAW ComdC, month and year; MAG-15 ComdCs for 1Jan-30Jun72, 1Jul-31Dec72, 1Jan-30Jun73, and 1Jul-31Dec73, hereafter MAG-15 ComdC, month and year; MAG-12 ComdCs for 1Jan-30Jun72, 1Jan-30Jun73, 1Jul-31Dec73, and 1Jul-31Dec74, hereafter MAG-12 ComdC, month and year; 1st MAW Task Force Delta After Action Report, May72-Sept73, entitled "The Rose Garden Story," hereafter Task Force Delta Report; VMA-311 ComdCs for 1Jan-30Jun72, 1Jul-31Dec72, 1Jan-30Jun73, and 1Jul-31Dec74, hereafter VMA-311 ComdC, month and year; VMA-211 ComdCs for 1Jan-30Jun72 and 1Jan-30Jun73, hereafter VMA-211 ComdC, month and year; 3d MarDiv ComdCs for 1Jan-30Jun73 and 1Jul-31Dec74, hereafter 3d MarDiv ComdC, month and year; and Company E, Marine Security Guard Battalion ComdC, 1Jul-31Dec73, hereafter Co E, MSG Bn ComdC. Also used in this chapter were *Senate Report Vietnam*; *Spring Victory*; Bernard C. Nalty, Comments on draft ms, dtd 24Oct88, hereafter Nalty Comments; Strickland Comments; LtCol Anthony A. Grimm, Comments on draft ms, dtd 28Nov88 (Comment File), hereafter Grimm Comments; and Strickland intvw.

1. Directorate for Information, Operations, and Reports, *Department of Defense Selected Manpower Statistics, Fiscal Year 1983* (Washington: Department of Defense, 1984), p. 128.
2. U.S. Embassy, DAO NavDivHistRpt, 29Mar73, p. 14.
3. *Senate Report Vietnam*, p. 20.

The Forces in Thailand

4. MAG 15 ComdC, 1Jan-30Jun72; Task Force Delta Report.
5. MAG-15 ComdCs, 1Jan-30Jun72 and 1Jul-31Dec72; Task Force Delta Report.
6. MAG-15 ComdCs, 1Jul72-31Dec72, 1Jan73-30Jun73, and 1Jul-31Dec73; Task Force Delta Report.
7. LtCol Horace W. Baker intvw, 1Sep76, Tape 6163 (Oral HistColl, MCHC), hereafter Baker intvw.
8. Ibid.
9. Grimm Comments.
10. Baker intvw.
11. LtCol Anthony A. Grimm intvw, 22Nov75, Tape 6191 (Oral HistColl, MCHC), hereafter Grimm intvw; Earl H. Tilford, *Search and Rescue in Southeast Asia, 1961-1975* (Washington: Office of Air Force History, 1980), pp. 127-128, hereafter *Search and Rescue in Southeast Asia*.
12. Grimm intvw.
13. Ibid.
14. Grimm intvw; Col John S. Roosma, USAF (Ret) intvw, 17Oct89, Tape 8990 (Oral HistColl, MCHC), hereafter Roosma intvw.
15. Roosma intvw; Benjamin M. Elson, "Command, Control Update Planned," *Aviation Week and Space Technology*, 6Mar78, pp. 52-54.

The Forces Afloat

16. *Spring Victory*, p. 25.
17. VAdm George P. Steele, USN, "The Seventh Fleet," *U.S. Naval Institute Proceedings*, Jan76, pp. 24-30.
18. Ibid.
19. Ibid.

The III Marine Amphibious Force

20. 1st MAW ComdCs, 1Jan-30Jun72, 1Jul-31Dec72, 1Jan-30Jun73, and 1Jul-31Dec73.
21. 1st MAW ComdC, 1Jan-30Jun72; MAG-12 ComdC, 1Jan-30Jun72; MAG-15 ComdC, 1Jan-30Jun72.
22. VMA-311 ComdCs, 1Jan-30Jun72, 1Jul-31Dec72, and 1Jan-30Jun73; VMA-211 ComdCs, 1Jan-30Jun72 and 1Jan-30Jun73.
23. 1st MAW ComdC, 1Jan-30Jun72; MAG-15 ComdCs, 1Jan-30Jun73 and 1Jul-31Dec73; Task Force Delta Report; MAG-12 ComdC 1Jul-31Dec73.
24. 1st MAW ComdCs, 1Jul-31Dec73 and 1Jul-31Dec74; MAG-12

ComdCs, 1Jul-31Dec73 and 1Jul-31Dec74; VMA-311 ComdC, 1Jul-31Dec74.
25. 1st MAW ComdCs, 1Jan-30Jun73 and 1Jul-31Dec73.
26. 3d MarDiv ComdC, 1Jan-30Jun73.
27. Ibid.
28. 3d MarDiv ComdC, 1Jul-31Dec74.

Americans Ashore

29. Baker intvw.
30. Strickland Comments.
31. *Senate Report Vietnam*, pp. 20-22.
32. Ibid.

The Marines in Vietnam

33. Strickland intvw.
34. Strickland Comments.
35. Col Nicholas M. Trapnell, Jr., Comments on draft ms, 12Nov88 (Comment File).
36. Maj Jaime Sabater, Jr., intvw, 30Apr76, Tape 6164 (Oral Hist-Coll, MCHC).
37. Strickland Comments.
38. Co E, MSG Bn ComdC.
39. Co E, MSG Bn ComdC, 1Jan-30Jun74.
40. Ibid.

CHAPTER 3
CONTINGENCY PLANNING

In preparing this chapter the following command chronologies were used: III MAF ComdCs for 1Jan-30Jun73, 1Jul-31Dec73, and 1Jul-31Dec74, hereafter III MAF ComdC, month and year; 31st MAU ComdCs 1Jan-31Dec73, 1Jan-31Dec74, and 1Jan-31May75, hereafter 31st MAU ComdC, month and year; 9th MAB ComdC, 1Jul-31Dec72, hereafter 9th MAB ComdC; and 1st Battalion, 9th Marines ComdC, 1Jul-31Dec74, hereafter 1/9 ComdC. Also used in this chapter were Col John F. Roche III, Comments on draft ms, 22Sept88 (Comment File), hereafter Roche Comments; and VAdm George P. Steele, USN, Comments on draft ms, 30Nov88 (Comment File), hereafter Steele Comments.

1. USMACThai/JUSMAGThai ComdHist 1973, 30Aug74, Bangkok, Thailand (OAB, NHD), hereafter USMACThai Hist.
2. Facts on File, *Facts on File Yearbook 1971*, 11-17 Nov 1971, pp. 897-898.
3. USMACThai Hist.
4. Ibid.
5. Gen Timothy F. O'Keefe, USAF intvw, 14-15Jun82 (Office of Air Force History, Washington, D.C.), p. 82.
6. Gen Timothy F. O'Keefe, USAF biography, dtd 1Nov73 (Office of Air Force History, Washington, D.C.), p. 30.

The Plan for Cambodia

7. CinCPac msg to CGIIIMAF, dtd 13Apr73, hereafter CinCPac msg.
8. Ibid.
9. Baker intvw.
10. Maj James B. Hicks intvw, 18Sept75, Tape No. 6146 (Oral Hist-Coll, MCHC), hereafter Hicks intvw.
11. CinCPac msg.
12. CGIIIMAF msg to CO, 31st MAU, dtd 15Apr73.
13. CGIIIMAF msg to CG, 3d MarDiv, dtd 20Apr73.

14. Hicks intvw.
15. MajGen Edward J. Bronars, Comments on draft chapter, 17Jan76 (Comment File).
16. Baker intvw.
17. Ibid.
18. Ibid.
19. Hicks intvw.
20. Baker intvw.
21. Hicks intvw.
22. Grimm intvw.
23. III MAF ComdC, 1Jan-30Jun73.
24. Baker intvw.
25. Ibid.
26. Hicks intvw.
27. III MAF ComdC, 1Jul-31Dec73; Maj James B. Hicks' Trip Report, Part IV (Vietnam File, 1973-75).
28. Grimm intvw.
29. Baker intvw.
30. Hicks intvw.
31. 31st MAU ComdC, Aug73.
32. Ibid.
33. 31st MAU ComdC, Sep73.
34. 31st MAU ComdC, Jun74.
35. Grimm intvw.
36. Ibid.

Vietnam

37. 9th MAB ComdC, 1Jul-31Dec74.
38. III MAF ComdC, 1Jul-31Dec74; Steele Comments.
39. III MAF ComdC, 1Jul-31Dec74.
40. Steele Comments.
41. Ibid.
42. III MAF ComdC, 1Jul-31Dec74.
43. LtCol James L. Cunningham intvw, 17Sep76, Tape 6189 (Oral HistColl, MCHC), hereafter Cunningham intvw.
44. Ibid.
45. 3d MarDiv ComdC, 1Jul-31Dec74.
46. Cunningham intvw.
47. 1/9 ComdC, 1Jul-31Dec74.
48. Ibid.
49. Cunningham intvw.

CHAPTER 4
THE FLEET MARINES ARE READIED

In preparing this chapter the following command chronologies were used: III MAF ComdC, 1Jan-30Jun73, hereafter III MAF ComdC, Jan-Jun73; III MAF ComdC, 1Jul-31Dec73, hereafter III MAF ComdC, Jul-Dec73; 31st MAU ComdCs, Jul73-Jun74, hereafter 31st MAU ComdC, month and year; 4th Marines ComdC, 1Jul-31Dec973, hereafter 4th Mar ComdC, 1Jul-31Dec73; and 9th Marines ComdCs, 1Jul-31Dec73, 1Jul-31Dec74, and 1Jan-30Jun75, hereafter 9th Mar ComdC, month and year. The cited messages are held in the Vietnam message binder (1973-75) in the archives at MCHC. Also used in this chapter were LtGen Stephen G. Olmstead, Comments on draft ms, 4Nov88 (Comment File), hereafter Olmstead Comments; MajGen Richard E. Carey, Comments on draft ms, 11May89 (Comment File), hereafter Carey Comments; Col Alexander S. Ruggiero, Comments on draft ms, 20Sept88 (Comment File), hereafter Ruggiero Comments; Col Peter M. Angle, Comments on draft ms, 4Nov88 (Comment File), hereafter Angle Comments;

Col Floyd A. Karker, Comments on draft ms, 21Sept88 (Comment File), hereafter Karker Comments; and LtCol Curtis G. Lawson, Comments on draft ms, 21Oct88 (Comment File), hereafter Lawson Comments.

The Air Contingency BLTs

1. CincPac msg to CGIIIMAF, dtd 13Apr73.
2. CGIIIMAF msg to CG, 3d MarDiv, dtd 15Apr73.
3. CO, CTG 79.4 msg to TG 79.4, dtd 17Apr73.
4. CGIIIMAF msg to CO, 31st MAU, dtd 20Apr73.
5. III MAF ComdC, Jan-Jun73.
6. Maj Henry C. Stackpole memo to CO, 9th Mar, Subj: Eagle Pull, dtd 29Sept73, p. 1 (Eagle Pull File).
7. 9th Mar ComdCs, Jul-Dec73 and Jul-Dec74.

The Eagle Pull Command Element

8. III MAF ComdC, Jul-Dec73.
9. Olmstead Comments; Angle Comments.
10. Lawson Comments.
11. Biographical sketch of LtGen John J. Burns, USAF (Office of Air Force History, Washington, D.C.).

The 31st MAU

12. Karker Comments.
13. 31st MAU ComdC, Jul73.
14. Ibid.
15. 31st MAU ComdC, Aug73.
16. Ibid.
17. Ibid., p. 6.
18. 31st MAU ComdC, Sep73.
19. 31st MAU ComdC, Oct73.
20. 31st MAU ComdC, Nov73.
21. 31st MAU ComdC, Dec73.
22. 31st MAU ComdC, Jan74.
23. 31st MAU ComdC, Feb74.
24. 31st MAU ComdC, Apr74.
25. 31st MAU ComdC, Jun74.
26. Capt Richard L. Jaehne intvw, 1Mar77, Tape 6192 (Oral Hist-Coll, MCHC).

The Other Contingency

27. 9th Mar ComdCs, Jul-Dec74 and Jan-Jul75.
28. Ibid.
29. Maj David A. Quinlan intvw, 16Mar76, Tape 6158 (Oral Hist-Coll, MCHC), hereafter Quinlan intvw; Carey Comments.
30. Carey Comments.

PART II
South Vietnam

CHAPTER 5
THE NORTH VIETNAMESE WINTER-SPRING OFFENSIVE, 1974-75: THE MORTAL BLOW

Unless otherwise noted the material in this chapter is derived from *Spring Victory*; "Final Assessment"; Col William E. Le Gro, USA, *Vietnam From Cease-Fire to Capitulation* (Washington: U.S. Army Center of Military History, 1981), hereafter *Cease-Fire to Capitulation*; Gen Cao Van Vien, *The Final Collapse* (Washington: U.S. Army Center of Military History, 1983), hereafter *Final Collapse*; Clark Dougan, David Fulghum, and editors, *The Fall of the South* (Boston: Boston Publishing Co., 1985), hereafter *Fall of the South*; David Butler, *The Fall of Saigon* (New York: Simon and Schuster, 1985), hereafter *Fall of Saigon*; Arnold R. Isaacs, *Without Honor* (Baltimore: John Hopkins University Press, 1983), hereafter *Without Honor*; and Col Harry G. Summers, Jr., *Vietnam Almanac* (New York: Facts on File Publications, 1985), hereafter *Vietnam Almanac*. Also used were LtCol Tran Ngoc Toan, Comments on draft ms, 16Mar90 (Comment File), hereafter Toan Comments; LtCol Edward A. Grimm, Comments on draft ms, 28Nov88 (Comment File), hereafter Grimm Comments.

The Collapse of the Central Highlands

1. *Spring Victory*, pp. 31-34; *Cease-Fire to Capitulation*, pp. 132-136.
2. *Final Collapse*, pp. 58-68.
3. Edward J. Marolda, Comments on draft ms, 6Jan89 (Comment File).
4. *Spring Victory*, pp. 23-26.
5. "Final Assessment," p. 5-1.
6. *Fall of the South*, pp. 46-49.
7. "Final Assessment," p. 1-10; *Fall of the South*, pp. 48-52.
8. *Spring Victory*, p. 44.
9. *Fall of the South*, p. 49; *Final Collapse*, pp. 69-70; *Cease-Fire to Capitulation*, pp. 147-149.
10. *Fall of the South*, pp. 49-50; *Final Collapse*, 70-72; *Cease-Fire to Capitulation*, 149-151.
11. *Fall of the South*, pp. 50-52; *Final Collapse*, 72-75; *Cease-Fire to Capitulation*, 151-152; *Spring Victory*, pp. 83-85.
12. *Fall of the South*, p. 54.
13. Ibid., pp. 54-63.
14. *Spring Victory*, p. 94.
15. *Cease-Fire to Capitulation*, p. 154.
16. *Without Honor*, p. 356.

Defeat in Military Region 1

17. "Final Assessment," p. 2-2.
18. *Cease-Fire to Capitulation*, pp. 156-157; *Fall of the South*, pp. 66-68; Toan Comments.
19. *Final Collapse*, p. 99; *Vietnam Almanac*, p. 79.
20. *Spring Victory*, p. 132.
21. "Final Assessment," p. 5-2.
22. *Spring Victory*, p. 132.
23. "Final Assessment," p. 1-9.

A Wasted Division

24. Ibid., p. 8-1.
25. Ibid.
26. Lukeman intvw.
27. Toan Comments.
28. "Final Assessment," p. 5-1.
29. "Final Assessment," pp. 8-1, 8-2.

CHAPTER 6
THE EVACUATION OF SOUTH VIETNAM'S NORTHERN PROVINCES

In preparing this chapter the following command chronologies were used: III MAF ComdC, 1Jan-30Jun75, hereafter III MAF

ComdC; 3d Marine Division ComdC, 1Jan-30Jun75, hereafter 3d MarDiv ComdC; 9th MAB ComdC, 25Mar-30Apr75, hereafter 9th MAB ComdC; 31st MAU ComdC, 1Jan-18Apr75, hereafter 31st MAU ComdC; 1st Battalion, 4th Marines ComdC, 1Jan-18Apr75, hereafter 1/4 ComdC; and HMM-165 ComdC, 1Jan-30Apr75, hereafter HMM-165 ComdC. Also used were: Steele Comments; Col Carl A. Shaver, Comments on draft ms, 20Apr89 (Comment File), hereafter Shaver Comments; Capt Charles J. Bushey, Comments on draft ms, 2Oct88 (Comment File), hereafter Bushey Comments; and LtCol Walter J. Wood, Comments on draft ms, 3Oct88 (Comment File), hereafter Wood Comments.

The Amphibious Evacuation RVN Support Group

1. III MAF ComdC.
2. 31st MAU ComdC.
3. 1/4 ComdC.
4. Quinlan intvw.
5. Ibid.
6. III MAF ComdC.
7. CO, CTF 76 msg to CO, Amphibious Evacuation RVN Support Group, dtd 30Mar75.

Initial Operations in Vietnamese Waters

8. 1/4 ComdC.
9. LtCol Charles E. Hester intvw, 10May75, Tape 6095 (Oral HistColl), hereafter Hester intvw; CWO2 Allen F. Kent intvw, 10May75, Tape 6060 (Oral HistColl, MCHC), hereafter Kent intvw.
10. Ibid.
11. 3d MarDiv ComdC.
12. 1/4 ComdC.
13. Ibid.
14. Ibid.

Military Sealift Command Operations

15. Ibid.
16. Ibid.
17. LtCol Gerald L. Berry, Comments on draft ms, dtd 3Oct88 (Comment File).
18. PacAF Office of History, "The Fall and Evacuation of South Vietnam," 30Apr78, pp. 63-67 (copy of pp. 63-67 in Vietnam File, 1973-75).
19. HMM-165 ComdC.
20. Bushey Comments.
21. Hester intvw.
22. Bushey Comments.

Meeting the Needs

23. 1/4 ComdC.
24. Ibid.
25. Hester intvw.

PART III
Operation Eagle Pull

CHAPTER 7
THE EVACUATION OF PHNOM PENH

In preparing this chapter the following command chronologies were used: 31st MAU ComdC, 1Jan-18Apr75, hereafter 31st MAU ComdC; III MAF ComdC, 1Jan-30Jun75, hereafter III MAF ComdC; III MAF ComdC, 1Jan-30Jun75, containing Trip Report of Col Sydney T. Batchelder, hereafter Batchelder Trip Report; HMH-463 ComdC, 1Jan-30Apr75, hereafter HMH-463 ComdC; and 11th MAB ComdC, 26Mar-5Apr75, hereafter 11th MAB ComdC. Additional sources for this section were derived from U.S. Senate Subcommittee on Foreign Assistance and Economic Policy, *Supplemental Assistance to Cambodia*, 94th Cong., 1st Sess. (Washington: GPO, 1975), hereafter Senate Subcmt Rpt Cambodia; U.S. House Subcommittee on Foreign Operations and Related Agencies, *Budget Amendment for Military Assistance to Cambodia, Foreign Assistance and Related Agencies Appropriations for 1975*, 94th Cong., 1st Sess. (Washington, GPO, 1975), hereafter House Subcmt Rpt Cambodia; U.S. Senate Committee on Foreign Relations, *U.S. Operations in Cambodia: April, 1973*, 93d Cong., 1st Sess., (Washington: GPO, 1973), hereafter Senate For Rel Cmt Rpt; and *Without Honor*. Also used were: Carey Comments; Steele Comments; Grimm Comments; Roche Comments; LtCol William R. Melton, Comments on draft ms, 14Nov88 (Comment File), hereafter Melton Comments; and LtCol John F. Guilmartin, Jr., USAF (Ret), Comments on draft ms, 27Sep88 (Comment File), hereafter Guilmartin Comments. Messages and after action reports are located in the Eagle Pull-Frequent Wind File.

The Khmer Rouge

1. Senate Subcmt Rpt Cambodia, p. 17.
2. Grimm intvw.
3. House Subcmt Rpt Cambodia.
4. House Subcmt Rpt Cambodia, pp. 48-49; Grimm intvw.
5. House Subcmt Rpt Cambodia, p. 10; Senate Subcmt Rpt Cambodia, p. 13; Grimm intvw.
6. Grimm intvw.
7. Ibid.
8. Senate For Rel Cmt Rpt.

The Khmer Communists' Last Dry Season Offensive

9. Ibid.
10. U.S. House Subcommittee on Foreign Operations and Related Agencies, *Foreign Assistance and Related Agencies Appropriations for 1975*, Hearings, Part 3, 94th Cong., 1st Sess. (Washington: GPO, 1975), pp. 9-12.
11. H. D. S. Greenway, "Convoy Brings Gas, Ammo to Phnom Penh," 28Jan75, p. 8, and "Mines in Mekong Tip Balance to Insurgents," 7Feb75, p. 18, *The Washington Post*.
12. Senate Subcmt Rpt, p. 31.
13. U.S. House Special Subcommittee on Investigations of the Committee on International Relations, *The Vietnam-Cambodia Emergency 1975, Part IV, Cambodian Evacuation: Testimony of Ambassador John Gunther Dean*, 94th Cong., 2d Sess. (Washington: GPO, 1976), p. 6634, hereafter Dean Testimony.
14. Ibid.

The Marines Move into Position

15. 31st MAU ComdC.
16. III MAF ComdC.
17. 31st MAU ComdC.
18. Batchelder Trip Report.
19. 31st MAU ComdC; Roche Comments.
20. Steele Comments.
21. Batchelder Trip Report.
22. HMH-463 ComdC.

23. 11th MAB ComdC.
24. Ibid.
25. Ibid.
26. Batchelder Trip Report.
27. 9th MAB AAR, 30Jun75, "Operation Frequent Wind."
28. 31st MAU ComdC.
29. HMH-463 ComdC.

Final Preparations Ashore

30. LtCol Curtis G. Lawson intvw, 26May75, Tape 6041 (Oral Hist-Coll, MCHC), hereafter Lawson intvw.
31. Batchelder Trip Report.
32. *Without Honor.*
33. Maj George L. Cates, unrecorded conversation with Maj David A. Quinlan, 1Jul76.
34. Lawson intvw.

Final Preparations at Sea

35. Col John F. Roche III intvw, 31May75, Tape 6130 (Oral Hist-Coll, MCHC), hereafter Roche intvw.
36. LtCol George P. Slade intvw, 4Jun75, Tape 6131 (Oral HistColl, MCHC), hereafter Slade intvw.
37. Roche Comments.
38. Slade intvw.
39. 31st MAU ComdC.
40. Ibid.
41. Ibid.

The Execution of Eagle Pull

42. Batchelder Trip Report.
43. 31st MAU ComdC.
44. Dean Testimony.
45. Roche intvw.
46. Maj William R. Melton intvw, 30Jun86, Tape 122 (Oral Hist-Coll, MCHC); Melton Comments.
47. Batchelder Trip Report.
48. 31st MAU ComdC.

PART IV
Ending an Alliance

CHAPTER 8
THE OTHER CONTINGENCY

In preparing this chapter the following materials were used: III MAF ComdC, 1Jan-30Jun75, hereafter III MAF ComdC; 31st MAU ComdC, 1Jan-30Apr75, hereafter 31st MAU ComdC; 9th MAB ComdC, 26Mar-30Apr75, hereafter 9th MAB ComdC; 4th Marines ComdC, 1Jan-30Jun75, hereafter 4th Marines ComdC; 1st Bn, 4th Marines Post-Exercise Report, Amphibious Evacuation RVN Support Group (CTG 79.9) dtd 30Apr75, hereafter 1/4 Post-Ex Rpt; VMGR-152 ComdC 1Jan-30Jun75, hereafter VMGR-152 ComdC; AESF ComdC, 17Apr-31May75, hereafter AESF ComdC; and Marine Corps Command Center Items of Significant Interest, hereafter MCCC ISA with date and enclosure. Also used were materials from Stephen Hosmer, Konrad Kellen, and Brian Jenkins, *The Fall of South Vietnam: Statements by Vietnamese Military and Civilian Leaders* (New York: Crane, Russak and Co., 1980), hereafter *Fall of South Vietnam: Statements*; LtCol Charles A. Barstow ltr to Gen Wallace M. Greene, Jr., dtd 18Dec73 (Vietnam File, 1973-75), hereafter Barstow ltr; *Fall of Saigon*; and *Cease-Fire to Capitulation*. Also Steele Comments and MSgt Michael A. McCormick, Comments on draft ms, 9Nov88 (Comment File), hereafter McCormick Comments.

1. Sun Tzu, *The Art of War*, Samuel B. Griffith, trans. (London: Oxford University Press, 1963), p. 77, hereafter *Art of War.*
2. *Fall of Saigon*, pp. 117-151.
3. Barstow ltr.
4. *Fall of South Vietnam: Statements*, p. 210.
5. Ibid., p. 211.

Marine Security Guard Detachment, Da Nang

6. Co C, MSG Bn ComdC, 1Jan-30Jun75.
7. SSgt Walter W. Sparks intvw, 7May75, Tape 6267 (Oral Hist-Coll, MCHC), hereafter Sparks intvw.
8. Ibid.
9. MCCC ISA, 3Mar75, with Encl 1: MCCC Talon Vise Message Summary (Vietnam File, 1973-75).
10. CG, Seventh Air Force msg to JCS, dtd 27Mar75 (Vietnam File, 1973-75).
11. MCCC ISA, 3Mar75, with Encl 1: MCCC Talon Vise Message Summary (Vietnam File, 1973-75).
12. Sparks Intvw.
13. Ibid.
14. MCCC ISA, 3Mar75, with Encl 1: MCCC Talon Vise Message Summary (Vietnam File, 1973-75).
15. Sparks Intvw.
16. Ibid.
17. Ibid.
18. Ibid.
19. Ibid.
20. Ibid.
21. Ibid.
22. Ibid.
23. Steele Comments.
24. MCCC ISA, 30Mar75, with Encl 1: MCCC Message Summary (Vietnam File, 1973-75).
25. 4th Marines ComdC.

Military Region 2: Nha Trang

26. *Fall of South Vietnam: Statements*, p. 199.
27. Ibid., p. 201.
28. MCCC ISA, 1Apr75, with Encl 1: MCCC Message Summary (Vietnam File, 1973-75).
29. Sgt Michael A. McCormick intvw, 16Jun86, Tape 120A (Oral HistColl, MCHC), hereafter McCormick intvw.
30. Ibid.

III MAF and the NVA Onslaught

31. MCCC ISA, 3Apr75, with Encl 1: MCCC Message Summary (Vietnam File, 1973-75).
32. Ibid.
33. ComPacInt message to CinCPac, dtd 3 Apr75, hereafter ComPacInt 3Apr75 msg.
34. ComSeventhFlt message to subordinate units, dtd 3Apr75.
35. ComPacInt 3Apr75 msg.
36. *Cease-Fire to Capitulation*, pp. 173-174.

9th MAB and Task Force 76

37. 9th MAB ComdC.
38. III MAF ComdC.

The Brigade

39. LtGen Richard E. Carey official biography (RefSec, MCHC).
40. III MAF ComdC.
41. 9th MAB ComdC.
42. Ibid.
43. III MAF ComdC.
44. Quinlan intvw.
45. 9th MAB ComdC.
46. VMGR-152 ComdC.
47. 9th MAB ComdC.
48. LtCol James L. Cunningham intvw, n.d., Tape 6189 (Oral Hist-Coll, MCHC), hereafter Cunningham intvw..
49. 9th MAB ComdC.

CHAPTER 9
PLANNING THE EVACUATION

In preparing this chapter the following command chronologies were used: 9th MAB ComdC, 26Mar-30Apr75, hereafter 9th MAB ComdC; 9th MAB BLSG ComdC, 19Apr-12May75, hereafter 9th MAB BLSG ComdC; RLT 4 ComdC, 27Mar-30Apr75, hereafter RLT 4 ComdC; and AESF ComdC, 17Apr-31May75, hereafter AESF ComdC. Also used were: LtGen Richard E. Carey, Comments on draft ms, 11May89 (Comment File), hereafter Carey Comments; Col Richard K. Young, Comments on draft ms, 27Sep88 (Comment File), hereafter Young Comments; Col Anthony A. Wood, Comments on draft ms, 23Feb90 (Comment File), hereafter Wood Comments; and LtCol John F. Guilmartin, Comments on draft ms, 27Sep88 (Comment File), hereafter Guilmartin Comments.

Brigade Planning and Liaison

1. 9th MAB, OPlans, "Frequent Wind" messages, 1975; and "Operation Frequent Wind, 1975, Postoperational Summary," dtd 5Aug75 (Frequent Wind File), hereafter Frequent Wind File.
2. Ibid.
3. Ibid.
4. Ibid.
5. 9th MAB ComdC.
6. Ibid.
7. Frequent Wind File.
8. Carey Comments.

The Restructured 9th Marine Amphibious Brigade

9. *Spring Victory*, p. 154.
10. 9th MAB ComdC.
11. Col Wylie W. Taylor intvw, 5Jun75, Tape 6163 (Oral HistColl, MCHC), hereafter Taylor intvw.
12. Young Comments.
13. Taylor intvw; Cunningham intvw.
14. Taylor intvw.
15. AESF ComdC.
16. 9th MAB ComdC.
17. Ibid.
18. RLT 4 ComdC.

The Concept

19. 9th MAB ComdC.
20. Ibid.
21. Quinlan intvw.

Additional Forces, Plans, and Liaison

22. *Search and Rescue*, pp. 142-143; Guilmartin Comments.
23. *Search and Rescue*.
24. 9th MAB ComdC.
25. Ibid.
26. 9th MAB BLSG ComdC.
27. Frequent Wind File.

DAO Planning: The SPG and Project Alamo

28. Col Anthony A. Wood intvw, 13Oct89, Tape 8910 (Oral Hist-Coll, MCHC), hereafter Wood intvw.
29. LtCol William E. McKinstry intvw, 6Apr76, Tape 6170 (Oral HistColl, MCHC), hereafter McKinstry intvw; Lukeman intvw.
30. Wood intvw.
31. CG, USSAG msg to JCS, dtd 4Apr75 (Vietnam File, 1973-75).
32. Wood intvw.
33. Ibid.
34. Ibid.
35. Ibid.
36. Ibid.
37. Ibid.
38. Ibid.
39. Wood Comments.
40. Wood intvw; Wood Comments.

CHAPTER 10
THE FINAL DAYS

In preparing this chapter the following materials were used: III MAF ComdC, 1Jan-30Jun75, hereafter III MAF ComdC; 31st MAU ComdC, 1Jan-30Apr75, hereafter 31st Mau ComdC; 9th MAB ComdC, 26Mar-30Apr75, hereafter 9th MAB ComdC; 4th Marines ComdC, 1Jan-30Jun75, hereafter 4th Mar ComdC; 1/4 Post-Ex Rpt; AESF ComdC, 17Apr-31May75, hereafter AESF ComdC; and Co C, MSG Bn ComdC, 1Jan-30Jun75. Also used were: *Art of War*; *Fall of South Vietnam: Statements*; *Fall of Saigon*; *Fall of the South*; *Spring Victory*; Carey Comments; MajGen Homer D. Smith, Jr., USA (Ret), Comments on draft ms, 30Oct88 (Comment File), hereafter Smith Comments; BGen James E. Livingston, Comments on draft ms, 20Oct88 (Comment File), hereafter Livingston Comments; Col Wylie W. Taylor, Comments on draft ms, 22Sep88 (Comment File), hereafter Taylor Comments; Col David A. Quinlan, Comments on draft ms, 13Feb89 (Comment File), hereafter Quinlan Comments; and Maj Charles J. Bushey, Comments on draft ms, 2Oct88 (Comment File), hereafter Bushey Comments.

The AESF

1. Maj David A. Quinlan intvw, 30Dec75, Tape 111A (Oral Hist-Coll, MCHC), hereafter Quinlan intvw, Tape 111A.
2. 9th MAB ComdC; Quinlan intvw, Tape 111A.
3. Quinlan Comments.
4. 4th Mar ComdC; 1/4 Post-Ex Rpt; AESF ComdC; Quinlan intvw, Tape 111A.
5. Quinlan intvw, Tape 111A.
6. LtCol Cyril V. Moyher, unrecorded conversation with author, 31Dec86.
7. AESF ComdC and Quinlan intvw, Tape 111A.
8. Ibid.

9. AESF ComdC.
10. Ibid.
11. Quinlan intvw, Tape 111A.
12. Ibid.
13. Bushey Comments.
14. AESF ComdC.

Xuan Loc Remembered

15. *Spring Victory*, p. 167.
16. *Fall of the South*, pp. 129-160.
17. *Spring Victory*, pp. 219-220; *Fall of the South*, pp. 157-158.
18. 9th MAB ComdC; Smith Comments; *Fall of South Vietnam: Statements*, pp. 245-247.
19. Smith Comments.
20. 9th MAB ComdC; Smith Comments; *Fall of Saigon*, pp. 390-392.
21. *Art of War*, p. 78.

Saigon and the Final Preparation Pieces

22. 9th MAB ComdC; Livingston Comments.
23. 9th MAB ComdC; McKinstry intvw.
24. 9th MAB ComdC; McKinstry intvw; Carey Comments; Taylor Comments.
25. 9th MAB ComdC; McKinstry intvw; Taylor Comments; Wood intvw.
26. Frequent Wind File.
27. Frequent Wind File; Wood intvw.
28. 9th MAB ComdC.

Consulate Marines

29. Co C, MSG Bn ComdC, 1Jan-30Jun75; *Fall of Saigon*, pp. 329-331, 360.
30. Co C, MSG Bn ComdC, 1Jan-30Jun75.
31. SSgt Boyette S. Hasty intvw, 23 May75, Tape 6344 (Oral Hist-Coll, MCHC), hereafter Hasty intvw.
32. Ibid.
33. Ibid.
34. Ibid.
35. Ibid.
36. AESF ComdC.
37. Hasty intvw.
38. Ibid.
39. Ibid.
40. Ibid.
41. Ibid.
42. Ibid.

PART V
Operation Frequent Wind and a New Beginning

CHAPTER 11
THE EVACUATION

In preparing this chapter the following materials were used: 9th MAB ComdC, 26Mar-30Apr75, hereafter 9th MAB ComdC; RLT 4 ComdC, 27Mar-30Apr75, hereafter RLT 4 ComdC; BLT 2/4 ComdC, 19Apr-30Apr75, hereafter BLT 2/4 ComdC; BLT 1/9 ComdC, 26Mar-30Apr75, hereafter BLT 1/9 ComdC; ProvMAG-39 ComdC, 19Apr-12May75, hereafter ProvMAG-39 ComdC; and 3d Battalion, 9th Marines ComdC 1Jan-30Jun75, hereafter BLT 3/9 ComdC. Also used were: MajGen John R. D. Cleland, Jr., USA, "Memorandum for the Chairman, Joint Chiefs of Staff: NEMVAC Survey Report," May 1975, hereafter Cleland Report; Frequent Wind File; Maj A. J. C. Lavalle, ed., *Last Flight From Saigon* (Washington: Office of Air Force History, 1985), hereafter *Last Flight*; and Ray L. Bowers, *The United States Air Force in Southeast Asia: Tactical Airlift* (Washington: Office of Air Force History, 1983), hereafter *Tactical Airlift*. Also, Gen Louis H. Wilson, Comments on draft ms, 26Sep88 (Comment File), hereafter Wilson Comments; MajGen Norman W. Gourley, Comments on draft ms, 1Mar89 (Comment File), hereafter Gourley Comments; Col Edwin F. Pelosky, Comments on draft ms, 21Sep88 (Comment File), hereafter Pelosky Comments; Carey Comments; Livingston Comments; Smith Comments; Taylor Comments; Wood Comments; Young Comments; and Guilmartin Comments.

1. Livingston Comments; McKinstry intvw.
2. Livingston Comments.
3. Wood intvw.

9th MAB

4. CinCPac msg to ComSeventhFlt, dtd 20Apr75 (Frequent Wind File).
5. CG 9th MAB msg to CO, CTF 76, dtd 29Apr75 (Frequent Wind File).
6. CO, CTG 76 msg to ComSeventhFlt, dtd 24Apr75 (Frequent Wind File).
7. Young Comments.
8. Carey Comments; *Last Flight*, pp. 76-82; *Tactical Airlift*, p. 643.
9. Capt John B. Heffernan intvw, 22Jul86, Tape 112A (Oral Hist-Coll, MCHC), hereafter Heffernan intvw.
10. CG 9th MAB msg to CO, RLT 4, dtd 28Apr75 (Frequent Wind File); Livingston Comments; Taylor Comments.
11. CinCPac msg to CG, USSAG/Seventh Air Force, dtd 29Apr75 (Frequent Wind File).

The DAO Compound

12. Frequent Wind AAR msg to CG, USSAG/Seventh Air Force and ComSeventhFlt, dtd 2May75 (Frequent Wind File), hereafter 9th MAB AAR.
13. Capt William R. Melton intvw, 28Jun86, Tape 115A (Oral Hist-Coll, MCHC), hereafter Melton intvw.
14. Capt Kurt A. Schrader, written comments on Operations Eagle Pull and Frequent Wind, dtd 9May88 (Frequent Wind File).
15. Heffernan intvw.
16. RLT 4 OPlan 3-75; RLT 4 ComdC (Frequent Wind File).
17. LtCol James L. Bolton intvw, 18Jun75, Tape 113A (Oral Hist-Coll, MCHC), hereafter Bolton intvw.
18. CO, CTG 76 msg to ComSeventhFlt, CG Seventh Air Force, and all participating forces, dtd 29Apr75 (Frequent Wind File).
19. GySgt Russell R. Thurmond intvw, 5Apr85, Tape 114A (Oral HistColl, MCHC).
20. 9th MAB ComdC.
21. CO, CTG 76 msg to ComSeventhFlt, CG Seventh Air Force, and participating forces, dtd 29Apr75, hereafter Frequent Wind Helo Time Schedule.
22. BLT 2/4 ComdC.
23. Melton intvw.
24. CTF 76 Special Situation Reports, Serial Numbers 1-72, to ComSeventhFlt, dtd 29Apr75 (Frequent Wind File), hereafter Spec SitReps.
25. Ibid.

26. 9th MAB ComdC.
27. USSAG/Seventh Air Force OPlan 5060V with revision 5, msg to all participating forces (Frequent Wind File), hereafter Frequent Wind OPlan.
28. Frequent Wind Helo Time Schedule; Col John J. Roosma, Jr. intvw, 17Oct89, Tape 8909 (Oral HistColl, MCHC).
29. Frequent Wind Helo Time Schedule.
30. Capt Edward J. Ritchie intvw, 16Jun86, Tape 116A (Oral HistColl, MCHC), hereafter Ritchie intvw.
31. 9th MAB AAR.
32. RLT 4 ComdC.
33. Smith Comments.
34. 9th MAB ComdC; Spec Sit Reps.
35. 9th MAB AAR; Melton intvw.
36. Melton intvw.
37. 9th MAB ComdC; RLT 4 ComdC; BLT 1/9 ComdC.
38. 9th MAB AAR.
39. Recorded tapes of radio transmissions of 9th MAB helicopters and ABCCC, 29Apr75 (Oral HistColl, MCHC).
40. Guilmartin Comments.
41. Spec Sit Reps.
42. BLT 3/9 ComdC.
43. Bloomer Comments.

The Embassy

44. Spec Sit Reps.
45. BLT 1/9 ComdC; RLT 4 ComdC.
46. 9th MAB ComdC; RLT 4 ComdC; BLT 1/9 ComdC.
47. 9th MAB AAR; BLT 1/9 ComdC.
48. JCS msg to CinCPac, dtd 24Apr75 (Frequent Wind File).
49. 9th MAB AAR.
50. Bolton intvw.
51. 9th MAB AAR; RLT 4 ComdC.
52. BLT 1/9 ComdC.
53. 9th MAB ComdC.
54. Ritchie intvw.
55. Carey Comments.
56. Wilson Comments.
57. Bolton intvw.
58. 9th MAB ComdC.
59. BLT 1/9 ComdC; LtCol Jon M. Walter intvw, 30Jun87, Tape 151A (OralHistColl, MCHC), hereafter Walter intvw.
60. Berry Comments; LtCol James H. Kean intvw, 23Oct88, Tape 8810 (Oral Hist Coll, MCHC), hereafter Kean intvw.
61. Walter intvw.
62. Kean intvw.
63. CG, 9th MAB msg to CinCPac, dtd 4May75 (Frequent Wind File); 9th MAB ComdC.
64. 9th MAB AAR; MSG Bn ComdC.
65. LtCol John W. Bowman, Jr., intvw, 30Jun87, Tape 150A (Oral HistColl, MCHC).
66. ProvMAG-39 ComdC; Spec Sit Reps.
67. Heffernan intvw.

CHAPTER 12
REFUGEE OPERATIONS

In preparing this chapter, the following materials were used: 9th MAB ComdC, 26Mar-30Apr75, hereafter 9th MAB ComdC; 4th Marines ComdC, 1Jan-30Jun75, hereafter 4th Mar ComdC; AESF ComdC, 17Apr-31May75, hereafter AESF ComdC; and ProvMAG-39 ComdC, 19Apr-30Apr75, hereafter ProvMAG-39 ComdC. Also used were Marine Barracks Guam AAR, dtd 10Nov75, hereafter MB Guam AAR; Operation New Arrival AAR, hereafter NewArr AAR; Operation New Arrival Phasedown Plan 1-75, dtd 15Sep75, hereafter OpNewArr PhPl; and Cleland Report. Also, VAdm George P. Steele, USN, Comments on draft ms, 30Nov88 (Comment File), hereafter Steele Comments; BGen Paul G. Graham, Comments on draft ms, 3Oct88 (Comment File), hereafter Graham Comments; BGen James A. Herbert, USA, Comments on draft ms, 6Nov88 (Comment File), hereafter Herbert Comments; Col Tullis J. Woodham, Comments on draft ms, 15Sep88 (Comment File), hereafter Woodham Comments; Col Nicholas M. Trapnell, Jr., Comments on draft ms, 12Nov88 (Comment File), hereafter Trapnell Comments; Capt James D. Tregurtha, USN, Comments on draft ms, 8Nov88 (Comment File), hereafter Tregurtha Comments; and Capt Michael T. Mallick, Comments on draft ms, 29Sep88 (Comment File), hereafter Mallick Comments.

1. OpNewArr PhPl.

A Link to Freedom: The Exodus and a New Beginning

2. USSAG/Seventh Air Force AAR, dtd 6Jun75 (Vietnam File, 1973-75), hereafter USSAG AAR; 9th MAB ComdC.
3. CinCPac message to all participating units, dtd 30Apr75 (Frequent Wind File).
4. AESF ComdC.
5. USSAG AAR.

Way Stations

6. U.S. Embassy Manila msg to Secretary of State, dtd 22Apr75 (Frequent Wind File).
7. CinCPacFlt msg to CinCPac, dtd 22Apr75 (Frequent Wind File).
8. JCS msg to CinCPac, dtd 27Apr75 (Frequent Wind File).
9. CinCPacRep Saigon msg to CinCPac, dtd 23 Apr75 (Frequent Wind File).
10. Steele Comments.

Preparations: 1st Battalion, 4th Marines and the Task Force

11. 4th Mar ComdC.
12. Thomas Bartlett, "Frequent Wind," *Leatherneck Magazine*, Nov75, p. 32.
13. Ibid.
14. Ibid., p. 31.
15. Ibid., pp. 31-32.
16. CinCPac msg to MAC and subordinate units, dtd 27Apr75 (Frequent Wind File).
17. CO, USS *Blue Ridge* msg to JCS and CinCPac, dtd 28Apr75 (Frequent Wind File).
18. CinCPac msg to JCS, CinCPacFlt, and Secretary of State, dtd 28Apr75 (Frequent Wind File).
19. Frequent Wind Situation Report 018, issued 29Apr75 (Frequent Wind File).

Evacuation and Passage: Frequent Wind and the AESF's Final Chapter

20. 1stLt Joseph J. Rogish, Jr., intvw, 7Jul75, Tape 6139 (Oral HistColl, MCHC), hereafter Rogish intvw.
21. Ibid.
22. Cleland Report.
23. 9th MAB ComdC; AESF ComdC.
24. Capt Cyril V. Moyher ltr to CG 3d MarDiv, dtd 4Jun75 (Vietnam File, 1973-75), hereafter Moyher ltr.

25. Tregurtha Comments.
26. Moyher ltr.
27. Ibid.
28. AESF ComdC.
29. CWO-2 J. C. Owens intvw, 16Jan87 (Memorandum for the Record, Vietnam File, 1973-75).
30. Mallick Comments.
31. Moyher ltr.
32. AESF ComdC.
33. 9th MAB ComdC; AESF ComdC.

A Vietnamese City in Guam

34. CinCPac msg to CinCPacRep Guam, dtd 23Apr75 (Frequent Wind File).
35. MB Guam AAR.
36. Ibid.
37. Marine Barracks Guam msg to CMC, dtd 28Apr75 (Vietnam File, 1973-75), hereafter MB Guam msg.
38. CinCPac msg to Marine Barracks Guam, dtd 23Apr75 (Vietnam File, 1973-75).
39. MB Guam msg.
40. MB Guam AAR.
41. Ibid.
42. Ibid.
43. Ibid.
44. Herbert Comments.
45. MB Guam AAR.
46. Ibid.
47. Ibid.
48. Ibid.
49. Ibid.

The Final Link: Camp Pendleton

50. BGen Paul G. Graham intvw, 30 Sept75, Tape 6154 (Oral Hist-Coll, MCHC), hereafter Graham intvw.
51. Ibid.
52. Ibid.
53. Ibid.
54. Ibid.
55. Ibid.
56. Ibid.
57. CMC msg to CG Camp Pendleton, dtd 29Apr75 (Vietnam File, 1973-75).
58. JCS msg to CMC, dtd 30Apr75 (Vietnam File, 1973-75).
59. Camp Pendleton New Arrival Operation Order 1-75, dtd 28Apr75 (Vietnam File, 1973-75), hereafter NewArr OpO 1-75.
60. CG MCAS El Toro msg to CMC, dtd 30Apr75 (Vietnam File, 1973-75).
61. CG 3d MAW msg to CG I MAF and CO MAG-16 (Vietnam File, 1973-75).
62. NewArr OpO 1-75.
63. Graham intvw.
64. NewArr AAR.
65. Ibid.
66. Ibid.
67. Ibid.
68. Ibid.
69. OpNewArr PhPl.
70. NewArr AAR.
71. Graham intvw.

PART VI
After 'Vietnam'

CHAPTER 13
RECOVERY OF THE SS *MAYAGUEZ*

In preparing this chapter the following sources were used: BLT 2/9 Koh Tang/*Mayaguez* Historical Report dtd 9Dec75, hereafter 2/9 Koh Tang Report; BLT 1/4 After Action Report on the Recovery of the *Mayaguez*, dtd 12Nov75, hereafter 1/4 AAR; DC/S Plans and Operations HQ PacAF, "Assault on Koh Tang," dtd 23Jun75 (Office of Air Force History, Washington, D.C.), hereafter "Assault on Koh Tang"; 1st Battalion, 9th Marines ComdC, 1Jan-30Jun75, hereafter 1/9 ComdC; Quinlan intvw, Tape 111A; and Col J. M. Johnson, LtCol R. W. Austin, and Maj D. A. Quinlan, "Individual Heroism Overcame Awkward Command Relationships, Confusion, and Bad Information Off the Cambodian Coast," *Marine Corps Gazette*, Oct77, pp. 24-34, hereafter "Individual Heroism." Additionally, copies of numerous messages were obtained from the Air Force Historical Research Center, Maxwell Air Force Base, Alabama, and are held in the *Mayaguez* message file, hereafter MMF. Another important source was U.S. House Committee on International Relations, *Seizure of the* Mayaguez, 94th Cong., 1st Sess., 1975, Pts I-IV, hereafter *Hearings on Seizure*. Also used were: Steele Comments; Carey Comments; Roche Comments; Strickland Comments; Grimm Comments; Guilmartin Comments; Wood Comments; 1stLt Terry L. Tonkin, Comments on draft ms, 13Mar89 (Comment File), hereafter Tonkin Comments; 2dLt Michael A. Cicere, Comments on draft ms, 9Nov88 (Comment File), hereafter Cicere Comments.

1. Capt C. T. Miller, "Seizure of the S.S. *Mayaguez* by Khmer Rouge Gunboat P128, Statement of Facts," 1975 (MMF), hereafter *Mayaguez* Master's statement.

The *Mayaguez* Crisis

2. Frances Levine, "Ship Seized," HQMC Public Affairs Division press release, dtd 12May75 (MMF).
3. Ibid.
4. "Individual Heroism."
5. *Hearings on Seizure*, pt I, pp. 3-5 and pt IV, p. 63; *History of Pacific Air Forces*, 1Jul74-31Dec75, (Air Force Historical Research Center, Maxwell AFB, Alabama), hereafter PacAF History (74-75).
6. Urey W. Patrick, "The *Mayaguez* Operation," (Center for Naval Analyses, Alexandria, Virginia), hereafter CNA *Mayaguez* Report.

The Initial Decisions

7. VAdm George P. Steele, USN (Ret), "The U.S. Seventh Fleet," *U.S. Naval Institute Proceedings*, Jan76 (U.S. Naval Institute, Annapolis, Maryland), p. 27, hereafter "U.S. Seventh Fleet"; *Hearings on Seizure*, pt I, pp. 3-6.
8. Ritchie intvw, Tape 121A.
9. *Hearings on Seizure*, pt I, pp. 3-6 and pt IV, pp. 87-88.
10. CG USSAG/Seventh Air Force msg to *Mayaguez* participants, dtd 13May75 (MMF), hereafter *Mayaguez* Surveillance Operation msg; Earl H. Tilford, Jr., *The United States Air Force Search and Rescue in Southeast Asia* (Office of Air Force History, Washington, D.C.), pp. 146-154.

NOTES

11. *Mayaguez* Surveillance Operation msg.
12. CinCPac msg to CG USSAG/Seventh Air Force, dtd 13May75 (MMF); *Mayaguez* Surveillance Operation msg.
13. Seventh Air Force SS *Mayaguez* SitRep 011 msg to CinCPac, dtd 13May75 (MMF); PacAF History (74-75).
14. CG USSAG/Seventh Air Force msg to CinCPac C/S, dtd 13May75 (MMF).
15. 2/9 Koh Tang Report; 1/4 AAR.
16. Ibid.
17. 1/4 AAR; Seventh Air Force SS *Mayaguez* SitRep 020 msg to CinCPac, dtd 14May75 (MMF).
18. Ibid.
19. 1/4 AAR; *Mayaguez* Surveillance Operation msg; CinCPacFlt msg to ComSeventhFlt, dtd 14May75 (MMF).
20. 2/9 Koh Tang Report.
21. Seventh Air Force SS *Mayaguez* SitRep 029 msg to CinCPac, dtd 14May75 (MMF).

Assault Preparations

22. *Hearings on Seizure*, Part IV, p. 76.
23. 2/9 Koh Tang Report; LtCol Randall W. Austin intvw dtd 15Dec84, Tape 112A (Oral HistColl, MCHC), hereafter Austin intvw.
24. 2/9 Koh Tang Report.
25. Austin intvw; 2/9 Koh Tang Report; Quinlan intvw, Tape 111A.
26. 1/4 *Mayaguez* Report.
27. 2/9 Koh Tang Report; CG USSAG/Seventh Air Force msg to units participating in recovery of *Mayaguez*, dtd 14May75 (MMF) hereafter USSAG *Mayaguez* Ops msg.
28. USSAG *Mayaguez* Ops msg.
29. 1/4 AAR.
30. "Assault on Koh Tang."

The First Assault Wave

31. Wood Comments.
32. Ibid.
33. Ibid.
34. 1/4 AAR.
35. "Assault on Koh Tang."
36. Ibid.
37. Utapao Command Post msg to PacAF, dtd 15May75 (MMF).
38. "Assault on Koh Tang."
39. 2/9 Koh Tang Report; "Assault on Koh Tang"; CNA *Mayaguez* Report.
40. Ibid.
41. 2/9 Koh Tang Report; Austin intvw.
42. 1/9 ComdC; Quinlan intvw, Tape 111A.
43. "Individual Heroism."
44. 2/9 Koh Tang Report; "Assault on Koh Tang."
45. Austin intvw.
46. "Assault on Koh Tang."
47. JCS msg to CinCPac, dtd 15May75 (MMF).

The Linkup

48. "Individual Heroism."
49. Ibid.
50. CNA *Mayaguez* Report.
51. 2/9 Koh Tang Report.
52. Ibid.

The Second Wave

53. "Individual Heroism."
54. CinCPac SitRep 001 msg to JCS and CG USSAG/Seventh Air Force, dtd 15May75 (MMF).
55. Col Robert R. Reed, End of Tour Report (Air Force Historical Research Center, Maxwell AFB, Alabama).
56. USSAG *Mayaguez* Ops msg.
57. "Assault on Koh Tang."
58. CO, 388 TFW, Korat RTAFB msg to CG USSAG/Seventh Air Force, dtd 15May75 (MMF).
59. Seventh Air Force SitRep 040 to CinCPac, dtd 15May75 (MMF).
60. "Assault on Koh Tang."
61. CNA *Mayaguez* Report.
62. Ibid.

The Retrograde

63. "Assault on Koh Tang"; CO, 388 TFW Korat RTAFB msg to CG, Seventh Air Force, dtd 15May75; Seventh Air Force SS *Mayaguez* SitRep 047 msg to CinCPac, dtd 15May75 (MMF).
64. "Assault on Koh Tang"; CNA *Mayaguez* Report; Seventh Air Force SS *Mayaguez* SitRep 046 msg to CinCPac, dtd 15May75 (MMF).
65. 2/9 Koh Tang Report.
66. Cicere Comments.
67. "Assault on Koh Tang"; Guilmartin Comments.
68. CNA *Mayaguez* Report.
69. 2/9 Koh Tang Report; "Individual Heroism"; PacAF History (74-75).
70. 2/9 Koh Tang Report.
71. Ibid.
72. CO, 388 TFW Korat RTAFB msg to CG Seventh Air Force, dtd 15May75 (MMF).
73. CNA *Mayaguez* Report; "Assault on Koh Tang"; *Mayaguez* Master's statement.
74. CinCPac Final SitRep msg to JCS, dtd 15May75 (MMF).
75. "U.S. Seventh Fleet," p. 27.
76. "Assault on Koh Tang."
77. Ibid.
78. Maj A. J. C. Lavelle, ed., *The Vietnamese Air Force, 1951-1975, An Analysis of its Role in Combat* and *Fourteen Hours at Koh Tang* (Office of Air Force History, Washington, D.C., 1985), hereafter *Fourteen Hours*.
79. "Assault on Koh Tang."
80. *Fourteen Hours*.
81. Maj Peter C. Brown Letter of Investigation to CG 3d MarDiv, n.d. (MMF), hereafter "*Mayaguez* Investigation"; "Assault on Koh Tang"; *Fourteen Hours*.
82. Pacific Intelligence Command msg to CinCPac, dtd 15May75 (MMF).
83. Seventh Air Force SitRep 049 msg to CinCPac, dtd 15May75 (MMF).

The Aftermath

84. "*Mayaguez* Investigation"; "Individual Heroism."
85. "*Mayaguez* Investigation."
86. CO, CTF 77 msg to ComSeventhFlt, dtd 15May75 (MMF); "Assault on Koh Tang."
87. "*Mayaguez* Investigation."

88. CO, 388 TFW Korat RTAFB msg to CG, Seventh Air Force, dtd 15May75 (MMF).
89. CG USSAG/Seventh Air Force inquiry msg to CO, USS *Henry B. Wilson*, dtd 17May75 (MMF).
90. "*Mayaguez* Investigation."
91. 2/9 Koh Tang Report; CNA *Mayaguez* Report; "Assault on Koh Tang."
92. U.S. Embassy, Bangkok msg to Secretary of State, dtd 14May75 (MMF).
93. 2/9 Koh Tang Report; Maj William L. Smith intvw, dtd 15Dec84, Tape 141A (Oral HistColl, MCHC).
94. "U.S. Seventh Fleet," p. 27.
95. JCS msg to *Mayaguez* Rescue Operation participants, dtd 16May75, extracted from "Assault on Koh Tang," footnote 38.
96. Steele Comments.
97. CNA *Mayaguez* Report.
98. 2/9 Koh Tang Report.
99. Carey Comments.

Appendix A
Command and Staff List, Southeast Asia 1973-1975

III MAF Headquarters, 1Apr73-30Jun75

CG	MajGen Michael P. Ryan	1Apr73-30Dec73
	MajGen Herman Poggemeyer, Jr.	31Dec73-30Dec74
	MajGen Carl W. Hoffman	31Dec74-31May75
	MajGen Kenneth J. Houghton	1Jun75-30Jun75
C/S	Col Paul B. Haigwood	1Apr73-9May73
	Col Jimmie W. Duncan	10May73-24Jun73
	Col John W. Clayborne	25Jun73-26Aug73
	Col Frank W. Harris III	27Aug73-19Jul74
	Col James G. Dionisopoulos	20Jul74-1Jun75
	Col John M. Johnson, Jr.	2Jun75-30Jun75
G-1	LtCol Jean P. White	1Apr73-18Sep73
	LtCol Joe B. Noble	19Sep73-11Sep74
	Maj Robert M. Reed	12Sep74-17Sep74
	LtCol Thomas L. Sullivan	18Sep74-30Jun75
G-2	LtCol Maurice Hunter	1Apr73-21Jul73
	LtCol Fred L. Edwards, Jr.	22Jul73-27Jul73
	Col Joseph A. Nelson	28Jul73-7Aug73
	LtCol Fred L. Edwards, Jr.	8Aug73-18Nov73
	LtCol Daniel Z. Boyd	19Nov73-14Jul74
	Col Emil W. Herich	15Jul74-22Aug74
	Maj James A. Marks	23Aug74-26Jun75
	LtCol Robert D. Rosecrans	27Jun75-30Jun75
G-3	Col Jimmie W. Duncan	1Apr73-9May73
	Col John W. Clayborne	10May73-24Jun73
	LtCol Jack A. Byrd	25Jun73-26Jul73
	Col Lavern W. Larson	27Jul73-17Aug73
	Col Robert N. Burhans	18Aug73-4Aug74
	Col John M. Johnson, Jr.	5Aug74-20Apr75
	Col John F. Roche III	21Apr75-1Jun75
	LtCol Billy F. Stewart	2Jun75-30Jun75
G-4	Col Louis A. Bonin	1Apr73-21May73
	LtCol Richard L. Etter	22May73-19Jun73
	LtCol Jimmie R. Phillips	20Jun73-13Jul73
	Col Anthony A. Monti	14Jul73-16Jun74
	LtCol Charles W. Schreiner, Jr.	17Jun74-6Aug74
	LtCol John I. Hopkins	7Aug74-15Aug74
	Col Hans G. Edebohls	16Aug74-26Jan75
	Col Emil W. Herich	27Jan75-30Jun75

1st Marine Aircraft Wing, 1Jan73-30Jun75

CG	MajGen Leslie E. Brown	1Jan73-17Apr73
	MajGen Frank C. Lang	18Apr73-8Apr74
	MajGen Victor A. Armstrong	9Apr74-17Jan75
	MajGen Norman W. Gourley	18Jan75-30Jun75

AWC	BGen Robert W. Taylor	1Jan73-13Aug73
	BGen Manning T. Jannell	14Aug73-8Aug74
	BGen Richard E. Carey	9Aug74-30Jun75
C/S	Col James W. Smith	1Jan73-31Aug73
	Col William P. Brown	1Sep73-3May74
	Col Kenny C. Palmer	4May74-12Sep74
	Col Erin D. Smith	13Sep74-20Sep74
	Col Herbert V. Lundin	21Sep74-19May75
	Col Norman B. McCrary	20May75-30Jun75
G-1	Col Clifford D. Corn	1Jan73-8Jun73
	Col Owen L. Owens	9Jun73-18May74
	LtCol David S. Twining	19May74-31May75
	Col George L. Bruser	1Jun75-30Jun75
G-2	LtCol John P. Reichert	1Jan73-25Jun73
	Maj Frank G. Castillo	25Jun73-24Aug73
	LtCol Morris G. Robbins	25Aug73-17Sep73
	Col Charles M. Wallace, Jr.	18Sep73-27Aug74
	Maj James R. Bryan	28Aug74-31Oct74
	LtCol John K. Hyatt, Jr.	1Nov74-30Jun75
G-3	Col John W. Parchen	1Jan73-10Jul73
	Col William R. Beeler	11Jul73-3Jul74
	Col Robert H. Schultz	4Jul74-15Jun75
	Col Eugene R. Howard, Jr.	15Jun75-30Jun75
G-4	Col Lonnie P. Baites	1Jan73-31Mar73
	LtCol Gregory A. Corliss	31Mar73-9Sep73
	Col Francis H. Thurston	10Sep73-23May74
	Col Erin D. Smith	24May74-15Jun75
	Col Richard L. Critz	16Jun75-30Jun75

3d Marine Division (Rein), 1Jul73-30Jun75

CG	MajGen Michael P. Ryan	1Jul73-31Aug73
	MajGen Fred E. Haynes, Jr.	1Sep73-22Aug74
	MajGen Kenneth J. Houghton	23Aug74-30Jun75
ADC	BGen Paul G. Graham	1Jul73-8Nov73
	BGen Donald H. Brooks	9Nov73-8May74
	BGen Harold L. Coffman	9May74-5Jun75
	BGen Edward J. Megarr	6Jun75-30Jun75
C/S	Col William J. Masterpool	1Jul73-23May74
	Col David M. Twomey	24May74-13Jul74
	Col William Plaskett, Jr.	14Jul74-30Jun75
G-1	Col Gordon M. B. Livingston	1Jul73-8May74
	Col Richard W. Goodale	9May74-31Oct74
	Col Wylie W. Taylor, Jr.	1Nov74-27Mar75
	LtCol Arthur A. Bergman	28Mar75-30Jun75

G-2	Col Val R. McClure	1Jul73-25Aug73
	LtCol James S. Wilson	26Aug73-22Sep73
	LtCol Darrell C. Danielson	23Sep73-28Jul74
	Maj Rafael A. Becerra, Jr.	29Jul74-13Aug74
	LtCol Charles E. Hester	14Aug74-2Jan75
	Maj Rafael A. Becerra, Jr.	3Jan75-5Mar75
	Col Howard M. Koppenhaver	6Mar75-20Jun75
	Col Morgan W. West	21Jun75-30Jun75
G-3	Col Heman J. Redfield III	1Jul73-25Jul73
	LtCol Conwill R. Casey	26Jul73-4Aug73
	Col Alexander S. Ruggiero	5Aug73-1May74
	Col Edward F. Fitzgerald	2May74-18Jul74
	Col Douglas T. Kane	19Jul74-13Aug74
	LtCol Thomas T. Glidden	14Aug74-1Sep74
	Col Robert E. Hunter, Jr.	2Sep74-30Jun75
G-4	Col George A. Merrill	1Jul73-22Jun74
	LtCol Albert Whalley	23Jun74-29Jul74
	Col Herbert G. Fischer	30Jul74-30Jun75

9th Marine Amphibious Brigade Headquarters Staff
1-30Apr75

CG	BGen Richard E. Carey	1-30Apr75
DepCmdr	Col Wylie W. Taylor	18Apr-30Apr75
C/S	Col Dan C. Alexander	1Apr-30Apr75
G-1	1stLt Robert B. Blose, Jr.	1Apr-11Apr75
	LtCol Edgar A. House	12Apr-30Apr75
G-2	Maj Charlton H. Blanks	1Apr-30Apr75
G-3	Maj Richard K. Young	1Apr-11Apr75
	LtCol Robert D. White	12Apr-30Apr75
G-4	Maj John F. Shea	1Apr-30Apr75

9th Marine Amphibious Brigade Subordinate Commands
7-10Apr75

31st Marine Amphibious Unit

CO	Col John F. Roche III
BLT 2/4	LtCol George P. Slade
LSU 2/4	Maj James A. Gallagher, Jr.
HMH-462	LtCol James L. Bolton

33d Marine Amphibious Unit

CO	Col Alfred M. Gray, Jr.
BLT 1/9	LtCol Royce L. Bond
LSU 1/9	Maj Donald O. Coughlin
HMM-165	LtCol James P. Kizer
HMH-463	LtCol Herbert M. Fix

35th Marine Amphibious Unit

CO	Col Hans G. Edebohls
BLT 3/9	LtCol Robert E. Loehe
LSU 3/9	Maj Fred L. Jones

Amphibious Evacuation RVN Support Group

BLT 1/4	LtCol Charles E. Hester

9th Marine Amphibious Brigade Subordinate Commands
19Apr-11May75

Regimental Landing Team 4 (RLT 4)

CO	Col Alfred M. Gray, Jr.
BLT 1/9	LtCol Royce L. Bond
BLT 2/4	LtCol George P. Slade
BLT 3/9	LtCol Robert E. Loehe

Provisional Marine Aircraft Group 39

CO	Col Frank G. McLenon
HMH-462	LtCol James L. Bolton
HMH-463	LtCol Herbert M. Fix
HMM-165	LtCol James P. Kizer
HML-367	LtCol James R. Gentry

Brigade Logistic Support Group

CO	Col Hans G. Edebohls
LSU 1/9	Maj Donald O. Coughlin
LSU 2/4	Maj James A. Gallagher, Jr.
LSU 3/9	Maj Fred L. Jones

Communications Company (-) (Rein)

CO	Maj Robert L. Turley

Amphibious Evacuation Security Force (AESF)

CO	Maj David A. Quinlan

Amphibious Evacuation Security Force (AESF)
17Apr-31May75

Locations: 18Apr75, Subic Bay, Philippines; 19-20Apr75, Enroute South Vietnam Coast; 20Apr-2May75, South Vietnam Coastal Waters; 2-4May75, Enroute Subic Bay; 4-14May75, Detachments to Guam; 4-27May75, Subic Bay.

CO	Maj David A. Quinlan
ExO/OpsO	Capt Charles J. Bushey
Control Group ExO	1stLt John W. Kinsel
LogO	1stLt Johnnie Johnson
PersO	1stLt Joseph J. Streitz

Detachments

Echo Det (12th Mar)	Capt Richard L. Reuter
USNS *Sgt Truman Kimbro*	19Apr-13May75
Foxtrot Det (12th Mar)	Capt John R. Page
USNS *Greenville Victory*	19Apr-23May75
Hotel Det (3d Engr)	Capt William H. Hackett, Jr.
USS *Dubuque*	18Apr-4May75
India Det (7th Comm)	Capt Cyril V. Moyher
SS *Pioneer Commander*	24Apr-7May75
Kilo Det*	1stLt Joseph J. Streitz
SS *Greenport*	6May-12May75
Mike Det*	1stLt Carl W. Fredricksen
SS *American Racer*	5-9May75

COMMAND AND STAFF LIST

November Det (3d Serv)   Capt Michael T. Mallick
SS *American Challenger*   25Apr-7May75

Papa Det (4th Mar)   Capt Richard M. Jessie, Jr.
SS *Greenport*   22Apr-6May75

Quebec Det*   1stLt Robert C. Koscheski
USS *Dubuque*   22Apr-13May75

Romeo Det*   1stLt Johnnie Johnson
USS *Dubuque*   22Apr-13May75

Sierra Det (HqBn)   Capt Edward R. Palmquist, Jr.
USNS *Sgt Andrew Miller*   22Apr-13May75

Tango Det (HqBn)   Capt Robert D. Amos, Jr.
SS *Green Forest*   24Apr-12May75

Uniform Det (3d Tk Bn)   Capt Steven A. Shepherd
SS *Green Wave*   24Apr-12May75

Victor Det (9th Mar)   Capt David A. Garcia
SS *Pioneer Contender*   22Apr-7May75

USS *Barbour County* Det*   1stLt David A. Kratochvil
USS *Barbour County*   27Apr-14May75

Det MP Co, 3dMarDiv**
1stLt Joseph J. Streitz   17Apr-31May75

Det 17th ITT**
CWO-2 Allen F. Kent   17Apr-31May75

Det 3d CIT**
Capt Charles J. Bushey   17Apr-31May75

*Units formed through reorganization 22Apr75
**Attached Units

Appendix B
Command Staff, BLT 2/4
29-30 April 1975

Battalion Landing Team
2d Battalion, 4th Marines

CO LtCol George P. Slade	29-30Apr75
S-1 2dLt Christopher J. Ford	29-30Apr75
S-2 2dLt Douglas E. Pickelsimer	29-30Apr75
S-3 Maj Robert R. Green	29-30Apr75
S-4 Capt Joseph A. Betta	29-30Apr75
CommO Capt Edward C. Gerstner	29-30Apr75
H&S Co Capt Michael G. Roth	29-30Apr75
E Co Capt Matthew E. Broderick	29-30Apr75
F Co Capt Thomas A. Keene	29-30Apr75
G Co Capt William R. Melton	29-30Apr75
H Co Capt Steven R. Bland	29-30Apr75

Btry H, 3d Bn, 12th Marines*

Capt David M. Hauntz	29-30Apr75

2d Plt, Co A, 1st Amtrac B*

1stLt James L. Wise	29-30Apr75

2d Plt, Co C, 3d Engr Bn*

2dLt Lagrant D. Velde	29-30Apr75

2d Plt, Co B, 3d Recon Bn*

1stLt Michael F. Clough	29-30Apr75

2d Plt, Co A, 3d Tank Bn*

2dLt James C. Lotito	29-30Apr75

---

*Attached Units

Appendix C
U.S. Marine Officers Serving in Billets in South Vietnam and USSAG, Thailand 1973-1975

Billets in Vietnam (other than Marine Security Guard Battalion)

Chief, Plans and Liaison Branch, Operations and Plans Division, DAO
Col William B. Fleming	Mar-Apr73
Col Nicholas M. Trapnell, Jr.	Apr73-Apr74
Col Paul L. Siegmund	Apr74- Feb75
Col Eugene R. Howard, Jr.	Jan75-Apr75

Chief, VNMC Logistics Support Branch, Navy Division, DAO
LtCol Walter D. Fillmore	Mar-Jun73
LtCol George E. Strickland	Jun73-Jun74
LtCol Anthony Lukeman	Jun74-Apr75

Operations Staff Officer, Readiness Section, Operations and Training Branch, Operations and Plans Division, DAO
Maj Richard F. Johnson	Mar73-Apr73
Maj Joseph F. Nardo	Apr73-Jul73
LtCol Charles A. Barstow	Jul73-Jul74
LtCol William E. McKinstry	Jul74-Apr75

Liaison Officer, Four Power Joint Military Commission, RVN
Maj Larry D. Richards	Mar73-May74
Maj Jaime Sabater, Jr.	May74-Apr75

Operations Officer (Forward, RVN), Joint Casualty Resolution Center
Capt James M. Strickland	Aug73-Aug74
Capt Anthony A. Wood	Aug74-Apr75

Billets in USSAG, Thailand (Nakhon Phanom)

Chief of Operations and Plans Division
Col George T. Balzer	Mar73-Jun73
Col Edward J. Bronars*	Jun73-Jun74

Director, Surface Operations
Col James P. Connolly II	Jun74-May75

Plans Action Officer
Maj John J. Carty	Mar73-May73
Maj Horace W. Baker	May73-Apr74
Maj Edward A. Grimm	Apr74-Apr75

Inspector, USSAG/Seventh Air Force
Col Melvin J. Steinberg	Jun74-May75

Operations Officer, Joint Casualty Resolution Center, Nakhon Phanom and Utapao (the Center moved to Samae San, just outside Utapao, in late 1974)
LtCol Charles Ward	Jun74-Jun75

---

*With Colonel Bronars' departure, USSAG discontinued the practice of making the senior Marine Corps officer the Chief, Operations and Plans Division, regardless of the seniority of the other members of the joint staff. Colonel Bronars' replacement, Colonel Connolly, was assigned to the Combat Operations Center.

Appendix D
Company C, Marine Security Guard Battalion January-April 1975

CO Maj James H. Kean		1Jan75-30Apr75
ExO Capt Robert C. Lewis		1Jan75-30Apr75
PersCh SSgt William J. Miller		1Jan75-30Apr75

MSG Detachment Saigon, RVN Personnel Roster
1Jan75-30Apr75

MSgt Juan J. Valdez
GySgt Vasco D. Martin
SSgt Colin D. Broussard
SSgt James J. Daisey
SSgt Clemon S. Segura, Jr.
SSgt Michael K. Sullivan

Sgt Phillip A. Babel
Sgt Terry J. Bennington
Sgt Martin J. Davenport
Sgt Robert L. Frain
Sgt Kenneth Geagley, Jr.
Sgt Duane R. Gevers
Sgt Paul J. Gozgit
Sgt Gregory E. Hargis
Sgt Steven E. Johnson
Sgt David M. Leet
Sgt Kevin M. Maloney
Sgt Dwight G. McDonald
Sgt Gary L. Mellinger
Sgt Helstead G. Murray III
Sgt William C. Newell
Sgt Donald R. Nicholas
Sgt Richard G. Paddock
Sgt Douglas D. Potratz
Sgt David Rose
Sgt Steven T. Schuller
Sgt Andre Stringer

Cpl Joseph F. Arata

Cpl Stephen Q. Bauer
Cpl Manuel A. Bispo
Cpl John L. Ghilain
Cpl Ronald A. Mayfield
Cpl Charles McMahon, Jr.
Cpl Robert E. Mondo
Cpl Joe B. Myes, Jr.
Cpl David E. Norman
Cpl Francis J. Richard
Cpl Carlos Silva
Cpl Randy C. Smith

LCpl Larry E. Beachy
LCpl Eric D. Boyd
LCpl Thomas E. Cole
LCpl Timothy B. Creighton
LCpl Kenneth E. Crouse
LCpl Thomas K. Dickson
LCpl Douglas G. Drummond
LCpl Clyde E. English, Jr.
LCpl William K. Fulton
LCpl Otis L. Holmes
LCpl Darwin D. Judge
LCpl Dennis R. Serbus
LCpl Patrick F. Short
LCpl John C. Stewart
LCpl S. K. Stratton
LCpl Walter M. Sweeny
LCpl Jerome Thomas
LCpl James V. Vaincourt
LCpl David B. Wilkie

MSG Detachment Bien Hoa
RVN Personnel Roster
1Jan75-27Apr75

GySgt Robert W. Schlager

Cpl Carlos R. Arraigna

Sgt Ronald E. Duffy
Sgt James M. Felber

MSG Detachment Can Tho
RVN Personnel Roster
1Jan75-30Apr75

SSgt Boyette S. Hasty
Sgt John W. Kirchner
Sgt John S. Moore

Sgt Terry D. Pate
Cpl Lee J. Johnson
Cpl Lawrence B. Killens

MSG Detachment Da Nang
RVN Personnel Roster
1Jan75-30Mar75

SSgt Walter W. Sparks
Sgt Lazaro Arriola
Sgt Venoy L. Rogers

Sgt William S. Spruce III
Cpl Ronald W. Anderson
Cpl Leonard A. Forseth

MSG Detachment Nha Trang
RVN Personnel Roster
1Jan75-23Apr75

SSgt Roger F. Painter
Sgt Michael A. McCormick
Cpl Robert L. Anderson

Cpl Levorn L. Brown
Cpl John G. Moya
Cpl Jimmie D. Sneed

MSG Phnom Penh
Cambodia Personnel Roster
1Jan75-12Apr75

GySgt Clarence D. McClenahan
SSgt Gilbert J. Feest*
Sgt Kenneth E. Armstrong
Sgt Robert L. Clark**
Sgt Russell H. Cutler
Sgt Marty L. Gray
Sgt James W. Shurtleff***
Sgt Ralph V. Simpson, Jr.
Sgt Gary Stanton

Cpl Gary N. Lindholm
LCpl Dean M. Kinzie

Sgt Maxie C. Wix**
Cpl James D. Cox
Cpl Allan W. Mitchell
Cpl David L. Ragland
Cpl Victor Sajka****
LCpl Allen J. Becker
LCpl Ronald C. C. Dumosch
LCpl Phillip D. Forsyth
LCpl Michael G. Miciotto

*Augmented from the Taipei Detachment
**Augmented from the Seoul Detachment
***Augmented from the Bangkok Detachment
****Augmented from the Hong Kong Detachment

Appendix E
Mayaguez Rescue Force (BLTs 2/9 and 1/4) 12-15 May 1975

Ground Security Force, CTG 79.9

CO	Col John M. Johnson, Jr.
Airlift Contingency, BLT 2/9, CTU 79.9.1	LtCol Randall W. Austin
S-3	Maj John B. Hendricks
AirO	Capt Barry L. Cassidy
Btry I, 3d Bn, 12th Mar (-)	1stLt Michael S. Eustis
FAC	1stLt Terry L. Tonkin
FAC	1stLt John J. Martinoli, Jr.
NGS Spotter Designee	2dLt Harry T. Williams

Assault Wave I, Co G

CO	Capt James H. Davis
ExO	1stLt James D. Keith
Plt Cmdr	2dLt James McDaniel
Plt Cmdr	2dLt Richard H. Zales
Plt Cmdr	2dtLt Michael A. Cicere
Plt Cmdr	2dLt Daniel J. Hoffman

Assault Wave II, Co E

CO	Capt Mykle E. Stahl
Plt Cmdr	2dLt James W. Davis, Jr.
Plt Cmdr	2dLt Robert E. King
Plt Cmdr	2dLt William L. Smith
81mm Mortar Plt (-)	2dLt Joseph J. McMenamin
EOD	Capt Raymond J. McManus

Mayaguez Boarding Party

Command Group Det

H&S Co, BLT 1/4, CTU 79.9.2	Maj Raymond E. Porter
Co D (-) (Rein), BLT 1/4	Capt Walter J. Wood

Marines Killed at Koh Tang, Cambodia

LCpl Gregory Copenhaver
LCpl Andres Garcia
LCpl Ashton N. Loney

PFC Daniel A. Benedett
PFC Lynn Blessing
PFC Walter Boyd
PFC Gary L. Hall
PFC Joseph N. Hargrove
PFC James J. Jacques
PFC James R. Maxwell
PFC Richard W. Rivenburgh
PFC Antonio R. Sandoval
PFC Kelton R. Turner

Pvt Danny G. Marshall

Navy Corpsmen Killed at Koh Tang, Cambodia

HM2 Bernard Gause, Jr.
HN Ronald J. Manning

Appendix F
Glossary of Terms and Abbreviations

A-1—Douglas Skyraider, a single-engine, propeller-driven attack aircraft.

A-4—Douglas Skyhawk, a single-seat, jet attack aircraft in service on board carriers of the U.S. Navy and with land-based Marine attack squadrons.

A-6—Grumman Intruder, a twin-seat, twin-jet attack aircraft specifically designed to deliver weapons on targets completely obscured by weather or darkness.

A-7—Vought Corsair, a single-seat, jet attack aircraft.

A-37—Cessna Dragonfly, a dual-seat, twin-jet light attack aircraft.

AAA—Antiaircraft Artillery.

ABCCC—Airborne Battlefield Command and Control Center, a U.S. Air Force aircraft equipped with communications, data link, and display equipment; it may be employed as an airborne command post or a communications and intelligence relay facility.

AC-47—Douglas Spooky, a twin-engine, propeller-driven gunship armed with four 7.62mm mini-guns and illumination.

AC-119—Fairchild Shadow and Stinger, a twin-engine, propeller-driven gunship armed with four 7.62mm mini-guns and illumination.

AC-130—Lockheed Spectre, a four-engine, turboprop gunship armed with 20mm and 40mm guns, illumination, and infrared capability.

ACCS—Airborne Command and Control Squadron.

ACBLT—Air Contingency Battalion Landing Team.

ADC—Assistant Division Commander.

AdminO—Administrative Officer.

AESF—Amphibious Evacuation Security Force.

AH-1J—Bell Sea Cobra, twin-engine, single rotor helicopter specifically designed for helicopter escort and gunship support with 20mm cannon, rockets, and illumination.

Air America—U.S. Government-sponsored proprietary air transport company.

AirO—Air officer.

AK-47—Kalashnikov-designed, gas-operated, air-cooled, magazine-fed, 7.62mm automatic rifle, with an effective range of 400 meters. Standard rifle of the North Vietnamese Army.

ALMAR—A Commandant of the Marine Corps bulletin directed to All Marines.

ALO—Air Liaison Officer, a naval aviator/flight officer attached to a ground unit who is the primary advisor to the ground commander on air operation matters.

AMC—Airborne Mission Commander.

ANGLICO—Air and Naval Gunfire Liaison Company, a unit composed of Marine and Navy personnel specially qualified for control of naval gunfire and close air support. ANGLICO personnel normally provide this service while attached to U.S. and allied units.

AO—Air Observer, an individual whose primary mission is to observe from light aircraft in order to adjust supporting arms fire and to obtain information.

AO—Area of Operations.

AOA—Amphibious Objective Area, a defined geographical area within which is located the area or areas to be captured by an amphibious task force.

AOE—Fast Combat Support Ship.

APC—Armored Personnel Carrier.

APD—Airborne Personnel Detector.

Arc Light—Codename for B-52 bombing missions in South Vietnam.

ARG—Amphibious Ready Group.

ARRS—Aerospace Rescue and Recovery Squadron.

Arty—Artillery.

ARVN—Army of the Republic of Vietnam (South Vietnam).

ASP—Ammunition Supply Point.

ASRT—Air Support Radar Team, a subordinate operational component of a tactical air control system which provides ground-controlled precision flight path guidance and weapons release for attack aircraft.

B-3—North Vietnamese military command established in the Central Highlands of South Vietnam to control military operations in Kontum, Dar Lac, and Pleiku Provinces.

B-40—Communist rocket-propelled grenade launcher.

B-52—Boeing Stratofortress, U.S. Air Force eight-engine, swept-wing, jet heavy bomber.

BA—Base Area.

Barrel Roll—Codename for air operations over Laos.

BDC—Base Defense Commander.

BGen—Brigadier General.

BLT—Battalion Landing Team.

Bn—Battalion.

Brig—Brigade.

C-5—Lockheed Galaxy, four-engine jet transport aircraft.

C-7—De Havilland Caribou, twin-engine, propeller-driven transport aircraft.

C-117—Douglas Skytrain, a twin-engine, propeller-driven transport aircraft. The C-117 was an improved version of the C-47, the military version of the DC-3.

C-123—Fairchild Provider, twin-engine, propeller-driven transport aircraft.

C-130—Lockheed Hercules, a four-engine, turboprop transport aircraft.

C-141—Lockheed Starlifter, a four-engine jet transport aircraft.

Capt—Captain.

CAS—Close Air Support.

CBU—Cluster Bomb Unit.

CCC—Combined Campaign Plan.

Cdr—Commander.

CEC—Construction Engineer Corps.

CG—Commanding General.

CH-46—Boeing Vertol Sea Knight, a twin-engine, tandem-rotor transport helicopter, designed to carry a four-man crew and 17 combat-loaded troops.

GLOSSARY

CH-47 — Boeing Vertol Chinook, a twin-engine, tandem-rotor transport helicopter, designed to carry a four-man crew and 33 combat-loaded troops.
CH-53 — Sikorsky Sea Stallion, a twin-engine, single-rotor, heavy transport helicopter with an average payload of 12,800 pounds. Carries crew of three and 38 combat-loaded troops.
CIA — Central Intelligence Agency.
CID — Criminal Investigation Division.
CinCPac — Commander in Chief, Pacific.
CinCPacFlt — Commander in Chief, Pacific Fleet.
CIT — Counter Intelligence Team.
Class I, II, III, et al. — Categories of military supplies, e.g., Class I, rations; Class II, petroleum-oil-lubricants; Class V, ammunition.
Claymore — M18A1 U.S. directional antipersonnel mine.
CMC — Commandant of the Marine Corps.
CMH — Center of Military History, U. S. Army.
CNO — Chief of Naval Operations.
CO — Commanding Officer.
COC — Combat Operations Center.
Col — Colonel.
ComdC — Command Chronology.
ComdHist — Command History.
Comm — Communications.
CommO — Communications officer.
ComNavForPac — Commander, Naval Forces, Pacific.
ComNavForV — Commander, Naval Forces, Vietnam.
ComUSMACV — Commander, U.S. Military Assistance Command, Vietnam.
ComUSMACThai — Commander, U.S. Military Assistance Command, Thailand.
COSVN — Central Office of South Vietnam, the nominal Communist military and political headquarters in South Vietnam.
CP — Command Post.
CPX — Command Post Exercise.
CRC — Control and Reporting Center, an element of the U.S. Air Force tactical air control system, subordinate to the Tactical Air Control Center, which conducts radar and warning operations.
CRIMP — Consolidated Republic of Vietnam Improvement and Modernization Plan.
CSC — Communications Service Company.
CV, CVA — Multipurpose Aircraft Carrier.

DAO — Defense Attache Office.
DASC — Direct Air Support Center, a subordinate operational component of the air control system designed for control of close air support and other direct air support operations.
DC-8 — McDonnell Douglas Jet Trader, a four-engine jet cargo and passenger transport aircraft.
D-Day — Day scheduled for the beginning of an operation.
DD — Destroyer.
DDG — Guided Missile Destroyer.
DE — Escort Destroyer.
DIA — Defense Intelligence Agency.
Div — Division.
DMZ — Demilitarized Zone separating North and South Vietnam.
DOD — Department of Defense.
DRV — Democratic Republic of Vietnam (North Vietnam).
Dtd — Dated.
Duster — Nickname for the U.S. M42 tracked vehicle which mounts dual 40mm automatic weapons.

EA-6 — Grumman Prowler, the electronic warfare version of the A-6A Intruder.
EB-66 — Douglas, a twin-engine jet, electronic warfare version of the B-66 Destroyer.
EC-130 — Lockheed, a four-engine, turbo-prop, electronic warfare and communications version of the C-130 Hercules.
ECC — Evacuation Control Center.
ECM — Electronic Countermeasures, a major subdivision of electronic warfare involving actions against enemy electronic equipment or to exploit the use of electromagnetic radiations from such equipment.
ECCM — Electronic Counter Countermeasures, the procedures and equipment used to protect communications and electronic equipment from interference or exploitation by an enemy.
ELINT — Electronic Intelligence, the intelligence information gained by monitoring radiations from enemy electronic equipment.
Engr — Engineer.
EOD — Explosive Ordnance Disposal.
EPC — Evacuation Processing Center.
ETA, ETD — Estimated Time of Arrival and Estimated Time of Departure.
ExO — Executive Officer.

F-4 — McDonnell Phantom II, a twin-engine, two-seat, long-range, all-weather jet interceptor and attack bomber.
F-5 — Northrop Freedom Fighter, a twin-engine, single-seat, jet fighter aircraft.
FAC — Forward Air Controller.
FAC(A) — Forward Air Controller (Airborne).
FANK — *Force Armee Nationale Khmer*, the Cambodian Army.
FDC — Fire Direction Center.
FMFPac — Fleet Marine Force, Pacific.
FO — Forward Observer.
FRC — Federal Records Center.
Front 4 — Communist headquarters subordinate to *MR-5* responsible for Quang Nam Province.
FSB — Fire Support Base.
FSCC — Fire Support Coordination Center, a single location involved in the coordination of all forms of fire support.
FSR — Force Service Regiment.
FWMF — Free World Military Force.
FY — Fiscal Year, for example "FY-74."

G-1, -2, et al. — Military staff positions on a general staff, e.g., G-1 refers to the staff member responsible for personnel; G-2, intelligence; G-3, operations; G-4, logistics; and G-5, civil affairs.
Gen — General.
Grenade Launcher — U.S. M79 or M203 single-shot, breech-loaded, shoulder weapon which fires 40mm projectiles and weighs approximately 6.5 pounds when loaded; it has a sustained rate of aimed fire of five to seven rounds per minute and an effective range of 375 meters.
GSF — Ground Security Force.
Gun, 175mm — U.S. M107 self-propelled gun which weighs 62,000 pounds and fires a 147-pound projectile to a maximum range of 32,800 meters. Maximum rate of fire is one round every two minutes.
GVN — Government of Vietnam (South Vietnam).

H&I — Harassing and Interdiction fires.
H&MS — Headquarters and Maintenance Squadron.
H&S Co — Headquarters and Service Company.
HC(A) — Helicopter Commander (Airborne).
HDC — Helicopter Direction Center.
HE — High Explosive.
HEALT — Helicopter Employment and Landing Table.
HH-3 — Sikorsky Sea King, a single-rotor helicopter used for combat search and rescue.
HH-53 — Sikorsky Sea Stallion, twin-engine, single-rotor assault helicopter in U.S. Navy and Air Force search and rescue configurations.
H-Hour — Specific time an operation begins.
HLZ — Helicopter Landing Zone.
HMH — Marine Heavy Helicopter Squadron.
HMM — Marine Medium Helicopter Squadron, also the basis of composite squadrons with deployed forces.
Howitzer, 8-inch — U.S. M55 self-propelled, heavy artillery piece with a maximum range of 16,900 meters and a rate of fire of one round every two minutes.
Howitzer, 105mm — U.S. M101A1 towed, general purpose light artillery piece with a maximum range of 11,000 meters and maximum rate of fire of four rounds per minute.
Howitzer, 155mm — U.S. M114A towed and M109 self-propelled medium artillery with a maximum range of 15,080 meters and a maximum rate of fire of three rounds per minute. The newer and heavier self-propelled M109 is largely road-bound, while the lighter, towed M114A can be moved either by truck or by helicopter.
HST — Helicopter Support Team.
Huey — Bell Iroquois UH-1 series of helicopters.
HQMC — Headquarters Marine Corps.

ICCS — International Commission of Control and Supervision, established by the Paris Peace Accords of 1973 to supervise the implementation of the accords. Composed of representatives from Canada, Hungary, Poland, Indonesia, and Iran.
I MAF — I Marine Amphibious Force.
Intel — Intelligence.
Intvw — Interview.
IOD — Integrated Observation Device.
ITT — Interrogation/Translator Team.

J-1, -2, et al. — Designation for members of a joint staff which includes members of several Services. J-1 refers to the staff member responsible for personnel; J-2, intelligence; J-3, operations; and J-4, logistics.
JCRC — Joint Casualty Resolution Center.
JCS — Joint Chiefs of Staff (U.S.).
JGS — Joint General Staff (South Vietnamese).
JMC — Joint Military Commission. The four-power JMC representing the United States, South Vietnam, North Vietnam, and the Provisional Revolutionary Government established by the 1973 Paris Peace Accords.
Jolly Green — Radio call sign for USAF HH-53 helicopters of 40th Aerospace Rescue and Recovery Squadron (40th ARRS).
JUSPAO — Joint U.S. Public Affairs Office.

KC-130 — Lockheed, in-flight refueling tanker configuration of the C-130 Hercules.

Khmer Rouge — Cambodian Communists.
KIA — Killed in Action.
Knife — Radio call sign for USAF CH-53 helicopters of 21st Special Operations Squadron (21st SOS).

LAAW — U.S. M72 light antitank assault weapon, also known as light antitank weapon (LAW).
LCC — Amphibious Command Ship.
LCM — Landing Craft, Mechanized, designed to land tanks, trucks, and trailers directly onto the beach. Also known as a "Mike boat."
LCPL — Landing Craft, Personnel, Large.
LCU — Landing Craft, Utility.
LCVP — Landing Craft, Vehicle, Personnel, a small craft with a bow ramp used to transport assault troops and light vehicles to the beach. Also known as a "Papa boat."
LGB — Laser Guided Bombs, commonly known as "smart bombs."
L-Hour — The specific time helicopters land in a helicopter landing zone (USMC); launch hour, when an aircraft leaves the ground (USAF).
Linebacker — Codename for the air and surface interdiction operations against North Vietnam in 1972.
LKA — Amphibious Cargo Ship.
LOC — Lines of Communication.
LogO — Logistics officer.
LORAN — Long Range Navigation, a system of radio stations at known positions used for air and sea guidance.
LPD — Amphibious Transport Dock, a ship designed to transport and land troops, equipment, and supplies by means of embarked landing craft, amphibious vehicles, and helicopters. It has both a submersible well deck and a helicopter landing deck.
LPH — Amphibious Assault Ship, a ship designed or modified to transport and land troops, equipment, and supplies by means of embarked helicopters.
LSA — Logistic Support Area.
LSD — Landing Ship Dock, a landing ship designed to combat load, transport, and launch amphibious crafts or vehicles together with crews and embarked personnel, and to provide limited docking and repair services to small ships and crafts. It lacks the helicopter landing deck of the LPD.
LST — Tank Landing Ship, a landing ship designed to transport heavy vehicles and to land them on a beach.
LSU — Logistics Support Unit.
Lt — Lieutenant.
LtCol — Lieutenant Colonel.
LTDS — Laser Target Designation System.
LtGen — Lieutenant General.
Ltr — Letter.
LVTC — Landing Vehicle, Tracked, Command, an amphibian vehicle fitted with radios for use as a command and control facility.
LVTE — Landing Vehicle, Tracked, Engineer, a lightly armored amphibian vehicle designed for minefield and obstacle clearance.
LVTP — Landing Vehicle, Tracked, Personnel, an amphibian vehicle used to land and/or transport personnel.
LZ — Landing Zone.

MAB — Marine Amphibious Brigade.
MABLEx — MAB Landing Exercise.
MABS — Marine Air Base Squadron.
MAC — Military Airlift Command.
Machine Gun, .50-Caliber — U.S. M2 belt-fed, recoil-operated, air-

cooled automatic weapon, which weighs approximately 80 pounds without mount or ammunition; it has a sustained rate of fire of 100 rounds per minute and an effective range of 1,450 meters.

Machine Gun, 7.62mm—U.S. M60 belt-fed, gas-operated, air-cooled automatic weapon, which weighs approximately 20 pounds without mount or ammunition; it has a sustained rate of fire of 100 rounds per minute and an effective range of 1,000 meters.

MACS—Marine Air Control Squadron, provides and operates ground facilities for the detection and interception of hostile aircraft and for the navigational direction of friendly aircraft in the conduct of support operations.

MACV—Military Assistance Command, Vietnam.

MAF—Marine Amphibious Force.

MAG—Marine Aircraft Group.

Main Force—Refers to organized Viet Cong battalions and regiments as opposed to local guerrilla groups.

Maj—Major.

MajGen—Major General.

MarDiv—Marine Division.

Marines—Designates an infantry regiment, e.g., 3d Marines.

MASS—Marine Air Support Squadron, provides and operates facilities for the control of aircraft operating in direct support of ground forces.

MAU—Marine Amphibious Unit, not to be confused with the Marine Advisory Unit of the Naval Advisory Group which administered the advisory effort to the South Vietnamese Marine Corps.

MarAdvU—Marine Advisory Unit.

MAW—Marine Aircraft Wing.

MCAF—Marine Corps Air Facility.

MCAS—Marine Corps Air Station.

MCCC—Marine Corps Command Center.

MCO—Marine Corps Order.

MCOAG—Marine Corps Operations Analysis Group, an organization of the Center for Naval Analyses in Washington, D.C.

MCSA—Marine Corps Supply Agency.

Medevac—Medical Evacuation.

MEDTC—Military Equipment Delivery Team, Cambodia.

MIA—Missing in Action.

MiG—Mikoyan-Gurevich designed Soviet aircraft.

MO—Mount Out, loaded and ready classes of supplies for contingency use by amphibious forces.

MOA—Mount Out Augmentation.

MODLOC—Modified Location, radius around a specified point from which naval ships may transit while waiting employment.

Mortar, 4.2 inch—U.S. M30 rifled, muzzle-loaded, drop-fired weapon consisting of tube, base-plate and standard; weapon weighs 330 pounds and has a maximum range of 4,020 meters. Rate of fire is 20 rounds per minute. Also known as the "Four-Deuce."

Mortar, 60mm—U.S. M19 smooth-bore, muzzle-loaded weapon which weighs 45.2 pounds when assembled; it has a maximum rate of fire of 30 rounds per minute and sustained rate of fire of 18 rounds per minute; the effective range is 2,000 meters.

Mortar, 81mm—U.S. M29 smooth-bore, muzzle-loaded weapon which weighs approximately 115 pounds when assembled; it has a sustained rate of fire of two rounds per minute and an effective range of 2,300-3,650 meters, depending upon ammunition used.

Mortar, 82mm—Communist smooth-bore, single-shot, high angle of fire weapon which weighs approximately 123 pounds; it has a maximum rate of fire of 25 rounds per minute and a maximum range of 3,040 meters.

Mortar, 120mm—Communist smooth bore, drop- or trigger-fired mortar which weighs approximately 600 pounds; it has a maximum rate of fire of 15 rounds per minute and a maximum range of 5,700 meters.

MR—Military Region. South Vietnamese army corps tactical zones were redesignated military regions in 1970, e.g., I Corps Tactical Zone became Military Region 1 (MR-1).

MR-5—Communist political and military sector in South Vietnam, including all of Military Region 1. NVA units in MR-5 did not report to COSVN.

Ms—Manuscript.

MSC—Military Sealift Command.

MSG—Marine Security Guard.

Msg—Message.

NAG—Naval Advisory Group.

NAIL—Radio call sign for USAF OV-10 aircraft.

NAS—Naval Air Station.

NATOPS—Naval Air Training and Operating Procedures Standardization.

NCC—Naval Component Commander.

NCO—Noncommissioned Officer.

NEmVac—Noncombatant Emergency Evacuation.

NGLO—Naval Gunfire Liaison Officer.

NGS—Naval Gunfire Support.

NKP—U.S. Air Force designation for Nakhon Phanom Air Base, Thailand.

NLF—National Liberation Front, the political arm of the Communist-led insurgency against the South Vietnamese Government.

NMCB—Naval Mobile Construction Battalion, whose members are known as "SeaBees."

NMCC—National Military Command Center.

NOD—Night Observation Device.

NPFF—National Police Field Force.

NSA—Naval Support Activity.

NSD—Naval Supply Depot.

Nui—Vietnamese word for hill or mountain.

Nung—Southeast Asian tribesman, of an ethnic group of probably Chinese origin.

NVA—North Vietnamese Army, the Peoples Army of Vietnam (PAVN); term often used by Americans to refer to a North Vietnamese soldier.

O-1—Cessna Bird Dog, a single-engine, propeller-driven observation aircraft.

O-2—Cessna Skymaster, a dual-engine, propeller-driven observation aircraft.

OH-6—Hughes Cayuse, single-rotor light helicopter used for armed reconnaissance and observation. Also known as a "Loach."

OH-58—Bell Kiowa, single-rotor light helicopter used for armed reconnaissance and observation.

OIC—Officer-in-Charge.

OpCon—Operational Control, the authority granted to a commander to direct forces assigned for specific missions or tasks which are usually limited by function, time, or location.

OpO—Operation Order, a directive issued by a commander to subordinate commanders for the execution of an operation.
OP—Observation Post.
OPlan—Operation Plan, a plan for a single or series of connected operations to be carried out simultaneously or in succession; directive issued by higher authority to permit subordinate commanders to prepare supporting plans and orders.
OpsO—Operations officer.
OpSum—Operational Summary.
OSJS (MACV)—Office of the Secretariat, Joint Staff (Military Assistance Command Vietnam).
OV-10—North American Rockwell Bronco, twin-engine, turboprop observation and light-attack aircraft.

P-3—Lockheed Orion, four-engine, turboprop naval patrol aircraft.
PATMA—Pacific Air Traffic Management Agency.
Pave Nail—Radio call sign for U.S. Air Force OV-10 with laser-designator to control precision-guided munitions.
PAVN—Peoples Army of Vietnam (North Vietnam). This acronym was dropped in favor of "NVA" (North Vietnamese Army).
PersO—Personnel officer.
PF—Popular Force, Vietnamese militia who were usually employed in the defense of their own communities.
PGM—Precision guided-munitions, so-called "smart bombs."
PIIC—Photo Imagery Interpretation Center.
POL—Petroleum, Oil, and Lubricants.
POW—Prisoner of war.
PRC25—Standard very-high-frequency radio used by Marine ground units in Vietnam for communication over distances up to 25 miles.
PRG—People's Revolutionary Government (Viet Cong).
ProvMAG—Provisional Marine Aircraft Group.
PSA—Province Senior Advisor.

QL—Vietnamese acronym for national highway.

R&R—Rest and Recreation.
Recoilless Rifle, 106mm—U.S. M40 single-shot, recoilless, breech-loaded weapon which weighs 438 pounds when assembled and mounted for firing; it has a sustained rate of fire of six rounds per minute and an effective range of 1,365 meters.
Regt—Regiment.
RF-4—Photographic-reconnaissance model of the F4B Phantom.
RF-8A—Vought reconnaissance version of the F-8 Crusader.
RF—Regional Force, Vietnamese militia who were employed in a specific region.
Rifle, M14—U.S. gas-operated, magazine-fed, air-cooled, semi-automatic, 7.62mm caliber shoulder weapon, which weighs 12 pounds with a full 20-round magazine; it has a sustained rate of fire of 30 rounds per minute and an effective range of 500 yards.
Rifle, M16—U.S. gas-operated, magazine-fed, air-cooled, automatic, 5.56mm caliber shoulder weapon, which weighs 3.1 pounds with a 20-round magazine; it has a sustained rate of fire of 12-15 rounds per minute and an effective range of 460 meters.
RLT—Regimental Landing Team.
ROK—Republic of Korea.
Rolling Thunder—Codename for initial U.S. air operations over North Vietnam.
ROE—Rules of Engagement.

RPG—Rocket Propelled Grenade.
RVN—Republic of Vietnam (South Vietnam).
RVNAF—Republic of Vietnam Armed Forces.
RZ—Reconnaissance Zone.

S-1, -2 et al.—Designations for staff positions at regimental and battalion levels. S-1 refers to the staff member responsible for personnel; S-2, intelligence; S-3, operations; S-4, logistics; and S-5, civil affairs.
SAC—Strategic Air Command.
SACC—Supporting Arms Control Center.
SAM—Surface to Air Missile.
SAR—Search and Rescue.
SATS—Short Airfield for Tactical Support, an expeditionary airfield used by Marine Corps aviation that includes a portable run-way surface, aircraft launching and recovery devices, and other essential components.
SCAMP—Sensor Control and Management Platoon.
SEATO—Southeast Asia Treaty Organization.
SecDef—Secretary of Defense.
SecState—Secretary of State.
SeventhAF—Seventh Air Force, the major U.S. Air Force command in Southeast Asia.
SeventhFlt—The U.S. Navy fleet assigned to the Western Pacific.
SID—Seismic Intrusion Device, sensor used to monitor movement through ground vibrations.
SitRep—Situation Report.
SKS—Simonov-designed, gas-operated, 7.62mm semiautomatic rifle.
SMA—Senior Marine Advisor.
Song—Vietnamese for river.
SOP—Standing Operating Procedure, set of instructions laying out standardized procedures.
Sortie—An operational flight by one aircraft.
SOS—Special Operations Squadron.
SOW—Special Operations Wing.
SPG—Special planning group.
SptRept—Spot Report.
SRF—Ship Repair Facility.

TA-4—Douglas, dual-seat version of the A-4 Skyhawk used as trainer and FAC/TAC platform.
T-39—North American Rockwell Sabreliner, twin-engine jet, used as trainer and passenger aircraft.
TAC(A)—Tactical Air Coordinator (Airborne), a designated aviator who controls and coordinates air support from an aircraft.
TACC—Tactical Air Control Center, the principal air operations installation for controlling all aircraft and air-warning functions of tactical air operations.
TACP—Tactical Air Control Party, a subordinate operational component of a tactical air control system designed to provide air liaison to land forces and for the control of aircraft.
TADC—Tactical Air Direction Center, an air operations installation under the Tactical Air Control Center, which directs aircraft and aircraft warning functions of the tactical air center.
TAFDS—Tactical Airfield Fuel Dispensing System, the expeditionary storage and dispensing system for aviation fuel at tactical air fields. It uses 10,000-gallon fabric tanks to store the fuel.
TAOC—Tactical Air Operations Center, a subordinate component

GLOSSARY

of the air command and control system which controls all air traffic and air defense operations.

Tank, M48—U.S. 50.7-ton tank with a crew of four; primary armament is a turret-mounted 90mm gun with one .30-caliber and one .50-caliber machine gun; has maximum road speed of 32 miles per hour and an average range of 195 miles.

TAOC—Tactical Air Operations Center, a subordinate component of the air command and control system which controls all air traffic and air defense operations.

TAOC—Tactical Area of Coordination.

TAOI—Tactical Area of Interest.

TAOR—Tactical Area of Responsibility, a defined area of land for which responsibility is specifically assigned to a commander for control of assigned forces and coordination of support.

TASS—Tactical Air Support Squadron.

TE—Task Element.

TF—Task Force.

TG—Task Group.

TO—Table of Organization.

TOE—Table of Equipment.

TOW—U.S. M220 Tube-launched, Optically-tracked, Wire-guided antitank missile system.

TU—Task Unit.

U-21—Beechcraft King Air, twin-engine, turboprop utility and passenger aircraft.

UCMJ—Uniform Code of Military Justice.

UH-1—Bell Iroquois, single-rotor light helicopter noted for its maneuverability and firepower; carries a crew of three; it can be armed with air-to-ground rocket packs and fuselage-mounted, electrically-fired machine guns. Also known as a "Huey."

USA—United States Army.

USAAG—U.S. Army Advisory Group.

USAF—United States Air Force.

USAID—U.S. Agency for International Development.

USARV—U.S. Army, Vietnam.

USASuppCom—U.S. Army Support Command.

USIA—U.S. Information Agency.

USMC—United States Marine Corps.

USN—United States Navy.

USSAG/SeventhAF—United States Support Activities Group/Seventh Air Force.

Viet Cong—Term used to refer to the Communist guerrillas in South Vietnam; a contraction of the Vietnamese phrase meaning "Vietnamese Communists."

VCI—Viet Cong Infrastructure.

VIS—Vietnamese Information Service (South Vietnam).

VMA—Marine Attack Squadron.

VMF(AW)—Marine Fighter Squadron (All-Weather).

VMFA—Marine Fighter Attack Squadron.

VMCJ—Marine Composite Reconnaissance Squadron.

VMGR—Marine Refueler Transport Squadron.

VMO—Marine Observation Squadron.

VNAF—Vietnamese Air Force.

VNMC—Vietnamese Marine Corps.

VNMC LSB—Vietnamese Marine Corps Logistics Support Branch, of the Navy Division, U.S. Defense Attache Office, Saigon.

VNN—Vietnamese Navy.

VT—Variably timed electronic fuze for an artillery shell which causes an airburst over the target area.

WestPac—Western Pacific.

WIA—Wounded in Action.

Wild Weasel—Codename for special techniques and aircraft used to suppress air defense electronic systems.

WFRC—Washington Federal Records Center.

Appendix G
Chronology of Significant Events 1973-1975

1973

27 January — The United States, Republic of Vietnam (South Vietnam), Democratic Republic of Vietnam (North Vietnam), and the Provisional Revolutionary Government of South Vietnam (Viet Cong) sign a peace agreement in Paris, France. The Paris Accords provided for three commissions to oversee the implementation of the agreements and resolve any differences. The commissions were the four-party Joint Military Commission (JMC) representing each of the belligerents, a two-party JMC representing North and South Vietnam, and an International Commission of Control and Supervision (ICCS) consisting of representatives from Canada, Poland, Hungary, and Indonesia.

27 March — The Marine Advisory Unit of the Naval Advisory Group in Vietnam is disestablished, and replaced by the U.S. Vietnamese Marine Corps Logistics Support Branch. This is the last day of the 60-day ceasefire period during which the North Vietnamese released American prisoners of war and in turn the United States turned over to the South Vietnamese its military bases and withdrew its last military forces from the RVN.

29 March — The U.S. Military Assistance Command, Vietnam (USMACV), officially ceases to exist, replaced at 1900 Saigon time by the U.S. Defense Attache Office (DAO).

13 June — The U.S., South Vietnam, North Vietnam, and the Viet Cong sign the implementation agreement to the Paris Accords.

30 June — Less than 250 U.S. military personnel, which includes the 50 at the DAO, remain in South Vietnam, the maximum allowed by the Paris Peace Accords.

1 July — New Fiscal Year begins with a reduction from 2.2 billion to 1.1 billion dollars in U.S. assistance to South Vietnam.

15 December — Communist troops ambush a JMC-sanctioned MIA recovery mission, killing a U.S. Army officer and wounding four American and several South Vietnamese soldiers.

1974

June — LtCol Anthony Lukeman replaces LtCol George E. Strickland as Chief, VNMC Logistic Support Branch, Navy Division, DAO.

1 July — Fiscal Year 1975 begins with funding for South Vietnamese military forces set at 700 million dollars, down from 1.1 billion dollars.

December — The North Vietnamese Army (NVA) *968th Division* moves into South Vietnam's Central Highlands from Laos, the first overt deployment of a North Vietnamese division into the south since the ceasefire agreement.

CHRONOLOGY

31 December	NVA units encircle Phuoc Long City (Song Be), capital of Phuoc Long Province, near the Cambodian border in Military Region 3.

1975

7 January	The NVA captures Phuoc Long Province.
27 January	The last allied Mekong River convoy from South Vietnam enters Phnom Penh. The Cambodian Communist Khmer Rouge have successfully halted resupply to the embattled Cambodian capital, threatening the downfall of the non-Communist Cambodian Government.
10 March	The NVA attacks Ban Me Thuot in the Central Highlands, marking the start of its 1975 Spring Offensive.
19 March	The South Vietnamese abandon Quang Tri City and Province.
24 March	Quang Ngai City and Tam Ky in I Corps fall to the advancing NVA.
25 March	Hue falls to the Communists.
26 March	The NVA captures the former U.S. Marine base of Chu Lai.
30 March	The NVA enters the major port city of Da Nang and captures the Da Nang Air Base.
12 April	Marines of the 9th Marine Amphibious Brigade (9th MAB) execute Operation Eagle Pull, the evacuation of American and other foreign nationals from Phnom Penh, just before the city falls to the Khmer Rouge.
21 April	Nguyen Van Thieu resigns as President of the Republic of Vietnam (South Vietnam) and departs Saigon four days later for Taiwan, leaving the control of the government in the hands of his vice president.
28 April	General Duong Van Minh becomes the new President of the Republic of Vietnam.
29 April	Marines of the 9th MAB execute Operation Frequent Wind, the evacuation of Americans, foreign nationals, and various Vietnamese officials and citizens associated with Americans from Saigon to ships of the Seventh Fleet.
30 April	The North Vietnamese Army enters Saigon and places General Minh and his cabinet under arrest. Organized South Vietnamese resistance to the NVA has collapsed.
12 May	A gunboat of the new Cambodian Khmer Rouge regime seizes an American ship, the SS *Mayaguez*, in the Gulf of Thailand.
14 May	Marines of BLT 2/9 in U.S. Air Force helicopters make a helicopter assault on Koh Tang Island off the Cambodian mainland where the crew of the *Mayaguez* is believed to be held. At the same time, Marines from Company D, 1st Battalion, 4th Marines board the *Mayaguez* only to find it deserted. The Cambodians in the meantime release the crew of the *Mayaguez* who later are recovered at sea by the U.S. destroyer *Wilson*.
15 May	With the recovery of both the *Mayaguez* and its crew, the Marines withdraw from Koh Tang Island. The American forces sustained total casualties of 15 killed, 3 missing in action (later declared dead), 49 wounded, and 23 other personnel killed in a related helicopter crash. U.S. forces inflicted an unknown number of casualties.

Appendix H
List of Reviewers

Gen Alfred M. Gray, USMC
Gen Louis H. Wilson, Jr., USMC, (Ret)

LtGen Edward J. Bronars, USMC (Ret)
LtGen Richard E. Carey, USMC (Ret)
LtGen Edwin J. Godfrey, USMC
LtGen Anthony Lukeman, USMC (Ret)
LtGen Carl E. Mundy, Jr., USMC (Ret)
LtGen Stephen G. Olmstead, USMC (Ret)
LtGen David M. Twomey, USMC (Ret)

MajGen George L. Cates, USMC
MajGen Gene A. Deegan, USMC
MajGen Norman W. Gourley, USMC (Ret)
MajGen Fred E. Haynes, Jr., USMC (Ret)
MajGen Carl W. Hoffman, USMC (Ret)
MajGen John I. Hopkins, USMC
MajGen Kenneth J. Houghton, USMC (Ret)
MajGen Herman Poggemeyer, Jr., USMC (Ret)
MajGen William R. Quinn, USMC (Ret)
MajGen Michael P. Ryan, USMC (Ret)
MajGen Henry C. Stackpole III, USMC

BGen William A. Bloomer, USMC (Ret)
BGen Harold L. Coffman, USMC (Ret)
BGen Walter D. Fillmore, USMC (Ret)
BGen Paul G. Graham, USMC (Ret)
BGen James E. Livingston, USMC
BGen William L. McCulloch, USMC (Ret)

Col Peter F. Angle, USMC (Ret)
Col Randall W. Austin, USMC (Ret)
Col Horace W. Baker, USMC (Ret)
Col George T. Balzer, USMC (Ret)
Col Charles A. Barstow, USMC (Ret)
Col Arthur A. Bergman, USMC (Ret)
Col Gerald L. Berry, USMC
Col John J. Carty, USMC (Ret)
Col Arthur B. Colbert, USMC (Ret)
Col Gerald L. Diffee, USMC (Ret)
Col Hans G. Edebohls, USMC (Ret)
Col Angelo Fernandez, USMC (Ret)
Col Herbert M. Fix, USMC (Ret)
Col Stephen R. Foulger, USMC (Ret)

Col Laurence R. Gaboury, USMC (Ret)
Col James R. Gentry, USMC (Ret)
Col Richard F. Johnson, USMC (Ret)
Col Fred L. Jones, USMC
Col James L. Jones, Jr., USMC
Col Douglas T. Kane, USMC (Ret)
Col Floyd A. Karker, Jr., USMC (Ret)
Col Burrell H. Landes, USMC (Ret)
Col Curtis G. Lawson, USMC (Ret)
Col Martin J. Lenzini, USMC
Col Robert E. Loehe, USMC (Ret)
Col Gene M. McCain, USMC (Ret)
Col William E. McKinstry, USMC (Ret)
Col Joseph F. Molineaux, Jr., USMC (Ret)
Col Robert M. Reed, USMC (Ret)
Col Alvin R. Ribbeck, Jr., USMC (Ret)
Col Edward J. Ritchie, USMC
Col John F. Roche III, USMC (Ret)
Col Jack D. Rowley, USMC (Ret)
Col Alexander S. Ruggiero, USMC (Ret)
Col Carl A. Shaver, USMC
Col Glenn J. Shaver, Jr., USMC (Ret)
Col Jerry L. Shelton, USMC (Ret)
Col George P. Slade, USMC (Ret)
Col Thomas J. Stevens, USMC (Ret)
Col Wylie W. Taylor, Jr., USMC (Ret)
Col Nicholas M. Trapnell, Jr., USMC (Ret)
Col Donald J. Verdon, USMC (Ret)
Col Jon M. Walters, USMC
Col Robert D. White, USMC (Ret)
Col Robert C. Wise, USMC (Ret)
Col Anthony A. Wood, USMC
Col Walter J. Wood, USMC
Col Tullis J. Woodham, Jr., USMC (Ret)
Col Richard K. Young, USMC (Ret)

LtCol Dwight R. Allen, Jr., USMC (Ret)
LtCol Daniel F. Bergen, USMC (Ret)
LtCol James L. Bolton, USMC (Ret)
LtCol Royce L. Bond, USMC (Ret)
LtCol John W. Bowman, Jr., USMC
LtCol Matthew E. Broderick, USMC
LtCol Kermit C. Corcoran, USMC (Ret)
LtCol James L. Cunningham, USMC (Ret)

REVIEWERS

LtCol James H. Davis, USMC (Ret)
LtCol Donald L. Evans, USMC (Ret)
LtCol James A. Gallagher, Jr., USMC (Ret)
LtCol David A. Garcia, USMC (Ret)
LtCol Charles W. Gobat, USMC (Ret)
LtCol Maurice O. V. Green, USMC (Ret)
LtCol Edward A. Grimm, USMC (Ret)
LtCol Ronald J. Gruenberg, USMC (Ret)
LtCol William H. Hackett, Jr., USMC (Ret)
LtCol Robert E. Hamilton, USMC (Ret)
LtCol William Harley, USMC
LtCol John B. Heffernan, USMC (Ret)
LtCol Charles E. Hester, USMC (Ret)
LtCol Robert T. Hickinbotham, USMC
LtCol Harry Jensen, Jr., USMC
LtCol James H. Kean, USMC (Ret)
LtCol Thomas A. Keene, USMC
LtCol James P. Kizer, USMC (Ret)
LtCol David A. Kratochvil, USMC
LtCol Bertram A. Maas, USMC (Ret)
LtCol Michael T. Mallick, USMC (Ret)
LtCol William R. Melton, USMC
LtCol Cyril V. Moyher, USMCR
LtCol Barry J. Murphy, USMC (Ret)
LtCol Ronald L. Owen, USMC (Ret)
LtCol Edward R. Palmquist, Jr., USMC
LtCol Charles E. Parker, USMC (Ret)
LtCol Jerome T. Paull, USMC (Ret)
LtCol Raymond E. Porter, USMC (Ret)
LtCol Richard L. Reuter, USMC
LtCol James P. Rigoulot, USMC (Ret)
LtCol Joseph J. Rogish, Jr., USMC
LtCol Howard P. Shores II, USMC
LtCol John F. Spangler, USMC (Ret)
LtCol Ronald E. Spratt, USMC
LtCol Mykle E. Stahl, USMC
LtCol Robert M. Stauffer, USMC (Ret)
LtCol Joseph J. Streitz, USMC
LtCol George E. Strickland, USMC (Ret)
LtCol Terry L. Tonkin, USMC
LtCol Richard H. Zales, USMC

Maj Robert D. Amos, Jr., USMC (Ret)
Maj Charles J. Bushey, USMC (Ret)
Maj Michael A. Cicere, USMC
Maj Donald O. Coughlin, USMC (Ret)
Maj Thomas W. Kinsell, USMC (Ret)
Maj Raymond J. McManus, USMC (Ret)
Maj Joseph J. McMenamin, USMC
Maj James L. O'Neill, USMC
Maj Steven A. Shepherd, USMC (Ret)

Maj Bruce P. Thompson-Bowers, USMC
Capt Eugene R. Hardman, USMC
Capt Richard M. Jessie, Jr., USMC
Capt Richard R. Page, USMC
Capt Charles R. Provini, USMC
Capt Russell R. Thurman, USMC (Ret)

1stLt Roger D. Gabelman, USMC
1stLt Johnnie Johnson, USMC

2dLt James McDaniel, USMC

CWO-4 Allen F. Kent, USMC (Ret)
CWO-2 J. C. Owens, USMC (Ret)

MSgt Michael A. McCormick, USMC
MSgt Juan J. Valdez, USMC (Ret)
GySgt Roger F. Painter, USMC (Ret)

Army

Gen Homer D. Smith, Jr., USA (Ret)
MajGen John E. Murray, USA (Ret)
BGen James A. Herbert, USA (Ret)
BGen William A. Stoftt, USA
Col Edwin Pelosky, USA (Ret)

Navy

Adm Noel A. M. Gayler, USN (Ret)
Adm Maurice F. Weisner, USN (Ret)
VAdm George P. Steele, USN (Ret)
RAdm Donald B. Whitmire, USN (Ret)
Capt Roy W. McLain, USN (Ret)
Capt James D. Tregurtha, USN (Ret)

Air Force

Gen William G. Moore, Jr., USAF (Ret)
Gen John W. Vogt, Jr., USAF (Ret)
LtGen John J. Burns, USAF (Ret)
LtGen Leroy Manor, USAF (Ret)
MajGen Andrew J. Evans, Jr., USAF (Ret)
LtCol John F. Guilmartin, USAF (Ret)
Lt David C. Jones, USAF (Ret)

Others

Hon. John Gunther Dean
Dr. Alfred Goldberg
Dr. Richard H. Kohn
Hon. Graham Martin
Dr. Ronald Spector
LtCol Tran Ngoc Toan, VNMC
Mr. Willard J. Webb

Appendix I
1st Battalion, 4th Marines Detachments 3-11 April 1975

USMC Security Detachments On Board MSC Ships

Military Sealift Command (MSC) ship*	Location	Estimated number of refugees on board	Date of USMC boarding	BLT 1/4 boarding detachment (officer in charge)
SS *Pioneer Contender*	Cam Ranh Bay	16,700	3 April	3d Plt, Co B (2dLt Robert E. Lee, Jr.)
SS *Pioneer Contender*	Phu Quoc Island	16,700	7 April	3d Plt, Co D (2dLt Joe Flores, Jr.)
SS *Trans Colorado*	Phan Rang	3,500	4 April	1st Plt, Co D (Unavailable)
SS *Green Port*	Phu Quoc Island	6,000 to 8,000	6 April	3d Plt, Co C (2dLt David L. Kiffer) 2d Plt, Co D (2dLt Edward R. Whitesides)
SS *American Challenger*	Phu Quoc Island	6,000	6 April	1st Plt, Co C 2d Plt, Co C (Capt Maurice O. V. Green)
USNS *Sgt Kimbro*	Ham Tan		9 April	3d Plt, Co A (Unavailable)

Source: Amphibious Evacuation RVN Support Group TG 79.9, Post-Exercise Report, 30 April 1975.

*All ships except the *Sgt Kimbro* were chartered by MSC.

Appendix J
Frequent Wind Forces

Summary of Forces Committed to Frequent Wind

U.S. Navy

Ships
- Carriers 2
- Amphibious 17
- Escorts 14
- Replenishment 11

Sea-based aircraft
- Fighter/Attack 125
- Support 33
- ASW Helos 12

U.S. Marine Corps

Sea-based ground forces (BLT plus security evacuation force) .... MAB
Land-based ground forces .... 3 BLTs
Sea-based helicopters
- Troop/Passenger lift 63
- Gunship 8
- Command and control 6

U.S. Air Force

Aircraft
- Fighter/Attack 193
- Support 112
- Troop/Passenger lift 69

Appendix K
Helicopter Flow Table for Frequent Wind

The helicopter time schedule as shown below was developed by Regimental Landing Team (RLT) 4 and Provisional Marine Aircraft Group (ProvMAG) 39 for movement of the ground security force from ships to the evacuation site, and is in fact a recap of the Helicopter Employment and Landing Table (HEALT) developed jointly by the RLT and ProvMAG:

Time	Ship	Event
L-2:00	*Hancock* (CVA 19)	Launch 6 CH-53s for troop pickup (3 to *Vancouver* [LPD 2], 3 to *Peoria* [LST 1183])
L-0:50	*Duluth* (LPD 6)	Land 1 CH-53 w/troops from *Okinawa* (LPH 3) for refuel
L-0:50	*Hancock* (CVA 19)	Land 3 CH-53s w/troops from *Vancouver* for refuel
L-0:50	*Peoria* (LST 1183)	Launch 1 CH-53 w/troops to *Mobile* (LKA 115) for refuel
L-0:50	*Peoria* (LST 1183)	Land 1 CH-53 for troop pickup and refuel
L-0:45	*Denver* (LPD 9)	Land 1 CH-53 w/troops from *Okinawa* for refuel
L-0:45	*Duluth* (LPD 6)	Land 1 CH-53 w/troops from *Okinawa* for refuel
L-0:40	*Mobile* (LKA 115)	Land 1 CH-53 w/troops from *Peoria* for refuel
L-0:40	*Okinawa* (LPH 3)	Load 4 CH-53s w/troops
L-0:30		Launch first wave of 12 CH-53s (4 from *Okinawa*, 2 each from *Dubuque* [LPD 8], *Denver*, and *Duluth*, and 1 each from *Mobile* and *Peoria*)
L-0:30	*Okinawa* (LPH 3)	Land 3 CH-53s for troop pickup and refuel
L-0:15		Launch second wave of 11 CH-53s (5 from *Hancock*, 3 from *Okinawa*, 2 from *Vancouver* and 1 from *Mount Vernon* [LSD 39])
L-1:25	*Peoria* (LST 1183)	Launch 1 CH-53 w/troops to *Hancock* for refuel
L-1:25	*Vancouver* (LPD 2)	Land 2 CH-53s for troop pickup and refuel
L-1:20	*Okinawa* (LPH 3)	Launch 4 CH-53s (2 w/troops to *Dubuque* for refuel, 2 to *Peoria* for troop pickup)

HELICOPTER FLOW TABLE FOR FREQUENT WIND

L-1:15	*Hancock* (CVA 19)	Land 3 CH-53s w/troops from *Peoria* for refuel
L-1:15	*Mount Vernon* (LSD 39)	Land 1 CH-53 w/troops from *Vancouver* for refuel
L-1:10	*Okinawa* (LPH 3)	Load 4 CH-53s w/troops
L-1:10	*Okinawa* (LPH 3)	Launch 4 CH-53s w/troops (2 to *Denver* for refuel, 2 to *Duluth* for refuel)
L-1:00	*Hancock* (CVA 19)	Launch 2 CH-53s to *Okinawa* for troop pickup and refuel
L-1:00	*Dubuque* (LPD 8)	Land 2 CH-53s w/troops from *Okinawa* for refuel
L-1:00	*Peoria* (LST 1183)	Land 1 CH-53 for troop pickup
L-0:50	*Denver* (LPD 9)	Land 1 CH-53 w/troops from *Okinawa* for refuel
L-1:50	*Vancouver* (LPD 2)	Land 2 CH-53s from *Hancock* for troop pickup
L-1:45	*Vancouver* (LPD 2)	Launch 2 CH-53s w/troops to *Hancock* for refuel
L-1:45	*Vancouver* (LPD 2)	Land 1 CH-53 from *Hancock* for troop pickup
L-1:40	*Vancouver* (LPD 2)	Launch 1 CH-53 w/troops to *Hancock* for refuel
L-1:40	*Hancock* (CVA 19)	Launch 3 CH-53s to *Vancouver* for troop pickup
L-1:40	*Peoria* (LST 1183)	Land 1 CH-53 for troop pickup
L-1:35	*Peoria* (LST 1183)	Launch 1 CH-53 w/troops to *Hancock* for refuel
L-1:35	*Peoria* (LST 1183)	Land 1 CH-53 for troop pickup
L-1:30	*Peoria* (LST 1183)	Launch 1 CH-53 w/troops to *Hancock* for refuel
L-1:30	*Okinawa* (LPH 3)	Load 2 CH-53s w/troops
L-1:30	*Vancouver* (LPD 2)	Land 1 CH-53 for troop pickup
L-1:30	*Peoria* (LST 1183)	Land 1 CH-53 for troop pickup
L-1:25	*Vancouver* (LPD 2)	Launch 1 CH-53 w/troops to *Mount Vernon* for refuel

INDEX

Key: **boldface type** = illustrations; *n* = footnotes

A Shau Valley, 10
Aduldet, King Phumiphol, Thailand, 40
Air America, 128, 174, 178-79, 181, 213. (*See also* Saigon.)
    Compound in Saigon, 145-46, 149, 153, 172, 178, 183, **191**, 192
    Vietnamese workers, 156
Air Force Bases
    Andersen, Guam, 221, 223
    Clark, Republic of the Philippines, 27, 206-7, 209
    Eglin, Florida, 214
    Travis, California, 156
Air Force Commands and Units
    Pacific Air Force (PacAF), 239
    Seventh Air Force, 11, 22, 26, 41, 44, 240
        Security Police Squadron, 108
    United States Support Activities Group/Seventh Air Force, 24-26, 36, 41-42, 44-45, 48, 55, 116, 143, 146, 151-52, 153-54, 181*n*, 182-83, 183*n*, 187, 239
    OPlan 2-75, 108
    Military Airlift Command, 140, 213
        3d Aerospace Rescue and Recovery Group, 26-27, 152
        Aerospace Rescue and Recovery Squadrons
            37th, 59, 59*n*
            40th, 26-27, 44, 59, 121*n*, 122-23, 152, 153*n*, 239
            56th, 26-27, 115
    Strategic Air Command, 25
    56th Special Operations Wing, 26, 152, 239
    307th Strategic Wing, 26
    374th Tactical Airlift Wing, 26
    347th Tactical Fighter Wing, 26
    388th Tactical Fighter Wing, 26
    432d Tactical Fighter Wing, 26
    7th Air Command and Control Squadron, 27
    23d Air Support Squadron, 122
    23d Tactical Air Support Squadron, 26-27
    34th Tactical Fighter Squadron, 26-27
    428th Tactical Fighter Squadron, 26
    429th Tactical Fighter Squadron, 26
    Special Operations Squadrons
        16th, 26-27
        21st, 26, 44, 153, 153*n*, 240
    Air Force Security Police, 240
    Pacific Air Traffic Management Agency, 25
Aircraft types
    fixed wing
        A-1, 13
        A-4, 14, **30**
        A-4E, 30
        A-6, **25**, 30, **32**
        A-6A, 14, 23*n*
        A-7, 14, 26
        A-37, 13, 168, 168*n*
        AC-47, 13
        AC-119, 13
        AC-130, 26-27, 153
        AC-130E, 26*n*
        AV-8A, 30
        B-52, 14, 26
        C-2, 163
        C-5, 140
        C-5A, 156
        C-7, 13
        C-47, 13
        C-119, 13
        C-123, 13
        C-130, 26, 44, 48, 80, 105, 109-10, 115, 141, 182, 188, 206, 213, 223
        C-130A, 13
        C-141, 159, 206, 213, 222, 241
        DC-8, 105
        EA-6, 110*n*; EA-6A, 14; EA-6B, **13**
        EB-66, 14
        EC-130F, 27
        F-4, 14, 23*n*, **25**, 26, **32**
        F-4B, 23*n*
        F-4J, 23*n*
        F-5, 168*n*; F-5A/B, 13
        F-111, 26
        HC-130, 26-27
        KC-130, **31**, 148, 162; KC-130F, 23*n*, 30
        KC-135, 26
        O-1, **211**
        OV-10, 26-27, 30, 44, 122, 257-58, 260
        RF-4, **29**, 110*n*
        T-39, 107
    rotary wing
        AH-1J, **28**, 30, 45, 61, 106, 110, 133, **133**, 181, 187, 201, 204
        CH-46, **28**, 44-45, 61-62, 86-87, 106, 110, 160, 187, 196, 200, 204, 216, 232
        CH-46D, 23*n*, 30, **33**, 133, 153
        CH-47, 13, 213
        CH-53, 44-45, 48, 61, 64, 106, 108, 111, 113, 119, 121, 152-53, 153*n*, 171, 185, 188, 196-97, 204, 240, 245*n*
        CH-53C, 26, 26*n*
        CH-53D, **3**, 30
        HH-53, 26-27, 44, 108, 122-23, 152-53, 185*n*, 239, 245
        UH-1, **12**, 13, 45
        UH-1E, **28**, 30, 61-62, 86, 89, 106, 110, 133, 187, 204, 212, 232
Alaska Barge and Transport Company, 128, 174
ALE-29 flare dispenser, 110-11
Alexander, Col Dan C., 87-89, 98, 131, 139, 162
Allen, LtCol Dwight R., 106
American Challenger (MSC ship), 97, 131, 166, 174, 205, 218-19, 221-22, 222*n*
American Operations

INDEX

Baby Lift, 156-57
Eagle Pull, 42, 53, 59, 84-85, 98, 105-106, 106n, 141-42
   development of fixed-wing plan, 109
   execution of, 121-24
   final stage of planning, 111
   insertion of command element, 110
   Marines committed to, 89
   Operation Order 2-73, 49, 61
   Operation Order 3-73, 49
   Operation Plan 1-73, 49
   order to execute, 116
   planning for, 43-46, 48-49, 51, 55-57, 61
   preparations for, 60-63, 107
End Sweep, 27, 44-45, 60
Fortress Journey, 53, 92, 138
Frequent Wind, 2, 141, 155, 159, 188, 195, 205, 213, 216-17
   casualties of, 169
   command relationships during, 192n, 194
   communications during, 192-93
   conclusion of, 200, 202
   decision to execute, 178
   deployment of naval forces at the start of, **186**
   execution of, 171, 184-85, 189
   first refugees delivered by, 191
   fixed wing evacuation, 169
   investigation of, 183n
   JCS investigation of, 204n
   L-Hour, 181, 181n, 182, 183n
   Operation Order 2-75, 148
   Option II, 182
   Option IV (rotary-wing evacuation), 169
      execution of, 183
   potential evacuation sites, **173**
Gallant Journey, 53, 138
New Life, 209, 222-23, 224, 226
Talon Vise, 53, 141
American Racer (MSC ship), 206, 219, 221
Amos, Capt Robert D., Jr., 165, **205**, 206
An Lao Valley, 15
An Loc
   veterans of, 69
   withdrawal from, 78
Anchorage (LSD 36), 138, 142
Anders, Col Loyd R., Jr., USAF, 152, 239-40, 244
Andersen, Sgt Carl C., 262-63
Anderson, Cpl Robert L., 132
Anderson, Cpl Ronald W., 127, 129
Androskaut, 1stLt David L., 201, **203**
Andrus, Lt Ken, MC, USN, 164
Angle, Maj Peter F., 57, 59
Appropriations Committee, House of Representatives, subcommittee of, 12
Apra Harbor, Guam, 218
Army Commands and Units
   25th Infantry Division, 42, 55
   Military Equipment Delivery Team, Cambodia, 46, 49, 61, 106
Arraigna, Cpl Carlos R., 174
Arriola, Sgt Lazaro, 127, 129
Austin, LtCol Randall W., 240, 242-43, 245, 250-51, 253-55, 256, 259-60
Austin, William D., 158

Ba Ra Mountain, 68
Ba Ria, 168
Babel, Sgt Philip A., **202**
Backlund, 1stLt Donald, USAF, 123n
Baker, Maj Horace W., 36, 43, 51
Balzer, Col George T., 36
Ban Bleik Pass, 74
Ban Me Thuot, 70-71, **71**, 72, 126, 156
   fall of, **72**, 73
      Montagnard involvement in, 72n
   plans for recapture of, 73-74
Banam, Cambodia, 105
Bangkok, Thailand, 40
Barbour County (LST 1195), 62, 64, 138, 164n, 217, 219
Barstow, LtCol Charles A., 38, 126, 126n
Basaae River, 176
Base Area 611, 266
Batchelder, Col Sydney H., Jr., **50-51**, 51, 59, 106-107, **108**, 110, 121-22, 147
Battaglia, Joseph, **231**
Bauer, Cpl Stephen Q., **202**
Baughn, BGen Richard M., USAF, 155
Be River, 68, 72
Belton, Capt E. H., CHC, USN, 22
Bennington, Sgt Terry J., **202**
Benton, RAdm Hugh G., USN, 146, 212
Bergen, Maj Daniel F., 38-39
Bernal, SSgt Serfino, Jr., 251n
Berry, Capt Gerald L., 199-201, 201n, 202
Bien Hoa, 13, 39, 133, 136, 160, 168
   Air Base, 30
   consulate, 173
   Front, 168
Binh Dinh Province, 15, 72, 76
   NVA assault on, 131
Binh Duong Front, 168
Binh Thuan Province, 131
Binh Thuy, 13
Bird Air Company, 102, 105, 112
Bishop, LCpl M. R., **219**
Bjorklund, Col Darrel E., 30
Bland, Capt Steven R., 119, 192
Bloomer, LtCol Walter A., 110n, 195, 195n
BLT Readiness Program, 34
Blue Ridge (LCC 19), 28, 61, 85n, 86, 88, 94, 138, 140, 145, 148, 163, 170-71, 172, 176, 178, 181, 184, 188, 198, 199n, 201n, 213, 215
Bo Duc, 69
Bolton, LtCol James L., 64-65, 105, 121, 148, 184, 189, 197, 199, 202
Bond, LtCol Royce Lynn, 53, 87, 109, 110, **110**, 140, 147, 148, 183
Boret, Prime Minister Long, 114, 114n
Borg, Ambassador Parker, 207, 209
Bowman, Capt John W., Jr., 201, **203**
Branson, LCpl Larry J., 255
Breyette, Sgt Ervin E., **122**
Brill, LtCol Arthur P., Jr., 234n
Bristol County (LST 1189), 64
Broderick, Capt Matthew E., 106, 191
Bronars, Col Edward J., 36, **45**, 46
Brown, Gen George S., USA, 264

Brown, Maj James R., Jr., 116
Brown, Cpl Levorn L., 132
Brush, Maj Martin C., 195
Bullard, Cdr L. D., USN, 22
Bunard Fire Support Base, 69
Burnett, SSgt Francis L., 255, 260
Burns, LtGen John J., USAF, 59, 106, 116, 128, 143, 146, 152-54, 181, 183, 187, 192, 192*n*, 194, 239-42, 245, 253, 255, 255*n*, 257-59
Bushey, Capt Charles J., 87, 89, 95-96, 164, 166

Calvert, Col Robert W., 228*n*, 233
Cam, Gen Tran Van, ARVN, 73-74
Cam Ranh, 73, 146
  Bay, 89-90, 92
Cambodia, 5*n*, 6, 40, 126, 267
  American Embassy, evacuation of, 113
  Banam, 105
  Boret, Prime Minister Long, 114, 114*n*
  conflict in, 101
  Dean, Ambassador John Gunther, 110-11, 114, 121-23, **124**
  defeat of government, 98
  evacuation of, 25, 42-43, 55-56, 89
  halt of U.S. air support in, 101
  Khmer Communists, 40, 50, 57, 123. (*See also* Khmer Rouge.)
  Khmer Republic, 100, 121
  Khmer Rouge, 57, 66, 100, 102, 111
    1975 Offensive, 102, **103**, 104. (*See also* Khmer Communists.)
  Khoy, President Saukham, **113**, 114, 122
  Koh Tang, 238, 240-41, **244**, **257**
    aerial reconnaissance of, 243*n*, 244
    assault on, 248, 248*n*, 249, 252-53, 253*n*, 254-55, 264-65
    communications during, 256
    enemy strength on, 248*n*
    extraction from, 255, 255*n*, 256, 259-61, 262-63
    helicopter landings on, 248, 248*n*, 251
    information on terrain, 243
    planning for assault on, 244-45
  Kompong Som, 50, 61, 64, 105-6, 121, 242
  last Marine helicopter to leave, 123
  Matak, Sirik, 114, 114*n*, 121
  Neak Loung, 104-5, 113
  neutrality of, 100
  Nol, President Lon, 100-101, 114, 114*n*
    government of, 50, 102, 104
  Parrot's Beak, 100
  pattern of conflict in, 100
  Phnom Penh, 39-40, 56-57, 98, 102, 106*n*, 107-8, 110, 119, 121, 142
    American Embassy landing zone, **58**
    evacuation of, 85, 114-15. (*See also* Eagle Pull, under American Operations.)
    evacuation sites, **112**
    landing zones in, 113
      Hotel, 116, **119-20**, 121-23
  Mekong supply line to, 104-5
  Phu My, mines in the Mekong at, 104
  Pochentong Airfield, 104-5, 109
    evacuation operation at, 111-12
  Point Oscar, 121-22
  political situation in, 64
  Poulo Wai Island, 238
  Sihanouk, Prince Norodom, 100
  tactical situation in, 116
  Toul Leap, 105
  U.S./South Vietnamese offensive in, 100
Cambodian Army (Force Armee Nationale Khmer [FANK]), 100, 105
Cambodian Navy, ability to sweep minefields, 104
Camp Asan, Guam, 222-23, 228
  refugee camp, 224, 226
Camp Fuji, Japan, 137, 141-42
Camp Plei Me, 16
Camp Talega, California, 228-29, 232
Camp Socio Refugee Camp, Guam, 226
Can Tho, 13, 39
  concept for evacuation of, 149
  consulate, 173
  evacuation of, 174, 176
  refugees, 174
Canada, as member of ICCS, 2, 4
Cang, VAdm Chung Tan, VNN, 15
Carey, BGen Richard E., 66, 98, 111*n*, 119, 138, **138**, 140-41, 143, **144**, 145-46, **147**, 147, 151, 153, 159, 163, 165, 181, 181*n*, 183-84, 187, 192, 192*n*, 194-95, 198-201, 201*n*, 204, 219, 265
Carmona, LCpl Ricardo, 97, 164
Carroll, RAdm Kent J., USN, 225, 226*n*
Carty, Maj John J., 36
Case-Church Amendment. (*See under* Foreign Military Sales Act.)
Cassidy, Capt Barry, 254-55
Catania, PFC Daniel N., 112
Cates, Maj George L., 51, **51**, 55, **55**, 107, 114
Cease-fire Agreement, 16, 21, 36
  violations of, 5
Central Highlands
  retreat from, 73-74
Charusathien, Interior Minister Gen Praphas, Thailand, 40
Chau Doc, 6
Cheo Reo, 74
Chu Lai, 126
  fall of, 79, 127
Cicere, 2dLt Michael A., 249, 251, 258, 258*n*
Cleland, BGen John R. D., Jr., USA, 46; MajGen, 183*n*, 217
Coffman, BGen Harold L., 109, 133, 164, 233*n*
Coker, Cpl C. R., 246
Colbert, LtCol Arthur B., 46
Colbert, Col Bruce A., 60-61
Committee to Denounce War Crimes, 5*n*
Con Son Island, 205
Conger, Capt C. N., USNR, 22
Connolly, Col James P., II, 36
Coral Sea (CVA 43), 50, 153, 163, 164*n*, 195, 239, 243*n*, 258-61
Corcoran, Capt Kermit C., 121
Coughlin, Maj Donald O., 140, 148
Cox, Maj David E., 147, 172, 194
Croizat, LtCol Victor J., 266
Cu Chi Front, 168
Cunningham, LtCol James L., 147, 181; Col, 53
Curcio, 2dLt Charles K., 94
Cushman, Gen Robert E., Jr., 30, 232

INDEX

Cuson, Capt C. E., USN, 22

Da Krong Valley, 266
Da Nang, 13, 30, 39, 52, 70, 76, 78, 82, 85*n*, **130**
  ARVN deserters in, 127
  consulate, 127
  defense of, 80, 84, 84*n*
  evacuation of, 53, 85-86, 89-92, 94, 127, 130-31, 154
    plans for, 87
    preparations for, 86, 89
  fall of, 78-79, 83*n*, 87, 128
  Francis, Consul General Albert A., 126-28, 128*n*
  Harbor, 204
  Marine House, 127
  NVA entrance into, 126
  refugees in, 83-84
Dalat, abandonment of, 133
DAO. (*See* Defense Attache Office (DAO), Saigon.)
Dao, BGen Le Minh, ARVN, 136, 168
Darlac Province, 15, 71-72
Davis, LtCol Charles E., Jr., 64
Davis, Capt James H., 57, 248, 252, 261-62
Dean, Ambassador John Gunther, 110-11, 114, 121-23, **124**
Deegan, LtCol Gene A., **52**, 53, 57
Defense Attache Office (DAO), Saigon, 2, 6-7, 16, 22, 25, 36-37, 132, 143, 145, 149, 151-53, 155, **155**, 157-59, 164, 169, 171, 171*n*, 172, **172**, 179
  Compound, 156, 160, 172, 178, 181-83, 185, 188-89, 191, **191**, 204, 217
    defense of, 159
    evacuation of, 192, 194, 194*n*, 195, 198, 198*n*, 199
  Evacuation Control Center (ECC), 147, 155-56, 178, 182
  Evacuation Processing Center (EPC), 155
  Special Planning Group (SPG), 155-56, 160, 170-72, 178
Demilitarized Zone (DMZ), 14, 52
Denver (LPD 9), 62, 138, 184, 195
Dien Bien Phu, 73
Diffee, Maj Gerald E., 38
Dittmar, Capt Charles A., **34**
Don Luan, 68-69
Dubuque (LPD 8), 85-88, 88*n*, 89, 93, 131, 138, 162-63, **163**, 164, 164*n*, 165-66, 184, 206, 216
Duc Co, 71
Duc Phong, 69
Duffy, Sgt Ronald E., 174
Duluth (LPD 6), 50, 62, **137**, 138, 184, 241
Dung, Gen Van Tien, NVA, 10-11, 68, 70, 70*n*, 71, 73-74, 78, 78*n*, 79, 146, 160, 168, 170
Durham (LKA 114), 85-86, 88-89, 93-94, 110, 138, 141

Ea Pa River, 74
East, MSgt William, 147, 172, 197
ECC. (*See* Evacuation Control Center (ECC) under Defense Attache Office (DAO), Saigon.)
Edebohls, Col Hans G., 142, 148
Edwards, Jerry, 36
Elfrink, 1stLt Ben C., USA, 7
Enders, Charge d'Affaires William K., 46
Enterprise (CVAN 65), 153

EPC. (*See* Evacuation Processing Center (EPC) under Defense Attache Office (DAO), Saigon.)
Esau, Maj Richard H., Jr., 38
Evans, MajGen Andrew J., USAF, 42-43
Evans, Maj Donald L., 39
Expo '76, 34

FANK. [Force Armee Nationale Khmer] (*See* Cambodian Army.)
Felber, Sgt James M., 175
Fernandez, Maj Angelo A., 61
Fillmore, LtCol Walter D., 22, 37-38
Fisk, TSgt Wayne, USAF, 262, 262*n*
Fix, LtCol Herbert M., 87, 108, 111, 121, 148, 184
Fleming, Col William B., 22, 38
Flores, 2dLt Joe, Jr., 97
Ford, President Gerald R., 52, 121*n*, 200, 228, 232, 238-40, 241*n*, 264
Ford, Mrs. Gerald, **231**
Foreign Military Sales Act
  Case-Church Amendment, 5, 5*n*, 40, 101
  Cooper-Church Amendment, 5, 5*n*
Forseth, Cpl Leonard A., 127, 129
Fort Chaffee, Florida, 214
Fort Fisher (LSD 40), 64
Foulger, LtCol Steven R., 62
Four-Power Joint Military Commission (JMC), 2, 4, 38, 155
Francis, Consul General Albert A., 126-28, 128*n*
Frederick (LSD 1184), 85-86, 88-90, 93, 110, 138, 141
Fredericksen, 1stLt Carl W., 206
Fresno (LST 1182), 64
Front Unifie pour la Liberation des Races Opprimees, 72*n*. (*See also* Montagnards.)
Funk, 1stSgt Lawrence L., 255

Gabelman, 1stLt Roger D., 226
Gaboury, LtCol Larry R., 61
GAIL. (*See* Glide Angle Indicator Light.)
Gallagher, Maj James A., 148
Garcia, Capt David A., 164, 174, 176, 206
Gayler, Adm Noel A. M., USN, 25, 42, 53, 53*n*, 57, 63, 105, 131, 133, 143, 164, 181, 183, 198-99, 204, 207, 211-14, 221-22, 224, 239-40, 255, 262
General Services Administration, 228
Gentry, LtCol James R., 142, 148
Gia Dinh, 135
Giselbreth, LCpl Charles A., 251*n*
Glide Angle Indicator Light (GAIL), 107
Gobat, LtCol Charles W., 222
Godfrey, LtCol Edwin J., 64
Gorman, MGySgt Charles C., USMC (Ret), 36
Gourley, MajGen Norman W., 66, 202*n*
Graham, BGen Paul G., 204, 228, 228*n*, 229, 229*n*, **231**, 232, 234*n*, 235, 238
Grande Island, Republic of the Philippines, 164, 209, 211, 214, 219
  refugee camp on, 212, **213**, 213
Gray, Col Alfred M., Jr., 86-87, 93, 110, 140, **145**, 146, **147**, 148, 163, 170, 178, 181*n*, 183-84, 187, 189, 192, 197-98
Grayback, 29
Green, Capt Maurice O. V., 88
Green Forest (MSC ship), 165, 205-206, 222
  conditions aboard, 219

Green Port (MSC ship), 205, 219, 221-22
Green Wave (MSC ship), 206, 222
Greene, Gen Wallace M., Jr., 126
Greenville Victory (MSC ship), **91**, 130-31, 163, 164*n*, 205, 218-19, 222, 241
  hijacking of, 91
Gridley (DLG 21), 163
Grimm, Maj Edward A., 36, 51; LtCol, 7*n*, 25, 26*n*, 106*n*; Col, 78*n*
Gruenberg, Maj Ronald J., 53
Guam, 28-29, 206, 209, 213-14, 218, 222
  Apra Harbor, 218
  arrival of refugees in, 219, 221-22
  Camp Asan Refugee Camp, 226, 228
  Camp Socio Refugee Camp, 224
  J&G Construction Refugee Camp, 224, 226
  Orote Point Refugee Camp, 224, 226
  refugees on, 212, 222-24, 227
  Tokyu Hotel Refugee Camp, 224, 226-27
Guilmartin, Maj John F., Jr., USAF, 121*n*, 153, 153*n*, 194, 194*n*, 197*n*, 257-58*n*, 262*n*; LtCol, 123*n*
Gulf of Thailand, 61, 63, 85, 105, 107, 110, 115, 121, 137-38, 239

Hai, Maj, adminstrative leader Camp Socio, Guam, 225
Hai Lang forest, 16
Hai Van Pass, 16, 78, 80
Haiphong Harbor, 44
Hall, PFC Gary C., 262-63
Hancock (CVA 19), 50, 87, 93, 108-10, 110*n*, 113, 138, **139**, 140-41, 143, 152-53, 171, 184, 188, 195, 201, 216, 216*n*, 239
Hanoi, 8
Hardman, Capt Eugene R., 222
Hargrove, LCpl Joseph N., 262-63
Harley, Capt William, 97
Harold E. Holt (DE 1074), 239, 241, 244-45, **246**, 246, 246*n*, 247, 249, 251, **253**, 260-61, 264
Hasty, SSgt Boyette S., 39, 174, 176
Hau Duc, 76
Haynes, MajGen Fred E., 57, 59
Heffernam, Capt John B., 202
Helicopter Employment and Landing Table (HEALT), 107, 116
Henry B. Wilson (DDG 7), 239, 258, 260, **261**, 261, 261*n*, 263-64
Herbert, BGen James A., USA (Ret), 225, 225*n*, 226, 226*n*
Hester, LtCol Charles E., 85-86, 88*n*, **96**, 98, 162-63, 207, 212
Hickinbotham, Capt Robert T., 88
Hicks, Maj James B., 46, 51
Highway
  Hwy 1, 76, 78-80, 136, 146, 168
  Hwy 4, 168
  Hwy 13, 168
  Hwy 14, 72-74
  Hwy 19, 72-73
  Hwy 20, 168
  Hwy 21, 72, 131
Ho Chi Minh Trail, 100, 267
Hoffman, 2dLt Daniel J., 255
Hoffman, MajGen Carl W., 85-86, 89, 109, 136, 138, 146, 160, 222, 240-41, 264
Hong Ngu, 6
Honshu, Japan, 30
Hopkins, LtCol John I., 106, **107**

Houghton, MajGen Kenneth J., 57, 66, 87, 90, 148, 160, 162, 164, **263**
Howard, Col Eugene R., Jr., 38, 143, 155-56, 159, 179
Hue, 16, 70, 76, 78, 82, 126, 266
  evacuation of, 127
Hungary, as member of ICCS, 2
Huong, Vice President Tran Van, RVN, 168
Huong Dien, 16, 80

Indochina Migration and Refugee Assistance Act, 232
Indonesia
  Jakarta, American Embassy in, 238
  Lombok Strait, 243*n*
  as member of ICCS, 2
Interagency Task Force (IATF) for Indochina Refugees, 225
International Commission of Control and Supervision (ICCS), 4
  Canada, 2
  Hungary, 2
  Indonesia, 2
  Poland, 2
  use of landing zone in evacuation of Da Nang, 128
Iran
  as member of ICCS, 4
  Pahlavi, Shah Mohammed Reza, 4
Iwakuni, Japan, 29-30

Jakarta, Indonesia, American Embassy in, 238
Japan
  agreement with U.S. on deployment of units to combat, 85
  Camp Fuji, 137, 141-42
  Honshu, 30
  Iwakuni, 29-30
  Numaza, 142
  Yokosuka, 28, 143
JCS. (*See* Joint Chiefs of Staff.)
Jensen, Capt Harry, Jr., 88
Jessie, Capt Richard M., Jr., 205
J&G Construction Refugee Camp, Guam, 224, 226
JGS. (*See* Joint General Staff (JGS), under South Vietnamese Armed Forces.)
JMC. (*See* Four-Power Joint Military Commission.)
John Paul Jones (DDG 32), 166
Johnson, Col John M., Jr., 52-53, 65, 147, 240, 240*n*, 241-42, 244-45, 255-56, 259
Johnson, 1stLt Johnnie, 166, 174, 222
Johnson, 1stLt Keith L., 226
Johnson, Cpl Lee J., 174
Johnson, Maj Richard F., 22, 38
Joint Chiefs of Staff (JCS), 24-25, 89, 108, 121*n*, 131, 183*n*, 196, 207, 214, 222, 229, 238-39, 245, 253, 255
  investigation of Frequent Wind, 204*n*
  National Military Command Center, 240
  plans for refugees, 211
Joint Commands and Units
  Joint Casualty Resolution Center, 155
  Joint Rescue Coordination Center, 27
Joint Operations Order 76.8/79.9, 87
Jones, Gen David C., USA, 239

INDEX

Jones, Maj Fred L., 142, 148
Jones, Capt James L., Jr., 57
Judge, LCpl Darwin D., 132, 169, 183, 201

Kampuchea. (*See* Cambodia.)
Kane, Col Douglas T., **50**, 51, 51*n*, 64
Kaohsiung, Taiwan, 62
Karker, LtCol Floyd A., Jr., 60
Kean, Capt James H., 39; Maj, 200-201
Keene, Capt Thomas A., **116**, 119, 192
Keith, 1stLt James D., 250-51, 253-55
Kennedy, Senator Edward M., 201
Kent, CWO Allen F., 87, 164, 222
Khang, LtGen Le Nguyen, VNMC, 14, 17, **80**
Khanh Hoa Province, 76, 131
Khe Sanh, 21, 266
Khmer Communists, 40, 44, 50, 123. (*See also* Khmer Rouge.)
Khmer Republic, Cambodia, 100, 121
Khmer Rouge, 57, 66, 100, 102, 111
    1975 Offensive, 102, **103**, 104. (*See also* Khmer Communists.)
Khoy, President Saukham, Cambodia, **113**, 114, 122
Kien Tuong Province, 16
Killens, Cpl Lawrence B., 174
Kinsell, 1stLt Thomas W., 65-66, 162, 164
Kinzie, LCpl Dean M., 174
Kirk (DE 1087), 201
Kissinger, Secretary of State Henry, 5, 101, 128, 169, 264
Kittikachorn, Premier Thanom, of Thailand, 40, 40*n*
Kizer, LtCol James P., 86, 94, 148
Koh Tang, Cambodia, 238-39, 240, **244**, 257
    aerial reconnaissance of, 243*n*, 244
    assault on, 248, 248*n*, 249, 252-53, 253*n*, 254-55, 264-65
    communications during, 256
    casualties, 263, 263*n*
    enemy strength on, 248*n*
    extraction from, 255, 255n, 259-63
    helicopter landings on, 248, 248*n*, 251
    information on terrain, 243
    planning for assault on, 244-45
Kompong Som, Cambodia, 50, 61, 64, 102, 105-6, 121, 242
Kontum, 74
    withdrawal from, 131
Korat, Thailand, 22, 138, 239-40
    Air Base, 26
Kratochvil, 1stLt David A., 164*n*, 219
Ky, Marshal Nguyen Cao, VNAF, **209**, 211; Vice President, South Vietnam, **234**
    arrival in States, 233

Lahiguera, Deputy Consul General Charles, Bien Hoa, 174
Lam, "Tony," 224
Lan, BGen Bui The, VNMC, 17-18, **18**, 19-21, **80**, 80, 83, 83*n*, 84, 84*n*; MajGen, **82**
Lan, Tran Van, South Vietnamese Senate leader, 216*n*
Landes, Maj Burrel H., 65
Lang, MajGen Frank C., 30, 60
Laos, 267
Lawson, LtCol Curtis G., 51, **51**, **59**, 59-60, 106-108, 111-12, 115, 121
Lee, 2dLt Robert E., Jr., 90-92

Lenzini, Maj Martin J., 109, 160
Lindholm, Cpl Gary N., 174
Livermore, SSgt Earle, 92
Livingston, Maj James E., 88*n*, 148, **170**, 170-71, 178, 183
Loc Ninh, 10
Loehe, LtCol Robert E., 85, 109, 141-42, 148, 195
Lombok Strait, Indonesia, 243*n*
Long, PO1 Paul, USN, 212
Long An Front, 168
Long Binh, 267
Long Hai, 166
Long Khang Province, 135, 160, 168
Long Thanh, 168
Long Xuyen, 6
Looney, LCpl Ashton N., 250, 261*n*, 263
Lotito, 2dLt Joseph C., 106
Lowenstein, James G., 100-101
Lukeman, LtCol Anthony, 11, **11**, 16, 21, 38, 83-84, 156, 195*n*, 266
Luong, LtCol, VNMC, **18**, 36
Lutes, Maj Morris W., 178
Ly, Col, 74

Maas, LtCol Bertram A., 61
MACThai. (*See* U.S. Military Assistance Command, Thailand.)
MACV. (*See* U.S. Military Assistance Command, Vietnam.)
Mallick, Capt Michael T., 166, 205, 221, 222*n*
Mang Yang Pass, 72
Manila, Republic of the Philippines, 206, 222
    American Embassy, 222
Manor, MajGen Leroy, USAF, 26
Marble Mountain, 83
    Airfield, 80
    use of in evacuation of Da Nang, 128
Marcos, President Ferdinand, Republic of the Philippines, 206
Marine Corps Air Stations and Facilities
    Air Facility, Camp Pendleton, California, 232
    El Toro, California, 204, 212, 228-29, 229*n*
    Futema (Futenma), Okinawa, 29*n*, 61, 162, 164
    Kadena, Okinawa, 140, 241
    Kaneohe, Hawaii, 137
Marine Corps Aviation Association
    Alfred A. Cunningham Award, 202
    General Keith B. McCutcheon Award, 202
Marine Corps Base, Camp Pendleton, California, 204, 212, 214, 228-29, 234*n*
    preparations for refugees, 218
    Refugee Processing Center, 229, 238
Marine Corps Commands and Units
    Headquarters Marine Corps, 228-29
        Command Center, 127
    Fleet Marine Force, Pacific (FMFPac), 56, 266
    Air
        Marine Aircraft Wings (MAW)
            1st MAW, 29, 29*n*, 56, 266
                Tactical Evaluation Board, 66
            3d MAW, 232
        Marine Aircraft Groups (MAG)
            MAG-12, 30
            MAG-15, 23, 23*n*, 24, 30
            MAG-16, 232

MAG-24, 31
MAG-32, 30
MAG-36, 29n, 30, 53, 65-66, 187
MAG-39 (Provisional), 148, 172, 187, 204, 204n
Headquarters and Maintenance Squadrons (H&MS)
    H&MS-36, 23n, 133
Marine Aerial Refueler Transport Squadrons (VMGR)
    VMGR-152, 23n, 29n, 30, 141, 148, 162, 164
Marine Air Base Squadrons (MABS)
    MABS-15, 30
    MABS-16, 266
Marine Air Support Squadron 2, 29n
Marine All Weather Attack Squadrons (VMA[AW])
    VMA(AW)-533, 23, 23n, 30
Marine Attack Helicopter Squadrons (HMA)
    HMA-369, 30, 148
Marine Attack Squadrons (VMA)
    VMA-211, 30
    VMA-311, 30
    VMA-324, 30
    VMA-513, 30
Marine Composite Reconnaissance Squadrons (VCMJ)
    VCMJ-1, 195, 195n
    VMCJ-1, 30, 110n
Marine Fighter Attack Squadrons (VMFA)
    VMFA-155, 23n
    VMFA-212, 23n
    VMFA-232, 23n
Marine Heavy Helicopter Squadrons (HMH)
    HMH-165, 216
    HMH-462, **3**, 30, 64-65, 93, 105-7, 109, 119, 121-22, 124, 137, 148, 184-85, 188, 191
    HMH-463, 87, 108, 111n, 113, 119, 119n, 138, 141, 148, 152, 184-85, 188, 202
Marine Light Helicopter Squadrons (HML)
    HML-367, 30, 133, 137, 142, 148
Marine Medium Helicopter Squadrons (HMM)
    HMM-164, 30, 51, 64, 106, 133
    HMM-165, 30, 60-61, 86-87, 92-94, 97, 137, 141, 148, 199-200
    HMM-362, 266
    HMM-369, 133
Task Force Delta, 23-24
Marine Air-Ground Task Forces (MAGTFs)
    III Marine Amphibious Force (III MAF), 29, 34, 42, 44-45, 53, 65, 73, 84-85, 89, 131, 133, 136-37, 143, 145, 148, 266
    1st Marine Brigade, 31
    9th Marine Expeditionary Brigade (9th MEB), 266
    Amphibious Evacuation RVN Support Group, 87, 88n, 89-90, 93, 95-96, 98, 131, 139, 160, 162, 204, 207
        3d Force Service Regiment (FSR), 30-31
        evacuation missions, 132
        training on Okinawa, 36
    Marine Amphibious Brigades (MAB)
        9th MAB, 2, 52, 62, 109, 136-38, 142, 145-46, 148, 156, 159, 171-72, 178, 181, 184, 187-88, 192, 198, 204, 217, 266
            Advance Command Element, 170-73
            Brigade Logistic Support Group, 148, 154-55
        11th MAB, 109-10, 133
    Marine Amphibious Units (MAU)

        31st MAU, 30, 34, **35**, 42-43, 45, 48-50, 55, 60-65, 85, 105-10, 115-16, **117**, 137-38, 141-42
        33d MAU, 86-87, 93, 110, 131, 140
        35th MAU, 142
Ground
    1st Marine Division, 228
    3d Marine Division, 29, 31, 43-44, 56, 90, 108
        Amphibious Evacuation Security Force (AESF), 148, 160, 162, 164-66, 168, 173-74, 176, 204, 212, 217, 219, 222
            Detachment E, 162, 166, 168, 206, 219
            Detachment F, 163, 164n, 205, 222
            Detachment H, 206, 219
            Detachment I, 163, 165, 205, 217, 221
            Detachment K, 164-66, 222
            Detachment M, 164-65, 206, 219, 221
            Detachment N, 166, 205, 222, 222n
            Detachment P, 165, 205, 221
            Detachment Q, 164-66, 216, 221
            Detachment R, 164-66, 216, 221
            Detachment S, 165, 205, 222
            Detachment T, 165, 205, 219, 222
            Detachment U, 206, 216, 222
            Detachment V, 164-65, 176, 206, 219
        Regimental Landing Team 4, 62, 148, 163, 172, 184
            Military Police Company, 87
            MP Company, 164
        3d Marines, 31, 212
            2d Battalion
                Company E, 227
                Company F, 227
        4th Marines, 31, 53, 55, 65, 140, 160
            Battalion Landing Team 1/4, 56, 60-61, 64
            Battalion Landing Team 2/4, 34n, 62, 64-65, 106-107, 109, 119, 122, 137, 148, 184-85, 189, 191-92, 197
            Battalion Landing Team 3/4, 64-65
            1st Battalion, 34n, 55, 85-88, 88n, 89-90, 93, 97-98, 131, 137, 139, 160, 162, 204, 207, 212, 252, 264
                Company A, 87
                Company B, 56, 87, 90
                Company C, 87
                Company D, 85n, 86, 240-41, 244-45, 246
                    1st Platoon, 94
                Security Force A, 88-89
                Security Force B, 88
                Security Force C, 88
                Security Force D, 88
            2d Battalion, 64, 85, 89, 115, 183, 241
                Company E, 106, 192
                Company F, 119, 192
                Company G, 119, 123, 192
                Company H, 119, 192
        9th Marines, 31, 34, 55, 57, 59, 65-66, 160
            Battalion Landing Team 1/9, 62, 87, 109, 140, 148, 192, 196
            Battalion Landing Team 2/9, 53, 57, 240, 242, 263-64
            Battalion Landing Team 3/9, 109, 137, 141-42, 148
            1st Battalion, 43n, 137, 183
                Company A
                    Sparrow Hawk teams, 187
                Company C
                    3d Platoon, 171, 196

INDEX

2d Battalion, 34n, 56, 251, 251n
   Company E, 252
   Company F, 56-57
   Company G, 56-57, 250, 252
      1st Platoon, 248
      2d Platoon, 250, 255, 258
      3d Platoon, 249, 255
3d Battalion, 34n, 85, 219
12th Marines, 31, 160
Other
  1st Force Service Regiment, 228
  3d Force Service Regiment, 29
  1st Amphibian Tractor Battalion, 31, 140, 160
  7th Communication Battalion, 160
  1st Engineer Battalion, 233
  3d Engineer Battalion, 87, 160
  7th Engineer Battalion, 233
  3d Medical Battalion, 97
  3d Motor Transport Battalion, 31, 57
  9th Motor Transport Battalion, 57, 140
  3d Reconnaissance Battalion, 31
  3d Service Battalion, 59, 160
  1st Shore Party Battalion, 233
  3d Shore Party Battalion, 31
  3d Tank Battalion, 160
  3d Counterintelligence Team (3d CIT), 87, 164
  17th Interrogator-Translator Team (17th ITT), 87-89, 164, 221
  Logistic Support Units (LSU)
    LSU 1/9, 140, 148
    LSU 2/4, 137, 148
    LSU 3/9, 137, 142, 148
  Marine Detachment, USS *Proteus* (AS 19), 224
  Marine Security Guard Battalion
    Company C, 39
    Company E, 38-39, **150**
    Marine Security Guard Detachments, 204
      Bien Hoa, 174
      Can Tho, 174-75
      Da Nang, 127, 129, 131
      Nha Trang, 132, 132n
      Saigon, 22, 39, 174, 196, 200
Marine Corps Exercises
  HeliLEx 1-75, 107
  HeloEx 1-73, 62
  HeloEx 2-73, 62
  MABLEx 2-75, 133, 136-37, 138
  Operation Pagasa II, 61-62, 109
  Operation Quick Jab II, 016
  ZAMEx 2-73, 62
Marine Corps Operations
  Dewey Canyon, 266
  New Arrival, 204, 232, 234, 234n, 235
Marine Corps Posts and Stations
  Camp Schwab, Okinawa, 241
  Marine Barracks
    Guam, 204, 209, 221-22, 224, 227
    Subic Bay, Republic of the Philippines, 140
Marine Corps Supply Depot, Barstow, California, 228
Marshall, Pvt Danny G., 262-63
Martin, Ambassador Graham A., 7n, 38-39, 52-53, 126-27, 143, 145-46, 159-60, 169, 171-72, 174, 178, 196-97, 207, 212, 217

evacuation of, 199, 199n, 200
Martinoli, 1stLt John J., Jr., 195
Matak, Sirik, 114, 114n, 121
Mayaguez, 239n, **246-47**, 253, **253**
  boarding of, 246-47
  capture of, 238
  location of crew, 243
  planning for recovery of, 241, 241n
  preparations for recovery, 240, 242-43, 243n
  recovery of, 245, 246n, 264-65
    command and control of operation, 245
    communications during, 245, 256
    management by JCS, 253n
  release of, 252
  seizure of, 239
McCain, Col Gene M., 222, 224-27
McClenahan, GySgt Clarence D., 39, **114**, 115
McCormick, Sgt Michael A., 132, 132n
McCulloch, BGen William L., 228
McDaniel, 2dLt James, 248, 250-51
McFall, Representative John J., 214
McKinstry, LtCol William E., 38, 155-56, 171, 178, 181, 195n
McLain, Capt Roy W., Jr., USN, 164, 216
McLenon, Col Frank G., **147**, 148, 187-88, 204
McMahon, Cpl Charles, Jr., 132, 169, 183, 201
McMahon, Col Richard L., USA, 15
McManus, Capt Raymond J., 147, 172, 197
McMenamin, 2dLt Joseph J., 254-55
McMonigle, LtCol Joseph, USAF, 153n
McNamara, Consul General Francis, Can Tho, 174, 176
McNemar, GySgt Lester, 261-62
MEDTC. (*See* Military Equipment Delivery Team, Cambodia under Army Commands and Units.)
Mekong Delta, 16, 70
Mekong River, 5-6, 102, 104-5, 113, 122
Melshen, 2dLt Paul, 87
Melton, Capt William R., 119, 123, 183, **184**, 192
Merrihew, Maj Ronald E., 30
Merrill, Col George A., 228n, 233, 234n
MIA accountability, 6-7
Midway (CVA 41), 29, **29**, 110, 110n, 133, 140-41, 143, 152-53, 153n, 185n, 192, 194-95, 195n, 197n, 198, 211, 239
Military Regions (South Veitnam)
  1, 10, 16, 52, 70, **77**, 78, 80, 126, 135, 138
    evacuation of, 53, 82-84, 95-97
    evacuees from, 91
    fall of, 127
    North Vietnamese offensive in
      U.S. assistance to refugees, 85
    placement of refugees from, 97
    South Vietnamese defeat in, 76
    withdrawal from, 79
  2, 15-16, 71-72, 131, 135, 138
    disposition of South Vietnamese forces in, 70
    evacuees from, 91
    NVA control of, 131, 133
  3, 10, 15-16, 68, 84
    disposition of South Vietnamese forces in, 70
    evacuation of, 133
  4, 16
    disposition of South Vietnamese forces in, 70

evacuation of, 133
Military Sealift Command (MSC), 88, 95, 146, 163, 166, 204, 214, 224
    in evacuation of Da Nang, 128, 131
    Marines aboard MSC ships, 89-90
    planning for use in evacuation of Saigon, 145
    use of ships for evacuation of refugees, 92-93
Miller, Capt Charles T., 238, 252
Minh, Gen Duong Van, ARVN, 168-69, 170
Minh, Cdr Hoang Co, VNN, 15
Minh, President Duong Van, South Vietnam, 267
Mo Tau Mountain, 16, 21
Mobile (LKA 115), 64, 138, 184-85
Molineaux, LtCol Joseph F., Jr., 140, 140*n*
Momyer, Gen William W., USAF, 13-14
Montagnards, involvement in the fall of Ban Me Thuot, 72*n*
Monticello (LSD 35), 64
Moore, Sgt John S., 174
Moore, LtGen William G., Jr., USAF, 240
Moose, Richard M., 100-101
Morrison, RAdm George F., USN, 224
Mount Vernon (LSD 39), 64, 138
Moya, Cpl John G., 132
Moyher, Capt Cyril V., 163, 165, 205, 217, 221
MSC. (*See* Military Sealift Command.
Murphy, Maj Barry J., 57
Murray, Maj John A., 170
Murray, MajGen John E., USA, 6-7, 16, **80**, 126
My Chanh, 79-80
    River, 79
My Tho, 70

Nakhon Phanom, Thailand, 22, 27, 36, 41, 46, 59, 106-107, 116, 133, 138, 145-46, 146*n*, 153*n*, 181, 239-40, 255
    Air Base, 26
Nam Bo, 146
Nam Phong, Thailand, **23**, 23-24, **24**, 30, **33**, 40
Nardo, Maj Joseph F., 38
National Military Command Center, 238
Naval Air Stations and Facilities
    Atsugi, Japan, 141
    Cubi Point, Republic of the Philippines, 29-30, 61, 86, 140, 147, 162, 164, 241
    Naha, Okinawa, 29-30
Naval Bases
    Subic Bay, Republic of the Philippines, 28, 138, 146, 162, 240
    Ship Repair Facility, 50, 226*n*
Navy Commands and Units
    Commander in Chief, Pacific (CinCPac), 25, 42, 44, 55, 63, 133, 137, 143, 153, 181, 198, 212, 219, 239
    Pacific Fleet, 53, 211
    First Fleet, 29
    Seventh Fleet, 2, 11, 27-29, 31, 53, 89, 137, 143, 181*n*, 183, 183*n*, 184, 199, 204, 212, 214, 239, 239*n*, 264
        Amphibious Force, 28
        Amphibious Ready Groups (ARG)
            ARG Alpha, 28-30, 34, 50, 53, 61-65, 85, 97, 105-6, 108, 110, 115, 121, 124, 137-38
            ARG Bravo, 28-29, 34, 53, 65, 85-86, 93, 108, 110, 131, 137-40

            ARG Charlie, 142
        Amphibious Squadrons (PhibRon)
            PhibRon 3, 64
            PhibRon 5, 64, 138, 141-42
            PhibRon 7, 64
        Landing Force, 28
        Operational Plan 1-75, 133
        Service Force, 166
        Task Force 72, 27-28, 242
        Task Force 73, 27
        Task Force 74, 28
        Task Force 75, 28
        Task Force 76, 28, 86-87, 139-40, 143, 146-47, 155, 164, 198, 198*n*, 204-5, 212
            position on 29-30 April, 1975, **180**
        Task Force 77, 28
        Task Force 79, 28-29, 143
        Task Group 76, 124
        Task Group 76.5, 166, 214*n*, 218
        Task Group 76.8, 93
        Task Group 79.9, 94, 98, 240-41
    U.S. Naval Forces, Vietnam, 22
    Naval Refugee Camps, Guam, 223
Neak Loung, Cambodia, 104-5, 113
Nelson, Col Neil A., 228*n*
Nessen, Presidential Press Secretary Ron, 238
New Horizon Coordination Center, 229
New Orleans (LPH 11), 64
Newport Pier, Saigon, 145-46, 148, **149**, 164, 178, 191
Nha Trang, 39, 74, 87, 89, 92, 128, 131
    abandonment of, 133
    defense of, 131
    fall of, 131-32
    Spear, Consul General Moncrieff, 131
Ninh Thuan Province, 131
Nixon, President Richard M., 4-5, 101, 266
Nol, President Lon, Cambodia, 100-101, 114, 114*n*
    government of, 102, 104
North Vietnam, 6, 70
    Campaign 275, 72
        battle plan, 71
    final offensive in the South, 71-72
        plan for, 70, 78
    Politburo, 11, 70, 78
North Vietnamese Army (NVA), 7-9, 11, 13, 15, 66, 68, 76, 89
    air defense, 14
    antiaircraft artillery regiments, 10
    assault of Saigon, 170
    assault on Binh Dinh Province, 131
    attack on Tan Son Nhut, 178, 182
    attack on Tan Son Nhut Airport, 189
    in Cambodia, 100
    capture of Phuoc Long Province, 69
    capture of Saigon, 168
    Commands and Units
        1st Corps, 168
        2d Corps, 168
        3d Corps, 168
        4th Corps, 168
        301st Corps, 68
        2d Division, 76

3d Division, 15, 68
    2d Regiment, 15
        2d Battalion, 15
5th Division, 16
6th Division, 136, 168
7th Division, 68, 136, 168
10th Division, 71-72, 146
316th Division, 71-72
320th Division, 71-72, 74
341st Division, 136, 168, 182n
968th Division, 16, 71-72
52d Brigade, 76
9th Regiment, 72
48th Regiment, 16
64th Regiment, 16
165th Regiment, 136
232d Tactical Force, 168
16th Antiaircraft Battalion, 15
control of Military Region 2, 131
entrance into Da Nang, 126
figures for final offensive on Saigon, 70n
final offensive in South, 133, 135-36, 160, 168
operations
    Easter Offensive, 1972, 8, 10, 14, 16, 19
    Tet Offensive, 1968, 8
tactics, 70
    blooming lotus, 69
Numaza, Japan, 142
Nystul, Capt William C., 201, 201n

Oakland, Lt John, MC, USN, 97, 164
O'Donnell, BGen Andrew W., 23n
O'Keefe, Gen Timothy F., USAF, 41, 53, 59-60, 62
Okinawa, 28, 42, 137, 141, 221, 241
    Camp Courtney, 140, 160
    Camp Schwab, 140, 142, 160, 241
    Ishikawa, 140
    Ora Wan Bay, 139
Okinawa (LPH 3), 62, 64, 106, 116, **117**, 119, 123-24, 138, **141**, 143, **144**, 151, 153, 184-85, 188, 191, 197, 201
    Helicopter Direction Center (HDC), 184
    position on 29-30 April, 1975, **180**
Oklahoma City (CLG 5), 29, 181n, 215
Olmstead, Col Stephen G., 45, **45**, 46, **50**, 51, 57, **57**, **58**, 59, 62-63
O'Neill, 1stLt James L., 107-8
Operation Plan 5060 (C), 109
Orote Point Refugee Camp, Guam, 224, 226
Oseola, 128n
Osgood, Cpl James R., Jr., 112
Owen, LtCol Ronald L., 51n, 61
Owens, Sgt J. C., 219
Owens, Sgt William J., 246, 248

Pacific Architect and Engineers, 159
Pacini, 1stLt Philip, USAF, 123n
Page, Capt Richard R., 163, 205
Pahlavi, Shah Mohammed Reza, of Iran, 4
Painter, SSgt Roger F., 39, 131-32
Palmquist, Capt Edward R., Jr., 205, **206**

Paris Conference on Vietnam, 2
Paris Peace Accords, 2, **3**, 6, 12-14, 19, 22, 25, 27, 29, 36-38, 40, 178
    alleged United States violations of, 5, 5n
    Article 3, 5
    Article 6, 5
    Article 8, 5-6
    enforcement of, 4
    Four-Power Joint Military Commission (JMC), 2
    International Commission of Control and Supervision (ICCS), 2
    Two-Power Joint Military Commission, 2
Parker, LtCol Charles E., 56
Parrot's Beak, Cambodia, 100
Pate, Sgt Terry D., 174
Paull, Maj Jerome T., 61
Pawnee, **93**
Pelosky, Col Edward, USA, 202n
Peoria (LST 1183), 106, 139, 184-85, 189
Peters, Consul General Richard, Bien Hoa, 173-74
Petry, Capt George, USA, 155, 159, 179, 197n
Phan Rang, 92-95
Phan Thiet, 92, 95
Philippines, Republic of the
    government, 222
    Grande Island, 209, 213, 219
        refugee camp on, 212
    Manila, 206, 222
    Subic Bay, 206-7, 209, 211, 213, 218, 222
Phnom Penh, Cambodia, 39-40, **47**, 56-57, 63, 98, 102, 107-108, 110, 119, 121, 142
    American Embassy landing zone, **58**
    evacuation of, 85, 114-15. (*See also* Eagle Pull, under American Operations.)
    evacuation sites, **49**, **112**
    landing zones in, 113
        Hotel, 116, **119-20**, 121-23
    Mekong supply line to, 104-5
Phong Dien, 16, 80
Phong Dinh Province, 39
Phu, MajGen Pham Van, ARVN, 71-74
Phu Bai Airfield, 16
Phu Bon, 74
Phu Cat Air Base, 15
Phu My, Cambodia, mines in the Mekong at, 104
Phu Quoc Island, 90, 94-95, 130, 174
    use as center for evacuees, 91-92, 98
Phuoc Long
    battle of, **69**
    City, 68, **68**, 69
    NVA assessment of victory at, 70
    Province, 10, 16, 68
        capture of, 69
    significance of battle for, 70
Phuoc Tong, 80
Phuong Dien
    defense of, 80
Phuong Duc, 72
Pioneer Commander (MSC ship), 205, 217-18, 219, 221, **221**
Pioneer Contender (MSC ship), 90-92, 95-96, 129-31, 165, 174, 176, 206, 218-19
Pleiku, 13, 73-74
    Province, 16, 71-72

withdrawal from, 131
Pochentong Airfield, Cambodia, 104-5, 109
    evacuation operation at, 111-12
Poggemeyer, MajGen Herman G., Jr., 52, 59, 64, 86
Poland, as member of ICCS, 2
Porter, Maj Raymond E., 240-41, 244-45
Poulo Wai Island, Cambodia, 238
PRC-77, 107
PRG. (*See* Provisional Revolutionary Government of South Vietnam.)
Project New Life, 213
Project Seven Hundred Million, 37
Proteus (AS 19), 224
Provini, Capt Charles R., 222, 224
Provisional Revolutionary Government of South Vietnam (PRG), 2, 7. (*See also* Viet Cong.)

QL-15 Front, 168
Quang Duc Province, 15
Quang Nai
    fall of, 79
Quang Ngai Province, 76
    fall of, 131
Quang Tri, 10
    City, 78
        abandonment of, 79
        evacuation of, 127
    Province, 21, 71, 76, 79, 83, 126
Quay, Col, political leader Camp Socio, Guam, 225-26
Que, Col Le Dinh, VNMC, 16, 18, **19**
Que Son Valley, 10
Qui Nhon, 87, 89, 92, 131
    abandonment of, 133
Quinlan, Maj David A., 148, 160, 162-66, 205, 222
Quinn, MajGen William R., 232

Rayong, Thailand, 251
Reasoner, 94
Reed, 1stLt Charles G., 30n
Reed, Maj Robert M., 140
Reed, Col Robert R., USAF, 256
Rees, Capt Richard M., USA, 7
Refugee Receiving Center, Camp Pendleton, 204
Refugees, 204, 204n, 205-6, 215, 218
    1973 resettlement efforts, 224
    in America, 232
    arrival in America, 229
    arrival in Guam, 219, 221-22
    conditions aboard ships, 219
    construction of camps for, 232
    desiring repatriation, 225, 226n
    disarming of, 218-19
    in Guam, 224
        repatriates, 226
    medical care for, 97
    numbers of, 217
    in the Philippines, 207, 209, 211-12, 222
        at Grande Island, 213
    placement of, 97-98
    preparations for in the States, 228-29
    way stations for, 207

Republic of Vietnam. (*See* South Vietnam.)
Reuter, Capt Richard L., 162-63, 166, 206, 219
Richards, Maj Larry D., 38
Rigoulot, Capt James P., 212
Ritchie, Capt Edward J., 188, 198, 239
Robinson, Col Kenneth J., Jr., 228n
Roche, Col John F. III, 48n, **50**, 51, 51n, 85, 106, **106**, 116, 119n, 121, 234
Rock Pile, the, 21
Rockefeller, Vice President Nelson, 216n
Rogers, Sgt Venoy L., 127, 129
Rogish, 1stLt Joseph J., 216-17
Roosma, Col John J., Jr, USAF, 188
Rose Garden. (*See* Nam Phong, Thailand.)
Routes
    1, 16, 135, 168
    2, 168
    7B, 73, **73**, 74
    20, 135
Rowley, Col Jack D., 65
Ruggiero, Col Alexander S., 57, 57n
Rumbaugh, SSgt Elwood, 248
Ryan, MajGen Michael P., **42**, 42-43, 52, 55-57, 59-60

Sabater, Maj Jaime, Jr., 38, 78, 155-56, 159, 179, 197n
Saigon, 16, 68, 133-34, 153, **158**, 267
    Air America Compound, 145-46, 149, 153, 178, 183, **191**, 192
    American Embassy, 52, 156, 176, 178, **195**, 204, 216
        closing of, 200
        concept for evacuation of, 151
        evacuation of, 195, 199, 217
    Defense Attache Office (DAO), 146, 149, 151-53, **155**, 157-59, 169, 171, 171n, 172, **172**, 179
        compound, 156, 160, 172, 178, 181-83, 185, 188-89, 191, **191**, 204, 216
        defense of, 159
        evacuation of, 192, 194, 194n, 195, 198, 198n, 199
        Evacuation Control Center (ECC), 147, 155-56, 178, 182
        Evacuation Processing Center (EPC), 155
        Special Planning Group (SPG), 155-56, 160, 170-72, 178
    evacuation of, 156, 169, 171-72, 179, 181, 183-84, 185
        by fixed-wing airlift, 182-83
        planning for, 143, 145-48
        Project Alamo, 155
        rules of engagement during, 154
    fall of, **167**, 170-71
    landing zones in, **186**
    Newport Pier, 145-46, 148, **149**, 164, 178, 191
    plans for evacuation of, 94-95
    River, 149, 164
Saigon River, 133
San Bernardino (LST 1189), 64
Schlager, GySgt Robert W., 39, 174
Schrader, Capt Kurt A., 184
Schuller, Sgt Steven T., **202**
Sea Lanes, 252
Sergeant Andrew Miller (MSC ship), 165, **165**, 205, **217**, 219, 222
Sergeant Truman Kimbro (MSC ship), 163, 166, 206, 219
Shaver, Maj Carl A., 88n, **96**, 97
Shaver, LtCol Glenn J., Jr., 51, 59

INDEX

Shea, 1stLt Michael J., 201
Sheffield, Capt Vernon, USAF, 197*n*
Shelton, LtCol Jerry L., 141-42
Shelton, LCpl Robert L., 255
Shepherd, Capt Steven A., 206
Shores, Capt Howard P. III, 225-26
Siegmund, Col Paul L., 38
Sihanouk, Prince Norodom, Cambodia, 5, 100
Singapore, 28, 216
Slade, LtCol George P., 64-65, 85, **115**, 119, 121, 123, 148, 183, **183**, 191
Smith, MajGen Homer D., Jr., USA, 38, 52, 143, 146, 155-57, 169, 172, 178-79, 183, 189, 195-6*n*
Sneed, Cpl Jimmie D., 132
Soc Trang, 266
Son Tay, 26*n*
Song Be, 72. (*See also* City, under Phuoc Long.)
Song Than, 16, **17**, 267
  Base Camp, 21
South China Sea, 16, 27, 102, 124, 133, 136, 138-39, 148-49, 152, 166
South Vietnam, 2
  evacuation of civilians from, 52-53
    planning for, 53
  government of, 5, 15
  military regions of, **75**. (*See also* Military Regions.)
South Vietnamese Armed Forces, 11-12, 15, 68
  advisors to, 2
  Air Force (VNAF), 10-11, 13-14, 80, 156, 213
    General Purpose Strategic Force, 17
    tactical air support provided by, 21
    weakness of, 69
  Army (ARVN), 8, 13
  defeat of in Military Region 1, 79
  disposition of in 1973, 70
  during evacuation of Saigon, 130
  inability to defend Military Region 1 coastal region, 126
  Joint General Staff (JGS), 14-16, 20, 69, 80, 168
  Marine Corps (VNMC), 8, 15-16, 79, 127, 266-67
    Advisors Program, termination of, 6
    area of operations
      1 January—15 March 1975, **77**
      15-31 March 1975, **81**
    employment of, 21
    in defense of Da Nang, 131
  Montagnards in, 72
  National Military Command Center, 131
  Navy (VNN), 82
  Popular Forces, 72-73
  Regional Forces, 72-73
South Vietnamese Commands and Units
  Army (ARVN)
    Corps
      I, 80, 83, 126
      II, 73-74, 76
      III, 78, 168
    Divisions
      1st, 16, 70, 127
      2d, 70, 76
      3d, 19, 70
      5th, 70
      7th, 70
      9th, 16, 70
      18th, 70, 136, 146, 160, 168, 170, 181
      21st, 70
      22d, 15, 70, 76, 131
      23d, 70, 72-73
      25th, 70
      Airborne, 76, 78-80, 126
    Brigades
      1st Airborne, 78, 168
      2d Airborne, 17
      3d Airborne, 76, 131
      1st Armored, 17, 70
      2d Armored, 70
      3d Armored, 70
      4th Armored, 70
    Groups
      20th Combat Engineer, 74
      4th Ranger, 70, 70*n*
      6th Ranger, 70, 70*n*
      7th Ranger, 70
      11th Ranger, 70
      12th Ranger, 70
      14th Ranger, 70
      15th Ranger, 16-17
      21st Ranger, 70
      22d Ranger, 70
      23d Ranger, 70, 74
      24th Ranger, 70
      25th Ranger, 70
      31st Ranger, 70
      32d Ranger, 70
      33d Ranger, 70
      81st Ranger, 69-70
    Regiments
      48th, 168
      52d, 168
      53d, 16, 72
    82d Ranger Battalion, 15
    108th Regional Force Battalion, 15
    263d Regional Force Battalion, 15
  Marine Corps (VNMC)
    Brigades
      147, 17, 80, 82
        4th Battalion, 80, 82, 82*n*
        5th Battalion, 80
        7th Battalion, 80
      258, 17, 79-80, 82-83
        3d Battalion, 82
      369, 17, 79-80, 82-83
      468, 17, 21, 78-80
    Battalions
      8th, 21
      14th, 21, 78
      16th, 21, 78
      18th, 21
    Logistic Support Branch, 36, 38
  Navy (VNN), 11, 14-15
    Coastal Surveillance Force, 89*n*
  Popular Forces, 17
    Regional Forces, 17

Sparkman, Senator John, 238
Sparks, SSgt Walter W., 39, 127-29, 204
Spear, Consul General Moncrieff, Nha Trang, 131
SPG. (*See* Special Planning Group (SPG) under Defense Attache Office (DAO), Saigon.)
Spratt, 1stLt Ronald E., 222
Spruce, Sgt William E., III, 127, 129
St. Louis (LKA 116), 64
Stadler, Capt R. F., Jr., USN, 22
Stahl, Capt Mykle E., 252, 253n, 262-63
Standfast, LCpl John S., 262
Stauffer, LtCol Robert M., 56
Steele, VAdm George P., USN, 52, 52n, 53, 53n, 56, 63, 88n, 105, 130, 133, 181, 181n, 196n, 198, 199n, 204, 212, 215, 239, 239n, 241, 241n, 243, 243n, 255n, 261, 261n, 264
Stevens, Col Thomas J., 42, 51n, 56
Streitz, 1stLt Joseph J., 87, 164
Strickland, LtCol George E., 7, 8-9, 16-17, **18**, 19, **19**, 20-21, **36**, 38, **80**
Subcommittee on U.S. Security Agreements and Commitments Abroad, U.S. Senate, 101
Subic Bay, Republic of the Philippines, 206-7, 209, 211, 213, 218, 222
Sullivan, SSgt Michael K., 39, **202**
Sun Tzu, 126, 169, 266
Swift boats, 89
Symington, Senator Stuart, 101

Tactics
    anti-surface-to-air missile tactics, 14
    electronic counter-measures, 14
Taft, Julia, 225
Taiwan, 168
    Kaohsiung, 62
Taiwanese Logistic Command, 20
Takhli, Thailand, 22
Tam, Capt, assistant political leader Camp Socio, Guam, 225-26
Tam Ky, 76
    fall of, 79
Tan Chau Naval Base, 6
Tan My, 82
Tan Son Nhut, 13, 147, 159, 168-69, 171, 178-79
    Air Base, 27, 146, 149, **154**, 156-57, 182
    Airport, 181, 192, 196, 196n, 213
        NVA attack on, 178, 189
Tat, Col Pham Van, ARVN, 73-74
Tay Nguyen, 10
Taylor, Col Wylie W., 146-47, 164, 170, 172, 183, 183n, 197n
Thach Han River, 16, 78-79
Thailand, 40, 213
    Aduldet, King Phumiphol, 40
    Air Force withdrawal from, 26
    American forces in, 22, 39
    Bangkok, 40
    Charusathien, Interior Minster Gen Praphas, 40
    formal protest against *Mayaguez* recovery operation, 264
    function of Air Force units in, 41
    Gulf of, 42, 61, 63, 85, 105, 107, 110, 115, 121, 137-38, 239
    Kittikachorn, Premier Thanom, 40
    Korat, 22, 138, 239-40
        Air Base, 26

Nakhon Phanom, 22, 27, 36, 41, 46, 59, 106-7, 116, 133, 138, 145-46, 146n, 153n, 181, 239-40, 255
    Air Base, 26
Nam Phong, **23**, 23-24, **24**, 30, **33**, 40
Phnom Penh, **47**, 63
    evacuation sites, **49**
Pochentong Airfield, 109
Rayong, 251
Takhli, 22
Thammasak, Premier Sanya, 40
Ubon, 22, 138
    Air Force Base, 109
Udorn, 22, 27, 138
    Air Base, 26
Utapao, 22, 26-27, 40n, 138, 152, 238, 240-42
    Air Base, 48, 116, 124
Thammasak, Premier Sanya, Thailand, 40
Thanh Hoa, 71
Thieu, President Nguyen Van, RVN, 5, 73-74, 76, 78, 126, 160, 168, 168n
Thompson-Bowers, 1stLt Bruce P., 171, 196
Thorne, Nicholas G., **231**, 232-33
Thuong Tin I (Vietnamese ship), 226, 226n, **227**
Thua Thien Province, 10, 16, 76, 80, 83, 126
Thurman, GySgt Russell R., 184, 200
Tien Phuoc, 76
Toan, LtGen Nguyen Van, ARVN, 78
Toan, LtCol Tran Ngoc, VNMC, **7**, 72n, 76n, 82, 82n, 84
Tokyu Hotel Refugee Camp, Guam, 226-27
Tong Le Chan, 15
Tonkin, 1stLt Terry L., 248n, 249, 254, **263**
Toul Leap, Cambodia, 105
Tra, Gen Tran Van, VC, 4-5, 5n
Transcolorado (MSC ship), 94, 206, 219
Trapnell, Col Nicholas M., Jr., 38, 38n, 229n
Trebil, PFC Timothy W., 249
Tregurtha, Capt James D., USN, 166, 214n, 218, 218n
Tri, Col, VNMC, 21
Tripoli (LPH 10), 45, 50, 61-62, 106
Trung, Lt Nguyen Thanh, VNAF, 168n
Truong, LtGen Ngo Quang, ARVN, 17, 76, **76**, 78, 80, **80**
Tuitele, SSgt Fofo T., 255, 260
Tulare (LKA 112), 64
Tuluga (AO 62), 61
Tuong Song, 10
Tuscaloosa (LST 1187), 62, 138, **166**
Tuy Hoa, 70
Two-Power Joint Military Commission, 2, 4
Twomey, Col David M., 45, **46**, 51n, 59, 61-64

Ubon, Thailand, 22, 138
    Air Force Base, 109
Udorn, Thailand, 22, 27, 138
    Air Base, 26
Undorf, Maj Robert W., USAF, 257n
U.S. Agency for International Development (USAID), 158
U.S. Military Assistance Advisory Group, Vietnam, 15
U.S. Military Assistance Command, Thailand (MACThai), 25, 41-42
U.S. Military Assistance Command, Vietnam (MACV), 25, 36, 266-67

INDEX

U.S.-Thai Accord, 40
USSAG. (*See* United States Support Activities Group/Seventh Air Force under Air Force Commands and Units.)
Utapao, Thailand, 22, 26-27, 40*n*, 138, 152, 238, 240-42
    Air Base, 48, 116, 124

Valdez, MSgt Juan J., 39, 132
Van Co Dong River, 135
Vancouver (LPD 2), 50, 119, 138, 174, 176, 184-85
Vehicles
    LVTP-5 amphibious tractor, 19-20
    LVTP-7, 87
    M-151 jeep, 19
    M170 ambulance jeep, 19
Verdon, LtCol Donald J., 147, 171-72
Vidaurri, PFC Charles, 92
Vien, Gen Cao Van, ARVN, 70, 70*n*
Viet Cong, 176, 266. (*See also* Provisional Revolutionary Government of South Vietnam.)
    in Cambodia, 100
    military units, 76
VNMC. (*See* Marine Corps [VNMC] under South Vietnamese Armed Forces.)
Vogt, Gen John W., Jr., USAF, 24, 26*n*, 41-44, 49, 53, 56, 60-61
Vung Tau, 16, 82-83, 92, 98, 102, 110, 130, 133, 141, 156, 164, 168, 267
    Light, **150**
    Peninsula, 145-47, 166, 195
        concept for evacuation from, 151

Walters, Capt Jon M., 200-1
Weapons and ordnance
    American
        105mm howitzer, 13
        106mm recoilless rifle, 87
        155mm howitzer, 13
        175mm gun, 13
        BLU-82, 182, 182*n*
        laser-guided weapons, 26
        M-48 tank, **35**
        M60 machine gun, 164, 176
        M72 LAW (light antitank weapon), 164
        M79 grenade launcher, 164

        TOW missile, 18-19, 82
    Khmer Rouge
        12.7mm machine gun, 102, 123
        107mm rocket, 102
        rocket-propelled grenade launcher (RPG), 102
    North Vietnamese
        85mm AAA gun, 10, 13
        100mm AAA gun, 10, 13
        122mm gun, 13
        130mm gun, 13, 82
        SA-2 surface-to-air missile, 10, 14, 194*n*
        SA-7 (Grail) surface-to-air missile, 10, 14, 110, 133, 153, 188
        T-54 tank (Soviet built), 10
        Type 59 tank (Chinese), 10
Weisner, Adm Maurice F., USN, 53, 105, 198-99, 211, 239, 241
Wemitt, PFC Jerome N., 251*n*
White, LtCol Robert D., 145
Whitmire, RAdm Donald E., USN, 86-87, 111*n*, 131, 139-41, 164, 181, 184, 187, 192, 198, 198*n*, 212, 214-15, 219, 221, 240
Wicker, GySgt Robert, 217-18
Williams, Lt Richard, MC, USN, 97
Willingham, TSgt Billy D., USAF, 258*n*
Wilson, 249, 252. (*See* Henry B. *Wilson* [DDG 7].)
Wilson, LtGen Louis H., Jr., 56-57, 108, 192*n*, 198-99
Wilson, Gen Louis L., Jr., USAF, 26*n*
Winkates, Dr. James E., 263*n*
Wise, LtCol Robert L., 65, 160
Wood, Capt Anthony A., 38, 155-56, 160, **178**, 179, 181*n*, 194*n*
Wood, Capt Walter J., 88, 241, 245-46, 246*n*, 252*n*; LtCol, 85*n*
Woodham, Col Tullis J., Jr., 228, 228*n*

Xuan Loc, 135-36, 146, 170, 182*n*
    abandonment of, 181
    battle for, 160, 164, 168
    fall of, **135**, 174

Yokosuka, Japan, 28, 143
Young, Capt L., USN, 22
Young, Maj Richard K., 146-47, 181
Youngman, Maj Thornton L., 191

Zales, 2dLt Richard H., 250-51, 253, 255

www.ingramcontent.com/pod-product-compliance
Lightning Source LLC
Chambersburg PA
CBHW080729300426
44114CB00019B/2521